Books for Elementary School Libraries

Books for Elementary School Libraries

An Initial Collection

Compiled and edited by

Elizabeth D. Hodges
Supervisor of Library Services, Retired
Board of Education of Baltimore County, Maryland

 American Library Association
Chicago, 1969

Standard Book Number 8389-0069-0 (1969)

Library of Congress Catalog Card Number 76-77273

Copyright © 1969 by the American Library Association

Printed in the United States of America

Consultants to the Editor

Miss MARY PHYLLIS BRINE
Librarian, Munsey Park School Library
Manhassett, New York

Miss MARY K. EAKIN
Associate Professor of Education
University of Northern Iowa
Cedar Falls, Iowa

Mrs. MARGARET H. MILLER
Supervisor, Elementary Libraries
City of Los Angeles Public Schools
Los Angeles, California

Mrs. PRISCILLA L. MOULTON
Director, School Library Service
Brookline, Massachusetts

Mrs. ALICE C. RUSK
Director of Library Services
Baltimore City Public Schools
Baltimore, Maryland

Mrs. MARION W. STOER
Librarian, Carney Elementary School Library
Baltimore County, Maryland

Miss OLIVIA R. WAY
Librarian, Ridge Elementary School Library
Ridgewood, New Jersey

Advisory-Steering Committee

ALA Editorial Committee Subcommittee on New Lists for School Libraries

ELEANOR AHLERS
Associate Professor
School of Librarianship
University of Washington
Seattle, Washington

LEILA A. DOYLE
Library Consultant
Gary Public Schools
Gary, Indiana

Mrs. MARY FRANCES K. JOHNSON
Assistant Professor
School of Education
University of North Carolina
Greensboro, North Carolina

DOROTHY McGINNISS
Associate Professor
School of Library Science
Syracuse University
Syracuse, New York

Mrs. DELLA THOMAS
Librarian, Curriculum Laboratory and
    Associate Professor of Library Science
Oklahoma State University
Stillwater, Oklahoma

JOHN ROWELL, *Chairman*
Director, Jennings-Lubrizol Program
    for School Libraries
School of Library Science
Case Western Reserve University
Cleveland, Ohio

Preface

Purpose. BOOKS FOR ELEMENTARY SCHOOL LIBRARIES: AN INITIAL COLLECTION is designed as a buying guide to a quality collection of books for initial library service to elementary pupils in kindergarten through eighth grade. It is closely geared to the elementary school curriculum and to the needs and interests of children. All books included in the list are recommended for first purchase to establish a first-year collection in new school libraries, and for addition to existing library collections. The list is not intended to describe a collection meeting minimum standards, but to provide a foundation upon which such a collection can be built.

Scope. Approximately 3080 books, with brief descriptive annotations and the most recent buying information, are listed. From the experience and recommendations of practicing school librarians, it has been found that at least 3000 separate titles are needed to give reasonably good support to the curriculum during the first year of the library's development, and that it is feasible to acquire and organize 3000 books within the library's first year of operation. The list is retrospective, but includes also many excellent recent publications. All books were in print at the time of the cut-off date, July 1, 1968.

Because this buying guide has been planned to cover the elementary curriculum in general, and not programs for exceptional students, emphasis is on books of general usefulness. However, many titles which can be used by beginning readers, children with reading problems, gifted students, and other special groups are included on the list, with notes to indicate their particular uses. Foreign-language books have been included only if they seem to be suitable for independent reading by pupils with considerable proficiency in the languages represented, or if they can be recommended for use by librarians and teachers with pupils. In the opinion of foreign-language teachers as well as of the selectors, books for foreign-language instruction are best selected by teachers to meet the particular requirements of their programs.

Excluded from this list are books out of print at the time of compilation, professional books to be used by teachers only, periodicals, pamphlets, and audio-visual materials. The editor and consultants endorse the American Association of School Librarians' concept of the school library as the center for all educational media; for a list of selection aids for nonprint materials and for aids helpful in building the book collection beyond this list, the reader is referred to the bibliography, "Professional Tools for Building Book Collections," on page 253. It is recommended that schools which include grades 7–8 supplement this buying guide with secondary lists, such as those named in the bibliography.

Books in this list are primarily hardbound editions; paperbacks are included only if hard-cover editions are not available. The selectors emphasize, however, that this policy is not to be interpreted as failure to recognize the value of paperbacks as a useful and economical type of material for the school library. The decision to give preference to hardbound books is based on the belief that a foundation collection should be durably bound. Since the purchase of multiple copies is a matter to be determined by the needs of the individual school, no recommendation is made on that point.

Curriculum Correlations. Examination of comprehensive curriculum studies and of curriculum guides from many parts of the country reveals the widest variation in content and method. Though there is little uniformity in curriculum offerings at stated levels, several trends in curriculum development in the elementary school seem fairly general. Among the most conspicuous are:

A shift from the deductive to the inductive method of learning, with greater emphasis on the discovery method and, therefore, on such techniques as observation, exploration, and drawing conclusions from valid evidence

The assumption that children can grasp abstract ideas if related to their own experience and that an understanding of abstraction at lower levels is essential to understanding at later levels

A filtering downward of subjects traditionally taught as disciplines in the upper grades and junior high school (for example, sociology, anthropology, archaeology, and economics)

An attempt to broaden the narrow Western viewpoint through better understanding of other countries and other cultures

Greater attention to literature, music, the arts, and other humanistic studies, to correct the imbalance in the curriculum resulting from recent emphasis on mathematics, technology, and science

Inclusion of additional courses on the duties and responsibilities of citizens in a democracy

More extensive consideration for individual differences in learning interests and capabilities, with greater opportunities for experimentation and independent study

Increasing acceptance of a curriculum content which reflects the diversity of knowledge as well as the tremendous growth in the amount of knowledge.

Because current offerings and experiments in the elementary curriculum vary so widely, materials to support the curriculum must be widely varied. Thus this list reflects both traditional content and newer trends. Such areas of current interest as the problems of minority groups and the inner city, the pressures of increasing populations, the pollution of air and water, and the effects of technology on employment have been recognized wherever suitable material could be found. Because simple concepts of complex subjects are frequently introduced in the primary grades and followed by more complex concepts in the middle and upper grades, many subjects are represented by books on several levels of difficulty.

Criteria. Choosing some 3080 books from the many thousands available was a difficult task. General criteria for evaluating the books were those familiar to all school and children's librarians: *excellence in literary quality and content,* offering positive values in terms of information and pleasure, and having ideas or facts that broaden children's understanding and knowledge; *suitability* of the subject matter, conceptual level, writing style, and treatment to the reader for whom the book is intended; *appeal* to the imagination and interest of the intended reader; *appropriateness of format,* in terms of attractiveness in design, artistic quality and aptness of illustrations, print and type size, satisfactory reproduction, and durability of paper and binding; and *inclusion in other standard selection aids,* not as a requirement for inclusion in this list but as recommendations by other specialists in children's books. To these criteria were added appropriateness to the purposes of this list and possibilities for support of the curriculum.

Additional criteria were applied for special types of literature and books in certain areas. Books for primary grades include those judged to have particular appeal for children in grades K–3 because of content, illustrations, or presentation. Some books in this group are intended for independent reading, others for use in storytelling or reading aloud; all were selected as the best in their respective groups.

Fiction was judged on the basis of children's interests, lively plot, excellent characterization, and literary quality. Adaptations of classic works (for example, *Little Women, Alice's Adventures in Wonderland,* and *Treasure Island*) were rejected in the belief that children should wait until they are ready to read the original versions, or that they should be introduced to the books through storytelling, reading aloud, or listening to recordings. Retellings of folk literature, however, have been accepted if the versions reflect the spirit of the age to which they belong and if the literary style of the retelling is acceptable. Wherever several editions of the same story were available, one or more of the editions considered best have been included.

Books in subject areas were judged for timeliness, accuracy, organization, and effectiveness and clarity of presentation. Books on several levels of reading difficulty were included wherever they were considered to be useful, but every effort was made to avoid those books in which oversimplification resulted in misleading concepts or loss of worthwhile content. In the opinion of the selectors, difficult concepts can sometimes be introduced more effectively through audio-visual materials than through oversimplified books. In all areas, inviting appearance and study aids (charts, diagrams, illustrations, indexes, and bibliographies) were considered valuable.

Sensitive subjects are represented by titles which present facts objectively and encourage attitudes of open-mindedness and intelligent inquiry. Books on religion emphasize the historical and factual aspects of the major religious faiths, without any attempt to influence the beliefs of the reader; racial and national minorities are presented as having the same worth and importance as more numerous groups; books on other countries stress understanding and appreciation of cultures other than our own. Books on sex present in an objective and dignified style the facts necessary to help boys and girls understand and respect their own bodies and to develop wholesome relationships with other young people.

Balance and Distribution. The editor regrets the necessity for omitting many fine books which could not be included within the limitations imposed by the purposes of this list. It must be recognized that for *a total but minimal collection of books which would make it possible to give initial library service to children in elementary schools (kindergarten through eighth grade)*, individual titles would need to be considered in relation to other titles available as well as to their own individual merits. Thus, not every subject need necessarily be represented by "a book" in order to be found in the collection, for material may be available variously, from coverage in a comprehensive reference work to a single-concept book. Where available materials could be recommended for school library purchase, their multiple values were considered favorably. Publishing gaps were left unfilled by marginal titles.

Balance was determined by many factors: frequent recurrence of a subject in the curriculum guides examined; availability of suitable materials; and usefulness of the materials as judged by the editor and the consultants. Distribution by grade levels is roughly 1000 books each for primary grades (K–3), intermediate grades (4–6), and upper grades (7–8). Grading is, of course, approximate and merely suggests the range of greatest usefulness of each title.

Arrangement. The titles are listed in a classified topical subject arrangement based on the Dewey Classification system. Since this list is intended as a buying guide to a *collection* of books, not as a cataloging aid or guide to shelf arrangement, considerable modifications were made in the Dewey scheme in order to bring books more closely together in groups according to their use in the curriculum. For example, all easy books with significant informational content have been grouped with other books on the same subjects; books on geography and history have been listed together by country instead of in two separate classes; pure and applied sciences have been combined; and books on holidays—whether story collections, plays, poetry, or other forms—have been grouped together. The many books equally useful in more than one area have been placed according to the best judgment of the editor, with additional curriculum correlations brought out in the index.

Entry. Entry in the body of the list is under the name of the author as it appears on the title page, and entries are numbered consecutively from 1–3077. When, after the completion of the manuscript, an occasional title was deleted or added, the corresponding number was omitted or a small-letter "a" was added to the previous number in order to insert the additional title in its proper position.

Prices. Prices are as listed in *Books in Print, 1967*, except for books too recent to be included therein. Prices for both trade editions and reinforced library editions are given whenever both are listed in *Books in Print*.

Acknowledgments. The editor gratefully acknowledges indebtedness to the many people who have assisted in the preparation of this list, chief among whom are: Miss Pauline Cianciolo, Assistant to Director, Publishing Department, American Library Association, who has guided the development of the list from an idea to a finished product; and seven consultants who gave generously of their time and talents at every step of the way by helping to develop cri-

teria; suggesting titles and subjects to be included; checking preliminary lists; advising about arrangement, annotating, and indexing; attending meetings and participating in the lively discussions which preceded decisions; and, most importantly, giving moral support and encouragement to the editor: Miss Mary Phyllis Brine, Miss Mary K. Eakin, Mrs. Margaret H. Miller, Mrs. Priscilla L. Moulton, Mrs. Alice C. Rusk, Mrs. Marion W. Stoer, and Miss Olivia R. Way.

Sincere thanks go also to the following assistants, who were indispensable to the preparation of the list: Mrs. Sara Claytor, Miss Barbara Moss, and Mrs. June Marr for cheerful and efficient preliminary typing and filing; Mrs. Myrta Neiheiser for painstakingly typing the final manuscript.

ELIZABETH D. HODGES

Contents

Contents

Symbols Used in This List

P   Primary level; suitable for use by and with pupils in grades K–3

I   Intermediate level; suitable for use by and with pupils in grades 4–6

U   Upper level; suitable for pupils in grades 7–8 and for advanced pupils in grade 6

R2–3, R3–4, etc. Suggested independent reading level as indicated in one or more of five lists of books tested for readability by reading specialists

Key to Abbreviations

arr.	arranged, arranger
comp.	compiled, compiler
diags.	diagrams
ed.	edited, edition, editor
enl.	enlarged
front.	frontispiece
illus.	illustrations, illustrated
introd.	introduced, introduction
K	Kindergarten
lib.	library
p.	pages
photos.	photographs
Pr.	Press
rev.	revised
sel.	selected, selector
tr.	translated, translator
unp.	unpaged
v.	volume, volumes

Reference Books

The following books are recommended as a minimum for ready reference during the first year of an elementary library's operation and as a foundation upon which a strong reference collection can be built. Each broad area of the curriculum is represented by one or more titles, supplemented by books in the circulating collection.

Encyclopedias and English-language dictionaries are listed in order of difficulty, other books alphabetically by author.

Encyclopedias

1   **New Book of Knowledge:** The Children's Encyclopedia. Grolier, 1966. 20v. $149.50. (P–I)

Contemporary educational content geared to the curriculum and interest needs of pupils in upper primary and intermediate grades. Controlled readability, inviting page make-up, colorful and informative illustrations, clear type. Alphabetical arrangement by subject with Fact-Index in each volume; bibliographies in a separate volume.

2   **Compton's Pictured Encyclopedia and Fact-Index.** Compton. 15v. $117. (I–U)

Long articles on broad subjects arranged alphabetically. Fact-Index in each volume analyzes smaller subjects and related material from all volumes, and gives brief information on subjects not entered in the body of the set. Text is written on varying levels of difficulty, providing the information needed at particular age and grade levels where the subject or interest usually arises. Maps, study outlines, bibliographies, and many illustrations. Continuous revision. Issued annually and supplemented by yearbook.

3   **World Book Encyclopedia.** Field Enterprises. 20v. $114. (I–U)

A comprehensive, general encyclopedia with text adapted to anticipated grade use.

Alphabetically arranged by short subjects, with many cross references and lists of related subjects. Bibliographies, outlines of longer articles, excellent maps, and numerous illustrations of many types. Continuous revision; issued annually and supplemented by yearbook. A Reading and Study Guide is available to schools.

4   **Lincoln Library of Essential Information** . . . rev. with each new printing. Frontier Pr. 2v. $39.50 (I-U)

Compact information on many subjects, arranged in 12 major subject fields with a detailed index in each volume. Includes maps, illustrations, tables, and bibliographies.

5   **Collier's Encyclopedia;** with Bibliography and Index. Crowell-Collier. 24v. $199.50. (U)

General encyclopedia presenting clearly and in attractive form accurate information on subjects most likely to be of interest to young people and adults in school, home, and work situations. Bibliographies, illustrations, maps, and a detailed index. Continuous revision; issued annually and supplemented by yearbook.

Dictionaries

6   **Webster's New World Dictionary.** elementary ed. World, 1961. 808p. $4.50. (I)

Approximately 45,000 words and 1700 pictures in one alphabetical arrangement. Open page, large print, clear definitions emphasizing modern usage.

7   World Book Dictionary. Field Enterprises, 1966. 2v. $50.20. (I–U)
Defines 180,000 words, with common meanings first; includes usage notes, word history, and illustrative phrases and sentences; employs pronunciation key adapted from the International Phonetic Alphabet. Includes sections on dictionary use, vocabulary study, and communication skills. Large, clear print; many illustrations.

8   American College Dictionary. Random, 1962. 1444p. $5.75; thumb-indexed $6.75. (U)
More than 132,000 words, including some 60,000 technical and scientific terms. Common meanings given first, usage levels indicated. Modified textbook pronunciation key at the bottom of each page; large, clear print; numerous small illustrations. Revised annually.

9   Webster's Third New International Dictionary of the English Language; unabridged. Merriam, 1961. 2662p. $47.50. (U)
Defines, pronounces, and illustrates usage of 450,000 entries, including 100,000 new words and new meanings. Presents language as living and flexible; omits labels indicating levels of acceptability.

10   Cassell's Spanish Dictionary: Spanish-English, English-Spanish. Funk & Wagnalls, 1960. 1477p. $7.50; thumb-indexed $8.50. (U)

11   New Cassell's German Dictionary: German-English, English-German. Funk & Wagnalls, 1962. 2v. in 1. $7.50; thumb-indexed $8.50. (U)

12   Larousse Modern French-English Dictionary. McGraw-Hill, 1960. 2v. in 1. $8.95. (U)
Includes an English-French Dictionary.

Annuals

13   Information Please Almanac. Simon & Schuster. Annual. $2.95. (I–U)
An up-to-date compilation of miscella-

neous facts and a review of important events for each year. Arranged in general classes and indexed by subject.

14   U.S. Government Organization Manual. Govt. Print. Off. Annual. $1.75. (I–U)
The official source book about the organization and functions of all branches of the United States government and their agencies. Gives names of officials and brief facts about their duties and responsibilities. Includes text of the U.S. Constitution.

15   World Almanac and Book of Facts. Newspaper Enterprise Assn.; for sale by Doubleday. Annual. $2.95; thumb-indexed $3.95; paper $1.75. (I–U)
Statistics and general miscellaneous information, including a summary of the year's events in every major field. Up-to-date, useful handbook, with alphabetical index in front.

Atlases

16   American Heritage. The American Heritage Pictorial Atlas of United States History. American Heritage, 1966. 424p. $16.50. (I–U)
Maps, charts, and contemporary prints are combined with authoritative text to illuminate American history from prehistoric times to the present. Special features are portfolios of colored maps and pictures showing battles of the Revolution and the Civil War, national parks, and nineteenth-century cities. Texts, maps, and illustrations are indexed.

17   Goode, John Paul. Goode's World Atlas. 12th ed. Rand McNally, 1964. 288p. $9.95. (I–U)
Political maps of the world plus more than 100 special maps showing products, resources, imports, exports, etc. Includes glossary of foreign geographical terms and a pronouncing index.

18   Odyssey World Atlas. Odyssey, 1966. 317p. $19.95. (U)
A new atlas with latest statistics and maps showing recently independent countries. The uncluttered, easily read maps include many small places, located through an index of 105,000 entries. Lists of largest countries, principal mountains, and other comparative information given in the appendix.

19 **World Book Atlas.** Field Enterprises, 1964. 392p. $19.95. (I–U)
Maps and geographical data for all countries of the world and for the states of the United States; also, space maps; star charts; railway, airline, and highway maps; and a travel guide. Includes index, table of abbreviations, glossary, and instructions for use.

Philosophy and Religion

20 **Bible.** The Holy Bible; containing the Old and New Testaments . . . Authorized King James Version. Oxford Univ. Pr. Prices vary. (I–U)

21 **Life** (Periodical). The World's Great Religions; by the editorial staff of Life. Special edition for young readers. Golden Pr., 1958. 192p. $4.95. (I–U)
Covers in condensed form the history, beliefs, and rituals of six major religions, with excerpts from religious writings and 200 photographs in brilliant color.

Social Studies

22 **Bailard, Virginia,** and **McKown, Harry C.** So You Were Elected! 3d ed. McGraw-Hill, 1968. 264p. $4.75; lib. ed. $4.24 net. (I–U)
Simplification of parliamentary procedures, intended especially for use in school clubs.

23 **Douglas, George William.** The American Book of Days: A Compendium of Information about Holidays, Festivals, Notable Anniversaries and Christian and Jewish Holy Days with Notes on Other American Anniversaries Worthy of Remembrance. 2d ed. rev. Wilson, 1948. 697p. $8. (I–U)
Arranged month by month and day by day. Indexed and illustrated.

24 **Gorsline, Douglas.** What People Wore: A Visual History of Dress from Ancient Times to Twentieth Century America. Viking, 1953. 266p. $10. (I–U)
Pictorial history of costume to 1925 with brief text and pictures reproduced from authentic sources. Especially good for information about cowboy and frontier dress.

25 **Post, Elizabeth L.** The Emily Post Book of Etiquette for Young People. Funk & Wagnalls, 1967. 238p. $5.95. (I–U)
Broad guidelines to behavior and personal development, reflecting the changing concepts about what is correct. Commonsense advice on everyday manners, grooming, correspondence, dating, travel, and entertaining. Indexed.

Pure and Applied Sciences

26 **Austin, Oliver L.** Birds of the World: A Survey of the Twenty-Seven Orders and One Hundred and Fifty-Five Families; illus. by Arthur Singer; ed. by Herbert S. Zim. Golden Pr., 1961. 316p. $14.95. (I–U)
Explains the origin and evolution of birds, their distribution, life histories, behavior, and relationships to one another and to their environments. Illustrated with colored pictures and with range and migration maps.

27 **Caidin, Martin.** The Man-in-Space Dictionary: A Modern Glossary. Dutton, 1963. 224p. $6.95. (I–U)
Brief definitions of nearly 2000 terms used in space travel, space medicine, and astronomy. Illustrated with photographs and drawings.

28 **Compton's Dictionary of the Natural Sciences.** Compton, 1966. 2v. $24.94. (I–U)
Part I identifies, defines, describes, and illustrates 2360 alphabetically arranged terms from 11 fields of earth and life sciences; Part II consists of 17 charts and tables on such subjects as classification of plants and animals, breeds of animals, and metallic elements; Part III is an index to the entire work, with definitions of some terms not included in Part I. Outstanding for coverage, clarity, and many colored illustrations.

29 **Comstock, Anna Botsford.** Handbook of Nature-Study. 24th rev. ed. Comstock, 1939. 937p. $6.75; text ed. $5. (I–U)
A comprehensive source of information on all aspects of nature study. Many maps and illustrations.

30 **Hegner, Robert.** Parade of the Animal Kingdom. Macmillan, 1935. 675p. $8.95. (I–U)
A popular survey of all forms of animal

life, organized by representative groups. Includes photographs, drawings, glossary, and suggestions for further reading.

31   **Macmillan Wild Flower Book;** descriptive text by Clarence J. Hylander. Macmillan, 1954. 480p. $9.95. (I–U)
Handsome colored illustrations of more than 400 wild flowers, arranged by families and described in brief text, with an identification guide in the appendix.

32   **Pearson, Gilbert T.** Birds of America. Doubleday, 1936. 3v. in 1. $8.95. (I–U)
Concise text organized by bird families and illustrated with numerous colored photographs and reproductions of bird pictures in the New York State Museum. Pictures of bird nests and bird eggs in actual size and color are useful for identification.

33   **Petrides, George A.** A Field Guide to Trees and Shrubs . . . Houghton, 1958. 431p. $4.50. (U)
Trees, shrubs, and woody vines of the Northeastern and North Central United States and Southeastern and South Central Canada are briefly described and shown in clear illustrations.

34   **Red Cross. U.S. American National Red Cross.** First Aid Textbook; prepared by the American National Red Cross for the instruction of first aid classes. 4th ed. rev. 249p. Doubleday, 1957. $1. (I–U)
Explicit instructions and clear illustrations for emergency procedures recommended by the Red Cross.

35   **Rombauer, Irma S.,** and **Becker, Marion Rombauer.** The Joy of Cooking. Bobbs-Merrill, 1962. 852p. $5.95. (I–U)
More than 4300 recipes and many reference features, such as nutrition, calorie charts, advice on table settings, and entertaining. Clear text and tested procedures. Fully indexed.

The Arts

36   **Concise Oxford Dictionary of Opera.** Oxford Univ. Pr., 1964. 446p. $6.50. (U)
Brief information on composers, librettists, conductors, performers, themes, and plots.

37   **Janson, H. W.,** and **Janson, Dora Jane.** The Story of Painting for Young People, from Cave Painting to Modern Times; with 245 reproductions including 32 in full color. Abrams, 1962. 259p. $5.95. (I–U)
Includes seldom-reproduced paintings as well as familiar masterpieces, chosen for appeal to children and young people. The discussion which interprets each painting's meaning and place in the history of art is scholarly yet concrete and simple.

38   **Scholes, Percy A.** The Oxford Junior Companion to Music. Oxford Univ. Pr., 1954. 435p. $6.75. (I–U)
Adapted from *The Oxford Companion to Music.* Brief articles on musicians, instruments, musical terms, and other topics of interest to young musicians. British emphasis. Includes a pronouncing glossary.

Sports and Recreation

39   **Hindman, Darwin A.** Complete Book of Games and Stunts. Prentice-Hall, 1956. 464p. $6.95. (I–U)
Book I, Indoor Games and Stunts; Book II, Active Games. Approximately 2000 games for all ages.

40   **Hunt, Sarah Ethridge.** Games and Sports the World Around. 3d ed. Ronald, 1964. 271p. $5. (I–U)
Games, sports, and play for developing an understanding of human relationships. Each activity is prefaced with headings indicating age level, number of players, playing area, necessary equipment, type, and intellectual appeal. Addressed to teachers and recreation leaders, but useful also to pupils.

41   **Menke, Frank G.** The Encyclopedia of Sports. 3d ed. rev. Barnes, 1963. 1044p. $15. (I–U)
Historical and current information about all major sports.

42   **Reinfeld, Fred.** A Catalogue of the World's Most Popular Coins. rev. ed. Doubleday, 1965. 288p. $7.50. (I–U)
Lists ancient and modern coins most in demand by collectors and readily available.

43   **Scott Publications, Inc.** Scott's Stan-

dard Postage Stamp Catalogue. 2v. in 1. Scott Publications, Inc. Annual. $12. (I–U)
Gives date of issue, color, shape, and value of all stamps ever printed.

Literature and Language

44   **Bartlett, John,** comp. Familiar Quotations. 13th and centennial ed. completely rev. Little, 1955. 1614p. $10. (U)
Passages from ancient and modern literature arranged chronologically by author. Indexed by key words.

45   **Benét, William Rose,** ed. The Reader's Encyclopedia: An Encyclopedia of World Literature and the Arts. 2d ed. Crowell, 1965. 1118p. $8.95; thumb-indexed $10. (I–U)
Brief definitions and articles, alphabetically arranged and illustrated. Includes plots, themes, biographical information, and nicknames. Emphasis is on literature, but music, art, and history are also covered.

46   **Bernstein, Theodore M.** The Careful Writer: A Modern Guide to English Usage. Atheneum, 1965. 487p. $7.95. (U)
A concise manual of more than 2000 alphabetized entries, covering use, meaning, grammar, punctuation, and style. Takes a middle position between the advocates of formal grammar and the structural linguists.

47   **Brewer's Dictionary of Phrase and Fable.** rev. ed. Harper, 1963. 970p. $7.50. (I–U)
A handbook of information on mythological and fictitious characters, abbreviations, authors, proverbs, etc., found in world literature. Alphabetically arranged.

48   **Brewton, John E.,** and **Brewton, Sara W.** Index to Children's Poetry. Wilson, 1942. 965p. $12; First Supplement. Wilson, 1954. 405p. $8; Second Supplement. Wilson, 1965. 453p. $10. (I–U)
A title, subject, author, and first-line index to poetry in collections for children and youth. Useful as a buying guide as well as for locating poems.

49   **Roget's International Thesaurus.** 3d ed. Crowell, 1962. 1258p. $5.95; thumb-indexed $6.95. (U)
A standard handbook to help the writer

or speaker locate the exact word needed. Contains 200,000 words and phrases, fully indexed.

50   **Sechrist, Elizabeth Hough,** comp. One Thousand Poems for Children. Macrae, 1946. 601p. $6.50. (I–U)
Divided into groups for younger and older children and subdivided by subject. Emphasis is on traditional poetry by the older poets. Indexed by author, title, and first line.

51   **Stevenson, Burton,** ed. The Home Book of Quotations: Classical and Modern; sel. and arr. by Burton Stevenson. 9th ed. Dodd, 1958. 2817p. $35. (I–U)
A subject arrangement of more than 70,000 quotations, indexed by author and leading words and phrases, with brief biographical information in the author index.

52   **Stevenson, Burton Egbert,** comp. The Home Book of Verse: American and English. 9th ed. Holt, 1953. 2v. 4013p. $30. (I–U)
An extensive collection arranged by broad subject. Indexed by author, title, and first line.

53   **Webster's Dictionary of Synonyms:** A Dictionary of Discriminated Synonyms, with Antonyms and Analogous and Contrasted Words. Merriam, 1951. 944p. $6. (I–U)
Alphabetical arrangement, with brief discussions and examples of correct use.

Mythology and Folklore

54   **Bulfinch, Thomas.** Bulfinch's Mythology: The Age of Fable; The Age of Chivalry; Legends of Charlemagne. Crowell, 1962. 992p. $5.95. (U)
A comprehensive source book of myths and legends.

55   **Guerber, H. A.** The Myths of Greece and Rome; rev. by Dorothy Margaret Stuart; with forty-nine reproductions from famous pictures and statues. London House, 1963. 957p. $4.75. (I–U)
A standard reference book for identification of names and allusions from classical mythology. Includes a genealogical table, a glossary, and an index.

Biography

56   Current Biography Yearbook. Wilson. Annual. $8. (I–U)

Biographical articles on important contemporary personalities compiled annually from monthly issues of *Current Biography* for the preceding year. A convenient source of information, much of which is not readily found elsewhere. Includes pronunciations of biographees' names, photographs, and brief bibliographies.

57   Fuller, Muriel, ed. More Junior Authors. Wilson, 1963. 235p. $6. (I–U)

Biographical or autobiographical sketches of 268 authors and illustrators of books for children and young people. Companion volume to *The Junior Book of Authors,* below.

58   Kunitz, Stanley J., and **Haycraft, Howard,** eds. The Junior Book of Authors. 2d ed. rev. Wilson, 1951. 309p. $6. (I–U)

Brief sketches, many autobiographical, of 289 authors and illustrators of children's books. Includes photographs and pronunciations.

59   Webster's Biographical Dictionary. Merriam, 1956. 1697p. $8.50. (I–U)

Lists and identifies more than 40,000 persons from all times and places. Pronunciations and concise biographies.

Geography and History

60   Webster's Geographical Dictionary. rev. ed. Merriam, 1962. 1352p. $8.50. (I–U)

An alphabetical arrangement of 40,000 place names, ancient and modern, with pronunciations and historical and geographical information.

61   Worldmark Encyclopedia of the Nations: A Practical Guide to the Geographic, Historical, Political, Social and Economic Status of All Nations, Their International Relationships and the United Nations System. 2d ed. Worldmark Pr., Harper, 1965. 5v. $49.95. (I–U)

Volumes are for the United Nations, Africa, The Americas, Asia and Australasia, and Europe. The volume on the United Nations is topically arranged and indexed; other volumes are alphabetically arranged by country.

Philosophy, Ethics, and Religion

62   Barnhart, Nancy. The Lord Is My Shepherd: Stories from the Bible Pictured in Bible Lands; arr. and illus. by Nancy Barnhart. Scribner, 1949. 263p. $5.95. (I–U)

Selections from the Old and New Testaments, retold with dignity and reverence and illustrated with black-and-white drawings.

63   Bible. Selections. Animals of the Bible; a picture book by Dorothy P. Lathrop; with text sel. by Helen Dean Fish from the King James Bible. Lippincott, 1937. 65p. $3.75; lib. ed. $3.59 net. (P–I)

Passages from the Bible describe animals mentioned in the Scriptures, and opposite pages show the animals and Holy Land flora in beautifully designed black-and-white pictures.

64   Bible. Selections. A First Bible; illus. by Helen Sewell. Walck, 1934. 109p. $4. (I–U)

Stories with special appeal for children, selected from the Old and New Testaments and presented in the words of the King James version. An excellent introduction to the Bible, enhanced by sensitive illustrations.

65   Bible. Selections. Small Rain: Verses from the Bible; chosen by Jessie Orton Jones; illus. by Elizabeth Orton Jones. Viking, 1943. unp. $3; lib. ed. $3.04. (P–I)

Verses from the Old and New Testaments reflecting the universal experiences of childhood, interpreted in pictures showing present-day children of all races in familiar situations.

66 **Bible.** Old Testament. Daniel. Shadrach, Meshach, and Abednego; from the Book of Daniel; illus. by Paul Galdone. McGraw-Hill, 1965. 32p. $2.75; lib. ed. $2.84 net. (P–I)

The story of the brave men who were thrown into the fiery furnace because they refused to obey King Nebuchadnezzar's command to kneel before an idol is dramatically illustrated in three colors. Text is from the King James Bible.

67 **Bible.** New Testament. Selections. The Christ Child; as told by Matthew and Luke; made by Maud and Miska Petersham. Doubleday, 1931. unp. $3.95. (P–I)

Beautiful illustrations by artists familiar with the Holy Land are combined with the Gospel text to make a distinguished picture book.

68 **Black, Algernon D.** The First Book of Ethics; drawings by Rick Schreiter. Watts, 1965. 66p. $2.65. (I–U)

The principles of right and wrong in human relationships are discussed in a thought-provoking treatment.

69 **Bowie, Walter Russell.** The Bible Story for Boys and Girls: New Testament. Abingdon, 1951. 160p. $3.50. (I–U)

Stories from the life of Christ told in dignified style and illustrated with colored plates and black-and-white drawings. Companion volume to *The Bible Story for Boys and Girls: Old Testament,* listed below.

70 **Bowie, Walter Russell.** The Bible Story for Boys and Girls: Old Testament. Abingdon, 1952. 224p. $3.50. (I–U)

Gives the history of Palestine before the birth of Christ and retells the stories of Abraham, Moses, Joseph, Esther, and other Old Testament characters. Illustrated with colored plates and black-and-white drawings. Companion volume and introduction to *The Bible Story for Boys and Girls: New Testament,* listed above.

71 **Branley, Franklyn M.** The Christmas Sky; illus. by Blair Lent. Crowell, 1966. unp. $3.75; lib. ed. $3.60 net. (I)

Basing his text on the annual Christmas show at New York's Hayden Planetarium, the author explains in simple language the various theories which astronomers have advanced to explain the Christmas star. A reverent and sensitive blend of religion and science. Appropriately illustrated in woodblock prints.

72 **De La Mare, Walter.** Stories from the Bible; illus. by Edward Ardizzone. Knopf, 1961. 420p. $4.95; lib. ed. $4.59 net. (I–U)

Thirty-four stories from the first nine books of the Bible retold in beautiful prose style. Included are stories of the Garden of Eden, Noah's Ark, and David and Goliath.

73 **De Regniers, Beatrice Schenk.** David and Goliath; illus. by Richard M. Powers. Viking, 1965. unp. $3.75; lib. ed. $3.59 net. (P–I)

Drawn from four books of the Bible, the story tells of David's encounter with the lion, the bear, and finally with the giant Goliath. Bold, colored illustrations match the drama of the story.

74 **Field, Rachel.** Prayer for a Child; pictures by Elizabeth Orton Jones. Macmillan, 1944. unp. $3.50; lib. ed. $3.24 net. (P)

In simple verses a child thanks God for the blessings of her small, safe world. Outstanding for freshness of expression and charm of illustrations.

75 **Fitch, Florence Mary.** One God: The Ways We Worship Him; photos. chosen by Beatrice Creighton. Lothrop, 1944. 144p. $3.50; lib. ed. $3.35 net. (I–U)

The beliefs and rituals of Judaism, Catholicism, and Protestantism are explained in reverent and objective text and illustrated with exceptionally fine photographs.

76 **Fitch, Florence Mary.** Their Search for God: Ways of Worship in the Orient; illus. with photos. sel. by Edith Bozyan, Beatrice Creighton, and the author. Lothrop, 1947. 160p. $3.50; lib. ed. $3.35 net. (I–U)

Five great religions of the East are described in a manner intended to help young people understand the people who follow them. Excellent photographs contribute to authenticity and attractiveness.

77 **Gaer, Joseph.** How the Great Religions Began. new and rev. ed. Dodd, 1956. 424p. $5. (U)

The history, beliefs, and rituals of 11

great religions told through the life stories of their founders.

78   **Jones, Jessie Orton.** This Is the Way: Prayers and Precepts from World Religions; chosen by Jessie Orton Jones; illus. by Elizabeth Orton Jones. Viking, 1951. 62p. $3.50;. lib. ed. $3.37 net. (P–I)

Prayers and precepts chosen to show likenesses in different religions and the universal need for worship, illustrated with pictures of small children of many lands. Though in picture-book format, the book will be useful to pupils in intermediate social studies classes.

79   **Palmer, Geoffrey.** Quest for the Dead Sea Scrolls; with illus. by Peter Forster. Day, 1965. 88p. lib. ed. $3.29 net. (U)

A lively account of the discovery of the 2000-year-old manuscripts, explaining what the scrolls are and their significance to religious history.

80   **Petersham, Maud,** and **Petersham, Miska.** Joseph and His Brothers; from the story told in the Book of Genesis. Macmillan, 1958. unp. $2.95. (P–I)

The familiar story retold with distinction and illustrated in color by the authors.

81   **Petersham, Maud,** and **Petersham, Miska.** Moses; from the story told in the Old Testament. Macmillan, 1958. unp. $2.50. (P–I)

The life story of Moses interpreted by colored pictures giving many background details.

82   **Petersham, Maud,** and **Petersham, Miska.** Ruth; from the story told in the Book of Ruth. Macmillan, 1958. unp. $2.50; lib. ed. $3.44 net. (P–I)

The Moabite Ruth who follows her husband's mother into the land of Judah is made very real in story and pictures.

83   **Smith, Ruth,** ed. The Tree of Life: Selections from the Literature of the World's Religions; with an introd. by Robert O. Ballou, and fourteen drawings by Boris Artzybasheff. Viking, 1942. 496p. $6; lib. ed. $5.63. (U)

Writings from the faiths of all times, showing how man has tried to explain the mysteries of creation and to establish a relationship with his Creator. Includes introductory notes and background material, a glossary, and an index.

Social Studies

Anthropology

84   **Baldwin, Gordon C.** Stone Age Peoples Today. Norton, 1964. 183p. $3.75; lib. ed. $3.48 net. (I–U)

Discusses the appearance, living conditions, and tribal organizations of 12 present-day peoples who have not advanced beyond the Stone Age. Illustrated with photographs.

85   **Clarke, Robin.** The Diversity of Man; with 28 plates, front. and 13 drawings by Elizabeth Winston. Roy, 1964. 62p. $3.25. (U)

An objective discussion of the relationship of climate to variations in skin color, body structure, hair, and other racial differences.

86   **Dickinson, Alice.** The First Book of Stone Age Man; pictures by Lorence Bjorklund. Watts, 1962. 82p. $2.65. (I)

Basing her story on archaeological research, the author describes the types of Stone Age men and reconstructs their world.

87   **Edel, May.** The Story of Our Ancestors; illus. by Herbert Danska. Little, 1955. 199p. $4.50. (I–U)

Describes how anthropologists have used fossil finds to piece together the story of man's evolution and discusses the various theories concerning the origin of man.

88   **Epstein, Sam,** and **Epstein, Beryl.** All about Prehistoric Cave Men; foreword by Carleton S. Coon; illus. by Will Huntington. Random, 1959. 137p. $2.50; lib. ed. $2.48 net. (I)

A readable account of the information gained about primitive peoples from archaeology and cave discoveries.

89   **Evans, Eva Knox.** All about Us; illus. by Vana Earle. Golden Pr., 1947. 95p. $3.95. (I)
An informal presentation of man's beginnings and development, explaining why different skin colors, languages, and customs have developed and stressing interracial understanding. (R2–3)

90   **Evans, Eva Knox.** People Are Important; illus. by Vana Earle. Golden Pr., 1947. 95p. $3.95. (I)
Explains differences in different races and nationalities, showing that what seems right to one group may seem strange to another and stressing that it is the people themselves—not their ways of doing things —that are important.

91   **Horizon Magazine.** The Search for Early Man; by John E. Pfeiffer and the eds. of Horizon Magazine. Consultant, Carleton S. Coon. American Heritage, 1963. American Heritage Junior Library, distributed by Harper. 153p. $4.95; lib. ed. $4.79 net. (U)
Describes the evidence of early man found by archaeologists and anthropologists in southern France and discusses the methods by which scientists reconstruct prehistory. Excellent photographs, paintings, drawings, and diagrams.

92   **Howell, F. Clark.** Early Man; by F. Clark Howell and the eds. of Life. Time, Inc., 1965. Life Nature Library, distributed by Silver Burdett. 200p. $4.95. (U)
A picture-history of man's development from earliest forms to modern man, with chapters on the "pioneers in prehistory," the tools of Stone Age man, and the present-day African bushmen. Illustrated with superb photographs, many in color, and with diagrams.

93   **Linton, Ralph,** and **Linton, Adelin.** Man's Way from Cave to Skyscraper; illus. by Raine Renshaw. Harper, 1947. 185p. lib. ed. $3.27 net. (U)
Broad coverage of man's origin and evolution, and of races, customs, and social organization.

94   **Mead, Margaret.** Anthropologists and What They Do. Watts, 1965. 209p. $3.95. (U)

A famous anthropologist explains the importance of anthropology, describes the work of anthropologists, and tells what students must do to prepare themselves for work in this field. Includes a glossary and a list for further reading.

95   **Mead, Margaret.** People and Places; illus. by W. T. Mars and Jan Fairservis and with photos. World, 1959. 318p. $5.95. (U)
Introduces the science of anthropology and shows what can be learned about man through the study of five groups: the Eskimo, the Plains Indian, the Balinese, the Minoans, and the Ashanti. Concludes by summarizing the ideas and needs common to all men and making a plea for world understanding and peace.

Negroes in American Society

96   **Bontemps, Arna.** 100 Years of Negro Freedom. Dodd, 1961. 276p. $4.25. (U)
Recounts the struggle of Negroes and their leaders to achieve the promise of the Emancipation Proclamation.

97   **Bontemps, Arna.** Story of the Negro; illus. by Raymond Lufkin. Knopf, 1958. 243p. lib. ed. $3.95 net. (I–U)
A history of the Negro in America from the beginning of slavery to the position of the Negro people in American life of the 1950's.

98   **Buckmaster, Henrietta.** Flight to Freedom: The Story of the Underground Railroad. Crowell, 1958. 217p. $3.75. (U)
An account of the formation and operation of the Underground Railroad by which so many slaves escaped to freedom, vitalized by fictionalized accounts of actual escapes. Includes information about the Abolitionist movement and biographical sketches of some of its leaders.

99   **Hughes, Langston,** and **Meltzer, Milton.** A Pictorial History of the Negro in America. new ed. rev. Crown, 1963. 337p. $5.95. (I–U)
A brief account of important people and events of Negro history.

100   **Johnston, Johanna.** Together in America: The Story of Two Races and One

Nation; illus. by Mort Kunstler. Dodd, 1965. 158p. $3.50. (I–U)

Discusses the contributions made by Negroes to the development of America and the attitudes toward the Negro in different parts of the country. Good background material for racial understanding.

101   Meltzer, Milton, ed. In Their Own Words: A History of the American Negro, 1619–1865. Crowell, 1964. 195p. $4.95. (U)

The first of a three-volume history of the American Negro, told through selections from speeches, letters, diaries, and other writings by Negroes. The author gives background and commentary for each selection, a calendar of Negro history to 1865, and an annotated list for further reading. Excellent reference material.

102   Meltzer, Milton, ed. In Their Own Words: A History of the American Negro, 1865–1916. Crowell, 1965. 180p. $4.95. (U)

103   Meltzer, Milton, ed. In Their Own Words: A History of the American Negro, 1916–1966. Crowell, 1967. 213p. $4.95. (U)

104   Schecter, Betty. The Peaceable Revolution. Houghton, 1963. 243p. $3.75. (U)

The influence of Thoreau and Gandhi on the nonviolent resistance movement in this country is discussed in an interestingly written account of protests against segregation and other injustices, prefaced by descriptions of protests in nineteenth-century Massachusetts and twentieth-century India.

Immigration and Emigration

105   Heaps, Willard A. The Story of Ellis Island. Seabury, 1967. 152p. $3.95. (U)

The history of Ellis Island from 1892 to 1932, when it was discontinued as the reception center for immigrants, is recounted in a lively narrative including interviews with immigrants who passed through the "Golden Door." Concludes with tables of statistics about immigration and a description of plans for making the island a historic monument.

106   Pei, Mario. Our National Heritage. Houghton, 1965. 183p. $2.95. (I–U)

An animated, thought-provoking discussion of the contributions of various ethnic groups to American life, emphasizing understanding and cooperation among all groups.

106a   Shippen, Katherine B. Passage to America: The Story of the Great Migrations. Harper, 1950. 211p. $3.50; lib. ed. $3.27 net. (U)

Comprehensive coverage of the nineteenth-century influx of people from other countries to the United States, discussing their reasons for leaving home, and how they changed this country and were changed by it.

Home and Community Life

FOOD AND COOKING

107   Ames, Gerald, and **Wyler, Rose.** Food and Life. Creative Educ. Soc., 1966. 144p. $5.95. (I)

A clearly written discussion of the sources of food, the nutritional values of various foods, and the necessity for conservation and research to ensure an adequate food supply for the world's burgeoning population. Fully illustrated.

108   Bendick, Jeanne. The First Book of Supermarkets; written and illus. by Jeanne Bendick. Watts, 1954. 40p. $2.65. (P–I)

A behind-the-scenes look at the big self-service stores, showing how they are organized and how they operate. (R3–4)

108a   Boyd-Orr, John. The Wonderful World of Food, the Substance of Life. Garden City, 1958. 67p. $2.95. (I)

A brief survey of food production, preservation, and distribution throughout the ages, including problems of nutrition and future food supply.

109   Buehr, Walter. Bread: The Staff of Life; written and illus. By Walter Buehr. Morrow, 1959. 80p. lib. ed. $2.94 net. (I)

An anecdotal history of bread from earliest times to the present: kinds of bread, baking methods, and the importance of bread to man.

110   Chapin, Cynthia. Dairyman Don; under the supervision of Jene Barr; pictures by Joe Rogers. Albert Whitman, 1964. unp. $1.95; lib. ed. $1.46 net. (P)

Easy-to-read text and bright pictures explain how milk and cheese products are produced and prepared for the market. (R2–3)

111 **Crocker, Betty.** New Good and Easy Cook Book; illus. by Rudi Trautman. Golden Pr., 1962. 192p. $1.95. (I–U)
Easy-to-prepare recipes based on the use of convenience foods. Organized in four parts: breakfast, lunch, dinner, and the fourth meal (between-meal snacks). Includes menus, useful charts, and helpful hints. Illustrated with color photographs and cartoons.

112 **Eberle, Irmengarde.** Basketful: The Story of Our Foods; illus. by Marion R. Kohs. Crowell, 1946. 256p. $3.95. (I)
A survey of all kinds of food, covering history, production, distribution, and modern methods of increasing or improving the food supply.

113 **Floethe, Louise Lee.** The Farmer and His Cows; with illus. by Richard Floethe. Scribner, 1957. unp. lib. ed. $3.31 net. (P)
Contrasts old and modern methods of operating a dairy farm in simple text and attractive colored illustrations.

114 **Hammond, Winifred.** Rice: Food for a Hungry World. Coward-McCann, 1961. 160p. $3.50. (I–U)
Gives the history of rice, its importance to the millions for whom it is the staple food, and methods of cultivating rice in different parts of the world.

115 **Joy, Charles R.** Race between Food and People: The Challenge of a Hungry World. Coward-McCann, 1961. 121p. $2.60. (I–U)
Shows how population growth is overtaking growth of the world's food supply and explores ways of providing sufficient food for the future. Illustrated with photographs.

117 **Perkins, Wilma Lord.** The Fannie Farmer Junior Cook Book. new and rev. ed. With illus. by Martha Powell Setchell. Little, 1957. 179p. $3.50. (I)
Standard recipes, based on those in the *Boston Cooking School Cook Book,* simplified and using inexpensive foods. Includes practical hints for the inexperienced cook.

118 **Perl, Lila.** Red-Flannel Hash and Shoo-Fly Pie: American Regional Foods

and Festivals; illus. by Eric Carle. World, 1965. 288p. $5.95. (I–U)
Explains why certain food specialties have developed in particular regions and tells the part which regional foods have played in the lives of the people. Includes typical recipes. Useful in the study of American history as well as in home economics classes.

119 **Riedman, Sarah R.** Food for People. rev. ed. Abelard-Schuman, 1961. 190p. $3.50. (I–U)
Primitive foods, food superstitions, and the development of modern ideas of nutrition through the work of many people, reviewed in readable text.

120 **Rombauer, Irma S.** A Cookbook for Girls and Boys; chapter headings by Marion Rombauer Becker. rev. ed. Bobbs-Merrill, 1952. 243p. $3.95. (I–U)
Defines cooking terms and processes, teaches correct methods of measuring and mixing, and gives hundreds of recipes for the new and the experienced cook.

121 **Scheib, Ida.** The First Book of Food; written and illus. by Ida Scheib. Watts, 1956. 65p. $2.65. (I)
Traces the development of food preservation by drying, canning, and freezing; describes present methods; and speculates about future developments.

122 **Schloat, G. Warren.** Milk for You. Scribner, 1951. 47p. lib. ed. $2.97 net. (P–I).
Clear photographs and brief text take the reader through the activities of a real milk farm: milking, testing, pasteurization, and distribution.

123 **Whitney, David C.** Let's Find Out about Milk; illus. by Gloria Gaulke. Watts, 1967. 48p. $2.65. (P)
The story of milk traced from the cow on the farm to milk products in the store. (R1–2)

124 **Zim, Herbert S.** Your Food and You; illus. by Gustav Shrotter. Morrow, 1957. 61p. $2.95; lib. ed. $2.94 net. (I)
The kinds and amounts of food needed for good health are briefly discussed. Includes charts, tables, and diagrams.

CLOTHING AND GROOMING

125 **Adler, Irving,** and **Adler, Ruth.** Fi-

bers. Day, 1964. 47p. lib. ed. $2.68 net. (I)
Natural and synthetic fibers are described and their manufacture and uses explained.

126   **Bendick, Jeanne,** and **Levin, Marcia O.** Pushups and Pinups; illus. by Jeanne Bendick. McGraw-Hill, 1963. 127p. $2.95; lib. ed. $2.96 net. (I–U)
Skin and body care, physical fitness, diets, and exercises for good health and good grooming.

127   **Bradley, Duane.** Sew It and Wear It; illus. by Ava Morgan. Crowell, 1966. 132p. $3.95. (U)
Clear directions and encouraging advice to beginning seamstresses for making simple garments without commercial patterns. Fundamental procedures are stressed in text and clear diagrams.

128   **Buehr, Walter.** Cloth from Fiber to Fabric; written and illus. by Walter Buehr. Morrow, 1965. 96p. lib. ed. $3.14 net. (I–U)
Presents the making of cloth from the first crude looms to a modern textile factory.

129   **Cavanna, Betty,** and **Harrison, George Russell.** The First Book of Wool. Watts, 1966. 60p. $2.65. (I)
Beginning with the animals which produce fleece, the author describes the processes of shearing, preparing wool for the loom, and weaving. Includes a glossary of words used in the wool trade.

130   **De Santis, Mallen.** Bubble Baths and Hair Bows: A Little Girl's Guide to Grooming; photographed by Martin Iger; Jean Ellen's clothes designed by Helen Lee. Doubleday, 1963. 63p. $3.50. (P)
Simple routines for cleanliness and good grooming are described and illustrated with attractive photographs.

131   **Glynne.** The American Girl Beauty Book; including answers to questions often asked by readers of The American Girl Magazine; illus. by J. Raymond Porter. Random, 1964. 186p. $1.95; lib. ed. $2.38 net. (I)
Common-sense advice to teens and pre-teens on grooming and personal hygiene.

132   **Leeming, Joseph.** The Costume Book; drawings by Hilda Richman. Lippincott, 1938. 123p. $4.95. (I–U)
Historical, folk, and fanciful costumes are described and illustrated, along with practical directions for making them. Use-

ful for history classes and for costuming plays and entertainments.

133   **Miller, Irene Preston,** and **Lubell, Winifred.** The Stitchery Book; drawings by Winifred Lubell. Doubleday, 1965. 96p. $4.95. (I–U)
Embroidery, from the Bayeux Tapestry to the present day, is the subject of a book including both history and explicit directions for basic stitches. Clear illustrations and suggestions for creative projects.

134   **Rogers, Matilda.** The First Book of Cotton; pictures by Mimi Korach. Watts, 1954. 68p. $2.65. (I)
The history and importance of cotton and its production and manufacture are discussed in a book useful in the study of clothing and of the southern states.

135   **Uggams, Leslie,** and **Fenton, Marie.** The Leslie Uggams Beauty Book. Prentice-Hall, 1966. 178p. $4.95. (U)
Good grooming, good health, charm, and manners for teen-age girls, with special hints for Negro girls.

136   **Wilcox, R. Turner.** Five Centuries of American Costume. Scribner, 1963. 207p. $6.50. (I–U)
Children's clothing, military uniforms, and everyday dress for each century in North and South America. Useful in history classes and for costuming plays.

137   **Wilson, Erica.** Fun with Crewel Embroidery. Scribner, 1965. 41p. $3.50; lib. ed. $3.41 net. (I–U)
Gives step-by-step instructions for embroidering with wool and suggests many simple articles which a beginner can design and make. Includes a chart of crewel embroidery stitches with instructions for working them. Many colorful illustrations.

SHELTER, ARCHITECTURE, BUILDINGS

138   **Adler, Irving,** and **Adler, Ruth.** Houses: From Caves to Skyscrapers. Day, 1964. 48p. lib. ed. $2.68 net. (P–I)
All kinds of houses in all times and places.

139   **Barr, George.** Young Scientist Looks at Skyscrapers: The How and Why of Construction for Sidewalk Superintendents; illus. by Mildred Waltrip. McGraw-Hill, 1963. 159p. $3.50; lib. ed. $3.06 net. (I–U)
All the steps in building a skyscraper,

from foundation to roof, are interestingly described and illustrated with informative drawings. Includes suggestions for home experiments to demonstrate the scientific principles involved in construction.

140   Bergere, Thea, and **Bergere, Richard.** From Stones to Skyscrapers: A Book about Architecture. Dodd, 1960. 91p. $3.50 net. (I–U)
A concise history of architecture from prehistoric to contemporary times, describing distinctive characteristics of different periods and places and commenting on the influences which shaped the various styles. Includes many clear line drawings and a glossary.

141   Bergere, Thea. Homes of the Presidents; illus. by Richard Bergere. Dodd, 1962. 94p. $3.50. (I–U)
The birthplace and family home of each President from Washington to Kennedy are briefly described and shown in detailed drawings. Includes the history of the White House and statistics about the Presidents.

142   Burns, William A. A World Full of Homes; pictures by Paula Hutchison. McGraw-Hill, 1953. 120p. $3.50; lib. ed. $3.06 net. (I–U)
Homes, from earliest times to the present, are described and illustrated. Special features include unusual homes, basic building materials, and directions for making models.

143   Downer, Marion. Roofs over America. Lothrop, 1967. 75p. $3.95; lib. ed. $3.70 net. (I–U)
Excellent full-page photographs show roofs of many styles, and the brief text explains the reason for each. Early American houses are shown, many parts of the country are represented, and modern roofs are included. A handsome book, useful for the study of architecture, art, and history.

144   Duggan, Alfred. The Castle Book; illus. by Raymond Briggs. Pantheon, 1961. 95p. lib. ed. $2.49 net. (I)
Reviews the origin and function of English castles from Norman times to their decline six centuries later, with emphasis on the castle as a fortress.

145   Hader, Berta, and **Hader, Elmer.** The Little Stone House: A Story of Building a House in the Country. Macmillan, 1944. unp. lib. ed. $3.94 net. (P)

When the Doe family decide to build a house themselves, they learn all the steps in its construction. So does the reader, through the story and handsome colored pictures. (R2–3)

146   Hiller, Carl E. From Tepees to Towers: A Photographic History of American Architecture. Little, 1967. 106p. $4.50 (U)
A chronological survey of architecture in the United States presented by more than a hundred photographs and brief text, noting Old World influences and the trends led by outstanding architects. Includes an illustrated glossary and an index of architects.

147   Hoag, Edwin. American Houses: Colonial, Classic, and Contemporary. Lippincott, 1964. 160p. $4.95. (U)
An overview of American domestic architecture showing how each style influences and is influenced by the way people live. Many excellent photographs. Useful as supplementary reading in American history.

148   Iger, Martin, and **Iger, Eve Marie.** Building a Skyscraper; photos. by Martin Iger. W. R. Scott, 1967. 72p. $4.50. (I)
Using a New York skyscraper as an example, the authors describe and illustrate basic steps in the construction of tall buildings. Each chapter explains one phase of the project, from foundation work to finishing. Includes a time chart and a glossary of construction terms.

149   Jackson, Kathryn. Homes around the World. Teaching suggestions: Alda Raulin. Silver Burdett, 1957. 144p. lib. ed. $2.04 net. (P)
The homes of children in all parts of the world are described and illustrated with photographs.

150   Lamprey, L. All the Ways of Building; illus. by Helène Carter. Macmillan, 1933. 304p. $5. (I–U)
A history of world achitecture with emphasis on the backgrounds out of which various styles grew.

151   Leacroft, Helen, and **Leacroft, Richard.** The Buildings of Ancient Egypt. W. R. Scott, 1963. 39p. $3.50. (I–U)
Family and community life among the Egyptians is revealed through descriptions and informative illustrations of their homes, tombs, and temples. Useful for the study of ancient civilizations.

152   **Leacroft, Helen,** and **Leacroft, Richard.** The Buildings of Ancient Greece. W. R. Scott, 1966. 40p. $3.50. (I–U)
Beautifully detailed drawings and clear text show the domestic and public architecture of Greece, from prehistoric times to 300 B.C., against a background of early Greek life.

153   **Wills, Royal Barry.** Tree Houses; with illus. by the author and Charles H. Crombie. Houghton, 1957. 66p. $3.50. (I)
Materials, tools, and plans for building two safe and comfortable tree houses are offered by a well-known architect.

ETIQUETTE

154   **Allen, Betty,** and **Briggs, Mitchell Pirie.** Mind Your Manners; illus. by Ann Atene. rev. ed. Lippincott, 1964. 262p. $4.25; lib. ed. $3.80 net. (U)
A teen-age etiquette book for school, home, and work. Includes chapters on choosing a vocational school or college.

155   **Beery, Mary.** Manners Made Easy. 3d ed. McGraw-Hill, 1966. 338p. $5.75; lib. ed. $4.72. (U)
A handbook of advice about correct social form and personal appearance, based on the assumption that good manners grow out of consideration for others. Includes a list for further reading.

156   **Bendick, Jeanne,** and **Warren, Marian.** What To Do: Everyday Guides for Everyone; illus. by Jeanne Bendick. McGraw-Hill, 1967. 160p. $3.95; lib. ed. $3.31 net. (I–U)
Common-sense advice in the form of "do's" and "dont's" on manners, getting along with the family, handling money, and correct behavior away from home. A simply written guide illustrated with cartoon-like drawings.

157   **Haupt, Enid A.,** ed. The Seventeen Guide to Your Widening World. Macmillan, 1965. 242p. $4.95. (U)
Advice for teen-age girls on budgets, behavior, boys, personality, appearance, party giving, and other vital matters. Agreeable style, modern tone.

158   **Joslin, Sesyle.** What Do You Do, Dear? Pictures by Maurice Sendak. W. R. Scott, 1961. unp. $2.75. (P)
A lighthearted guide to correct behavior for young ladies and gentlemen. Advice is made memorable by being presented in astonishing situations and humorous pictures.

159   **Joslin, Sesyle.** What Do You Say, Dear? Pictures by Maurice Sendak. W. R. Scott, 1958. unp. $2.75. (P)
Gives correct responses in such unlikely dilemmas as being introduced to a baby elephant or bumping into a crocodile.

160   **Leaf, Munro.** Manners Can Be Fun. rev. ed. Lippincott, 1958. 47p. $3.25; lib. ed. $3.11 net. (P)
The idea that "having good manners is really just living with other people pleasantly" is given a light touch in advice on proper behavior in many situations. Illustrated with humorous stick figures.

161   **Lee, Tina.** Manners To Grow On: A How-To-Do-Book for Boys and Girls; pictures by Manning Lee. Doubleday, 1955. 93p. $3.50. (I)
Advice on how to behave at home, in school, when visiting, and in public places is given in an informal manner. Many illustrations and an index add to the book's usefulness.

162   **Slobodkin, Louis.** Excuse Me! Certainly! Vanguard, 1959. unp. $2.95. (P)
A picture book in rhyme tells how "Willie White who was not polite" learned better manners. Amusing illustrations by the author. (R2–3)

163   **Slobodkin, Louis.** Thank You—You're Welcome. Vanguard, 1957. unp. $3.95. (P)
Jimmie gets tired of always saying "Thank you" and wants to say "You're welcome" sometimes. This rhymed story, humorously illustrated by the author, tells how he learned that one must earn the right to say "You're welcome." (R2–3)

CITY AND COUNTRY

164   **Gregor, Arthur S.** How the World's First Cities Began; illus. by W. T. Mars. Dutton, 1967. 64p. $3.75; lib. ed. $3.71 net. (I)
The gradual transition from wandering bands of hunters, to small farming villages, to the concentration of people in cities is traced in simple text and informative pictures.

165   **Howard, Robert West.** Farms. Watts, 1967. 64p. $2.65. (I)
Contrasts farm life today with farming in the past, emphasizing the changes brought about by modern machinery. Illustrated with photographs.

166   **Ipcar, Dahlov.** One Horse Farm. Doubleday, 1950. unp. $3.50. (P)
Big Betty faithfully did her share of the farm work until a tractor replaced her and she was retired. The author's striking illustrations in color bring farm scenes to life.

167   **Ipcar, Dahlov.** Ten Big Farms; written and illus. by Dahlov Ipcar. Knopf, 1958. unp. lib. ed. $3.29 net. (P)
A city family tours the country looking for a farm to buy. After seeing ten big specialty farms—poultry, fruit, dairy, tobacco, etc.—they decide to buy a small farm that has a little of everything. Text and bright pictures give a good idea of the diversity of farming.

168   **Lavine, David.** Under the City; photos. by Ira Mandelbaum. Doubleday, 1967. 128p. $3.50. (I–U)
The subterranean world of New York City is explored in informative text and remarkable photographs showing subways, telephone cables, bank vaults, and other underground marvels.

169   **Lenski, Lois.** The Little Farm. Walck, 1942. unp. $2.75. (P)
The author's realistic illustrations show Farmer Small doing all the daily and seasonal chores of farm routine. (R2–3)

170   **Schneider, Herman,** and **Schneider, Nina.** Let's Look under the City; illus. by Bill Ballantine. W. R. Scott, 1954. 70p. $2.75. (P–I)
A tour through the pipes and cables which bring water, electricity, and telephone service to the city and carry away its wastes. (R2–3)

171   **Schwartz, Alvin.** The Night Workers; photos. by Ulli Steltzer. Dutton, 1966. 64p. $3.95. (P–I)
The city employees who work at night are introduced in brief text and excellent photographs.

172   **Tensen, Ruth M.** Come to the City. Reilly & Lee, 1951. 37p. $2.95. (P)
Short sentences, large print, and many photographs give this book appeal for beginning readers studying about city life. (R2–3)

173   **Tensen, Ruth M.** Come to the Farm. Reilly & Lee, 1949. 35p. $2.95. (P)
Children visit a farm and talk to the animals. An easy-to-read photographic study of farm animals. (R2–3)

COMMUNITY AGENCIES AND HELPERS

174   **Barr, George.** Young Scientist and the Fire Department; illus. by Mildred Waltrip. McGraw-Hill, 1966. 143p. $3.50; lib. ed. $3.06 net. (I–U)
With the cooperation of the New York City Fire Department the author describes up-to-date methods of fire prevention and fire fighting, relates them to scientific principles, and gives rules for fire prevention and survival.

175   **Barr, George.** Young Scientist and the Police Department; illus. by Mildred Waltrip. McGraw-Hill, 1967. 176p. $3.95; lib. ed. $3.26 net. (I–U)
Explores the role of science in law enforcement, describes the well-trained policeman, and explains modern methods of traffic control and crime detection through the use of radar, television, computers, and medical analysis.

176   **Bartlett, Susan.** A Book To Begin on Libraries; illus. by Giola Fiammenghi. Holt, 1964. unp. $2.95; lib. ed. $2.92. (P–I)
Libraries, from ancient Nineveh's library of clay tablets to the libraries of today, are described in an enthusiastic introduction to the history and functions of an important community agency.

177   **Brewster, Benjamin.** The First Book of Firemen; pictures by Jeanne Bendick. Watts, 1951. unp. $2.65. (P)
Easy text and informative pictures introduce the fire department, describing the training, equipment, and duties of firemen and the methods used in fighting fires in the city, the country, the forest, and on the water. (R2–3)

178   **Buchheimer, Naomi.** Let's Go to a Post Office; illus. by Ruth Van Schiver. rev. ed. Putnam, 1964. 47p. lib. ed. $1.97 net. (P)
Follows mail through sorting, canceling, loading, and delivery.

179   **Chase, Francine.** A Visit to the Hospital; written by Francine Chase; pictures by James Bama. Prepared under the supervision of Lester L. Coleman, with an introd. by Flanders Dunbar. Grosset, 1957. 68p. $1.95; lib. ed. $2.59 net. (P)
Written to reassure the child facing a stay in the hospital, the book takes a visitor on a friendly tour of admission routines, preparation for an operation, and postoperative care.

180   **Coy, Harold.** The First Book of Hospitals; illus. with photographs. Watts, 1964. 81p. $2.65. (I)
Explains the work of each department of a modern hospital. Includes sources of career information and a glossary of hospital terms.

181   **De Leeuw, Adèle.** The Girl Scout Story; illus. by Robert Doremus. Garrard, 1965. 95p. $2.32. (P–I)
A simply written history of the Girl Scout movement, stressing its importance in promoting international good will. (R3–4)

182   **Grant, Bruce.** The Boy Scout Encyclopedia; text and illus. prepared under the direction of the Boy Scouts of America; illus. by Fiore and Jackie Mastri and William Timmins. new rev. ed. Rand McNally, 1965. 168p. $3.95. (I–U)
An alphabetically arranged guide to all Scout groups, from Cub Scouts to Explorers, and to their organization and activities.

183   **Greene, Carla.** Where Does a Letter Go? Illus. by Leonard Kessler. Harvey House, 1966. 45p. $2.75; lib. ed. $2.89 net. (P)
Traces the journey of a letter from California to Maine.

184   **Jackson, Kathryn.** Schools around the World; by Kathryn Jackson and others. Teaching suggestions: Alda Raulin. Silver Burdett, 1965. 160p. lib. ed. $2.13 net. (P–I)
Describes typical schools and school activities in the United States, Canada, Europe, Africa, the East, and Australia.

185   **Jupo, Frank.** Any Mail for Me? 5,000 Years of Postal Service; written and illus. by Frank Jupo. Dodd, 1964. 64p. lib. ed. $2.99 net. (I)
A lively survey from the days when couriers were condemned to death when the news was bad, through packet-boat and Pony Express service, to today's mechanized postal service.

186   **Landin, Les.** About Policemen around the World; pictures by Lucy and John Hawkinson. Melmont, 1964. 45p. $2.50. (P)
Simple text and clear pictures show how police uniforms, duties, and ways of working differ in different parts of the world. (R2–3)

187   **Lenski, Lois.** The Little Fire Engine. Walck, 1946. unp. $2.75. (P)
All the equipment of the fire department is featured in the author's bright pictures as Fireman Small goes about his work. (R2–3)

188   **Lenski, Lois.** Policeman Small. Walck, 1962. unp. $2.75. (P)
The author describes and illustrates a busy day in the life of traffic Policeman Small as he helps children across the street, leads a parade, directs traffic, and stops speeders. (R2–3)

189   **Miner, Irene.** The True Book of Policemen and Firemen; pictures by Irene Miner and Mary Salem. Childrens Pr., 1954. 44p. $2.50. (P)
An easy-to-read explanation of the training and work of these community helpers. (R2–3)

190   **Miner, O. Irene Sevry.** The True Book of Our Post Office and Its Helpers; pictures by Irene Miner and Mary Salem. Childrens Pr., 1955. 43p. $2.50. (P)
A simple account of postal service, intended for independent reading in primary grades. (R2–3)

191   **Shay, Arthur.** What Happens When You Mail a Letter? Reilly & Lee, 1967. unp. $2.95. (P)
Photographs and brief explanations make processing of mail interesting to primary children. Includes information on the Zip Code.

192   **Slobodkin, Louis.** Read about the Busman; illus. by Louis Slobodkin. Watts, 1967. 70p. $2.65. (P–I)
An amusingly illustrated story of the duties, past and present, of the bus driver, intended to encourage respect for an important community helper. (R2–3)

193   **Slobodkin, Louis.** Read about the

format and informal style should attract older slow readers.

244 **Purdy, Ken W.** Young People and Driving: The Use and Abuse of the Automobile; foreword by Stirling Moss. Day, 1967. 92p. $3.50. (U)

A practical guide to good driving and safety, covering characteristics of good and poor drivers, the effects of drinking on the driver, the responsibilities of the driver, and tips for handling an automobile in emergency situations.

245 **Shuttlesworth, Dorothy.** ABC of Buses; illus. by Leonard Shortall. Doubleday, 1965. unp. $3.25. (P)

All kinds of buses presented in rhymes and gay pictures.

246 **Stambler, Irwin.** Automobiles of the Future. Putnam, 1966. 95p. lib. ed. $3.29 net. (I–U)

Describes and illustrates experimental models being tested today and speculates on future developments in engineering and design. Photographs and labeled diagrams add information and interest.

247 **Stevens, Leonard A.** Trucks That Haul by Night; illus. by John Kaufmann. Crowell, 1966. unp. $3.50; lib. ed. $3.40 net. (P–I)

Simple text and clear drawings dramatize long-distance trucking from loading to delivery. Appealing to the automotive-minded and useful for the study of transportation and community helpers.

248 **Tunis, Edwin.** Wheels: A Pictorial History; written and illus. by Edwin Tunis. World, 1955. 96p. $5.95. (I–U)

A history of land transportation beginning with earliest use of the wheel and extending through modern vehicles. Emphasizes wagons, carriages, and coaches rather than the automobile and accompanies all types by detailed drawings.

AIR

249 **American Heritage.** The History of Flight; from the American Heritage History of Flight; by the eds. of American Heritage, The Magazine of History . . . Adapted for young readers by Sarel Eimerl. Golden Pr., 1964. 102p. $3.95. (U)

An informative and profusely illustrated review of man's efforts to fly, with emphasis on military rather than on commercial aviation.

250 **Burchard, Peter.** Balloons: From Paper Bags to Skyhooks; designed and illus. by the author; with photos. Macmillan, 1960. 48p. $1.95; lib. ed. $3.27 net. (I)

An introduction to ballooning, from eighteenth-century experiments to the space balloon, illustrated with drawings and photographs.

251 **Colby, Carroll B.** Jets of the World: New Fighters, Bombers, and Transports. new rev. ed. Coward-McCann, 1966. 48p. lib. ed. $2.68 net. (I–U)

Commercial and military jets are briefly described and illustrated with photographs.

252 **Delear, Frank J.** The New World of Helicopters; illus. with photos. Dodd, 1967. 80p. $3; lib. ed. $2.79. (I–U)

Discusses the history of the helicopter, the principles on which it operates, and its usefulness in peace and war.

253 **Feravolo, Rocco V.** Junior Science Book of Flying; illus. by Denny McMains. Garrard, 1960. 65p. $2.19. (P–I)

Simple text, large print, and uncomplicated illustrations and experiments give this explanation of the basic facts of flying an appeal for primary readers and older slow readers. (R3–4)

254 **Hyde, Margaret O.** Flight Today and Tomorrow; foreword by Glenn O. Blough; illus. by Clifford N. Geary. rev. ed. McGraw-Hill, 1962. 139p. $3.25; lib. ed. $3.01 net. (U)

Describes the parts of a plane, explains why a plane flies, and gives instructions on how to fly a plane. Includes a discussion of space flight and a list for further reading.

255 **Jacobs, Lou.** SST—Plane of Tomorrow: The Story of America's Supersonic Transport; foreword by J. C. Maxwell. Golden Gate, 1967. 95p. $3.95; lib. ed. $3.79 net. (I–U)

A photographic account of the supersonic transport, due for service in the 1970's, including problems of engineering, construction, and operation.

256 **Kettelkamp, Larry.** Gliders; written and illus. by Larry Kettelkamp. Morrow, 1961. 46p. $2.95; lib. ed. $2.94 net. (P–I)

Explains the principles of glider flight

and gives directions for making model gliders.

257   **Lenski, Lois.** The Little Airplane. Walck, 1938. unp. $2.75. (P)
Mr. Small takes his airplane on a flight, explained in a simple story and pictures by the author. (R2–3)

258   **Paust, Gil.** How a Jet Flies. Sterling, 1962. 72p. lib. ed. $2.99 net. (I–U)
An interesting discussion of jet propulsion: its history, scientific principles, advantages, and disadvantages.

259   **Richards, Norman.** Giants in the Sky. Childrens Pr., 1967. 141p. lib. ed. $5. (I–U)
An informal history of lighter-than-air craft, with chapters on the Graf Zeppelin, the Shenandoah, the Hindenburg, and other famous dirigibles, including sketches of the men who designed and flew them. Breezy, anecdotal style; many photographs.

SPACE

260   **American Heritage.** Americans in Space; by the eds. of American Heritage, The Magazine of History; author, John Dille; consultant, Philip S. Hopkins. American Heritage, 1965. American Heritage Junior Library, distributed by Harper. 153p. $4.95; lib. ed. $4.79 net. (I–U)
A history of rocket research and experimentation, beginning with Robert Goddard's work and extending through the flights of Project Mercury. Especially valuable for numerous illustrations, many in color.

261   **Asimov, Isaac.** Satellites in Outer Space; illus. by John Polgreen. rev. ed. Random, 1964. 61p. $1.95; lib. ed. $2.29 net. (P–I)
A simple but authoritative account of satellites from Sputnik to Apollo.

262   **Bendick, Jeanne.** The First Book of Space Travel; written and illus. by Jeanne Bendick. rev. and rewritten. Watts, 1963. 93p. $2.65. (I)
An introductory overview of space travel, well organized and illustrated with animated drawings.

263   **Bergaust, Erik.** Space Stations. Putnam, 1962. 48p. lib. ed. $2.68 net. (I)
Explains the need for space stations and surveys plans for space platforms and observatories. Includes information supplied by the National Aeronautics and Space Administration, many photographs, and a glossary.

264   **Bergwin, Clyde R.,** and **Coleman, William T.** Animal Astronauts: They Opened the Way to the Stars. Prentice-Hall, 1963. 207p. $4.95. (I–U)
Discusses the contribution which animals have made to space research and experiment.

265   **Bova, Benjamin.** The Uses of Space; illus. by George Giusti. Holt, 1965. 144p. $3.50; lib ed. $3.27 net. (I–U)
An enlightening discussion of a subject not adequately treated in most books on space—the reason for man's exploration of space and the benefits to be derived therefrom. Clear explanations supported by diagrams and photographs.

266   **Branley, Franklyn M.** A Book of Astronauts for You; illus. by Leonard Kessler. Crowell, 1963. unp. $3.95; lib. ed. $3.85 net. (P)
The testing, training, and performance of astronauts are presented in simple language, illustrated with drawings on almost every page. (R2–3)

267   **Branley, Franklyn M.** A Book of Moon Rockets for You; illus. by Bill Sokol. rev. ed. Crowell, 1964. unp. $3.95; lib. ed. $3.85 net. (P)
Author and artist combine their talents to present complex concepts to young children, explaining the purpose and mechanism of rockets and describing some of the experiments by which they are tested. (R2–3)

268   **Branley, Franklyn M.** Experiments in the Principles of Space Travel; illus. by Jeanyee Wong. Crowell, 1955. 119p. $3.50. (I–U)
Applies the basic laws of science to space travel to help pupils distinguish between fiction and fact about interplanetary travel. Suggests simple experiments requiring minimum equipment.

269   **Branley, Franklyn M.** Rockets and Satellites; illus. by Bill Sokol. Crowell, 1961. unp. $3.25; lib. ed. $2.96 net. (P)
Describes simply and clearly how rockets and satellites work and how they differ. (R2–3)

270   **Coombs, Charles.** Aerospace Pilot; illus. with photos. Morrow, 1964. 224p. $3.95. (U)

A review in story form of the training of a test pilot, for future astronauts and aviation enthusiasts. Authentic text and informative photographs.

271   **Coombs, Charles.** Lift-Off: The Story of Rocket Power; illus. by R. H. Foor. Morrow, 1963. 96p. $3.25; lib. ed. $3.14 net. (I)

Explains what rocket power is, reviews the history of rocketry, shows how rockets are designed and constructed, and considers the future of rocketry. Illustrated with diagrams and photographs.

272   **Coombs, Charles.** Project Apollo: Mission to the Moon; with 34 photographic illus. Morrow, 1965. 96p. $3.25; lib. ed. $3.14 net. (I)

Describes the three-part spacecraft designed to land on the moon and then reenter the earth's atmosphere, emphasizing the problems and planning of the enterprise.

273   **Freeman, Mae,** and **Freeman, Ira.** You Will Go to the Moon; illus. by Robert Patterson. Beginner Books, 1959. 54p. $1.95; lib. ed. $2.29 net. (P)

An introduction to space travel for the beginning reader. (R2–3)

274   **Hyde, Wayne.** The Men behind the Astronauts. Dodd, 1965. 128p. $3.50. (U)

Using the Mercury Project as an example, the author describes the work of the scientists, engineers, technicians, and others essential to the space program. Illustrated with photographs.

275   **Sasek, M.** This Is Cape Kennedy. Macmillan, 1964. 60p. $3.50; lib. ed. $3.74 net. (P–I)

The author's captioned pictures in color give an impressionistic view of the "Space Capital of the World."

276   **Stambler, Irwin.** Project Gemini. Putnam, 1964. 64p. $2.95; lib. ed. $2.86 net. (I–U)

Explains the need for rendezvousing capsules as an intermediate step between the Mercury and the Apollo projects, describes the design and construction of the Gemini capsule, and discusses the selection and training of the astronauts.

Holidays and Celebrations

277   **Anglund, Joan Walsh.** Christmas Is a Time of Giving. Harcourt, 1961. unp. $1.95. (P)

Expresses the true spirit of Christmas in terms a young child can understand. A tiny, simply written book with delicate, stylized illustrations by the author.

278   **Association for Childhood Education International.** Told under the Christmas Tree: Stories and Poems from around the World; selections by the Literature Committee of the Association for Childhood Education; illus. by Maud and Miska Petersham. Macmillan, 1948. 304p. $2.95; lib. ed. $3.74 net. (P–I)

Arranged in three parts: miscellaneous poems and stories; stories and poems about Christmas in many lands; and stories about Hanukkah and the Jewish Festival of Lights.

279   **Borten, Helen.** Halloween; written and illus. by Helen Borten. Crowell, 1965. unp. $2.95; lib. ed. $2.85 net. (P–I)

Explains the origin of Halloween customs and relates them to today's celebrations.

280   **Brewton, Sara,** and **Brewton, John E.,** comps. Birthday Candles Burning Bright: A Treasury of Birthday Poetry; decorations by Vera Bock. Macmillan, 1960. 199p. $3.95. (I)

Poetry to celebrate birthdays and the fun that goes with them. A useful collection of pleasant verse, suitable for reading aloud to younger children. Author, title, and first-line index.

281   **Brewton, Sara,** and **Brewton, John E.,** comps. Christmas Bells Are Ringing: A Treasury of Christmas Poetry; sel. by Sara and John E. Brewton; illus. by Decie Merwin. Macmillan, 1951. 114p. lib. ed. $3.74 net. (P–I)

Christmas shopping, the suspense of waiting for Santa Claus, decorating the house, the coming of the Christ Child, and the excitement of Christmas morning are the themes of poems in this well-organized and fully indexed anthology.

282   **Bulla, Clyde Robert.** St. Valentine's

Day; illus. by Valenti Angelo. Crowell, 1965. $2.95; lib. ed. $2.85 net. (P–I)

An attractively illustrated book giving the history of the holiday and telling how it is celebrated today.

283   **Cone, Molly.** Purim; illus. by Helen Borten. Crowell, 1967. unp. $2.95; lib. ed. $2.85 net. (P–I)

Through a simple retelling of the story of Esther, the author explains the origin and significance of Purim, followed by a description of the special foods and ceremonies with which the Jewish day of rest is celebrated.

284   **Cooney, Barbara.** Christmas; written and illus. by Barbara Cooney. Crowell, 1967. unp. $2.95; lib. ed. $2.85 net. (P–I)

The story of the Nativity and a description of the Christian and non-Christian legends and festivities related to the season, distinguished by beautiful illustrations featuring Christmas red and green.

285   **Dalgliesh, Alice,** comp. Christmas: A Book of Stories Old and New; illus. by Hildegard Woodward. Scribner, 1962. 244p. $3.50; lib. ed. $3.31 net. (I–U)

Poems as well as stories are included in this four-part anthology: Christmas Stories and Wonder Tales; The First Christmas; Christmas in Old-Time America; and Christmas in Other Lands.

286   **Dalgliesh, Alice.** The Fourth of July Story; illus. by Marie Nonnast. Scribner, 1956. unp. $3.25; lib. ed. $3.12 net. (P–I)

A compact and readable account of the writing and signing of the Declaration of Independence, intended to help children understand the significance of the Fourth of July holiday. Illustrated with full-page colored illustrations. (R2–3)

287   **Dalgliesh, Alice.** The Thanksgiving Story; with illus. by Helen Sewell. Scribner, 1954. unp. $3.25; lib. ed. $3.12 net. (P)

Follows the Hopkins family to America on the "Mayflower," through the hardships of the first year, to the joyous first Thanksgiving. Especially appealing to young children because of the simplicity of language, the dramatic pictures, and the children in the story. (R2–3)

288   **Eaton, Anne Thaxter,** comp. Welcome Christmas! A Garland of Poems; decorated by Valenti Angelo. Viking, 1955. 128p. $3.50; lib. ed. $3.37 net. (P–I)

A useful anthology of poems, old and new, expressing the meaning of Christmas. Indexed by author, title, and subject.

289   **Ehret, Walter.** The International Book of Christmas Carols; musical arrangements by Walter Ehret; tr. and notes by George K. Evans; illus. by Don Martinetti; foreword by Norman Luboff. Prentice-Hall, 1963. 388p. $13.95. (P–I–U)

A comprehensive collection of carols from many countries and an essay on Christmas music.

290   **Emberley, Ed.** The Parade Book; written and illus. by Ed Emberley. Little, 1962. 28p. $3.25; lib. ed. $3.14 net. (P)

Gay scenes from parades in celebration of Mardi Gras, the Chinese New Year, the Tournament of Roses, and others showing street decorations, marchers, and spectators.

291   **Epstein, Morris.** A Pictorial Treasury of Jewish Holidays and Customs. Ktav, 1959. 200p. $5.95. (U)

Jewish religious holidays, ceremonial occasions, and family customs are shown in authentic photographs.

292   **Fisher, Aileen.** Arbor Day; illus. by Nonny Hogrogian. Crowell, 1965. unp. $2.95; lib. ed. $2.85 net. (P–I)

Tells how a special day for planting trees is observed throughout the United States.

293   **Fisher, Aileen.** Holiday Programs for Boys and Girls. Plays, 1958. 374p. $5. (I–U)

A collection of easily produced, royalty-free plays, poems, readings, and recitations, suitable for classroom and assembly programs. Includes production notes.

294   **Gaer, Joseph.** Holidays around the World; drawings by Anne Marie Jauss. Little, 1953. 212p. $3.95. (I–U)

Introduces the world's five great religions by describing and comparing their holidays. Lists also holidays observed in the United States.

295   **Guilfoile, Elizabeth.** Valentine's Day; illus. by Gordon Laite. Garrard, 1965. 62p. $2.32. (P–I)

Information on the origin and celebration of Valentine's Day, attractively illustrated and easy to read. (R3–4)

296   **Harper, Wilhelmina,** comp. Easter Chimes: Stories for Easter and the Spring

Season; illus. by Hoot von Zitzewitz. new rev. ed. Dutton, 1965. 253p. $4.50; lib. ed. $4.45 net. (I)

A new edition of a serviceable anthology.

297 **Harper, Wilhelmina,** comp. Ghosts and Goblins: Stories for Halloween; illus. by William Wiesner. new rev. ed. Dutton, 1965. 250p. $4.50. (I–U)

Three stories and four poems have been added to this familiar anthology, now in a new format.

298 **Harper, Wilhelmina,** comp. Harvest Feast: Stories of Thanksgiving Yesterday and Today; illus. by W. T. Mars. new rev. ed. Dutton, 1965. 256p. $4.50; lib. ed. $4.45 net. (I–U)

A newly illustrated and designed edition of a standard anthology, with several poems and stories added.

299 **Harper, Wilhelmina,** comp. Merry Christmas to You: Stories for Christmas; illus. by Fermin Rocker. new rev. ed. Dutton, 1965. 254p. $4.50; lib. ed. $4.45 net. (I–U)

Stories and poems for the celebration of Christmas around the world, with new illustrations and new format.

300 **Jennings, Gary.** Parades! Celebrations and Circuses on the March. Lippincott, 1966. 150p. $4.95. (U)

The history and lore of parades in many parts of the world, from the Changing of the Royal Guards at Buckingham Palace in London to the May Day parade in Moscow, with a chapter on "Music To March To." Illustrated with photographs and prints. Adds a colorful note of atmosphere to the study of other countries.

301 **Johnson, Lois S.** Happy Birthdays round the World; illus. by Genia. Rand McNally, 1963. 128p. $2.95. (I)

Describes birthday celebrations in 24 countries. Useful in the study of the countries represented.

302 **Johnson, Lois S.** Happy New Year round the World; illus. by Lili Cassel Wronker. Rand McNally, 1966. 176p. $2.95. (I)

New Year celebrations in 25 countries and New Year's greetings in 24 languages, with a pronunciation guide.

303 **Langstaff, John,** comp. On Christmas Day in the Morning! Carols gathered by John Langstaff; illus. by Anthony Groves-Raines; piano settings by Marshall Woodbridge. Harcourt, 1959. unp. $3.25; lib. ed. $3.26 net. (P–I–U)

After a brief introduction describing the possibilities for dramatizing carols, the compiler gives words and music of four traditional Christmas carols. Illustrations in jewel-like colors are reminiscent of medieval manuscripts.

304 **Larrick, Nancy,** ed. Poetry for Holidays; drawings by Kelly Oechsli. Garrard, 1966. 64p. $2.32. (P)

Familiar poetry for ten holidays, especially suitable for use by and with young children.

305 **Les Tina, Dorothy.** Flag Day; illus. by Ed Emberley. Crowell, 1965. unp. $2.95; lib. ed. $2.85 net. (P–I)

Gives the history of the United States flag, the origin of Flag Day, and rules for handling and displaying the flag.

306 **Luckhardt, Mildred C.,** ed. Thanksgiving: Feast and Festival; illus. by Ralph McDonald. Abingdon, 1966. 352p. $5.95. (I)

Stories, poems, and prayers arranged in two parts: "The Pilgrims and Thanksgiving" and "Thanksgiving and Harvest Time Near and Far."

307 **McGinley, Phyllis.** The Year without a Santa Claus; pictures by Kurt Werth. Lippincott, c1957. unp. $3. (P–I)

A story poem about the year Santa decided he was too tired to bother with Christmas, but changed his mind when the children of the world brought presents to him.

308 **McSpadden, J. Walker.** The Book of Holidays; illus. by Robert Galster. rev. ed. Crowell, 1958. 246p. $3.50. (I)

Discusses the customs and superstitions related to holidays in many lands.

309 **Millen, Nina.** Children's Festivals in Many Lands; illus. by Janet Smalley. Friendship Pr., 1964. 191p. $3.95. (I)

Religious and folk festivals around the world.

310 **Moore, Clement C.** The Night before Christmas; illus. by Arthur Rackham. Lippincott, 1954. 32p. $2.50. (P–I)

The well-loved Christmas poem illustrated by a great English artist.

311   **Patterson, Lillie.** Halloween; illus. by Gil Miret. Garrard, 1963. 63p. $2.32. (P)

An easy-to-read account of Halloween customs from the ancient Celts and Romans to the present day. (R2–3)

312   **Pauli, Hertha.** Silent Night: The Story of a Song; illus. by Fritz Kredel. Knopf, 1943. 81p. lib. ed. $3.19 net. (I)

The story behind a favorite Christmas carol and the words and music of the carol itself.

313   **Preston, Carol.** A Trilogy of Christmas Plays for Children. Music selected by John Langstaff. Harcourt, 1967. 135p. $3.95. (I–U)

Three Nativity plays adapted from the Scriptures, the medieval miracle plays, and folk material. Carols to accompany the action are designated, and full production notes are included. Outstanding for quality and suitability to school production.

314   **Rollins, Charlemae,** comp. Christmas Gif'; line drawings by Tom O'Sullivan; book design by Stan Williamson. Follett, 1963. 119p. $4.95. (I–U)

Christmas poems, songs, and stories written by and about Negroes are collected in an attractively illustrated anthology, along with several unusual Christmas recipes.

315   **Sawyer, Ruth.** Joy to the World: Christmas Legends; illus. by Trina Schart Hyman. Little, 1966. 102p. $3.95; lib. ed. $3.97 net. (I)

A collection of Christmas legends, told by a gifted storyteller and not available in other books, especially suited to reading aloud. Each story is preceded by a carol.

316   **Sechrist, Elizabeth Hough,** comp. Christmas Everywhere: A Book of Christmas Customs of Many Lands; illus. by Elsie Jane McCorkell. new rev. ed. Macrae, 1962. 186p. $3.95; lib. ed. $3.73 net. (I–U)

Christmas customs in 20 different countries.

317   **Sechrist, Elizabeth Hough,** comp. Heigh-Ho for Halloween! Written and comp. by Elizabeth Hough Sechrist; illus. by Guy Fry. Macrae, 1948. 240p. $4.50; lib. ed. $4.21 net. (I–U)

Traces the origin of Halloween and contains stories, poems, games, and plays suitable for the occasion. Gives ideas for parties, costumes, and entertainments and suggests plans for community celebration.

318   **Sechrist, Elizabeth Hough,** and **Woolsey, Janette,** comps. It's Time for Brotherhood; illus. by Clifford Schule. Macrae, 1962. 222p. $4.25. (I–U)

Stories of people and organizations whose work exemplifies the theme of responsibility to one's neighbors and promotion of world peace.

319   **Sechrist, Elizabeth Hough,** and **Woolsey, Janette,** comps. It's Time for Christmas; decorations by Reisie Lonette. Macrae, 1959. 256p. $4.95; lib. ed. $4.68 net. (I–U)

Emphasizing Christmas as Christ's birthday instead of the commercial aspects of the holiday, the authors tell the story of the Nativity and give legends, symbols, poems, and carols suitable to the theme.

320   **Sechrist, Elizabeth Hough,** and **Woolsey, Janette,** comps. It's Time for Easter; illus. by Elsie Jane McCorkell. Macrae, 1961. 255p. $5.50. (I–U)

Gives a shortened version of the Easter story as told in the Gospels and describes the origin and significance of Easter symbols and their use in celebrations around the world. Includes legends, stories, poems, and music.

321   **Sechrist, Elizabeth Hough,** and **Woolsey, Janette,** comps. It's Time for Thanksgiving; decorations by Guy Fry. Macrae, 1957. 251p. $4.75; lib. ed. $4.48 net. (I–U)

Fresh holiday material including poems, plays, stories, games, and recipes, in addition to the usual information on the origin and history of Thanksgiving Day.

322   **Sechrist, Elizabeth Hough,** comp. Poems for Red Letter Days; illus. by Guy Fry. Macrae, 1951. 349p. $4.95; lib. ed. $4.63 net. (I–U)

An anthology of old and new poems, arranged by season and holiday and indexed by author, title, and first lines.

323   **Sechrist, Elizabeth Hough,** comp. Red Letter Days: A Book of Holiday Customs; illus. by Elsie Jane McCorkell. rev.

ed. Macrae, 1965. 253p. $4.25; lib. ed. $3.97 net. (I–U)

A chronological arrangement of special days, their historical significance, and the customs associated with them in different parts of the world.

324 **Simon, Norma.** Hanukkah; illus. by Symeon Shimin. Crowell, 1966. unp. $2.95; lib. ed. $2.85 net. (P–I)

The origin of the Jewish Feast of Lights and the customs observed in its celebration are described with simplicity and dignity.

325 **Simon, Norma.** Passover; illus. by Symeon Shimin. Crowell, 1965. unp. $2.95; lib. ed. $2.85 net. (P–I)

Background and traditions of this Jewish holiday are presented in readable and attractive form.

326 **Smith, Elva Sophronia,** and **Hazeltine, Alice Isabel,** comps. The Christmas Book of Legends & Stories. Lothrop, 1944. 429p. $4.50. (I–U)

Varied material chosen for literary merit, religious significance, and appeal to children.

327 **Tudor, Tasha.** Take Joy! The Tasha Tudor Christmas Book; sel., ed., and illus. by Tasha Tudor. World, 1966. 157p. $4.95; lib. ed. $4.61 net. (I)

Selections and illustrations reflect the nostalgic and sentimental celebration of Christmas as observed by the author.

328 **The Twelve Days of Christmas;** in pictures by Ilonka Karasz. Harper, 1949. unp. $3.50; lib. ed. $3.27 net. (P–I)

The exuberance of the old folk song is caught in lovely illustrations with a medieval setting. The melody is given at the end.

329 **Woolsey, Janette,** and **Sechrist, Elizabeth Hough,** comps. New Plays for Red Letter Days; illus. by Guy Fry. Macrae, 1953. 310p. lib. ed. $4.67 net. (I–U)

Twenty-five nonroyalty, easy-to-produce plays for special days celebrated in the schools. Includes notes on production.

330 **Wyndham, Lee.** Thanksgiving; illus. by Hazel Hoecker. Garrard, 1963. 64p. $2.32. (P)

History and customs of Thanksgiving Day in the United States and harvest festivals around the world. (R2–3)

Politics and Government

331 **Commager, Henry Steele.** The Great Constitution: A Book for Young Americans. Bobbs-Merrill, 1961. 128p. $3.75; lib. ed. $3.25 net. (U)

Describes the events leading to the Constitutional Convention and the writing and adoption of the Constitution. Enlivened by comments on the framers of the Constitution and by period illustrations.

332 **Cooke, David C.** Your Treasury Department. Norton, 1964. 93p. $3.50; lib. ed. $3.28 net. (I–U)

A photographic survey of the organization and functions of the Treasury Department, covering collection of taxes; printing of money; work of the Secret Service, Coast Guard, Bureau of Narcotics, etc.

333 **Elting, Mary,** and **Gossett, Margaret.** We Are the Government; illus. by Angie Culfogienis. rev. ed. Doubleday, 1967. 96p. $2.95. (I)

A brief, illustrated overview of all departments of the United States government. Includes a map of Washington and a list of international organizations.

334 **Johnson, Gerald W.** The Cabinet; illus. by Leonard Everett Fisher. Morrow, 1966. 160p. $3.50; lib. ed. $3.32 net. (I–U)

The growth and development of the Cabinet and its role in United States government are explained in clear, lively text.

335 **Johnson, Gerald W.** Communism: An American's View; illus. by Leonard Everett Fisher. Morrow, 1964. 160p. $3.50; lib. ed. $3.32 net. (I–U)

Traces the history of communism from Marx to Khrushchev, noting both strengths and weaknesses; contrasts Russian communism with democracy; and emphasizes the importance of understanding communism in order to combat it.

336 **Johnson, Gerald W.** The Congress; illus. by Leonard Everett Fisher. Morrow, 1963. 128p. $3.25; lib. ed. $3.14 net. (I–U)

Sketches the history of the U.S. Congress; explains its functions; discusses the system of checks and balances; and lists Vice-Presidents, speakers of the House, and standing committees of the House and Senate.

27

337   **Johnson, Gerald W.** The Presidency; illus. by Leonard Everett Fisher. Morrow, 1962. 128p. $3.25; lib. ed. $3.14 net. (I–U)

A readable analysis of the executive branch of the United States government, showing how its functions and influence have changed over the years and discussing the impact of six strong Presidents on the office.

338   **Johnson, Gerald W.** The Supreme Court; illus. by Leonard Everett Fisher. Morrow, 1962. 127p. $3.25; lib. ed. $3.14 net. (I–U)

Explains how the Supreme Court functions and, through analysis of important decisions, shows how it affects the lives of citizens.

339   **Kuhn, Ferdinand.** The Story of the Secret Service; foreword by James J. Rowley. rev. ed. Random, 1965. 174p. $1.95; lib. ed. $2.48 net. (I)

The history and work of the Secret Service, including case histories based on official Secret Service reports.

340   **Lindop, Edmund.** The First Book of Elections; illus. by Gustave E. Nebel. Watts, 1968. 63p. $2.65. (I–U)

Voting laws and practices are clearly explained, with emphasis on the election of a President.

341   **McGuire, Edna.** The Peace Corps: Kindlers of the Spark; introd. by Donovan V. McClure. Macmillan, 1966. 224p. $3.95; lib. ed. $3.94 net. (U)

After describing the beginning of the Peace Corps and the training of its applicants, the author shows through firsthand observations and photographs Peace Corps activities in five countries.

342   **Morris, Richard B.** The First Book of the Constitution; pictures by Leonard Everett Fisher. Watts, 1958. 68p. $2.65. (I–U)

The evolution of the U.S. Constitution, from the Philadelphia Convention through the Bill of Rights and amendments, is presented in clear and vigorous style.

343   **Newman, Shirlee Petkins,** and **Sherman, Diane Finn.** About the People Who Run Your City; illus. by James David Johnson. Melmont, 1963. 47p. $2.50. (P)

An introduction to city government, explaining the responsibilities of the officials who work in its various departments.

344   **Ross, George E.** Know Your Government; illus. by Seymour Fleishman. Rand McNally, 1959. 72p. $1.95; lib. ed. $2.79 net. (I–U)

Basic information about the United States government, including charts and tables to show organization and functions of the different branches.

345   **Scholastic Magazines.** What You Should Know about Communism and Why; by the eds. of Scholastic Magazines; adapted by Matthew Mestrovic. rev. junior ed. McGraw-Hill, 1964. 128p. $2.95; lib. ed. $2.96 net. (U)

A useful guide to the study of communism, describing the Communist system, Stalin's reign of terror, Khrushchev's command of the party, training of youth in Communist countries, and communism in the United States.

346   **Scholastic Magazines.** What You Should Know about Democracy and Why; by the eds. of Scholastic Magazines. Four Winds, 1964. 189p. $3.50. (U)

This companion volume to *What You Should Know about Communism and Why,* above, traces the growth of democracy and contrasts democracy and totalitarianism.

347   **Schwartz, Alvin.** The City and Its People: The Story of One City's Government. Photos. by Sy Katzoff. Dutton, 1967. 64p. $3.95; lib. ed. $3.91 net. (I–U)

Using Trenton, New Jersey, as an example, the author briefly outlines municipal government, emphasizing its complications and problems.

348   **Wagner, Ruth H.** Put Democracy to Work. rev. ed. Abelard-Schuman, 1961. 160p. $3.50. (I–U)

A useful presentation of the privileges and responsibilities of the citizen in a democracy, focusing on the duty of each person to help make democracy work at home and abroad. Includes a list for further reading.

349   **Whitehead, Don.** The FBI Story; foreword by J. Edgar Hoover. Young readers' ed. Random, 1963. 172p. $3.95; lib. ed. $3.87 net. (I–U)

Crime-fighting techniques of the Federal Bureau of Investigation are examined through actual cases in this adaptation of a book for adults. Includes a chapter on the selection, training, and work of FBI agents.

350 Wines, Emma M., and **Card, Marjory W.** "Come to Order!" Essentials of Parliamentary Practice and Group Discussion. enl. ed. Odyssey, 1941. 122p. $1.20. (I–U)
A simplified guide to parliamentary procedure.

CIVIL LIBERTIES

351 Cavanah, Frances. Our Country's Freedom; illus. by Dorothy Bayley Morse. Rand McNally, 1966. 97p. $3.50; lib. ed. $3.47 net. (P–I)
Traces the development of freedom from Colonial times to the present, stressing the idea that liberty is a hard-won blessing requiring continual vigilance in its defense.

352 Commager, Henry Steele. Crusaders for Freedom; illus. by Mimi Korach. Doubleday, 1962. 240p. $3.95. (I–U)
Discusses the significance of civil liberties and sketches the lives of the men and women who have helped to win them.

353 Commager, Henry Steele. The Great Proclamation: A Book for Young Americans. Bobbs-Merrill, 1960. 112p. $3.75; lib. ed. $3.25 net. (I–U)
Background for the Emancipation Proclamation and the Thirteenth Amendment to the Constitution is given largely in Lincoln's own words and the words of his contemporaries. Illustrated with photographs and old prints.

354 Hoffman, Edwin D. Pathways to Freedom: Nine Dramatic Episodes in the Evolution of the American Democratic Tradition. Houghton, 1964. 213p. $3.75. (I–U)
Describes Peter Zenger's trial which established freedom of the press, the Philadelphia strike of 1835 which gained the right for labor to organize, and other incidents by which American civil liberties were won.

355 Miers, Earl Schenck. Freedom. Grosset, 1965. 192p. $4.95; lib. ed. $4.98 net. (I–U)
Surveys the struggles of Americans to guarantee freedom of the press, religious freedom, women's suffrage, and other rights enjoyed by today's citizens.

356 Sterling, Dorothy. Forever Free: The

Story of the Emancipation Proclamation; illus. by Ernest Crichlow. Doubleday, 1963. 208p. $3.95. (U)
A record of slavery in the United States from 1607 to 1863, with emphasis on the conditions and events which led to the Emancipation Proclamation.

357 Sterne, Emma Gelders. I Have a Dream; illus. by Tracy Sugarman. Knopf, 1965. 229p. $3.95; lib. ed. $3.39 net. (U)
Traces the Negroes' struggle for full citizenship through the lives of nine leaders of the civil rights movement. Includes a list for further reading.

ARMED FORCES

358 Baldwin, Hanson W. The New Navy. Dutton, 1964. 191p. $4.95. (U)
An overview of the U.S. Navy focusing on recent technological advances in ships, weapons, planes, and equipment. Illustrated with photographs.

359 Blassingame, Wyatt. U.S. Frogmen of World War II; illus. with photos. and maps. Random, 1964. 171p. $1.95; lib. ed. $2.48 net. (I–U)
A spirited account of the history and training of the Navy's frogmen and their remarkable feats of demolition in World War II.

360 Caidin, Martin. The Winged Armada: The Story of the Strategic Air Command; illus. with photos. Dutton, 1964. 182p. $3.50. (U)
A lively account of the purpose, equipment, and operation of the SAC.

361 Castillo, Edmund L. The Seabees of World War II; foreword by Ben Moreell; illus. with official U.S. Navy photos. Random, 1963. 190p. $2.50; lib. ed. $2.48 net. (I)
The story of the exploits of the U.S. Navy Construction Battalions in World War II is told in vigorous style.

362 Colby, C. B. Air Force Academy: Cadets, Training, and Equipment. Coward-McCann, 1962. 48p. lib. ed. $2.48 net. (I)
A photographic study of Air Force cadets from basic training to graduation. Simple text geared to official photographs.

363 Colby, C. B. Annapolis: Cadets, Training, and Equipment. Coward-McCann, 1964. 48p. lib. ed. $2.48 net. (I)

Companion volume to *Air Force Academy,* above.

364   **Colby, C. B.** Signal Corps Today: Its Role in Modern Warfare. Coward-McCann, 1966. 48p. lib. ed. $2.48 net. (I)
Captioned photographs give the history and work of the branch of the Army responsible for communications and enemy surveillance in wartime.

365   **Colby, C. B.** Special Forces: The U.S. Army's Experts in Unconventional Warfare. Coward-McCann, 1964. 48p. lib. ed. $2.86 net. (I-U)
The training, equipment, and purpose of the Army's guerrilla fighters are explained in brief text and many photographs.

366   **Colby, C. B.** Survival: Training in Our Armed Services. Coward-McCann, 1965. 48p. lib. ed. $2.86 net. (I)
Photographs and brief text show survival training given members of the armed services.

367   **Colby, C. B.** West Point: Cadets, Training, and Equipment. Coward-McCann, 1963. 48p. lib. ed. $2.86 net. (I)
Companion volume similar in coverage and format to *Air Force Academy* and *Annapolis,* above.

368   **Cooke, Donald E.** For Conspicuous Gallantry . . . : Winners of the Medal of Honor; illus. by Jack Woodson. Hammond, 1966. 93p. $3.50; lib. ed. $3.39 net. (U)
A history of the Medal of Honor and descriptions of some of the acts of heroism for which it has been awarded in war and peace. Includes a list of medal winners, pictures of the medal, and a glossary.

369   **Hunt, George P.** The Story of the U.S. Marines; illus. with official U.S. Marine photos. Random, 1951. 192p. $1.95; lib. ed. $2.48 net. (I)
A stirring account of the Marine Corps from its beginning to the present, told through representative incidents in each period of United States history.

370   **Reeder, Red.** Medal of Honor Heroes; illus. by Gil Walker. Random, 1965. 180p. $1.95; lib. ed. $2.48 net. (I-U)
Describes the heroic acts of 17 twentieth-century servicemen who have received the Medal of Honor. Easier reading than *For*

Conspicuous Gallantry, above, and less comprehensive coverage.

371   **Weller, George.** The Story of the Paratroops. Random, 1958. 149p. $1.95; lib. ed. $2.48 net. (I)
Begins with a brief general account of parachuting, followed by the story of paratroops in World War II.

INTERNATIONAL ORGANIZATIONS

372   **Ellis, Harry B.** The Common Market. World, 1965. 204p. $4.95. (U)
A clear presentation of the historical background, objectives, and problems of the organization which attempts to unite Europe economically. Illustrated with photographs.

373   **Epstein, Beryl.** The Story of the International Red Cross. Nelson, 1963. 183p. $3.50; lib. ed. $3.31 net. (I-U)
Summarizes the history, organization, and work of the Red Cross, including Clara Barton's role in the American Red Cross.

374   **Epstein, Edna.** The United Nations. 4th rev. ed. Watts, 1966. 94p. $2.65. (I)
Many photographs enhance this concise explanation of the purposes, organization, and operation of the United Nations. Includes a glossary.

375   **Galt, Tom.** How the United Nations Works; illus. by Ava Morgan. 3d ed. Crowell, 1965. 248p. $3.75. (I-U)
Information on committees, commissions, specialized agencies, and peace-keeping operations, as well as on the history and operation of the UN.

376   **Karen, Ruth.** Neighbors in a New World: The Organization of American States. World, 1966. 188p. $4.95. (U)
A survey of the history, purposes, structure, and activities of the OAS, with emphasis on its efforts to promote trade and to stop the spread of communism.

377   **Sasek, M.** This Is the United Nations. Macmillan, 1968. 60p. $4.95. (P-I)
A pictorial tour of the United Nations Headquarters and a simple explanation of the work done there and by UN agencies around the world. Striking colored pictures show furnishings, costumes, flags, and other details especially interesting to children.

378   **Seegers, Kathleen Walker.** Alliance for Progress: The Challenge of the Western Hemisphere. Coward-McCann, 1964. 120p. $2.60. (I–U)
Explains how 19 countries work together to raise the standard of living in Latin America. Includes a pronouncing guide for foreign names.

379   **Shippen, Katherine B.** The Pool of Knowledge: How the United Nations Share Their Skills; illus. with photos. new and rev. ed. Harper, 1965. 99p. lib. ed. $2.92 net. (I–U)
Discusses the work of the UN Technical Assistance Program in underdeveloped countries, describing projects in such fields as health, education, and agriculture.

380   **Speiser, Jean.** UNICEF and the World. Day, 1965. 94p. lib. ed. $3.96 net. (I)
A photographic account of the work done by the United Nations Children's Fund in caring for the health and education of children around the world.

381   **Teltsch, Kathleen.** Getting To Know the United Nations Peace Forces; illus. by Marvin Besunder. Coward-McCann, 1966. 64p. lib. ed. $2.68. (I)
Tells how the international UN Emergency Force has helped to stop fighting in Egypt, the Congo, and Cyprus. Includes a pronunciation guide to foreign names.

Economics

MONEY AND BANKING

382   **Buehr, Walter.** Treasure: The Story of Money and Its Safeguarding; written and illus. by Walter Buehr. Putnam, 1955. 64p. lib. ed. $2.92 net. (I)
An introductory history of exchange, from primitive barter to today's complex monetary system.

383   **Floherty, John J.** Money-Go-Round. rev. ed. Lippincott, 1964. 192p. $3.95. (U)
Explains various methods of exchange, from earliest days to the present, including information on banking and credit systems, international finance, the Marshall Plan, and the functions of the U.S. Treasury Department.

384   **Lowenstein, Dyno.** Money; pictures by Adolar. Watts, 1963. 68p. $2.95. (U)
"Discusses the theory of money, government controls, banking, printing, and spending," and describes American coins and paper money.

385   **Paradis, Adrian A.** The Bulls and the Bears: How the Stock Exchange Works; illus. with drawings by Alan Moyler and photos. Hawthorn, 1967. 94p. $3.50 (I)
This introduction to the stock exchange follows the steps taken by an inventor to raise capital for the production and marketing of his product. Covers formation of a company, issuance of stocks, a stockholders' meeting, and activities of the stock exchange. Includes a glossary, a list of stock exchanges, and a plan for studying the stock market.

386   **Wade, William W.** From Barter to Banking: The Story of Money. Crowell-Collier, 1967. 136p. $3.50. (I)
Reviews the history of money and banking in lively, anecdotal style and gives advice on personal money management. Illustrated with photographs.

387   **Wood, James Playstead.** What's the Market? The Story of the Stock Exchange. Duell, 1966. 179p. $3.95. (U)
The history of trade from classical times to the formation of stock exchanges in France, Britain, and the United States. Includes sketches of the financial barons of early days and explains how to buy stocks.

COMMERCE AND INDUSTRY

388 **American Heritage.** The Story of Yankee Whaling; by the eds. of American Heritage, The Magazine of History; narrative by Irwin Shapiro in consultation with Edouard A. Stackpole. American Heritage, 1959. American Heritage Junior Library, distributed by Harper. 153p. $4.95; lib. ed. $4.79 net. (I–U)
An exciting narrative of whaling ships, men, and whaling expeditions, using material from whalers' logbooks, letters, and journals, and lavishly illustrated with contemporary prints and paintings.

389   **Buehr, Walter.** The Magic of Paper; written and illus. by Walter Buehr. Morrow, 1966. 95p. $3.25; lib. ed. $3.14 net. (I)
A clear, well-organized account of the history, manufacture, and uses of paper,

including new developments in the paper industry.

390   **Buehr, Walter.** Oil . . . Today's Black Magic; written and illus. by Walter Buehr. Morrow, 1957. 96p. lib. ed. $2.94 net. (I)

Traces the flow of petroleum from the oil fields, through the refining and distribution processes, to its many uses.

391   **Buehr, Walter.** Rubber: Natural and Synthetic; written and illus. by Walter Buehr. Morrow, 1964. 96p. lib. ed. $3.14 net. (I)

Beginning with the discovery of rubber in the Amazon jungle, the author describes the procedures for preparing natural rubber for use, the manufacture of synthetic rubber, and the growth of the giant rubber industry.

392   **Epstein, Sam,** and **Epstein, Beryl.** The First Book of Glass; pictures by Bette Davis. Watts, 1955. 63p. $2.65. (I–U)

The history of glass and glassmaking, with especially good chapters on the use of glass in telescopes, microscopes, and eyeglasses.

393   **Harrison, C. W.** The First Book of Commercial Fishing; illus. with photos. by the author. Watts, 1964. 73p. $2.65. (I–U)

Describes the methods of saltwater fishing and discusses the importance of the industry and the necessity for conservation.

394   **Lewis, Alfred.** The New World of Plastics; illus. with photos. Dodd, 1963. 79p. lib. ed. $2.79 net. (I–U)

Provides a tour through a plastic research center where the director answers questions about the development, manufacture, and uses of plastics.

395   **Paradis, Adrian A.** Business in Action. Messner, 1962. 191p. $3.95; lib. ed. $3.64 net. (U)

Explains the American system of free enterprise and the role of government, industry, labor, and agriculture in the United States economy.

396   **Shippen, Katherine B.** Miracle in Motion: The Story of America's Industry. Harper, 1955. 150p. $2.95; lib. ed. $2.92 net. (I–U)

From the pre-Revolutionary agricultural society, through the industrial revolution, to the coming of the age of automation, the author describes the development of American industry, with attention to the growth of corporations, the rise of organized labor, and the need for government controls.

LABOR

397   **Hirsch, S. Carl.** This Is Automation; illus. by Anthony Ravielli. Viking, 1964. 128p. $3.75; lib. ed. $3.56 net. (I–U)

An overview of automation, discussing its development, the machines which make it possible, and its impact on labor and society.

398   **Paradis, Adrian A.** The Hungry Years: The Story of the Great American Depression. Chilton, 1967. 183p. $4.25. (I–U)

A graphic picture of the Depression, covering its causes, its effects on people, the social legislation enacted to relieve it, and the impact of new laws on present-day laboring classes. Told in the form of case histories and illustrated with photographs of bread lines, apple vendors, and ragged children.

399   **Shippen, Katherine B.** This Union Cause: The Growth of Organized Labor in America. Harper, 1958. 180p. $3.50; lib. ed. $3.27 net. (U)

Traces the rise of labor unions from the early craft guilds to today's powerful organizations, highlighting the leaders of the movement and the problems they have faced.

400   **Spencer, Cornelia.** Keeping Ahead of Machines: The Human Side of the Automation Revolution. Day, 1965. 128p. lib. ed. $3.29 net. (U)

After a brief survey of the factors which have led to the development of automation, the author discusses the effect of machines on people, stressing the need for retraining, adjustment to the new order, and better use of the leisure time made possible by automation.

401   **Werstein, Irving.** The Great Struggle: Labor in America. Scribner, 1965. 190p. lib. ed. $3.63 net. (U)

Emphasis is on the men and milestones in the long fight for better working and living conditions for laboring classes. Illustrated with reproductions of historical pictures.

Languages

Picture dictionaries only are included here; dictionaries for intermediate and upper grades are listed on pages 1–2.

402 **Alexander, Arthur.** The Magic of Words; illus. by R. S. Alexander. Prentice-Hall, 1962. 71p. $3.50. (P–I)
An informal introduction to the development of written and spoken language, covering gestures, signs, symbols, codes, and other means by which man has attempted to express himself.

403 **Cahn, William,** and **Cahn, Rhoda.** The Story of Writing: From Cave Art to Computer; illus. by Anne Lewis; reviewed for scientific accuracy by Rhys Carpenter. Harvey House, 1963. 128p. $3.95; lib. ed. $3.79 net. (I)
Surveys the development of written communication: alphabets, number systems, invention of paper, and the use of mechanical aids, such as pen and ink, typewriter, and printing press. Includes a glossary and a bibliography.

404 **Courtis, Stuart A.,** and **Watters, Garnette.** The Courtis-Watters Illustrated Golden Dictionary for Young Readers. Allen Walker Read, consultant on pronunciation. rev. and expanded. Golden Pr., 1965. 666p. $3.95. (P)
Defines and illustrates in sentences and pictures more than 10,000 words. Phonetically spelled pronunciation system.

405 **Epstein, Sam,** and **Epstein, Beryl.** The First Book of Words: Their Family Histories; pictures by László Roth. 62p. Watts, 1954. $2.65. (I)
A stimulating introduction to the study of language, showing how words originate, how they are used, and how they change with the times. Includes a chart showing the development of the alphabet through Phoenician, Greek, and Roman forms.

406 **Frasconi, Antonio.** See and Say, Guarda e Parla, Mira y Habla, Regarde et Parle; woodcuts by Antonio Frasconi. Harcourt, 1955. unp. $3.25; lib. ed. $3.56 net. (P–I)
A picture book in four languages—English, Italian, Spanish, and French—with terms printed in a different color for each language and illustrated with bold, imaginative pictures. Words are chosen from children's vocabularies and phonetically pronounced.

407 **Ogg, Oscar.** The 26 Letters. Crowell, 1961. 262p. $5.50. (U)
From picture writing to the linotype, history of how writing has developed. Enlivened with anecdotes and drawings.

408 **Pei, Mario.** All about Language; decorations by Donat Ivanovsky. Lippincott, 1954. 186p. $2.95. (I–U)
Traces the evolution of language from its beginnings to the great language branches, with emphasis on the English language.

409 **Rand, Ann,** and **Rand, Paul.** Sparkle and Spin: A Book about Words. Harcourt, 1962. unp. $3.25; lib. ed. $3.36 net. (P)
Through rhythmic text and stylized pictures, author and artist introduce children to the fascination of words. An original and provocative book, useful to encourage an awareness of the variety and color of words.

410 **Sparke, William.** Story of the English Language; illus. with drawings by Wayne Gallup and with photos. Abelard-Schuman, 1966. 190p. $3.95. (U)
An introduction to the history of the English language, discussing its variations in different countries and among different classes, the changes in language influenced by mass media, and the principles of linguistics which have shaped its development.

411 **Wiese, Kurt.** You Can Write Chinese. Viking, 1945. unp. $3; lib. ed. $2.96 net. (P–I)
Brief explanations and the author's ingenious illustrations introduce Chinese characters and explain their origin. Useful in the study of China.

412 **Wright, Wendell W.,** and **Laird,**

Helen. The Rainbow Dictionary; illus. by Joseph Low. World, 1959. 433p. $5.95; lib. ed. $5.28 net. (P)

A picture dictionary containing 2300 entries based on words most frequently occurring in a consolidation of eight word lists for young children. Uncluttered pages, large type, and many colored pictures.

Pure and Applied Sciences

General Science

413   **Adler, Irving.** The Tools of Science: From Yardstick to Cyclotron; illus. by Ruth Adler. Day, 1958. 128p. lib. ed. $3.49 net. (I–U)

Explains the basic principles and purposes of the tools used by the modern scientist.

414   **American Heritage.** Men of Science and Invention; by the eds. of American Heritage, The Magazine of History; narrative by Michael Blow, in consultation with Robert P. Multhauf. American Heritage, 1960. American Heritage Junior Library, distributed by Harper. 153p. $4.95; lib. ed. $3.79 net. (I–U)

A survey of the scientific and technological advances made in America from Colonial times to the present, centered around the work of pioneering scientists and profusely illustrated with old prints and photographs.

415   **Barr, George.** Research Ideas for Young Scientists; illus. by John Teppich. McGraw-Hill, 1958. 142p. $3.50; lib. ed. $3.06 net. (I–U)

Provides easy-to-do experiments in many fields of science, with instructions on how to make accurate measurements, record and interpret data, construct graphs, and use experimental controls. Includes practical ideas for science clubs and science fairs.

416   **Barr, George.** Young Scientist Takes a Walk: A Guide to Outdoor Observation; illus. by Jeanne Bendick. McGraw-Hill, 1959. 160p. $3.50; lib. ed. $3.06 net. (I–U)

An exercise in observation intended to make the young reader more aware of his immediate environment.

417   **Beeler, Nelson F.,** and **Branley, Franklyn M.** Experiments in Science; illus. by Ruth Beck. rev. enl. ed. Crowell, 1955. 144p. $3.50. (I)

Two science teachers describe 45 experiments which can be done at home or in school with inexpensive, easily obtained materials and equipment.

418   **Bendick, Jeanne.** All around You: A First Look at the World; written and illus. by Jeanne Bendick; foreword by Glenn O. Blough. McGraw-Hill, 1951. 48p. $3.50; lib. ed. $3.06 net. (P)

A science picture book which encourages observation to answer questions of "how" and "why." (R2–3)

419   **Cooper, Elizabeth K.** Science in Your Own Back Yard; with illus. by the author. Harcourt, 1958. 192p. $3. (I)

Gives directions for exploring natural objects and phenomena around the child's own home and for setting up a home laboratory.

420   **Farb, Peter.** Face of North America: The Natural History of a Continent; introd. by Stewart L. Udall; illus. by Bob Hines and Jerome Connolly. Young Readers' ed. Harper, 1964. 254p. $4.50; lib. ed. $4.11 net. (U)

An absorbing account of the physical features of North America and the plant and animal life of the continent, profusely illustrated with maps, diagrams, drawings, and photographs. Includes a list of outstanding natural areas and suggestions for further reading.

421   **Freeman, Mae,** and **Freeman, Ira.** Fun with Scientific Experiments. Random, 1960. 58p. $1.95; lib. ed. $2.07 net. (I)
Simple experiments with inexpensive materials enable a child to prove basic laws of science.

442   **Herbert, Don.** Mr. Wizard's Experiments for Young Scientists: illus. by Dan Noonan. Doubleday, 1959. 187p. $3.50. (I)
Thirteen experiments introduce scientists in various fields and allow the experimenter to prove the theory developed by each.

423   **Horizon Magazine.** The Universe of Galileo and Newton; by the eds. of Horizon Magazine. Author, William Bixby; consultant, Giorgio de Santillana . . . American Heritage, 1964. A Horizon Caravel Book, distributed by Harper. 153p. $4.95; lib. ed. $4.79 net. (I–U)
A history of seventeenth-century science focusing on the struggles of Galileo and Newton to gain acceptance for their revolutionary theories. Excerpts from the writings of the two men and their contemporaries and voluminous photographs and period prints throw light on the seventeenth-century world.

424   **Milgrom, Harry.** Explorations in Science: A Book of Basic Experiments; illus. by Anne Marie Jauss from original drawings by the author. Dutton, 1961. 127p. $3.25. (I)
Clearly described experiments which demonstrate scientific principles and are fun to do. Illustrated with diagrams.

425   **Parker, Bertha Morris.** The Golden Book of Science; illus. by Harry McNaught. rev. ed. Golden Pr., 1963. 103p. $3.95. (P)
Very brief treatment of 66 varied topics of interest to young children, illustrated with inviting pictures in color. (R4–5)

426   **Parker, Bertha Morris.** The Golden Treasury of Natural History. Golden Pr., 1952. 216p. $4.95. (I)
Concise text and numerous illustrations provide an overview of natural history, ranging from geology and paleontology to biology and astronomy. (R4–5)

427   **Pratt, Fletcher.** All about Famous Inventors and Their Inventions; illus. by Rus Anderson. Random, 1955. 141p. $2.50; lib. ed. $2.48 net. (I)
An introductory survey of great inventions, past and present, and brief sketches of their inventors. Readable style, clear type, many illustrations. (R4–5)

428   **Schneider, Herman,** and **Schneider, Nina.** Follow the Sunset; pictures by Lucille Corcos. Doubleday, 1952. 43p. $3.75. (P)
The readers—or listeners—"follow the sunset" to find answers to questions such as "Where does the sun go when it sets?" and "What makes the night come after the day?"

429   **Schneider, Herman,** and **Schneider, Nina.** How Big Is Big? From Stars to Atoms; with illus. by Symeon Shimin. new ed. unp. W. R. Scott, 1950. $3. (P)
The concept of size is presented in relation to the child's own size, in text geared to the child's experiences, and illustrated with cartoon-like pictures.

430   **Stepp, Ann.** Setting Up a Science Project; illus. by Polly Bolian. Prentice-Hall, 1966. 56p. $3.50. (I)
Clear, practical suggestions for selecting, planning, and presenting a science project which will illustrate a scientific principle. Includes suggestions about materials and safety measures and a checklist for evaluating the project.

431   **Stock, Robert.** Natural Wonders of the World. Parents Mag. Pr., 1966. 94p. $3.95; lib. ed. $3.34 net. (I)
An informal account of 13 natural wonders, including the Sahara Desert, the Grand Canyon, and the Dead Sea. Excellent photographs.

432   **Waller, Leslie.** A Book To Begin on American Inventions; illus. by Ed Emberley. Holt, 1963. unp. $2.75; lib. ed. $2.78 net. (P–I)
An introduction to American inventors and inventions, from Benjamin Franklin to Robert Goddard.

Mathematics

433   **Adler, Irving.** The Giant Golden Book of Mathematics: Exploring the World of Numbers and Space; illus. by Lowell Hess; with a foreword by Howard F. Fehr. Golden Pr., 1960. 91p. $3.95. (I)
Presents basic concepts of arithmetic, al-

gebra, geometry, and trigonometry and discusses applications of each to daily life. Short topics, brightly illustrated.

434   Adler, Irving, and **Adler, Ruth.** Numerals: New Dresses for Old Numbers. Day, 1964. 48p. lib. ed. $2.68 net. (I–U)
A clear introduction to methods of counting on different bases. Explains how to translate from base ten and back again, and gives problems for each operation.

435   Adler, Irving, and **Adler, Ruth.** Sets. Day, 1967. 48p. lib. ed. $2.68 net. (I)
A step-by-step explanation of the use of sets in solving problems of arithmetic, beginning with sets of familiar objects and proceeding to sets composed of symbols. Includes practice exercises.

436   Asimov, Isaac. Quick and Easy Math. Houghton, 1964. 180p. $3. (U)
Short cuts, based on fundamental mathematical principles, for the four arithmetic operations, using whole numbers, fractions, and decimals.

437   Asimov, Isaac. Realm of Algebra; diags. by Robert Belmore. Houghton, 1961. 230p. $3.50. (U)
Presents the concepts of algebra in terms comprehensible to the older pupil with some background in mathematics. Lists algebraic symbols, explains basic operations, and discusses the use of algebra in everyday life and in science.

437a   Asimov, Isaac. Realm of Measure; diags. by Robert Belmore. Houghton, 1960. 186p. $3.25. (U)
The publisher states that "this book explains the underlying theories of measure and also describes the history of man's gradual refinement of tools and techniques." Starting with simple units of measure, such as feet, inches, and miles, the explanation proceeds to the more complex units used to measure force, energy, and viscosity.

438   Asimov, Isaac. Realm of Numbers; diags. by Robert Belmore. Houghton, 1959. 200p. $3.50 (U)
An informal explanation of the meaning and uses of numbers, combining the history of mathematics with an explanation of mathematical principles and procedures.

438a   Bendick, Jeanne. How Much and How Many: The Story of Weights and Measures. McGraw-Hill, 1947. 188p. $3.25; lib. ed. $3.01 net. (I)
Traces the origin of different types of measurement and explains how they have been used in science, industry, and everyday life. Includes many tables of measurement and numerous clarifying illustrations.

439   Bendick, Jeanne, and **Levin, Marcia.** Take a Number: New Ideas + Imagination = More Fun; pictures by Jeanne Bendick. McGraw-Hill, 1961. 63p. $2.75; lib. ed. $2.84 net. (I)
The history and theory of numbers are made interesting by means of tricks, games, and clever illustrations.

440   Bendick, Jeanne, and **Levin, Marcia.** Take Shapes, Lines, and Letters: New Horizons in Mathematics; pictures by Jeanne Bendick. McGraw-Hill, 1962. 79p. $2.95; lib. ed. $2.96 net. (I–U)
This companion book to *Take a Number,* above, deals with mathematical ideas and relationships rather than with numbers, explaining the concepts of lines, curves, angles, planes, and shapes. A fresh, stimulating introduction to geometry, with eye-catching illustrations.

441   Diggins, Julia E. String, Straightedge, and Shadow: The Story of Geometry; illus. by Corydon Bell. Viking, 1965. 160p. $5; lib. ed. $4.53. (U)
Relates how early scientists used only three simple tools—the string, the straightedge, and the shadow—to discover the basic principles of geometry, and tells how these discoveries affected the civilizations of ancient Egypt, Greece, and Mesopotamia.

441a   Epstein, Sam, and **Epstein, Beryl.** The First Book of Measurement; pictures by Walter Buehr. Watts, 1960. 60p. $2.65. (P–I)
An introduction to the methods, systems, and instruments used to measure weight, distance, temperature, time, etc. Proceeds from early to present-day methods and emphasizes the need for standardization.

442   Hogben, Lancelot. The Wonderful World of Mathematics; art by André Charles Keeping and Kenneth Symonds; maps by Marjorie Saynor. Doubleday, 1955. 69p. $2.95. (U)
A readable and generously illustrated history of mathematics, showing how man

has used mathematical principles to advance his civilization.

442a Irwin, Keith Gordon. The Romance of Weights and Measures; illus. by Johannes Troyer. Viking, 1960. 144p. lib. ed. $3.56. (U)

Against a background of various periods, the author tells how men in each age have developed systems of measurement, from the time of ancient Egypt up to today's modern systems.

443 Jonas, Arthur. New Ways in Math; illus. by Aliki. Prentice-Hall, 1962. 70p. $3.50. (I)

Surveys the development of mathematical theory from earliest times to today's binary systems, computers, and sets. Enlivened by illustrative cartoons and mathematical puzzles.

444 Kohn, Bernice. Computers at Your Service; illus. by Aliki. Prentice-Hall, 1962. 72p. $3.50. (I)

After a brief explanation of how a computer works, the author discusses the use of computers in the space program, research, and everyday life. Intended to arouse interest in the subject rather than to overwhelm the reader with technical detail.

445 Lewis, Alfred. The New World of Computers. Dodd, 1965. 79p. $3; lib. ed. $2.79 net. (I)

Concentrates on the amazing things a computer can do: helping with a medical diagnosis, sending an astronaut into space, cataloging books, keeping records, etc.

446 Ravielli, Anthony. An Adventure in Geometry; written and illus. by Anthony Ravielli. Viking, 1957. 117p. $3.75; lib. ed. $3.56. (I–U)

The outstandingly beautiful drawings, showing how geometrical shapes abound in nature, are the distinguishing feature of this clear and readable introduction to geometry.

447 Rogers, James T. The Pantheon Story of Mathematics for Young People; designed by Will Burtin. Pantheon, 1966. 122p. $4.95; lib. ed. $4.39 net. (I–U)

A history of mathematics told through the lives of great mathematicians and dramatized by striking design and illustrations. An inviting browsing volume.

448 Russell, Solveig Paulson. Lines and Shapes: A First Look at Geometry; illus. by Arnold Spilka. Walck, 1965. 31p. $3.25. (P–I)

Correct mathematical names are applied to geometrical shapes in nature and pointed out to the young child in simple explanations and informative pictures.

448a Schlein, Miriam. Heavy Is a Hippopotamus; pictures by Leonard Kessler. W. R. Scott, 1954. unp. $3.25. (P)

In an approach similar to her *Fast Is Not a Ladybug* (see No.488), the author and artist lead the young child to think of weights and measures in relation to familiar objects. (R2–3)

449 Vorwald, Alan, and **Clark, Frank.** Computers! From Sand Table to Electronic Brain; illus. by Frank Aloise. rev. ed. McGraw-Hill, 1964. 176p. $3.95; lib. ed. $3.31 net. (U)

A detailed explanation of computer principles and operation, including memory devices, the use of punch cards, and other technical devices. Gives directions for building a simple computer.

450 Whitney, David C. Let's Find Out about Addition; pictures by Harriet Sherman. Watts, 1966. unp. $2.65. (P)

Introduces numbers, the number line, and sets with clear explanations and attractive illustrations intended to clarify the young child's understanding of beginning arithmetic.

Astronomy

451 Asimov, Isaac. The Kingdom of the Sun; illus. with diags. rev. ed. Abelard-Schuman, 1963. 159p. $3.50. (U)

Discusses the theories about the solar system from Babylonian times to the present and explains the laws governing its bodies. For the advanced student with sufficient background to assimilate the wealth of information included.

452 Branley, Franklyn M. The Big Dipper; illus. by Ed Emberley. Crowell, 1962. unp. $3.25; lib. ed. $2.96 net. (P)

This book for the youngest skywatchers gives directions for locating the Big Dipper and the Little Dipper, explains how they show direction, and relates facts and legends concerning the two constellations. (R1–2)

453   **Branley, Franklyn M.** The Earth: Planet Number Three; illus. by Helmut K. Wimmer. Crowell, 1966. 151p. $4.50; lib. ed. $4.40 net. (U)

A readable survey of investigations, historical and current, about the earth: its origin, composition, motions, forces, and radiation belts. Illustrative materials include photographs, charts, graphs, and a data table. For the advanced older student.

454   **Branley, Franklyn M.** Experiments in Skywatching; illus. by Helmut K. Wimmer. Crowell, 1959. 111p. $3.95. (U)

Clearly demonstrates how to locate objects in the sky without the use of telescopes and gives directions for constructing simple devices for skywatching. Suggests experiments on the principles revealed in the observations. Helpful diagrams, good index, and a list for further reading.

455   **Branley Franklyn M.** Mars: Planet Number Four; illus. by Helmut K. Wimmer. rev. ed. Crowell, 1962. 116p. $4.50; lib. ed. $4.40 net. (I–U)

Incorporates the most up-to-date information about the origin, temperature, canals, and the possibilities of life on this interesting planet. An authoritative and readable account, supplemented by clarifying illustrations, a table of planetary data, a good index, and a list for further reading.

456   **Branley, Franklyn M.** The Moon: Earth's Natural Satellite; illus. by Helmut K. Wimmer. Crowell, 1960. 114p. $3.75; lib. ed. $4.40 net. (U)

The physical characteristics of the moon, its motion and forces, and the theories and legends associated with it are explained in clear, but somewhat technical, language and illustrated with diagrams and photographs.

457   **Branley, Franklyn M.** The Nine Planets; illus. by Helmut K. Wimmer. Crowell, 1958. 77p. $3.50; lib. ed. $4.40 net. (U)

An introduction to the solar system, with one chapter describing each of the nine planets in detail.

458   **Branley, Franklyn M.** The Sun: Our Nearest Star; pictures by Helen Borten.

Crowell, 1961. unp. $3.25; lib. ed. $2.96 net. (P)

A first book on the sun, explaining its size, shape, and other characteristics and pointing out our dependence on it. (R2–3)

459   **Chamberlain, Joseph Miles,** and **Nicholson, Thomas D.** Planets, Stars, and Space; in co-operation with the American Museum of Natural History. Creative Educ. Soc., 1962. 222p. $5.95. (I–U)

Broad coverage of astronomy, written in nontechnical language and illustrated with good photographs.

460   **Fenton, Carroll Lane,** and **Fenton, Mildred Adams.** Worlds in the Sky; illus. by the authors. rev. ed. Day, 1963. 96p. lib. ed. $3.29 net. (I)

Fundamental facts and principles of astronomy, covering the planets, seasons, eclipses, and other celestial phenomena. Crisp, clear writing; good organization; and illuminating illustrations.

461   **Freeman, Mae,** and **Freeman, Ira.** Fun with Astronomy. Random, 1953. 57p. $1.95; lib. ed. $2.07 net. (I)

Stimulates interest and encourages experimentation by suggesting projects and experiments by which the reader can demonstrate the principles involved in day and night, the seasons, and other aspects of astronomy. Excellent photographs and diagrams.

462   **Gallant, Roy A.** Exploring the Moon; illus. by Lowell Hess. Garden City, 1955. 63p. $3.75. (I)

A large, lavishly illustrated book describing in concise text the theories about the origin and nature of the moon and explaining tides and eclipses.

463   **Gringhuis, Dirk.** Stars on the Ceiling; illus. by the author. Meredith, 1967. 96p. $4.95. (I)

Pictures and text trace the development of the planetarium and the astronomical instruments which make knowledge of the heavens possible.

464   **Lauber, Patricia.** All about the Planets; foreword by Harlow Shapley; illus. by Arthur Renshaw. Random, 1960. 139p. $2.50; lib. ed. $2.48 net. (I)

Describes each planet and tells what is known about it as distinguished from unproven conjectures.

465   **Reed, W. Maxwell.** Patterns in the Sky: The Story of the Constellations; illus. by D. F. Levett Bradley. Morrow, 1951. 125p. $4. (I–U)
Clear explanations and 25 star charts show how to locate the most familiar constellations. Names, facts, and myths are given for each.

466   **Rey, H. A.** Find the Constellations. Houghton, 1954. 72p. $3.95; lib. ed. $3.57 net. (I)
Informal style and clear charts explain how to find the constellations of the Northern Hemisphere. Quizzes, time charts, and stories from mythology make this a good choice for the hobbyist.

467   **Rey, H. A.** The Stars: A New Way To See Them. rev. ed. Houghton, 1967. 160p. $6. (I)
Charts and line drawings which make the constellations look like the mythological characters for which they are named simplify locating them from any place at any time. A second section of the book explains phases of the moon, celestial movement, equinoxes, etc.

468   **Sagan, Carl,** and **Leonard, Jonathan Norton.** Planets; by Carl Sagan, Jonathan Norton Leonard, and the eds. of Life. Time, Inc., 1966. Life Science Library, distributed by Silver Burdett. 200p. $4.95. (U)
A pictorial guide to the planets, written in cooperation with the editors of Life, with emphasis on the earth and its moon, Venus, Mars, and Jupiter. Includes statistical charts, diagrams, and a list of books for further reading.

469   **Schloat, G. Warren.** Andy's Wonderful Telescope. Scribner, 1958. 48p. lib. ed. $2.97 net. (I)
An introduction to astronomy and telescopes, illustrated with vivid photographs of objects as they are seen through a telescope.

470   **Zim, Herbert S.** Comets; illus. by Gustav Schrotter. Morrow, 1957. 64p. $2.95; lib. ed. $2.94 net. (I)
A clear, concise statement of known facts and current speculations about comets, along with descriptions of some of the most famous ones. Clear diagrams and pictures.

471   **Zim, Herbert S.** Shooting Stars; illus. by Gustav Schrotter. Morrow, 1958. 64p. $2.95; lib. ed. $2.94 net. (I)

A simple introduction to meteors and meteorites, profusely illustrated with informative pictures.

472   **Zim, Herbert S.,** and **Baker, Robert G.** Stars: A Guide to the Constellations, Sun, Moon, Planets, and Other Features of the Heavens; illus. by James Gordon Irving. rev. ed. Golden Pr., 1956. 160p. $3.95. (I–U)
This field guide condenses a wealth of information into a small space for quick reference. Illustrated with charts, diagrams, and colorful pictures.

473   **Zim, Herbert S.** The Sun; illus. by Larry Kettelkamp. Morrow, 1953. 51p. $2.95; lib. ed. $2.94 net. (I)
Concise information about the sun and its effects on earth, including the possibility of harnessing solar energy. Illustrated with clear, well-labeled pictures.

474   **Zim, Herbert S.** The Universe; illus. by Gustav Schrotter. Morrow, 1961. 63p. $2.95; lib. ed. $2.94 net. (I)
A clear description of the expanding universe, from Ptolemy to Palomar, and an explanation of modern methods of extending knowledge about it.

TIME AND CALENDARS

475   **Adler, Irving.** Time in Your Life; illus. by Ruth Adler. Day, 1955. 127p. lib. ed. $3.49 net. (I–U)
Considers all the ways of telling time: the rhythms of nature, the behavior of astronomical bodies, the coloring of a fiddler crab, and clocks and calendars. Includes directions for making a perpetual calendar.

476   **Bendick, Jeanne.** The First Book of Time. Watts, 1963. 69p. $2.65. (I)
Relates time to space and motion and explains time zones, the development of the modern calendar, and plant and animal "clocks."

477   **Bradley, Duane.** Time for You; illus. by Anne Marie Jauss. Lippincott, 1960. 110p. lib. ed. $2.69 net. (I)
The many devices men have used to measure time are described in this introduction to the history of time and calendars.

478   **Brindze, Ruth.** The Story of Our Calendar; illus. by Helene Carter. Vanguard, 1949. 63p. $3.95. (I)

An interesting, beautifully illustrated history of the calendar from Babylonian times to the present, including information on the Greenwich meridian, the International Date Line, and proposed changes in the calendar.

479   **Tannenbaum, Beulah,** and **Stillman, Myra.** Understanding Time: The Science of Clocks and Calendars; illus. by William D. Hayes. McGraw-Hill, 1958. 143p. $3.25; lib. ed. $3.01 net. (U)

Describes the devices by which man has measured time and discusses the standardization of time and the relationship between time and space. Includes anecdotes about clocks and watches and experimental projects.

480   **Zarchy, Harry.** Wheel of Time; illus. by René Martin. Crowell, 1957. 133p. $3.75. (I–U)

Traces the development of time-measuring devices and calendars: the lunar calendars of Babylonia and Greece, the solar calendar of Egypt, the Julian and Gregorian calendars, and the proposed thirteen-month and world calendars.

Physics

GENERAL CONCEPTS

481   **Adler, Irving.** Fire in Your Life; illus. by Ruth Adler. Day, 1955. 128p. lib. ed. $3.49 net. (I–U)

The history of fire: the mythology of its origin; man's efforts to produce, control, and measure it; and its role in present-day life.

482   **Adler, Irving.** The Wonders of Physics: An Introduction to the Physical World; illus. by Cornelius De Witt. Golden Pr., 1966. 165p. $4.95. (U)

A popular survey of matter and its governing laws: the forms of matter, its measurement, motion, radiation, and other characteristics, including relativity and the smashing of the atom.

483   **Huey, Edward G.** What Makes the Wheels Go Round: A First-Time Physics; with illus. by Elmer Loemker. Harcourt, 1952. 176p. $3. (I–U)

Simple explanations of physical phenomena and their application to everyday life.

484   **Irwin, Keith Gordon.** The Romance of Physics; illus. by Anthony Ravielli. Scribner, 1966. 240p. $4.95; lib. ed. $4.37 net. (U)

A history of physics, tracing each branch of the subject through the work of famous physicists. Readable style, informative illustrations, chronology, glossary, and index.

486   **Pine, Tillie S.,** and **Levine, Joseph.** Friction All Around; illus. by Bernice Myers. McGraw-Hill, 1960. 46p. $2.50; lib. ed. $2.63 net. (P)

Explains friction in terms young children can understand and gives directions for experiments which they can do themselves. (R3–4)

487   **Pine, Tillie S.,** and **Levine, Joseph.** Gravity All Around; illus. by Bernice Myers. McGraw-Hill, 1963. 48p. $2.75; lib. ed. $2.84 net. (P)

Similar in presentation and format to *Friction All Around,* above; a simple account of the effects of gravity in everyday life. (R3–4)

488   **Schlein, Miriam.** Fast Is Not a Ladybug: A Book about Fast and Slow Things; illus. by Leonard Kessler. W. R. Scott, 1953. unp. $3.25. (P)

Amusing illustrations and simple text present the concept that speed is relative. (R2–3)

490   **Schneider, Nina,** and **Schneider, Herman.** Let's Find Out: A Picture Science Book; pictures by Jeanne Bendick. W. R. Scott, 1946. 38p. $3.25. (P)

This first experiment book encourages the child to find answers to his questions about physical phenomena through easy-to-do experiments requiring only the simplest materials. (R3–4)

491   **Valens, E. G.** Motion; photos. by Berenice Abbott. World, 1965. 77p. $3.50; lib. ed. $3.41 net. (I)

Explains the laws of motion and provides thought-provoking questions, excellent photographs, and experiments to aid understanding.

FORCE AND ENERGY

492   **Blackwood, Paul.** Push and Pull: The Story of Energy; illus. by William D.

Hayes. rev. ed. McGraw-Hill, 1966. 192p.
$3.95; lib. ed. $3.31 net. (U)

A well-organized treatment of the various
kinds of energy—solar, electrical, radiant,
and kinetic—and their uses. Includes many
easy experiments and a glossary.

493   Branley, Franklyn M. Solar Energy;
illus. by John Teppich. Crowell, 1957. 117p.
$3.95. (I–U)

The author discusses the sun as the source
of all energy, describes the ways in which
man is now making use of solar energy, and
considers some future possibilities, such as
controlled photosynthesis. Devices for harnessing the sun's energy are clearly explained in the text and in excellent diagrams.

494   Harrison, George Russell. The First
Book of Energy; illus. with line drawings
and photos. Watts, 1965. 81p. $2.65. (I–U)

Explains the nature, kinds, and uses of
energy and the ways in which man controls
and measures it. Many explanatory diagrams, drawings, and photographs and a
glossary.

495   Hogben, Lancelot. The Wonderful
World of Energy. Artists: Eileen Aplin
(and others). Garden City, 1957. 69p. $2.95.
(I–U)

A concise, profusely illustrated presentation of energy in all its forms and uses,
emphasizing the scientific principles underlying its development and control. No index.

496   Podendorf, Illa. The True Book of
Energy; illus. by George Wilde. Childrens
Pr., 1963. 47p. $1.95; lib. ed. $2.50 net. (P)

A very simple description of the energy
of heat, running water, and sunlight and an
explanation of how man controls and uses
different forms of energy.

497   Ruchlis, Hy. Orbit: A Picture Story
of Force and Motion; drawings by Alice
Hirsh. Harper, 1958. 147p. $3.96; lib. ed.
$3.79 net. (U)

The author reviews Newton's laws of inertia, acceleration and momentum, action
and reaction, and gravity and resistance
and applies them to the space age. Diagrams and photographs aid understanding.

498   Ruchlis, Hy. The Wonder of Heat
Energy: A Picture Story of the Vital Part
Heat Plays in Our World; drawings by

Alice Hirsh. Harper, 1961. 186p. lib. ed.
$3.79 net. (U)

A thought-provoking overview of the
ways in which the sun's heat is converted
into energy to operate engines, turbines,
and jets, and of how heat affects every aspect of everyday life.

Magnetism, Electricity, and Electronics

499   Adler, Irving. Electricity in Your
Life; illus. by Ruth Adler. Day, 1965. 128p.
lib. ed. $3.49 net. (I–U)

The essentials about electricity and how
it is used in industry and science are explained in clear language and illustrated
with informative pictures.

500   Adler, Irving, and **Adler, Ruth.** Magnets. Day, 1966. 48p. lib. ed. $2.68 net. (I)

Introduces and explains magnets of all
kinds: the sun, the moon, the earth, and
the more familiar bar and horseshoe magnets. Well-placed, well-captioned drawings
augment the text.

501   Beeler, Nelson F., and **Branley,
Franklyn M.** Experiments with Electricity;
illus. by A. W. Revell. Crowell, 1949. 145p.
$3.95. (I)

Clear directions for 25 experiments, with
explanations of the principles demonstrated
and a list of equipment needed. Includes
interest-catching projects, such as making
a secret door lock and wiring a dancing doll.

502   Bendick, Jeanne. Electronics for
Young People; written and illus. by Jeanne
Bendick; new 4th ed. including nuclear energy, automation, computers, miniaturiza-
tion and more. McGraw-Hill, 1960. 190p.
$3.50; lib. ed. $3.06 net. (I–U)

Basic information about electronics and
its many applications in present-day life,
including an introduction to atomic theory
and nuclear power.

503   Branley, Franklyn M., and **Vaughan,
Eleanor K.** Mickey's Magnet; drawings by
Crockett Johnson. Crowell, 1956. unp.
$2.50; lib. ed. $2.69 net. (P)

A science book for the youngest, explaining what a magnet is, what it will do, and
how to make one.

504   Branley, Franklyn M. North, South,
East, and West; illus. by Robert Galster.
Crowell, 1966. unp. $3.25; lib. ed. $2.96 net.
(P)

A simple explanation of the compass and how to tell directions by shadows, including experiments which a child can perform with only sunlight, paper, crayon, and a few stones.

505   Epstein, Sam, and Epstein, Beryl. The First Book of Electricity; illus. by R. G. Amann. Watts, 1966. 68p. $2.65. (I)
A clear explanation, with experiments, of what electricity is, how it is generated and controlled, and how it is used.

506   Feravolo, Rocco V. Junior Science Book of Electricity; illus. by Evelyn Urbanowich. Garrard, 1960. 61p. $2.19. (P–I)
Interesting experiments with easy directions and informative illustrations clarify the basics of a complex subject for young children. Useful also with older slow readers. (R3–4)

507   Feravolo, Rocco V. Junior Science Book of Magnets; illus. by Evelyn Urbanowich. Garrard, 1960. 64p. $2.19. (P–I)
Simple experiments and clear explanations help the child to understand the properties and uses of magnets. Directions for making a magnet, a compass, and an electromagnet are given. Easy reading. (R3–4)

508   Klein, H. Arthur. Masers and Lasers; Helen Hale, editorial consultant; illus. by Frank Aloise. Lippincott, 1963. 184p. $3.95. (U)
Two of the newest developments in electronics are traced in clearly written text and excellent diagrams and photographs. For the advanced science student.

509   Knight, David C. Let's Find Out about Magnets; illus. by Don Miller. Watts, 1967. 64p. $2.65. (P)
An easy-to-understand explanation of the nature and uses of magnets, including a few simple experiments.

510   Morgan, Alfred. A First Electrical Book for Boys; illus. by the author. 3d ed. Scribner, 1963. 280p. $4.95; lib. ed. $4.37 net. (I–U)
Following a brief history of electricity, the author explains its nature and uses and gives explicit directions for performing interesting experiments.

511   Pine, Tillie S., and Levine, Joseph. Electricity and How We Use It; illus. by Bernice Myers. McGraw-Hill, 1962. 48p. $2.75; lib. ed. $2.84 net. (P)

A first book about electricity with simple explanations of circuits, switches, conductors, etc., and of how they function in everyday life. Includes easy experiments. (R2–3)

512   Pine, Tillie S., and Levine, Joseph. Magnets and How To Use Them; illus. by Anne Marie Jauss. McGraw-Hill, 1958. 47p. $2.75; lib. ed. $2.84 net. (P)
Introduces magnets, shows how they are used, and gives instructions for easy experiments. (R2–3)

513   Valens, E. G. Magnet; photos. by Berenice Abbott. World, 1964. unp. $3; lib. ed. $2.96 net. (I–U)
Facts about magnets are presented in lucid text and clear photographs of actual experiments demonstrating attraction and repulsion, magnetic poles, electromagnetism, etc.

Atomic Energy

514   Asimov, Isaac. Inside the Atom; illus. by John Bradford. rev. ed. Abelard-Schuman, 1966. 197p. $4. (U)
A study of the atomic theory and its applications, clearly written and illustrated with diagrams.

515   Bronowski, Jacob, and Selsam, Millicent. Biography of an Atom; illus. with pictures by Weimer Pursell and with photos. Harper, 1965. 43p. $3.50; lib. ed. $3.27. (I–U)
A simply written and attractively illustrated account of the structure, origin, and unchanging cycle of the carbon atom.

516   Freeman, Mae, and Freeman, Ira. The Story of the Atom; illus. by René Martin. Random, 1960. 81p. $1.95; lib. ed. $2.29 net. (I)
A simplified account of the structure and splitting of the atom, emphasizing peacetime uses of atomic energy. Illustrations are informative and well placed.

517   Grey, Vivian. Secret of the Mysterious Rays: The Discovery of Nuclear Energy; illus. by Ed Malsberg. Basic Books, 1966. 120p. $3.95. (I–U)
Covers the period from the discovery of X-rays in 1895 to the discovery of nuclear fission in 1939 and discusses the scientists involved in advancing knowledge about nuclear energy.

518   Hyde, Margaret O. Atoms Today and Tomorrow; illus. by Clifford N. Geary.

3d ed. McGraw-Hill, 1966. 160p. $3.50; lib. ed. $3.06 net. (U)

After briefly explaining what atomic energy is and how it is produced, the author discusses its uses in medicine, transportation, agriculture, and other peacetime pursuits. A stimulating overview of the atomic age.

Machines, Tools, and Engines

519   **Adler, Irving,** and **Adler, Ruth.** Machines. Day, 1964. 47p. lib. ed. $2.68 net. (I)

Explains wheels, pulleys, levers, and other simple devices and shows how they are used in more complex machinery.

520   **Adler, Irving.** Tools in Your Life; illus. by Ruth Adler. Day, 1956. 128p. lib. ed. $3.49 net. (I)

A history of tools, showing how the development of tools has paralleled the advance of civilization and has enabled man to conquer his environment.

521   **Bechdolt, Jack.** Going Up: The Story of Vertical Transportation; pictures by Jeanne Bendick. Abingdon, 1948. 128p. $3. (I)

The ladder, the pulley, the elevator, the escalator, and the airplane are explained as stages in man's efforts to climb ever higher.

522   **Beim, Jerrold.** Tim and the Tool Chest; illus. by Tracy Sugarman. Morrow, 1951. unp. lib. ed. $2.94 net. (P)

Tim's father teaches him how to use tools correctly and then gives him a tool chest of his own. A first book about tools with large print and many pictures. (R1–2)

523   **Burns, William A.** Man and His Tools; pictures by Paula Hutchison. McGraw-Hill, 1956. 158p. $3.95; lib. ed. $3.31 net. (I)

Beginning with the discovery or invention of basic tools—the hammer, the knife, the wheel, etc.—the author traces the development of each group to its present-day form.

524   **Mann, Martin.** How Things Work; illus. by Ava Morgan. Crowell, 1960. 146p. $3.50. (I)

Explains the "how" and "why" of ten modern machines in clear text and helpful illustrations.

525   **Meyer, Jerome S.** Engines; illus. by John Teppich. World, 1962. 78p. $2.95; lib. ed. $2.88 net. (I)

Distinguishes between the engine and the machine and discusses the evolution and working principles of internal-combustion, steam, and jet engines.

526   **Meyer, Jerome S.** Machines; illus. by John Polgreen. World, 1958. 63p. $2.95; lib. ed. $2.88 net. (I)

Shows how wheels, axles, screws, levers, and wedges are used in such machines as steam shovels, railroad engines, and nutcrackers.

527   **Pine, Tillie S.,** and **Levine, Joseph.** Simple Machines and How We Use Them; illus. by Bernice Myers. McGraw-Hill, 1965. 48p. $2.75; lib. ed. $2.84 net. (P–I)

Describes simple machines, such as the wheel and axle, lever, pulley, wedge, and screw, and discusses their application in doing the world's work. Basic information presented in simple text and many pictures. (R3–4)

528   **Saunders, F. Wenderoth.** Machines for You. Little, 1967. 58p. $3.95; lib. ed. $3.97 net. (P–I)

The author's dramatic pictures in bright colors augment simple explanations of how heavy machinery works. Describes the service to the community of the branch clipper, the snowfighter, and the leaf-sucker-up, as well as more familiar machines.

529   **Schneider, Herman.** Everyday Machines and How They Work; pictures by Jeanne Bendick. McGraw-Hill, 1950. 192p. $3.95; lib. ed. $3.31 net. (I)

Author and artist present an informative and entertaining explanation of how common household machines work.

530   **Schneider, Herman,** and **Schneider, Nina.** More Power to You: A Short History of Power from the Windmill to the Atom; illus. by Bill Ballentine. W. R. Scott, 1953. 119p. $3.50. (I)

Clear explanations, diagrams, and experiments show how man has captured the power of the sun, wind, water, and steam and has used it it machines and engines.

531   **Schneider, Herman,** and **Schneider, Nina.** Now Try This To Move a Heavy Load: Push, Pull, and Lift; with illus. by Bill Ballentine. W. R. Scott, 1947. 40p. $3.25. (P–I)

Step-by-step directions and clear diagrams for simple experiments demonstrating how loads can be lifted by friction, levers, inclined planes, and wheels. (R3–4)

532   **Sharp, Elizabeth N.** Simple Machines and How They Work; illus. by Ida Scheib. Random, 1959. 83p. $1.95; lib. ed. $2.29 net. (P–I)
Describes how the oldest machines (the wheel, pulley, screw, inclined plane, lever, and wedge) work in such familiar implements as pencil sharpeners and egg beaters. Includes easy experiments requiring only the simplest materials.

533   **Tunis, Edwin.** Weapons: A Pictorial History; written and illus. by Edwin Tunis. World, 1954. 151p. $6.95; lib. ed. $5.96 net. (I–U)
Traces the history of weapons from the stone thrower to the atomic bomb, explaining the mechanism of each device in readable text and informative sketches. Useful for the hobbyist and for history and science classes.

534   **Yates, Raymond F.** The Boys' Book of Tools. Harper, 1957. 173p. $3.95; lib. ed. $3.79 net. (I–U)
An introductory guide to basic tools and how to select and use them.

Engineering

535   **Billings, Henry.** Bridges; written and illus. by Henry Billings. Viking, 1956. 159p. $3.75; lib. ed. $3.56 net. (U)
Famous bridges, the men who designed and built them, and the problems of their construction are effectively discussed in a book focusing on three types of bridges: steel arch, cantilever, and suspension.

536   **Boardman, Fon W.** Roads. Walck, 1958. 143p. $3.75. (U)
Gives a brief history of roads from Roman days to the present and discusses modern methods of building them.

537   **Boardman, Fon W.** Tunnels. Walck, 1960. 144p. $3.75. (U)
Natural and man-made tunnels, past and present, are described and shown in photographs.

538   **Buehr, Walter.** Underground Riches: The Story of Mining; written and illus. by Walter Buehr. Morrow, 1958. 95p. lib. ed. $2.94 net. (I)
Covers the kinds of minerals mined, their uses, the means by which they are extracted, and the engineering problems involved in the process.

539   **Colby, C. B.** Historic American Forts: From Frontier Stockade to Coastal Fortress. Coward-McCann, 1963. 47p. lib. ed. $2.86 net. (I)
A survey of 15 early fortifications, describing the construction and present condition of each. Illustrated with maps and photographs. Useful in American History classes.

540   **Cooke, David C.** How Superhighways Are Made. Dodd, 1958. 64p. lib. ed. $2.79 net. (I)
Each step in planning and construction of a modern expressway is briefly explained and illustrated with a photograph facing the explanation.

541   **Farb, Peter.** The Story of Dams: An Introduction to Hydrology; foreword by E. C. Itschner; illus. by George Kanelous; reviewed for scientific accuracy by the U.S. Army Corps of Engineers. Harvey House, 1961. 127p. $3.95; lib. ed. $3.79 net. (I–U)
Describes the principal types and uses of dams, explains their construction, and discusses some famous American dams. Includes a guide to the location of 200 United States dams, a list for further reading, and many diagrams and photographs.

542   **Ley, Willy.** Engineers' Dreams; diags. and maps by Willy Ley; illus. by Isami Kashiwagi. rev. ed. Viking, 1954. 280p. $4.50; lib. ed. $4.13 net. (U)
A provocative account of nine engineering projects which have been dreamed of for years but never accomplished, including such unusual feats as irrigating the Iranian desert, tapping volcanic power, and lowering the level of the Mediterranean Sea.

543   **Markun, Patricia Maloney.** The First Book of Mining; pictures by Mildred Waltrip. Watts, 1959. 69p. $2.65. (I)
An introduction to the history of mines and mining, discussing types of mines and the techniques of mining.

544   **Peet, Creighton.** The First Book of Bridges. rev. ed. Watts, 1966. 72p. $2.65. (I)
Covers the history of bridges since prehistoric times, the engineering problems of

bridge building, types of bridges, and brief sketches of some famous bridges. Illustrated with photographs. Includes a glossary.

545 **Peterson, Harold L.** Forts in America; illus. by Daniel D. Feaser. Scribner, 1964. 61p. lib. ed. $3.31 net. (I–U)
Eleven forts, from the sixteenth century to the present, are described and pictured in detailed drawings. Notes which forts can be visited. Useful in American history classes.

SOUND AND ULTRASONICS

546 **Freeman, Ira M.** All about Sound and Ultrasonics; illus. with drawings and diags. by Irving Geis and with photos. Random, 1961. 141p. $2.50; lib. ed. $2.48 net. (U)
The science of sound is explored in clear text and excellent illustrations. Includes a few experiments.

547 **Irving, Robert.** Sound and Ultrasonics; illus. by Leonard Everett Fisher. Knopf, 1959. 146p. lib. ed. $3.09 net. (U)
Contents: The Nature of Sound; Sound Makers; The Musical Scale; Sound Bends and Bounces; Animal Sounds; How We Hear; Sound Recording and Transmission; Sounds We Cannot Hear; Faster than Sound.

548 **Murray, Don.** The World of Sound Recording. Lippincott, 1965. 128p. $3.50. (U)
Reviews the development of sound recording and discusses how recordings are made and how they are used. Useful in science classes and as vocational material.

549 **Pine, Tillie S.,** and **Levine, Joseph.** Sounds All Around; illus. by Bernice Myers. McGraw-Hill, 1958. 47p. $2.50; lib. ed. $2.63 net. (P)
Simply written text and interesting activities help the young child to grasp the basic principles of sound. (R3–4)

550 **Podendorf, Illa.** The True Book of Sounds We Hear; illus. by Chauncy Maltman. Childrens Pr., 1955. 46p. $2.50. (P)
Describes the sounds made by different animals and shows how sounds convey meaning. An easy-to-read introduction to sound. (R2–3)

551 **Showers, Paul.** The Listening Walk; illus. by Aliki. Crowell, 1961. unp. $3.25; lib. ed. $2.96 net. (P)
Makes the young child aware of sounds by describing the many different sounds he could hear when taking a walk. An interesting first science book with possibilities for class participation. (R2–3)

552 **Sootin, Harry.** Science Experiments with Sound; illus. by Frank Aloise. Norton, 1964. 95p. $3.25; lib. ed. $3.03 net. (U)
Step-by-step directions for performing experiments to demonstrate the principles of sound. Helpful illustrations, glossary, and bibliography. Recommended for the serious science student.

553 **Windle, Eric.** Sounds You Cannot Hear; illus. by John Kaufmann. Prentice-Hall, 1963. 69p. $3.50. (I)
The many interesting facets of ultrasonics are discussed in a well-written book: how bats fly at night, how sonar works, etc.

LIGHT AND COLOR

554 **Adler, Irving.** Color in Your Life; illus. by Ruth Adler. Day, 1962. 127p. lib. ed. $3.49 net. (I)
Discusses reflection, diffraction, and polarization of light and the importance of color in nature and industry. Diagrams, some in color, clarify the text.

555 **Beeler, Nelson F.,** and **Branley, Franklyn M.** Experiments with Light; illus. by Anne Marie Jauss. Crowell, 1957. 159p. $3.50. (U)
Explanations and experiments to interest the student in the nature of light and to encourage him to discover its characteristics for himself. Covers the working of lenses, polarization, and the speed of light and includes plans for making a simple lens, a light meter, a polaroid viewer, and other devices.

556 **Feravolo, Rocco V.** Junior Science Book of Light; illus. by George Wilde. Garrard, 1961. 62p. $2.19. (P–I)
A simple presentation of the basic principles of light and its motion in space, geared to everyday experiences such as changing shadows. Contains a few easy-to-do experiments. Recommended for primary grades and the older slow reader. (R3–4)

557 **Freeman, Mae,** and **Freeman, Ira.** Fun and Experiments with Light; illus. by

Anne Marie Jauss. Crowell, 1957. 159p. $1.95; lib. ed. $2.07 net. (U)

Experiments on the nature of light, the working of lenses, the speed of light, etc.

558   **Harrison, George Russell.** The First Book of Light. Watts, 1962. 85p. $2.65. (I)

After giving general information about light, the author discusses the development and operation of arc, incandescent, and fluorescent lamps; the relation of light waves to the total radio-wave spectrum; and other special aspects of the subject. Illustrated with diagrams and photographs.

559   **Hellman, Harold.** The Art and Science of Color; illus. by Mark Binn. McGraw-Hill, 1967. 175p. $4.50; lib. ed. $3.99 net. (U)

A comprehensive treatment of color, from the physics of light to the modern use of color in art, science, and technology. Entertainingly written and illustrated with diagrams and color photographs. Useful with advanced students in art and science.

560   **Kettelkamp, Larry.** Shadows; written and illus. by Larry Kettelkamp. Morrow, 1957. 63p. lib. ed. $2.94 net. (P–I)

Shadow plays and games introduce a discussion of shadows on the moon, X-rays, eclipses, sundials, and other manifestations of shadows.

561   **Meyer, Jerome S.** Prisms and Lenses; illus. by John Polgreen. World, 1959. 63p. $2.75; lib. ed. $2.73 net. (I)

An introduction to the science of optics, with emphasis on the theory behind prisms and lenses and their use by scientists and in everyday life.

562   **Tannenbaum, Beulah,** and **Stillman, Myra.** Understanding Light: The Science of Visible and Invisible Rays; illus. by Gustav Schrotter. McGraw-Hill, 1960. 144p. $3.25; lib. ed. $3.01 net. (U)

Wide coverage of the history, nature, and uses of light. Illustrated with diagrams, drawings, and photographs.

Chemistry

563   **Asimov, Isaac.** Building Blocks of the Universe. rev. ed. Abelard-Schuman, 1961. 280p. $3.50. (U)

An advanced but nontechnical discussion of the 102 known chemical elements, explaining the structure, form, and uses of each.

564   **Carona, Philip.** The True Book of Chemistry: What Things Are Made Of; pictures by George Wilde. Childrens Pr., 1962. 46p. $1.95; lib. ed. $2.50 net. (P–I)

An introduction to chemical elements and their symbols, compounds, chemical changes, and other basic concepts of chemistry.

565   **Freeman, Mae,** and **Freeman, Ira.** Fun with Chemistry. new rev. ed. Random, 1962. 58p. $1.95. (I)

Simple experiments with easily obtained materials. (R4–5)

566   **Goldin, Augusta.** Salt; illus. by Robert Galster. Crowell, 1965. unp. $3.25; lib. ed. $2.96 net. (P)

An explanation in simplest terms of the properties, sources, and uses of salt and of how to make salt crystals. Bold, clear illustrations add interest and information.

567   **Irwin, Keith Gordon.** The Romance of Chemistry: From Ancient Alchemy to Nuclear Fission; illus. by Anthony Ravielli. Viking, 1959. 148p. lib. ed. $3.56 net. (U)

An advanced history of chemistry centering around the lives and work of such pioneer scientists as Boyle, Priestley, Lavoisier, and the Curies.

568   **Morgan, Alfred Powell.** First Chemistry Book for Boys and Girls; illus. by Bradford Babbitt and Terry Smith. Scribner, 1950. 179p. $3.95; lib. ed. $3.63 net. (I)

A brief introduction to chemistry followed by 64 easy experiments demonstrating the principles of chemistry, including combustion, elements and symbols, acids, bases, etc. Illustrations clarify instructions.

570   **Roberson, Paul.** Chemistry by Experiment; illus. by Eric Thomas. Day, 1965. 48p. lib. ed. $2.52 net. (I)

Experiments with simple materials and equipment, designed to encourage independent exploration.

571   **Wohlrabe, Raymond A.** Crystals; Helen Hale, editorial consultant. Lippincott, 1962. 128p. $3.50. (U)

A serious discussion of the nature of crystals, their structure, and uses, including instructions for growing and studying crystals at home.

572 **Woodburn, John H.** Radioisotopes; Helen Hale, editorial consultant. Lippincott, 1962. 128p. $3.50. (U)

For the advanced student, a lucid introduction to radioisotopes, explaining the meaning of isotopes and how they are made and discussing their uses in medicine, farming, industry, and research.

Earth Sciences

LAND FORMATIONS

573 **Adler, Irving,** and **Adler, Ruth.** Coal. Day, 1965. 47p. lib. ed. $2.68 net. (I)

Explains the origin, chemistry, mining, and uses of coal in well-organized text and informative pictures.

574 **Ames, Gerald,** and **Wyler, Rose,** in cooperation with the American Museum of Natural History. The Earth's Story. Creative Educ. Soc., 1962. 224p. $5.95 (I)

A study of the earth's crust, showing how it was formed, what it is made of, and how it has changed through the ages. Illustrated with photographs and drawings.

575 **Bendick, Jeanne.** The Shape of the Earth. Rand McNally, 1965. 72p. $2.95; lib. ed. $3.08 net. (I)

Describes the evolution of the earth, the formation of mountains and oceans, the composition of the earth's crust, and the effect of the earth's shape on climate and weather.

576 **Cormack, M. B.** The First Book of Stones; pictures by M. K. Scott. Watts, 1950. 93p. $2.65. (I)

Brief information about the characteristics of common rocks and advice about collecting and studying them.

577 **Fenton, Carroll Lane,** and **Fenton, Mildred Adams.** The Land We Live On. rev. ed. Doubleday, 1966. 96p. $3.50. (I)

Concise text and many photographs about mountains, deserts, mesas, and other features of the earth's surface; also, a discussion of the need for conservation.

578 **Fenton, Carroll Lane,** and **Fenton,**

Mildred Adams. Riches from the Earth; illus. by the authors. Day, 1953. 159p. $3.75. (I)

Surveys the history, properties, mining, and uses of rocks, ores, and mineral resources.

579 **Fenton, Carroll Lane,** and **Fenton, Mildred Adams.** Rocks and Their Stories. Doubleday, 1951. 112p. $3.50. (I)

An introduction to petrology, distinguishing rocks, stones, and minerals; explaining methods of identification; and discussing 40 basic minerals.

580 **Goetz, Delia.** Deserts; illus. by Louis Darling. Morrow, 1956. 64p. lib. ed. $2.94 net. (I)

Describes the desert lands that cover a third of the earth and discusses the adaptations made by desert fauna and flora. Large type, easy reading, many well-placed illustrations.

581 **Goetz, Delia.** Grasslands; illus. by Louis Darling. Morrow, 1959. 62p. lib. ed. $2.94 net. (I)

A discussion of prairies, steppes, and savannas, similar to *Deserts,* above, in presentation and format.

582 **Goetz, Delia.** Islands in the Ocean; illus. by Louis Darling. Morrow, 1964. 64p. $2.95; lib. ed. $2.94 net. (I)

Another title in this author's series explains the difference between continental and oceanic islands; the formation of islands; and the influence of an island environment on plant, animal, and human life.

583 **Goetz, Delia.** Mountains; illus. by Louis Darling. Morrow, 1962. 64p. lib. ed. $2.94 net. (I)

Continuing this well-written and well-illustrated series, the author explains the formation of mountains, their values, and some of the problems of mountain life.

584 **Goetz, Delia.** Tropical Rain Forests; illus. by Louis Darling. Morrow, 1957. 64p. lib. ed. $2.94 net. (I)

Describes the climate, vegetation, animals, and primitive people of the rain forests of the world.

585 **Hamilton, Elizabeth.** The First Book of Caves; illus. by Bette J. Davis. Watts, 1956. 62p. $2.65. (I)

An active spelunker describes cave formation, the strange plant and animal life found in caves, and the uses made of caves in prehistoric and modern times. Includes information about well-known caves and rules for cave exploration.

586   **Hoke, John.** The First Book of the Jungle; pictures by Russell Peterson. Watts, 1964. 64p. $2.65. (I)

Using the Guiana jungle as an example, the author explains the jungle, explodes mistaken ideas about it, and describes the types of life supported by it.

587   **Huntington, Harriet E.** The Yosemite Story. Doubleday, 1967. 96p. $3.50. (I–U)

In a beautifully illustrated and interestingly written account of the Yosemite Valley, the author discusses its geological history, discovery, and conversion into a national park.

588   **Hyde, Margaret O.** Exploring Earth and Space; illus. by Clifford N. Geary. 4th ed. McGraw-Hill, 1967. 159p. $3.95; lib. ed. $3.31 net. (U)

Describes the research undertaken in the International Geophysical Year, 1957–1958, and later explorations of the Antarctic, the Continental Shelf, the ocean, and space.

589   **Irving, Robert.** Volcanoes and Earthquakes; illus. by Ruth Adler and with photos. Knopf, 1962. 123p. lib. ed. $3.29 net. (I–U)

An authoritative discussion of the scientific basis for volcanoes and earthquakes and descriptions of some of the most disastrous ones. Diagrams and photographs reinforce the lucid text.

590   **Knight, David C.** The First Book of Deserts: An Introduction to the Earth's Arid Lands; illus. with drawings and photos. Watts, 1964. 88p. $2.65. (I)

Locates the most famous deserts, describes types of deserts, and explains how they were formed and what kinds of life exist in them.

591   **Lauber, Patricia,** All about the Planet Earth; illus. with drawings by Lee J. Ames and with photos. Random, 1962. 142p. $2.50; lib. ed. $2.48 net. (I)

Facts and theories about the origin and evolution of the earth, the formation of mountains and oceans, the causes of earth-

quakes and volcanoes, and other aspects of the earth's story.

592   **Lauber, Patricia.** The Junior Science Book of Volcanoes; illus. by Matthew Kalmenoff. Garrard, 1965. 64p. $2.19. (P–I)

An introductory book on the causes and behavior of volcanoes, beginning with the dramatic story of Parícutin, Mexico. Suggested for older pupils with reading problems. (R3–4)

593   **Life** (Periodical). The World We Live In; by the editorial staff of Life and Lincoln Barnett. Text especially adapted by Jane Werner Watson from the original version. Golden Pr., 1956. 216p. $4.95. (U)

A colorfully illustrated panorama of the earth: its formation, structure, history, plant and animal life, and place in the universe.

594   **Loomis, Frederick Brewster.** Field Book of Common Rocks and Minerals: For Identifying the Rocks and Minerals of the United States and Interpreting Their Origins and Meanings; rev. With 47 colored specimens and over 100 illus. from photos. by W. E. Corbin and drawings by the author. Putnam, 1948. 352p. $3.95. (U)

A standard handbook for the serious student and collector.

595   **Pine, Tillie S.,** and **Levine, Joseph.** Rocks and How We Use Them; illus. by Bernice Myers. McGraw-Hill, 1967. 48p. $3.50. (P)

In very simple text and cartoon-like pictures, author and artist show that rocks are everywhere and serve many useful purposes. Includes easy experiments to encourage young children to become aware of rocks. (R2–3)

596   **Podendorf, Illa.** The True Book of Rocks and Minerals; illus. by George Rhoads. Childrens Pr., 1958. 48p. $2.50. (P)

An introduction to the subject, written in controlled vocabulary and illustrated with informative pictures. Defines such scientific terms as "igneus," "metamorphic," "sedimentary," "petrified," "fossil," and "crystal." (R2–3)

597   **Pond, Alonzo.** Deserts: Silent Lands of the World. Norton, 1965. 157p. $3.95; lib. ed. $3.73 net. (I–U)

From his exploration of deserts in many

parts of the world the author writes of the geology, geography, and life of deserts, stressing the importance of deserts as a possible future home for the world's teeming population. Highly readable and packed with unusual facts.

598   **Poole, Lynn,** and **Poole, Gray.** Deep in Caves and Caverns. Dodd, 1962. 158p. $3.50. (U)
An interesting account of the formation, exploration, and inhabitants of caves, including information about the work of speleologists. Enlivened by anecdotes and photographs.

599   **Ravielli, Anthony.** The World Is Round; written and illus. by Anthony Ravielli. Viking, 1963. 45p. $3.50; lib. ed. $3.37 net. (P–I)
A beautiful science picture book explaining why the earth seems flat and how scientists have determined its true shape.

600   **Selsam, Millicent E.** Birth of an Island; pictures by Winifred Lubell. Harper, 1959. 42p. $2.95; lib. ed. $2.92 net. (P)
The story of how a mass of volcanic rock in the ocean weathers, develops soil, and acquires plant and animal life is told simply but engrossingly. Striking colored illustrations add information and appeal.

601   **Shuttlesworth, Dorothy E.** The Story of Rocks; illus. by Su Zan N. Swain. rev. ed. Garden City, 1966. 57p. $3.50. (I)
Discusses rocks, minerals, gems, and fossils in concise text, extended by many illustrations in color. Includes information on locating, identifying, collecting, and displaying rocks and lists books for further reading.

602   **Sootin, Harry** and **Sootin, Laura.** The Young Experimenters' Workbook: Treasures of the Earth; illus. by Frank Aloise. Norton, 1965. 59p. $3.25; lib. ed. $3.03 net. (I)
Experiments designed to demonstrate basic facts about rocks and minerals. Includes a glossary and a reading list.

603   **Sperry, Armstrong.** All about the Jungle; written and illus. by Armstrong Sperry. Random, 1959. 141p. $2.50; lib. ed. $2.48 net. (I)
Locates and describes the three main jungle regions of the world, discusses plant and animal life in the areas, and gives advice on survival in the jungle.

604   **Sterling, Dorothy.** The Story of Caves; illus. by Winifred Lubell. Doubleday, 1956. 121p. $3.50. (I)
In addition to basic information about the formation and history of caves, the author tells how stalactites and stalagmites are formed, relates superstitions about caves, discusses cave paintings, and gives a list of American caves. Interestingly written and illustrated.

605   **Zim, Herbert S.,** and **Shaffer, Paul R.** Rocks and Minerals; illus. by Raymond Perlman. Golden Pr., 1957. 160p. $3.95. (I)
A guide to rock and mineral identification, illustrated with color plates and drawings.

OCEANS AND INLAND WATERS

606   **Archer, Sellers G.** Rain, Rivers, and Reservoirs: The Challenge of Running Water. Coward-McCann, 1963. 120p. lib. ed. $2.60 net. (U)
Explains the water cycle sources of water, water pollution, and plans for ensuring a supply of pure water for the future.

607   **Bartlett, Margaret Farrington.** The Clean Brook; illus. by Aldren A. Watson. Crowell, 1960. 40p. $3.25; lib. ed. $2.96 net. (P)
A science picture book telling how nature filters the water and keeps the brook clean and clear.

608   **Brindze, Ruth.** The Gulf Stream; illus. by Helene Carter. Vanguard, 1945. 62p. $3.95. (I)
Flowing pictures in three colors dramatize the story of the great ocean-river and its effects on the discovery and exploration of America and on climate, weather, and navigation.

609   **Brindze, Ruth.** The Rise and Fall of the Seas: The Story of Tides; illus. with photos. and diags. by Felix Cooper. Harcourt, 1964. 96p. $3.50. (I)
Tells "how sun and moon draw up the ocean to produce the tides and their amazing variations in height and depth, how tides are measured and predicted, how men have made use of them in the past and may in the future . . . "

610   **Carson, Rachel.** The Sea around Us. rev. ed. Oxford Univ. Pr., 1961. 237p. $5.75. (U)

A noted biologist writes a thoroughly scientific, yet poetic, account of the sea in all its aspects. A rewarding adult book for the gifted student.

611   Clarke, Arthur C. The Challenge of the Sea; illus. by Alex Schomburg; introd. by Wernher von Braun. Holt, 1960. 167p. lib. ed. $3.59 net. (U)
In a blend of science and science fiction the author discusses what is known about the ocean's history, geology, and geography; its plant and animal life; and its mineral and food resources, then speculates about its future uses as a dwelling place and source of food and wealth for man.

612   Coggins, Jack. Hydrospace: Frontier beneath the Sea; illus. by the author. Dodd, 1966. 96p. lib. ed. $3.23 net. (I–U)
Surveys the possibilities of obtaining food, water, power, mineral resources, and living space in the ocean and describes the equipment which makes undersea exploration possible.

613   Coombs, Charles. Deep-Sea World: The Story of Oceanography. Morrow, 1966. 256p. $4.95. (U)
Oceanographic research—stressing the work of oceanographers and their equipment—is discussed in a well-organized text illustrated with diagrams and photographs. Includes a chapter on oceanography as a career.

614   Engel, Leonard. The Sea; adapted by the eds. of Silver Burdett from a volume in the Life Nature Library by Leonard Engel and the eds. of Life. Silver Burdett, 1964. 190p. $4.95. (I–U)
Broad coverage, concise text, many illustrations in color.

615   Epstein, Sam, and **Epstein, Beryl.** The First Book of the Ocean; pictures by Walter Buehr. Watts, 1961. 72p. $2.65. (I)
A simply written, well-illustrated introduction to oceans.

616   Gans, Roma. Icebergs; illus. by Bobri. Crowell, 1964. unp. $3.25; lib. ed. $2.96 net. (P)
Easy text and clarifying pictures explain for the young child what icebergs are, where they come from, and the dangers they present to ships.

617   Goldin, Augusta. The Bottom of the Sea; illus. by Ed Emberley. Crowell, 1967. unp. $3.25; lib. ed. $2.96 net. (P)
Beginning concepts of oceanography and underwater topography are explained in language understandable to primary children and illustrated with interest-catching pictures.

618   Greenhood, David. Watch the Tides; illus. by Jane Castle. Holiday, 1961. unp. lib. ed. $2.95 net. (P)
Encourages the young child to observe the ebb and flow of tides, explains the causes and effects of tides, and tells what to look for at high and low tide.

619   Halacy, D. S. The Water Crisis; illus. with drawings by George H. Buehler and with photos. Dutton, 1966. 192p. $4.95; lib. ed. $4.90 net. (U)
A survey of the world's water supply and the problems of pollution, conservation, and future sources. Includes a bibliography and a list of agencies offering positions in hydrology.

620   Helfman, Elizabeth S. Rivers and Watersheds in America's Future; illus. with a map and 24 photos. McKay, 1965. 244p. $4.95; lib. ed. $4.19 net. (U)
Sources of water, past and current use and abuse of streams and rivers, and water-supply problems are discussed in a timely book.

621   Lane, Ferdinand C. All about the Sea; illus. by Fritz Kredel. Random, 1953. 148p. $2.50; lib. ed. $2.48 net. (I)
An inviting account of the sea, the life within it, and how man explores and exploits it. (R4–5)

622   Lauber, Patricia. Junior Science Book of Icebergs and Glaciers. Garrard, 1961. 64p. $2.19. (P–I)
Beginning with the sinking of the "Titanic" and the establishment of the International Ice Patrol, the author explains the formation of glaciers and icebergs, the ice ages of the past, and the possibility of a future ice age. Written and designed for readers with limited skills. (R3–4)

623   Meeks, Esther M. Jeff and Mr. James' Pond; illus. by Paul Galdone. Lothrop, 1962. unp. $3.25; lib. ed. $3.13 net. (P)
This science picture book tells how a small boy helps a farmer keep his pond

fresh and clear by maintaining the balance of nature.

624 Meyer, Jerome S. Water at Work; illus. with photos. and diags. by John Polgreen. World, 1963. 92p. $3.50. (I)

Discusses the water cycle, sources of water, and the vital role of water in all life.

625 Naden, Corinne J. The First Book of Rivers; illus. with maps by Dick Urso. Watts, 1967. 73p. $2.65. (I)

A general discussion of rivers and their importance and a chart of facts about the principal rivers of the world.

626 Poole, Lynn, and **Poole, Gray.** Danger! Icebergs Ahead! Random, 1961. 61p. $1.95; lib. ed. $2.29 net. (I)

Similar in coverage to the Lauber book, above, but on a higher level. Illustrated with photographs, maps, and diagrams.

627 Riedman, Sarah R. Water for People; illus. by Bunji Tagawa. rev. ed. Abelard-Schuman, 1961. 156p. $3. (U)

Discusses the importance of water as a natural resource and the many uses which it serves. Includes information about water engineering and conservation.

628 Shannon, Terry, and **Payzant, Charles.** Project Sealab: The Story of the United States Navy's Man-in-the-Sea Program; illus. with photos. and diags. Golden Gate, 1966. 96p. $3.95; lib. ed. $3.79 net. (I–U)

An informal but authoritative explanation of the purposes, procedures, and equipment of the Navy's underseas research project off the coast of La Jolla, California.

629 Spilhaus, Athelstan. The Ocean Laboratory. Creative Educ. Soc., 1967. 112p. $5.95. (U)

A readable survey of the history, physical geography, and ecology of the ocean, with emphasis on recent oceanographic research and conservation measures. Illustrated with photographs, maps, and explanatory drawings. Includes a glossary.

630 White, Anne Terry. All about Great Rivers of the World; illus. by Anne Terry White. Random, 1957. 150p. $2.50; lib. ed. $2.48 net. (I)

Explains what rivers are, how they originated, and how they affect man, then describes at length the Nile, the Amazon, the

Yangtze, the Volga, and the Mississippi.

631 Woodbury, David O. Fresh Water from Salty Seas. Dodd, 1967. 96p. $3.50; lib. ed. $3.23 net. (I–U)

A timely story of desalination, considering the pros and cons of each possible method and discussing the need for new sources of water supply, the role of the Office of Saline Water, and the proposed floating desalting plant. Illustrated with photographs and diagrams. Useful in social studies as well as in science.

ATMOSPHERE, WEATHER, AND SEASONS

632 Adler, Irving, and **Adler, Ruth.** Air. Day, 1962. 48p. lib. ed. $2.68 net. (I)

An introductory book on air, covering its characteristics and functions.

633 Adler, Irving. Weather in Your Life; illus. by Peggy and Ruth Adler. Day, 1959. 126p. lib. ed. $3.49 net. (I–U)

Explains how the effects of air, water, land, and the sun's heat are combined to produce changes in the weather. A well-organized book illustrated with photographs and diagrams.

634 Bell, Thelma Harrington. Snow; with drawings by Corydon Bell. Viking, 1954. 55p. $3; lib. ed. $3.04 net. (I)

An interesting account of the formation of snow and other frozen precipitation, explaining how they are both helpful and dangerous to man. Illustrations in soft blue and white show the delicate shapes of the snow crystals.

635 Bell, Thelma Harrington. Thunderstorm; illus. by Corydon Bell. Viking, 1960. 128p. $3.25; lib. ed. $3.19 net. (U)

Explains thunderstorms, lightning, thunder, and clouds and describes the work of scientists who investigate them. Includes anecdotes and weather superstitions.

636 Bendick, Jeanne. The Wind; written and illus. by Jeanne Bendick. Rand McNally, 1964. 80p. $2.95; lib. ed. $3.08 net. (I)

Scientific facts, myths, superstitions, and sayings about the wind. Simply written and profusely illustrated with maps, diagrams, and drawings.

637 Branley, Franklyn M. Air Is All

around You; illus. by Robert Galster. Crowell, 1962. unp. $3.25; lib. ed. $2.96 net. (P)

Very simple explanations and illustrations help the young child to understand that air is everywhere, even though he cannot see it. Includes three experiments.

638   **Branley, Franklyn M.** Flash, Crash, Rumble, and Roll; illus. by Ed Emberley. Crowell, 1964. unp. $3.25; lib. ed. $2.96 net. (P)

This reassuring book makes thunderstorms interesting instead of frightening by explaining their causes, nature, and effects. Includes safety rules and directions for telling how far away a storm is.

639   **Branley, Franklyn M.** Snow Is Falling; illus. by Helen Stone. Crowell, 1963. unp. $3.25; lib. ed. $2.96 net. (P)

A picture science book about the beauty, usefulness, and dangers of snow, including an experiment to prove that snow retains warmth.

640   **Craig, M. Jean.** Spring Is Like the Morning; illus. by Don Almquist. Putnam, 1965. 61p. lib. ed. $2.68 net. (P)

A small boy discovers the delights of spring as he watches the earth wake from its winter sleep. Expressive pictures reinforce the mood of wonder inherent in the simple text.

641   **Fox, Charles Phillip.** When Autumn Comes; story and photos. by Charles Phillip Fox. Reilly & Lee, 1966. unp. $2.95. (P)

Appealing photographs with brief, easy-to-read captions show signs of approaching autumn. (R1–2)

642   **Fox, Charles Phillip.** When Spring Comes; story and photos. by Charles Phillip Fox. Reilly & Lee, 1964. unp. $2.95. (P)

Presents facts about what happens in the plant and animal world in springtime through beautiful photographs and simple text. (R1–2)

643   **Fox, Charles Phillip.** When Summer Comes; story and photos. by Charles Phillip Fox. Reilly & Lee, 1966. unp. $2.95. (P)

Photographs and easy text introduce the young child to typical summer scenes. (R1–2)

644   **Fox, Charles Phillip.** When Winter Comes; story and photos. by Charles Phillip Fox. Reilly & Lee, 1962. 29p. $2.95 (P)

In the same format as the three books above, the author presents factual information about how animals live in winter. (R1–2)

645   **Gallant, Roy A.** Exploring the Weather; illus. by Lowell Hess. Garden City, 1957. 64p. $3.50. (I)

Numerous charts, diagrams, and pictures, many in color, distinguish this survey of weather phenomena and weather forecasting. Includes a discussion of recent and possible future developments in meteorology and a reading list.

646   **Irving, Robert.** Hurricanes and Twisters; foreword by Ernest J. Christie; illus. by Ruth Adler and with photos. Knopf, 1955. 143p. lib. ed. $3.39 net. (I)

A straightforward discussion of the causes, nature, and destructive results of hurricanes and tornadoes, including information about the hurricane season and stories of some famous hurricanes.

647   **Kavaler, Lucy.** Dangerous Air; illus. by Carl Smith. Day, 1967. 143p. $3.95. (U)

Discusses the causes and effects of air pollution and measures to combat it.

648   **Knight, David C.** The First Book of Air: A Basic Guide to the Earth's Atmosphere; illus. with photos. and drawings. Watts, 1961. 67p. $2.65. (I)

Explains the composition of the air, its movement, and its importance to man, emphasizing weather. Includes experiments.

649   **Laird, Charles,** and **Laird, Ruth.** Weathercasting. Prentice-Hall, 1955. 163p. $4.95. (U)

An introduction to the science of weather observation and forecasting: terminology, symbols, instruments, and methods. Includes charts and tables to encourage interpretation of weather reports and gives detailed directions for building and using weather-indicating devices.

650   **Lewis, Alfred.** Clean the Air! Fighting Smoke, Smog, and Smaze across the Country; illus. with photos. McGraw-Hill, 1965. 96p. $3.50; lib. ed. $3.06 net. (U)

The author gives the essential facts about the causes and control of air pollution in concise text, illustrated with excellent photographs.

651   **Podendorf, Illa.** The True Book of Weather Experiments; pictures by Felix Palm. Childrens Pr., 1961. 47p. $2.50. (P)

Easy experiments to help the primary pupil learn about the weather, climate, seasons, and other aspects of meteorology. (R2–3)

652   **Schneider, Herman.** Everyday Weather and How It Works; pictures by Jeanne Bendick. rev. ed. McGraw-Hill, 1961. 194p. $3.50; lib. ed. $3.06 net. (I)

A useful explanation of weather and climate, including instructions for building and using simple meteorological devices.

653   **Sootin, Harry.** The Long Search: Man Learns about the Nature of Air; illus. by Frank Aloise. Norton, 1967. 262p. $4.50; lib. ed. $4.36 net. (I–U)

Clear explanations and informative illustrations trace the development of man's understanding of the nature of air. Includes a discussion of the problems of pollution.

654   **Tannehill, Ivan Ray.** All about the Weather; illus. by Rene Martin. Random, 1953. 149p. $2.50; lib. ed. $2.48 net. (I–U)

Discusses weather, the work of meteorologists, and the functions of the U.S. Weather Bureau.

655   **Thompson, Phillip D.** Weather; by Phillip D. Thompson and the eds. of Life. Time, Inc., 1965. Life Science Library, distributed by Silver Burdett. 200p. $4.95. (U)

A survey of weather and weather forecasting, generously illustrated with colored photographs.

656   **Zim, Herbert S.** Lightning and Thunder; illus. by James Gordon Irving. Morrow, 1952. 58p. $2.95; lib. ed. $2.94 net. (I)

Basic principles of electrical storms, lightning, and thunder are simply explained.

Biology

GENERAL CONCEPTS

657   **Cadbury, B. Bartram.** The Community of Living Things in Fresh and Salt Water, by B. Bartram Cadbury, in co-operation with The National Audubon Society. Creative Educ. Soc., 1960. unp. $5.95. (P–I)

Introduces the plants and animals found in water, describes their relationship to one another, and stresses the importance of keeping water clean. Colorfully illustrated with drawings and photographs.

658   **Carson, Rachel.** The Edge of the Sea; with illus. by Bob Hines. Houghton, 1955. 276p. $5.50. (U)

Describes the typical community of plants and animals found in each of three coastal habitats: "The Rocky Shore," "The Rim of Sand," and "The Coral Coast." A beautifully written and thought-provoking book for the superior reader.

659   **Clemons, Elizabeth.** Tide Pools & Beaches; illus. by Joe Gault. Knopf, 1964. 78p. $2.95; lib. ed. $3.09 net. (P–I)

A simply written book explaining how to identify, collect, and preserve the commonest sea animals and plants found along the seashore. Warns about dangerous preservatives and shows specimens in clear drawings.

660   **Collins, Stephen.** The Community of Living Things in Forest and Woodland, by Stephen Collins, in co-operation with The National Audubon Society. Creative Educ. Soc., 1960. unp. $5.95. (P–I)

The natural history and ecology of forests are presented in simple text and many beautiful photographs.

661   **Darling, Lois,** and **Darling, Louis.** The Science of Life; written and illus. by Lois and Louis Darling. World, 1961. 256p. $4.95. (U)

An excellent introduction to biology for the superior student. Organized into five sections: "The Basis of Life," "The Organization of Life," "The Reproduction of Life," "The History of Life," and "The Web of Life." Includes maps, drawings, and a reading list.

662   **Frankel, Edward.** DNA—Ladder of Life; illus. by Anne Marie Jauss. McGraw-Hill, 1964. 127p. $2.95; lib. ed. $2.96 net. (U)

After giving essential chemical background information, the author reviews current information and research about the molecule that determines the nature of all living things, explaining the role of DNA in heredity and its possibilities for creating life.

663   **Huntington, Harriet E.** Let's Go Out-

doors; illus. by Preston Duncan. Doubleday, 1939. 88p. $3.50. (P–I)

Photographs and simple text encourage the young child to observe the plants and small creatures in his own neighborhood.

664   Huntington, Harriet E. Let's Go to the Brook; illus. with photos. by the author. Doubleday, 1952. 88p. $3.50. (P–I)

Exceptionally fine photographs show the plant and animal life to be found along the brook. Text is lively and clear.

665   Huntington, Harriet E. Let's Go to the Desert; illus. with photos. by the author. Doubleday, 1949. 90p. $3.50. (P–I)

Snakes, lizards, scorpions, and desert-loving plants are introduced in brief text and fine photographs.

666   Klein, H. Arthur. Bioluminescence; Helen Hale, editorial consultant; illus. by the author and Lewis Zacks. Lippincott, 1965. 184p. $4.25. (U)

A readable account of the emission of light by plants and animals, augmented by photographs, diagrams, and drawings.

667   Klots, Alexander B., and **Klots, Elsie B.** The Community of Living Things in the Desert, by Alexander and Elsie B. Klots, in co-operation with The National Audubon Society. Creative Educ. Soc., 1960. unp. $5.95. (P–I)

Beautiful photographs make this study of desert life especially appealing. The readable text explains how plant and animal life adapts to the harsh living conditions of the desert.

668   Lemmon, Robert S. The Community of Living Things in Parks and Gardens; by Robert S. Lemmon in co-operation with The National Audubon Society. Creative Educ. Soc., 1960. unp. $5.95. (P–I)

A profusely illustrated, simply written survey of plant and animal life in areas around one's own home.

669   Life (Periodical). The Wonders of Life on Earth; by the eds. of Life and Lincoln Barnett. Text especially adapted by Sarel Eimerl from the original version. Golden Pr., 1960. 215p. $4.95. (I–U)

Explores the effects of heredity and environment on the development of life, with chapters on Darwin's journey, Mendel's experiments, and the recent research on DNA. The many beautiful photographs and other illustrations are included in the detailed index.

670   Peattie, Donald Culross. The Rainbow Book of Nature; illus. by Rudolf Freund. World, 1957. 319p. $5.95. (I)

A well-written and beautifully illustrated introduction to the natural world, concentrating on living things and the conditions necessary to different forms of life. Included is a list of nature books, films, and recordings.

671   Ress, Etta Schneider, ed. The Community of Living Things in Field and Meadow, by Etta Schneider Ress, in co-operation with The National Audubon Society. Creative Educ. Soc., 1960. unp. $5.95. (P–I)

A picture story of how plants and animals live together.

672   Riedman, Sarah R. Naming Living Things: The Grouping of Plants and Animals; illus. by Jerome P. Connolly. Rand McNally, 1964. 128p. $3.50. (U)

Traces the development of biological nomenclature from Aristotle to Darwin. Well organized, well written, and well illustrated.

673   Selsam, Millicent. See through the Forest; pictures by Winifred Lubell. Harper, 1956. unp. $2.95; lib. ed. $2.92. net. (P)

Likens the forest to a building and explains that animals and plants live on the "floor" best suited to their needs. Simple text and attractive pictures.

674   Selsam, Millicent. See through the Jungle; pictures by Winifred Lubell. Harper, 1957. 52p. $2.95; lib. ed. $2.92 net. (P)

Using the same approach as in *See through the Forest,* above, the author describes the plants and animals that inhabit the various layers of the tropical rain forest. Illustrations are in vivid jungle colors.

675   Shippen, Katherine B. Men, Microscopes, and Living Things; illus. by Anthony Ravielli. Viking, 1955. 192p. $3.50; lib. ed. $3.37 net. (U)

A history of biology from Aristotle to the present, centering around the lives of great scientists. Readable style and attractive illustrations.

676   Zim, Herbert S. How Things Grow;

illus. by Gustav Schrotter. Morrow, 1960. 64p. lib. ed. $2.94 net. (P–I)

The mental, emotional, and social growth of man is explained in relation to the growth of plants and animals, showing that all living things grow, each according to its own pattern, and that each reproduces its own kind. Animated style and illustrations.

677 **Zim, Herbert S.**, and **Ingle, Lester.** Seashores: A Guide to Animals and Plants along the Beaches; illus. by Dorothea and Sy Barlowe; sponsored by The Wildlife Management Institute. Golden Pr., 1955. 160p. $3.95. (I)

After giving general information about the seas, tides, and waves, the author describes typical plants, animals, and shells to be found on the beach. A good pocket guide to identification, with simple text and informative pictures.

ECOLOGY AND CONSERVATION

678 **Adler, Irving**, and **Adler, Ruth.** Irrigation: Changing Deserts into Gardens. Day, 1964. 48p. lib. ed. $2.68 net. (I)

A brief history of man's efforts to water the desert is followed by a discussion of modern methods of irrigation in many parts of the world. Illustrated with photographs, drawings, and maps.

679 **Farb, Peter.** Ecology; by Peter Farb and the eds. of Life. Time, Inc., 1963. Life Nature Library, distributed by Silver Burdett. 192p. $4.95. (U)

The interrelationships of all life are presented through explanations of natural selection, the balance in nature, the influence of environment, and other factors which affect the survival of species.

680 **Farb, Peter.** The Land and Wildlife of North America; by Peter Farb and the eds. of Life. Time, Inc., 1964. Life Nature Library, distributed by Silver Burdett. 200p. $4.95. (U)

The author describes the original natural resources of North America, tells how they have been squandered, and explains the efforts being made to conserve them. A strong plea for conservation, illustrated with handsome photographs, many in color. Includes an annotated list of principal national parks and national monuments in Canada and the United States.

681 **Gates, Richard.** The True Book of Conservation; written and illus. by Richard Gates. Childrens Pr., 1959. 46p. $2.50. (P)

An introduction to conservation, explaining the balance of nature, showing how it has been disturbed by wasteful and unwise use of natural resources, and discussing the efforts now being made to restore it. (R2–3)

682 **Green, Ivah.** Wildlife in Danger; with introd. by Robert Porter Allen. Coward-McCann, 1959. 128p. lib. ed. $3.29 net. (P–I)

Twenty-nine extinct or near-extinct birds and animals are described and pictured in excellent photographs, along with reasons for their disappearance and suggested measures for conservation.

683 **Harrison, C. William.** Conservationists and What They Do. Watts, 1963. 170p. $3.95. (U)

Covers the need for conservationists and their training and career opportunities in forestry, flood control, soil conservation, wildlife research and management, etc. Includes a list of schools and colleges offering training in conservation.

684 **Harrison, C. William.** The First Book of Wildlife Sanctuaries; illus. with photos. Watts, 1963. 61p. $2.65. (I)

Discusses the destruction of wildlife in the United States and describes the attempts to restore it by means of fish hatcheries, game preserves, bird sanctuaries, etc. Lists some of the country's wildlife refuges and gives some of the federal wildlife preservation laws.

685 **Hirsch, S. Carl.** The Living Community: A Venture into Ecology; illus. by William Steinel. Viking, 1966. 128p. $3.75; lib. ed. $3.56 net. (U)

A clear presentation of the relationship of all living things to one another and to their environment, emphasizing the importance of maintaining the balance of nature. Includes a reading list.

686 **Hogner, Dorothy Childs.** Conservation in America; decorations by Nils Hogner. Lippincott, 1958. 240p. $3.95. (U)

Begins with the history of conservation, then describes the efforts of the government, industry, and private agencies to protect and restore our remaining natural resources.

687   **Hyde, Margaret O.** This Crowded Planet; illus. by Mildred Waltrip. McGraw-Hill, 1961. 59p. $3.50; lib. ed. $3.06 net. (U)
A timely and interesting discussion of the population problem, pointing out the need for conservation and scientific research to provide adequate natural resources for the future.

688   **Raskin, Edith.** The Pyramid of Living Things; illus. by Joseph Cellini. McGraw-Hill, 1967. 192p. $4.50; lib. ed. $3.99 net. (U)
The interdependence of plant and animal life in eight ecological communities is described in smoothly written text and illustrated with diagrams, drawings, and maps. The author likens life to a pyramid with the lowest forms at the bottom and man at the top, shows that man and animals take much from and return little to the balance of nature, and emphasizes the need for conservation.

689   **Shippen, Katherine B.** The Great Heritage; illus. by C. B. Falls. Viking, 1962. 228p. $4.50; lib. ed. $4.13 net. (U)
The once-bountiful resources of the United States—a chapter each for furs, gold, cotton, oil, etc.—are discussed in a vividly written survey of our natural wealth and the men and women who developed or exploited it. Stresses the need for conservation and lists related books and recordings.

690   **Silverberg, Robert.** The Auk, the Dodo, and the Oryx: Vanished and Vanishing Animals. Crowell, 1967. 246p. $3.95. (U)
In a plea for conservation of rare animals, the author describes extinct and almost-extinct birds and animals and tells how many have been rescued from oblivion. A deftly written narrative with effective illustrations and a reading list.

691   **Smith, F. C.** The First Book of Conservation; pictures by Rene Martin. Watts, 1954. 68p. $2.65. (I)
An introductory book giving a brief general survey of the need for conservation and what is being done about it.

692   **Stoutenburg, Adrien.** A Vanishing Thunder: Extinct and Threatened American Birds; illus. by John Schoenherr. Published for the American Museum of Natural History by Natural History Press. Doubleday, 1967. 124p. $3.50. (I–U)

A dramatic account of the passenger pigeon, the ivory-billed woodpecker, the great auk, the whooping crane, and other rare or extinct North American birds. A simpler account than the Silverberg book, above, designed to interest young people in conservation.

693   **Talley, Naomi.** To Save the Soil. Dial, 1965. 79p. $2.95. (I)
A former employee of the Soil Conservation Service writes about the work of soil conservationists from early days to the present, describing erosion problems and ways of controlling them through legislation, government agencies, and private efforts. Illustrated with photographs.

MICROSCOPES AND MICROBES

694   **Beeler, Nelson F.,** and **Branley, Franklyn M.** Experiments with a Microscope; illus. by Anne Marie Jauss. Crowell, 1957. 154p. $3.50. (I–U)
Explains how to use a microscope, how to stain and photograph specimens, and how to keep records of investigations. Well-illustrated directions for experiments with blood, molds, yeasts, and other ordinary materials.

695   **Disraeli, Robert.** New Worlds through the Microscope. Viking, 1960. 175p. lib. ed. $4.13 net. (I–U)
Provides in text and microphotographs a look at the wonderful world which can be seen through a microscope. Tells what to look for, how to mount specimens, and how to interpret what is seen.

696   **Grant, Madeleine P.** Wonder World of Microbes; illus. by Clifford N. Geary. new 2d ed. McGraw-Hill, 1964. 174p. $3.50; lib. ed. $3.06 net. (I)
After explaining what microbes are, the author discusses both useful and harmful types and gives instructions for experiments to show how penicillin is made, why milk is pasteurized, etc. Helpful drawings, short sentences, and simple vocabulary make the book useful for slow readers.

697   **Schneider, Leo.** Microbes in Your Life; illus. with drawings by Henri A. Fluchere and with photos. Harcourt, 1966. 154p. $3.75. (U)
Makes the point that life could not exist without microorganisms and describes algae, protozoa, fungi, bacteria, and viruses.

Discusses harmful and beneficial microbes and explains how they are studied.

698 **Schwartz, Julius.** Through the Magnifying Glass: Little Things That Make a Big Difference; pictures by Jeanne Bendick. McGraw-Hill, 1954. 142p. $3.75; lib. ed. 3.26 net. (I)

A hobby book for the science-minded, telling how to use a hand lens to make ordinary objects look strange and wonderful. A good introduction to the world of microscopic science.

699 **Selsam, Millicent E.** Greg's Microscope; pictures by Arnold Lobel. Harper, 1963. 64p. $1.95; lib. ed. $2.19 net. (P)

An accurate introduction to microscopy for the beginning independent reader. Greg finds out about salt crystals, hair, thread, cell formations, and many other wonders. (R2–3)

BOTANY

Plants in General

700 **Beck, Barbara L.** The First Book of Fruits; pictures by Page Cary. Watts, 1967. 64p. $2.65. (I)

Following an introduction discussing seeds and other means of plant propagation, the author gives botanical and historical facts about the major families of edible fruits, telling where they are grown and how they are harvested and distributed. Colorfully illustrated.

701 **Brooks, Anita.** The Picture Book of Grains. Day, 1962. 96p. lib. ed. $3.29 net. (I)

Excellent photographs and concise text present the major grain-producing areas of the world, covering planting, cultivation, and harvesting of crops and describing the agricultural research back of improved strains and methods.

702 **Dickinson, Alice.** The First Book of Plants; pictures by Paul Wenck. Watts, 1953. 71p. $2.65. (I)

An introduction to botany discussing seed plants, bacteria, fungi, algae, mosses, and ferns. Includes a few experiments and many informative illustrations.

704 **Fenton, Carroll Lane,** and **Kitchen, Hermine B.** Fruits We Eat; illus. by Carroll Lane Fenton. Day, 1961. 128p. $3.75. (I–U)

Tells where various types of fruit originated, how they were introduced into other regions, how they look and taste, and how they have been improved through research. Beautiful illustrations show rare as well as common fruits.

705 **Fenton, Carroll Lane,** and **Kitchen, Hermine B.;** illus. by Carroll Lane Fenton. Plants That Feed Us: The Story of Grains and Vegetables. Day, 1956. 95p. lib. ed. $3.49 net. (I)

Information on the origin and use of many food plants, with a clear drawing for each.

705a **Frisch, Rose E.** Plants That Feed the World; pictures by Denny McMains. Van Nostrand, 1966. 104p. $3.95; lib. ed. $3.78 net. (I)

Edible plants—their characteristics, values, and deficiencies as food, and their cultivation—are discussed in simple text and illustrated with diagrams and photographs. Includes a list of suggested projects, addresses of state agricultural stations, and a glossary.

706 **Guilcher, J. M.,** and **Noialles, R. H.** A Fruit Is Born. Sterling, 1960. 111p. $2.95; lib. ed. $3.39 net. (I)

Unusually fine, enlarged photographs show the life cycle of fruit. The brief text explains and shows in diagrams the structure of a pistil, follows the development of the fruit from flower to seed, and explains seed dispersal.

707 **Hutchins, Ross E.** The Amazing Seeds; photos. by the author. Dodd, 1965. 159p. $3.50; lib. ed. $3.23 net. (I–U)

The structure, varieties, dispersal, dormancy, and germination of seeds are lucidly described and shown in remarkable close-up photographs.

708 **Hutchins, Ross E.** Plants without Leaves: Lichens, Fungi, Mosses, Liverworts, Slimemolds, Algae, Horsetails; photos. by the author. Dodd, 1966. 152p. $3.75; lib. ed. $3.46 net. (I–U)

Informative text and excellent photographs introduce cryptogams: their structure, reproduction, means of survival, and importance in nature.

709 **Hutchins, Ross E.** Strange Plants and Their Ways; with 60 photos. by the

author. Rand McNally, 1958. 96p. $3.50.
(U)

An intriguing photographic study of such curious plants as the Mexican jumping bean, the tumbleweed, and the Venus flytrap.

710   **Hutchins, Ross E.** This Is a Leaf; photos. by the author. Dodd, 1962. 121p. $3.50; lib. ed. $3.23 net. (U)

Photographs, diagrams, and interesting text provide information about the structure and types of leaves, their manufacture of food, growth, movement, and change of color.

711   **Kavaler, Lucy.** The Wonders of Algae; illus. with photos. and with drawings by Barbara Amlick and Richard Ott. Day, 1961. 96p. lib. ed. $3.29 net. (I–U)

Describes how this most primitive of plants serves man in many important ways: as a source of food, as fuel for the space age, and in medicine. Discusses the uses of plankton, gives a recipe for algae cookies, and includes suggestions for a science fair.

712   **Kavaler, Lucy.** The Wonders of Fungi; illus. with photos. and with drawings by Richard Ott. Day, 1964. 128p. lib. ed. $3.64 net. (I–U)

Smooth text and many illustrations introduce the study of molds, mushrooms, yeasts, and other kinds of fungi, explaining their useful and harmful effects in food and medicine.

713   **Lubell, Winifred,** and **Lubell, Cecil.** Green Is for Growing. Rand McNally, 1964. 64p. $2.95; lib. ed. $3.08 net. (P)

This gay and engaging little book provides a pleasant, scientifically accurate introduction to the plant world for young children, explaining the amazing variety of plants, their growth patterns, and their usefulness to man.

714   **Podendorf, Illa.** The True Book of Plant Experiments; pictures by Bill Armstrong. Childrens Pr., 1960. 48p. $2.50. (P)

An easy-to-read text and helpful pictures describe simple experiments and show how to set up a terrarium. (R2–3)

715   **Selsam, Millicent E.** The Plants We Eat; illus. by Helen Ludwig. Morrow, 1955. 123p. lib. ed. $2.94 net. (I)

Discusses man's dependence on plants and describes the kinds of food plants: roots,

stems, leaves, flowers, and fruits. Interestingly written and well illustrated.

716   **Selsam, Millicent E.** Play with Plants; illus. by James MacDonald. Morrow, 1949. 62p. lib. ed. $2.94 net. (I)

Experiments to demonstrate the response of plants to heat, light, and moisture, presented in detailed instructions and clear diagrams.

717   **Selsam, Millicent E.** Play with Seeds; illus. by Helen Ludwig. Morrow, 1957. 93p. lib. ed. $2.94 net. (I)

Explains how modern plants have evolved from seaweed, how flowers form seeds, and how seeds are dispersed. Includes simple experiments.

718   **Selsam, Millicent E.** Seeds and More Seeds; pictures by Tomi Ungerer. Harper, 1959. 60p. $1.95; lib. ed. $2.19 net. (P)

In this easy science book, Benny learns by observation and experimentation what seeds are, how they grow, and how they produce more seeds. Brightly colored illustrations. (R1–2)

719   **Sterling, Dorothy.** The Story of Mosses, Ferns, and Mushrooms; photos. by Myron Ehrenberg. Garden City, 1955. 159p. $3.25. (U)

Discusses plant evolution, describes the flowerless plants of the world, and explains the difference between edible and poisonous mushrooms. Many excellent photographs.

720   **Uhl, Melvin John.** About Grasses, Grains, and Canes; illus. by Carol Rogers. Melmont, 1964. 47p. $2.50. (P–I)

Information about the growth, distribution, and uses of cereal grasses, canes, bamboo, and some of the wild grasses.

721   **Webber, Irma E.** Bits That Grow Big: Where Plants Come From; illus. by Su Zan Noguchi Swain. W. R. Scott, 1949. 64p. $2.75. (P)

Plant reproduction by means of seeds, spores, cuttings, grafts, leaves, and roots is clearly explained and graphically illustrated. Includes simple experiments.

722   **Webber, Irma E.** Travelers All: The Story of How Plants Go Places; written and drawn by Irma E. Webber. W. R. Scott, 1944. unp. $2.50. (P)

Beautiful colored illustrations and simple text explain seed dispersal by wind, land, water, and animals.

723 **Webber, Irma E.** Up Above and Down Below. W. R. Scott, 1943. unp. $2.50. (P)

The parts of plants above ground and those below are shown in clear pictures and described in simple text.

724 **Went, Frits W.** The Plants; by Frits W. Went and the eds. of Life. Time, Inc., 1963. Life Nature Library, distributed by Silver Burdett. 194p. $4.95. (U)

A beautifully illustrated introduction to botany, covering its history and development and discussing all the major aspects of the subject. For the superior student.

725 **Zim, Herbert S.** Plants: A Guide to Plant Hobbies; illus. by John W. Brainerd. Harcourt, 1947. 398p. $4.75. (U)

A survey of the plant kingdom with many suggestions for plant hobbies. Includes a list of places in the United States of special interest to plant enthusiasts.

Garden Crops

726 **Baker, Samm Sinclair.** The Indoor and Outdoor Grow-It Book; illus. by Eric Carle. Random, 1966. 65p. $2.95; lib. ed. $2.99 net. (P–I)

This first gardening book, with explicit directions and pictures on every page, encourages the young child to try a variety of activities with plants and suggests the many ways in which his products can be put to use.

727 **Kirkus, Virginia.** The First Book of Gardening; pictures by Helene Carter. Watts, 1956. 69p. $2.65. (I)

A practical guide to soil preparation, planting, caring for, and harvesting flowers and vegetables. Includes tips on selecting a garden spot, using tools, and choosing and arranging plants.

728 **Selsam, Millicent E.** How To Grow House Plants; illus. by Kathleen Elgin. Morrow, 1960. 96p. lib. ed. $2.94 net. (I)

After explaining the structure of a plant and the functions of its parts, the author gives advice on selecting house plants, where to buy them, how to care for them, and how to propagate them.

Flowers

729 **Dowden, Anne Ophelia T.** Look at a Flower; illus. by the author. Crowell, 1963. 120p. $4.50. (I–U)

After explaining the classification of plants, the author examines their structure and methods of pollination and describes the parts of flowers. A well-written, well-organized introduction to botany, illustrated with accurate colored pictures.

730 **Hausman, Ethel Hinckley.** Beginner's Guide to Wild Flowers; illus. by the author. Putnam, 1955. 376p. $3.95. (U)

A standard field guide to wild flowers, arranged by flower colors. For each species there is a clear line drawing, accompanied by its Latin and common names, size, range, and other characteristics.

731 **Hutchins, Ross E.** This Is a Flower; photos. by the author. Dodd, 1963. 152p. $3.50; lib. ed. $3.23. (U)

A detailed study of flowers, illustrated with well-captioned, close-up photographs.

732 **Podendorf, Illa.** The True Book of Weeds and Wild Flowers; pictures by Mary Gehr. Childrens Pr., 1955. 47p. $2.50. (P)

Explains how to tell a weed from a flower, describes and illustrates many common weeds and wild flowers, and tells why wild flowers should be protected. (R2–3)

733 **Stupka, Arthur.** Wildflowers in Color; with the assistance of Donald H. Robinson. Harper, 1965. 144p. $5.95. (I–U)

A combination field guide to identification and full-color picture book portraying 250 species common in the eastern United States, with full botanical information and an excellent color photograph of each.

734 **Zim, Herbert S.,** and **Martin, Alexander C.** Flowers: A Guide to Familiar American Wildflowers; illus. by Rudolf Freund; sponsored by The Wildlife Management Institute. Golden Pr., 1950. 157p. $3.95. (I–U)

A field guide, arranged by color, giving complete information on many species. Illustrated with drawings and 134 plates in full color.

Trees

735 **Baker, Laura Nelson.** A Tree Called Moses; drawings by Penelope Naylor. Atheneum, 1966. 69p. $3.50; lib. ed. $3.41 net. (I)

The life story of a giant sequoia on the western slopes of the Sierra Nevada, describing its slow growth from seed to maturity and recounting some of the dramatic incidents in its history. Useful for nature and conservation study.

736   Buff, Mary, and **Buff, Conrad.** Big Tree. Viking, 1946. 79p. $3.50; lib. ed. $3.37 net. (I)

Through the story of Wawona, a giant sequoia, the authors symbolize the grandeur and antiquity of the sequoias and communicate the need for their preservation. A poetic and beautifully illustrated book which complements the more straightforward Baker book, above.

737   Bulla, Clyde Robert. A Tree Is a Plant; illus. by Lois Lignell. Crowell, 1960. unp. $3.25; lib. ed. $2.96 net. (P)

This first book about trees tells very simply what trees are, how they reproduce, and how their different parts function, using an apple tree as an example. An attractively illustrated book for independent reading in primary grades. (R1–2)

738   Cormack, M. B. The First Book of Trees; pictures by Helene Carter. Watts, 1951. 93p. $2.65. (I)

Describes the structure and life cycle of trees and for each species shows general outline, leaf, flower, fruit, and bark in green-and-brown illustrations. A small map on each page shows where the tree grows.

739   Fenton, Carroll Lane, and **Pallas, Dorothy Constance.** Trees and Their World; illus. by Carroll Lane Fenton. Day, 1957. 96p. lib. ed. $3.29 net. (I)

Explanatory drawings and well-written text give the essential facts about trees: how leaves manufacture food, the function of the root system, how seeds develop, etc.

740   Guilcher, J. M., and **Noailles, R. H.** A Tree Is Born. Sterling, 1960. 100p. $2.95; lib. ed. $3.39 net. (I)

Presents the life cycle of four trees—horse chestnut, oak, walnut, and pine—in interesting text and excellent close-up photographs.

741   Hutchins, Ross E. This Is a Tree; photos. by the author. Dodd, 1954. 159p. $3.50; lib. ed. $3.23 net. (U)

In addition to explaining all phases of a tree's life, the author discusses tree rings, state trees, superstitions about trees, male and female trees, and other topics not always covered in other books. Illustrated with fine photographs.

742   Kieran, John. An Introduction to Trees; illus. by Michael H. Bevans. new ed. Doubleday, 1966. 77p. $4.50. (I)

This book for beginners "is offered as a help in learning to recognize and name the more common trees of our city streets, suburban lawns, country lanes, valley farms, and the great forests of North America." Gives identifying facts and shows tree, leaves, and seeds in color paintings.

743   Mathews, F. Schuyler. Field Book of American Trees and Shrubs . . . with numerous reproductions of water color, crayon, and pen and ink sketches from nature by the author. Putnam, 1915. 465p. $4.95. (U)

A standard identification handbook, with maps showing the distribution of species.

744   Milne, Lorus J., and **Milne, Margery.** Because of a Tree; drawings by Kenneth Gosner. Atheneum, 1963. 152p. $3.95; lib. ed. $3.81 net. (I)

Emphasis is on the interdependence of all things in nature, showing how eight different kinds of trees help to support the life around them. Includes a reading list.

745   Podendorf, Illa. The True Book of Trees; illus. by Richard Gates. Childrens Pr., 1954. 43p. $2.50. (P)

An introduction to common American trees: structure, functions of parts, uses, and need for conservation. Designed for independent reading in primary grades. (R2–3)

746   Wall, Gertrude Wallace. Gifts from the Grove; photos. by John Calvin Towsley and others. Scribner, 1955. 96p. lib. ed. $3.31 net. (I)

After giving a brief history of citrus fruits and telling how they were introduced into the United States, the author describes how they are grown, harvested, and distributed. Illustrated with excellent photographs and maps.

747   Zim, Herbert S., and **Martin, Alexander C.** Trees: A Guide to Familiar American Trees; sponsored by The Wildlife Management Institute. rev. ed. Golden Pr., 1956. 160p. $3.95. (I)

A useful pocket guide to tree identification, with concise descriptions and color drawings of 140 species of trees. Includes distribution maps.

Forests and Forestry

748   Buehr, Walter. Timber! Farming Our Forests; written and illus. by Walter Buehr. Morrow, 1960. 96p. lib. ed. $3.14 net. (I–U)

After giving essential facts about the structure and growth of trees, the author reviews the history of lumbering, emphasizing the conservation of forests through tree farming.

749   Floethe, Louise Lee. The Story of Lumber; with pictures by Richard Floethe. Scribner, 1962. unp. lib. ed. $3.31 net. (P)

Informative colored drawings extend this simple story of how forest trees are selected for harvesting, cut, transported to sawmills, sawn, and finished.

750   Hyde, Wayne. What Does a Forest Ranger Do? Illus. with photos. Dodd, 1964. 64p. lib. ed. $2.79 net. (I–U)

An introduction to forestry as a profession: qualifications, training, duties, and job opportunities. Includes rules for what to do when lost in the woods. (R4–5)

751   Lauber, Patricia. Our Friend the Forest: A Conservation Story; illus. by Anne Marie Jauss. Doubleday, 1959. 61p. $2.75. (P–I)

Beginning with a description of the forest community, the author surveys the many ways in which trees are useful to man and stresses the need for forest conservation.

752   Life (Periodical). The Forest; by Peter Farb and the eds. of Life; adapted by the eds. of Silver Burdett. Silver Burdett, 1964. 192p. $4.95. (U)

A comprehensive, well-illustrated study of forests and their inhabitants, with emphasis on the ecology of forest life. Includes tree records, a guide to tree identification, and a glossary.

ZOOLOGY

Zoology in General

753   Barker, Will. Winter-sleeping Wildlife; illus. by Carl Burger; foreword by Ernest F. Swift. Harper, 1958. 136p. $3.95; lib. ed. $3.79 net. (U)

Describes the life cycles and characteristics of mammals, birds, reptiles, insects, and other creatures who have periods of dormancy, defining and contrasting hibernation, estivation, and diapause. Informative illustrations.

754   Berrill, Jacqueline. Wonders of Animal Migration; illus. by the author. Dodd, 1964. 96p. lib. ed. $2.79 net. (I)

A study of the homing instincts of animals and birds and the mysterious sense by which birds, fish, and other animals navigate.

755   Bridges, William. Zoo Babies. Morrow, 1953. 94p. lib. ed. $3.14 net. (I)

Thirteen true stories about animal babies at New York's Bronx Zoo. Engaging photographs.

756   Buchsbaum, Ralph. Animals without Backbones: An Introduction to the Invertebrates. rev. ed. Univ. of Chicago Pr., 1948. 405p. $9.50; text ed. $7. (U)

Each group of invertebrates "is used to illustrate some principle of biology or some level in the evolution of animals from simple to complex forms." More than 500 photographs and 327 drawings. For the advanced student.

757   Buff, Mary, and **Buff, Conrad.** Elf Owl. Viking, 1958. 72p. $3.50; lib. ed. $3.37 net. (P)

A pair of tiny elf owls living in a giant cactus are the central characters in this story of life around a water hole in an American desert. Illustrated with handsome sepia drawings.

758   Dorian, Edith, and **Wilson, W. N.** Animals That Made U.S. History. McGraw-Hill, 1964. 112p. $3.75; lib. ed. $3.26 net. (I)

An intriguing story of how wild and domestic animals have affected the history, politics, and language of this country, centering on 11 animals of special importance: the whale, the buffalo, the beaver, the mule, etc. Equally useful in science and in history classes.

759   Huntington, Harriet E. Let's Go to the Seashore; illus. with photos. by the author. Doubleday, 1941. 88p. $3. (P–I)

Photographs full of interesting detail extend the simple text of this book about the small creatures a child might find on the beach.

760   Hyde, Margaret O. Animal Clocks and Compasses: From Animal Migration to Space Travel; illus. by P. A. Hutchison. McGraw-Hill, 1960. 157p. $3.50; lib. ed. $3.06 net. (U)

A thought-provoking study of the marvelous sense of time and direction by which animals migrate, hibernate, mate, and perform other functions of their life cycles. Includes interesting sidelights, such as the possibility of hibernation in space travel, and suggests experiments which can be done at home.

761   **Mason, George F.** Animal Clothing. Morrow, 1955. 94p. lib. ed. $2.94 net. (I)
A straightforward discussion, illustrated with informative line drawings by the author, of the protective covering of animals: fur, feathers, scales, hair, shells, and external skeletons.

762   **Mason, George F.** Animal Homes. Morrow, 1947. 96p. lib. ed. $2.94 net. (I)
Describes and shows in the author's full-page, detailed drawings the almost endless variety of shelters constructed by animals: nests, lodges, burrows, dens, etc. A guide for locating and studying wildlife in the field makes this book especially useful to Scouts and naturalists.

763   **Mason, George F.** Animal Sounds. Morrow, 1948. 96p. lib. ed. $2.94 net. (I)
Bird songs, the roars of lions, the sounds made by singing mice, insect music—the author describes these and other animal sounds and discusses how and why they are made. Illustrations by the author show some of the mechanisms which produce the sounds.

764   **Mason, George F.** Animal Tails. Morrow, 1958. 95p. $2.95; lib. ed. $2.94 net. (I)
Explains the many uses of animal tails: to grasp, to swim, to fight, to warn, etc. Many illustrations by the author.

765   **Mason, George F.** Animal Tools. Morrow, 1951. 94p. lib. ed. $2.94 net. (I)
The author describes and illustrates the ingenious "tools" by which animals perform such specialized tasks as gathering honey, building nests, and constructing dams, and shows their relationship to man-made tools.

766   **Mason, George F.** Animal Tracks. Morrow, 1943. 95p. lib. ed. $2.94 net. (I)
In this handy guide to animal tracks, the author describes and shows in line drawings the tracks made by many common North American animals. The illus-

trations show the perfect track, with dimensions, and the track as it appears when the animal is moving.

767   **Mason, George F.** Animal Weapons. Morrow, 1949. 94p. lib. ed. $2.94 net. (I)
Accurate drawings and clear text explain how animals' defensive mechanisms develop and how they are used.

768   **Murie, Olaus J.** A Field Guide to Animal Tracks; illus. by the author. Houghton, 1954. 374p. $4.95. (U)
A comprehensive guide to the tracks, droppings, and other signs of an animal's presence, for the experienced naturalist. Covers many mammals, birds, insects, reptiles, and amphibians of the Western Hemisphere.

769   **Podendorf, Illa.** The True Book of Animal Babies; illus. by Pauline Adams. Childrens Pr., 1955. 44p. $2.50. (P)
Interesting facts about an appealing subject in a brightly illustrated, easy-to-read book. (R2–3)

770   **Selsam, Millicent.** All about Eggs and How They Change into Animals; illus. by Helen Ludwig. W. R. Scott, 1952. unp. $3.50. (P)
Simple text and many pictures explain the many kinds of eggs and the animals that grow from them, including eggs that grow inside the mother's body.

771   **Selsam, Millicent E.** Animals as Parents; illus. by John Kaufmann. Morrow, 1965. 96p. $2.95; lib. ed. $2.94 net. (I–U)
After giving an overview of parental behavior among animals, the author describes how various species of fish, reptiles, birds, and mammals care for their young. An absorbing account, based on scientific research and effectively illustrated.

772   **Selsam, Millicent E.** Benny's Animals and How He Put Them in Order; pictures by Arnold Lobel. Harper, 1966. 60p. $1.95; lib. ed. $2.19 net. (P)
A very simple book introducing some very complex concepts: observation, comparison, and classification. Benny, with the help of a zoologist friend, learns to arrange his sea shells and animal pictures according to the major divisions of zoology. (R2–3)

773   **Selsam, Millicent E.** How Animals

Tell Time; illus. by John Kaufmann. Morrow, 1967. 94p. $2.95; lib. ed. $2.94 net. (I–U)

In this lucid study of biological clocks, the author reports on scientific studies of animal activity rhythms as related to tidal, lunar, and seasonal rhythms. Well organized and effectively illustrated. Includes a reading list.

774 Selsam, Millicent E. How To Be a Nature Detective; pictures by Ezra Jack Keats. Harper, 1966. 46p. $2.95; lib. ed. $2.92 net. (P)

In this science picture book the reader learns that by observing footprints he can tell what animal went by, what he did, and how fast he was going. A good introduction to observation and deduction. (R2–3)

775 Selsam, Millicent E. The Language of Animals; illus. by Kathleen Elgin. Morrow, 1962. 96p. lib. ed. $2.94 net. (I)

Basing her study on recent research, the author examines the means by which animals communicate emotion and information, stressing the fallacy of thinking that animals communicate in the same manner and for the same purposes as human beings.

776 Simon, Seymour. Animals in Field and Laboratory: Science Projects in Animal Behavior; illus. by Emily McCully. McGraw-Hill, 1967. 160p. $4.95. (I)

Interesting projects in the study of animal behavior—using common animals and insects, simple laboratories, and inexpensive, easily obtained materials—are clearly described and pictured. Includes a list of supply houses.

777 Tensen, Ruth M. Come to the Zoo. Reilly & Lee, 1954. 41p. $2.95. (P)

This visit to the zoo is written in controlled vocabulary and illustrated with appealing photographs. (R1–2)

778 Webb, Addison. Song of the Seasons; illus. by Charles L. Ripper. Morrow, 1950. 127p. $3.75. (P–I)

A beautiful book about the year-round doings of familiar animals, describing spring as the season for babies, summer for learning, autumn for feasting, and winter for resting.

779 Ylla. Animal Babies; story by Arthur

Gregor; designed by Luc Bouchage. Harper, 1959. unp. $3.50; lib. ed. $3.29 net. (P)

Some of the most endearing pictures of a famous photographer of animals are brought together in this handsome book. A few lines of text identify the animal in each photograph.

Amphibians and Reptiles

780 Bronson, Wilfred S. Turtles; written and illus. by Wilfred S. Bronson. Harcourt, 1945. unp. $2.75. (P)

An accurate and amusing introduction to tortoises, terrapins, and sea turtles, telling how to study them and how to care for turtles as pets. Lively pictures on every page.

781 Carr, Archie. The Reptiles; by Archie Carr and the eds. of Life. Time, Inc., 1963. Life Nature Library, distributed by Silver Burdett. 192p. $4.95. (U)

Advanced text and a section of outstanding photographs with simpler commentary trace the rise and fall of the reptiles: their evolution, rise to dominance, subsequent decrease, and doubtful future.

782 Conant, Roger. A Field Guide to Reptiles and Amphibians of the United States and Canada East of the 100th Meridian; illus. by Isabelle Hunt Conant. Houghton, 1958. 366p. $4.95. (U)

A comprehensive guide giving identification, characteristics, habitat, ecology, and natural history of each species. Excellent illustrations (many in full color), distribution maps, glossary, and bibliography.

783 Darling, Lois, and **Darling, Louis.** Turtles. Morrow, 1962. 64p. lib. ed. $2.94 net. (I)

A simply written and beautifully illustrated history of turtles from the days of dinosaurs to the present, stressing the importance of turtles as food and as insect eaters. (R4–5)

784 Ditmars, Raymond L. Reptiles of the World: The Crocodilians, Lizards, Snakes, Turtles, and Tortoises of the Eastern and Western Hemispheres. new rev. ed. Macmillan, 1933. 321p. $8.50. (I–U)

Broad coverage of the class of reptiles as a whole, illustrated with photographs from the files of the New York Zoological Society.

785   **Hoke, John.** The First Book of Snakes; illus. by Paul Wenck. Watts, 1952. 67p. $2.65. (P–I)
Facts and myths about snakes are presented in a simply written and informatively illustrated introduction to the subject.

786   **Holling, Holling Clancy.** Minn of the Mississippi; written and illus. by Holling Clancy Holling. Houghton, 1951. 85p. $3.75. (I–U)
A snapping turtle named Minn takes a 2500-mile trip down the Mississippi River. Handsome, full-page pictures in color and many marginal drawings provide a wealth of information about Minn and the Mississippi.

787   **McClung, Robert M.** Buzztail: The Story of a Rattlesnake; written and illus. by Robert M. McClung. Morrow, 1958. 64p. lib. ed. $2.94 net. (P–I)
A narrative account of a timber rattlesnake, telling how to recognize him, what his habits are, and what to do if bitten.

788   **Selsam, Millicent E.** Let's Get Turtles; drawings by Arnold Lobel. Harper, 1965. 62p. $1.95; lib. ed. $2.19 net. (P)
Two small boys buy turtles for pets, and with the help of a friend at the zoo, they learn how to care for them. Conversational style, easy vocabulary, and many amusing pictures. (R1–2)

789   **Zim, Herbert S.** Alligators and Crocodiles; illus. by James Gordon Irving. Morrow, 1952. 62p. $2.95; lib. ed. $2.94 net. (P–I)
Distinguishes alligators from crocodiles, tells where both species are found, and describes their habits and peculiarities. Illustrations add interest and information.

790   **Zim, Herbert S.** Frogs and Toads; illus. by Joy Buba. Morrow, 1950. unp. lib. ed. $2.94 net. (P–I)
A lively and well-illustrated discussion of frog and toad life.

791   **Zim, Herbert S.,** and **Smith, Hobart M.** Reptiles and Amphibians: A Guide to Familiar American Species; illus. by James Gordon Irving; sponsored by The Wildlife Management Institute. rev. ed. Golden Pr., 1956. 160p. $3.95. (I)
An identification guide to more than 100 species, devoting approximately one page

to each. Color illustrations, distribution maps, and bibliography.

792   **Zim, Herbert S.** Snakes; illus. by James Gordon Irving. Morrow, 1949. unp. $2.95; lib. ed. $2.94 net. (P–I)
An introductory book, covering in simple text and clear illustrations the structure, life cycle, habits, and identification of snakes and giving suggestions for keeping snakes as pets.

Birds

793   **Adrian, Mary.** The American Eagle; illus. by Genevieve Vaughan-Jackson. Hastings, 1963. 59p. $3.50. (P–I)
Recounts the life cycle of a pair of bald eaglets, representatives of a fast-disappearing species, urging the preservation of this symbol of American power.

794   **Blough, Glenn O.** Bird Watchers and Bird Feeders; pictures by Jeanne Bendick. McGraw-Hill, 1963. 48p. $3.25; lib. ed. $3.01 net. (P–I)
Lively text and colorful drawings introduce bird observation and study to young readers. Covers types of feeders, food, banding, migration, and state birds. (R3–4)

795   **Bosiger, E.,** and **Guilcher, J. M.** A Bird Is Born; photos. by E. Hoskins and R. H. Noailles. Sterling, 1960. 92p. $2.95; lib. ed. $3.39 net. (P–I)
Exceptionally interesting close-up and X-ray photographs show the development of a chicken embryo and the stages of growth of several species of birds. Accompanying text is scientific and smoothly written.

796   **Boulton, Rudyerd.** Traveling with the Birds: A Book on Bird Migration; illus. by Walter Alois Weber. Donohue, 1933. 96p. $3.95. (I)
A large book with full-page colored illustrations and readable text.

797   **Darling, Louis.** Gull's Way; photos. and illus. by the author. Morrow, 1965. 96p. $6.50; lib. ed. $5.49 net. (I–U)
From his own observation of a pair of herring gulls on an island off the coast of Maine, the author describes and illustrates the life cycle and habits of the species. Superior nature writing and illustrating. Includes a reading list.

798   **Darling, Louis.** Penguins. Morrow, 1956. 64p. lib. ed. $2.94 net. (I)
An accurate, amusing discussion of the

Adélie penguins, emphasizing their adaptation to their environment. Excellent drawings add information and appeal.

799 **Earle, Olive L.** Birds and Their Beaks; written and illus. by Olive L. Earle. Morrow, 1965. 64p. $2.95; lib. ed. $2.94 net. (I)

Forty-six birds are alphabetically listed, illustrated, and briefly described, with special attention to their beaks.

800 **Earle, Olive L.** Birds and Their Nests. Morrow, 1952. 60p. lib. ed. $2.94 net. (I)

Describes and shows in detailed drawings 42 kinds of birds, their nesting areas, and their nests.

801 **Earle, Olive L.** Robins in the Garden; illus. by the author. Morrow, 1953. 63p. lib. ed. $2.94 net. (P)

Large print and many pictures make this simple story of a pair of robins especially useful with primary grades. Follows the robins from their arrival in March, through mating, nest building, hatching of eggs, care of baby birds, and migration in the fall.

802 **Fenton, Carroll Lane,** and **Pallas, Dorothy Constance.** Birds and Their World; illus. by Carroll Lane Fenton. Day, 1954. 94p. $3.50. (I)

Each chapter deals with one particular aspect of bird study—feathers, sight, etc.— as it relates to a particular bird and to birds in general. A good overview of many different kinds of birds.

803 **Fox, Charles Philip.** Birds Will Come to You; photos. by the author. Reilly & Lee, 1963. 86p. $3.50. (I)

Interesting suggestions for attracting birds, including construction of birdhouses and feeding stations, planting, and a chart with specifications for 20 houses for different birds.

804 **Friskey, Margaret R.** The True Book of Birds We Know; color plates by Anna Pistorius. Childrens Pr., 1954. 47p. $2.50. (P)

Very brief text and bright pictures introduce familiar birds to the small child, tell him something of their habits, and help him to identify them. (R2–3)

805 **Gans, Roma.** It's Nesting Time; illus.

by Kazue Mizumura. Crowell, 1964. unp. $3.25; lib. ed. $2.96 net. (P)

Encourages the child to watch birds building nests and to help them by putting out suitable materials. Nests of the robin, oriole, hummingbird, and other species are shown in clearly drawn pictures, many in color.

806 **Gilliard, E. Thomas.** Living Birds of the World; photos. by Eliot Porter (and others). Doubleday, 1958. 400p. $12.50. (U)

A comprehensive identification guide to approximately 1000 species. More than 200 full-color illustrations and additional pictures in black and white.

807 **Goudey, Alice E.** Graywings; illus. by Marie Nonnast. Scribner, 1964. unp. lib. ed. $2.97 net. (P–I)

A herring gull and her mate serve to demonstrate the life cycle of this species. Simple text and soft black-and-white pictures appeal to beginning bird watchers.

808 **Hess, Lilo.** Pigeons Everywhere. Scribner, 1967. 62p. $3.50; lib. ed. $3.31 net. (I)

The history of pigeons, their characteristics and habits, and their use in science, industry, and the Armed Forces are covered in brief text and excellent photographs by the author. Includes information on breeding and raising pigeons and on training racing homers.

809 **Kieran, John.** An Introduction to Birds; illus. by Don Eckelberry. new ed. Doubleday, 1965. 77p. $4.50. (I–U)

An informal guide to the more common birds, filled with entertaining anecdotes and illustrated with more than 100 full-color pictures.

810 **McClung, Robert M.** Honker: The Story of a Wild Goose; illus. by Bob Hines. Morrow, 1965. 63p. lib. ed. $2.94 net. (P–I)

Honker is a great gander who leads a flock of Canadian geese on their annual migrations. This is the story of one season in the life of Honker and his mate and their goslings, with glimpses of the wildlife refuges in which they find shelter.

811 **McClung, Robert M.** Ruby Throat: The Story of a Humming Bird; written and illus. by Robert M. McClung. Morrow, 1950. unp. lib. ed. $2.94 net. (P)

The marvel of the tiny hummingbird who

can fly from Central America across the Gulf of Mexico to his summer home in the north is brought out in a simple story with pictures on every page.

812 **McClung, Robert M.** Whooping Crane; illus. by Lloyd Sanford. Morrow, 1959. 63p. lib. ed. $2.94 net. (P–I)
A simply written and accurately illustrated life history of the rare whooping crane, emphasizing the efforts now being made to save it from extinction.

813 **Mowat, Farley.** Owls in the Family; illus. by Robert Frankenberg. Little, 1961. 103p. $3.50. (I)
Billy learns a great deal about owls in this true story of two owl pets.

814 **Peterson, Roger Tory.** The Birds; by Roger Tory Peterson and the eds. of Life. Time, Inc., 1963. Life Nature Library, distributed by Silver Burdett. 192p. $4.95. (U)
A noted ornithologist discusses the evolution of birds and all facets of bird life. Colored photographs, diagrams, and drawings are outstanding.

815 **Peterson, Roger Tory.** How To Know the Birds: An Introduction to Bird Recognition. 2d ed. . . . Endorsed by The National Audubon Society. Houghton, 1962. 168p. $3.75. (U)
A useful handbook on bird identification by silhouette without the use of field glasses, divided into five sections: general characteristics and terminology; drawings by family; habitats; silhouettes of common species; and index.

816 **Schloat, G. Warren.** The Wonderful Egg. Scribner, 1952. unp. lib. ed. $2.97 net. (P–I)
A photographic picture book in which two boys tour a poultry farm and learn about egg production and marketing. One sequence of photographs shows the development of the chick within the egg, and another shows the actual hatching.

817 **Selsam, Millicent E.** Egg to Chick; pictures by Frances Wells. International, 1946. unp. $1.95. (P)
A picture-book introduction to embryology, explaining and illustrating the development of the chick from the time the egg is laid until it is hatched.

818 **Webb, Addison.** Birds in Their Homes; pictures by Sabra Mallett Kimball. Garden City, 1947. 66p. $3.50. (P)
A beautiful picture book describing 54 birds, their nests, and how they care for their young.

819 **Welty, Susan F.** Birds with Bracelets: The Story of Bird-Banding; illus. by John Kaufmann. Prentice-Hall, 1965. 72p. $3.50. (I)
Traces the practice of birdbanding back to the early Greeks, describes modern techniques of trapping and banding, and states the requirements for becoming a bander. Includes maps of important flyways.

820 **Williamson, Margaret.** The First Book of Birds; written and illus. by Margaret Williamson. Watts, 1951. 69p. $2.65. (I)
A lively account of the daily lives of birds, illustrated with interesting marginal drawings and bird pictures on every page.

821 **Zim, Herbert S.,** and **Gabrielson, Ira N.** Birds: A Guide to the Most Familiar American Birds; illus. by James Gordon Irving; sponsored by The Wildlife Management Institute. Golden Pr., 1956. 160p. $3.95. (I)
Descriptive text and 125 pictures in full color enable the reader to identify 250 birds. Includes a table of data for each bird illustrated.

822 **Zim, Herbert S.** Homing Pigeons. Morrow, 1949. 64p. lib. ed. $2.94 net. (I)
Following a short history of the homing pigeon, the author discusses the raising, training, flying, and racing of pigeons and gives a list of organizations of pigeon fanciers. Includes an account of the U.S. Signal Corps' pigeon service during World War I.

823 **Zim, Herbert S.** Parrakeets; illus. by Larry Kettelkamp. Morrow, 1953. 59p. lib. ed. $2.94 net. (I)
Everything the young person needs to know about breeding, raising, and training parrakeets, including how to teach them to talk and how to build the right kind of cage for them.

Crabs, Spiders, Worms

824 **Hogner, Dorothy Childs.** Earthworms; illus. by Nils Hogner. Crowell, 1953. 51p. $3.50; lib. ed. $3.40 net. (I)

Explains how earthworms eat, see, and hear and discusses their importance to agriculture. Includes instructions for setting up an earthworm farm. Easy text and clear illustrations.

825 **Holling, Holling Clancy.** Pagoo; illus. by the author and Lucille Webster Holling. Houghton, 1957. 86p. $4.50; lib. ed. $3.90 net. (I)
The story of the hermit crab and his tide-pool neighbors is told in a fictionalized account, illustrated with handsome, scientifically accurate pictures.

826 **Lavine, Sigmund A.** Wonders of the Spider World. Dodd, 1966. 64p. $3; lib. ed. $2.79 net. (I–U)
An informal account of the history, legends, anatomy, and habits of spiders, stressing their importance as insect eaters and giving suggestions for observing spiders.

827 **Milne, Lorus J.,** and **Milne, Margery.** The Crab That Crawled Out of the Past; drawings by Kenneth Gosner. Atheneum, 1965. 84p. $3.50; lib. ed. $3.41 net. (I–U)
Two biologists examine a living fossil—the horseshoe crab—and describe its history, appearance, habits, and life cycle.

828 **Shuttlesworth, Dorothy E.** The Story of Spiders; illus. by Su Zan N. Swain. Garden City, 1959. 55p. $3.50. (I)
Explains the difference between spiders and insects, dispels some of the misconceptions about spiders, and discusses their characteristics, habits, spinning abilities, and value to man.

Fishes (Including Aquariums)

829 **Bendick, Jeanne.** The First Book of Fishes. Watts, 1965. 72p. $2.65. (P–I)
An introductory book about familiar and unfamiliar fish: "what they look like, where they live, how they protect themselves, what they eat, and how they reproduce." Animated illustrations by the author.

830 **Broekel, Ray.** The True Book of Tropical Fishes; illus. by Rocco Dante Navigato. Childrens Pr., 1956. 46p. $2.50. (P)
A beginning book on aquariums, telling how to set up and care for an aquarium and what kinds of fish to put into it. (R2–3)

831 **Hess, Lilo.** Sea Horses; story and photos. by Lilo Hess. Scribner, 1966. 46p. $3.25; lib. ed. $3.12 net. (P–I)
Close-up photographs and simple text introduce the sea horse and suggest how to keep sea horses as pets.

832 **Morgan, Alfred.** Aquarium Book for Boys and Girls; illus. with drawings by the author, and with photos. Scribner, 1959. 209p. $3.95; lib. ed. $3.63 net. (I–U)
A comprehensive handbook giving detailed instructions for setting up, stocking, and maintaining both fresh- and salt-water aquariums for fish, turtles, and amphibians.

833 **National Geographic Society.** Wondrous World of Fishes. National Geographic Soc., 1965. 366p. $8.75. (I–U)
Handsome colored photographs illustrate this broad coverage of fishes and fishing, written by authorities on the subject.

834 **Ommanney, F. D.** The Fishes; by F. D. Ommanney and the eds. of Life. Time, Inc., 1963. Life Nature Library, distributed by Silver Burdett. 192p. $4.95. (U)
A profusely illustrated survey of the evolution, natural history, ecology, diversity, and economic importance of fishes.

835 **Phleger, Fred.** Red Tag Comes Back; pictures by Arnold Lobel. Harper, 1961. 64p. $1.95; lib. ed. $2.19 net. (P)
An easy-to-read story about a Pacific salmon, marked by a fishery research group, who goes to sea and then returns to her home stream to lay her eggs. (R2–3)

836 **Selsam, Millicent.** Plenty of Fish; with illus. by Erik Blegvad. Harper, 1960. 61p. $1.95; lib. ed. $2.19 net. (P)
A simple story about a small boy who learns the biological facts about fish by observing his two goldfish. (R2–3)

837 **Selsam, Millicent E.** Underwater Zoos; illus. by Kathleen Elgin. Morrow, 1961. 96p. lib. ed. $2.94 net. (I)
Explains how to collect specimens, set up salt- and fresh-water aquariums, and care for the different kinds of animals in them. Includes a list of supply houses.

838 **Zim, Herbert S.,** and **Shoemaker, Hurst H.** Fishes: A Guide to Fresh- and Salt-Water Species; illus. by James Gordon Irving. Golden Pr., 1956. 160p. $3.95. (I)

A pocket identification guide with suggestions for collecting, classifying, and photographing fishes.

839   Zim, Herbert S. Goldfish; pictures by Joy Buba. Morrow, 1947. unp. $2.95; lib. ed. $2.94 net. (P–I)
A simple but scientifically sound guide to the selection and care of goldfish.

Insects

840   Barker, Will. Familiar Insects of America; illus. by Carl Burger; schematic drawings by Nancy Lloyd; foreword by Hilary J. Deason. Harper, 1960. 236p. $5.95; lib. ed. $5.11 net. (U)
After an introduction explaining the evolution, classification, and habits of insects in general, the author discusses in detail various classes of insects, such as ants, wasps, bees, butterflies, skippers, and moths. Includes a glossary and a reading list.

841   Bronson, Wilfrid S. The Grasshopper Book; illus. by the author. Harcourt, 1943. 127p. $3.50. (I)
Grasshoppers and their relatives are discussed in entertaining text and shown in informative pictures.

842   Doering, Harald. A Bee Is Born; tr. and adapted by Dale S. Cunningham. Sterling, 1962. 96p. $2.95; lib. ed. $3.39 net. (I–U)
Excellent magnified and close-up photographs augment this life history of bees: hatching of eggs, development of the several classes of bees, social structure of the bee community, and activities in the hive.

843   Farb, Peter. The Insects; by Peter Farb and the eds. of Life. Time, Inc., 1962. Life Nature Library, distributed by Silver Burdett. 192p. $4.95. (U)
Expertly written, scientifically accurate text and numerous photographs and drawings present the world of insects in its many interesting aspects.

844   Goudey, Alice E. Butterfly Time; illus. by Adrienne Adams. Scribner, 1964. unp. $3.25; lib. ed. $3.12 net. (P)
A beautiful picture book about 12 commonly seen butterflies, showing them in four-color illustrations and describing their life cycles and habitats. (R2–3)

845   Goudey, Alice E. Here Come the

Bees! Illus. by Garry MacKenzie. Scribner, 1960. 94p. lib. ed. $3.12 net. (P)
An introduction to social insects through the life of the honeybee. Well illustrated and easy to read. (R2–3)

846   Harris, Louise Dyer, and **Harris, Norman Dyer.** Flash: The Life Story of a Firefly; illus. by Henry B. Kane. Little, 1966. 57p. $2.95; lib. ed. $2.97 net. (P–I)
Traces the life of the firefly through the stages of egg, glowworm, pupa, and beetle in simple text and informative pictures.

847   Hogner, Dorothy Childs. Butterflies; illus. by Nils Hogner. Crowell, 1962. 69p. $3.50; lib. ed. $3.40 net. (P)
In this "butterfly-watching book" a young reader may learn the essential facts about butterflies and find out how to raise caterpillars that change into butterflies.

848   Hogner, Dorothy Childs. Grasshoppers and Crickets; illus. by Nils Hogner. Crowell, 1960. 61p. $3.50; lib. ed. $3.40 net. (P)
Explains how to tell grasshoppers from locusts and crickets and describes the characteristics, habits, and behavior of each species. Labeled diagrams aid the reader to follow the simple text.

849   Hussey, Lois J., and **Pessino, Catherine.** Collecting Cocoons; illus. by Isabel Sherwin Harris. Crowell, 1953. 73p. $3.50; lib. ed. $3.20 net. (I)
An introductory book on where to look for cocoons, how to collect and care for them, and how to keep records. Includes identification information for 19 moths.

850   Hutchins, Carleen Maley. Moon Moth; illus. by Douglas Howland. Coward-McCann, 1965. unp. $2.75; lib. ed. $2.68 net. (P–I)
The life story of the beautiful night-flying luna moth is told from the time she emerges from her brown cocoon until she lays her eggs and dies.

851   Hutchins, Ross E. Caddis Insects: Nature's Carpenters and Stonemasons; illus. with photos. by the author. Dodd, 1966. 80p. $3.25; lib. ed. $2.99 net. (I)
Describes the life cycle and habits of the unique caddis insects—builders of protective cases of twigs and pebbles—and tells where to obtain caddis flies for aquariums. Close-up photographs show many types of cases.

852 **Lavine, Sigmund A.** Wonders of the Anthill; illus. by Ernest H. Hart. Dodd, 1960. 64p. lib. ed. $2.79 net. (I)

Investigates the characteristics and activities of ants, showing how their social organization parallels man's in some respects. Includes suggestions for making an observation nest.

853 **Lutz, Frank E.** Field Book of Insects of the United States and Canada, Aiming To Answer Common Questions. 3d ed. rewritten to include much additional material; with about 800 illus., many in color. Putnam, 1935. 510p. $4.50. (U)

A standard handbook, useful in science, nature study, and for the entomologist.

854 **McClung, Robert M.** Caterpillars and How They Live; written and illus. by Robert M. McClung. Morrow, 1965. 63p. lib. ed. $2.94 net. (P)

Tells what a caterpillar is, how it lives, and how it benefits or harms man. Useful in identifying the different species of caterpillars and for caterpillar-raising projects. Large type, helpful illustrations. (R3–4)

855 **McClung, Robert M.** Ladybug; illus. by Robert M. McClung. Morrow, 1966. 48p. $2.95; lib. ed. $2.94 net. (P)

Large type, simple text, and many colorful illustrations make this story of the little insect-eating ladybug popular with primary children. (R3–4)

856 **McClung, Robert M.** Moths and Butterflies and How They Live; illus. by Robert M. McClung. Morrow, 1966. 63p. $2.95; lib. ed. $2.94 net. (P)

A clear explanation of how moths and butterflies differ, what they eat, and how they live, presented in style and format similar to the McClung books listed above. (R3–4)

857 **Phillips, Mary Geisler.** Dragonflies and Damselflies; illus. by Anne Marie Jauss. Crowell, 1960. 95p. $3.50. (I)

Begins by explaining the scientific names of living things, then compares and contrasts two closely related insects and tells where to find them and how to collect and preserve them.

858 **Phillips, Mary Geisler.** The Makers of Honey; illus. by Elizabeth Burckmyer. Crowell, 1956. 163p. $3. (I)

Explores the characteristics, life cycle, social organization, and activities of bees. Includes a list of books on beekeeping.

859 **Poole, Lynn,** and **Poole, Gray.** Fireflies in Nature and the Laboratory; illus. by Christine Sapieha. Crowell, 1965. 149p. $3.95. (I–U)

In addition to giving an account of fireflies in history, legend, and nature, the authors introduce the subject of bioluminescence and show how fireflies are used in the study of light emission from living things.

860 **Selsam, Millicent E.** Terry and the Caterpillars; pictures by Arnold Lobel. Harper, 1962. 64p. $1.95; lib. ed. $2.19 net. (P)

A little girl finds three caterpillars, puts them into a jar, and watches all the stages of their life: caterpillar to cocoon to moth to egg and back to caterpillar again. Large type, short sentences, many illustrations. (R1–2)

861 **Shuttlesworth, Dorothy E.** The Story of Ants; illus. by Su Zan N. Swain. Doubleday, 1964. 60p. $3.95. (I)

Describes the organization of an ant colony and the characteristics and behavior of its inhabitants, including such fascinating aspects as slavery among ants and ant armies. Lavishly illustrated in color, with figures in actual size beside magnified drawings for clearer detail.

862 **Teale, Edwin Way.** Grassroots Jungle: A Book of Insects; illus. with one hundred and thirty photographs by the author. rev. ed. Dodd, 1953. 240p. $6.50. (U)

An authoritative account of the common insects of lawn, garden, and field, illustrated with exceptionally fine photographs.

863 **Tibbets, Albert B.** The First Book of Bees; pictures by Helene Carter. Watts, 1952. 68p. $2.65. (P–I)

A good introduction to bees and beekeeping. (R2–3)

864 **Williamson, Margaret.** The First Book of Bugs; written and illus. by Margaret Williamson. Watts, 1949. 44p. $2.65. (P–I)

Many pictures and brief text are combined to provide information about mosquitoes, daddy longlegs, spiders, ants, and many other common bugs. (R2–3)

865   **Zim, Herbert S.,** and **Cottam, Clarence.** Insects: A Guide to Familiar American Insects; illus. by James Gordon Irving; sponsored by The Wildlife Management Institute. Golden Pr., 1956. 160p. $3.95. (U)

An identification guide to 225 species with brief descriptions, colored pictures, and range maps.

Mammals (Other Than Man)

866   **Adamson, Joy.** Born Free: A Lioness of Two Worlds. Pantheon, 1960. 220p. $4.95. (U)

The remarkable story of a lioness, raised by the wife of a Kenya game warden, and the unique relationship between this half-wild animal and the world of human beings. Important as a different kind of animal story and for exceptionally interesting photographs.

867   **Adamson, Joy.** Elsa . . . Pantheon, 1963. rev. ed. unp. $2.95; lib. ed. $3.09 net. (P–I)

Photographs, some from *Born Free,* above, and a simplified story of Elsa are combined in a book for younger children.

868   **Andrews, Roy Chapman.** All about Whales; illus. by Thomas W. Voter. Random, 1954. 148p. $2.50; lib. ed. $2.48 net. (I)

An authoritative account of the major groups of whales, based on the author's extensive voyages to study these largest of creatures. Includes chapters on the evolution of whales and their relatives and on the whaling industry. (R3–4)

869   **Bronson, Wilfred S.** Coyotes (Ki′yotes or Ki-yo′tays); written and illus. by Wilfred S. Bronson. Harcourt, 1946. unp. $2.95. (P–I)

An easy, sympathetic account of these often-maligned wild dogs of the West. Large type and many illustrations.

870   **Buff, Mary,** and **Buff, Conrad.** Dash and Dart. Viking, 1942. 73p. $3.25; lib. ed. $3.19 net. (P)

An especially lovely picture book about a year in the life of twin fawns, the brief, rhythmic text interpreted in soft sepia pictures and four color double spreads, one for each season.

871   **Darling, Louis.** Kangaroos and Other Animals with Pockets; written and illus. by

Louis Darling. Morrow, 1958. 64p. lib. ed. $2.94 net. (I)

Introduces the marsupial mammals of the world in concise text and informative pictures, explaining why most of them are found only in Australia. (R4–5)

872   **Earle, Olive L.** Camels and Llamas; written and illus. by Olive L. Earle. Morrow, 1961. 63p. lib. ed. $2.94 net. (P–I)

In simple text and many pictures the author recounts the evolution, history, habits, and domestication of these animals, stressing their usefulness to man.

873   **Earle, Olive L.** Squirrels in the Garden; written and illus. by Olive L. Earle. Morrow, 1963. 63p. lib. ed. $2.94 net. (P–I)

One squirrel, from birth until he finds a mate, is used to demonstrate the characteristics and habits of the species. Excellent line drawings throughout.

874   **Eberle, Irmengarde.** Bears Live Here. Doubleday, 1966. 61p. $3.25. (P)

Describes one year in the life of a black bear family in readable text and shows their activities in full-page color photographs. Useful as a read-aloud story or for animal study in primary grades.

875   **Eberle, Irmengarde.** A Chipmunk Lives Here; with drawings by Matthew Kalmenoff. Doubleday, 1966. 60p. $3.25. (P)

In the same style as *Bears Live Here,* above, the author tells the dramatic story of a chipmunk's life. In addition to excellent color photographs, there are cutaway drawings showing the chipmunk's burrow.

876   **Eberle, Irmengarde.** Fawn in the Woods; photos. by Lilo Hess. Crowell, 1962. 42p. $3.50; lib. ed. $3.36 net. (P)

A photographic study of one year in the life of a fawn, covering physical characteristics, habits, training, and means of survival.

877   **Goudey, Alice E.** Here Come the Bears! Illus. by Garry MacKenzie. Scribner, 1954. 92p. lib. ed. $3.12 net. (P)

Easy text and informative pictures introduce four families of American bears: grizzly, polar, Alaskan brown, and black. (R2–3)

878   **Goudey, Alice E.** Here Come the Beavers! Illus. by Garry MacKenzie. Scribner, 1957. 94p. lib. ed. $3.12 net. (P)

The life story, illustrated with excellent drawings, of a pair of beavers, stressing their dam-building activities. (R2–3)

879   **Goudey, Alice E.** Here Come the Cottontails! Illus. by Garry MacKenzie. Scribner, 1965. 93p. lib. ed. $3.12 net. (P)
The first year in the life of one litter of rabbits is described in easy, attractively illustrated text. (R2–3)

880   **Goudey, Alice E.** Here Come the Dolphins! Illus. by Garry MacKenzie. Scribner, 1961. 94p. lib. ed. $3.12 net. (P)
An appealing story of a baby dolphin and his herd, covering habits, intelligence, and the use of dolphins in research. (R2–3)

881   **Goudey, Alice E.** Here Come the Elephants! Illus. by Garry MacKenzie. Scribner, 1955. 92p. lib. ed. $3.12 net. (P)
Compares African and Indian elephants and describes the behavior and habitats of both, in the same easy, copiously illustrated style as in the Goudey books, above. (R2–3)

882   **Hess, Lilo.** Rabbits in the Meadow; story and photos. by Lilo Hess. Crowell, 1963. 42p. $3.50; lib. ed. $3.36 net. (P)
Working from a blind, the author photographed a family of three baby rabbits and their mother in all aspects of their family life. The simple, narrative text is informative and closely coordinated with the pictures.

883   **Liers, Emil E.** An Otter's Story; illus. by Tony Palazzo. Viking, 1953. 191p. $3.75; lib. ed. $3.56 net. (I)
Out of his own experience, the author writes the life story of a pair of otters, their parents, and their cubs. Filled with interesting incidents and illustrated with excellent drawings.

884   **Life** (Periodical). The Mammals; by the eds. of Life; text by Richard Carrington. Time, Inc., 1963. Life Nature Library, distributed by Silver Burdett. 192p. $4.95. (U)
Excellent photographs and advanced but nontechnical style are combined in a survey of mammals for the browser or advanced reader.

885   **National Geographic Society.** Wild Animals of North America. National Geographic Soc., 1960. 400p. $7.75. (I–U)
After an introduction on the evolution and characteristics of animals in general, the authors discuss each of the orders represented in North America: the hoofed animals, carnivores, gnawing animals, "survivors of ancient orders," and ocean dwellers. Written by specialists and lavishly illustrated with color photographs and drawings.

886   **North, Sterling.** Rascal: A Memoir of a Better Era; illus. by John Schoenherr. Dutton, 1963. 189p. $3.95; lib. ed. $3.91 net. (U)
The true story of the author's pet raccoon and the good times the two had together in a Wisconsin village in 1918.

887   **Ripper, Charles L.** Bats; written and illus. by Charles L. Ripper. Morrow, 1954. 63p. lib. ed. $2.94 net. (I)
Dispels many of the misconceptions about bats and describes their appearance, habits, and family life.

888   **Rue, Leonard Lee.** The World of the Beaver; text and photos. by Leonard Lee Rue III. Lippincott, 1964. 158p. $4.95. (U)
From his own observations, the author gives a comprehensive account of the beaver's life and habits. Illustrated with excellent photographs. For the superior reader.

889   **Sanderson, Ivan T.** Living Mammals of the World; photos. by John Markham (and others). Doubleday, 1955. 303p. $12.50. (U)
Advanced text and excellent photographs give comprehensive coverage of most species of living mammals.

890   **Tee-Van, Helen Damrosch.** Small Mammals Are Where You Find Them; illus. by the author. Knopf, 1966. 148p. $3.50; lib. ed. $3.39 net. (I)
Thumbnail sketches of mice, moles, squirrels, chipmunks, and other common small animals, illustrated with drawings and a range map for each species.

891   **Williamson, Margaret.** The First Book of Mammals; written and illus. by Margaret Williamson. Watts, 1957. 62p. $2.65. (I)
An introduction to mammals, defining terms and giving basic facts common to the group.

892   **Ylla.** The Little Elephant; story by Arthur Gregor; designed by Luc Bouchage.

Harper, 1956. unp. $3.50; lib. ed. $3.27 net.
(P)

A very simple story ties together exceptionally appealing photographs of a small Indian elephant who led a festival parade decked out in holiday regalia.

893   Zim, Herbert S. The Great Whales; illus. by James Gordon Irving. Morrow, 1951. unp. $2.95; lib. ed. $2.94 net. (P–I)

Elementary text and excellent illustrations present interesting and authentic facts about the ancestors, adaptations, characteristics, and habits of whales. (R3–4)

894   Zim, Herbert S., and **Hoffmeister, Donald F.** Mammals: A Guide to Familiar American Species; sponsored by The Wildlife Management Institute. Golden Pr., 1955. 160p. $3.95. (I)

In addition to surveying each major family of North American animals, the authors provide a list of zoos and museums, a glossary, and a reading list. The description of each animal is accompanied by a picture and a range map.

895   Zim, Herbert S. Mice, Men, and Elephants: A Book about the Mammals; illus. with drawings by James MacDonald, and with photos. Harcourt, 1942. 215p. $5.95. (I)

Discusses the evolution and classification of mammals and explains the characteristics which separate them from the rest of the animal kingdom.

896   Zim, Herbert S. Monkeys; illus. by Gardell D. Christensen. Morrow, 1955. unp. $2.95; lib. ed. $2.94 net. (I)

Monkeys and marmosets are discussed in simple text and shown in clear pictures. Covers various species, their similarities to man, and keeping monkeys as pets. (R3–4)

Domestic Animals and Pets

897   Anderson, C. W. C. W. Anderson's Complete Book of Horses and Horsemanship; with over 50 drawings by the author. Macmillan, 1963. 182p. $4.95; lib. ed. $4.54 net. (I–U)

Beginning with the history and development of the horse, the author discusses breeds of horses, selection, care and training, and techniques of riding. Enthusiastic style and anatomically correct drawings.

898   Buck, Margaret Waring. Small Pets from Woods and Fields; written and illus.

by Margaret Waring Buck. Abingdon, 1960. 72p. $3. (I)

Identifies and gives directions for the capture and care of small wild pets. Includes many suggestions for children's nature projects and a reading list.

899   Burger, Carl. All about Cats; illus. with photos; with a foreword by William Bridges. Random, 1966. 143p. $1.95; lib. ed. $2.48 net. (I)

The evolution of the cat, his role in history and folklore, and his characteristics and personality are discussed in an entertaining and informative book. Includes a classification table, a chart of the cat's family tree, and a bibliography.

900   Carter, Gordon. Willing Walkers: The Story of Dogs for the Blind; with an introd. by Arthur J. Phillipson. Abelard-Schuman, 1965. 95p. $3.25; lib. ed. $3.19. (I–U)

Discusses the training and use of Seeing Eye dogs and relates stories of some unusual dogs.

901   Chrystie, Frances N. Pets: A Complete Handbook on the Care, Understanding, and Appreciation of All Kinds of Pets. new rev. ed. With illus. by Gillett Good Griffin. Little, 1964. 274p. $4.95. (I–U)

Comprehensive coverage and practical advice, including a chapter on first aid and common diseases.

902   Henry, Marguerite. Album of Horses; illus. by Wesley Dennis. Rand McNally, 1951. 112p. $3.95; lib. ed. $3.97 net. (I)

A handsomely illustrated volume describing 20 breeds of horses, from the Shetland pony to the thoroughbred race horse, anecdotal in style and including many little-known facts.

903   Henry, Marguerite. All about Horses; with photos. by Walter D. Osborne. Random, 1967. 129p. $3.95. (I–U)

The evolution of the horse and his wild relatives, the place of the horse in history, and the best-known breeds are discussed in horseman's language and illustrated with excellent photographs.

904   Henry, Marguerite. Mustang: Wild Spirit of the West; illus. by Robert Lougheed. Rand McNally, 1966. 222p. $3.95; lib. ed. $3.79 net. (I–U)

The true story of America's wild horses

and of one woman's battle to save them from extinction, telling how "Wild Horse Annie's" efforts led to protective legislation and wild-horse refuges.

905   Ipcar, Dahlov. World Full of Horses. Doubleday, 1955. unp. $3.25. (P)

Horses, past and present, are presented in a picture book combining unusual colors and simple text. (R2–3)

906   Lauber, Patricia. The Story of Dogs; foreword by Konrad Lorenz; illus. with photos. Random, 1966. 64p. $1.95; lib. ed. $2.29 net. (P–I)

A simply written history of dogs, telling how they may have been domesticated and how different breeds have developed. Photographs show many species.

907   Levin, Jane Whitbread. Bringing Up Puppies: A Child's Book of Dog Breeding and Care; photos. by Mary Morris Steiner. Harcourt, 1958. 62p. $2.95. (I)

A practical guide, with many appealing photographs, based on the author's own experience.

908   Morgan, Alfred. A Pet Book for Boys and Girls; illus. by the author and by Ruth King. Scribner, 1949. 246p. $3.95; lib. ed. $3.63 net. (I–U)

Interestingly presented information about how to choose a pet; how to provide proper shelter for him; and how to feed, treat, and train him.

909   Tensen, Ruth M. Come to the Pet Shop. Reilly & Lee, 1954. 41p. $2.95. (P)

Appealing photographs and the simplest of texts tell the story of two boys who go to the pet shop to choose a birthday present. (R1–2)

910   Weil, Ann. Animal Families; based on a text by Ann Weil; illus. by Roger Vernam. Childrens Pr., 1956. 29p. $2.75. (P)

Shows in colored illustrations the male, female, and young of several species of farm animals and tells the correct name of each (bull, cow, calf, etc.).

911   Williams, Garth. Baby Farm Animals. Golden Pr., 1959. unp. $1. (P)

For the very youngest, a book of engaging colored pictures with a minimum of text.

912   Zim, Herbert S. Golden Hamsters; illus. by Herschel Wartik. Morrow, 1951. 63p. $2.95; lib. ed. $2.94 net. (I)

Gives a brief history of Syrian hamsters and explains the responsibilities of keeping them as pets. (R3–4)

913   Zim, Herbert S. Rabbits; pictures by Joy Buba. Morrow, 1958. 57p. lib. ed. $2.94 net. (I)

Simple text and accurate pictures give information about wild rabbits and tell how to raise tame ones. (R3–4)

Mollusks and Shells

914   Abbott, R. Tucker. Sea Shells of the World: A Guide to the Better-known Species: under the editorship of Herbert S. Zim; illus. by George and Marita Sandström. Golden Pr., 1962. 160p. $3.95. (I)

A guide for identification, collecting, and preservation of sea shells, with 790 colored illustrations of 562 species.

915   Dudley, Ruth H. Sea Shells; illus. by Phoebe Erickson. Crowell, 1953. 149p. $3.50; lib. ed. $3.40 net. (I)

Describes the lives of five common mollusks and gives suggestions for shell collecting. Includes a list of shell clubs. (R3–4)

916   Earle, Olive L. The Octopus; illus. by the author. Morrow, 1955. 62p. lib. ed. $2.94 net. (I)

In a lively, factual text and excellent drawings, the author presents a much-maligned animal in a favorable light, explaining how he moves, catches his prey, and defends himself.

917   Goudey, Alice E. Houses from the Sea; illus. by Adrienne Adams. Scribner, 1959. unp. $3.25; lib. ed. $3.12 net. (P)

An unusually beautiful picture story of two children who gather shells on the beach and learn about the animals who inhabited them. Pictures identifying the shells are repeated at the end of the book.

918   Hogner, Dorothy Childs. Snails; illus. by Nils Hogner. Crowell, 1958. 81p. $3.50; lib. ed. $3.40 net. (I)

Describes the characteristics and habits of several species of land and water snails and their relatives and gives instructions for building a snailery.

919   Podendorf, Illa. The True Book of Pebbles and Shells; pictures by Mary Gehr. Childrens Pr., 1964. 47p. $2.50. (P)

An easy-to-read, effectively illustrated introduction to the pebbles and shells found along the seashore. (R2–3)

920   **Rogers, Julia Ellen.** The Shell Book . . . 8 plates in color and 96 in black and white mostly from photos. by A. R. Dugmore. rev. ed. Branford, 1951. 503p. $8.50. (U)

A comprehensive authority on shells of the world.

921   **Verrill, A. Hyatt.** The Shell Collector's Handbook. Putnam, 1950. 228p. $4.95. (U)

Describes typical shells of the world in an informal, well-illustrated study and gives instructions for building a shell collection.

MAN

Anatomy and Physiology

922   **Adler, Irving,** and **Adler, Ruth.** Your Ears; illus. by Peggy Adler Walsh. Day, 1963. 48p. lib. ed. $2.68 net. (I)

Describes the structure of the ear, explains how the ears convert vibrations into sound, and discusses deafness and some famous deaf people who have overcome the handicap. Readable text and clear illustrations.

923   **Adler, Irving,** and **Adler, Ruth.** Your Eyes. Day, 1962. 48p. lib. ed. $2.68 net. (I)

In style and format similar to *Your Ears,* above, the authors discuss the structure and functions of the eyes, defects of vision, care of the eyes, and education of the blind.

924   **Aliki.** My Five Senses. Crowell, 1962. unp. $3.25; lib. ed. $2.96 net. (P)

Bright pictures and simple text help the young child to understand his senses and how he learns through them.

925   **Asimov, Isaac.** The Human Body: Its Structure and Operation; illus. by Anthony Ravielli. Houghton, 1963. 340p. $5.95. (U)

Places man in the classification of living things and describes his skeleton, muscles, and major anatomical systems and their functions.

926   **Cosgrove, Margaret L.** Wonders of Your Senses; illus. by the author. Dodd, 1958. 64p. lib. ed. $2.79 net. (I)

Covers the same material as the Aliki book, above, but in more detail.

927   **De Schweinitz, Karl.** Growing Up: How We Become Alive, Are Born, and Grow. 4th ed. Macmillan, 1965. 54p. $3.50. (I)

A straightforward, dignified presentation of reproduction, birth, and growth among animals and human beings. Useful to teachers and parents as well as to older children.

928   **Glemser, Bernard.** All about the Human Body; illus. by Felix Traugott. Random, 1958. 136p. $1.95; lib. ed. $2.48 net. (I)

Organized by bodily functions: respiration, digestion, circulation, etc. Clear diagrams of organs support the simply written text.

929   **Goldenson, Robert M.** All about the Human Mind; illus. with photos. and diags. Random, 1963. 143p. $2.50; lib. ed. $2.48 net. (I–U)

A psychologist writes about the brain and how it governs thinking and behavior in man and animals.

930   **Gruenberg, Sidonie Matsner.** The Wonderful Story of How You Were Born; illus. by Hildegard Woodward. rev. ed. Doubleday, 1952. 38p. $2.95. (P–I)

For younger children than the De Schweinitz book, above, a picture book answering the child's first questions about where he came from.

931   **Hyde, Margaret O.** Your Brain: Master Computer; illus. by P. A. Hutchison. McGraw-Hill, 1964. 154p. $3.50; lib. ed. $3.06 net. (U)

Describes the human brain and its functioning and compares it with mechanical "brains." Includes a glossary and a reading list.

932   **Kettelkamp, Larry.** Song, Speech, and Ventriloquism; illus. by Larry Kettelkamp. Morrow, 1967. 96p. $2.95; lib. ed. $2.94 net. (I–U)

The speech organs and their functions are described, with particular attention to voice control and projection. Gives explicit instructions for ventriloquism, supported by experiments, labeled drawings, and charts. Includes a glossary.

933   **Lauber, Patricia.** Your Body and How It Works; drawings by Stephen Rogers Peck; photos. by Florence Burns. Random, 1962. 77p. $1.95; lib. ed. $2.29 net. (I)

An introduction to bodily functions and the organs which control them.

934   Lerner, Marguerite Rush. Red Man, White Man, African Chief: The Story of Skin Color; illus. by George Overlie. Medical Books for Children, 1960. unp. $2.95. (I)

A clear explanation of why different people have different skin coloring. Includes definitions and pronunciations of technical terms and a chapter for parents and teachers.

935   Ravielli, Anthony. Wonders of the Human Body; written and illus. by Anthony Ravielli. Viking, 1954. 125p. $3; lib. ed. $2.96 net. (I)

Smooth writing and effective illustrations introduce human anatomy and physiology, using scientific terms and comparing the functioning of the body to the working of machines.

936   Riedman, Sarah R. The World through Your Senses; preface by John F. Fulton; illus. by Ruth Levin. rev. ed. Abelard-Schuman, 1962. 189p. $3. (U)

Discusses the nervous system, the five senses which it controls, and such familiar sensations as hunger, fear, and pain.

937   Schloat, G. Warren. Your Wonderful Teeth. Scribner, 1954. unp. lib. ed. $2.79 net. (P)

Two boys visit their dentists and learn about their teeth and how to care for them.

938   Schneider, Herman, and **Schneider, Nina.** How Your Body Works; introd. by Milton R. Levine; with illus. by Barbara Ivins. W. R. Scott, 1949. 160p. $3.50. (I)

A first physiology book discussing the preadolescent body and explaining how it can be kept healthy. Includes simple experiments.

939   Schneider, Leo. Lifeline: The Story of Your Circulatory System; illus. by Jere Donovan. Harcourt, 1958. 127p. $2.95. (I)

In addition to describing the composition of the blood and the circulatory system, the author discusses how the blood cells fight disease, how the electrocardiograph works, and how surgeons repair damaged hearts.

940   Schneider, Leo. You and Your Cells; illus. with drawings by Henri A. Fluchere

and with photos. Harcourt, 1964. 157p. $3.75. (U)

Explains the structure, types, and functions of cells, beginning with the amoeba and proceeding to the cellular biology of man.

941   Weart, Edith Lucie. The Story of Your Blood; illus. by Z. Onyshkewych. Coward-McCann, 1960. 64p. $3.50; lib. ed. $3.29 net. (I–U)

An introduction to the composition, functions, and circulation of the blood, and to blood groups and transfusions, illustrated with clarifying drawings. Glossary.

942   Weart, Edith Lucie. The Story of Your Bones; illus. by Jan Fairservis. Coward-McCann, 1966. 63p. lib. ed. $3.29 net. (I–U)

Man's skeleton is described and accurately pictured, the function of bones is explained, and the importance of bones in the study of prehistoric life is discussed.

943   Weart, Edith Lucie. The Story of Your Brain and Nerves; illus. by Alan Tompkins. Coward-McCann, 1961. 64p. $3.50; lib. ed. $3.29 net. (I–U)

The complex control system of the body is explained in terms understandable to children and illustrated with clear drawings. Glossary.

944   Weart, Edith Lucie. The Story of Your Respiratory System; illus. by Jan Fairservis. Coward-McCann, 1964. 62p. lib. ed. $3.29 net. (I–U)

Illustrations and diagrams augment a lucid discussion of each part of the respiratory system. Similar in treatment and format to the three Weart books, above. Glossary.

945   Zim, Herbert S. Our Senses and How They Work; illus. by Herschel Wartik. Morrow, 1956. 64p. $2.95; lib. ed. $2.94 net. (I)

The five senses by which man becomes aware of the world are explained in concise text and illustrated with clear drawings.

946   Zim, Herbert S. Your Heart and How It Works; illus. by Gustav Schrotter. Morrow, 1959. 63p. $2.95; lib. ed. $2.94 net. (I)

Describes simply the heart and its functions, traces the development of the human heart from lower forms, and describes some of the diseases to which the heart is subject. Drawings and diagrams aid understanding.

Health and Safety

947   Antonacci, Robert J., and **Barr, Jene.** Physical Fitness for Young Champions; illus. by Charles Geer. McGraw-Hill, 1962. 160p. $3.95; lib. ed. $3.31 net. (I–U)

Beginning with two physical-fitness tests, the authors give a series of exercises for developing and maintaining fitness with sports and home-built equipment. Includes a chapter for girls and for the handicapped.

948   Asimov, Isaac. The Chemicals of Life: Enzymes, Vitamins, Hormones. Abelard-Schuman, 1954. 159p. $3.50. (U)

An introduction to biochemistry, explaining the chemical reactions necessary to life and health and discussing the use of wonder drugs to correct deficiencies.

949   Bendick, Jeanne. The Emergency Book; written and illus. by Jeanne Bendick. Rand McNally, 1967. 144p. $3.95. (I–U)

Tells clearly and simply what to do in case of fire, robberies, injuries, and other emergencies, and gives common-sense advice on preventing emergencies. Cartoon-like illustrations and an excellent index.

950   Cain, Arthur H. Young People and Drinking: The Use and Abuse of Alcohol. Day, 1963. 94p. $3.50. (U)

An honest and objective discussion of drinking, intended to help young people understand the dangers of alcohol and to make an intelligent decision about its use. Will be helpful to counselors as well as to older pupils.

951   Cain, Arthur H. Young People and Smoking: The Use and Abuse of Cigarette Tobacco. Day, 1964. 94p. $3.50. (U)

Both sides of the controversy over cigarette smoking are considered in this survey of research on the relationship of smoking to health, including a summary of the Surgeon General's report. Useful in physical education, science, and guidance.

952   Epstein, Sam, and **Epstein, Beryl.** The First Book of the World Health Organization; illus. with photos. Watts, 1964. 82p. $2.65. (I)

Describes the purposes, structure, and

some of the world-wide accomplishments of WHO in improving health and preventing disease.

953   Faber, Doris. The Miracle of Vitamins. Putnam, 1964. 158p. lib. ed. $3.29 net. (U)

Traces the development of information about vitamins and their use in treating vitamin-deficiency diseases and stresses the importance of a vitamin-rich diet. Includes a vitamin chart and a bibliography.

954   Hillcourt, William. Physical Fitness for Boys; illus. by Frank Bolle. Golden Pr., 1967. 64p. $1.95. (I–U)

Chapters on nutrition, sleep, rest, and good health habits, followed by exercises and sports for body building. Explicit instructions illustrated with detailed drawings.

955   Hillcourt, William. Physical Fitness for Girls; illus. by Frank Bolle. Golden Pr., 1967. 64p. $1.95. (I–U)

Common-sense principles of good health and a program of exercises for developing a sound and attractive body. Similar in presentation and format to *Physical Fitness for Boys,* above.

955a   Hyde, Margaret O., ed. Mind Drugs. McGraw-Hill, 1968. 150p. $4.50. (U)

An informed and unemotional survey of drug use, in which specialists in medicine, psychiatry, social psychology, and public health discuss the findings of research and give their views on the effects of marijuana, alcohol, LSD, heroin, and other drugs on the mind, health, and personality of users. Laws pertaining to drugs are stated, terms are defined, and the credentials of the contributors are given. Includes a list for further reading, a section on "Where to Find Help in New York City," and an index.

956   Jacobs, Helen Hull. Better Physical Fitness for Girls; photos. by E. Peter Schroeder. Dodd, 1964. 63p. $3; lib. ed. $2.79 net. (I–U)

The exercises described in the text and demonstrated by a teen-age model are intended to "guide girls wisely in the development of bodily strength, suppleness, agility, and grace without over-exercise." Eating and sleeping habits are discussed in a concluding chapter.

957   MacDonald, Golden. Red Light,

Green Light; illus. by Leonard Weisgard. Doubleday, 1944. unp. $3.50. (P)

Rhythmic text and bold illustrations in appropriate colors introduce the young child to traffic signals and their meaning.

958 **Shapp, Martha,** and **Shapp, Charles.** Let's Find Out about Safety; pictures by László Roth. Watts, 1964. 42p. $2.65. (P)

An easy-to-read story about safety at home, at school, and on the streets. (R1–2)

959 **Wilson, Pat.** The Young Sportsman's Guide to Water Safety. Nelson, 1966. 96p. $2.75; lib. ed. $2.78 net. (I–U)

Safe practices for boating, swimming, water skiing, and scuba diving are described and illustrated with photographs. Includes a checklist on what to do and why to do it and a chapter on lifesaving.

Medicine

960 **Caidin, Martin,** and **Caidin, Grace.** Aviation and Space Medicine: Man Conquers the Vertical Frontier. Dutton, 1962. 215p. $4.25. (U)

Explains the effects on bodily functions of flights at altitudes of more than 10,000 feet and describes the equipment developed to combat lack of oxygen, cold, weightlessness, and other problems of space flight. Illustrated with photographs.

961 **Calder, Ritchie.** The Wonderful World of Medicine. Diags. by Isotype Institute. Art by A. Bailey (and others). Garden City, 1958. 67p. $2.95. (I)

Reviews man's efforts to learn about himself, to find ways to prevent and cure disease, and to prolong life. Many striking illustrations add interest and information.

962 **Coy, Harold.** Doctors and What They Do. Watts, 1956. 183p. $3.95. (U)

Introduces the medical profession: the many branches of medicine, clinics, hospitals, public health, and other aspects of the subject and explains the doctor's role in each. Includes a glossary, an outline of educational requirements, and a list of medical specialties. Good vocational material.

963 **Dietz, David.** All about Great Medical Discoveries; illus. by Ernest Kurt Barth. Random, 1960. 140p. $2.50. (I)

Great medical discoveries and the men who made them, from Vesalius to Dr. Salk, are discussed in readable text and illustrated with clear pictures.

964 **Dodge, Bertha S.** The Story of Nursing; illus. by Barbara Corrigan. rev. ed. Little, 1964. 244p. $4.50. (I–U)

Part I is a history of nursing centered around the lives of such pioneer nurses as Florence Nightingale, Dorothea Dix, and Clara Barton; Part II describes the striking changes which have since occurred in the profession and explores the many career opportunities which it offers. Useful in guidance and health as well as for general reading.

965 **Eberle, Irmengarde.** Modern Medical Discoveries. new rev. ed. Crowell, 1968. 206p. $4.50. (I)

Forceful style and simple language characterize this review of the medical research which developed the sulfa drugs, penicillin, vaccines, machine substitutes for body organs, and other lifesaving agents.

966 **Greene, Carla.** Doctors and Nurses —What Do They Do? Pictures by Leonard Kessler. Harper, 1963. 64p. $1.95; lib. ed. $2.15. (P)

Easy text and bright pictures introduce these professions to young children: the training, work, hospital routines, and health care. (R2–3)

967 **Hyde, Margaret O.** Medicine in Action: Today & Tomorrow; foreword by Charles Philamore Bailey; illus. by Clifford N. Geary. rev. ed. McGraw-Hill, 1964. 160p. $3.50; lib. ed. $3.06 net. (I–U)

A dramatic overview of medical research and the role which doctors, nurses, technicians, pharmacologists, and therapists play in battling disease. Lists career opportunities and sources of further information.

968 **Reinfeld, Fred.** Miracle Drugs and the New Age of Medicine. Sterling, 1962. 126p. $3.95; lib. ed. $3.99 net. (U)

Begins with a brief history of medicine and the establishment of the germ theory of disease and continues with a survey of the research which has produced antibiotics and is seeking to extend knowledge in this field. Excellent illustrations.

969 **Silverberg, Robert.** The Dawn of Medicine; illus. by Frank Aloise. Putnam, 1967. 192p. lib. ed. $3.49 net. (U)

Traces the evolution of medicine from earliest times, showing how the practice of magic gradually gave way to science.

970   **Sutherland, Louis.** Magic Bullets: The Story of Man's Valiant Struggle against Enemy Microbes; with illus. by Harper Johnson. Little, 1956. 148p. $3.50. (U)

Graphic illustrations and smoothly writ-ten text provide information about the germs which science combats in the cause of public and individual health and about the modern discoveries which are helping to win the fight. Includes a reading list, a pronunciation guide, and an index.

The Arts

Art

ASPECTS OF ART

971   **Ayer, Margaret.** Made in Thailand; illus. by Margaret Ayer and with photos. Knopf, 1964. 237p. $3.95; lib. ed. $3.59 net. (U)

The many arts and crafts of Thailand are described against a background of Thai history, religion, and culture. Useful in art and social studies.

972   **Bailey, Carolyn Sherwin.** Pioneer Art in America; with lithographs by Grace Paull. Viking, 1944. 221p. lib. ed. $4.13 net. (I)

A readable story of Early American arts and crafts and the people who produced them, illustrated with historically accurate lithographs.

973   **Borten, Helen.** Do You See What I See? Written and illus. by Helen Borten. Abelard-Schuman, 1959. unp. $2.95; lib. ed. $2.89 net. (P)

The author introduces line, shape, and color in terms a young child can understand and extends her text with multicolor woodcuts.

974   **Chase, Alice Elizabeth.** Looking at Art. Crowell, 1966. 119p. $4.50. (I–U)

In this introduction to art appreciation, the author discusses what the artist sees and what he attempts to convey in his work. More than 100 reproductions show art of many different periods and styles.

975   **Craven, Thomas.** The Rainbow Book of Art. World, 1956. 256p. $5.95. (U)

An animated history of world art and artists, illustrated with hundreds of reproductions, 32 in full color.

976   **Glubok, Shirley.** The Art of Africa; designed by Gerard Nook; special photos. by Alfred H. Tamarin. Harper, 1965. 48p. $4.50; lib. ed. $4.11 net. (I–U)

African arts and crafts as they reflect African civilization are presented in a beautifully designed book combining brief, interesting text with excellent color photographs against backgrounds of complementary or contrasting colors.

977   **Glubok, Shirley.** The Art of Ancient Egypt; designed by Gerard Nook. Atheneum, 1962. 48p. $3.95; lib. ed. $3.79 net. (I–U)

In style and format similar to *The Art of Africa*, above, the author introduces the art of ancient Egypt, describing and showing in color and black-and-white photographs objects of special interest to children: a mechanical toy, a hand mirror, a sphinx.

978   **Glubok, Shirley.** The Art of Ancient Greece; designed by Oscar Krauss. Atheneum, 1963. 48p. $3.95; lib. ed. $3.79 net. (I–U)

Thumbnail sketches of Greek gods and goddesses and superior photographs of Greek vases, statues, and other art objects reflecting everyday life are combined in a handsome book.

979   **Glubok, Shirley.** The Art of Ancient Mexico; designed by Gerard Nook; special photos. by Alfred H. Tamarin. Harper, 1968. 41p. $4.50; lib. ed. $4.11 net. (I–U)

Carefully selected and dramatically arranged art objects from the culture of ancient Mexico are shown in excellent photographs and described in brief but significant text.

980   Glubok, Shirley. The Art of Ancient Rome; designed by Oscar Krauss. Harper, 1965. 40p. $4.50; lib. ed. $4.11 net. (I–U)

Another in this author's series of art books, showing buildings, statuary, mosaics, and other art forms of ancient Rome and relating them to Roman life.

981   Glubok, Shirley. The Art of the Eskimo; designed by Oscar Krauss; special photos. by Alfred H. Tamarin. Harper, 1964. 48p. $4.50; lib. ed. $4.11 net. (P–I)

Bone carvings, masks, and other art objects of the Eskimos are effectively arranged against colored backgrounds and photographed. The concise text reveals many aspects of life among the Eskimos.

982   Glubok, Shirley. The Art of the Etruscans; designed by Gerard Nook; special photos. by Alfred H. Tamarin. Harper, 1967. 40p. $4.50; lib. ed. $4.11 net. (I–U)

An intriguing ancient civilization is presented through a brief but informative text and excellent photographs of artifacts found in the sealed tombs of the Etruscans. Gold jewelry, terra-cotta statues, and vases are shown as evidence of the highly developed culture of a little-known people.

983   Glubok, Shirley. The Art of the North American Indian; designed by Oscar Krauss; special photography by Alfred H. Tamarin. Harper, 1964. 48p. $4.50; lib. ed. $4.11 net. (P–I)

The author describes and shows in colored photographs the varied and beautiful arts of the Indian, explaining the part each object played in the life of the tribe.

984   Hughes, Langston. The First Book of Rhythms; pictures by Robin King. Watts, 1954. 63p. $2.65. (I–U)

This introduction to rhythm in everyday life as well as in art and music makes the reader aware of the cadences all around him.

985   MacAgy, Douglas, and **MacAgy, Elizabeth.** Going for a Walk with a Line: A Step into the World of Modern Art. Doubleday, 1959. unp. $3.95. (P–I)

From Henri Rousseau to Paul Klee, modern artists and their work are introduced through 43 contemporary masterpieces, shown in excellent reproductions and discussed in a text explaining new ways of seeing and creating art.

986   Price, Christine. Made in Ancient Greece; illus. with photos. and drawings. Dutton, 1967. 160p. $5.95; lib. ed. $5.89 net. (U)

Lively text and effective illustrations present Greek arts and crafts from the eighth to the second century B.C., with emphasis on their diversity and the qualities of Greek life which made them possible. Useful for reference, but principally an invitation to the enjoyment of Greek art.

987   Price, Christine. Made in the Middle Ages; illus. by Christine Price. Dutton, 1961. 118p. $3.75; lib. ed. $3.71 net. (U)

A well-illustrated, well-written survey of the varied objects made by medieval artists and craftsmen: paintings, carvings, books, jewelry, armor, tapestries, etc. Companion volume to *Made in the Renaissance,* below.

988   Price, Christine. Made in the Renaissance: Arts and Crafts of the Age of Exploration; written and illus. by Christine Price. Dutton, 1963. 120p. $3.75; lib. ed. $3.71 net. (U)

A narrative account of the exciting period between 1450 and 1650 as reflected in Renaissance arts and crafts. Companion volume to *Made in the Middle Ages,* above.

989   Ruskin, Ariane. The Pantheon Story of Art for Young People. Pantheon, 1964. 157p. $6.95; lib. ed. $5.69 net. (I–U)

The history of art from cave paintings to the present, with attention to the motives and ideas which inspired the art of each period, illustrated with 68 full-color reproductions and 90 in black and white.

990   Schwartz, Alvin. Museum: The Story of America's Treasure Houses. Dutton, 1967. 256p. $5.95; lib. ed. $5.89 net. (U)

Art museums and museums of history, science, and technology are included in a comprehensive discussion covering their history, collecting, organizing, financing, and educational programs. A final chapter is devoted to museum career training and opportunities.

991   Spencer, Cornelia. Made in Japan; illus. by Richard Powers and with photos. Knopf, 1963. 210p. lib. ed. $3.59 net. (U)

The author surveys Japanese arts and

products from prehistoric times to the present, devoting entire chapters to painting, ceramics, and porcelains. Includes an outline of Japanese history and 28 photographs.

992   Weisgard, Leonard. Treasures To See: A Museum Picture-Book. Harcourt, 1956. unp. $3.50. (P–I)

Explains the purpose and organization of a fine arts museum, showing in the author's full-color illustrations the objects most likely to interest a child. Useful when preparing children for a field trip.

PAINTING, DRAWING, AND DESIGN

993   Borten, Helen. A Picture Has a Special Look. Abelard-Schuman, 1961. unp. $2.95; lib. ed. $2.89 net. (P)

The various media (pencil, crayon, watercolor, collage, etc.) which can be used to create a picture are discussed in simple text and illustrated with the author's effective pictures. Useful to show young children the possibilities in different materials and to encourage art appreciation and diversification in art work.

994   Chase, Alice Elizabeth. Famous Paintings: An Introduction to Art; with 184 plates, including 54 in full color. Platt & Munk, 1962. 120p. $6.95. (I–U)

Selections cover a span of 5000 years and include both familiar and less-well-known works; text analyzes each full-color picture in relation to other pictures of the same type, period, or artist. Excellent for browsing or class use.

995   Downer, Marion. Discovering Design; illus. with photos. and drawings. Lothrop, 1947. 104p. $3.50; lib. ed. $3.35 net. (I–U)

Nine branches of design are discussed, showing how patterns in nature have inspired designs in textiles, furniture, ceramics, and other arts and crafts. Principles of design are stressed and illustrated in color, encouraging observation and the development of critical judgment.

996   Downer, Marion. The Story of Design. Lothrop, 1963. 216p. $4.95. (U)

In this companion volume to *Discovering Design*, above, the author shows in museum photographs a discriminating selection of prehistoric, ancient, and contemporary art objects and points out in illuminating text

the qualities which make each an example of excellent design.

997   Hawkinson, John. Collect, Print, and Paint from Nature. Albert Whitman, 1963. 38p. $2.95. (P–I)

Clear instructions for art projects based on natural designs: leaves, trees, flowers. Encourages observation and the use of varied techniques.

998   Holme, Bryan. Drawings To Live With. Viking, 1966. 155p. $4.50; lib. ed. $4.13 net. (I–U)

A handsome book introducing great artists and discussing the styles and techniques of drawing for which they are noted. Lively text illustrated with 140 drawings, well reproduced in black and white.

999   Holme, Bryan, ed. Pictures To Live With. Viking, 1959. 152p. $4.95; lib. ed. $4.53 net. (I–U)

This discriminatingly selected and interestingly grouped collection of 150 well-reproduced paintings and drawings (eight in color), accompanied by illuminating commentary, is excellent for art appreciation. Many periods are represented in such categories as "Fur and Feather," "Sports and Athletes," "The Oldest and the Newest."

1000   Seidelman, James E., and **Mintonye, Grace.** Creating with Paint; illus. by Peter Landa. Crowell-Collier, 1967. 58p. $3.95. (I–U)

Clear instructions for the beginning painter on papers, brushes, kinds of paint, and step-by-step procedures. The authors introduce various techniques of working with paint, but leave the artist free to create his own effects. Illustrated with photographs and two-color pictures.

1001   Spilka, Arnold. Paint All Kinds of Pictures. Walck, 1963. unp. $4.25. (P)

A picture book designed to encourage the young child to express his own ideas in painting. The author's imaginative colored illustrations are perfect examples of variety and self-expression in art.

1002   Ungerer, Tomi. Snail, Where Are You? Harper, 1962. unp. $2.50; lib. ed. $2.57 net. (P)

A first lesson in observation, in which the child is stimulated to find the snail design in each of the author's striking colored illustrations. No text.

1003 Weiss, Harvey. Paint, Brush, and Palette. W. R. Scott, 1966. 64p. $4.50. (I–U)

An art teacher discusses the fundamentals of painting, describes the materials needed, gives instructions for various techniques, and suggests practice exercises, illustrating his discussion with full-color reproductions of paintings and with drawings.

1004 Weiss, Harvey. Pencil, Pen, and Brush: Drawing for Beginners. W. R. Scott, 1961. 63p. $3.95. (I–U)

Creative expression in drawing is stressed in this introduction to basic techniques and media. The author suggests various ways of achieving desired effects and shows different interpretations of the same idea in reproductions of drawings by well-known artists.

CRAFTS

1005 Araki, Chiyo. Origami in the Classroom. Tuttle, 1965. 40p. $3.25. (I–U)

Japanese paper folding is adapted to American celebrations with 11 origami patterns of graduated difficulty for Columbus Day, Halloween, Christmas, and parties, with clear instructions, lists of materials, and time required.

1006 Brock, Virginia. Piñatas; illus. by Anne Marie Jauss. Abingdon, 1966. 112p. $3. (I–U)

A handicraft book useful for many occasions, giving the history of these Mexican decorations, stories about them, and explicit instructions and diagrams for making piñatas of many kinds. Includes a glossary and a pronouncing guide.

1007 Carlson, Bernice Wells. Make It Yourself! Handicraft for Boys and Girls; illus. by Aline Hansens. Abingdon, 1950. 160p. $2.50. (I)

Each chapter of this book is devoted to things made from a particular material: paper, boxes, scraps, and other easily obtained supplies. Projects include gifts, toys, party favors, and holiday decorations; instructions are easy to follow and clearly illustrated.

1008 Cutler, Katherine N. Junior Flower Arranging; photos. by Roche; drawings by Joan Lucas. Barrows, 1954. 179p. $3.50. (I–U)

Basic principles of selecting, keeping, and arranging flowers for the home, parties, and flower shows.

1009 Hautzig, Esther. Let's Make Presents: 100 Gifts for Less Than $1.00; illus. by Ava Morgan. Crowell, 1962. 191p. $4.50. (I)

Easy-to-follow instructions and helpful illustrations for making gifts—belts, aprons, ornaments, cookies, candy, and many others—from inexpensive materials.

1010 Hirsch, S. Carl. Printing from a Stone: The Story of Lithography. Viking, 1967. 111p. $3.75; lib. ed. $3.56 net. (U)

Lithography as a medium for works of art and as a method of commercial printing is discussed in an animated account of the history, techniques, and uses of the process. Illustrated with photographs.

1011 Hunt, Kari, and **Carlson, Bernice Wells.** Masks and Mask Makers. Abingdon, 1961. 67p. $3. (I–U)

Masks, their significance and uses in many parts of the world at many times, are discussed in an unusual book which includes also instructions for making a mask. Illustrated with photographs of masks in museums and in Kari Hunt's collection. Useful in ethnology, drama, and art.

1012 Johnson, Lillian. Papier-mâché. McKay, 1958. 88p. $4.95. (P–I–U)

A guide to creating papier-mâché toys, dolls, puppets, masks, and many other objects, some simple enough for primary children, others more complicated.

1013 Maginley, C. J. Historic Models of Early America, and How To Make Them; illus. with numerous diags. by James MacDonald. Harcourt, 1947. 156p. $2.75. (I–U)

Exact specifications, working diagrams, and clear instructions for making Early American models grouped in four categories: transportation, farms, homes, and villages. Especially useful for history projects.

1014 Massoglia, Elinor Tripato. Fun-Time Paper Folding; pictures by George Rhoads. Childrens Pr., 1959. 31p. $2.50. (P)

Primary children can follow the simple

directions and diagrams for 13 objects made of paper.

1015 Seidelman, James E., and Mintonye, Grace. Creating Mosaics; illus. by Harriet Sherman. Crowell-Collier, 1967. 56p. $3.95. (I)

Explicit instructions and two-color line drawings encourage the beginner to create mosaics from many types of easily obtained materials. Includes suggestions for collecting, storing, and handling materials and for working safely. Emphasis is on creative expression rather than on copying.

1016 Seidelman, James E., and Mintonye, Grace. Creating with Clay; illus. by Robert William Hinds. Crowell-Collier, 1967. 56p. $3.95. (I)

A guide to clay modeling covering tools, materials, basic instructions, a glossary of claying terms, and a special section on firing, glazing, and painting the finished product. Illustrated with photographs, diagrams, and colored line drawings.

1017 Weiss, Harvey. Ceramics: From Clay to Kiln. W. R. Scott, 1963. 63p. $3.95. (I–U)

After describing the basic materials, tools, and methods of working with clay, the author gives instructions for making specific objects, progressing from the very simple to the more difficult. Photographs of museum pieces and line drawings augment the instructions. Includes a glossary.

1018 Weiss, Harvey. Clay, Wood, and Wire: A How-To-Do-It Book of Sculpture. W. R. Scott, 1956. 48p. $3.95. (I–U)

An introductory book on sculpture with clear directions for handling materials and techniques for creating a variety of models. Helpful illustrations.

1019 Weiss, Harvey. Paper, Ink, and Roller: Print-making for Beginners. W. R. Scott, 1958. 64p. $3.95. (I–U)

Instructions and illustrations for making prints from linoleum blocks, potatoes, cardboard, and other inexpensive materials. More complicated techniques, such as woodcuts, silk screen, and lithography, are discussed, without instructions, in a final section.

1020 Zarchy, Harry. Mobiles; illus. by Harry Zarchy. World, 1966. 47p. $1.95; lib. ed. $2.53 net. (I–U)

Simple directions for making mobiles out of inexpensive materials. Illustrated with drawings and color photographs.

Music

1021 Balet, Jan. What Makes an Orchestra; story and pictures by Jan Balet. Walck, 1951. 41p. $4. (I)

Each instrument of the orchestra is pictured on a separate page, described, and shown as it is played, one by one joining the group until the entire orchestra is assembled. A witty and colorful introduction to the orchestra, designed to arouse interest.

1022 Bauer, Marion, and Peyser, Ethel. How Music Grew; with an introd. by William J. Henderson; with 64 illus. rev. ed. Putnam, 1939. 647p. $6. (U)

A comprehensive and smoothly written history of music, supplemented by biographical sketches of seven famous composers and lists of composers arranged by forms of composition.

1023 Bertail, Inez, ed. and arr. Complete Nursery Song Book; illus. by Walt Kelly. Lothrop, 1947. 150p. $4.50; lib. ed. $4.14 net. (P)

Simple piano arrangements and words for more than 150 nursery songs, some familiar, others less well known. Versions most popular with American children are used, and directions are given for playing singing games.

1024 Boni, Margaret Bradford, ed. The Fireside Book of Favorite American Songs; sel. and arr. by Margaret Bradford Boni; arr. for the piano by Norman Lloyd; illus. by Aurelius Battaglia; introd. by Anne Brooks; with a foreword by Carl Van Doren. Simon & Schuster, 1952. 359p. $6. (P–I–U)

Includes a wide range of ballads, sentimental songs, gospel hymns, and ragtime songs.

1025 Browne, C. A. The Story of Our National Ballads; rev. by Willard A. Heaps. Crowell, 1960. 314p. $4.50. (I–U)

Text of each song is followed by the circumstances of its composition and biographical notes about its author. Significant for history as well as for music classes.

1026 **Bulla, Clyde Robert.** Stories of Favorite Operas; illus. by Robert Galster. Crowell, 1959. 276p. $4.95. (I)

Plots of 23 operas are retold in direct, uncomplicated style and accompanied by notes on composers and first performances.

1027 **Carmer, Carl,** comp. America Sings: Stories and Songs of Our Country's Growing; collected and told by Carl Carmer. Knopf, 1942. 243p. lib. ed. $5.99 net. (I–U)

Music and legends of America's work heroes—cowboys, lumberjacks, cotton pickers, railroad men, and others—in an anthology useful in history, music, and literature.

1028 **Dietz, Betty Warner,** and **Olatunji, Michael Babatunde.** Musical Instruments of Africa: Their Nature, Use, and Place in a Deeply Musical People; illus. by Richard M. Powers. Day, 1965. 115p. $5.95. (U)

Designed to interest young people in African culture through music, this book describes and illustrates indigenous African musical instruments and tells how they are used in native life. Important in the study of the African people and of music and crafts. Includes a list of records, a long-playing record, a glossary, and a reading list.

1029 **Grimm, William,** and **Grimm, Jacob.** Hansel and Gretel: A Story of the Forest; music by Engelbert Humperdinck and illus. by Warren Chappell. Knopf, 1944. unp. lib. ed. $3.39 net. (I)

Easy piano versions of four familiar airs from the opera accompany the story. Illustrated with brooding forest scenes.

1030 **Hughes, Langston.** The First Book of Jazz; pictures by Cliff Roberts; music sel. by David Martin. Watts, 1955. 65p. $2.65. (I–U)

Traces the history of jazz from African drums, blues, and jubilee songs to modern forms, centering the account around the life of Louis Armstrong, the most famous exponent of jazz. Lists outstanding recordings.

1031 **Huntington, Harriet E.** Tune Up: The Instruments of the Orchestra and Their Players; illus. with photos. by the author; foreword by Ernest La Prade. Doubleday, 1942. 76p. $3.25. (I–U)

Introduces the instruments of the orchestra through brief descriptions and photographs.

1032 **Kettelkamp, Larry.** Drums, Rattles, and Bells; written and illus. by Larry Kettelkamp. Morrow, 1960. 47p. $2.95; lib. ed. $2.94 net. (I–U)

The history and design of percussion instruments are presented in simple text and informative illustrations. Includes directions for making rattles, drums, and a water-glass carillon.

1033 **Kettelkamp, Larry.** Flutes, Whistles, and Reeds; written and illus. by Larry Kettelkamp. Morrow, 1962. 48p. lib. ed. $2.94 net. (I–U)

In a companion volume to *Drums, Rattles, and Bells,* above, the author discusses wind instruments—their history, construction, and place in the orchestra—and gives directions for making simple pipes and whistles.

1034 **Kettelkamp, Larry.** Horns; written and illus. by Larry Kettelkamp. Morrow, 1964. 48p. $2.95; lib. ed. $2.94 net. (I–U)

Another in this author's series describes the development of the modern horn family from tusks, shells, and animal horns and suggests experiments with horns.

1035 **Kettelkamp, Larry.** Singing Strings; written and illus. by Larry Kettelkamp. Morrow, 1958. 48p. lib. ed. $2.94 net. (I–U)

Four groups of stringed instruments are briefly discussed and pictured: harps and the piano, guitar, and violin families. Includes instructions for making simplified stringed instruments and a glossary of musical terms.

1036 **Landeck, Beatrice,** comp. Songs To Grow On: A Collection of American Folk Songs for Children . . . E. B. Marks, distributed by Morrow, 1950. 125p. $4.50. (P–I)

Background notes, text, piano settings, and rhythm arrangements for 60 American folk songs, grouped by grade levels and including suggested activities.

1037 **Lomax, John A.,** and **Lomax, Alan.** Cowboy Songs, and Other Frontier Ballads. rev. and enl. Macmillan, 1938. 431p. $8.95. (I–U)

Music, words, and background notes for songs of the trail, the round-up, the campfire, and other aspects of frontier life. A comprehensive collection by noted folklorists.

1038 Lomax, John A., and **Lomax, Alan.**
Folk Song U.S.A.; collected, adapted, and
arr. by John Lomax and Alan Lomax; Alan
Lomax, ed.; Charles Seeger and Ruth Crawford Seeger, music eds. Duell, 1948. 407p.
$10. (I–U)

A spirited introduction precedes each
group of songs: Spirituals, Railroad Songs,
Farmers' Tunes, Lumberjack Ballads, Sailors' Chanteys, Love Songs, Work Songs,
and Cowboy Ditties. Includes piano and
guitar music, a selected list of records, and
a reading list.

1039 Mandell, Muriel, and **Wood, Robert
E.** Make Your Own Musical Instruments;
illus. by Margaret Krivak. Sterling, 1957.
126p. $2.95; lib. ed. $3.39 net. (I–U)

Clear directions and illustrations for
making a variety of musical instruments
from things around the house and suggestions for forming a rhythm and a calypso
band. Ingenious projects for music or hand-
icrafts.

1040 One Wide River To Cross (Folk
Song). One Wide River To Cross; adapted
by Barbara Emberley; illus. by Ed Emberley. Prentice-Hall, 1966. unp. $3.95. (P)

The old folk song about Noah's Ark, illustrated with imaginative woodcuts against
boldly colored backgrounds, tells of the animals entering the Ark "two by two."

1041 Posell, Elsa Z. This Is an Orchestra;
illus. with over 30 photos. Houghton, 1950.
94p. lib. ed. $2.90 net. (I–U)

In addition to describing and showing
the instruments of the orchestra in excellent photographs, this book contains important supplementary information on choosing and buying an instrument, finding a
teacher, establishing good practice habits,
and building a home record collection, as
well as a chapter on famous instrument
makers and a seating chart of the orchestra.

1042 Prokofieff, Serge. Peter and the Wolf.
Watts, 1962. unp. lib. ed. $3.39 net. (P)

Frans Haacken's bold, full-page illustrations dramatically interpret the Russian
fairy tale about the boy who outwitted the
wolf. Includes the musical themes repre-
senting the characters.

1043 Ritchie, Jean, comp. From Fair to
Fair: Folk Songs of the British Isles;
photos. by George Pickow; piano arrange-

ments by Edward Tripp. Walck, 1966. 93p.
$5.95. (I)

Sixteen folk songs of Ireland, Scotland,
and England, given an imaginary setting
as a minstrel wanders from fair to fair.
Words, music, and guitar notations are
given for each; photographs show appropriate scenes and activities.

1044 Rublowsky, John. Music in America.
Crowell-Collier, 1967. 185p. $3.50. (U)

Surveys American music: its history,
development, and the influences which
shaped it. Chapters on Indian music, the
madrigals of Appalachia, Negro songs, jazz,
and American music today. Illustrated with
photographs and old prints.

1045 Schackburg, Richard. Yankee Doodle; woodcuts by Ed Emberley; notes by
Barbara Emberley. Prentice-Hall, 1965.
unp. $3.75. (P–I)

A vigorous interpretation in red, white,
and blue woodcuts of the stirring Revolutionary song, with informative notes on the
historical background. Includes both words
and music.

1046 Seeger, Ruth Crawford. American
Folk Songs for Children in Home, School,
and Nursery School: A Book for Children,
Parents, and Teachers; illus. by Barbara
Cooney. Doubleday, 1948. 190p. $4.95.
(P–I–U)

Beginning with a discussion of the value
of folk songs and how to use them with
children, the author provides words, simple
piano accompaniments, and suggested activities for 90 songs of all kinds from all
parts of the country. Indexed by titles,
first lines, and classes of songs. Recommended for music and physical education
classes and for recreational groups.

1047 Seligman, Jean Hortense, and **Dan-
ziger, Juliet.** The Meaning of Music: The
Young Listener's Guide; illus. by Donald
Leake. World, 1966. 128p. $4.50; lib. ed.
$4.28 net. (U)

An interestingly written guide to the understanding and appreciation of music, covering its forms, language, patterns, and
composers.

1048 Shippen, Katherine B., and **Seidlova,
Anca.** The Heritage of Music; illus. by Otto
van Eersel. Viking, 1963. 311p. $6; lib. ed.
$5.63 net. (U)

An anecdotal history of music centered

around the lives of great composers and covering all periods and many forms and fashions.

1049 Sloane, Eric. The Sound of Bells. Doubleday, 1966. 58p. $2.75. (I–U)

Written to encourage bell ringing on Independence Day, this book describes the many kinds of bells used in early America, including the Liberty Bell; tells how they were used; and urges the revival of the custom of ringing bells on the Fourth of July.

1050 Updike, John. The Ring; music by Richard Wagner; adapted and illus. by John Updike and Warren Chappell. Knopf, 1964. unp. $3.50; lib. ed. $3.39 net. (I–U)

This retelling of *Siegfried*, the third of the four operas in Wagner's Ring cycle, is accompanied by musical themes and appropriate illustrations. An aid in understanding the music and arousing interest in reading the Siegfried legend.

1051 Wessells, Katharine Tyler. The Golden Song Book; sel. and arr. by Katharine Tyler Wessells; illus. by Gertrude Elliott. Golden Pr., 1945. 69p. $1.95. (P–I)

Words and music for 56 favorite songs for children, with suggestions for singing games.

1052 Wheeler, Opal. Sing Mother Goose; music by Opal Wheeler; illus. by Marjorie Torrey. Dutton, 1945. 102p. $5.95. (P)

Fifty-two Mother Goose rhymes set to rollicking tunes and illustrated with gaily colored pictures.

1053 Wilder, Alec. Lullabies and Night Songs; music by Alec Wilder; pictures by Maurice Sendak. Harper, 1965. 77p. $6.95; lib. ed. $5.79 net. (P)

Mood songs for quiet time are presented with simple, pleasing melodies and endearing illustrations. The 56 songs range from nursery rhymes to the poems of Blake, Kipling, and De La Mare.

1054 Winn, Marie, ed. The Fireside Book of Children's Songs; collected and ed. by Marie Winn; musical arrangements by Alan Miller; illus. by John Alcorn. Simon & Schuster, 1966. 192p. $6.95. (P–I)

Simple piano accompaniments and guitar chords for more than 100 songs grouped under five headings: Good Morning and Good Night, Birds and Beasts, Nursery Songs, Silly Songs, and Singing Games and Rounds. Brightly illustrated and indexed by title and first line.

Theater Arts

1055 Adair, Margaret Weeks. Do-It-in-a-Day Puppets for Beginners: How To Make Your Puppets, Create Your Script, and Perform—All in One Day. Day, 1964. 89p. $3.98; lib. ed. $3.95 net. (P–I)

Everything necessary for instant production of three puppet plays: scripts, directions for making easy puppets and constructing a stage, and production notes. The plays are: *Three Billy Goats Gruff, King Midas and the Golden Touch,* and *The Three Little Pigs.*

1056 American Heritage. Great Days of the Circus; by the eds. of American Heritage, The Magazine of History; narrative by Freeman Hubbard, in consultation with Leonard V. Farley. 2d ed. American Heritage, 1962. American Heritage Junior Library, distributed by Harper. 153p. $4.95; lib. ed. $4.79 net. (I–U)

A profusely illustrated history of the circus in the United States, enlivened by a biographical sketch of Phineas T. Barnum and by numerous anecdotes of circus life and a description of a typical day at the circus.

1057 Berk, Barbara. The First Book of Stage Costume and Make-up; pictures by Jeanne Bendick. Watts, 1954. 45p. $2.65. (I–U)

Practical help for amateur actors.

1058 Berk, Barbara, and **Bendick, Jeanne.** How To Have a Show; pictures by Jeanne Bendick. Watts, 1957. 63p. $2.95. (P–I)

Simple text, charts, and diagrams provide suggestions for impromptu entertainment by amateurs. Emphasis is on resourcefulness and ingenuity.

1059 Carlson, Bernice Wells. Act It Out; illus. by Laszlo Matulay. Abingdon, 1956. 160p. $2.50. (I)

An introductory book on dramatics for children, covering the fundamentals of acting and many suggestions for puppet plays, acting games, dramatic stunts, and other skits for amateurs.

1060 Chappell, Warren. The Nutcracker; adapted and illus. by Warren Chappell. Knopf, 1958. unp. $2.95; lib. ed. $3.39 net. (I)

Main themes from the Tchaikovsky ballet are included in this airily illustrated version of the Nutcracker and the Mouse King.

1061 Chute, Marchette. An Introduction to Shakespeare. Dutton, 1951. 123p. $3.25. (U)

Describes the theaters of Shakespeare's London and tells how his plays were costumed, produced, and acted. Notes on each play give source, theme, and plot.

1062 De Mille, Agnes. The Book of the Dance; illus. by N. M. Bodecker. Golden Pr., 1963. 252p. $14.95. (U)

A large, lavishly illustrated book tracing the history of the dance from primitive rituals to modern precision dancing. Chapters on the ballet include stories of famous dancers and interviews with great choreographers.

1063 Draper, Nancy, and **Atkinson, Margaret F.** Ballet for Beginners. Knopf, 1951. 115p. $3.95; lib. ed. $3.79 net. (I)

Lucid text, photographs, diagrams, and music introduce ballet to children.

1064 Hodges, C. Walter. Shakespeare's Theatre; written and illus. by C. Walter Hodges. Coward-McCann, 1964. 103p. $4.95. (U)

Traces the development of the Elizabethan theater from the early medieval religious dramas to Shakespeare's day. A beautifully illustrated book explaining and depicting exactly how stage effects were achieved and culminating in a description of a performance of *Julius Caesar* at the Globe Theatre.

1065 Jennings, Gary. The Movie Book; illus. with photos. Dial, 1963. 212p. $3.95. (U)

A history of the moving-picture industry: mechanical devices; types of pictures; famous actors, directors, and producers; and subsidiary personnel. Illustrated with photographs and portraits.

1066 Pels, Gertrude. Easy Puppets: Making and Using Hand Puppets; illus. by Albert Pels. Crowell, 1951. 104p. $3.95; lib. ed. $3.76 net. (P–I)

A simple, practical guide to making puppets out of such materials as apples, bottle caps, clothespins, and other odds and ends. Clear directions and diagrams for designing and making the puppets, constructing the stage, and giving the plays.

1067 Streatfeild, Noel. The First Book of the Ballet; pictures by Moses Soyer. Watts, 1953. 93p. $2.65. (I)

Outlines the training of a ballet dancer, emphasizing the hard work necessary for success, and gives a brief history of the ballet and sketches of some of its stars. Includes a pronouncing guide to ballet terms.

1068 Tensen, Ruth M. Come To See the Clowns; illus. by Dianne Dengel. Reilly & Lee, 1963. 35p. $2.95. (P)

Funny pictures with easy-to-read captions show clowns going through their antics. (R1–2)

Sports and Recreation

Baseball

1069 Antonacci, Robert J., and **Barr, Jene.** Baseball for Young Champions; foreword by Yogi Berra; illus. by Rus Anderson. McGraw-Hill, 1956. 156p. $3.95; lib. ed. $3.31 net. (I–U)

A practical guide to learning and practicing the game, with tips on training, pitching, hitting, catching, etc.

1070 Cooke, David C. Better Baseball for Boys. Dodd, 1959. 64p. $3; lib. ed. $2.79 net. (I–U)

Basic plays, rules of the game, and techniques are explained in detail and pictured in action photographs. Includes advice on care of equipment and a glossary.

1071 DiClementi, Frank F., ed. Baseball. Advisory eds.: Theodore A. Sanford, Otto Kuehn, (and) Harold Schmickley. Creative Educ. Soc., 1962. 256p. $5.95. (I–U)

Traces the origin and development of baseball and describes playing techniques in detail. Includes a code of ethics, a glossary, and a reading list. Profusely illustrated with diagrams and photographs.

1072 Jackson, C. Paul. How To Play Better Baseball; illus. by Leonard Kessler. Crowell, 1963. 151p. $3.50. (I)

A guide to the game, useful to observers as well as to players. Informal style and lively illustrations.

1073 Robinson, Ray. Greatest World Series Thrillers; illus. with photos. Random, 1965. 181p. $1.95; lib. ed. $2.48 net. (I–U)

Graphic descriptions of plays which won or lost memorable games. Good bait for the reluctant older reader.

Basketball

1074 Antonacci, Robert J., and **Barr, Jene.** Basketball for Young Champions; illus. by Richard Leach. McGraw-Hill, 1960. 160p. $3.95; lib. ed. $3.31 net. (I–U)

Rules, drills, and exercises for aspiring basketball players.

1075 Hutton, Joe, and **Hoffman, Vern B.** Basketball. Advisory eds.: Everett S. Dean, Vern Mikkelsen, (and) Joe Lapchick. Creative Educ. Soc., 1962. 255p. $5.95. (I–U)

A brief history of the sport is followed by a clear explanation of rules and playing techniques, illustrated with drawings, diagrams, and photographs. Includes a code of ethics, a glossary, and a reading list.

Football

1076 Antonacci, Robert J., and **Barr, Jene.** Football for Young Champions; illus. by

Rus Anderson. McGraw-Hill, 1958. 159p. $3.25; lib. ed. $3.01 net. (I–U)

A practical handbook for players and spectators.

1077 Cooke, David C. Better Football for Boys. Dodd, 1958. 64p. $3; lib. ed. $2.79 net. (I–U)

Concise text and action photographs explain proper playing techniques for sandlot football and organized teams, including 20 different plays.

1078 Otto, J. R. "Bob." Football. Advisory eds.: William C. Pace, U. G. Montgomery, M. F. Sprunger. Creative Educ. Soc., 1962. 256p. $5.95. (I–U)

History and fundamentals of football are presented in informative text, illustrated with photographs, diagrams, and drawings. Emphasizes sportsmanship and includes a glossary and a bibliography.

Other Sports

1079 Barr, George. Young Scientist and Sports: Featuring Baseball, Football, and Basketball; illus. by Mildred Waltrip. McGraw-Hill, 1962. 159p. $3.50; lib. ed. $3.06 net. (I–U)

Applies such scientific principles as action and reaction, gravity, and inertia to sports in general and the three major sports in particular. Useful in science classes as well as in sports.

1080 Boy Scouts of America. Field Book for Boy Scouts, Explorers, Scouters, Educators, (and) Outdoorsmen. 1967. Distributed by McGraw-Hill. 565p. $4.95; lib. ed. $4.24 net. (I–U)

A readable guide to outdoor life, including chapters on equipment, maps and compasses, first aid, survival, and conservation. Illustrated with photographs and line drawings.

1081 Brown, Conrad. Skiing for Beginners: A Complete and Simple Method for Children and Their Parents; photos. by Nancy Graham. Scribner, 1951. 63p. $3.50. (I)

Fundamentals of skiing, emphasizing the Arlberg technique, presented in text and photographs, with each maneuver carefully demonstrated.

1082 Brownell, Clifford L., and **Moore, Roy B.,** eds. Recreational Sports. Creative Educ. Soc., 1962. 256p. $5.95. (I–U)

Covers history, equipment, playing fields, rules, and basic playing techniques for ten recreational sports. Readable text and many illustrations.

1083 Colby, C. B. First Camping Trip; written and illus. by C. B. Colby . . . Coward-McCann, 1955. 48p. lib. ed. $2.52 net. (I)

Offers practical advice on choosing a site, using equipment, organizing recreation, and preventing and caring for emergencies.

1084 Cooke, David C. Better Bowling for Boys. Dodd, 1963. 64p. $3; lib. ed. $2.79 net. (I–U)

Rules and techniques of the game are presented in clear instructions and a sequence of diagrams and photographs.

1085 Dypwick, Otis J. Golf, by Otis J. Dypwick. Swimming by Einar A. Olsen. Tennis by Helen Hull Jacobs. Advisory eds.: Charles (Chick) Evans, Jr., Charles E. Forsythe, (and) Paul D. Waldorf. Creative Educ. Soc., 1962. 256p. $5.95. (I–U)

Basic instruction in text and pictures for each of the three sports, and supplementary information about tournaments and scholarship opportunities. Includes glossaries and bibliographies.

1086 Frey, Shaney. The Complete Beginner's Guide to Skin Diving; foreword by C. B. Momsen. Doubleday, 1965. 116p. $3.50. (I–U)

An experienced skin and scuba diver describes the equipment and techniques of skin diving and suggests diving activities. Excellent photographs, a list of safety rules, and a reading list are valuable features.

1087 Harrison, C. William. The First Book of Hiking; illus. by E. Frank Habbas. Watts, 1965. 59p. $2.65. (I–U)

Practical suggestions about what to wear, how to assemble and pack equipment and supplies, how to avoid accidents, and what to do in emergencies. Names and describes famous hiking trails in the United States and Canada and suggests special hikes to historical spots, bird walks, etc.

1088 Keith, Harold. Sports and Games. new rev. ed. Crowell, 1960. 375p. $5.50. (I–U)

Alphabetically arranged descriptions of 15 games, giving history and rules for playing each.

1089 Kramp, Harry, and **Sullivan, George.** Swimming for Boys and Girls. Follett, 1966. 96p. $1; lib. ed. $1.98 net. (I–U)

Basic instructions for safe swimming, floating, diving, and competition swimming.

1090 Mason, Bernard S. The Junior Book of Camping and Woodcraft; drawings by Frederick H. Kock. Ronald, 1943. 120p. $4.50. (I)

Practical advice for safe and enjoyable outdoor activities.

1091 Myers, Earl "Bud," and **Hacker, Rich.** Track and Field. Advisory eds.: W. J. McConnell, Cliff Harper, (and) James J. Pursell. Creative Educ. Soc. 1962. 256p. $5.95. (I–U)

Describes and gives a brief history of 13 sports and discusses some of the outstanding athletes in these fields. Includes a glossary and a bibliography.

1092 Pearsall, William. Junior Skipper. Norton, 1965. 99p. $3.50; lib. ed. $3.28 net. (I–U)

A guide to safety and skills in handling a boat, with a glossary of boating terms and a queston-and-answer section on correct procedures.

1093 Scott, Barbara Ann, and **Kirby, Michael.** Skating for Beginners. Knopf, 1953. 106p. lib. ed. $3.99 net. (I–U)

Step-by-step directions for ice skating, supported by photographs and diagrams.

1094 Slaughter, Jean. Horsemanship for Beginners: Riding, Jumping, and Schooling; photos. by Michael J. Phillips. Knopf, 1952. 118p. $3.95; lib. ed. $3.99 net. (I–U)

Everything the novice needs to know about handling a horse, riding, and participating in horse shows.

1095 Walsh, John. The First Book of the Olympic Games; illus. with photos. Watts, 1963. 55p. $2.65. (I)

The story of the Olympic games from their beginning to the present, and information about some of the great competitors and their records.

1096 Zarchy, Harry. Let's Go Boating; written and illus. by Harry Zarchy. Knopf, 1952. 154p. $3.25; lib. ed. $3.09 net. (I)

Tells the beginner about rowboats, sailboats, and canoes: how to handle them and how to care for them.

Games and Amusements

1097 Bley, Edgar S. The Best Singing Games for Children of All Ages; drawings by Patt Willen; piano arrangements by Margaret Chase. Sterling, 1957. 96p. $3.95; lib. ed. $3.99 net. (P–I–U)

More than 50 musical games, jump-rope jingles, and play party games, with words, musical scores, and directions for action. Arranged by age levels and illustrated with helpful drawings.

1098 Cerf, Bennett. Bennett Cerf's Book of Riddles; illus. by Roy McKie. Beginner Books, 1960. 62p. $1.95; lib. ed. $2.27 net. (P–I–U)

Easy-to-read riddles selected to please the young child's special sense of humor. (R1–2)

1099 Chrystie, Frances N. The First Book of Jokes and Funny Things; pictures by Ida Scheib. Watts, 1951. unp. $2.65. (P–I)

Jokes, riddles, games, tongue twisters, and funny things to make and do, with illustrations as laughable as the contents.

1100 De Regniers, Beatrice Schenk. The Abraham Lincoln Joke Book; illus. by William Lahey Cummings. Random, 1965. 92p. $2.95; lib. ed. $2.99 net. (I–U)

Witty anecdotes told by and about Lincoln reveal his human side and his sense of humor. Includes a chronology of Lincoln's life.

1101 Downer, Marion. Kites: How To Make and Fly Them. Lothrop, 1959. 64p. $3.50; lib. ed. $3.35 net. (I)

Patterns, diagrams, and explicit instructions for making several kinds of kites, along with lists of tools and materials and directions for kite contests and tournaments.

1102 Freeman, Lois M. Betty Crocker's Parties for Children; illus. by Judy and Barry Martin. Golden Pr., 1964. 163p. $1.95. (P–I–U)

After giving advice on planning and organizing parties, the author discusses decorations, invitations, themes, refreshments, and party favors. Colorful illustrations and directions for playing more than 150 games, including games for handicapped children.

1103 Grayson, Marion. Let's Do Fingerplays; illus. by Nancy Weyl. Luce, 1962. 109p. $5.25; lib. ed. $4.24 net. (P)

Approximately 200 rhymes and songs, with directions for accompanying finger plays, are organized under such headings as Animal Antics, Counting and Counting Out, and Holidays and Special Occasions. Attractively illustrated and indexed by title and first line.

1104 Helfman, Harry. Tricks with Your Fingers; illus. by Robert Bartram. Morrow, 1967. 46p. $2.95; lib. ed. $2.94 net. (I)

An activity book containing a collection of sleight-of-hand tricks and instructions for making finger puppets.

1105 Kettelkamp, Larry. Magic Made Easy; written and illus. by Larry Kettelkamp. Morrow, 1954. 63p. lib. ed. $2.94 net. (P–I)

Directions for tricks, ranging in difficulty from very simple to more complicated, are clearly written and illustrated; materials are simple and easily obtained.

1106 Kohl, Marguerite, (and) Young, Frederica. Jokes for Children; illus. by Bob Patterson. Hill & Wang, 1963. 116p. $3. (I)

More than 650 jokes, puns, and riddles, including many selected by children themselves.

1107 Leeming, Joseph. Fun with Magic: How To Make Magic Equipment; How To Perform Many Tricks, Including Some of the Best Tricks of Professional Magicians and How To Give Successful Magic Shows; drawings by Jessie Robinson. Lippincott, 1943. 86p. $4.75. (I–U)

More comprehensive than the Kettelkamp book, above. Includes a list of dealers in magicians' supplies.

1108 Leeming, Joseph. Fun with Puzzles . . . Drawings by Jessie Robinson. Lippincott, 1946. 128p. $3.95. (I–U)

Brain teasers, anagrams, and puzzles with coins, matches, and numbers—all with answers in the back of the book.

1109 Millen, Nina, ed. Children's Games from Many Lands; illus. by Allan Eitzen.

new and rev. ed. Friendship Pr., 1951. 192p. $3.95. (I)

Instructions for playing 260 games from 55 countries and words and music for many national songs.

1110 Morrison, Lillian, comp. Black Within and Red Without: A Book of Riddles; illus. by Jo Spier. Crowell, 1953. 120p. $2.95; lib. ed. $2.92 net. (I)

An unusually varied collection of 200 riddles from many countries, some drawn from folklore, some from primitive chants and Elizabethan lyrics.

1111 Withers, Carl, and **Benet, Sula.** The American Riddle Book; illus. by Marc Simont. Abelard-Schuman, 1954. 157p. $3. (I)

More than 1000 riddles, conundrums, and other nonsense, collected by two anthropologists and arranged in categories such as Arithmetic Riddles, Bible Riddles, and Riddles from Other Lands.

Hobbies

1112 Braverman, Robert, and **Neumann, William.** Here Is Your Hobby: Slot Car Racing. Putnam, 1966. 128p. $3.25; lib. ed. $2.95 net. (I–U)

Two authorities discuss the popular hobby of slot-car racing, giving detailed instructions for building model cars and tracks and providing a list of manufacturers and a glossary of terms.

1113 Browin, Frances. Coins Have Tales To Tell: The Story of American Coins. Lippincott, 1966. 152p. $4.95. (I–U)

This coin book, interesting to history classes as well as to hobbyists, relates American coins to the circumstances under which they were issued and gives a brief history of United States mints and mint marks. Illustrated with photographs.

1114 Hoke, John. The First Book of Photography; illus. by Peter Plasencia. Watts, 1965. 81p. $2.65. (I–U)

Gives a brief history of photography, explains how different kinds of cameras work, states general principles for taking good pictures, and includes a bibliography. Illustrated with photographs.

1115 Hoyt, Edwin Palmer. One Penny Black: The Story of Stamp Collecting. Duell, 1965. 122p. $3.50. (U)

Beginning with the issuance of the first postage stamp, the English One Penny Black, the author traces in breezy, anecdotal style the history of stamp collecting and describes unusual and rare stamps and colorful stamp collectors and dealers.

1116 Kohn, Eugene. Photography: A Manual for Shutterbugs; illus. by Peter Plasencia. Prentice-Hall, 1965. 64p. $3.50. (I)

Offers practical advice on choosing a camera, regulating light, focusing, developing film, and other essentials of good photography.

1117 Lopshire, Robert. A Beginner's Guide to Building and Flying Model Airplanes. Harper, 1967. 128p. $4.95; lib. ed. $4.43 net. (I–U)

Step-by-step instructions, clear diagrams, a list of necessary tools and materials, and a glossary of terms answer most of the novice's questions about building and flying model airplanes.

1118 Petersham, Maud, and **Petersham, Miska.** America's Stamps: The Story of One Hundred Years of U.S. Postage Stamps. rev. ed. Macmillan, 1965. 144p. $5.50. (I–U)

Of interest to history students and hobbyists, a beautifully illustrated survey of United States postage stamps and the people and events they commemorate.

1119 Reinfeld, Fred. Fun with Stamp Collecting; illus. by W. T. Mars. Garden City, 1957. 88p. $3.95. (I–U)

Concise information on the history of postal systems, rare stamps, what stamps to buy, where to buy them, and how to organize them. Includes a glossary and a list of stamp dealers.

1120 Reinfeld, Fred. How To Build a Coin Collection. rev. ed. Sterling, 1966. 159p. $2.95; lib. ed. $3.39 net. (I–U)

A practical guide for the beginning collector of United States coins, covering issues to collect, points for judging coins, and suggestions for arrangement. Includes a glossary and a price list of United States and foreign coins.

1121 Reinfeld, Fred, and **Hobson, Burton.** Picture Book of Ancient Coins. Sterling, 1963. 64p. lib. ed. $2.29 net. (I–U)

The history of Egypt, Greece, and Rome as revealed through ancient coins.

1122 Yates, Raymond F. The Boys' Book of Model Railroading; illus. with drawings by the author and photos. Harper, 1951. 172p. $3.50; lib. ed. $3.27 net. (I-U)

Explains the electrical principles by which model trains are run and tells how to set up and operate a model railroad. Glossary.

Literature—General

Anthologies

1123 Arbuthnot, May Hill, comp. The Arbuthnot Anthology of Children's Literature; illus. by Arthur Paul (and others) . . . rev. ed. Scott, Foresman, 1961. 3v. in 1. 207, 418, 459p. $14.50. (P-I-U)

Combines *Time for Poetry, Time for Fairy Tales,* and *Time for True Tales* in a single volume convenient for teachers and librarians to use with children. Includes helpful notes and background materials.

1124 Gagliardo, Ruth, comp. Let's Read Aloud: Stories and Poems; illus. by Valenti Angelo. Lippincott, 1962. 256p. $4.95. (I)

A discriminating choice of stories, poems, and excerpts from outstanding children's books, excellent for introducing good reading to children.

1125 Gruenberg, Sidonie Matsner, ed. Favorite Stories Old and New. rev. and enl. ed.; illus. by Kurt Wiese. Doubleday, 1955. 512p. $4.95. (P-I-U)

Many excellent stories and poems, chosen for appeal to children of all ages, useful for storytelling and reading aloud.

1126 Henry, Ralph, and **Pannell, Lucile,** comps. My American Heritage . . . with an introd. by Marguerite Henry; illus. by John Dukes McKee. Rand McNally, 1949. 318p. $2.95. (I-U)

A collection of songs, poems, speeches, and sayings reflecting America's national spirit.

1127 Lines, Kathleen, comp. A Ring of Tales; illus. by Harold Jones. Watts, 1958. 239p. $3.95. (I)

Folk tales, poems, and excerpts from children's books in a well-designed and illustrated collection, suitable for reading aloud or for independent reading in the middle grades.

1128 Morrison, Lillian, comp. A Diller, a Dollar: Rhymes and Sayings for the Ten O'Clock Scholar; illus. by Marjorie Bauernschmidt. Crowell, 1955. 150p. $3.50. (I-U)

Rhymes and sayings of school children, gathered from old books and the recollections of older people and arranged by school subjects. Very funny and very appealing to today's children.

1129 Morrison, Lillian, comp. Yours Till Niagara Falls; illus. by Marjorie Bauernschmidt. Crowell, 1950. 182p. $2.95. (I-U)

A collection of verses from old albums and present-day yearbooks.

1130 Poe, Edgar Allan. Tales and Poems of Edgar Allan Poe; illus. by Russell Hoban; afterword by Clifton Fadiman. Macmillan, 1963. 338p. $4.95. (I-U)

Seventeen stories and several of Poe's best-known poems in an attractive edition.

1131 Thoreau, Henry David. Henry David Thoreau: A Man for Our Time; selections and drawings by James Daugherty. Viking, 1967. 111p. $4.50; lib. ed. $4.13 net. (U)

A selection of Thoreau's writings, chosen to illustrate his views on such current concerns as individual liberty, civil disobedience, and respect for the individual. James Daugherty's handsome illustrations perfectly reflect Thoreau's sturdy, independent spirit.

1132 Whitman, Walt. Walt Whitman's America: Being selections from *Leaves of Grass, Democratic Vistas, Specimen Days,* and *Portraits of Lincoln,* by James Daugherty. World, 1964. 110p. $3.95. (U)

An excellent introduction to Whitman's poetry and prose, illustrated with James Daugherty's dramatic pictures.

Writing

1133 Jacobson, Helen, and **Mischel, Florence.** The First Book of Letter Writing; pictures by László Roth. Watts, 1957. 62p. $2.65. (I–U)

A practical guide to writing letters of all kinds.

1134 Joslin, Sesyle. Dear Dragon . . . ; illus. by Irene Haas. Harcourt, 1962. unp. $2.25; lib. ed. $2.38 net. (P)

In a spirit of imaginative playfulness, the author and artist provide "useful letter forms for young ladies and gentlemen engaged in everyday correspondence" by giving correct letter forms for thank-you notes, get-well notes, and other types of correspondence occasioned by wildly absurd situations. A good take-off point for an entertaining exercise in letter writing.

1135 Yates, Elizabeth. Some Day You'll Write. Dutton, 1962. 94p. $2.75; lib. ed. $2.72 net. (I–U)

Advice and encouragement for the young person interested in creative writing, covering research, plot construction, character development, dialogue, and good writing habits.

Poetry

1136 Adshead, Gladys L., and **Duff, Annis,** comps. An Inheritance of Poetry; with decorations by Nora S. Unwin. Houghton, 1948. 415p. $5. (P–I–U)

A distinguished anthology of poems from all times and for all ages, designed to instill a love of poetry in the child. Excellent for reading aloud. Full index includes sources of poems and musical settings.

1137 Aiken, Conrad. Cats and Bats and Things with Wings: Poems; drawings by Milton Glaser. Atheneum, 1965. unp. $4.50; lib. ed. $4.29 net. (P)

Witty poems about 16 different animals, illustrated with highly imaginative illustrations done in 16 different styles.

1138 Aldis, Dorothy. All Together: A Child's Treasury of Verse . . . illus. by Helen D. Jameson, Marjorie Flack, and Margaret Freeman. Putnam, 1952. 192p. $3.95. (P)

Simple, childlike poems chosen by the author from four of her earlier volumes.

1139 Arbuthnot, May Hill, comp. Time for Poetry; illus. by Arthur Paul . . . general ed. rev. Scott, Foresman, 1961. 227p. $8.75. (P–I–U)

A collection of more than 700 poems for all ages, with an introduction for teachers and parents on reading poetry to children and using poetry in verse choirs. An excellent source to use with children, fully indexed.

1140 Association for Childhood Education International. Sung under the Silver Umbrella: Poems for Children; sel. by the Literature Committee of the Association for Childhood Education International; illus. by Dorothy Lathrop. Macmillan, 1935. 211p. $2.95; lib. ed. $2.94 net. (P)

A subject grouping of about 200 tried and true poems for young children, with an introduction about poetry by Padraic Colum. Author and first-line index.

1141 Behn, Harry. Cricket Songs: Japanese Haiku; tr. by Harry Behn; with pictures sel. from Sesshu and other Japanese masters. Harcourt, 1964. unp. $2.50; lib. ed. $2.67 net. (P–I–U)

A small, exquisite book of Japanese nature poems illustrated by Japanese paintings, perfect for reading aloud or to inspire creative writing of poetry.

1142 Behn, Harry. The Golden Hive: Poems and Pictures. Harcourt, 1966. 61p. $3.25. (I)

Nature poems predominate in these rhymed and unrhymed verses.

1143 Behn, Harry. The Little Hill. Harcourt, 1949. 58p. $3. (P–I)

Rhythm and humor make the 29 poems in this volume especially suitable for reading aloud in primary grades.

1144 Benét, Rosemary, and **Benét, Stephen Vincent.** A Book of Americans; illus. by

Charles Child. Rinehart, 1933. 114p. $3.95; lib. ed. $3.59 net. (P–I)

Fifty-six lighthearted poems introduce characters from American history, from Columbus to Woodrow Wilson, pointing up the brave or tragic or humorous quality for which each is memorable. Recommended for enlivening history classes.

1145 **Beyond the High Hills:** A Book of Eskimo Poems; photos. by Guy Mary-Rousselière. World, 1961. 32p. $3.95; lib. ed. $4.09 net. (I–U)

These songs and chants of the Eskimos of the Hudson Bay region and the Musk Ox people of the Copper Country, collected by a Danish explorer and translated by an Oblate priest, express the joys and sorrows of an interesting people. Handsome color photographs form an appropriate background and add to the book's usefulness in both social studies and literature.

1146 **Blishen, Edward,** comp. Oxford Book of Poetry for Children; with illus. by Brian Wildsmith. Watts, 1964. 167p. $7.95. (P–I)

A sprightly collection of English verse selected to encourage a love of poetry, brilliantly illustrated in full color.

1147 **Brewton, John E.,** comp. Gaily We Parade: A Collection of Poems about People, Here, There & Everywhere; illus. by Robert Lawson. Macmillan, 1940. 218p. $4.95. (I–U)

Poems about neighbors, relatives, sailors, fairies, royalty, and funny folk, by authors as diverse as Blake, Keats, Rachel Field, and Elizabeth Madox Roberts.

1148 **Brewton, John E.,** comp. Under the Tent of the Sky: A Collection of Poems about Animals Large and Small; with drawings by Robert Lawson. Macmillan, 1937. 205p. lib. ed. $3.74 net. (P–I–U)

There's something for children of all ages in this anthology of poems about zoo, circus, and farm animals—and even about animals that exist only in the imagination. Indexed by author, title, and first line.

1149 **Brewton, Sara,** and **Brewton, John E.,** comps. Bridled wtih Rainbows: Poems about Many Things of Earth and Sky; decorations by Vera Bock. Macmillan, 1949. 191p. $3.95; lib. ed. $3.94 net. (P–I–U)

A subject arrangement of about 200 poems, indexed by author, title, and first line.

1150 **Brewton, Sara,** and **Brewton, John E.,** comps. Sing a Song of Seasons: Poems about Holidays, Vacation Days, and Days To Go to School; decorations by Vera Bock. Macmillan, 1955. 200p. $4.50; lib. ed. $3.94 net. (P–I–U)

A useful collection, arranged by seasons and special occasions and fully indexed.

1151 **Brown, Margaret Wise.** Nibble Nibble: Poems for Children; illus. by Leonard Weisgard. unp. W. R. Scott, 1959. $3.95. (P)

Twenty-five gently cadenced nature poems, beautifully illustrated in black, white, and garden green.

1152 **Browning, Robert.** The Pied Piper of Hamelin; illus. by Kate Greenaway. Warne, 1899. 48p. $4.95. (I–U)

This famous poem, illustrated by a distinguished nineteenth-century English artist, is a charming read-aloud period piece.

1153 **Chaucer, Geoffrey.** A Taste of Chaucer: Selections from The Canterbury Tales; chosen and ed. by Anne Malcolmson; illus. by Enrico Arno. Harcourt, 1964. 184p. $3.75; lib. ed. $3.81 net. (U)

Following a brief introduction to Chaucer's life and times, the editor provides a selection of tales chosen for appeal to young people. The slightly modified verse translation is accompanied by background notes and a glossary.

1154 **Ciardi, John.** I Met a Man; illus. by Robert Osborn. Houghton, 1961. 74p. $3.25; lib. ed. $3.07 net. (P)

Using only the words in two first-grade word lists, a well-known poet wrote these verses for his first-grade daughter to read for herself. In them he makes a game of poetry, introducing riddles and plays on words to lure the reader on. (R1–2)

1155 **Cole, William,** comp. The Birds and the Beasts Were There: Animal Poems; sel. by William Cole; woodcuts by Helen Siegl. World, 1963. 320p. $4.95. (I–U)

Twelve categories of poems about all kinds of animals, ranging in time from the Bible to Ogden Nash and including many poets who deserve to be better known—for example, John Clare. Author and title index.

1156 **Cole, William,** ed. I Went to the Animal Fair: A Book of Animal Poems; illus.

by Colette Rosselli. World, 1958. 45p. $2.95; lib. ed. $2.88 net. (P)

Thirty-five animal poems in a read-aloud picture book for young children.

1157 **Cole, William,** comp. Oh, What Nonsense! Poems sel. by William Cole; drawings by Tomi Ungerer. Viking, 1966. 80p. $4. (P–I)

A fresh collection of nonsense verses, including counting rhymes, jump-rope rhymes, and words to folk songs, illustrated with droll black-and-white drawings.

1158 **De La Mare, Walter,** ed. Come Hither: A Collection of Rhymes & Poems for the Young of All Ages; decorations by Warren Chappell. new and rev ed. Knopf, 1957. 777p. $7.95. (P–I–U)

A distinguished anthology compiled by a distinguished English poet, with an introduction and background notes. Notes, authors, titles, and first lines are indexed.

1159 **De La Mare, Walter.** Rhymes and Verses: Collected Poems for Children; with drawings by Elinore Blaisdell. Holt, 1947. 344p. $6. (I–U)

All of De La Mare's poems for children in a beautifully designed and printed volume.

1160 **Dickinson, Emily.** Poems for Youth; ed. by Alfred Leete Hampson; foreword by May Lamberton Becker; illus. by George and Doris Hauman. Little, 1934. unp. $4.50. (I–U)

Seventy-eight poems written by Emily Dickinson for her young niece and nephews serve as an excellent introduction to the poet. Indexed by first lines.

1161 **Doane, Pelagie,** comp. A Small Child's Book of Verse; comp. and illus. by Pelagie Doane. Walck, 1948. 142p. $5.95. (P)

A selection of the compiler-illustrator's favorite poems for children, especially recommended for reading aloud in primary grades.

1162 **Dunbar, Paul Lawrence.** Little Brown Baby; selections with biographical sketch by Bertha Rodgers; illus. by Erick Berry. Dodd, 1940. 106p. $2.75. (I–U)

This collection of poems, some in dialect, provides a good introduction to the well-known Negro poet.

1163 **Dunning, Stephen,** and others. Reflections on a Gift of Watermelon Pickle . . . and Other Modern Verse. Lothrop, 1967. 139p. $3.95; lib. ed. $3.70 net. (U)

Modern poems chosen for excellence and appeal to young people, illustrated with unusual photographs with a contemporary feeling. A fresh collection with special relevance to today's world.

1164 **Farjeon, Eleanor.** The Children's Bells: A Selection of Poems; illus. by Peggy Fortnum. Walck, 1960. 212p. $5. (I–U)

Poems, selected by the author from her previous books for children, sing of the seasons, of magic, of kings and heroes, and of other matters of the child's world. Arranged by subject and indexed by title.

1165 **Ferris, Helen,** ed. Favorite Poems, Old and New; sel. for boys and girls; illus. by Leonard Weisgard. Doubleday, 1957. 598p. $5.95. (P–I–U)

A standard anthology of more than 700 poems, arranged in 18 sections related to children's interests and indexed by author, title, and first line. A large volume, better for reading aloud than for use by children.

1166 **Field, Rachel.** Taxis and Toadstools; verses and decorations by Rachel Field. Doubleday, 1926. 129p. $3.25. (P–I)

Gay poems about all sorts of things that children enjoy in the city and the country.

1167 **Fisher, Aileen.** Cricket in a Thicket; illus. by Feodor Rojankovsky. Scribner, 1963. 63p. $2.95; lib. ed. $2.97 net. (P)

Cheerful verses and soft charcoal drawings about the world outdoors.

1168 **Fisher, Aileen.** Going Barefoot; illus. by Adrienne Adams. Crowell, 1960. unp. $3.95; lib. ed. $3.79 net. (P)

A happy read-aloud poem about a little boy who loves going barefoot and envies the animals who do not have to wear shoes. Especially appealing to kindergarten and first grade.

1169 **Fisher, Aileen.** In the Middle of the Night; illus. by Adrienne Adams. Crowell, 1965. unp. $3.95; lib. ed. $3.76 net. (P)

A nocturnal walk as a birthday present delights a little girl who discovers for the first time the beauty and magic of a country night. Illustrations evoke the mood and combine with the gentle verses to reassure the small child about nighttime.

1170 **Fisher, Aileen.** In the Woods, in the Meadow, in the Sky; illus. by Margot Tomes. Scribner, 1965. 64p. lib. ed. $3.12 net. (P)

Lilting rhymes about wild creatures, trees, stars, and other outdoor wonders.

1171 **Fisher, Aileen.** Listen, Rabbit; illus. by Symeon Shimin. Crowell, 1964. unp. lib. ed. $3.12 net. (P–I)

A small boy watches a wild rabbit, longing to make it his friend, but when it produces a nest full of baby rabbits, he realizes that he must be satisfied to let it live its own life while he continues to watch. A long narrative poem with expressive illustrations.

1172 **Fisher, Aileen.** Where Does Everyone Go? Illus. by Adrienne Adams. Crowell, 1961. unp. $3.95; lib. ed. $3.76 net. (P)

A picture book in rhyme answering children's questions about what happens to small creatures when winter approaches. A good seasonal book for the youngest, enhanced by sensitive illustrations in fall colors.

1173 **Frost, Robert.** You Come Too: Favorite Poems for Young Readers; with wood engravings by Thomas W. Nason. Holt, 1959. 94p. $3.50; lib. ed. $3.27 net. (I–U)

A perceptive foreword introduces Frost's own selection of his poems to be read to and by young people.

1174 **Fyleman, Rose.** Fairies and Chimneys. Doubleday, 1920. 62p. $3.25. (P–I)

The "poet of fairyland" is at her best in these fanciful poems about fairies and their delicate magic.

1175 **Geismer, Barbara Peck,** and **Suter, Antoinette B.** Very Young Verses; illus. by Mildred Bronson. Houghton, 1945. 210p. $3.50. (P)

A subject arrangement of poems enjoyed by young children, compiled by two nursery-school teachers out of their own experience. No index.

1176 **Huffard, Grace Thompson,** comp. My Poetry Book: An Anthology of Modern Verse for Boys and Girls. rev. ed. Sel. and arr. by Grace Thompson Huffard and Laura Mae Carlisle in collaboration with Helen Ferris; introd. by Marguerite de Angeli; illus. by Willy Pogány. rev. ed. Winston, 1956. 504p. $4.50. (P–I–U)

More than 500 poems arranged in categories reflecting children's interests and indexed by author, title, and first line. Includes a glossary of difficult words.

1177 **Hughes, Langston.** The Dream Keeper, and Other Poems; with illus. by Helen Sewell. Knopf, 1932. 77p. lib. ed. $2.79 net. (I–U)

The author's own selection of his poems, including lyrics, songs, and several typical Negro blues.

1178 **Larrick, Nancy.** Piper, Pipe That Song Again! Poems for Boys and Girls; illus. by Kelly Oechsli. Random, 1965. 85p. $2.95; lib. ed. $2.99 net. (P–I)

About 70 poems selected for their appeal to primary-grade children.

1179 **Lear, Edward.** The Complete Nonsense Book . . . ed. by Lady Strachey; introd. by the Earl of Cromer. Dodd, 1948. 430p. $5. (P–I–U)

All the daft limericks and nonsense verses, with the author's own illustrations.

1180 **Lewis, Richard,** ed. In a Spring Garden; pictures by Ezra Jack Keats. Dial, 1965. unp. $3.95; lib. ed. $3.69 net. (P–I)

Arresting pictures in collage, watercolor, and line drawing illustrate this selection of 23 Japanese *haiku,* chosen for appeal to young children.

1181 **Lewis, Richard,** comp. Miracles: Poems by Children of the English-speaking World. Simon & Schuster, 1966. 215p. $4.95. (P–I–U)

Poems by children between the ages of four and thirteen show the power of imagination and talent for creative expression of which young people are capable. Useful to encourage creative writing.

1182 **Lewis, Richard,** ed. The Moment of Wonder: A Collection of Chinese and Japanese Poetry; illus. with paintings by Chinese and Japanese masters. Dial, 1964. 138p. $3.95. (P–I–U)

A collection of exquisite poems, some written 2000 years ago, expressing the poets' delight in the small miracles of nature.

1183 **Lindsay, Vachel.** Johnny Appleseed, and Other Poems; illus. by George Richards. Macmillan, 1928. 144p. $3.50. (I–U)

A representative selection of Lindsay's poetry, including nonsense rhymes, poems of history, and selections from "The Congo" and "The Chinese Nightingale."

1184 Longfellow, Henry Wadsworth. Paul Revere's Ride; illus. by Paul Galdone. Crowell, 1963. unp. $3.50; lib. ed. $3.76 net. (I)

Dramatic colored illustrations set the scene and capture the excitement of the historic ride in a picture book which can be used to vitalize the Revolutionary period.

1185 Love, Katherine, comp. A Little Laughter; illus. by Walter H. Lorraine. Crowell, 1957. 114p. $2.95; lib. ed. $2.90 net. (I)

Humorous verses and rhymes with laughable illustrations.

1186 McCord, David. All Day Long: Fifty Rhymes of the Never Was and Always Is; drawings by Henry B. Kane. Little, 1966. 104p. $3.50. (I)

Poems—some nonsensical, some thoughtful—about the everyday interests and experiences of childhood. Companion volume to *Far and Few*, below.

1187 McCord, David. Far and Few: Rhymes of the Never Was and Always Is; drawings by Henry B. Kane. Little, 1952. 99p. $3.75. (I)

The author states that these verses reflect "a child's self-reliance, his instinctive interest in nature." The 60 poems are varied in rhythm, verse form, imagery, and theme.

1188 McFarland, Wilma, ed. For a Child: Great Poems Old and New; collected by Wilma McFarland; illus. by Ninon. Westminster, 1947. 96p. $3.95. (P–I)

Home, family, pets, nature, and childhood experiences are the subjects of these poems, presented in a gay picture-book format.

1189 Merriam, Eve. It Doesn't Always Have To Rhyme; drawings by Malcolm Spooner. Atheneum, 1964. 83p. $3.25; lib. ed. $3.07 net. (P–I)

The author demonstrates in fresh and amusing verse patterns that poetry "doesn't always have to rhyme." Should encourage pupils to try writing their own poems.

1190 Millay, Edna St. Vincent. Edna St. Vincent Millay's Poems Selected for Young

People; illus. and decorations by J. Paget-Fredericks. Harper, 1951. 113p. $2.95; lib. ed. $2.92 net. (I–U)

An attractively illustrated introduction to Millay, for the true poetry lover.

1191 Milne, A. A. Now We Are Six; with decorations by Ernest H. Shepard. Dutton, 1955. 104p. $3.50; lib. ed. $3.46 net. (P)

Companion volume to *When We Were Very Young,* below.

1192 Milne, A. A. When We Were Very Young; with decorations by Ernest H. Shepard. Dutton, 1952. 102p. $3.50; lib. ed. $3.46 net. (P)

Whimsical verses written to amuse the author's son, Christopher Robin—poems full of nonsense, surprises, and moments of tenderness. Companion volume to *Now We Are Six,* above.

1193 Morrison, Lillian, comp. Sprints and Distances: Sports in Poetry and the Poetry in Sport; illus. by Clare and John Ross. Crowell, 1965. 211p. $4.95. (I–U)

Light and serious poetry is combined in an unusual anthology celebrating sports and the sportsman. Indexed by author, title, first line, and type of sport.

1194 Nash, Ogden, ed. The Moon Is Shining Bright as Day: An Anthology of Good-humored Verse; sel. with an introd. by Ogden Nash; with drawings by Rose Shirvanian. Lippincott, 1953. 177p. $3.95. (P–I)

More than 175 poems, old and new, serious and silly, for reading to or by children.

1195 O'Neill, Mary. Hailstones and Halibut Bones: Adventures in Color; illus. by Leonard Weisgard. Doubleday, 1961. 59p. $3.25. (P–I)

Poems about color—each illustrated in the proper color—tell what thoughts and moods each suggests to the poet and stimulate the child to add his own reactions. Can be used to help children become aware of color and to encourage creative writing.

1196 Parker, Elinor, ed. 100 Story Poems; sel. by Elinor Parker; illus. by Henry C. Pitz. Crowell, 1951. 499p. $5. (I–U)

Old ballads and modern narrative poems about heroes, romance, chivalry, the sea, and magic make up the greater part of this useful anthology. Indexed by author, title, and first line.

1197 **Parker, Elinor,** comp. The Singing and the Gold: Poems Translated from World Literature; wood engravings by Clare Leighton. Crowell, 1965. 223p. $4.50. (U)

A discriminating selection of world poems organized by the themes of war and death, love, seasons and nature, solitude, and worship and praise. Excellent translations, many hard-to-find poems; indexed by author, title, first line, translator, source, and language.

1198 **Peterson, Isabel J.,** ed. The First Book of Poetry; pictures by Kathleen Elgin. Watts, 1954. 114p. $2.65. (I)

Eighty poems, favorites with children, in an attractively illustrated, fully indexed volume.

1199 **Plotz, Helen,** comp. Imagination's Other Place: Poems of Science and Mathematics; illus. with wood engravings by Clare Leighton. Crowell, 1955. 200p. $3.95. (U)

Poems about scientists and science, selected to show the part imagination plays in scientific achievement. Should appeal to the future scientist, the poetry lover, and the science fiction fan. Indexed by poet, title, and first line.

1200 **Plotz, Helen,** comp. Untune the Sky: Poems of Music and the Dance; illus. with wood engravings by Clare Leighton. Crowell, 1957. 162p. $3.95. (U)

An unusual collection of poems, ranging from the humorous to the serious, celebrating the power of music and dancing. Indexed by poet, title, and first line.

1201 **Read, Herbert,** ed. This Way Delight: A Book of Poetry for the Young; illus. by Juliet Kepes. Pantheon, 1956. 155p. lib. ed. $3.69 net. (I–U)

Poems chosen to lead the reader into enjoyment of poetry, the editor's "Afterthought" explaining the nature of poetry and encouraging young people to read and write it. The table of contents is at the back, along with an index of authors and first lines.

1202 **Richards, Laura E.** Tirra Lirra: Rhymes Old and New; foreword by May Hill Arbuthnot; with illus. by Marguerite Davis. Little, 1955. 194p. $3.75. (P–I)

Nonsense rhymes full of made-up words and absurd situations provide fun for listeners in primary and intermediate grades.

1203 **Roberts, Elizabeth Madox.** Under the Tree; illus. by F. D. Bedford. enl. ed. Viking, 1930. 85p. $3; lib. ed. $2.96 net. (P)

The simplicity and directness of these poems about a child's everyday world reveal the poet's genius for seeing through a child's eyes and her ability to communicate with children.

1204 **Rossetti, Christina G.** Sing-Song: A Nursery Rhyme Book for Children; illus. by Marguerite Davis. Macmillan, 1924 88p. $2.50. (P)

A collection of lilting verses which provide the young child with a happy introduction to lyric poetry.

1205 **Sandburg, Carl.** Wind Song; illus. by William A. Smith. Harcourt, 1960. 217p. $3. (I–U)

Eighty poems chosen by the poet for children and young people.

1206 **Smith, William Jay.** Laughing Time; illus. by Juliet Kepes. Little, 1955. 55p. lib. ed. $3.14 net. (P)

A book of very funny nonsense verses for the very young.

1207 **Stevenson, Robert Louis.** A Child's Garden of Verses; illus. by Tasha Tudor. Walck, 1947. unp. $4.25. (P)

The softly colored illustrations in this edition portray young Robert Louis Stevenson himself as the boy in the pictures.

1208 **Thayer, Ernest Lawrence.** Casey at the Bat; illus. by Paul Frame. Prentice-Hall, 1964. unp. $3.25. (I)

A picture-book edition of the famous baseball poem interpreted in broadly humorous pictures in harmony with the burlesque tone of the situation.

1209 **Thompson, Blanche Jennings,** ed. All the Silver Pennies; combining *Silver Pennies* and *More Silver Pennies;* illus. by Ursula Arndt. Macmillan, 1967. 224p. $4.95. (P–I)

Time-tested poems for children, organized into Part I for the young child and Part II for older children. Includes an introduction, notes for individual poems, and author, title, and first-line indexes.

1210 **Untermeyer, Louis,** ed. The Golden Treasury of Poetry; sel. and with a commentary by Louis Untermeyer; illus. by

Joan Walsh Anglund. Golden Pr., 1959. 324p. $4.95. (P–I–U)

A wide-ranging selection of poems for all ages and from all times, selected with a poet's discrimination and presented in inviting format. Arranged by themes, annotated by the editor, and indexed by author, title, and first line.

1211 Untermeyer, Louis, ed. Rainbow in the Sky; collected and ed. by Louis Untermeyer; illus. by Reginald Birch. Harcourt, 1935. 498p. $5.75. (P–I)

An introduction on the nature and delights of poetry is followed by a subject arrangement of poems selected for children from six to twelve. Fully indexed.

1212 Untermeyer, Louis, ed. This Singing World: An Anthology of Modern Poetry for Young People; illus. by Florence Wyman Ivins. Harcourt, 1923. 445p. $4.75. (I–U)

Forty-nine English and American poets are represented in this classic collection of 321 poems. Author, title, and first-line indexes.

Drama

1213 Chute, Marchette. Stories from Shakespeare. World, 1956. 351p. $3.95; lib. ed. $4.09 net. (I–U)

The introduction to this book states that its purpose is "to give the reader a preliminary idea of each of the thirty-six plays by telling the stories and explaining in a general way the intentions and points of view of the characters." An excellent preparation for appreciating the plays themselves.

1214 Plays, The Drama Magazine for Young People. Children's Plays for Creative Actors. Plays, 1967. 368p. $4.50. (I–U)

Thirty-five plays on various subjects, easy to produce and suitable for school occasions.

1215 Plays, The Drama Magazine for Young People. One Hundred Plays for Children; ed. by A. S. Burack. Plays, 1949. 886p. $7.95. (I–U)

A useful collection of one-act plays, easy to produce and royalty-free.

1216 Plays, The Drama Magazine for Young People. Plays from Famous Stories and Fairy Tales: Royalty-Free Dramatizations of Favorite Children's Stories. Plays, 1967. 463p. $7.95. (I)

Excellent dramatizations and production notes for 28 well-known stories.

1217 Smith, Moyne Rice. Plays & How To Put Them On; illus. by Don Bolognese. Walck, 1961. 169p. $4.50. (I–U)

Scripts for seven plays with helpful notes on planning, rehearsing, and producing plays. Includes suggestions for stories suitable for dramatization and lists of plays recommended for production by children and young people.

Literature—Traditional and Folk

Mythology

1218 Asimov, Isaac. Words from the Myths; decorations by William Barss. Houghton, 1961. 225p. $3.50. (U)

Traces pertinent English words to their origins in Greek myths and discusses the myths from which they were derived. Provides insight into word connotations and affords a fresh view of mythology. Includes a mythological index.

1219 Aulaire, Ingri d', and **Aulaire, Edgar Parin d'.** Norse Gods and Giants. Doubleday, 1967. 154p. $5.95. (I)

A handsomely illustrated collection of Norse myths, reflecting the rugged spirit of the characters, both evil and benign. Pronunciations are given within the stories and repeated, with definitions and explanatory notes, at the end of the book.

1220 Benson, Sally. Stories of the Gods and Heroes; illus. by Steele Savage. Dial, 1940. 256p. $3.50. (I–U)

Stories taken from Bulfinch's *Age of Fable,* edited or rewritten by the author with fidelity to the spirit of the originals.

1221 Bulfinch, Thomas. A Book of Myths: Selections from Bulfinch's *Age of Fable*; with illus. by Helen Sewell. Macmillan, 1942. 126p. $3.95; lib. ed. $3.94 net. (I–U)

Beautiful illustrations suggesting classical sculpture and vase paintings illuminate 30 slightly adapted Greek myths.

1222 Colum, Padraic. The Children of Odin: The Book of Northern Myths; illus. by Willy Pogány. Macmillan, 1920. 271p. $4.50. (I–U)

Norse myths, from the twilight of the gods to the destruction of Asgard, retold in a connected narrative distinguished by fine literary style and fanciful illustrations.

1223 Coolidge, Olivia. Greek Myths; illus. by Edouard Sandoz. Houghton, 1949. 243p. $3.75. (U)

Discriminating choice of titles, spirited retelling, and effective illustrations mark these 27 famous stories. Includes a list of proper names, with pronunciations.

1224 Coolidge, Olivia E. Legends of the North; illus. by Edouard Sandoz. Houghton, 1951. 260p. $3.75. (U)

In the same vigorous style as in *Greek Myths,* above, the author retells the stories of Thor, Baldur, Odin, the Valkyries, Beowulf, and other northern gods and heroes. Lists proper names, with pronunciations.

1225 Graves, Robert. Greek Gods and Heroes; illus. by Dimitris Davis. Doubleday, 1960. 160p. $3.75. (U)

These Greek myths, retold with wit and a modern flavor and illustrated with attractive drawings, will appeal to older readers.

1226 Hamilton, Edith. Mythology; illus. by Steele Savage. Little, 1942. 497p. $5.95. (U)

A source book for Greek, Roman, and Norse myths with versions close to the originals and introductory background notes.

1227 Hawthorne, Nathaniel. A Wonder Book and Tanglewood Tales, for Girls and Boys; with pictures by Maxfield Parrish. Dodd, 1938. 358p. $4.50. (I)

Greek myths retold as fairy tales for nineteenth-century children, lighter in tone and with moral implications, suitable as an introduction to classical mythology for younger children.

1228 Hosford, Dorothy. Thunder of the Gods; illus. by Claire and George Louden. Holt, 1952. 115p. lib. ed. $2.52 net. (I–U)

An animated retelling of the Norse myths, especially well suited to storytelling or reading aloud.

1229 Lum, Peter. The Stars in Our Heaven: Myths and Fables; illus. by Anne Marie Jauss. Pantheon, 1948. 245p. lib. ed. $3.99 net. (U)

Myths and legends from many lands about the stars and constellations, with charts to help the observer locate the heavenly bodies.

1230 Sellew, Catharine F. Adventures with the Giants; illus. by Steele Savage. Little, 1950. 132p. $3.95; lib. ed. $3.79 net. (I)

Fourteen stories from Norse mythology retold in language easy enough for independent reading in the middle grades. Large print, flavorful style and illustrations. Includes a pronouncing index of names.

1231 Sellew, Catharine F. Adventures with the Gods; with illus. by George and Doris Hauman. Little, 1945. 114p. $3.75; lib. ed. $3.58 net. (I)

Sixteen stories of Greek gods and goddesses, similar in presentation and format to *Adventures with the Giants,* above.

Hero Tales and Epics

1232 Baldwin, James. The Story of Roland; illus. by Peter Hurd. Scribner, 1930. 347p. $5. (I–U)

The age-old story of Roland, nephew of Charlemagne and the greatest hero of the Middle Ages, is told in a stirring narrative and illustrated with richly colored paintings.

1233 Baldwin, James. The Story of Siegfried; with pictures by Peter Hurd. Scribner, 1931. 279p. $5. (I–U)

A continuous narrative, drawn from many

sources, of Siegfried, or Sigurd, the great Germanic hero whose adventures were the inspiration of Wagner's Ring cycle.

1234   Church, Alfred J. The Aeneid for Boys and Girls: Told from Virgil in Simple Language; with 12 illus. in color. Macmillan, 1908. 300p. $2.95; lib. ed. $3.24 net. (U)

A prose version of the *Aeneid,* telling the story of the wanderings of King Aeneas on his journey from Troy.

1235   Church, Alfred J. The Iliad and the Odyssey of Homer, Retold; illus. by Eugene Karlin; afterword by Clifton Fadiman. Macmillan, 1964. 277p. $3.95. (I–U)

Combines the story of the Trojan War with Ulysses' adventures on his way home in a faithful rendering of events in their proper sequence.

1236   Colum, Padraic. The Children's Homer: Adventures of Odysseus and the Tale of Troy; illus. by Willy Pogány. Macmillan, 1918. 247p. $3.95; lib. ed. $3.94 net. (I–U)

Another version of the epic stories told in vigorous, rhythmical prose and beautifully illustrated.

1237   Colum, Padraic. The Golden Fleece and the Heroes Who Lived before Achilles; illus. by Willy Pogány. Macmillan, 1921. 317p. $3.95; lib. ed. $3.94 net. (I–U)

Jason's voyage in search of the golden fleece is interwoven with other myths and legends of Greece. Spirited prose and excellent illustrations.

1238   Deutsch, Babette. Heroes of the Kalevala: Finland's Saga; illus. by Fritz Eichenberg. Messner, 1940. 238p. $3.95. (U)

An excellent retelling in prose of the great Finnish collection of heroic poetry.

1239   Gaer, Joseph. The Adventures of Rama; illus. by Randy Monk. Little, 1954. 210p. $3.95. (U)

This story of the great Hindu epic Ramayana relates the adventures of Prince Rama, an incarnation of the god Vishnu, who with his wife Sita fled from his enemies and endured many dangers.

1240   Green, Roger Lancelyn. Heroes of Greece and Troy; retold from the ancient authors by Roger Lancelyn Green; with drawings by Heather Copley and Christopher Chamberlain. Walck, 1961. 337p. $6.50. (U)

Spirited, continuous account of the exploits of Achilles, Hector, Perseus, Heracles, Theseus, and others. Two maps and a list of Greek and Roman names help the reader to follow the story.

1241   Hazeltine, Alice E., ed. Hero Tales from Many Lands; illus. by Gordon Laite. Abingdon, 1961. 475p. $5.95. (I–U)

Thirty tales of such heroes as Fionn, Odysseus, Ogier the Dane, and Tristram are presented in vivid retellings, with background notes, a pronunciation guide, and a list for further reading. An excellent introduction to heroic literature, recommended for reading aloud and storytelling.

1242   Hosford, Dorothy. By His Own Might: The Battles of Beowulf; drawings by Laszlo Matulay. Holt, 1947. 69p. lib. ed. $2.92 net. (I–U)

A rousing retelling of this oldest of English epics, in which Beowulf slays the monster Grendel and his wicked mother, becomes king of the Danes, and finally meets his death in combat with a dragon.

1243   McLean, Mollie, and **Wiseman, Anne.** Adventures of the Greek Heroes; illus. by Witold T. Mars. Houghton, 1961. 174p. $3.95. (I)

Easy versions of the stories of Hercules, Perseus, Theseus, Orpheus, Meleager, and Jason, presented in a format designed to attract independent readers. (R5–6)

1244   Malory, Sir Thomas. The Boy's King Arthur: Sir Thomas Malory's History of King Arthur and His Knights of the Round Table; ed. for boys with an introd. by Sidney Lanier; illus. by N. C. Wyeth. Scribner, 1952. 321p. $5. (I–U)

The Arthurian legend retold with fidelity to Malory and illustrated with pictures in glowing color.

1245   Picard, Barbara Leonie. The Iliad of Homer; retold by Barbara Leonie Picard; illus. by Joan Kiddell-Monroe. Walck, 1960. 208p. $4.50. (U)

Relates the incidents which took place in the ninth year of the Trojan War, centering around Achilles' quarrel with Agamemnon and the death of Patroclus. Includes a prologue and an epilogue and a list of names, with identifications.

1246 **Pyle, Howard.** Some Merry Adventures of Robin Hood of Great Renown in Nottinghamshire; written and illus. by Howard Pyle. Scribner, 1954. 212p. $2.95; lib. ed. $2.97 net. (I–U)

Twelve stories selected and adapted by Pyle from his longer account of Robin Hood's adventures and illustrated with the author's classic pictures.

1247 **Pyle, Howard.** The Story of King Arthur and His Knights; written and illus. by Howard Pyle. Scribner, 1903. 312p. $6. (I–U)

An introduction to the loftiest of medieval romances, worthy in style and illustrations of its noble theme: Book of King Arthur; Winning of a Sword; Winning of a Queen; Story of Merlin; Story of Sir Pellias; Story of Sir Gawaine.

1248 **Sellew, Catharine F.** Adventures with the Heroes; with illus. by Steele Savage. Little, 1954. 145p. $3.95; lib. ed. $3.79 net. (I)

A retelling of the Völsunga Saga in which the Norse heroes come to life for readers in middle grades. Useful in the literature program and as background for Wagner's Ring cycle. Includes a pronouncing glossary. (R5–6)

American Legendary Heroes

The following tall tales of America's work heroes are a colorful expression of the American spirit, equally valuable for reading aloud, storytelling, independent reading, and supplementary reading for history classes.

1249 **Blair, Walter.** Tall Tale America: A Legendary History of Our Humorous Heroes; illus. by Glen Rounds. Coward-McCann, 1944. 262p. lib. ed. $3.49 net. (I–U)

Developing the theme of hardship's role in "raising up heroes," the author tells with gusto the stories of Paul Bunyan, Davy Crockett, Captain Stormalong, Windwagon Smith, and other legendary and near-legendary characters who have helped to shape the nation and the national character.

1250 **Bowman, James Cloyd.** Pecos Bill: The Greatest Cowboy of All Time; pictures by Laura Bannon. Whitman, 1937. 296p. $3.50. (I–U)

Humorous tales of Pecos Bill's marvelous doings, from his childhood with the coyotes to his career as a famous cowpuncher.

1251 **Felton, Harold W.** John Henry and His Hammer; illus. by Aldren A. Watson. Knopf, 1950. 82p. lib. ed. $3.29 net. (I–U)

John Henry, the work giant who helped to build the nation's railroads, met his death in a contest with a steam drill. A vigorous tale suitable for storytelling.

1252 **Felton, Harold W.** Mike Fink, Best of the Keelboatmen . . . Tastefully amplified and illus. by Aldren A. Watson. Dodd, 1960. 159p. $3.25. (I–U)

The author claims that his story contains facts, anecdotes, history, legend, and folklore of the unique and justly famed hero who was half "hoss" and half alligator and could outrun, outjump, and outfight any man who challenged him. Told in dialect and illustrated with humorously exaggerated pictures.

1253 **Keats, Ezra Jack.** John Henry: An American Legend; story and pictures by Ezra Jack Keats. Pantheon, 1965. unp. $3.50; lib. ed. $3.39 net. (P–I)

A greatly simplified story of John Henry, the famous pile driver, embellished with large, bold pictures in color.

1254 **McCormick, Dell J.** Paul Bunyan Swings His Axe. Caxton, 1936. 111p. $3.50. (I)

Paul, the mighty logger, and his blue ox, Babe, loom larger than life in this hilarious tale of their exploits.

1255 **Malcolmson, Anne.** Yankee Doodle's Cousins; illus. by Robert McCloskey. Houghton, 1941. 267p. $4.50. (I)

Johnny Darling, Captain Kidd, Joe Magarac, and Old Stormalong are among the real and legendary characters in this humorously told and illustrated collection of tales.

1256 **Peck, Leigh.** Pecos Bill and Lightning; illus. by Kurt Wiese. Houghton, 1940. 68p. lib. ed. $3.57 net. (I)

Cartoon-like pictures and easy text give

this story of the famous cowboy and his horse appeal for reluctant readers.

1257 Shapiro, Irwin. Heroes in American Folklore; illus. by James Daugherty and Donald McKay. Messner, 1962. 256p. $4.95. (I–U)

Tall tales about Casey Jones, Old Stormalong, John Henry, Steamboat Bill, and Joe Magarac.

1258 Wadsworth, Wallace. Paul Bunyan and His Great Blue Ox; retold by Wallace Wadsworth; illus. by Enrico Arno. Doubleday, 1926. 205p. $3.50. (I–U)

A choice collection of stories about the mythical lumberjack of the North woods.

Fables

1259 Aesop. Aesop's Fables; ed. and illus. with wood engravings by Boris Artzybasheff. Viking, 1933. 86p. $3.50; lib. ed. $3.37 net. (P–I)

A lively version of 90 Aesop fables, illustrated with striking woodcuts.

1260 Aesop. The Fables of Aesop; sel., told anew, and their history traced by Joseph Jacobs; illus. by David Levine; afterword by Clifton Fadiman. Macmillan, 1964. 115p. $2.95; lib. ed. $3.29 net. (P–I)

A short history of the Aesop fables precedes 80 of the tales in an attractively illustrated edition.

1261 Brown, Marcia. Once a Mouse . . . A Fable Cut in Wood. Scribner, 1961. unp. $3.25; lib. ed. $3.12 net. (P–I)

A fable from the folklore of India, in which a frightened mouse is changed into larger and larger animals until his increasing pride brings about his downfall. Notable for action woodcuts in color.

1262 Gaer, Joseph. The Fables of India; illus. by Randy Monk. Little, 1955. 176p. $3.95. (I)

Fables selected from the Jatakas, the Panchatantra, and other East Indian sources, retold in informal style suitable for storytelling.

1263 The Hare and the Tortoise; pictures by Paul Galdone. McGraw-Hill, 1962. unp. $2.50; lib. ed. $2.63 net. (P)

A picture-book version of the famous race interpreted with humorous illustrations.

1264 La Fontaine. The Lion and the Rat: A Fable; illus. by Brian Wildsmith. Watts, 1963. unp. lib. ed. $3.95 net. (P)

A retelling of the fable in which the grateful rat rescues the mighty lion, illustrated in glowing colors.

1265 La Fontaine. The North Wind and the Sun: A Fable; illus. by Brian Wildsmith. Watts, 1964. unp. lib. ed. $3.95 net. (P)

The fable about the contest between the wind and the sun to see which could make a man take off his coat is simply retold and imaginatively illustrated in brilliant colors.

1266 La Fontaine. The Rich Man and the Shoe-maker: A Fable; illus. by Brian Wildsmith. Watts, 1965. unp. lib. ed. $3.95 net. (P)

Another colorful picture-book presentation of a La Fontaine fable, this one about the shoemaker who decides it is better to be poor and happy than rich and miserable.

Folk and Fairy Tales

1267 Aardema, Verna. Tales from the Story Hat; illus. by Elton Fax; introd. by Augusta Baker. Coward-McCann, 1960. 72p. lib. ed. $3.29 net. (I)

Nine African tales of clever animals who outwit their adversaries are retold with zest and illustrated with humor. Helpful notes for the storyteller, a glossary, and a bibliography are included.

1268 Andersen, Hans Christian. The Emperor's New Clothes; designed and illus. by Virginia Lee Burton. Houghton, 1949. 43p. $3.50; lib. ed. $3.23 net. (P–I)

The familiar story of the vain emperor and his deceitful court is presented in a handsome picture book, delightfully illustrated with humorous pictures. Lends itself equally well to looking, listening, and discussion.

1269 Andersen, Hans Christian. It's Perfectly True, and Other Stories; tr. from the Danish by Paul Leyssac; illus. by Richard Bennett. Harcourt, 1938. 305p. $3.50. (I–U)

Twenty-eight Andersen tales, including some less-familiar ones, in an attractive edition.

1270 Andersen, Hans Christian. The Nightingale; tr. by Eva Le Gallienne; designed and illus. by Nancy Ekholm Burkert. Harper, 1965. 32p. $3.95; lib. ed. $3.99 net. (P–I)

Elaborately beautiful illustrations in jewel tones bring to life the Chinese background of this story-hour favorite.

1271 Andersen, Hans Christian. Seven Tales; tr. from the Danish by Eva Le Gallienne; pictures by Maurice Sendak. Harper, 1959. 127p. $3.95; lib. ed. $3.99 net. (I)

Translator and artist show understanding and appreciation of Andersen's poignant stories. Charming illustrations, large print, and open page invite independent reading.

1272 Andersen, Hans Christian. The Steadfast Tin Soldier; tr. by M. R. James; illus. by Marcia Brown. Scribner, 1953. unp. lib. ed. $3.12 net. (P–I)

The story of the faithful tin soldier and his love for the little dancing girl is presented in picture-book format.

1273 Andersen, Hans Christian. Thumbelina; tr. by R. P. Keigwin; illus. by Adrienne Adams. Scribner, 1961. unp. $3.50; lib. ed. $3.31 net. (P–I)

Tiny Thumbelina and her miniature world are shown in delicate watercolors.

1274 Andersen, Hans Christian. The Ugly Duckling; tr. by R. P. Keigwin; illus. by Adrienne Adams. Scribner, 1965. unp. $3.50; lib. ed. $3.31 net. (P–I)

Soft watercolor pictures interpret the story of the ugly duckling who became a beautiful swan.

1275 Andersen, Hans Christian. The Wild Swans; tr. by M. R. James; illus. by Marcia Brown. Scribner, 1963. 80p. $3.50; lib. ed. $3.31 net. (P–I)

Soft gray-and-pink illustrations reflect the sad and gentle mood of the princess who tries to free her brothers from a wicked enchantment.

1276 Arabian Nights. Arabian Nights; collected and ed. by Andrew Lang; illus. by

Vera Bock; with a foreword by Mary Gould Davis. McKay, 1946. 303p. $3.95; lib. ed. $3.59 net. (I–U)

Scheherazade's tales of Arabia and the East in an edition with readable type and beautiful illustrations.

1277 Asbjørnsen, Peter Christen, and **Moe, Jørgen E.** East of the Sun and West of the Moon, and Other Tales; illus. by Tom Vroman; afterword by Clifton Fadiman. Macmillan, 1963. 136p. $2.95; lib. ed. $3.24 net. (I)

Twelve of the best-loved folk and fairy tales of the Scandinavian countries retold by two folklorists and illustrated in color.

1278 Asbjørnsen, Peter Christen, and **Moe, Jørgen E.** The Three Billy Goats Gruff; pictures by Marcia Brown. Harcourt, 1957. unp. $3.25; lib. ed. $3.40 net. (P)

The hideous troll and the three billy goats are shown in imaginative pictures which capture all the drama of the old Norse tale.

1279 Baldwin, James. Favorite Tales of Long Ago; retold by James Baldwin; illus. by Lili Réthi. Dutton, 1955. 150p. $3. (I)

Very simple versions of familiar stories and some hard-to-find favorites, such as those about King Alfred and the cakes, Alexander and Bucephalus, King Canute, and Robert Bruce and the spider.

1280 Barbeau, Marius. The Golden Phoenix, and Other French-Canadian Fairy Tales; retold by Michael Hornyansky; illus. by Arthur Price. Walck, 1967. 144p. $3.50. (I)

Eight fairy tales, with background notes and stylized illustrations.

1281 Belpré, Pura. Perez and Martina: A Portorican Folk Tale; illus. by Carlos Sanchez. Warne, 1960. unp. $2.95. (P–I)

The romantic tale of the lovely Spanish cockroach who rejected all her suitors except the gallant mouse, Perez, pictured against an authentic Puerto Rican background.

1282 Belpré, Pura. The Tiger and the Rabbit, and Other Tales; illus. by Tomie de Paola. Lippincott, 1965. 127p. $2.95; lib. ed. $2.82 net. (I)

Excellent retellings of Puerto Rican folk tales reflecting the characteristics of the island and its people.

1283   Belting, Natalia. The Sun Is a Golden Earring; illus. by Bernarda Bryson. Holt, 1962. unp. $3.50; lib. ed. $3.27 net. (I)

Folk sayings from around the world about the sun, the wind, and other natural phenomena that primitive people have tried to explain are illustrated with delicate, imaginative pictures.

1284   Brenner, Anita. The Boy Who Could Do Anything & Other Mexican Folk Tales; retold by Anita Brenner; illus. by Jean Charlot. W. R. Scott, 1942. 134p. $3.95. (I)

Style and illustrations of these 25 tales evoke the flavor of Mexico and throw light on the customs and beliefs of the Mexican people.

1285   Brooke, L. Leslie. The Golden Goose Book: Being the Stories of *The Golden Goose, The Three Bears, The Three Little Pigs, Tom Thumb*; with numerous drawings in color and black and white. Warne, 1905. unp. $3.95. (P)

Open format and humorous illustrations make this especially suited for primary grades.

1286   Brown, Marcia. Backbone of the King: The Story of Paka'a and His Son Ku. Scribner, 1966. 180p. $4.50; lib. ed. $4.05 net. (I–U)

This story of a courageous Hawaiian boy who helped to restore his father to his rightful place in the King's court is told in distinguished style and illustrated with stunning linoleum prints by the author. Suggested for reading aloud at story time, or as background reading in the study of the fiftieth state. Includes a pronunciation guide.

1287   Brown, Marcia. Dick Whittington and His Cat; told and cut in linoleum by Marcia Brown. Scribner, 1950. unp. lib. ed. $3.12 net. (P)

The old story of Dick Whittington who, with the help of his cat, became Lord Mayor of London is simply told and effectively illustrated.

1288   Brown, Marcia. Stone Soup: An Old Tale; told and pictured by Marcia Brown. Scribner, 1947. unp. lib. ed. $4.12 net. (P)

Three French soldiers beguile the villagers into contributing their hidden vegetables to make "stone soup," thereby converting suspicion into friendliness. Witty drawings help to tell the story.

1289   Carpenter, Frances. Tales of a Chinese Grandmother; illus. by Malthé Hasselriis. Doubleday, 1937. 261p. $4.50. (I)

Chinese character and customs are revealed in these age-old tales.

1290   Chase, Richard, ed. Grandfather Tales; American-English Folk Tales sel. and ed. by Richard Chase; illus. by Berkeley Williams, Jr. Houghton, 1948. 239p. $5. (I)

Stories, rhymes, and songs gathered from Southern mountain people and retold in the vernacular of the region are brought together in a volume especially recommended for reading aloud and storytelling. Includes background notes, music, and humorous illustrations.

1291   Chase, Richard, ed. Jack Tales . . . ; set down from these sources and ed. by Richard Chase; with an appendix comp. by Herbert Halpert; and illus. by Berkeley Williams, Jr. Houghton, 1943. 201p. $3.75. (I)

Authentic folk tales of the Appalachian Mountains, collected from natives of the region and told with gusto and humor. The scholarly appendix gives sources and parallels.

1292   Colum, Padraic. The Stone of Victory, and Other Tales of Padraic Colum; foreword by Virginia Haviland; illus. by Judith Gwyn Brown. McGraw-Hill, 1966. 119p. $3.75; lib. ed. $3.31 net. (I)

Thirteen Irish tales chosen by the author from his earlier collections and effectively illustrated in black and white.

1293   Courlander, Harold, and **Herzog, George.** The Cow-Tail Switch and Other West African Stories; drawings by Madye Lee Chastain. Holt, 1947. 143p. lib. ed. $3.27 net. (I)

Folk tales of the Ashanti people and other West African tribes, rich in humor and native wisdom, told with verve and illustrated with atmospheric pictures.

1294   Courlander, Harold. The King's Drum, and Other African Stories; illus. by Enrico Arno. Harcourt, 1962. 125p. $3. (I)

These 29 tales come from all parts of Africa and reflect the beliefs and traditions of the people. Short, dramatic versions with excellent notes, useful for the storyteller.

1295 **Curry, Jane Louise.** Down from the Lonely Mountain: California Indian Tales; retold by Jane Louise Curry; illus. by Enrico Arno. Harcourt, 1965. 128p. $3. (I)

Creation myths and legends told in dramatic style and illustrated with amusing pictures.

1296 **Dalgliesh, Alice,** ed. The Enchanted Book; stories sel. by Alice Dalgliesh; illus. by Concetta Cacciolo. Scribner, 1947. 246p. $5. (I)

Spells and enchantments are freely cast in this collection of 21 tales from many countries.

1297 **De La Mare, Walter.** Tales Told Again; illus. by Alan Howard. Knopf, 1927. 207p. lib. ed. $3.39 net. (I)

Nineteen folk and fairy tales told in fine literary style, well suited to reading aloud and storytelling.

1298 **Elkin, Benjamin.** Six Foolish Fishermen; based on a folk tale in Ashton's *Chap-Books of the Eighteenth Century*, 1882; illus. by Katherine Evans. Childrens Pr., 1957. unp. $2.75. (P)

Six brothers go fishing and assume that one has drowned when each can count only five, forgetting himself. Colorful illustrations in a mystery whose solution primary children can anticipate.

1299 **Fenner, Phyllis R.,** comp. Giants and Witches and a Dragon or Two; illus. by Henry C. Pitz. Knopf, 1943. 208p. lib. ed. $3.49 net. (I)

Seventeen delightfully scary folktales, including the popular "Molly Whuppie" and "Baba Yaga." Especially appropriate for Halloween.

1300 **Fillmore, Parker.** The Shepherd's Nosegay: Stories from Finland and Czechoslovakia; retold by Parker Fillmore; ed. by Katherine Love; illus. by Enrico Arno. Harcourt, 1958. 192p. $3. (I)

Eighteen lively tales for reading and telling.

1301 **Fisher, Anne B.** Stories California Indians Told; illus. by Ruth Robbins. Parnassus, 1958. 109p. $3.25. (I)

Stories telling how the Great Spirit created California; how light, fire, and the mountains were made; and how the god Coyote helped the people overcome the hardship of their lives.

1302 **Frost, Frances,** ed. Legends of the United Nations. McGraw-Hill, 1943. 323p. $3.95; lib. ed. $3.31 net. (P–I)

Favorite stories from many nations.

1303 **Gilstrap, Robert,** and **Estabrook, Irene.** The Sultan's Fool, and Other North African Tales; illus. by Robert Greco. Holt, 1958. 95p. lib. ed. $3.27 net. (P–I)

Talking beasts, dishonest merchants, foolish husbands, and many other interesting characters appear in these varied stories.

1304 **Gray, J. E. B.** India's Tales and Legends; retold by J. E. B. Gray; illus. by Joan Kiddell-Monroe. Walck, 1961. 230p. $4.50. (U)

These tales, selected and adapted from India's folklore and literature, include Buddhist birth stories, animal fables, and selections from the Mahabharata and the Ramayana. For storytelling or independent reading by advanced pupils.

1305 **Grimm, Jacob.** The Bremen Town Musicians; from the Collection of the Brothers Grimm; Paul Galdone drew the pictures. McGraw-Hill, 1968. 32p. $3.75; lib. ed. $3.51 net. (P)

The old tale of the three abandoned animals who routed a band of robbers with their ear-splitting "music" is given additional drollery by Paul Galdone's robust pictures.

1306 **Grimm, Jacob.** Household Stories; from the Collection of the Brothers Grimm; tr. from the German by Lucy Crane, and done into pictures by Walter Crane. McGraw-Hill, 1966. 269p. $3.25; lib. ed. $3.01 net. (P–I)

The publishers state that this is an unabridged republication of the work first published by Macmillan in 1886. It includes 50 stories in a translation which preserves the flavor of the original and is illustrated by a famous nineteenth-century artist.

1307 **Grimm, Jacob.** More Tales from Grimm; freely tr. and illus. by Wanda Gág. Coward-McCann, 1947. 257p. $3.95. (I)

Thirty-one of the best-loved tales retold and illustrated with zest and humor.

1308 **Grimm, Jacob.** The Shoemaker and the Elves; by the Brothers Grimm; illus. by Adrienne Adams. Scribner, 1960. unp. $3.25; lib. ed. $3.12 net. (P)

The tale of the kind shoemaker and the elves who helped him is presented in a smooth translation interpreted by exceptionally lovely pictures.

1309 Grimm, Jacob. The Sleeping Beauty: A Story by the Brothers Grimm; with pictures by Felix Hoffmann. Harcourt, 1960. unp. $3.95. (P)

The well-loved story of the beautiful princess awakened from an enchanted sleep by a handsome prince has been made into a handsome picture book by a noted Swiss artist.

1310 Grimm, Jacob. Snow-White and Rose-Red; illus. by Adrienne Adams. Scribner, 1964. unp. $3.50; lib. ed. $3.31 net. (P)

Delicately colored illustrations interpret the action in this story of the two sisters and the enchanted prince.

1311 Grimm, Jacob. Tales from Grimm; freely tr. and illus. by Wanda Gág. Coward-McCann, 1936. 237p. $3.75. (I)

The simplicity and clarity of the telling and the humorous, flavorsome illustrations make these 16 familiar tales especially suitable for independent reading in the middle grades.

1312 Grimm, Jacob. The Wolf and the Seven Little Kids: A Story by the Brothers Grimm; with pictures by Felix Hoffmann. Harcourt, 1959. unp. $3.95. (P)

An old tale made into a beautiful picture book by a fine Swiss artist.

1313 Hardendorff, Jeanne B., comp. Tricky Peik, and Other Picture Tales; illus. by Tomie de Paola. Lippincott, 1967. 122p. $3.25; lib. ed. $3.11 net. (I)

Twenty tales selected from the "Picture Tales" series, now out of print, represent China, France, Holland, India, Italy, Mexico, Spain, and Scandinavia with humorous stories admirably suited to the story hour.

1314 Harman, Humphrey, comp. Tales Told near a Crocodile: Stories from Nyanza; illus. by George Ford. Viking, 1967. 185p. $3.95; lib. ed. $3.77 net. (I)

The compiler of these tales has recorded them just as he heard them from storytellers living near the shores of Lake Victoria in Kenya. The result is authentic African folklore reflecting the character and culture of the people, especially suited to reading aloud.

1315 Harris, Joel Chandler. Brer Rabbit: Stories from Uncle Remus; adapted by Margaret Wise Brown with the A. B. Frost pictures redrawn for reproduction by Victor Dowling. Harper, 1941. 132p. $2.95; lib. ed. $2.92 net. (P–I)

Twenty-four animal stories from *Nights with Uncle Remus* and *Uncle Remus: His Songs and Sayings,* with modified dialect and without the characters of Uncle Remus and the little boy.

1316 Haviland, Virginia. Favorite Fairy Tales Told in Czechoslovakia; retold by Virginia Haviland; illus. by Trina Schart Hyman. Little, 1966. 90p. $2.95; lib. ed. $2.97 net. (P–I)

1317 Haviland, Virginia. Favorite Fairy Tales Told in England; retold from Joseph Jacobs, by Virginia Haviland; illus. by Bettina. Little, 1959. 88p. $2.95; lib. ed. $2.97 net. (P–I)

1318 Haviland, Virginia. Favorite Fairy Tales Told in France; retold from Charles Perrault and other French storytellers, by Virginia Haviland; illus. by Roger Duvoisin. Little, 1959. 91p. $2.95; lib. ed. $2.97 net. (P–I)

1319 Haviland, Virginia. Favorite Fairy Tales Told in Germany; retold from the Brothers Grimm, by Virginia Haviland; illus. by Susanne Suba. Little, 1959. 83p. $2.95; lib. ed. $2.97 net. (P–I)

1320 Haviland, Virginia. Favorite Fairy Tales Told in Ireland; retold from Irish storytellers by Virginia Haviland; illus. by Arthur Marokvia. Little, 1961. 91p. $2.95; lib. ed. $2.97 net. (P–I)

1321 Haviland, Virginia. Favorite Fairy Tales Told in Italy; retold by Virginia Haviland; illus. by Evaline Ness. Little, 1965. 90p. $2.95; lib. ed. $2.97 net. (P–I)

1322 Haviland, Virginia. Favorite Fairy Tales Told in Japan; retold by Virginia Haviland; illus. by George Suyeoka. Little, 1967. 89p. $2.95; lib. ed. $2.97 net. (P–I)

1323 Haviland, Virginia. Favorite Fairy Tales Told in Norway; retold from Norse folklore by Virginia Haviland; illus. by Leonard Weisgard. Little, 1961. 88p. $2.95; lib. ed. $2.97 net. (P–I)

1324 **Haviland, Virginia.** Favorite Fairy Tales Told in Poland; retold by Virginia Haviland; illus. by Felix Hoffmann. Little, 1963. 90p. $2.95; lib. ed. $2.97 net. (P–I)

1325 **Haviland, Virginia.** Favorite Fairy Tales Told in Russia; retold from Russian storytellers by Virginia Haviland; illus. by Herbert Danska. Little, 1961. 86p. $2.95; lib. ed. $2.97 net. (P–I)

1326 **Haviland, Virginia.** Favorite Fairy Tales Told in Scotland; retold by Virginia Haviland; illus. by Adrienne Adams. Little, 1963. 92p. $2.95; lib. ed. $2.97 net. (P–I)

1327 **Haviland, Virginia.** Favorite Fairy Tales Told in Spain; retold by Virginia Haviland; illus. by Barbara Cooney. Little, 1963. 87p. $2.95; lib. ed. $2.97 net. (P–I)

1328 **Haviland, Virginia.** Favorite Fairy Tales Told in Sweden; retold by Virginia Haviland; illus. by Ronni Solbert. Little, 1966. 92p. $2.95; lib. ed. $2.97 net. (P–I)

This author has retold the best-loved fairy tales from many lands. The stories—five to eight to a volume—are drawn from authentic sources and retold in slightly simplified versions to suit the abilities of children in the middle grades, where interest in fairy tales is at its peak. The style is literate and faithful to the originals; the books are of medium size, beautifully designed and illustrated by well-known artists; and the print is clear and generously leaded.

1329 **Hitchcock, Patricia.** The King Who Rides a Tiger, and Other Folk Tales from Nepal; with illus. by Lillian Sader. Parnassus, 1966. 133p. $3.75. (I)

Sprightly tales of the Nepalese people, based on familiar folktale themes and exemplifying national characteristics and customs. Includes background notes and a glossary.

1330 **Hodges, Margaret.** The Wave; adapted from Lafcadio Hearn's *Gleanings in Buddhafields;* illus. by Blair Lent. Houghton, 1964. 45p. $3.50; lib. ed. $3.23 net. (I)

The story of the old Japanese who burned his mountain rice fields to warn the people of a coastal village that a tidal wave was approaching is interpreted in rhythmic pictures whose somber colors have dramatic impact.

1331 **Hoge, Dorothy.** The Black Heart of Indri; adapted by Dorothy Hoge; illus. by

Janina Domanska. Scribner, 1966. unp. $3.50; lib. ed. $3.31 net. (I)

Indri is a froglike creature who can be redeemed only by living nine days and nights in the presence of goodness. How his transformation is accomplished is told in this nineteenth-century Chinese folk tale, sensitively illustrated with full-page color pictures.

1332 **Ish-Kishor, Judith.** Tales from the Wise Men of Israel; with an introd. by Harry Golden and drawings by W. T. Mars. Lippincott, 1962. 219p. $4. (I–U)

A treasury of Jewish folk tales reflecting the history, character, and customs of the Jews and introducing some of their heroes.

1333 **Jacobs, Joseph,** comp. English Folk and Fairy Tales; illus. by John D. Batten. 3d ed. rev. Putnam, n.d. 277p. $2.95. (I)

Forty-one stories retold in colloquial, conversational style, with background notes for the storyteller. Stories which are strictly English are combined with English versions of tales from other lands.

1334 **Jacobs, Joseph.** Johnny-Cake; illus. by Emma L. Brock. Putnam, 1933. unp. lib. ed. $2.52 net. (P)

A simple, repetitive story illustrated with pictures reflecting the folk quality of the tale, perfect for storytelling in kindergarten and first grade.

1335 **Jagendorf, M. A.** Noodlehead Stories from around the World; with illus. by Shane Miller. Vanguard, 1957. 302p. $3.95. (I)

Fools and funny fellows go through their comic escapades in a collection of tales from many countries.

1336 **Jagendorf, M. A.** Upstate, Downstate: Folk Stories of the Middle Atlantic States; illus. by Howard Simon; introd. by Henry W. Shoemaker. Vanguard, 1949. 299p. $3.95. (I–U)

Tall tales from the Atlantic seaboard.

1337 **Jewett, Eleanore M.** Which Was Witch? Tales of Ghosts and Magic from Korea; illus. by Taro Yashima. Viking, 1953. 160p. $3.25; lib. ed. $3.19 net. (I)

The folk wisdom of the Korean people is inherent in these stories of the supernatural, especially appropriate for Halloween.

1338 **Kelsey, Alice Geer.** Once the Hodja;

illus. by Frank Dobias. Longmans, 1943. 170p. lib. ed. $3.94 net. (I)

Humorous stories of a Turkish character who gets himself into ridiculous situations through foolish behavior, but gets himself out by his wits. Recommended for reading aloud or storytelling.

1339 Kelsey, Alice Geer. Once the Mullah; Persian Folk Tales; retold by Alice Geer Kelsey; illus. by Kurt Werth. Longmans, 1954. 137p. $3.75. (I)

The Mullah, a combination priest-teacher-judge, is both wise and foolish, but, like the Hodja, he always manages to extricate himself from the predicaments created by his bad judgment. Tales and illustrations accentuate the comic situations in which the Mullah finds himself.

1340 Lang, Andrew, ed. The Green Fairy Book; collected and ed. by Andrew Lang; illus. by Dorothy Lake Gregory; with a foreword by Mary Gould Davis. Longmans, 1948. 355p. $3.95; lib. ed. $3.59 net. (I)

One of the famous "color" fairy books with 37 of the author's tales from many lands.

1341 Lang, Andrew, ed. The Red Fairy Book; collected and ed. by Andrew Lang; with a foreword by Mary Gould Davis. Longmans, 1948. 364p. $3.95; lib. ed. $3.59 net. (I)

Twenty-nine tales of princesses and peasant boys, fairies and witches, gathered from the world's best stories and retold by a master storyteller.

1342 Leach, Maria. How the People Sang the Mountains Up: How and Why Stories; illus. by Glen Rounds. Viking, 1967. 159p. $3.75; lib. ed. $3.56 net. (P–I)

Eighty brief stories from primitive cultures giving imaginative answers to such questions as: How was the sun made? Why do lions live in the forest? Why does the peacock look at his tail? Sources and background notes are given at the end.

1343 Leach, Maria. The Rainbow Book of American Folk Tales and Legends; illus. by Marc Simont. World, 1958. 318p. $5.95. (I–U)

A noted folklorist presents a wide selection of tales from all parts of the United States, along with notes on local customs, state flowers and birds, and folkways peculiar to different parts of the country.

1344 Lent, Blair. John Tabor's Ride; story and pictures by Blair Lent. Little, 1966. 48p. $3.75; lib. ed. $3.79 net. (P)

Humorous pictures with the tang of salt interpret this tall tale of a shipwrecked New Englander who rode home on the back of a whale.

1345 Manning-Sanders, Ruth. A Book of Dragons; drawings by Robin Jacques. Dutton, 1965. 128p. $3.50; lib. ed. $3.40 net. (I)

Dragons, famous and infamous, parade through these 14 well-told and humorously illustrated stories.

1346 Mehdevi, Anne Sinclair. Persian Folk and Fairy Tales; retold by Anne Sinclair Mehdevi; illus. by Paul E. Kennedy. Knopf, 1965. 117p. $3.50; lib. ed. $3.39 net. (I)

Tales told to the author by a Persian nurse are here retold with a true folk flavor and illustrated with drawings suggestive of Persian art.

1347 Nic Leodhas, Sorche. All in the Morning Early; illus. by Evaline Ness. Holt, 1963. unp. $3.50; lib. ed. $3.27 net. (P)

A picture-book version of an old Scottish tale about a miller's adventures on the way to the mill. The story, part in prose and part in verse, and the colored illustrations are in true folk style.

1348 Nic Leodhas, Sorche. Always Room for One More; illus. by Nonny Hogrogian. Holt, 1965. unp. $3; lib. ed. $2.96 net. (P)

A picture book based on an old Scottish folk song about hospitable Lachie Mac-Lachlan, who invited in so many guests that his little house finally burst. Rhymed text, humorous illustrations touched with heather lavender, a glossary of Scottish words, and music for the tune are combined into an effective whole.

1349 Nic Leodhas, Sorche. Gaelic Ghosts; illus. by Nonny Hogrogian. Holt, 1964. 110p. $3.50; lib. ed. $3.27 net. (I–U)

Scottish ghosts, both friendly and fearsome, are the principal characters in this collection of ten tales, ideal for Halloween or campfire telling. Handsome woodcuts carry out the folk quality of the stories.

1350 Nic Leodhas, Sorche. Ghosts Go Haunting; illus. by Nonny Hogrogian.

Holt, 1965. 128p. $3.75; lib. ed. $3.45 net. (I–U)

More Scottish ghost tales, based on stories the author heard at clan outings, made more humorous and eerie by harmonious woodcuts.

1351 Nic Leodhas, Sorche. Heather and Broom: Tales of the Scottish Highlands; illus. by Consuelo Joerns. Holt, 1960. 128p. lib. ed. $3.07 net. (I–U)

Eight tales told by wandering Scottish storytellers, effectively retold, with notes on the special qualities of the Highland folk tale.

1352 Old Woman and Her Pig; pictures by Paul Galdone. McGraw-Hill, 1960. 32p. $2.50; lib. ed. $2.63 net. (P)

The popular cumulative tale about the old woman's difficulties in getting her pig to market is enlivened with droll action pictures on every page.

1353 Perrault, Charles. Cinderella; or, The Little Glass Slipper; with pictures by Marcia Brown. Scribner, 1954. unp. $3.25; lib. ed. $3.12 net. (P–I)

The old fairy tale is interpreted in delicately colored pictures which create a fairyland world and suggest the elegance of the French court. A beautiful picture book for use at the story hour or for independent reading.

1354 Perrault, Charles. Complete Fairy Tales; tr. from the French by A. E. Johnson and others; with illus. by W. Heath Robinson. Dodd, 1961. 183p. $3.75. (I)

Fourteen tales, including "Blue Beard," "Little Red Riding Hood," and "Tom Thumb," by Perrault and other French storytellers.

1355 Perrault, Charles. Puss in Boots; a free translation from the French; with pictures by Marcia Brown. Scribner, 1952. unp. lib. ed. $3.12 net. (P)

All the wit, humor, and drama of the fairy tale are captured in the beautiful colored illustrations in this handsome picture book.

1356 Price, Christine. The Valiant Chattee-Maker: A Folktale of India Retold. Warne, [1965]. unp. $2.95. (P)

A poor potter becomes a hero by capturing a tiger one dark night, thinking it is his lost donkey.

1357 Quigley, Lillian. The Blind Men and the Elephant: An Old Tale from the Land of India; illus. by Janice Holland. Scribner, 1959. unp. lib. ed. $3.31 net. (P)

Stylized pictures with an Oriental flavor interpret this simple retelling of a familiar folktale which primary pupils will enjoy dramatizing.

1358 Rackham, Arthur, comp. Arthur Rackham Fairy Book: A Book of Old Favorites with New Illustrations. Lippincott, 1950. 286p. $4.75. (P–I)

Twenty-three tales from Andersen, Grimm, Perrault, and others, notable for subtly beautiful illustrations.

1359 Robbins, Ruth. Baboushka and the Three Kings; illus. by Nicolas Sidjakov; adapted from a Russian folk tale. Parnassus. 1960. unp. $2.95. (P–I)

A reverent retelling of the story of Baboushka who was too busy to go with the three kings to seek the Christ Child, and who spent the rest of her life in her own search. A beautifully designed book, illustrated with richly colored, stylized pictures. Words and music of the old folk song are given at the back of the book.

1360 Rushmore, Helen. The Dancing Horses of Acoma, and Other Acoma Indian Stories; by Helen Rushmore with Wolf Robe Hunt. World, 1963. 163p. $4.50; lib. ed. $4.28 net. (I–U)

These 12 legends, recorded in collaboration with an Acoma chief, reflect the traditions and beliefs of the Pueblo Indians.

1361 Sawyer, Ruth. Journey Cake, Ho! Illus. by Robert McCloskey. Viking, 1953. 45p. $3.25; lib. ed. $3.19 net. (P)

An American version of *The Johnnycake,* in which a journey cake leads a farm boy a merry chase. Big, humorous pictures vitalize this new version of an old story.

1362 Sherlock, Philip M. Anansi, the Spider Man: Jamaican Folk Tales; told by Philip M. Sherlock; illus. by Marcia Brown. Crowell, 1954. 112p. $3.75. (I)

Fifteen West Indian tales centering around Anansi, who could change himself into a spider to escape punishment for his mischief-making.

1363 Siddiqui, Ashraf, and **Lerch, Marilyn.** Toontoony Pie, and Other Tales of

Pakistan; illus. by Jan Fairservis. World, 1961. 157p. $3.50. (P–I)

The marvelous toontoony bird, the clever jackal, and other unusual animal characters appear in these tales of magic and Oriental lore.

1364   **Singer, Isaac B.** Zlateh the Goat, and Other Stories; pictures by Maurice Sendak; tr. from the Yiddish by the author and Elizabeth Shub. Harper, 1966. 90p. $4.50; lib. ed. $4.11 net. (I–U)

Seven tales drawn from middle-European Jewish village life, with illustrations which extend the humor and subtlety of the situations.

1365   **Small, Ernest.** Baba Yaga; illus. by Blair Lent. Houghton, 1966. 48p. $3.50; lib. ed. $3.23 net. (P)

Stories of Baba Yaga, a traditional witch in Russian folklore, and her little house on chicken legs are illustrated with pictures wonderfully evocative of the haunted forest.

1366   **Story of the Three Bears:** A Picture Book by William Stobbs. McGraw-Hill, 1965. 32p. $2.75; lib. ed. $2.84 net. (P)

Engaging pictures in red, green, and brown are the special feature of this simple retelling of a favorite tale.

1367   **Story of the Three Little Pigs:** A Picture Book by William Stobbs. McGraw-Hill, 1963. unp. $2.75; lib. ed. $2.84 net. (P)

Stout little pigs outrace the wolf in this picture book for the very youngest.

1368   **Sturton, Hugh.** Zomo, the Rabbit; drawings by Peter Warner. Atheneum, 1966. 128p. $3.95; lib. ed. $3.81 net. (I)

Tales told by Nigerian storytellers about the cunning and unscrupulous Zomo, the African ancestor of the American Br'er Rabbit.

1369   **Tashjian, Virginia A.** Once There Was and Was Not: Armenian Tales Retold by Virginia Tashjian; based on stories by H. Toumanian; illus. by Nonny Hogogrian. Little, 1966. 83p. $3.50; lib. ed. $3.27 net. (P–I)

These seven tales, recreated by an author and an illustrator of Armenian extraction, reveal the lore and character of the common people. Interesting variants of such familiar tales as "The Brave Little Tailor" and "Mighty Mikko" are included.

1370   **Thompson, Vivian L.** Hawaiian Myths of Earth, Sea, and Sky; illus. by Leonard Weisgard. Holiday, 1966. 83p. $4.50. (I)

Twelve stories about the gods and goddesses of Hawaii and the beliefs of the people about the creation of the earth, the stars, volcanoes, and other phenomena of nature. Beautiful illustrations in island colors add atmosphere and background scenes. Useful in the study of Hawaii.

1371   **Tom Tit Tot.** Tom Tit Tot: An English Folk Tale; illus. by Evaline Ness. Scribner, 1965. unp. $3.25; lib. ed. $3.12 net. (P)

This lively variant of the tale of Rumpelstiltskin, the horrid little creature who sought to outwit a stupid country girl, is handsomely illustrated in humorous and witty woodcuts.

1372   **Tresselt, Alvin.** The Mitten: An Old Ukrainian Folktale; retold by Alvin Tresselt; illus. by Yaroslava; adapted from the version by E. Rachev. Lothrop, 1964. unp. $2.95; lib. ed. $2.84 net. (P)

On the coldest day of the year a little Ukrainian boy loses his fur-lined mitten, which becomes so overcrowded with animals seeking a snug shelter that it finally bursts. Brightly colored pictures show the animals dressed in typical Ukrainian costumes.

1373   **Uchida, Yoshiko.** The Sea of Gold, and Other Tales from Japan; adapted by Yoshiko Uchida; illus. by Marianne Yamaguchi. Scribner, 1965. 136p. $3.50; lib. ed. $3.31 net. (I–U)

Distinctively Japanese tales, many with universal themes, are skillfully retold and effectively illustrated.

1374   **Wiesner, William.** Joco and the Fishbone: An Arabian Nights Tale; retold and illus. by William Wiesner. Viking, 1966. 46p. $3.50; lib. ed. $3.37 net. (P–I)

When a poor hunchback of Baghdad gets a fishbone in his throat and falls unconscious, he is the cause of much amusing commotion. A flavorful and funny picture book.

1375   **Zemach, Margot.** The Three Sillies: A Folk Tale; illus. by Margot Zemach. Holt, 1963. unp. $2.95; lib. ed. $3.07 net. (P)

The ridiculous story of the stupid fellow

who would not marry his sweetheart until he found three people sillier than the girl and her parents makes a hilarious picture book, with all the silliness accented in the illustrations.

Mother Goose and Nursery Rhymes

1376 Lines, Kathleen, comp. Lavender's Blue: A Book of Nursery Rhymes; pictured by Harold Jones. Watts, 1954. 180p. $7.95. (P)

A discriminating collection of English nursery rhymes illustrated with expressive pictures in color.

1377 Mother Goose. Brian Wildsmith's Mother Goose: A Collection of Nursery Rhymes. Watts, 1965. 80p. $4.95; lib. ed. $4.46 net. (P)

Illustrations in brilliant watercolor distinguish this collection of 86 familiar rhymes.

1378 Mother Goose. The House That Jack Built; pictures by Paul Galdone. McGraw-Hill, 1961. 32p. $2.75; lib. ed. $2.84 net. (P)

Humorous pictures interpret this cumulative action story in verse.

1379 Mother Goose. Marguerite de Angeli's Book of Nursery and Mother Goose Rhymes. Doubleday, 1954. 192p. $5.95. (P)

Nearly 400 familiar and less-well-known rhymes in an oversized book. Exceptionally fine illustrations, many in color.

1380 Mother Goose. Mother Goose; 77 verses, with pictures by Tasha Tudor. Walck, 1944. 87p. $3.95. (P)

A small book with delicate, old-fashioned illustrations, especially suited for handling by young children.

1381 Mother Goose. Mother Goose and Nursery Rhymes; wood engravings by Philip Reid. Atheneum, 1963. 57p. $4.95; lib. ed. $4.57 net. (P)

Precisely drawn six-color illustrations with an eighteenth-century flavor interpret the 66 rhymes in this handsomely designed book.

1382 Mother Goose. The Mother Goose Treasury; illus. by Raymond Briggs. Cow-

ard-McCann, 1966. 217p. $8.95; lib. ed. $6.87 net. (P)

Iona and Peter Opie, eminent folklorists, selected the 408 verses in this collection. The artist's full-color illustrations are suitably robust and humorous.

1383 Mother Goose. Old Mother Hubbard and Her Dog; pictures by Paul Galdone. McGraw-Hill, 1960. 32p. $2.95; lib. ed. $2.96 net. (P)

A familiar nursery rhyme enlivened by droll illustrations. Excellent for audience-participation story hour with young children.

1384 Mother Goose. A Pocket Full of Posies: A Merry Mother Goose. Doubleday, 1961. 30p. $2.50. (P)

A selection of 77 rhymes from Marguerite de Angeli's *Book of Nursery and Mother Goose Rhymes,* with the original illustrations.

1385 Mother Goose. The Real Mother Goose; with introd. by May Hill Arbuthnot; illus. by Blanche Fisher Wright. Rand McNally, 1965. 128p. lib. ed. $3.95 net. (P)

A fiftieth-anniversary edition of a favorite collection of more than 300 rhymes, illustrated with clear, simple pictures in color.

1386 Mother Goose. Ring o' Roses: A Nursery Rhyme Picture Book; with numerous drawings in colour and black-and-white by L. Leslie Brooke. Warne, n.d. unp. $3.95. (P)

Open pages and gay pictures by a noted nineteenth-century English artist make this an excellent selection for use with young children.

1387 Mother Goose. The Tall Book of Mother Goose; pictured by Feodor Rojankovsky. Harper, 1942. 120p. $1.95; lib. ed. $2.39 net. (P)

The unusual shape of this book and its humorous illustrations with a modern touch give the book great appeal for children ready to enjoy it independently.

1388 Petersham, Maud, and **Petersham, Miska,** comps. The Rooster Crows: A Book of American Rhymes and Jingles. Macmillan, 1945. unp. $3.95; lib. ed. $3.74 net. (P)

Counting-out rhymes, jump-rope jingles, and other verses which children have chanted for generations are brought together and illustrated with humorous colored pictures.

1389 **Potter, Charles Francis,** comp. Tongue Tanglers; illus. by William Wiesner. World, 1962. 42p. $2.95; lib. ed. $2.88 net. (P)

Hard-to-say rhymes, old and new, for word lovers or just for fun.

1390 **Wood, Ray,** comp. The American Mother Goose; with a foreword by John A. Lomax; illus. by Ed Hargis. Lippincott, 1940. 109p. $4.25; lib. ed. $3.99 net. (P–I)

These homespun American folk rhymes, illustrated with cartoon-like pictures, are filled with backwoods humor.

Biography

Collective Biography

Arranged alphabetically by author.

1391 **American Heritage.** Captains of Industry; by the eds. of American Heritage, The Magazine of History. Author, Bernard A. Weisberger; consultant, Alan Nevins. American Heritage, 1966. American Heritage Junior Library, distributed by Harper. 153p. $4.95; lib. ed. $4.79 net. (I–U)

Brief biographies of ten industrial giants of the late nineteenth and early twentieth centuries, emphasizing their personalities and accomplishments and touching lightly on their personal lives. Excellent contemporary photographs and prints and a list for further reading.

1392 **Angell, Pauline K.** To the Top of the World: The Story of Peary and Henson; illus. with portraits and maps. Rand McNally, 1964. 288p. $4.50. (U)

A dual biography of Robert Peary and his little-known Negro companion, Matthew Henson, centering on the contribution which each of the two widely different men made to Arctic exploration.

1393 **Asimov, Isaac.** Breakthroughs in Science; illus. by Karoly and Szanto. Houghton, 1959. 197p. $4. (U)

The work of pioneers in the biological and physical sciences, from Archimedes to Goddard, who made important discoveries upon which modern science is based, is discussed in 26 lively essays.

1394 **Atkinson, Margaret F.,** and **Hillman,**

May. Dancers of the Ballet: Biographies. Knopf, 1955. 174p. lib. ed. $3.99 net. (U)

The personalities, training, and careers of 40 of the principal ballerinas of the United States, England, and France. Glossary of ballet terms.

1395 **Bailey, Bernadine.** Famous Latin-American Liberators; illus. by Gerald McCann. Dodd, 1960. 158p. $3.50. (I–U)

The inspiring and dramatic lives of these ten heroes provide a good introduction to Latin-American history.

1396 **Bailey, Carolyn Sherwin.** Children of the Handcrafts; with lithographs by Grace Paull. Viking, 1935. 192p. lib. ed. $3.37 net. (I–U)

Seventeen young people of early America, including Paul Revere, Duncan Phyfe, and Henry Thoreau, who became master craftsmen are the subjects of a lively book, useful in social studies and art classes.

1397 **Bakeless, Katherine Little.** Story-Lives of American Composers. rev. ed. Lippincott, 1962. 291p. $4.75. (I–U)

Nineteen brief biographies, recommended for independent reading or for use in music classes.

1398 **Bakeless, Katherine Little.** Story-Lives of Great Composers. rev. ed. Lippincott, 1962. 265p. $4.75. (I–U)

Similar to *Story-Lives of American Composers,* above, but limited to nineteenth-century musicians.

1399 **Beard, Annie E. S.** Our Foreign-born Citizens. 6th ed. Crowell, 1968. 276p. $4.50. (I–U)

Short biographies of distinguished Americans of foreign extraction who have made important contributions to our national life.

1400 Beard, Charles A. Charles A. Beard's The Presidents in American History; brought forward since 1948 by William Beard. rev. ed. Messner, 1961. 182p. $3.50; lib. ed. $3.34 net. (U)

An eminent historian assesses the lives and accomplishments of United States Presidents from Washington to Kennedy.

1401 Benét, Laura. Famous Poets for Young People. Dodd, 1964. 160p. $3.50. (I–U)

Brief biographies and samplings of the poetry of 24 British and American poets of the nineteenth and twentieth centuries, chosen for special appeal to young people. Indexed.

1402 Bixby, William. Great Experimenters. McKay, 1964. 182p. $4.25. (U)

The lives and scientific achievements of nine scientists and inventors are discussed in clear, readable essays.

1403 Bolton, Sarah K. Famous Men of Science. 4th ed. rev. by Barbara Lovett Cline. Crowell, 1960. 326p. $3.95. (I–U)

Accurate, interesting sketches of 22 scientists, including Enrico Fermi and Jonas Salk, who have made major contributions to the advancement of science.

1404 Bontemps, Arna. Famous Negro Athletes; illus. with photos. Dodd, 1964. 155p. $3.50. (I–U)

Brief biographical sketches of Negroes outstanding in boxing, basketball, track, baseball, football, and tennis.

1405 Burch, Gladys. Modern Composers for Young People. Dodd, 1941. 207p. $3.50. (I–U)

Style, rather than period, classifies the nineteenth- and twentieth-century composers introduced in these brief biographies.

1406 Burlingame, Roger. Inventors behind the Inventor; illus. with photos. Harcourt, 1947. 211p. $3.75. (I–U)

Stories of unheralded scientists who laid the foundation for the work of popularly acclaimed inventors.

1407 Burlingame, Roger. Scientists behind the Inventors. Harcourt, 1960. 192p. $3.25. (I–U)

The importance of pure scientific research is emphasized in sketches of seven men, from Joseph Black to Einstein, whose discoveries changed the world.

1408 Carr, Albert. Men of Power: A Book of Dictators; illus. by Marc Simont. rev. ed. Viking, 1956. 298p. $4. (U)

The meaning and methods of totalitarianism are explored through the lives of 12 dictators from the sixteenth century to the present.

1409 Chandler, Anna Curtis. Story-Lives of Master Artists; with 23 reproductions from paintings. rev. ed. Lippincott, 1953. 255p. $4.75. (I–U)

Biographies of 21 artists, from Giotto to Winslow Homer.

1410 Chandler, Caroline A. Famous Men of Medicine. Dodd, 1950. 140p. $3.50. (I–U)

Interesting biographical sketches of physicians, from ancient times to the present, whose achievements blazed the path of medical progress.

1411 Chase, Alice Elizabeth. Famous Artists of the Past; with 177 reproductions, 44 in full color. Platt & Munk, 1964. 120p. $6.95. (I–U)

A museum lecturer discusses the lives and works of 26 master artists, illustrating each biography with a group of well-reproduced examples of the artist's work. An index of artists, pictures, and owners is provided.

1412 Coolidge, Olivia E. Lives of Famous Romans; illus. with photos. Houghton, 1965. 248p. $3.50. (U)

Profiles of 12 famous Romans from about 86 B.C. to the death of Constantine.

1413 Daugherty, Sonia. Ten Brave Men: Makers of the American Way . . . with drawings by James Daugherty. Lippincott, 1951. 152p. $3.95. (I–U)

Brief biographies of ten Americans whose courageous actions in times of crisis helped to establish the principles upon which the nation is founded. Excellent background reading for American history.

1414 Daugherty, Sonia. Ten Brave Women . . . with drawings by James Daugherty. Lippincott, 1953. 147p. $3.95. (I–U)

Significant incidents in the lives of ten

women, from Anne Hutchinson to Eleanor Roosevelt, highlighting their influence on the development of American ideals. The brief, dramatic stories are well suited to reading aloud.

1415 **Epstein, Sam,** and **Epstein, Beryl.** Baseball Hall of Fame: Stories of Champions; illus. by Ken Wagner. Garrard, 1965. 96p. $2.32. (I–U)
Profiles of the first five players to be named to the Baseball Hall of Fame. Subject, format, and reading level make this useful for older reluctant or retarded readers. (R3–4)

1416 **Evans, I. O.** Inventors of the World; illus. by Drake Brookshaw. Warne, 1962. 191p. $2.95. (U)
The lives and work of 13 inventors, from Archimedes to the age of radar and jet propulsion, are briefly sketched.

1417 **Fanning, Leonard M.** Fathers of Industries; illus. by Albert Orbaan. Lippincott, 1962. 256p. $4.75. (I–U)
Sketched here are the lives of 25 men whose ideas changed the world, including James Watt, Eli Whitney, Robert Fulton, Cyrus McCormick, and Willis Carrier.

1418 **Farjeon, Eleanor.** Mighty Men; with an introd. by C. C. Barnes; pictures by Hugh Chesterman. Appleton, 1954. 213p. $2.60. (I)
A book of heroes briefly covering the lives of such mighty men as Achilles, Julius Caesar, Beowulf, and William the Conqueror.

1419 **Fleming, Alice.** Doctors in Petticoats. Lippincott, 1964. 159p. $3.50. (I–U)
Semifictionalized stories of ten women who helped to break the barrier against women in medicine or who made important contributions in their field.

1420 **Fleming, Alice.** Great Women Teachers. Lippincott, 1965. 157p. $3.50. (I–U)
Ten pioneer teachers in all fields of education are the subjects of lively, conversational sketches.

1421 **Freedgood, Lillian.** Great Artists of America. Crowell, 1963. 253p. $5.95. (U)
A concise history of American painting presented through the lives of 15 representative painters, from Gilbert Stuart to Jackson Pollock. One example of the work of each is shown in well-reproduced color.

1422 **Halacy, D. S.** They Gave Their Names to Science. Putnam, 1967. 160p. lib. ed. $3.29 net. (U)
Ten short biographies of scientists whose names are more familiar than their lives—for example, Hans Geiger.

1423 **Heuman, William.** Famous American Athletes. Dodd, 1963. 152p. $3.50. (I–U)
Sixteen outstanding professional athletes in various fields are informally sketched in brief, easily read biographies, especially recommended for older boys. Illustrated with photographs.

1424 **Higdon, Hal.** Heroes of the Olympics; illus. by Paul Frame. Prentice-Hall, 1965. 63p. $3.50. (I)
Nurmi, Didrickson, and Owens are among the ten Olympic gold-medal winners sketched in this book.

1425 **Hughes, Langston.** Famous American Negroes. Dodd, 1954. 147p. $3.50. (I–U)
The lives of 17 Negroes, some little known, who have distinguished themselves in American life are briefly sketched by a Negro author. Photographs and index.

1426 **Hughes, Langston.** Famous Negro Heroes of America; illus. by Gerald McCann. Dodd, 1958. 202p. $3.50. (I–U)
Sixteen American Negro patriots—explorers, slave leaders, war heroes, etc.—are presented in brief, interesting biographies.

1427 **Hume, Ruth Fox.** Great Men of Medicine; illus. by Robert Frankenberg. Random, 1961. 192p. $2.50; lib. ed. $2.48 net. (I–U)
Dramatic stories of ten men who have pioneered in the conquest of disease and pain. Bibliography.

1428 **Kaula, Edna M.** Leaders of the New Africa; illus. by the author. World, 1965. 180p. 3.75; lib. ed. $3.61 net. (I–U)
Animated accounts of the lives and accomplishments of prominent twentieth-century African leaders, emphasizing the ideals, issues, and problems of the emerging nations. A chart giving date of independence and head of each state and a pronunciation guide to names are useful features.

1429 Kennedy, John F. Profiles in Courage. Harper, 1964. 287p. $5; lib. ed. $4.43 net. (U)

A memorial edition with a foreword by Robert F. Kennedy. Vignettes of crises in American public life and the men who faced them at great risk to themselves.

1430 Lawson, Robert. They Were Strong and Good; written and illus. by Robert Lawson. Viking, 1940. unp. 3.50; lib. ed. $3.37 net. (I)

The author relates the stories of his parents and his four grandparents with pride, not because they were great and famous, but because they were strong and good. American ideals are inherent in the story and the superb drawings.

1431 McNeer, May, and **Ward, Lynd.** Armed with Courage. Abingdon, 1957. 112p. $2.50. (I)

Biographies of seven courageous men and women who dedicated their lives to the service of mankind: Florence Nightingale, Father Damien, George Washington Carver, Jane Addams, Wilfred Grenfell, Mahatma Gandhi, and Albert Schweitzer.

1432 McNeer, May. Give Me Freedom; drawings by Lynd Ward. Abingdon, 1964. 128p. $3. (I–U)

Stories of seven men and women who stood up for freedom; illustrated with dramatic black-and-white drawings.

1433 National Geographic Society. Our Country's Presidents; by Frank Friedel; introd. by Lyndon B. Johnson; foreword by Melville Bell Grosvenor. National Geographic Soc., 1966. 248p. $4.25. (U)

A profusely illustrated survey of the lives and administrations of all United States Presidents.

1434 Petersham, Maud, and **Petersham, Miska.** Story of the Presidents of the United States of America. rev. ed. Macmillan, 1965. 80p. $3.95; lib. ed. $3.94 net. (P–I)

Facts about the Presidents, from Washington to Lyndon Johnson, entertainingly presented and colorfully illustrated.

1435 Plutarch. Ten Famous Lives; the Dryden translation rev. by Arthur Hugh Clough; further rev. and ed. for young readers and with an introd. by Charles Alexander Robinson, Jr. Dutton, 1962. 170p. $3.75. (U)

Skillful editing retains Plutarch's style and omits only matter not likely to interest young people. An excellent introduction to the personalities and civilization of Greece and Rome.

1436 Poole, Lynn, and **Poole, Gray.** Scientists Who Work with Astronauts; with a foreword by Hugh L. Dryden. Dodd, 1964. 172p. $3.50. (I–U)

The work of the National Aeronautics and Space Administration is described through the contributions of its key scientists and engineers. The importance of coordinated research in many fields is stressed, and possible future applications are suggested.

1437 Posell, Elsa Z. American Composers. Houghton, 1963. 183p. $3.50. (I–U)

Emphasis is on the lives rather than on the music of these 29 composers. Portraits.

1438 Richardson, Ben. Great American Negroes; rev. by William A. Fahey; illus. by Robert Hallock. Crowell, 1956. 339p. $4.50. (I–U)

Short chapters about the early lives of twentieth-century Negroes who have made important contributions in music, entertainment, sports, politics, civil rights, and other fields.

1439 Riedman, Sarah R. Shots without Guns: The Story of Vaccination; illus. with 45 photos. Rand McNally, 1960. 232p. $4.50. (I–U)

Biographical information about the men who developed vaccines for the prevention of disease. Useful for general reading and in science and health classes.

1440 Rollins, Charlemae Hill. They Showed the Way: Forty American Negro Leaders. Crowell, 1964. 165p. $3. (I–U)

Brief biographical sketches about Negroes who have been the first to achieve success in their field.

1441 Ross, Nancy Wilson. Heroines of the Early West; illus. by Paul Galdone. Random, 1960. 232p. $2.50; lib. ed. $2.48 net. (I)

The hardships and dangers endured by such pioneer women as Sacajawea, Narcissa Whitman, and Sister Mary Loyola are vividly narrated in an account based on diaries, letters, and other contemporary sources.

1442　**Simon, Charlie May.** Art in the New Land: Stories of Some American Artists and Their Work; decorations by James McDonald, and 45 plates. Dutton, 1945. 207p. $5.50. (U)

Beginning with a chapter on unknown artists and ending with one on new artists, the selection includes American painters from Colonial days to the present. A well-written and well-illustrated book, useful in social studies and in art classes.

1443　**Stratton, Madeline Robinson.** Negroes Who Helped Build America; preface by Joseph E. Penn. Ginn, 1965. 165p. $3. (I–U)

Fourteen Negroes who have made important contributions in various fields are briefly sketched, along with chapters summarizing the work of Negroes in science, education, the fine arts, and other areas. Illustrated with photographs and drawings. Includes a list for further reading.

1444　**Sullivan, Navin.** Pioneer Astronomers; drawings by Eric Fraser. Atheneum, 1964. 156p. $3.75. (I–U)

The history of astronomy told through the lives and work of 18 scientists outstanding in the field. Includes information about latest advances in astronomy and a reading list and index-glossary.

1445　**Sullivan, Navin.** Pioneer Germ Fighters; illus. by Eric Fraser. Atheneum, 1962. 164p. $3.75. (I–U)

Brief biographies of scientists whose work in bacteriology has contributed to the control of disease. Shows how present-day scientists build upon earlier discoveries.

1446　**U.S. Congress. Senate. Committee on Aeronautical and Space Sciences.** United States Astronauts. Govt. Print. Off., 1963. 79p. $1.60. (I–U)

Brief information and photographs of astronauts selected from 1959 to 1963.

1447　**Webb, Robert N.** Leaders of Our Time; Series 1. Watts, 1964. 150p. $3.95. (U)

Brief biographies and portraits of 12 men who have influenced recent world history: Adenauer, Ben-Gurion, Castro, De Gaulle, John F. Kennedy, Khrushchev, Macmillan, Mao Tse-Tung, Nasser, Nehru, Nkrumah, U Thant.

1448　**Webb, Robert N.** Leaders of Our Time; Series 2. Watts, 1965. 152p. $3.95. (U)

Adds 13 sketches of world leaders to Series 1, above: Queen Elizabeth II, Ludwig Erhard, Emperor Hirohito, Lyndon Baines Johnson, Martin Luther King, Robert Gordon Menzies, Pope Paul VI, Hyman G. Rickover, Sargent Shriver, Achmed Sukarno, Josip Broz Tito, Earl Warren, Harold Wilson.

1449　**Webb, Robert N.** Leaders of Our Time; Series 3. Watts, 1966. 116p. $3.95. (U)

Brings Series 1 and 2 up to date with biographies of Leonid Brezhnev, Arthur Goldberg, Hubert Humphrey, Robert F. Kennedy, Mohammed Ayub Khan, Aleksei Kosygin, John Lindsay, Thurgood Marshall, Robert McNamara, Lester Pearson, Walter Reuther, George Romney.

Individual Biography

Arranged alphabetically by biographee.

JOHN QUINCY ADAMS

1450　**Lomask, Milton.** John Quincy Adams: Son of the American Revolution. Farrar, 1965. 147p. $2.95. (U)

A well-written, interesting picture of the President, the important people around him, and the times in which they lived.

JANE ADDAMS

1451　**Judson, Clara Ingram.** City Neighbor: The Story of Jane Addams; illus. by Ralph Ray. Scribner, 1951. 130p. lib. ed. $2.97 net. (I–U)

The story of the founder of Hull House and her work among the immigrants of Chicago is based on authentic sources, though told in fiction form.

LOUIS AGASSIZ

1452　**Peare, Catherine Owens.** A Scientist of Two Worlds. Lippincott, 1958. 188p. $3.50. (U)

Louis Agassiz, the Swiss-born naturalist who proposed the Ice Age theory, is the subject of a readable biography emphasizing Agassiz' American career as a naturalist.

LOUISA MAY ALCOTT

1453 **Meigs, Cornelia Lynde.** Invincible Louisa: The Story of the Author of Little Women. Alcott centennial ed. With a new introd. by the author. illus. Little, 1968. 195p. $4.95. (U)

The intellectual world of nineteenth-century New England forms the background for this biography of the author of *Little Women*. New format, new jacket, and a new introduction by the author.

1454 **Papashvily, Helen Waite.** Louisa May Alcott; illus. by Bea Holmes. Houghton, 1965. 183p. $2.95. (I)

Personal anecdotes, quotations, and fictionalized dialogue enliven this brief, attractive picture of Louisa May Alcott and her family.

ALEXANDER THE GREAT

1455 **Gunther, John.** Alexander the Great; illus. by Isa Barnett. Random, 1953. 183p. $2.50; lib. ed. $2.48 net. (I–U)

An introduction to the adventurous life of the first world conqueror, whose exploits have great appeal for boys. Exciting story and inviting format recommend this as supplementary reading for reluctant students of world history.

1456 **Horizon Magazine.** Alexander the Great; by the eds. of Horizon Magazine. Author, Charles Mercer; consultant, Cornelius C. Vermeule, III. American Heritage, 1962. A Horizon Caravel Book, distributed by Harper. 153p. $4.95; lib. ed. $4.79 net. (I–U)

Many interpretations of the great military genius and empire builder are given in this portrayal of his life. Excellent illustrations of paintings, mosaics, and sculpture make this useful in art as well as in history.

ETHAN ALLEN

1457 **Holbrook, Stewart Hall.** America's Ethan Allen; pictures by Lynd Ward. Houghton, 1949. 95p. $4.50; lib. ed. $3.90 net. (I–U)

A spirited biography of the hero of Fort Ticonderoga and his Green Mountain Boys. Beautifully illustrated.

HANS CHRISTIAN ANDERSEN

1458 **Collin, Hedvig.** Young Hans Christian Andersen; written and illus. by Hedvig Collin. Viking, 1955. 216p. $3.75; lib. ed. $3.56 net. (I–U)

The ugly duckling who became a famous storyteller is brought to life in this sensitive story of Andersen's boyhood and his later life in Copenhagen.

MARIAN ANDERSON

1459 **Newman, Shirlee P.** Marian Anderson: Lady from Philadelphia. Westminster, 1966. 175p. $3.75. (U)

Marian Anderson's difficulties in getting a musical education and establishing herself as a singer, her work in promoting racial understanding, and her service as a delegate to the United Nations are the focal points of an inspiring biography. Illustrated with photographs.

ARCHIMEDES

1460 **Bendick, Jeanne.** Archimedes and the Door of Science; pictures by the author. Watts, 1962. 143p. $2.95. (U)

The discoveries and inventions of this Greek mathematician and physicist opened the door to the modern scientific method. Clear explanation and lively style make this a good introduction to one of the great men of science.

JOHN JAMES AUDUBON

1461 **Kieran, Margaret,** and **Kieran, John.** John James Audubon; illus. by Christine Price. Random, 1954. 182p. $2.50; lib. ed. $2.48 net. (I)

A moving account of the young artist's struggles to achieve perfection in his bird paintings despite poverty and other difficulties.

SIR ROBERT BADEN-POWELL

1462 **Blassingame, Wyatt.** Baden-Powell: Chief Scout of the World. Garrard, 1967. 80p. $2.32. (P–I)

This story of the man who gave up his career in the British Army to become founder of the Boy Scouts will appeal especially to Scouts with limited reading ability. (R3-4)

VASCO NÚÑEZ DE BALBOA

1463 **Syme, Ronald. Balboa:** Finder of the Pacific; illus. by William Stobbs. Morrow, 1956. 96p. lib. ed. $2.94 net. (I)
A stirring chronicle, supported by vigorous illustrations, of the young Spanish explorer's amazing exploits.

SIR FREDERICK GRANT BANTING

1464 **Levine, Israel E.** The Discoverer of Insulin: Dr. Frederick G. Banting. Messner, 1959. 192p. $3.50; lib. ed. $3.34 net. (I-U)
Dr. Banting's research in various fields of medicine, as well as his discovery of insulin, is covered in a well-written biography. Index and bibliography.

CLARA HARLOWE BARTON

1465 **Boylston, Helen Dore.** Clara Barton: Founder of the American Red Cross; illus. by Paula Hutchison. Random, 1955. 182p. $1.95; lib. ed. $2.28 net. (I-U)
Brings out Clara Barton's pioneer work in education, nursing, and humanitarian service in the Civil War in addition to her role as founder of the American Red Cross.

ALEXANDER GRAHAM BELL

1466 **Shippen, Katherine B.** Mr. Bell Invents the Telephone; illus. by Richard Floethe. Random, 1952. 183p. $2.50; lib. ed. $2.48 net. (I-U)
Bell's work with the deaf, his invention of the telephone, and his difficulties in getting it accepted are the highlights of a readable biography.

DAVID BEN-GURION

1467 **Samuels, Gertrude.** B-G, Fighter of Goliaths: The Story of David Ben-Gurion; photos. by the author. Crowell, 1961. 279p. $4.50. (U)
The history of modern Israel is interwoven with this life of the remarkable man who guided the new state in its early days.

LEONARD BERNSTEIN

1468 **Ewen, David.** Leonard Bernstein: A Biography for Young People. Chilton, 1960. 174p. $4.25. (I-U)

The many-faceted life of an immensely talented musician makes absorbing reading for young people, whether music lovers or not. An appendix lists Bernstein's compositions and recordings, and there is a bibliography and an index.

MARY MCLEOD BETHUNE

1469 **Carruth, Ella Kaiser.** She Wanted To Read: The Story of Mary McLeod Bethune; illus. by Herbert McClure. Abingdon, 1966. 80p. $2.25. (I)
The personality and work of a woman who dedicated her life to Negro education and civil rights are sketched in a simple biography, useful for slow readers in the upper grades as well as for pupils in grades 4 and 5.

1470 **Sterne, Emma Gelders.** Mary McLeod Bethune; illus. by Raymond Lufkin. Knopf, 1957. 268p. lib. ed. $3.79 net. (U)
Treats the subject in greater depth than the Carruth biography, above, does and gives a perceptive view of America's social growth from Reconstruction days to the present.

ELIZABETH BLACKWELL

1471 **Baker, Rachel.** The First Woman Doctor: The Story of Elizabeth Blackwell, M.D.; illus. by Corinne Malvern. Messner, 1944. 246 p. $3.50; lib. ed. $3.34 net. (U)
In the 1840's, when prejudice barred women from medical school, Elizabeth Blackwell defied convention to become the first woman in modern times to graduate in medicine. Her fight to enable other women to become physicians, and her work in nursing education and public health, are interestingly described in a biography especially recommended as career material.

SIMÓN BOLÍVAR

1472 **Whitridge, Arnold.** Simón Bolívar: The Great Liberator; illus. by Dirk Gringhuis. Random, 1954. 179p. $2.50; lib. ed. $2.48 net. (I-U)
The history of South America is reflected in this story of the man who fought for the colonies' independence from Spain and their eventual federation.

DANIEL BOONE

1473 **Daugherty, James.** Daniel Boone;

with original lithographs in color by the author. Viking, 1939. 94p. $4.50. (I–U)

Vigorous illustrations in forest colors are in complete harmony with this zestful story of the rugged pioneer who broke the trail to the West. Frontier frolic, hunting expeditions, and encounters with Indians are described in exciting detail.

1474 Meadowcraft, Enid La Monte. On Indian Trails with Daniel Boone; illus. by Lloyd Coe. Crowell, 1947. 136p. $3.75. (I)

This biography follows the Boone family from North Carolina to Kentucky and relates their struggle to protect their new home in the wilderness from Indian raids.

1475 Wilkie, Katharine E. Daniel Boone: Taming the Wilds; illus. by E. Harper Johnson. Garrard, 1960. 72p. $2.19. (P–I)

A very brief story covering the main events in Boone's life and designed especially for the slow reader. (R3–4)

NATHANIEL BOWDITCH

1476 Latham, Jean Lee. Carry On, Mr. Bowditch; illus. by John O'Hara Cosgrave. Houghton, 1955. 251p. $3.50. (I–U)

Facts about a self-taught New England boy who became a famous navigator are presented in fiction form. Life at sea in the late eighteenth century is realistically described, as are Bowditch's pioneer efforts to teach navigation to his crew and his writing of *The American Practical Navigator,* still used today.

JAMES BOWIE

1477 Garst, Shannon. James Bowie and His Famous Knife. Messner, 1955. 192p. $3.50; lib. ed. $3.34 net. (I–U)

The author re-creates an exciting period in her story of the man who invented the Bowie knife, fought Indians and Mexicans, and died at the Alamo.

ROBERT BOYLE

1478 Sootin, Harry. Robert Boyle: Founder of Modern Chemistry; pictures by Gustav Schrotter. Watts, 1962. 133p. $2.95. (I–U)

In this biography of the seventeenth-century English chemist and physicist, emphasis is on his experimental work which led to modern research methods. Diagrams clarify the more difficult experiments.

LOUIS BRAILLE

1479 DeGering, Etta. Seeing Fingers: The Story of Louis Braille; illus. by Emil Weiss. McKay, 1962. 115p. $3.25; lib. ed. $3.11 net. (I–U)

Musician, teacher, and inventor of the Braille system of reading and writing, blind Louis Braille was one of the great benefactors of mankind. This sympathetic biography emphasizes his childhood adjustment to blindness and his youth, during which some of his most important work was accomplished.

JAMES BRIDGER

1480 Garst, Shannon. Jim Bridger: Greatest of the Mountain Men; illus. by William Moyers. Houghton, 1952. 242p. $3.75. (I–U)

No adventure story could be more exciting than the life of Jim Bridger, beaver trapper, Indian fighter, and founder of Fort Bridger. Maps and a list for further reading are useful features.

LAURA DEWEY BRIDGMAN

1481 Hunter, Edith Fisher. Child of the Silent Night; illus. by Bea Holmes. Houghton, 1963. 124p. $2.75. (I)

The story of the first blind deaf-mute to be successfully educated is told in an easily read biography centering on Laura Bridgman's childhood and her life at the Perkins Institute for the Blind.

TABITHA MOFFATT BROWN

1482 Lampman, Evelyn Sibley. Wheels West: The Story of Tabitha Brown; illus. by Gil Walker. Doubleday, 1965. 226p. $3.50. (I–U)

An indomitable 68-year-old grandmother stirs things up on the family's trip to Oregon by covered wagon. A fine pioneer story with a remarkable central character.

RALPH JOHNSON BUNCHE

1483 Kugelmass, J. Alvin. Ralph J. Bunche: Fighter for Peace. Messner, 1962. 178p. $3.50; lib. ed. $3.34 net. (U)

From a childhood of poverty and discrimination Ralph Bunche rose to a position of influence in world affairs. His early struggles for an education and his later career in the U.S. State Department and the United

Nations, culminating in his being awarded the Nobel Prize, make an inspiring story.

1484 Young, Margaret B. The Picture Life of Ralph J. Bunche. Watts, 1967. 47p. $2.65. (P–I)

Excellent photographs and a simply written account of Bunche's life are combined in a biography for beginning readers or older slow readers. (R2–3)

JOHN BURROUGHS

1485 Swift, Hildegarde Hoyt. The Edge of April: A Biography of John Burroughs; illus. by Lynd Ward. Morrow, 1957. 316p. $4.95. (U)

A well-written and strikingly illustrated biography of the American nature essayist, especially recommended for good older readers.

RICHARD EVELYN BYRD

1486 Steinberg, Alfred. Admiral Richard E. Byrd; illus. by Charles Beck. Putnam, 1960. 128p. lib. ed. $3.29 net. (U)

The character traits which enabled Admiral Byrd to accomplish his hazardous feats of Antarctic exploration are emphasized in this account of his life.

CAIUS JULIUS CAESAR

1487 Horizon Magazine. Caesar; by the eds. of Horizon Magazine. Author, Irwin Isenberg; consultant, Richard M. Haywood . . . American Heritage, 1964. A Horizon Caravel Book, distributed by Harper. 151p. $4.95; lib. ed. $4.79 net. (U)

The foreword states that "this book brings together the facts and the myths of Caesar's life with pertinent art, documents, and photographs and reconstruction of significant sites." Included also is much information about the Roman soldier and the political intrigues of the period.

ROY CAMPANELLA

1488 Schoor, Gene. Roy Campanella: Man of Courage. Putnam, 1959. 190p. lib. ed. $3.29 net. (I–U)

An informal biography of the Dodgers' most valuable player from his early days on a Negro baseball team to the automobile accident which ended his career.

ANDREW CARNEGIE

1489 Shippen, Katherine B. Andrew Carnegie and the Age of Steel; illus. with photos. and with drawings by Ernest Kurt Barth. Random, 1958. 183p. $2.50; lib. ed. $2.48 net. (I–U)

The poor Scottish boy who rose to be a steel magnate and one of the world's great philanthropists is the subject of a sympathetic biography. A success story emphasizing the importance of ambition and hard work and including much information about the development of the steel industry.

CHRISTOPHER CARSON

1490 Bell, Margaret E. Kit Carson: Mountain Man; illus. by Harry Daugherty. Morrow, 1952. 71p. lib. ed. $2.94 net. (I–U)

Trader, trapper, and Indian fighter, Kit Carson embodies the most romantic ideas of the mountain man. This clearly written story makes the most of his extraordinary exploits.

1491 Campion, Nardi Reeder. Kit Carson: Pathfinder of the West. Garrard, 1963. 219p. $2.19. (P–I)

Because of his reckless bravery and adventurous life, Kit Carson has strong appeal for boys. This story of his life can be read by advanced pupils in upper primary grades and by older slow readers. (R3–4)

JACQUES CARTIER

1492 Syme, Ronald. Cartier: Finder of the St. Lawrence; illus. by William Stobbs. Morrow, 1958. 95p. lib. ed. $2.94 net. (I)

The intrepid Frenchman's attempts to find a water passage to the Pacific are recreated in a biography enlivened by imaginary conversations and quotations from Cartier's journals. Maps and virile illustrations add interest and information.

GEORGE WASHINGTON CARVER

1493 Aliki. A Weed Is a Flower: The Life of George Washington Carver; written and illus. by Aliki. Prentice-Hall, 1965. unp. $4.25. (P)

A picture-biography of the famous Negro scientist, centering on his work with plants. (R2–3)

1494 Graham, Shirley, and **Lipscomb, George D.** Dr. George Washington Carver, Scientist; illus. by Elton C. Fax. Messner, 1944. 248p. $3.50; lib. ed. $3.34 net. (U)

The early struggles of a delicate Negro boy, son of a slave girl, to obtain an education and his later work in carrying out the experiments which were to transform the agriculture of the South are detailed in an appreciative biography, written and illustrated by members of his own race. Chronology, bibliography, and index.

1495 White, Anne Terry. George Washington Carver: The Story of a Great American; illus. by Douglas Gorsline. Random, 1953. 182p. $2.50; lib. ed. $2.48 net. (I–U)

A brief but readable and accurate biography for less-able readers than is the Graham book, above.

SAMUEL DE CHAMPLAIN

1496 Syme, Ronald. Champlain of the St. Lawrence; illus. by William Stobbs. Morrow, 1952. 189p. $3.25. (I)

The heroic Father of New France emerges as a three-dimensional figure in this simple, forcefully illustrated biography. His explorations of Canada, his relations with the Indians, and his settlement of Quebec highlight the story.

JOHN CHAPMAN

1497 Aliki. The Story of Johnny Appleseed. Prentice-Hall, 1963. unp. $3.95. (P)

Charming illustrations help the primary child to visualize the adventures of the folk hero who planted apple seeds throughout the Middle West. (R2–3)

1498 Hunt, Mabel Leigh. Better Known as Johnny Appleseed; decorations by James Daugherty. Lippincott, 1950. 212p. $3.95. (I–U)

The many legends centering around John Chapman—pioneer, missionary, and apple lover—are incorporated in a story of the eccentric character who wandered through the Middle West making friends with the Indians, preaching, and planting apple seeds. Adds a picturesque note to the study of the Westward movement.

CHARLEMAGNE

1499 Komroff, Manuel. Charlemagne. Messner, 1964. 191p. $3.50; lib. ed. $3.34 net. (U)

A vivid portrait of the greatest of medieval rulers, centering on his conquests, his efforts to spread Christianity, and his political reforms. An excellent picture of the times, recommended for independent or collateral reading in social studies.

FRÉDÉRIC FRANÇOIS CHOPIN

1500 Seroff, Victor. Frédéric Chopin. Macmillan, 1964. 118p. $3.95; lib. ed. $3.74 net. (I–U)

The personal life and musical career of Chopin are related to the important persons and events of his times in a knowledgeable biography for the serious student of music.

CHRISTOPHE, HENRI, KING OF HAITI

1501 Newcomb, Covelle. Black Fire: A Story of Henri Christophe; illus. by Avery Johnson. Longmans, 1940. 275p. $4.95. (U)

Henri Christophe, born a slave on a plantation of the British West Indies, took part in the Haitian rebellion against France and later became its king. A dramatic story told with zest.

SIR WINSTON LEONARD SPENCER CHURCHILL

1502 Reynolds, Quentin. Winston Churchill; illus. with photos. Random, 1963. 183p. $2.50; lib. ed. $2.48 net. (I–U)

The many facets of Sir Winston's personality and career are brought out in a smoothly written biography, ending with his resignation as prime minister in 1955. Photographs include pictures of his funeral.

GEORGE ROGERS CLARK

1503 Nolan, Jeannette Covert. George Rogers Clark: Soldier and Hero (November 19, 1752—February 13, 1818); illus. by Lee Ames. Messner, 1954. 190p. $3.50; lib. ed. $3.34 net. (U)

Pioneer, Indian fighter, and soldier, George Rogers Clark played an important part in early American history. This biography records his adventurous career and delineates his character with accuracy and color.

SAMUEL LANGHORNE CLEMENS

1504 McNeer, May. America's Mark Twain; with illus. by Lynd Ward. Houghton, 1962. 159p. $3.75; lib. ed. $3.40 net. (I–U)

A beautifully illustrated account of Mark Twain's early life, his career as an author, and the tragedies of his later life. As an introduction to his books, excerpts from six of his stories are included.

1505 **Proudfit, Isabel.** River-Boy: The Story of Mark Twain; illus. by W. C. Nims. Messner, 1940. 247p. $3.50; lib. ed. $3.34 net. ((I–U)

The picturesque early life of Mark Twain receives the emphasis in a biography that reads almost like fiction. Bibliography and maps.

COCHISE, APACHE CHIEF

1506 **Wyatt, Edgar.** Cochise: Apache Warrior and Statesman; illus. by Allan Houser. McGraw-Hill, 1953. 192p. $3.25; lib. ed. $3.01 net. (I–U)

Both sides of the Indian problem are shown in a thought-provoking biography of the Apache chief who tried to live in peace with the white man but was forced into war by dishonorable dealings.

WILLIAM FREDERICK CODY

1507 **Aulaire, Ingri d', and Aulaire, Edgar Parin d'.** Buffalo Bill. Doubleday, 1952. unp. $3.50. (P–I)

Large, colorful lithographs illustrate the equally colorful life of this Western personality.

1508 **Garst, Shannon.** Buffalo Bill; illus. by Elton C. Fax. Messner, 1948. 214p. $3.50. (I–U)

A fast-moving story of Buffalo Bill's eventful life and an authentic picture of the West of his day.

CHRISTOPHER COLUMBUS

1509 **Aulaire, Ingri d', and Aulaire, Edgar Parin d'.** Columbus. Doubleday, 1955. 56p. $3.95. (P–I)

A picture-story of Columbus' early life, his voyages, and his disappointing old age.

1510 **Dalgliesh, Alice.** The Columbus Story; pictures by Leo Politi. Scribner, 1955. unp. $3.25; lib. ed. $3.12 net. (P)

A brief biography highlighting the events in Columbus' life most likely to interest children and planned for reading aloud.

Use of the Admiral's own words and handsome colored illustrations add authenticity and vitality. (R2–3)

1511 **Sperry, Armstrong.** The Voyages of Christopher Columbus; written and illus. by Armstrong Sperry. Random, 1950. 186p. $2.50; lib. ed. $2.48 net. (I–U)

This account of the four voyages of Columbus reads like a brisk sea story, with storms, mutinous crews, and other dangers to give suspense. Historically accurate and vigorously illustrated.

1512 **Syme, Ronald.** Columbus: Finder of the New World; illus. by William Stobbs. Morrow, 1952. 70p. lib. ed. $2.94 net. (I)

The important events of Columbus' life are compressed into a suspenseful story, illustrated with bold drawings.

JAMES COOK

1513 **Sperry, Armstrong.** Captain Cook Explores the South Seas; written and illus. by Armstrong Sperry. Random, 1955. 184p. $2.50; lib. ed. $2.48 net. (I–U)

Smoothly written narrative and action-filled pictures tell the story of Cook's explorations in the South Seas.

1514 **Syme, Ronald.** Captain Cook: Pacific Explorer; illus. by William Stobbs. Morrow, 1960. 96p. lib. ed. $2.94 net. (I)

Captain Cook's adventures, including an attack by Maori warriors and imprisonment on the Great Barrier Reef, make exciting reading in a well-written and profusely illustrated biography.

HERNANDO CORTÉS

1515 **Syme, Ronald.** Cortés of Mexico; illus. by William Stobbs. Morrow, 1951. 191p. lib. ed. $3.25 net. (I)

A fast-paced and authentic account of Cortés' conquest of Mexico, attributing the destruction of the Aztec civilization to the men under Cortés, rather than to the explorer himself.

JACQUES-YVES COSTEAU

1516 **Dugan, James.** Undersea Explorer: The Story of Captain Costeau; with a message to young people by Captain Jacques-Yves Costeau; illus. with photos. and diagrams. Harper, 1957. 143p. $3.95; lib. ed. $3.79 net. (U)

An associate on Costeau's famous undersea expeditions writes the story of their amazing adventures in oceanography. Beautiful photographs and clear diagrams of the aqualung and other diving equipment.

CRAZY HORSE, OGLALA INDIAN

1517 **Garst, Shannon.** Crazy Horse: Great Warrior of the Sioux; illus. by William Moyers. Houghton, 1950. 260p. $3.75. (U)
A thrilling tale of true adventure about the great Sioux chief's fight for his people's own land and freedom, presented from the Indians' point of view.

1518 **Meadowcraft, Enid La Monte.** Crazy Horse: Sioux Warrior; illus. by Cary. Garrard, 1965. 80p. $2.19. (P–I)
This simple story of a bold Indian warrior with its numerous illustrations and large print should attract older slow readers as well as advanced primary pupils. (R3–4)

DAVID CROCKETT

1519 **Holbrook, Stewart.** Davy Crockett; illus. by Ernest Richardson. Random, 1955. 179p. $2.50; lib. ed. $2.48 net. (I–U)
The half-legendary hero of the Alamo appears larger than life in a story interweaving fact and tall tale. Covers Crockett's life as a frontiersman, politician, and soldier and includes a list of Crockett memorials.

MARIE SKLODOWSKA CURIE

1520 **Curie, Eve.** Madame Curie: A Biography; tr. by Vincent Sheean. Doubleday, 1937. 412p. $5.95. (U)
The life of the great woman scientist, codiscoverer of radium, is told with objectivity and affection by her daughter. Madame Curie's life in Poland, her collaboration with her scientist husband, and the discoveries which brought her acclaim are the focus of the story.

GEORGE ARMSTRONG CUSTER

1521 **Reynolds, Quentin.** Custer's Last Stand; illus. by Frederick T. Chapman. Random, 1951. 185p. $2.50; lib. ed. $2.48 net. (I–U)
The flamboyant "Yellow Hair" is the ideal hero to attract older slow readers. The massacre at the Little Big Horn, when Custer fell with all his troops, is the tragic climax of an exciting biography.

FATHER DAMIEN

1522 **Roos, Ann.** Man of Molokai: The Life of Father Damien; illus. by Raymond Lufkin. Lippincott, 1943. 254p. $3.75. (U)
An inspiring story of the man who dedicated his life to work among the lepers of Molokai, Hawaii.

CHARLES ROBERT DARWIN

1523 **Gregor, Arthur S.** Charles Darwin. Dutton, 1966. 189p. $4.75; lib. ed. $4.70 net. (U)
The character and work of Darwin are presented against a background of nineteenth-century science, with emphasis on Darwin's scientific theories and their impact on the world of science. Bibliography, chronology, and glossary.

CHARLES DICKENS

1524 **Becker, May Lamberton.** Introducing Charles Dickens; illus. by Oscar Ogg. Dodd, 1940. 250p. $4. (U)
The character and personality of Dickens and the social conditions about which he wrote some of his greatest novels come to life in a revealing study of the man and his times.

RAYMOND LEE DITMARS

1525 **Wood, L. N.** Raymond L. Ditmars: His Exciting Career with Reptiles, Animals, and Insects; illus. with photos. Messner, 1944. 272p. 58 plates. $3.50; lib. ed. $3.34 net. (I–U)
The experiences—some alarming, some laughable—of the man who collected snakes in his own household share emphasis with Ditmars' contributions to medical and natural science.

THOMAS A. DOOLEY

1526 **Dooley, Thomas A.** Doctor Tom Dooley: My Story. new and rev. ed. Farrar, 1962. 160p. $3.25. (I–U)
Dr. Dooley's own story, written especially for young people, tells movingly of his work among the sick and poor of Laos and Vietnam. An epilogue gives an account of his last months and death in 1961.

FREDERICK DOUGLASS

1527 **Bontemps, Arna.** Frederick Douglass: Slavefighter—Freeman; illus. by Harper Johnson. Knopf, 1959. 177p. lib. ed. $3.19 net. (I–U)

Frederick Douglass, born a slave, overcame almost insurmountable odds to gain his freedom and to rise to greatness as abolitionist, orator, journalist, and statesman. A straightforward biography, with emphasis on Douglass' character and personality as well as on his achievements.

1528 **Patterson, Lillie.** Frederick Douglass: Freedom Fighter; illus. by Gray Morrow. Garrard, 1965. 80p. $2.19. (P–I)

For younger or less-able readers, a simply written biography covering the significant events in Douglass' life. (R3–4)

SIR FRANCIS DRAKE

1529 **Latham, Jean Lee.** Drake: The Man They Called a Pirate; illus. by Frederick T. Chapman. Harper, 1960. 278p. $3.95; lib. ed. $3.79 net. (I–U)

Colorful style and astute choice of incidents make this a highly readable biography of a great mariner, from his early days at sea to his defeat of the Spanish Armada in 1588.

AMELIA EARHART

1530 **Garst, Shannon.** Amelia Earhart: Heroine of the Skies; illus. by Joseph Dreamy. Messner, 1947. 191p. $3.50; lib. ed. $3.34 net. (U)

The early life and flying career of the first woman to fly the Atlantic, ending with her disappearance over the Pacific in 1937. Includes a chronology and a bibliography.

WYATT BERRY STAPP EARP

1531 **Lake, Stuart N.** The Life and Times of Wyatt Earp; illus. by John McCormick. Houghton, 1956. 271p. $3.95. (U)

This story of how Wyatt Earp brought law and order to the West is based on interviews with the famous frontier marshal and includes his own accounts of some of his exploits.

THOMAS ALVA EDISON

1532 **Cousins, Margaret.** The Story of Thomas Alva Edison; illus. with photos.

and map. Random, 1965. 175p. $2.50; lib. ed. $2.48 net. (I)

A readable biography of one of America's greatest inventors, with emphasis on his part in the development of the phonograph, the incandescent light, and motion pictures.

1533 **North, Sterling.** Young Thomas Edison; illus. with photos.; decorations, diags., and maps by William Barss. Houghton, 1958. 182p. $2.95. (I–U)

Covering much the same material as the Cousins biography, above, but for somewhat more mature readers. Includes a list of Edison historic sites.

ALBERT EINSTEIN

1534 **Beckhard, Arthur J.** Albert Einstein; illus. by Charles Beck. Putnam, 1959. 126p. lib. ed. $3.29 net. (I–U)

In this story of the great mathematician and physicist, Einstein is presented as a humanitarian as well as a scientist. His scientific theories are explained in brief general terms.

ELIZABETH I, QUEEN OF ENGLAND

1535 **Winwar, Frances.** Queen Elizabeth and the Spanish Armada; illus. by C. Walter Hodges. Random, 1954. 184p. $2.50; lib. ed. $2.48 net. (I–U)

Queen Elizabeth's life story, culminating in the defeat of the Spanish Armada by England's tiny navy, is told against a background of court life and social conditions in sixteenth-century England.

ELIZABETH II, QUEEN OF ENGLAND

1536 **Parker, Elinor.** Most Gracious Majesty: The Story of Queen Elizabeth II; illus. with photos. rev. ed. Crowell, 1962. 197p. $4.50. (I–U)

An admiring informal biography, illustrated with engaging family photographs.

JOHN ERICSSON

1537 **Latham, Jean Lee.** Man of the Monitor: The Story of John Ericsson; pictures by Leonard Everett Fisher. Harper, 1962. 231p. $3.95; lib. ed. $3.79 net. (I)

The mechanical genius who invented the ironclad "Monitor," which took part in the celebrated battle with the Confederate "Merrimac" during the Civil War, is portrayed in a lively biography.

SIR ARTHUR JOHN EVANS

1538 **Honour, Alan.** Secrets of Minos: Sir Arthur Evans' Discoveries at Crete. Foreword by John H. Young; illus. with photos. and line drawings. McGraw-Hill, 1961. 189p. $3.25. (I–U)

A brisk biography of the British archaeologist whose excavations uncovered evidence of the ancient civilization of the Minoans. Sir Arthur's early life, his explorations at Knossos, and the significance of his discoveries to the study of European prehistory are covered.

MICHAEL FARADAY

1539 **Sootin, Harry.** Michael Faraday: From Errand Boy to Master Physicist. Messner, 1954. 180p. lib. ed. $3.34 net. (U)

The British scientist whose discovery of electromagnetic induction revolutionized the world of industry is the subject of an informal biography stressing Faraday's life rather than his theories.

CYRUS WEST FIELD

1540 **Latham, Jean Lee.** Young Man in a Hurry: The Story of Cyrus W. Field; pictures by Victor Mays. Harper, 1958. 238p. $3.50; lib. ed. $3.27 net. (I–U)

Field's work in laying the Atlantic cable in 1858 is the focus of a biography emphasizing the energy, enthusiasm, and hard work which made the achievement possible.

ALICE FITZGERALD

1541 **Noble, Iris.** Nurse around the World: Alice Fitzgerald. Messner, 1964. 191p. $3.50; lib. ed. $3.34 net. (U)

The story of the nineteenth-century debutante who helped to make nursing respectable for women by becoming a nurse and serving with distinction in World War I and in the Far East. A semifictionalized account with much invented conversation.

SIR ALEXANDER FLEMING

1542 **Rowland, John.** The Penicillin Man: The Story of Sir Alexander Fleming. Roy, 1957. 155p. $3.25. (U)

The story of the accidental discovery of penicillin and its later development through cooperative effort is the high point of this account of Alexander Fleming's life.

HENRY FORD

1543 **Neyhart, Louise Albright.** Henry Ford: Engineer; illus. by Joshua Tolford. Houghton, 1950. 210p. $4.25. (U)

A dual treatment of the development of the Ford automobile and of the man who produced it.

AMOS FORTUNE

1544 **Yates, Elizabeth.** Amos Fortune: Free Man; illus. by Nora S. Unwin. Dutton, 1950. 181p. $3.50; lib. ed. $3.46 net. (I–U)

After buying his own freedom, Amos Fortune devoted the rest of his life to freeing other slaves. This moving story of his life depicts a great and dedicated man who won the respect and admiration of both races.

STEPHEN COLLINS FOSTER

1545 **Purdy, Claire Lee.** He Heard America Sing: The Story of Stephen Collins Foster; pictures by Dorothea Cook. Messner, 1940. 236p. $3.50; lib. ed. $3.34 net. (I–U)

The colorful aspects of American life which inspired the songs of Stephen Foster form the background for this semifictionalized biography. Includes music for 28 songs.

BENJAMIN FRANKLIN

1546 **American Heritage.** The Many Worlds of Benjamin Franklin; by the authors of American Heritage, The Magazine of History. Author, Frank R. Donovan; consultant, Whitfield J. Bell. 3d ed. American Heritage, 1963. American Heritage Junior Library, distributed by Harper. 152p. $4.95; lib. ed. $4.79 net. (I–U)

Excellent illustrative material is combined with an informative text to present the "Renaissance Man of eighteenth-century America." Includes a list for further reading.

1547 **Aulaire, Ingri d', and Aulaire, Edgar Parin d'.** Benjamin Franklin. Doubleday, 1950. 48p. $3.95. (P–I)

Incidents chosen for special appeal to young children make up this picture-biography of Franklin. The large, colored lithographs and marginal drawings dramatize the story and add details of eighteenth-century American life. (R3–4)

1548 **Daugherty, James.** Poor Richard; illus. with lithographs in two colors by the author. Viking, 1941. 158p. $5.95. (U)

Franklin's personality and his contributions to American life receive the emphasis in this revealing biography.

ROBERT FULTON

1549 **Judson, Clara Ingram.** Boat Builder: The Story of Robert Fulton; illus. by Armstrong Sperry. Scribner, 1940. 121p. lib. ed. $2.97 net. (I–U)

For mechanically minded boys, a nontechnical story of Fulton's inventions which led to the construction of the first commercial steamboat, the torpedo, and the first successful submarine.

GALILEO GALILEI

1550 **Rosen, Sidney.** Galileo and the Magic Numbers; illus. by Harve Stein. Little, 1958. 212p. $3.95. (I–U)

Galileo's conflicts with the church and his struggles to gain acceptance of his revolutionary theories are balanced with personal history and accounts of conditions in the scientific world of the sixteenth and seventeenth centuries.

THOMAS HOPKINS GALLAUDET

1551 **DeGering, Etta.** Gallaudet: Friend of the Deaf; illus. by Emil Weiss. McKay, 1964. 177p. $3.75; lib. ed. $3.44 net. (I–U)

The early life and later achievements of the man who founded the first school for the deaf in America are recounted against a background of nineteenth-century New England family life.

VASCO DA GAMA

1552 **Syme, Ronald.** Vasco da Gama; Sailor toward the Sunrise; illus. by William Stobbs. Morrow, 1959. 95p. lib. ed. $2.94 net. (I)

The rise and fall of the Portuguese empire, and the part played in it by the intrepid navigator who discovered the western sea route from Portugal to India, are depicted in a straightforward biography.

MOHANDAS KARAMCHAND GANDHI

1553 **Eaton, Jeanette.** Gandhi: Fighter without a Sword; illus. by Ralph Ray. Morrow, 1950. 253p. $3.95. (U)

Gandhi emerges as hero, saint, and man from this simply written story of his life, centering on his labors to free India from English rule.

LOU GEHRIG

1554 **Graham, Frank.** Lou Gehrig: A Quiet Hero. Putnam, 1942. 250p. $3.95. (I–U)

This is more than a biography of a baseball great; it is the story of a great human being who faced tragedy with dignity and courage.

GERONIMO, APACHE CHIEF

1555 **Wyatt, Edgar.** Geronimo: The Last Apache War Chief; illus. by Allan Houser. McGraw-Hill, 1952. 188p. $2.95; lib. ed. $2.96 net. (I–U)

A thrilling story of the Indian war chief, bringing out the reasons for Geronimo's hatred of the white man. Includes a guide to pronunciation of Indian names.

ROBERT HUTCHINGS GODDARD

1556 **Verral, Charles Spain.** Robert Goddard: Father of the Space Age; illus. by Paul Frame. Prentice-Hall, 1963. 83p. $3.50. (I)

Despite illness and lack of funds, Robert Goddard built and fired a liquid-fuel rocket more than 50 years ago. His life story is an important chapter in the development of the modern rocket.

GEORGE WASHINGTON GOETHALS

1557 **Fast, Howard M.** Goethals and the Panama Canal; illus. by Rafaello Busoni. Messner, 1942. 230p. $3.50; lib. ed. $3.34 net. (I–U)

This able biography of the U.S. Army engineer in charge of building the Panama Canal brings out Goethals' dynamic personality and describes the engineering feats accomplished in the project. Includes a bibliography and maps.

VINCENT VAN GOGH

1558 **Ripley, Elizabeth.** Vincent van Gogh: A Biography; with drawings and paintings by Vincent van Gogh. Walck, 1954. 68p. $4. (I–U)

Text and illustrations are integrated in a revealing biography of a troubled genius. Includes a bibliography.

SAMUEL GOMPERS

1559 Selvin, David F. Sam Gompers: Labor's Pioneer. Abelard-Schuman, 1964. 159p. $3. (I–U)

Recounts the remarkable accomplishments of a poor boy who founded the American Federation of Labor and became a powerful figure in the life of the nation.

WILLIAM CRAWFORD GORGAS

1560 Judson, Clara Ingram. Soldier Doctor: The Story of William Gorgas; with illus. by Robert Doremus. Scribner, 1942. 151p. lib. ed. $3.31 net. (U)

Without the work of the American doctor who freed the Canal Zone of yellow-fever-carrying mosquitoes, the Panama Canal might never have been built. A lively story of a pioneer in public health work.

NATHAN HALE

1561 Brown, Marion Marsh. Young Nathan; decorated by Don McDonough. Westminster, 1949. 191p. $3.25. (I)

A fictionalized biography of the young hero spy of the Revolution.

WILLIAM STEWART HALSTEAD

1562 Beckhard, Arthur J., and **Crane, William D.** Cancer, Cocaine, and Courage: The Story of Dr. William Halstead. Messner, 1960. 191p. $3.50; lib. ed. $3.34 net. (U)

Pioneer surgeon and first advocate of aseptic medicine, Dr. Halstead made brilliant contributions to medical science. This account of his experiments with cocaine as an anesthetic, leading to his own addiction, and his courageous fight to break the habit has special significance for today's young people.

ALEXANDER HAMILTON

1563 Crouse, Anna Erskine, and **Crouse, Russel.** Alexander Hamilton and Aaron Burr: Their Lives, Their Times, Their Duel; illus. by Walter Buehr. Random, 1958. 184p. $2.50; lib. ed. $2.48 net. (I–U)

This competent dual biography of two brilliant men whose parallel lives ended in tragedy for both is set against a vivid background of eighteenth-century social and political conditions.

DAG HAMMARSKJÖLD

1564 Levine, I. E. Champion of World Peace: Dag Hammarskjöld. Messner, 1962. 190p. $3.50; lib. ed. $3.34 net. (U)

The Swedish statesman and world diplomat is presented as an able and courageous peacemaker in his role as secretary-general of the United Nations. A good picture of the development of the UN from 1945 to 1961 as well as an inspiring biography of a dedicated man.

PATRICK HENRY

1565 Campion, Nardi Reeder. Patrick Henry: Firebrand of the Revolution; illus. by Victor Mays. Little, 1961. 261p. $3.95. (I–U)

The country boy who failed in most of his early undertakings but rose to national prominence as an orator and a statesman comes to life in an animated biography. Excellent background reading for the Colonial and Revolutionary periods.

JAMES BUTLER HICKOK

1566 Holbrook, Stewart. Wild Bill Hickok Tames the West; illus. by Ernest Richardson. Random, 1952. 179p. $2.50; lib. ed. $2.48 net. (I)

A man of many careers—member of the Underground Railroad, Union spy, stage driver, and plainsman—Wild Bill Hickok is best remembered as the man who brought law and order to the West. A readable biography emphasizing the man rather than the times.

HIPPOCRATES

1567 Goldberg, Herbert S. Hippocrates: Father of Medicine. Watts, 1963. 107p. $2.95. (U)

The versatility and genius of Hippocrates are brought out in this biography of the physician who, four hundred years before Christ, transformed medical practice from quackery into science.

OLIVER WENDELL HOLMES

1568 Judson, Clara Ingram. Mr. Justice Holmes; illus. by Robert Todd. Follett, 1956. 192p. $3.95; lib. ed. $4.17 net. (U)

The qualities which made Justice Holmes a character respected as much for his integrity as for his achievements receive attention in this biography. Includes considerable information about the U.S. Supreme Court.

HERBERT CLARK HOOVER

1569 **Peare, Catherine Owens.** The Herbert Hoover Story. Crowell, 1965. 247p. $4.50. (U)

A well-rounded biography of the 31st President, devoting much of the story to his early life, mining career, and humanitarian services. Bibliography and index.

SAMUEL HOUSTON

1570 **Latham, Jean Lee.** Retreat to Glory: The Story of Sam Houston. Harper, 1965. 274p. $3.95; lib. ed. $3.79 net. (U)

Facts and legends about the Texas hero are blended in a readable story of Houston's life, not omitting his shortcomings.

1571 **Latham, Jean Lee.** Sam Houston: Hero of Texas. Garrard, 1965. 80p. $2.19. (P–I)

A simpler story of Houston's life. Large print and numerous illustrations recommend this to readers with limited skills. (R3–4)

SAMUEL GRIDLEY HOWE

1572 **Meltzer, Milton.** A Light in the Dark: The Life of Samuel Gridley Howe. Crowell, 1964. 239p. $3.50. (U)

The life of the Boston doctor who established the Perkins Institute for the Blind is vividly delineated against a background of nineteenth-century New England social conditions. This account of his pioneer work with the blind, the deaf, the feeble-minded, and the delinquent makes inspiring reading. Includes a bibliography and a chronology.

HENRY HUDSON

1573 **Syme, Ronald.** Henry Hudson; illus. by Ronald Syme. Morrow, 1955. 190p. $3.25. (I)

An enjoyable beginning biography of the English mariner who explored the northeastern coast of America.

ISHI

1574 **Kroeber, Theodora.** Ishi: Last of His Tribe; drawings by Ruth Robbins. Parnassus, 1964. 209p. $4.25. (I–U)

Ishi, the sole survivor of his tribe of California Yana Indians, is forced by loneliness and starvation into the world of the twentieth century. Befriended by an anthropologist, he finds a home in a museum, where he demonstrates his now-disappearing crafts to visitors. A quietly tragic story told with sensitivity and restraint.

ANDREW JACKSON

1575 **Coit, Margaret L.** Andrew Jackson; illus. by Milton Johnson. Houghton, 1965. 154p. $3.50. (U)

This forceful biography of the tough, hotheaded Jackson will help young people to grasp the issues of his period and to understand Jacksonian democracy. The facts are entirely accurate, covering both strengths and weaknesses of his character and his administration.

1576 **Vance, Marguerite.** The Jacksons of Tennessee; illus. by Nedda Walker. Dutton, 1953. 181p. $3.75. (U)

A more informal biography centering on both Rachel and Andrew Jackson and their troubled life together, with special appeal for girls.

THOMAS JONATHAN JACKSON

1577 **Daniels, Jonathan.** Stonewall Jackson; illus. by William Moyers. Random, 1959. 183p. $2.50; lib. ed. $2.48 net. (I–U)

The early life, teaching career, and military exploits of a great soldier are recounted by a Southern writer, with Jackson's famous Valley Campaign described in detail.

THOMAS JEFFERSON

1578 **American Heritage.** Thomas Jefferson and His World; by the eds. of American Heritage, The Magazine of History; narrative by Henry Moscow, in consultation with Dumas Malone. American Heritage, 1960. American Heritage Junior Library, distributed by Harper. 153p. $4.95; lib. ed. $4.79 net. (I–U)

Thomas Jefferson's many talents—as statesman, farmer, scientist, architect, inventor, educator—earned him the title "Sage of Monticello." This biography, illustrated with paintings, prints, drawings, and photographs of the period, is an excellent interpretation of the man and his times. Includes a list for further reading.

1579 **Judson, Clara Ingram.** Thomas Jefferson: Champion of the People; illus. by Robert Frankenberg. Follett, 1952. 224p. $3.95; lib. ed. $4.17 net. (U)

The author has successfully carried out her purpose of presenting Jefferson's "philosophy of government, his ideal of freedom, his faith in man" to young Americans.

MARY JEMISON

1580 **Lenski, Lois.** Indian Captive: The Story of Mary Jemison; written and illus. by Lois Lenski. Lippincott, 1941. 269p. lib. ed. $4.82 net. (I–U)

This story of a white child's capture by and life with the Seneca Indians in the eighteenth century is based on records of the time and a study of Seneca Indian customs.

JENGHIS KHAN

1581 **Lamb, Harold.** Genghis Khan and the Mongol Horde; illus. by Elton Fax. Random, 1954. 182p. $2.50; lib. ed. $2.48 net. (I–U)

A dramatic story of the great Mongol chieftain who led his conquering tribe from the Gobi Desert through China, Iran, Russia, and Mongolia.

EDWARD JENNER

1582 **Eberle, Irmengarde.** Edward Jenner & Smallpox Vaccination; pictures by Henry S. Gillette. Watts, 1962. 153p. $2.95. (I–U)

Edward Jenner's trials in gaining acceptance for his theory of vaccination against smallpox are graphically recounted in a readable biography.

JOAN OF ARC

1583 **Horizon Magazine.** Joan of Arc; by the eds. of Horizon Magazine. Author, Jay Williams; consultant, Charles Wayland Lightbody. American Heritage, 1963. A Horizon Caravel Book, distributed by Harper. 153p. $4.95; lib. ed. $4.79 net. (I–U)

The facts of Joan of Arc's life and the legends surrounding her inspired leadership of the French armies are presented in a copiously illustrated biography, useful in art as well as in social studies. Includes a list for further reading.

JOHN PAUL JONES

1584 **Sperry, Armstrong.** John Paul Jones: Fighting Sailor; written and illus. by Armstrong Sperry. Random, 1953. 180p. $2.50; lib. ed. $2.48 net. (I–U)

Direct and forceful writing, well suited to the character and life of the naval hero of the Revolution, marks this somewhat fictionalized but historically accurate account of his career.

BENITO PABLO JUÁREZ

1585 **Baker, Nina Brown.** Juárez: Hero of Mexico. Vanguard, 1942. 122p. $3.95. (U)

A competent biography of the liberator and first civilian president of Mexico, covering both his personal life and his military and political careers.

HELEN ADAMS KELLER

1586 **Peare, Catherine Owens.** The Helen Keller Story. Crowell, 1959. 183p. $3.50. (I–U)

This story of a remarkable woman reflects changes in attitudes and conditions for education of the handicapped, as well as follows the painful steps by which a deaf and blind child became aware of her world. Includes an index and diagrams explaining the finger alphabet.

1587 **Waite, Helen E.** Valiant Companions: Helen Keller and Anne Sullivan Macy. Macrae, 1959. 223p. $3.75. (U)

Anne Sullivan Macy shares this story with her famous pupil. Pioneer methods of communicating with the blind-deaf are interestingly described.

JOHN FITZGERALD KENNEDY

1588 **Levine, I. E.** Young Man in the White House: John Fitzgerald Kennedy. Messner, 1964. 196p. $3.50; lib. ed. $3.34 net. (I–U)

Takes Kennedy from his childhood, through his school days, World War II experiences, and his political career to his assassination.

JOHANN KEPLER

1589 **Knight, David C.** Johannes Kepler & Planetary Motion. Watts, 1963. 186p. $2.95. (U)

A well-written account of the life and achievements of the German astronomer and mathematician who was one of the founders of modern astrophysics. Describes the many discouragements in Kepler's life and explains his three planetary laws.

MARTIN LUTHER KING

1590 **Clayton, Ed.** Martin Luther King: The Peaceful Warrior; illus. by David Hodges. enl. ed. Prentice-Hall, 1964. 87p. $3.50. (I–U)

Dr. King's fight to gain civil rights for Negroes in peaceful ways dominates this story of his life.

1591 **Young, Margaret B.** The Picture Life of Martin Luther King, Jr. Watts, 1967. 45p. $2.65. (P)

An easy-to-read photographic study of the famous Negro civil rights leader and winner of the Nobel Peace Prize, with brief facts, a chronology, and many photographs. (R2–3)

MARY HENRIETTA KINGSLEY

1592 **Syme, Ronald.** African Traveler: The Story of Mary Kingsley; illus. by Jacqueline Tomes. Morrow, 1962. 191p. $3.50. (I)

On an expedition to find new specimens of fish for the British Museum, Mary Kingsley traveled into the unexplored jungles of West Africa, "armed with nothing but curiosity, a sense of humor, and a British umbrella." This entertaining story of her adventures stresses her courage and her talent for establishing good relationships with the native peoples.

RUDYARD KIPLING

1593 **Manley, Seon.** Rudyard Kipling: Creative Adventurer. Vanguard, 1965. 256p. $4.95. (U)

A semifictionalized story of Kipling's life, showing how his stories and poems grew out of his colorful experiences in India and England. Descriptions of his major works and a list for further reading should entice advanced readers to explore further.

ROBERT KOCH

1594 **Dolan, Edward F.** Adventure with a Microscope: A Story of Robert Koch. Dodd, 1964. 240p. $3.50. (U)

A warm biography centering on Koch's experiments proving that specific microbes cause specific diseases.

LAFAYETTE, MARIE JOSEPH PAUL YVES ROCH GILBERT DU MOTIER, MARQUIS DE

1595 **Graham, Alberta Powell.** Lafayette: Friend of America; illus. by Ralph Ray. Abingdon, 1952. 127p. $2.25. (I)

Lafayette's role in the American Revolution is stressed in this story of the young Frenchman's life.

JEAN LAFITTE

1596 **Tallant, Robert.** The Pirate Lafitte and the Battle of New Orleans; illus. by John Chase. Random, 1951. 186p. $2.50; lib. ed. $2.48 net. (I–U)

The slave smuggler and privateer who became a hero by helping to win the Battle of New Orleans in the War of 1812 is the subject of an exciting biography.

ROBERT CAVELIER LA SALLE, SIEUR DE

1597 **Syme, Ronald.** La Salle of the Mississippi; illus. by William Stobbs. Morrow, 1953. 184p. $3.25. (I–U)

An authentic picture of the seventeenth-century Frenchman who explored the lands along the Mississippi River.

ANTOINE LAURENT LAVOISIER

1598 **Riedman, Sarah R.** Antoine Lavoisier: Scientist and Citizen. Abelard-Schuman, 1967. 192p. $4.50. (U)

The many theories and experiments of "the father of modern chemistry" are explored in a biography for serious students of science.

THOMAS EDWARD LAWRENCE

1599 **MacLean, Alistair.** Lawrence of Arabia; illus. by Gil Walker. Random, 1962. 177p. $2.50; lib. ed. $2.48 net. (I–U)

A partial biography of the legendary British officer who led guerrilla troops in the Arabian desert in World War I, concentrating on his military exploits.

ROBERT EDWARD LEE

1600 **Commager, Henry Steele,** and **Ward, Lynd.** America's Robert E. Lee. Houghton, 1951. 111p. $4.25; lib. ed. $3.73 net. (I–U)

An eminent historian and a talented artist have collaborated to produce a beautiful and unbiased account of Lee's personal life and his military leadership. A brief summary of the Civil War is vitalized by descriptions of battles and stunning colored pictures of battle scenes.

1601 **Freeman, Douglas Southall.** Lee of Virginia. Scribner, 1958. 256p. $4.50; lib. ed. $4.05 net. (U)

The author based this outstanding biography for older boys and girls on the extensive research done for his four-volume life of Lee. Superior command of material and lucid writing style are employed to delineate Lee the man as well as Lee the general.

LEIF ERICSSON

1602 **Aulaire, Ingri d', and Aulaire, Edgar Parin d'.** Leif the Lucky. Doubleday, 1941. 61p. $3.95. (P–I)

The Viking explorations of Greenland and America come to life in this picture-biography of Leif Ericsson.

1603 **Janeway, Elizabeth.** The Vikings; illus. by Henry C. Pitz. Random, 1951. 175p. $2.50; lib. ed. $2.48 net. (I)

Fact and fiction are combined in this story of Eric the Red and his son, Leif the Lucky, in Iceland, Greenland, and Vinland.

1604 **Shippen, Katherine B.** Leif Eriksson: First Voyager to America. Harper, 1951. 150p. $2.95; lib. ed. $2.92 net. (I–U)

Rich details of Viking life, trade, and customs, drawn from the Icelandic sagas, are incorporated in a rousing story of hardihood and daring.

LEONARDO DA VINCI

1605 **Horizon Magazine.** Leonardo da Vinci; by the eds. of Horizon Magazine. Author, Jay Williams; Consultant, Bates Lowry . . . American Heritage, 1965. A Horizon Caravel Book, distributed by Harper. 153p. $4.95; lib. ed. $4.79 net. (U)

Leonardo's life and work in art, science, and engineering are authoritatively treated in a biography useful in art classes and as background for the Renaissance. Copious illustrations include reproductions (many in color) of all paintings known to be Leonardo's.

LILIUOKALANI, QUEEN OF THE HAWAIIAN ISLANDS

1606 **Wilson, Hazel.** Last Queen of Hawaii; illus. by W. T. Mars. Knopf, 1963. 176p. $3.25; lib. ed. $3.09 net. (I–U)

A moving chapter in the history of the Hawaiian Islands is the background for Liliuokalani's life story. Includes a pronouncing glossary of Hawaiian words.

ABRAHAM LINCOLN

1607 **Aulaire, Ingri d', and Aulaire, Edgar Parin d'.** Abraham Lincoln. Doubleday, 1957. unp. $3.95. (P–I)

A handsomely illustrated introductory biography of Lincoln up to, but not including, his assassination. Homely details of Lincoln's early life are pictured with humor, later scenes with dignity and tenderness.

1608 **Judson, Clara Ingram.** Abraham Lincoln: Friend of the People; pen drawings by Robert Frankenberg; kodachromes of the Chicago Historical Society dioramas. Follett, 1950. 206p. $3.95; lib. ed. $4.17 net. (U)

The author's deep feeling for Lincoln and her careful research of recent material make this an exceptionally fine portrait.

1609 **McNeer, May.** America's Abraham Lincoln; illus. by Lynd Ward. Houghton, 1957. 119p. $3.75; lib. ed. $3.40 net. (I–U)

A brief biography told with dignity and warmth and strikingly illustrated.

1610 **Sandburg, Carl.** Abe Lincoln Grows Up; with illus. by James Daugherty. Harcourt, 1956. 222p. $3.75. (U)

The first 27 chapters of Sandburg's adult biography, *The Prairie Years,* covering Lincoln's childhood and youth up to his departure for New Salem. Rugged illustrations exactly reflect the frontier setting. Recommended for reading aloud or for independent reading by advanced students.

JENNY LIND

1611 **Kyle, Elizabeth.** The Swedish Nightingale: Jenny Lind. Holt, 1965. 223p. $3.75; lib. ed. $3.45 net. (U)

The famous Swedish singer emerges as a warm and generous person as well as a great musician in a fictionalized biography with special appeal for older girls.

CHARLES A. LINDBERGH

1612 Dalgliesh, Alice. Ride on the Wind; told by Alice Dalgliesh from the *Spirit of St. Louis* by Charles A. Lindbergh; pictures by Georges Schreiber. Scribner, 1956. unp. lib. ed. $3.12 net. (P–I)

Spacious colored pictures help to tell the story of Lindbergh's solo flight across the Atlantic.

CARL VON LINNÉ

1613 Stoutenburg, Adrien, and **Baker, Laura Nelson.** Beloved Botanist: The Story of Carl Linnaeus. Scribner, 1961. 192p. $2.95; lib. ed. $2.97 net. (U)

A well-written biography of the eighteenth-century Swedish naturalist who laid the foundation for modern systemic botany.

JOSEPH LISTER, BARON

1614 Farmer, Laurence. Master Surgeon: A Biography of Joseph Lister. Harper, 1962. 141p. lib. ed. $3.11 net. (U)

In a day when wound infection was prevalent and little understood, a nineteenth-century English surgeon introduced the germ theory of infectious diseases and gained acceptance of antiseptic methods in surgery against heavy opposition from the doctors of his day. A well-organized study of Lister's life and medical career and a shocking picture of the hospital conditions under which he worked.

DAVID LIVINGSTONE

1615 Eaton, Jeanette. David Livingstone: Foe of Darkness; illus. by Ralph Ray. Morrow, 1947. 256p. $3.75. (U)

The adventurous life of the nineteenth-century Scottish missionary who spent 30 years on a little-known continent to bring Christianity and science to native Africans.

HENRY WADSWORTH LONGFELLOW

1616 Peare, Catherine Owens. Henry Wadsworth Longfellow: His Life; illus. by Margaret Ayer. Holt, 1953. 116p. lib. ed. $3.07 net. (I)

A warm biography of "the good grey poet," covering his childhood, school days, travels abroad, and teaching and writing careers. Includes background notes and text of some of his poems.

JULIETTE LOW

1617 Pace, Mildred Mastin. Juliette Low; with drawings by Jane Castle. Scribner, 1947. 186p. $3.50; lib. ed. $3.31 net. (I–U)

This life story of the charming and brilliant Southern belle who founded the Girl Scouts of America will appeal to older girls, whether Scouts or not. Approved by the Girl Scout organization.

1618 Radford, Ruby L. Juliette Low: Girl Scout Founder. Garrard, 1965. 80p. $2.32. (I)

A brief, easily read biography for girls with limited reading ability. (R3–4)

MARTIN LUTHER

1619 McNeer, May, and **Ward, Lynd.** Martin Luther. Abingdon, 1953. 95p. $3.50. (I–U)

This well-told and strikingly illustrated story of the man who led the Protestant Reformation places him against an authentic historical background.

DOUGLAS MACARTHUR

1620 Archer, Jules. Front-Line General: Douglas MacArthur. Messner, 1963. 191p. $3.50; lib. ed. $3.34 net. (I–U)

A sympathetic biography of the soldier who served his country in both peace and war, giving the weak as well as the strong points in his character and personality.

SIR ALEXANDER MACKENZIE

1621 Syme, Ronald. Alexander Mackenzie: Canadian Explorer; illus. by William Stobbs. Morrow, 1964. 96p. lib. ed. $2.94. (I)

Sir Alexander Mackenzie's adventures and difficulties in finding an overland route to open new fur-trading territory in the West are recounted in a brief biography based on Mackenzie's journals.

ANNE SULLIVAN MACY

1622 Brown, Marion Marsh, and **Crone, Ruth.** The Silent Storm; illus. by Fritz Kredel. Abingdon, 1963. 250p. $3.25. (I–U)

In spite of her own dreary background as a child in an almshouse, Anne Sullivan became the inspired teacher of Helen Keller and made important contributions to the education of the blind-deaf. A touching account of her devotion to her pupil and an admiring portrait of a dedicated woman.

FERDINAND MAGELLAN

1623 **Syme, Ronald.** Magellan: First around the World; illus. by William Stobbs. Morrow, 1953. 71p. lib. ed. $2.94 net. (I)

Another brief, brisk biography of an explorer by this author-artist team, picturing in story and illustrations the storms, mutinies, and other disasters that beset Magellan's voyage around the world.

CHARLES MICKEY MANTLE

1624 **Silverman, Al.** Mickey Mantle: Mister Yankee. Putnam, 1963. 224p. lib. ed. $3.29 net. (I–U)

The qualities of courage and loyalty which helped to make Mickey Mantle the Yankees' most valuable player are stressed in this story of his career in the major leagues.

GUGLIELMO MARCONI

1625 **Coe, Douglas.** Marconi: Pioneer of Radio; illus. by Kreigh Collins. Messner, 1943. 272p. $3.50; lib. ed. $3.34 net. (U)

Marconi's life and work are reviewed as a chapter in the development of radio.

FRANCIS MARION

1626 **Brown, Marion Marsh.** The Swamp Fox. Westminster, 1950. 185p. $3.25. (I)

An action-filled tale of Francis Marion and his guerrilla fighters in the swamps of South Carolina during the Revolution.

JACQUES MARQUETTE

1627 **Kjelgaard, Jim.** Explorations of Père Marquette; illus. by Stephen J. Voorhies. Random, 1951. 181p. $2.50; lib. ed. $2.48 net. (I)

This story of Father Marquette and Louis Joliet who explored the Great Lakes and Mississippi regions is based on Marquette's journals.

JOHN MARSHALL

1628 **Tucker, Caroline.** John Marshall: The Great Chief Justice. Farrar, 1962. 209p. $3.25. (I–U)

A narrative biography tracing the life of the first Chief Justice of the Supreme Court from the age of ten to his death.

MARTIN DE PORRES

1629 **Bishop, Claire Huchet.** Martin de Porres, Hero; illus. by Jean Charlot. Houghton, 1954. 120p. $3.95 (I–U)

Martin de Porres, a Negro-Spanish child born in poverty and subjected to prejudice and mistreatment, devoted his life to work with the underprivileged in sixteenth-century Peru. An inspiring story of dedication and self-sacrifice.

MARY STUART, QUEEN OF THE SCOTS

1630 **Vance, Marguerite.** Scotland's Queen: The Story of Mary Stuart; illus. by J. Luis Pellicer. Dutton, 1962. 158p. $3.50. (U)

Political intrigue and religious controversy in England, France, and Scotland swirled around Mary Stuart. This story of her life, covering her years at the French court, her life in Scotland, and her imprisonment and execution in England, reveals a beautiful and charming woman destroyed by her personal ambitions.

CHARLES HORACE MAYO AND WILLIAM JAMES MAYO

1631 **Clapesattle, Helen.** The Mayo Brothers; illus. by Karoly and Szanto. Houghton, 1962. 180p. $2.95. (I)

A joint biography of the two great Minnesota physicians who established the clinic at Rochester, written by the author of an adult biography of the Mayos.

WILLIE HOWARD MAYS

1632 **Einstein, Charles.** Willie Mays: Coast to Coast Giant. Putnam, 1963. 191p. lib. ed. $3.69 net. (I–U)

A fast-paced story of Willie Mays's baseball career, from rookie to the highest-paid Giant in history.

MICHELANGELO BUONARROTI

1633 **Ripley, Elizabeth.** Michelangelo: A Biography; with drawings, paintings, and sculpture by Michelangelo. Walck, 1953. 68p. $4. (I–U)

Thirty-one photographs of Michelangelo's work, placed to coincide exactly with the author's commentary, are an outstanding feature of this authoritative life story.

RALPH MOODY

1634 **Moody, Ralph.** Little Britches; illus. by Edward Shenton. Norton, 1950. 261p. $4.95; lib. ed. $4.51 net. (U)

The author tells the story of his boyhood on a Colorado ranch where his large family struggled to establish a home. A warm family story with excellent father-son relationships.

SIR HENRY MORGAN

1635 **Syme, Ronald.** Sir Henry Morgan: Buccaneer; illus. by William Stobbs. Morrow, 1965. 96p. $2.95; lib. ed. $2.94 net. (I)

Part pirate, part patriot, Morgan gained fame and knighthood by raiding Spanish-held cities in the Caribbean. Text and pictures are well suited to the character of the bold, dashing buccaneer.

SAMUEL FINLEY BREESE MORSE

1636 **Hays, Wilma Pitchford.** Samuel Morse and the Electronic Age. Watts, 1966. 114p. $2.95. (I–U)

Emphasis is on Morse's invention of the telegraph and its effect on communication. Includes a chapter on communications in the electronic age.

LUCRETIA COFFIN MOTT

1637 **Sterling, Dorothy.** Lucretia Mott: Gentle Warrior. Doubleday, 1964. 237p. $3.50. (U)

Lucretia Mott's many activities — as Quaker preacher, abolitionist, crusader for women's rights, and wife and mother — are related in a lively biography of one of the most remarkable women of the nineteenth century.

JOHANN CHRYSOSTOM WOLFGANG AMADEUS MOZART

1638 **Mirsky, Reba Paeff.** Mozart; illus. by W. T. Mars. Follett, 1960. 144p. $3.95; lib. ed. $4.17 net. (I)

An entertaining biography of Mozart's life and work, including excerpts from his letters.

JOHN MUIR

1639 **Swift, Hildegarde Hoyt.** From the Eagle's Wing: A Biography of John Muir; illus. by Lynd Ward. Morrow, 1962. 287p. $4.50. (U)

Portrays the life and character of the naturalist who championed the cause of conservation and helped to establish national parks and forests. Muir's love of beauty and dedication to his mission are sensitively interpreted, often through quotations from his own writings.

STANLEY FRANK MUSIAL

1640 **Robinson, Ray.** Stan Musial: Baseball's Durable "Man." Putnam, 1963. 192p. lib. ed. $3.69 net. (I–U)

Tributes from Musial's colleagues are included in this appreciative biography of the National League's champion batter.

NAPOLEON I, EMPEROR OF THE FRENCH

1641 **Komroff, Manuel.** Napoleon. Messner, 1954. 189p. $3.50; lib. ed. $3.34 net. (I–U)

The rise and fall of the great military genius are chronicled in a dramatic account of Napoleon's life. Bibliography.

JAWAHARLAL NEHRU

1642 **Apsler, Alfred.** Fighter for Independence: Jawaharlal Nehru. Messner, 1963. 191p. $3.50; lib. ed. $3.34 net. (U)

Against the turbulent background of Indian history and politics, Nehru's part in winning independence from England and his accomplishments as prime minister are examined. Includes a glossary of Indian words and a bibliography.

HORATIO NELSON

1643 **Whipple, A. B. C.** Hero of Trafalgar: The Story of Lord Nelson; illus. by William Hofmann. Random, 1963. 186p. $2.50; lib. ed. $2.48 net. (U)

This biography, devoted mainly to Nelson's spectacular career in the British navy, gives exciting accounts of his sea battles and touches only lightly on his personal life.

ISAAC NEWTON

1644 **Tannenbaum, Beulah,** and **Stillman, Myra.** Isaac Newton: Pioneer of Space Mathematics; illus. by Gustav Schrotter. McGraw-Hill, 1959. 128p. $3; lib. ed. $2.96 net. (U)

A lively picture of Newton and the scientists around him, explaining his theories of light, gravitation, and motion which form the basis of modern scientific thought.

FLORENCE NIGHTINGALE

1645 Nolan, Jeannette Covert. Florence Nightingale; illus. by George Avison. Messner, 1946. 209p. $3.50; lib. ed. $3.34 net. (U)

Florence Nightingale's service in the Crimean War and her work to raise the standards of nursing and public health in England dominate this story of her life. Good vocational material for older girls.

CABEZA DE VACA, ALVAR NÚÑEZ

1646 Syme, Ronald. First Man To Cross America: The Story of Cabeza de Vaca; illus. by William Stobbs. Morrow, 1961. 190p. $3.25. (I–U)

A concise account of the Spanish explorer's eight years of search for the "cities of gold," which took him from Florida to Mexico and Arizona. An absorbing story of a little-known character in early American history.

OSCEOLA, SEMINOLE CHIEF

1647 McNeer, May. War Chief of the Seminoles; illus. by Lynd Ward. Random, 1954. 180p. $2.50; lib. ed. $2.48 net. (I)

The tragic story of Osceola, the Indian chief who led his warriors through the swamps of Florida in his fight against the encroachments of the white man.

SIR WILLIAM OSLER

1648 Noble, Iris. The Doctor Who Dared: William Osler. Messner, 1959. 192p. lib. ed. $3.34 net. (I–U)

Canadian-born William Osler led the crusade for improved medical education and practice in Canada, America, and England. This sympathetic account of his life and career is an interesting chapter in history of medicine.

THOMAS PAINE

1649 Gurko, Leo. Tom Paine: Freedom's Apostle; illus. by Fritz Kredel. Crowell, 1957. 231p. $4.50. (U)

Both strengths and weaknesses of the controversial writer whose ideas of freedom

influenced the thinking of Revolutionary thinkers are presented in a biography for mature older readers.

LOUIS PASTEUR

1650 Grant, Madeleine P. Louis Pasteur: Fighting Hero of Science. McGraw-Hill, 1959. 220p. $3.25. (U)

A warm story of Pasteur's life and an account of his career and achievements, stressing his work in crystals, microbes, fermentation, and vaccines.

ANNA PAVLOVA

1651 Malvern, Gladys. Dancing Star: The Story of Anna Pavlova; illus. by Susanne Suba. Messner, 1942. 280p. $3.50; lib. ed. $3.34 net. (U)

Shows Pavlova as an interesting personality as well as a great ballerina and gives a realistic picture of her training with the Russian ballet and her later world triumphs.

ROBERT EDWIN PEARY

1652 Lord, Walter. Peary to the Pole. Harper, 1963. 141p. $3.50; lib. ed. $3.27 net. (I–U)

Peary's six unsuccessful attempts to reach the North Pole are lightly sketched and his final effort is described in exciting detail.

WILLIAM PENN

1653 Aliki. The Story of William Penn; written and illus. by Aliki. Prentice-Hall, 1964. unp. $3.75. (P–I)

This picture-story of Penn's adult life, emphasizing his belief in brotherly love, introduces Penn to young children. (R2–3)

1654 Gray, Elizabeth Janet. Penn; illus. by George Gillett Whitney. Viking, 1938. 298p. $4.50; lib. ed. $4.13 net. (U)

Penn's early life and conversion to the Quaker religion, his persecution for his religious beliefs, and his life as founder and proprietor of Pennsylvania are related in a sympathetic biography stressing the character traits which governed his life.

PRUDENCE CRANDALL PHILLEO

1655 Yates, Elizabeth. Prudence Crandall: Woman of Courage; illus. by Nora S. Unwin. Dutton, 1955. 246p. $3.95. (U)

In 1833 a Quaker schoolmistress admitted

Negro girls to her classes and stood firm against the persecutions of her outraged Connecticut neighbors. A quiet story of courage, particularly relevant to today's world. Suggested for discussion groups.

AUGUSTE PICCARD AND JEAN FELIX PICCARD

1656   **Honour, Alan.** Ten Miles High, Two Miles Deep: The Adventures of the Piccards; illus. with photos. and with line drawings by Charles Geer. McGraw-Hill, 1957. 206p. $3.95; lib. ed. $3.31 net. (U)
Describes the mechanisms by which the French twins explored the atmosphere and the ocean depths and tells of the brothers' many daring experiments.

ZEBULON MONTGOMERY PIKE

1657   **Keating, Bern.** Zebulon Pike: Young America's Frontier Scout; illus. by Frank Aloise. Putnam, 1965. 159p. lib. ed. $3.29 net. (I–U)
A born adventurer, Zebulon Pike was sent as a young Army officer to promote peace and good will among the Indians living in the territory acquired by the Louisiana Purchase. The story of his adventures on this assignment and of his discovery of the Rocky Mountain peak named for him should be of especial interest to boys.

FRANCISCO PIZARRO

1658   **Syme, Ronald.** Francisco Pizarro: Finder of Peru; illus. by William Stobbs. Morrow, 1963. 96p. lib. ed. $2.94 net. (I)
A dramatic story of Pizarro and his ruthless followers who destroyed the Inca empire, emphasizing the brutality and greed of the Spaniards rather than the civilization of the Incas.

POCAHONTAS

1659   **Aulaire, Ingri d',** and **Aulaire, Edgar Parin d'.** Pocahontas; by Ingri & Edgar Parin d'Aulaire. Doubleday, 1946. 44p. $3.95. (P–I)
Large colored lithographs show many details of Indian life in this picture-biography of the little Indian girl who befriended the Jamestown colony. The brief story begins with Pocahontas' childhood in the Virginia wilderness and ends with her death in England.

MARCO POLO

1660   **Buehr, Walter.** The World of Marco Polo; illus. by the author. Putnam, 1961. 91p. lib. ed. $2.97 net. (I)
The reader follows Marco Polo's fabulous journey to China and his sojourn at the court of Kublai Khan in a concise biography of one of the world's great travelers.

1661   **Horizon Magazine.** Marco Polo's Adventures in China; by the eds. of Horizon Magazine. Author, Milton Rugoff; consultant, L. Carrington Goodrich . . . American Heritage, 1964. A Horizon Caravel Book, distributed by Harper, 153p. $4.95; lib. ed. $4.79 net. (I–U)
Good background material about the known world in the thirteenth century and the Mongol empire. Illustrations show Oriental art and artifacts and contemporary maps and paintings of Venice and other parts of Europe.

JUAN PONCE DE LEÓN

1662   **Baker, Nina Brown.** Juan Ponce de León; illus. by Robert Doremus. Knopf, 1957. 145p. lib. ed. $3.07 net. (I–U)
Ponce de León is portrayed as less ruthless than many of the Spanish conquistadors in his conquest and rule of Puerto Rico and Haiti and in his Florida explorations.

SIR WALTER RALEIGH

1663   **De Leeuw, Adèle.** Sir Walter Raleigh; illus. by Adolph Le Moult. Garrard, 1964. 96p. $2.32. (P–I)
This very simple story of the colorful life and tragic death of Sir Walter Raleigh is designed to attract good readers in the primary grades and slow middle-grade pupils. (R3–4)

1664   **Syme, Ronald.** Walter Raleigh; illus. by William Stobbs. Morrow, 1962. 96p. $2.95; lib. ed. $2.94 net. (I)
Shows that the many-talented Raleigh served his queen well in spite of his faults and helped to push back the boundaries of the sixteenth-century world. A well-written and vigorously illustrated story of an adventurous life.

WALTER REED

1665   **Wood, Laura N.** Walter Reed: Doctor in Uniform; illus. by Douglas Duer.

Messner, 1943. 277p. $3.50; lib. ed. $3.34 net. (I–U)

The U.S. Army doctor whose experiments proved that yellow fever is transmitted by mosquitoes is the subject of a competent biography covering his personal life and medical career. An index, a bibliography, and a brief history of yellow fever make the book useful for reference.

HERMANZOON VAN RIJN REMBRANDT

1666 **Ripley, Elizabeth.** Rembrandt: A Biography; with drawings, etchings, and paintings by Rembrandt. Walck, 1955. 68p. $4. (I–U)

Well-placed black-and-white reproductions of Rembrandt's work illustrate the author's comments on his paintings. A brief but authoritative introduction to the Dutch master.

PAUL REVERE

1667 **Fisher, Dorothy Canfield.** Paul Revere and the Minute Men; illus. by Norman Price. Random, 1950. 181p. $2.50; lib. ed. $2.48 net. (I–U)

Against an authentic setting of pre-Revolutionary Boston, the author tells Paul Revere's life story, bringing it to a climax with a detailed description of his famous ride.

1668 **Forbes, Esther.** America's Paul Revere; pictures by Lynd Ward. Houghton, 1946. 46p. lib. ed. $4.23 net. (I)

The author of an adult biography of Paul Revere has made a discriminating choice of incidents in this story for children. Text and dramatic colored pictures re-create the turbulent times and bring to life a dynamic personality.

LINDA RICHARDS

1669 **Baker, Rachel.** America's First Trained Nurse: Linda Richards; born July 27, 1841; died April 16, 1930. Messner, 1959. 192p. $3.50; lib. ed. $3.34 net. (U)

Gives a good picture of hospital conditions in the late nineteenth and early twentieth centuries and describes the obstacles Linda Richards faced in her pursuit of a nursing education.

JACKIE ROBINSON

1670 **Robinson, John Roosevelt,** and **Duckett, Alfred.** Breakthrough to the Big League: The Story of Jackie Robinson. Harper, 1965. 178p. $3.50; lib. ed. $3.27 net. (I–U)

A candid account of Jackie Robinson's early life and his career in baseball, focused on his problems in breaking the race barrier in the Big Leagues and his trials in winning the acceptance of his teammates. Illustrated with photographs.

ELEANOR ROOSEVELT

1671 **Eaton, Jeanette.** The Story of Eleanor Roosevelt; illus. with photos. Morrow, 1956. 251p. $4.95. (I–U)

An appreciative biography of the shy girl who became a famous world figure.

FRANKLIN DELANO ROOSEVELT

1672 **Peare, Catherine Owens.** The FDR Story. Crowell, 1962. 245p. $3.75. (U)

The author delineates Roosevelt's character and personality with fairness and describes his political career objectively. A well-organized, well-balanced picture of his life and times.

THEODORE ROOSEVELT

1673 **Judson, Clara Ingram.** Theodore Roosevelt: Fighting Patriot; front. and pencil drawings by Lorence F. Bjorklund. Follett, 1953. 218p. $3.95; lib. ed. $4.17 net. (I–U)

A well-researched and readable story of Roosevelt's frail childhood, his life in the West, and his Army and political careers, stressing his many services to his country.

BENJAMIN RUSH

1674 **Douty, Esther M.** Patriot Doctor: The Story of Benjamin Rush. Messner, 1959. 192p. $3.50. (U)

The Revolutionary physician, signer of the Declaration of Independence, "father of American psychiatry," and front-line doctor is vividly pictured in a setting of eighteenth-century Philadelphia.

SACAGAWEA

1675 **Farnsworth, Frances Joyce.** Winged Moccasins: The Story of Sacagawea; illus. by Lorence F. Bjorklund. Messner, 1954. 189p. $3.50; lib. ed. $3.34 net. (I–U)

The Indian girl who led the Lewis and Clark expedition into the newly acquired Louisiana territory is pictured as a brave and intelligent guide and an asset in establishing peaceful relations with the Indian tribes. The scant historical evidence has been supplemented with plausible conjecture to produce a readable story.

JONAS SALK

1676 **Rowland, John.** The Polio Man: The Story of Dr. Jonas Salk. Roy, 1961. 128p. $3.25. (U)
  Dr. Salk's research and experimentation with polio vaccine are the focus of a biography touching only lightly on his personal life.

HAYM SALOMON

1677 **Fast, Howard.** Haym Salomon: Son of Liberty; illus. by Eric M. Simon. Messner, 1941. 243p. $3.50; lib. ed. $3.34 net. (U)
  A fictionalized biography of the Polish-Jew immigrant who devoted his hard-won fortune to financing the Revolution and stabilizing the new government. A little-known aspect of the period which should interest mature readers.

CARL SANDBURG

1678 **Sandburg, Carl.** Prairie-Town Boy; taken from *Always the Young Strangers*; illus. by Joe Krush. Harcourt, 1955. 179p. $3.25. (U)
  Nostalgic reminiscences of Sandburg's childhood and youth in the Swedish community of Galesburg, Illinois.

HEINRICH SCHLIEMANN

1679 **Braymer, Marjorie.** The Walls of Windy Troy: A Biography of Heinrich Schliemann; illus. with photos. Harcourt, 1960. 189p. $3.50. (U)
  Following clues in Homer's *Iliad*, Schliemann devoted his fortune and ten years of his life to discovering the location of Troy. This account of his early life and explorations is excellent background reading for the Homeric epics and good fare for the serious archaeology buff.

FRANZ PETER SCHUBERT

1680 **Wheeler, Opal,** and **Deucher, Sybil.** Franz Schubert and His Merry Friends; illus. by Mary Greenwalt. Dutton, 1939. 124p. $3.50; lib. ed. $3.46 net. (I)
  Excerpts from Schubert's best-known compositions are included in this story of his early life for younger musicians.

ALBERT SCHWEITZER

1681 **Gollomb, Joseph.** Albert Schweitzer: Genius in the Jungle. Vanguard, 1949. 249p. $3.95. (U)
  A serious and laudatory study of Schweitzer's missionary and medical work in the jungles of Africa, showing how his philosophy of reverence for life shaped his career.

JUNÍPERO SERRA

1682 **Politi, Leo.** The Mission Bell. Scribner, 1953. unp. lib. ed. $3.31 net. (P–I)
  The author's beautiful colored illustrations are the perfect extension of his reverent story of Father Junípero Serra, who traveled by mule from Mexico to found the first mission in California.

SITTING BULL, DAKOTA CHIEF

1683 **Garst, Shannon.** Sitting Bull: Champion of His People; illus. by Elton Fax. Messner, 1946. 189p. $3.50; lib. ed. $3.34 net. (I–U)
  A narrative biography of the Dakota chief's early life and his courageous but unavailing battle against the depredations and injustices of the white man. Records a shameful chapter of American history which young people should know.

JOHN SMITH

1684 **Syme, Ronald.** John Smith of Virginia; illus. by William Stobbs. Morrow, 1954. 192p. $3.25. (I–U)
  Relates John Smith's adventures as leader of the Jamestown colony, explorer, and map maker, in direct style supplemented by vigorous illustrations.

HERNANDO DE SOTO

1685 **Syme, Ronald.** De Soto: Finder of the Mississippi; illus. by William Stobbs. Morrow, 1957. 96p. lib. ed. $2.94 net. (I)
  An exciting story of De Soto's explorations in the New World, including, in addition to his discovery of the Mississippi River, his expeditions into Florida and Peru.

SQUANTO, WAMPANOAG INDIAN

1686 **Bulla, Clyde Robert.** Squanto: Friend of the White Man; illus. by Peter Burchard.

Crowell, 1954. 106p. $3.50; lib. ed. $3.40 net. (P–I)

Open pages, large print, and lively illustrations attract reluctant readers in the middle grades to this story of the remarkable Indian youth who befriended the Pilgrim colony. (R2–3)

JOSEPH STALIN

1687 **Archer, Jules.** Man of Steel: Joseph Stalin. Messner, 1965. 191p. $3.50; lib. ed. $3.34 net. (U)

The rise and fall of Joseph Stalin are recounted against the background of the twentieth-century world conditions in which he played so prominent a part. His character, ambitions, and achievements in the industrialization of Russia are convincingly portrayed.

SIR HENRY MORTON STANLEY

1688 **Hall-Quest, Olga.** With Stanley in Africa. Dutton, 1961. 157p. $3.50. (U)

Henry Morton Stanley, an American journalist, went to Africa in search of David Livingtone and stayed to become an explorer himself. A well-told adventure tale with special appeal for older boys.

CHARLES PROTEUS STEINMETZ

1689 **Miller, Floyd.** The Electrical Genius of Liberty Hall: Charles Proteus Steinmetz. McGraw-Hill, 1962. 126p. $3.50; lib. ed. $3.06 net. (I–U)

Concentrates on the human side of the electrical wizard whose work transformed the field of electrical engineering.

ROBERT LOUIS STEVENSON

1690 **Peare, Catherine Owens.** Robert Louis Stevenson: His Life; illus. by Margaret Ayer. Holt, 1962. 128p. lib. ed. $3.07 net. (I)

An introduction to Stevenson and his works, with much attention to his early life and personality and to the people who influenced him most.

PETER ILYICH TCHAIKOVSKY

1691 **Wheeler, Opal.** Peter Tschaikowsky and the Nutcracker Ballet; illus. by Christine Price. Dutton, 1959. 95p. $3.50. (I)

A story-biography for younger children telling of Tchaikovsky's early life and education, his travels, and his most famous

compositions. Piano arrangements for some of his best-known works are included.

JAMES FRANCIS THORPE

1692 **Schoor, Gene, and Gilfond, Henry.** The Jim Thorpe Story: America's Greatest Athlete. Messner, 1951. 186p. $3.50; lib. ed. $3.34 net. (U)

The Indian athlete who starred in track, baseball, and football but who was ruled ineligible for his Olympic trophies is portrayed in an exciting story.

ARTURO TOSCANINI

1693 **Ewen, David.** The Story of Arturo Toscanini. rev. and enl. ed. Holt, 1960. 142p. lib. ed. $3.27 net. (U)

This story of the great conductor's musical life includes an essay on the art of the conductor, a bibliography on Toscanini, and a discography, making it especially useful to music classes and to serious students of music.

PIERRE DOMINIQUE TOUSSAINT L'OUVERTURE

1694 **Scherman, Katharine.** The Slave Who Freed Haiti: The Story of Toussaint L'Ouverture; illus. by Adolf Dehn. Random, 1954. 182p. $2.50; lib. ed. $2.48 net. (I–U)

A fast-paced biography of the slave who led the Haitian revolt against French rule in the eighteenth century.

HARRY S. TRUMAN

1695 **Steinberg, Alfred.** Harry S. Truman. Putnam, 1963. 223p. lib. ed. $3.29 net. (U)

Following an account of Truman's early life, the author discusses his political career, including both failures and successes, and draws the conclusion that Truman grew in office to become a strong president.

HARRIET TUBMAN

1696 **Petry, Ann.** Harriet Tubman: Conductor of the Underground Railroad. Crowell, 1955. 247p. $3.95. (U)

Harriet Tubman, the "Moses of her people," led more than three hundred Negroes from slavery in Maryland to freedom in the North. A moving picture of an indomitable woman and the antislavery movement of which she was a part.

JOHN UNITAS

1697   Greene, Lee. The Johnny Unitas Story. Putnam, 1962. 183p. lib. ed. $3.29 net. (I–U)

This story of the Baltimore Colts' great quarterback covers his high school and college days, his experiences as a professional football player, and some of his most exciting games.

AMERIGO VESPUCCI

1698   Baker, Nina Brown. Amerigo Vespucci; illus. by Paul Valentino. Knopf, 1956. 143p. lib. ed. $3.09 net. (I)

The new world bears the name of this scholar, merchant, and explorer who sailed for love of adventure and new scientific knowledge rather than for fame and riches. A readable account of his life as an aristocrat in sixteenth-century Florence and of his voyages.

WERNHER VON BRAUN

1699   Walters, Helen B. Wernher Von Braun: Rocket Engineer; introd. by Wernher Von Braun; illus. with photos. Macmillan, 1964. 187p. $4.50; lib. ed. $4.34 net. (U)

Briefly sketches the German-born scientist's life and describes in detail his development of the liquid-fuel rocket. Includes a photographic survey of his life, a glossary, a chronology of parallel events, and a bibliography.

BOOKER TALIAFERRO WASHINGTON

1700   Graham, Shirley. Booker T. Washington: Educator of Hand, Head, and Heart; front. and jacket by Donald W. Lambo. Messner, 1955. 192p. $3.50; lib. ed. $3.34 net. (I–U)

A sympathetic story of the slave who overcame tremendous difficulties to establish the Tuskegee Normal and Industrial School for the education of his people.

GEORGE WASHINGTON

1701   Aulaire, Ingri d', and Aulaire, Edgar Parin d'. George Washington. Doubleday, 1936. unp. $3.95. (P–I)

Appealing incidents and gay, colored illustrations make this a particularly attractive first biography of Washington.

1702   Judson, Clara Ingram. George Washington: Leader of the People; illus. by Rob-

ert Frankenberg. Follett, 1951. 224p. $3.95; lib. ed. $4.17 net. (I–U)

The author portrays Washington's youth, home life, and public career with warmth and authority and emphasizes the character traits which made him a great general and President.

1703   North, Sterling. George Washington: Frontier Colonel; illus. by Lee Ames. Random, 1957. 184p. $2.50; lib. ed. $2.48 net. (I)

Washington's early life and his experiences during the French and Indian War, based largely on his letters and journals, are the focus of this biography, which ends when he became President.

MARTHA DANDRIDGE CUSTIS WASHINGTON

1704   Vance, Marguerite. Martha, Daughter of Virginia: The Story of Martha Washington; illus. by Nedda Walker. Dutton, 1947. 190p. $3.75. (I)

A pleasant story of the First Lady, combining romance, history, and biography in approximately equal proportions.

BENJAMIN WEST

1705   Henry, Marguerite, and Dennis, Wesley. Benjamin West and His Cat Grimalkin. Bobbs-Merrill, 1947. 147p. $3.50; lib. ed. $3.25 net. (I)

An ingenious blending of cat story and biography, in which Grimalkin encourages Benjamin to paint in spite of his Quaker family's disapproval. After seeing the paintings done with a cat-hair brush, the parents relent and Benjamin becomes a famous court painter in England.

MARCUS WHITMAN

1706   Daugherty, James. Marcus and Narcissa Whitman: Pioneers of Oregon. Viking, 1953. 158p. $3.95; lib. ed. $3.77 net. (I–U)

In 1836 a young doctor and his schoolteacher bride made the hazardous journey to Oregon to establish a mission among the Indians. This is a graphic account, based on the Whitmans' letters and journals, of the hardships and dangers of the journey and the difficulties of establishing the mission, ending with the Indian raid in which the couple were massacred.

WOODROW WILSON

1707   Peare, Catherine Owens. The Woodrow Wilson Story: An Idealist in Politics. Crowell, 1963. 277p. $4.50. (U)

The author sketches the early life, teaching and political careers, and the post-World War I activities of the President, devoting much of the story to an interpretation of Wilson's ideals and to his unsuccessful efforts to establish the League of Nations.

ORVILLE WRIGHT AND
WILBUR WRIGHT

1708 **Reynolds, Quentin.** The Wright Brothers: Pioneers of American Aviation; illus. by Jacob Landau. Random, 1950. 183p. $1.95; lib. ed. $2.48 net. (I)

This story of two brothers who invented, built, and flew the first heavier-than-air craft at Kitty Hawk, North Carolina, in 1903, is a lively chapter in the history of flight, with special appeal for boys.

JOHN PETER ZENGER

1709 **Galt, Tom.** Peter Zenger: Fighter for Freedom; illus. by Ralph Ray. Crowell, 1951. 242p. $4.50. (U)

One man's fight for freedom of the press is dramatized in a story of the printer who defied the governor of New York by printing articles critical of the administration. A vivid picture of Colonial New York and a detailed report on Zenger's trial (based on Zenger's own account), which established freedom of the press in America and England.

Geography and History

Atlases and Maps

1710 **Epstein, Sam,** and **Epstein, Beryl.** The First Book of Maps and Globes; pictures by Lászlo Roth. Watts, 1959. 63p. $2.65. (P–I)

A very simple explanation of map symbols and terminology and concise information on how to use maps of different kinds.

1711 **Hammond (C. S.) and Co., Inc.** The First Book Atlas; by the eds. and cartographers of C. S. Hammond and Co. rev. ed. Watts, 1968. 96p. $2.65. (P–I)

Includes a map of every country in the world, with population figures and descriptions.

1712 **Hirsch, S. Carl.** The Globe for the Space Age; illus. by Burt Silverman. Viking, 1963. 88p. $3.75; lib. ed. $3.56 net. (I–U)

Presents the globe as the best means of understanding the earth and explains how it is used in communication, weather-casting, telling time, and space exploration.

1713 **Moore, Patrick,** and **Brinton, Henry.**

Exploring Maps; illus. by Cyril Deakins. Hawthorn, 1967. 95p. $3.50. (I–U)

Explains the development of map making and the different kinds of maps now in use.

1714 **Tannenbaum, Beulah,** and **Stillman, Myra.** Understanding Maps: Charting the Land, Sea, and Sky; illus. by Rus Anderson. McGraw-Hill, 1957. 144p. $3.50; lib. ed. $3.06 net. (I–U)

An informal discussion of the problems of map making and the instruments and methods used in drawing different kinds of maps. Clarifying diagrams and experiments aid understanding.

Exploration and Discovery

1715 **American Heritage.** Pirates of the Spanish Main; by the eds. of American Heritage, The Magazine of History; narrative by Hamilton Cochran, in consultation with Robert I. Nesmith. American Heritage, 1961. American Heritage Junior Library, distributed by Harper. 153p. $4.95; lib. ed. $4.79 net. (I–U)

A rousing account of the Spanish, Dutch, French, British, and American buccaneers who roamed the Spanish Main during the sixteenth and seventeenth centuries, and a discussion of pirates in art and literature. Illustrated with a wealth of maps, prints, paintings, coins, and weapons. Bibliography.

1716 Clark, William R. Explorers of the World; with paintings by Hans Schwarz. Published for the American Museum of Natural History by the Natural History Press. Doubleday, 1964. 252p. $5.95. (U)

A smoothly written historical survey of geographic and scientific explorations, profusely illustrated with maps, photographs, and paintings, many in color.

1717 Duvoisin, Roger. They Put Out to Sea: The Story of the Map; written and illus. by Roger Duvoisin. Knopf, 1944. 171p. lib. ed. $3.49 net. (I)

A dramatic tale of the great seafarers of early times who helped to unroll the map, illustrated with spirited pictures.

1718 Heyerdahl, Thor. Kon-Tiki: Across the Pacific by Raft; tr. by F. H. Lyon. Rand McNally, 1950. 304p. $5.95. (U)

To prove his theory that civilization had come to the South Seas from South America, the author built a primitive raft and set out with five companions and a parrot to drift across the Pacific Ocean. This is his vivid record of that 100-day, 4300-mile voyage.

1719 Horizon Magazine. Captain Cook and the South Pacific; by the eds. of Horizon Magazine. Author, Oliver Warner; consultant, J. C. Beaglehole . . . American Heritage, 1963. A Horizon Caravel Book, distributed by Harper. 153p. $4.95; lib. ed. $4.79 net. (U)

The three voyages which the intrepid British explorer made to survey and map the islands of the South Pacific are absorbingly described, and the personality and character of Captain Cook are pictured with fairness. Lavishly illustrated with maps and pictures of the period.

1720 Price, Christine. Cities of Gold and Isles of Spice: Travel to the East in the Middle Ages; maps and decorations by the author. McKay, 1965. 208p. $4.25. (I–U)

Beginning with the Arab merchants and

geographers of the eighth and ninth centuries and ending with the first voyage of Vasco da Gama, the author relates the story of the European adventurers, merchants, pilgrims, and emissaries who made the perilous journey to the fabled East.

1721 Selsam, Millicent E. The Quest of Captain Cook; illus. by Lee J. Ames. Doubleday, 1962. 128p. $3.50. (I)

Describes Cook's voyages, his search for the legendary Northwest Passage, his circumnavigation of the Antarctic, and his discovery of Hawaii and other Pacific islands.

1722 Stockton, Frank R. Buccaneers & Pirates of Our Coasts. Macmillan, 1967. [new ed.] 248p. $4.50. (I–U)

Pirates, famous and infamous, are introduced and their exploits recounted in this new edition of an old favorite. Illustrated with old prints and engravings.

1723 Walsh, Richard J. Adventures and Discoveries of Marco Polo; illus. by Cyrus LeRoy Baldridge. Random, 1953. 183p. $2.50; lib. ed. $2.48 net. (I)

A simplified story of Marco Polo's travels across Asia to visit the court of Kublai Kahn, based on Marco Polo's own account. Vivid descriptions of the wonders of the Mongol world, skillful selection of incidents of interest to young people, and inviting format recommend this as a colorful adventure story as well as good background reading in history.

Prehistoric Archaeology

For the origin and evolution of man, see Anthropology, pages 8–9.

1724 Andrews, Roy Chapman. All about Dinosaurs; illus. by Thomas W. Voter. Random, 1953. 146p. $1.95; lib. ed. $2.48 net. (I)

A noted scientist and fossil hunter tells how the world of the dinosaurs has been reconstructed from remains found by archaeologists and describes the various species of dinosaurs. An authoritative and readable account, enlivened by the author's own experiences and by accurate illustrations.

1725 **Baity, Elizabeth Chesley.** America before Man; illus. with drawings, maps, charts, and diags. by C. B. Falls and with 31 pages of photos. Viking, 1953. 224p. $5; lib. ed. $4.53 net. (U)

A chronological account of the development of geological and life forms in the Western Hemisphere, covering fossils, reptiles, and mammals from the beginning through the Ice Age. For the superior upper-grade reader.

1726 **Baldwin, Gordon C.** Race against Time: The Story of Salvage Archaeology; introd. by Robert L. Stephenson. Putnam, 1966. 191p. lib. ed. $3.29 net. (U)

Describes recent efforts to save prehistoric American remains from destruction by construction projects, stressing the urgency of the movement and the need for public awareness and support. Illustrated with photographs.

1727 **Baumann, Hans.** The Caves of the Great Hunters; newly illus. and rev. ed. Pantheon, 1962. 183p. lib. ed. $3.99 net. (I–U)

Equally interesting for art and history classes is this true story of the discovery by four boys of beautiful cave paintings in southern France.

1728 **Braidwood Robert J.** Archaeologists and What They Do. Watts, 1960. 180p. $3.95. (U)

An eminent archaeologist discusses the purposes and methods of archaeology and the qualifications and training required for the profession, making his explanations vivid by taking the reader on an imaginary expedition to excavate a site in Iran.

1729 **Christie, Trevor L.** Legacy of a Pharaoh: The United Effort To Save Abu Simbel. Lippincott, 1966. 122p. $3.95. (U)

A remarkable archaeological feat of the present day—the cooperative effort to save the temples of Rameses II from the waters of the Aswan High Dam—is described in an absorbing account.

1730 **Clark, Mary Lou.** The True Book of Dinosaurs; illus. by Chauncey Maltman. Childrens Pr., 1955. 47p. $1.95; lib. ed. $2.50 net. (P)

A very simple, colorfully illustrated first book on dinosaurs, for independent reading in primary grades. (R2–3)

1731 **Colbert, Edwin H.** Millions of Years Ago: Prehistoric Life in North America; illus. by Margaret M. Colbert. Crowell, 1958. 153p. $3.95. (I)

Takes the reader on a fossil-hunting expedition to see how paleontologists find, recover, and preserve remains from the past, and how they learn from their finds. North American fishes, dinosaurs, and other ancient animals are described and pictured.

1732 **Cottrell, Leonard.** Digs and Diggers: A Book of World Archaeology; illus. with photos. World, 1964. 285p. $4.95. (U)

A history of archaeology told through the methods and achievements of famous archaeologists. Includes a reading list.

1733 **Darling, Lois.** Before and after Dinosaurs; written and illus. by Lois and Louis Darling. Morrow, 1959. 95p. lib. ed. $2.94 net. (I)

Traces the evolution of vertebrate animals through the geologic ages. Excellent pictures and evolutionary charts.

1734 **De Borhegyi, Suzanne.** Ships, Shoals, and Amphoras: The Story of Underwater Archaeology; illus. by Alex Schomburg. Holt, 1961. 176p. lib. ed. $3.59 net. (U)

Discusses the rich underwater archaeological treasures and describes the equipment and methods by which they are recovered.

1735 **Dickinson, Alice.** The First Book of Prehistoric Animals; pictures by Helene Carter. Watts, 1954. 92p. $2.65. (I)

Traces the development of land, air, and sea animals and relates each stage of their evolution to changing conditions on earth.

1736 **Epstein, Sam,** and **Epstein, Beryl.** Prehistoric Animals; pictures by W. R. Lohse. Watts, 1956. 210p. $3.95. (U)

This more detailed treatment of the subject than the books listed above reconstructs each prehistoric period and describes the life in each, showing how the various species evolved, adapted to changing conditions, and survived or became extinct.

1737 **Fenton, Carroll Lane.** Prehistoric World: Stories of Animal Life in Past Ages; with drawings by the author; color plates by James E. Allen. Day, 1954. 126p. $3.75. (I)

An introduction to typical prehistoric animals and the evolutionary eras in which they lived, clarified by informative drawings and a chart of prehistoric ages.

1738   Fenton, Carroll Lane. Tales Told by Fossils. Doubleday, 1966. 182p. $4.95. (I–U)

An enthusiastic discussion of fossil hunting, what can be learned through fossils, and the methods by which they are studied. Lists museums with collections of fossils, and includes a glossary and a reading list.

1739   Holden, Raymond. Famous Fossil Finds: Great Discoveries in Paleontology; illus. by John Martinez. Dodd, 1966. 100p. $3.50; lib. ed. $3.23 net. (I–U)

Describes nine important fossil finds (dinosaur eggs, Peking man, La Brea tar pits, etc.) and the men who made them. An interestingly written introduction to paleontology, including maps, pictorial reconstructions of prehistoric animals, and a reading list.

1740   Holsaert, Eunice, and Gartland, Robert. A Book To Begin on Dinosaurs. Holt, 1959. unp. $2.75; lib. ed. $2.78 net. (P)

An introduction to dinosaurs, describing each species by the meaning of its name (i.e., "Three-horned Face") and telling how they lived and why they disappeared. A generously illustrated book, somewhat more difficult than Clark's *The True Book of Dinosaurs,* above.

1741   Jessup, Ronald. The Wonderful World of Archaeology; art by Norman Battershill and Kenneth Symonds; diags. by Isotope Institute. Doubleday, 1956. 65p. $2.95. (I)

This large book with more than 250 pictures in color is designed to stimulate interest in archaeology by describing how and where scientists have found evidence of the past and how they interpret it to help solve the mysteries of the ancient world.

1742   Kubie, Nora Benjamin. The First Book of Archaeology; illus. by the author. Watts, 1957. 63p. $2.65. (I)

A concise overview of archaeology covering its history, purpose, methods, and accomplishments.

1743   Poole, Lynn, and Poole, Gray. Carbon 14, and Other Science Methods That Date the Past; illus. by P. A. Hutchison. McGraw-Hill, 1961. 160p. $3.95; lib. ed. $3.06 net. (U)

A readable account of the new methods by which scientists date artifacts from the past, concentrating on the Carbon 14 method and giving examples of its application.

1744   Rhodes, Frank H. T.; Zim, Herbert S.; (and) Shaffer, Paul R. Fossils: A Guide to Prehistoric Life; illus. by Raymond Perlman. Golden Pr., 1962. 160p. $3.95. (I–U)

A colorful, informative handbook on fossils and fossil collecting.

1745   Scheele, William E. The First Mammals; written and illus. by William E. Scheele. World, 1955. 128p. $5.95. (U)

The Curator of the Cleveland Museum of Natural History describes and illustrates the evolution of mammals, with the exception of men and apes, arranging text and pictures by geologic eras. Includes a bibliography.

1746   Scheele, William E. Prehistoric Animals; written and illus. by William E. Scheele. World, 1954. 125p. $5.95; lib. ed. $5.28 net. (U)

In a companion volume to *The First Mammals,* above, the author tells a word-and-picture story of the first 500 million years of life on earth.

1747   Shippen, Katherine B. Portals to the Past: The Story of Archaeology; illus. by Mel Silverman. Viking, 1963. 255p. $4.50. (U)

A history of archaeology incorporating newer methods of research and showing how the science has moved beyond the early sites at Greece and Rome.

1748   Suggs, Robert C. Modern Discoveries in Archaeology; illus. by Leonard Everett Fisher. Crowell, 1962. 117p. $3.50. (I–U)

Discusses dating methods; recent digs in Crete, Iraq, and other areas; discovery of the Dead Sea Scrolls; and investigation of sunken ships in the Mediterranean.

1749   White, Anne Terry. All about Archaeology; drawings by Tom O'Sullivan; with a 12-page photo. section. Random, 1959. 148p. $2.50; lib. ed. $2.48 net. (I)

Lively style and many illustrations make this a particularly interesting account of early archaeological discoveries.

1750 **White, Anne Terry.** Lost Worlds: Adventures in Archaeology. Random, 1941. 316p. $3.95; lib. ed. $3.99 net. (U)

A more complete, more advanced study of archaeology than the author's *All about Archaeology*, above, describing how scientists discovered the four great ancient civilizations: Troy and Crete, Egypt, Assyria, and the Mayan Indian of Yucatan.

1751 **White, Anne Terry.** Prehistoric America; illus. by Aldren Watson. Random, 1951. 182p. $1.95; lib. ed. $2.48 net. (I–U)

Re-creates the America of the brontosaurus, the saber-toothed tiger, and the eohippus and tells how the Colorado River was first explored and the culture of the Basket Weavers and Mound Builders investigated.

Ancient Civilizations

1752 **Asimov, Isaac.** The Greeks: A Great Adventure. Houghton, 1965. 326p. $4.50. (U)

A concise history of the Greek people from the beginning to the Christian era, concluding with a brief account of recent history. City states, wars, political affairs, and famous people are discussed in conversational style. Includes maps and a table of dates.

1753 **Baumann, Hans.** The World of the Pharaohs; colour photos. by Albert Burges; line drawings by Hans Peter Renner. Pantheon, 1960. 255p. lib. ed. $4.29 net. (U)

Within the framework of a story, the author reconstructs the civilization of ancient Egypt and describes the archaeological research which revealed it. Packed with historical detail and illustrated with excellent line drawings and color photographs.

1754 **Chubb, Thomas Caldecot.** The Byzantines; illus. by Richard M. Powers. World, 1959. 126p. $3.95; lib. ed. $3.86 net. (U)

Eleven centuries of Byzantine history are described in all their glory in an exciting account of life in the great empire.

1755 **Cottrell, Leonard.** Crete: Island of Mystery; illus. by W. T. Mars. Prentice-Hall, 1965. 71p. $3.50. (U)

The ancient Minoan civilization of Knos-

sos, as revealed by archaeological digs in Crete, is re-created in an account which blends myth with evidence. Special attention is given to the procedures by which archaeologists deduced their theories.

1756 **Cottrell, Leonard.** Land of the Pharaohs; illus. by Richard M. Powers. World, 1960. 127p. $3.95; lib. ed. $3.86 net. (U)

After describing how King Tutankhamen's tomb was discovered, the author takes the reader on a tour of ancient Eypt, re-creating the life of the period and discussing the Rosetta Stone, the Valley of the Kings, and other significant aspects of Egyptian life.

1757 **Downey, Glanville.** Stories from Herodotus: A Panorama of Events and Peoples of the Ancient World; sel. and tr. by Glanville Downey; illus. by Enrico Arno. Dutton, 1965. 158p. $3.95; lib. ed. $3.91 net. (U)

These slightly adapted stories give children a vivid picture of the struggle between Greece and Persia. People, places, and deities are identified in a glossary.

1758 **Fairservis, Walter A.** Egypt: Gift of the Nile; illus. with photos. and with drawings by Jan Fairservis. Macmillan, 1963. 146p. $4.50. (U)

Reconstructs the daily life of ancient Egypt through concise text and 42 pages of photographs. Includes tables of historical information, a glossary, a bibliography, and an index.

1759 **Fairservis, Walter A.** Mesopotamia: The Civilization That Rose Out of Clay; illus. with photos., and with drawings and maps by Jan Fairservis. Macmillan, 1964. 126p. $4.50. (U)

This companion volume to *Egypt: Gift of the Nile*, above, surveys the customs, government, religion, and arts of the Sumerian, Babylonian, Assyrian, and Chaldean civilizations in a photographic essay and a dramatic narrative. Includes a chronology, a bibliography, and a glossary.

1760 **Falls, C. B.** The First 3000 Years: Ancient Civilizations of the Tigris, Euphrates, and Nile River Valleys, and the Mediterranean Sea; written and illus. by C. B. Falls. Viking, 1960. 220p. $5.95; lib. ed. $5.63 net. (U)

Broad coverage of historical events and daily life in the Tigris and Euphrates valleys from earliest times to A.D. 14, presented in an enthusiastic narrative and striking colored maps and pictures. Includes a bibliography and an index.

1761   Foster, Genevieve. Augustus Caesar's World: A Story of Ideas and Events from B.C. 44 to 14 A.D.; illus. by the author. Scribner, 1947. 330p. $5.95; lib. ed. $5.09 net. (U)

The author relates the Golden Age of Rome to events in other parts of the known world and shows how religious, social, and political forces from many parts of the world were converging to produce a new era. Many informative illustrations.

1762   Glubok, Shirley. Discovering Tut-Ankh-Amen's Tomb; abridged and adapted from *The Tomb of Tut-Ankh-Amen,* by Howard Carter and A. C. Mace; foreword by Eric Young, Associate Curator, Department of Egyptian Art, The Metropolitan Museum of Art; designed by Gerard Nook. Macmillan, 1968. 143p. $6.95. (U)

The thrilling story of a fabulous archaeological discovery is skillfully adapted for young people and illustrated with photographs of the tomb and its treasures, taken by a museum photographer. The narrative describes the expedition in detail and interprets Egyptian life through its findings.

1763   Hall, Jennie. Buried Cities; rev. under the editorship of Lily Poritz; introd. by Katharine Taylor. Macmillan, 1964. 116p. $3.50. (I–U)

Pompeii, Herculaneum, Olympia, and Mycenae are the lost cities discovered through archaeology and vividly described in this book.

1764   Horizon Magazine. Pharaohs of Egypt; by the eds. of Horizon Magazine. Author, Jacquetta Hawkes; consultant, Bernard V. Bothmer . . . American Heritage, 1965. A Horizon Caravel Book, distributed by Harper. 153p. $4.95; lib. ed. $4.79 net. (U)

Describes the beginnings of civilization in the Nile Valley, with emphasis on the period of the New Kingdom when the Pharaohs were at the height of their power. Notable for illustrations of wall paintings, sculptures, reliefs, and monuments of the period.

1765   Meadowcroft, Enid La Monte. The Gift of the River: A History of Ancient Egypt; introd. by Kirk Meadowcroft; illus. adapted from Egyptian sources by Katharine Dewey. Crowell, 1937. 235p. $3.95. (I)

A history of Egypt from 3400 B.C. to 609 B.C., centering around the people, both great and lowly, and the contributions which they made to world civilization.

1766   Quennell, Marjorie, and Quennell, C. H. B. Everyday Life in Roman and Anglo-Saxon Times: Including Viking and Norman Times. rev. ed. Putnam, 1959. 235p. $3.50. (U)

Two volumes in one, describing the contributions of various invading peoples to British life and culture.

1767   Robinson, Charles Alexander. The First Book of Ancient Greece; pictures by Lili Réthi. Watts, 1960. 61p. $2.65. (I)

Discusses the contributions made by the first democracy to government, art, and literature, and describes the religion, social life, and festivals of the Greek people.

1768   Robinson, Charles Alexander. The First Book of Ancient Mesopotamia and Persia. Watts, 1962. 61p. $2.65. (I)

An introduction to the earliest civilizations—Sumeria, Babylonia, Assyria, and Persia—in readable text and informative photographs and drawings.

1769   Robinson, Charles Alexander. The First Book of Ancient Rome. rev. ed. Watts, 1964. 66p. $2.65. (I)

A concise history of Rome, covering the Republic and the Empire and stressing its contributions to Western civilization.

1770   Sobol, Donald J. The First Book of the Barbarian Invaders, A.D. 373–511; pictures by W. Kirtman Plummer. Watts, 1962. 63p. $2.65. (I–U)

The barbarians who destroyed the Roman Empire are vividly described and pictured in a survey covering the reasons for their migrations, their methods of fighting, their daily lives, and some of their leaders.

Middle Ages, 476-1453

1771   Boardman, Fon W. Castles. Walck, 1957. 104p. $3.75. (I)

In an accurate and interesting study, the

author discusses feudalism and the castles which were its strongholds, animating his narrative with anecdotes, diagrams, and 33 photographs of castles as they appear today.

1772 Brooks, Polly Schoyer, and Walworth, Nancy Zinsser. The World of Walls: The Middle Ages in Western Europe. Lippincott, 1966. 256p. $6.95. (U)

This history of medieval times from the fifth to the fourteenth century combines sketches of famous men of the period with a stirring chronicle of events to give a vivid picture of the social, political, and religious life of the era.

1773 Buehr, Walter. Chivalry and the Mailed Knight; written and illus. by Walter Buehr. Putnam, 1963. 93p. lib. ed. $2.97 net. (I)

Describes the training and duties of knights, their weapons, coats of arms, and some of the famous orders of knighthood, concluding with a chapter on the Battle of Crécy, which marked the beginning of the end of knighthood.

1774 Buehr, Walter. Heraldry: The Story of Armorial Bearings; written and illus. by Walter Buehr. Putnam, 1964. 96p. lib. ed. $2.79 net. (I)

Traces the origin of heraldry from the Middle Ages, when battle dress distinguished friend from foe, to the formal codes prescribed by the College of Heralds today; describes, explains, and pictures the symbols used for armorial bearings; and explains how to create a coat of arms.

1775 Buehr, Walter. Knights, Castles, and Feudal Life. Putnam, 1957. 72p. lib. ed. $2.97 net. (I)

The organization of the feudal system and life within and without the castle are clearly described and illustrated with the author's informative pictures.

1776 Hartman, Gertrude. Medieval Days and Ways. Macmillan, 1937. 332p. $5.95. (I–U)

Comprehensive coverage of the medieval period in a picturesque narrative built around the types of people: lords, vassals, knights, pages, minstrels, monks, artisans, and others.

1777 Horizon Magazine. Knights of the Crusades; by the eds. of Horizon Magazine. Author, Jay Williams, in consultation with

Margaret B. Freeman. American Heritage, 1962. A Horizon Caravel Book, distributed by Harper. 153p. $4.95; lib. ed. $4.79 net. (I–U)

A history of the Crusades from 1095 to 1270, focused on the knights who led them and rich in reproductions of medieval art. An excellent reference for world-history, art, and literature classes, as well as an interesting browsing volume.

1778 Williams, Jay. Life in the Middle Ages; art work by Haig and Regina Shekerjian, together with many old prints, paintings, and illuminations. Random, 1966. 160p. $4.95; lib. ed. $4.99 net. (I–U)

An anecdotal history of social life in the Middle Ages, organized into chapters on the village, the castle, the military camps, the church, etc. A handsome and absorbing introduction to the period.

Modern Period, 1453-Present

General Works

1779 Brooks, Polly Schoyer, and Walworth, Nancy Zinsser. The World Awakes: The Renaissance in Western Europe. Lippincott, 1962. 224p. $5.95. (U)

Events, rulers, and famous personalities of Renaissance France, England, Spain, and Italy are brought to life in informed text and reproductions of contemporary maps and art. Useful in art classes as well as in social studies.

1780 Chamberlin, Eric Russell. Everyday Life in Renaissance Times; drawings by Helen Nixon Fairfield. Putnam, 1966. 200p. $3.50. (U)

Surveys the social and cultural awakening of Europe during the period from 1455 to 1648 in smoothly written text illustrated with many drawings.

1781 Foster, Genevieve. Abraham Lincoln's World; written and illus. by Genevieve Foster. 1809-1865. Scribner, 1944. 347p. $5.95; lib. ed. $5.09 net. (U)

A popular, effectively illustrated overview of world events during Abraham Lincoln's lifetime, useful to provide background for the period and as a basis for understanding world history.

1782 **Foster, Genevieve.** George Washington's World; written and illus. by Genevieve Foster. Scribner, 1941. 348p. $5.95; lib. ed. $5.09 net. (U)

World events of Washington's period are interrelated in a study similar in style and format to *Abraham Lincoln's World*, above.

1783 **Foster, Genevieve.** The World of Captain John Smith; written and illus. by Genevieve Foster. Scribner, 1959. 406p. $5.95; lib. ed. $5.09 net. (U)

The stirring events occurring all over the world in John Smith's lifetime are described in interesting text and pictured in dramatic illustrations.

1784 **Foster, Genevieve.** The World of Columbus and Sons; illus. by the author. Scribner, 1965. 406p. $5.95; lib. ed. $5.09 net. (U)

In a companion volume to the three books listed above, the author scans the world of Renaissance and the Reformation, building her story around the extraordinary characters of the period: Columbus and his sons, Diego and Ferdinand; Prince Henry the Navigator; Ferdinand and Isabella; Leonardo da Vinci; and many others.

1785 **Gottlieb, Gerald.** The First Book of the Mediterranean; pictures by Lili Réthi. Watts, 1960. 60p. $2.65. (I)

A concise account of "how men have used the Mediterranean Sea—for adventure, for trade, for war, and for pleasure," from the time of King Minos to the present.

1786 **Morris, James.** Cities. Harcourt, 1963. 375p. $6.95. (U)

Lively descriptions of 74 cities in all parts of the world which the author visited from 1951 to 1961.

1787 **Silverberg, Robert.** 15 Battles That Changed the World; illus. by Lewis Zacks. Putnam, 1963. 194p. $3.50. (U)

The author gives the historical background for each battle, describes the issue over which it was fought, follows the course of the fighting, and explains the significance of the outcome. Included, among others, are the battles of Marathon, Hastings, Waterloo, Gettysburg, and Stalingrad.

1788 **Trease, Geoffrey.** This Is Your Century. Harcourt, 1966. 343p. $6.95. (U)

World events of the first two thirds of the twentieth century are described, inter-related, and pictured in signficant photographs. Excellent to give perspective on recent world history.

WORLD WAR I

1789 **Bowen, Robert Sidney.** They Flew to Glory: The Story of the Lafayette Flying Corps. Lothrop, 1965. 160p. $3.50; lib. ed. $3.35 net. (I–U)

An action-filled account of the American fighter pilots who flew for France during the early years of World War I, describing planes, methods of combat, and exploits of individual fliers.

1790 **Gurney, Gene.** Flying Aces of World War I; illus. with photos. Random, 1965. 185p. $1.95; lib. ed. $2.48 net. (I–U)

Recounts the exploits of the famed Flying Aces of World War I, who, in their frail single-seated planes, made aviation history. American, British, French, and German fliers are included, with a list of 58 high-scoring pilots.

1791 **Reeder, Red.** The Story of the First World War. Duell, 1962. 243p. $3.95. (U)

A compact history of World War I, reviewing causes, leaders, theaters of action, battles, and stories of individual heroism.

1792 **Snyder, Louis L.** The First Book of World War I; maps by Leonard Derwinski. Watts, 1958. 94p. $2.65. (I)

After outlining the events which led up to the war, the author discusses the victories, defeats, and mistakes on both sides and shows how the failures of World War I led to World War II. Illustrated with photographs.

WORLD WAR II

1793 **American Heritage.** Air War against Hitler's Germany; by the eds. of American Heritage, The Magazine of History. Author, Stephen W. Sears; consultant, Marvin W. McFarland. American Heritage, 1964. American Heritage Junior Library, distributed by Harper. 150p. $4.95; lib. ed. $4.79 net. (U)

A competent review of the United States daylight bombing campaign against Nazi Germany, incorporating the contributions of the Allied air arms and describing Germany's defense. Illustrated with numerous combat photographs and with the work of war artists.

1794 American Heritage. D-Day: The Invasion of Europe; by the eds. of American Heritage, The Magazine of History. Narrative by Al Hine; consultant, S. L. A. Marshall. American Heritage, 1962. American Heritage Junior Library, distributed by Harper. 153p. $4.95; lib. ed. $4.79 net. (U)

Eloquently describes Operation Overlord, the Allied plan to invade France and liberate Western Europe from Nazi Germany. Accounts of preparations, landing, and air coverage are made more graphic by a wealth of photographs, maps, and paintings.

1795 Bliven, Bruce. From Casablanca to Berlin: The War in North Africa and Europe: 1942–1945; illus. with photos. Random, 1965. 180p. $1.95; lib. ed. $2.48 net. (I–U)

Carries the war from the American landing in North Africa to the unconditional surrender of Nazi Germany. Illustrated with maps and photographs.

1796 Bliven, Bruce. From Pearl Harbor to Okinawa: the War in the Pacific: 1941–1945; maps by Fritz and Stephen Kredel. Random, 1960. 192p. $1.95; lib. ed. $2.48 net. (I–U)

An exciting story of air, sea, and land combat in the Pacific theater of the war, covering all major battles and stressing the heroism of the troops as well as the horrors of war. Illustrated with photographs and maps.

1797 Bliven, Bruce. The Story of D-Day: June 6, 1944; illus. by Albert Orbaan. Random, 1956. 180p. $1.95; lib. ed. $2.48 net. (I)

The turning point in the war came with the successful invasion of Normandy on June 6, 1944. A brief, dramatic account of D-Day, recommended for reluctant older readers.

1798 Davis, Russell G. Marine at War. Little, 1961. 258p. $3.95. (U)

This candid account of the author's experiences in the campaigns of Peleliu and Okinawa gives an honest picture of life in the Marines and the reactions of ordinary men in war.

1799 Frank, Anne. The Diary of a Young Girl; tr. from the Dutch by B. M. Mooyaart-Doubleday; with an introd. by Eleanor Roosevelt. Doubleday, 1952. 285p. $4.50. (U)

A moving account of a young Jewish girl, in hiding with two families in occupied Holland, records an adolescent's growing awareness of the people around her and her reflections on the injustices of war.

1800 Leckie, Robert. The Story of World War II; illus. with photos. and maps. Random, 1964. 193p. $3.95; lib. ed. $3.99 net. (I–U)

A fair, over-all picture of the war on all fronts, but with special attention to the war in the Pacific.

1801 Loomis, Robert D. Great American Fighter Pilots of World War II. Random, 1961. 208p. $1.95; lib. ed. $2.48 net. (I–U)

The air battles of outstanding fighter pilots of the Army, Navy, and Marine Corps are described in exciting detail, and their planes are shown in three-view silhouettes.

1802 Reynolds, Quentin. The Battle of Britain; illus. by Clayton Knight. Random, 1953. 182p. $1.95; lib. ed. $2.48 net. (I)

A war correspondent's eyewitness account of the defeat of Germany's air invasion of Britain after 83 days of gallant defense by the R.A.F. and the English people.

1803 Snyder, Louis L. The First Book of World War II. Watts, 1958. 94p. $2.65. (I)

This companion volume to *The First Book of World War I* (see No.1792) is a concise, readable overview of the war and its political and military leaders, illustrated with maps and photographs.

1804 Tregaskis, Richard. John F. Kennedy and PT-109. Random, 1962. 192p. $1.95; lib. ed. $2.48 net. (I)

A swift-paced story of PT-boat operations in the Solomon Islands and of Kennedy's rescue of his crew after his boat was wrecked. Illustrated with photographs and maps.

North America

Indians of North America

1805 American Heritage. The American Indian; adapted for young readers by Anne Terry White . . . Random, 1963. 200p. $5.95; lib. ed. $5.29 net. (I–U)

A skillful adaptation of William Brandon's *The American Heritage Book of Indians,* retaining the exceptionally fine illustrations of the adult book and considering all aspects of Indian life from prehistoric times to the present.

1806   Baity, Elizabeth Chesley. Americans before Columbus; illus. with drawings and maps by C. B. Falls and with 32 pages of photos. Viking, 1961. 272p. lib. ed. $4.13 net. (U)

The earliest inhabitants of the American continent are discussed in a semifictional style intended to hold the interest of young readers. Includes the Aztecs, the Incas, and the Mayas as well as tribes of the North American continent.

1807   Bleeker, Sonia. The Apache Indians: Raiders of the Southwest; illus. by Althea Karr. Morrow, 1951. 157p. $2.95; lib. ed. $2.94 net. (I)

This author has written a number of books about specific Indian tribes, all of which follow the same pattern, discussing history, home life, beliefs and customs, occupations and crafts, special characteristics, and present-day conditions. All are smoothly written, accurate, and illustrated with informative drawings. A sampling of the series follows:

1808   Bleeker, Sonia. The Cherokee: Indians of the Mountains; illus. by Althea Karr. Morrow, 1952. 159p. $2.95; lib. ed. $2.94 net. (I)

1809   Bleeker, Sonia. The Delaware Indians: Eastern Fishermen and Farmers; illus. by Patricia Boodell. Morrow, 1953. 160p. $2.95. (I)

1810   Bleeker, Sonia. Horsemen of the Western Plateaus: The Nez Percé Indians; illus. by Patricia Boodell. Morrow, 1957. 157p. $2.95. (I)

1811   Bleeker, Sonia. The Navajo: Herders, Weavers, and Silversmiths; illus. by Patricia Boodell. Morrow, 1958. 159p. lib. ed. $2.94 net. (I)

1812   Bleeker, Sonia. The Seminole Indians; illus. by Althea Karr. Morrow, 1954. 156p. lib. ed. $2.94 net. (I)

1813   Brindze, Ruth. The Story of the Totem Pole; illus. by Yeffe Kimball. Vanguard, 1951. 62p. $3.95. (I)

The totem poles carved by the American Indians of the Northwest are described and their symbolism explained in interesting text and authentic illustrations.

1814   Clark, Ann Nolan. The Desert People; illus. by Allan Houser. Viking, 1962. 59p. $3; lib. ed. $3.04 net. (P–I)

Daily life among the Papago Indians and their desert home are described by a young Indian boy and depicted in stylized illustrations in vivid colors.

1815   Clark, Ann Nolan. In My Mother's House; illus. by Velino Herrera. Viking, 1951. 56p. $3.50; lib. ed. $3.37 net. (P–I)

Rhythmic prose and illustrations using tribal designs tell the story of life among the Tewa Indians of the Southwest.

1816   Dorian, Edith, and **Wilson, W. N.** Hokahey! American Indians Then and Now. McGraw-Hill, 1957. 112p. $4.50; lib. ed. $3.99 net. (U)

Groups American Indians by geographical regions; briefly describes their probable origin, history, migrations, language, and culture; and discusses their influence on American life today.

1817   Floethe, Louise Lee. The Indian and His Pueblo; with pictures by Richard Floethe. Scribner, 1960. unp. lib. ed. $3.31 net. (P)

An attractive picture book describing life among the Pueblo Indians, past and present.

1818   Harris, Christie. Raven's Cry; illus. by Bill Reid. Atheneum, 1966. 193p. $3.95; lib. ed. $3.81 net. (U)

Basing her story on extensive study of the Haida Indians of Queen Charlotte Islands, the author describes tribal beliefs and customs and analyzes the conflict between the civilization of the Indian and that of the white man. Illustrations in authentic Haida style are by a Canadian artist of Haida descent.

1819   Hofsinde, Robert. The Indian and His Horse; written and illus. by Robert Hofsinde (Gray-Wolf). Morrow, 1960. 96p. lib. ed. $2.94 net. (I)

This author's books on various aspects of Indian life are carefully researched, simply written, and well illustrated. The following books are similar in presentation and format:

1820 **Hofsinde, Robert.** Indian Fishing and Camping; written and illus. by Robert Hofsinde (Gray-Wolf). Morrow, 1963. 92p. lib. ed. $2.94 net. (I)

1821 **Hofsinde, Robert.** Indian Games and Crafts; written and illus. by Robert Hofsinde (Gray-Wolf). Morrow, 1957. 126p. $2.95. (I)

1822 **Hofsinde, Robert.** Indian Hunting; written and illus. by Robert Hofsinde (Gray-Wolf). Morrow, 1962. 96p. lib. ed. $2.94 net. (I)

1822a **Hofsinde, Robert.** The Indian Medicine Man; written and illus. by Robert Hofsinde (Gray-Wolf). Morrow, 1966. 94p. $2.95; lib. ed. $2.94 net. (I)

1823 **Hofsinde, Robert.** Indian Picture Writing; written and illus. by Robert Hofsinde (Gray-Wolf). Morrow, 1959. 96p. lib. ed. $2.94 net. (I)

1824 **Hofsinde, Robert.** Indian Sign Language; written and illus. by Robert Hofsinde (Gray-Wolf). Morrow, 1956. 96p. lib. ed. $2.94 net. (I)

1825 **Hofsinde, Robert.** Indian Warriors and Their Weapons; written and illus. by Robert Hofsinde (Gray-Wolf). Morrow, 1965. 96p. lib. ed. $2.94 net. (I)

1826 **Hofsinde, Robert.** Indians at Home; written and illus. by Robert Hofsinde (Gray-Wolf). Morrow, 1964. 96p. lib. ed. $2.94 net. (I)

1827 **Hunt, W. Ben.** The Golden Book of Indian Crafts and Lore. Golden Pr., 1954. 111p. $2.95. (I–U)
Describes and illustrates Indian clothes, homes, dances, and crafts and gives directions and patterns for making costumes and ornaments. Includes a table of pronunciation and maps showing distribution of the tribes. Excellent for Scouts and campers.

1828 **Kirk, Ruth.** David, Young Chief of the Quileutes: An American Indian Today; photos. by Ruth Kirk. Harcourt, 1967. 59p. $3.25; lib. ed. $3.30 net. (I)
An eleven-year-old Quileute Indian of Washington State has been chief of his tribe since the age of three. This photographic study shows David at school, where his life is much like that of other boys, and at home, where many of the old ceremonies (including a potlach for his eleventh birthday) are observed.

1829 **McNeer, May.** The American Indian Story; with lithographs by Lynd Ward. Farrar, 1963. 95p. $4.25. (I)
Stunning lithographs in color dramatize these stories of important people and incidents in Indian history.

1830 **Mason, Bernard S.** The Book of Indian Crafts and Costumes; drawings by Frederic H. Kock. Ronald, 1946. 118p. $5.50. (I–U)
Describes the costumes and crafts of Indian tribes in all parts of the country and gives directions for making various items of clothing and adornment. Excellent for Scouts and campers.

1831 **National Geographic Society on Indians of the Americas;** a color-illus. record (by) Matthew W. Stirling, with contributions by Hiram Bingham (and others) . . . Foreword by John Oliver La Gorce. National Geographic Soc., 1961. 431p. $7.50. (U)
Comprehensive coverage of Indian history, customs, arts and crafts, religion, and government in an authoritative and profusely illustrated volume. Indians of South and Central America are included.

1832 **Rounds, Glen.** Buffalo Harvest; written and illus. by Glen Rounds. Holiday, 1952. 141p. $3.25. (I)
A graphic account of the importance of the buffalo to the Plains Indians and of the autumn hunts by which the tribes supplied themselves with food, clothing, and shelter.

1833 **Scheele, William E.** The Mound Builders; written and illus. by William E. Scheele. World, 1960. 64p. $2.95; lib. ed. $2.88 net. (I)
Discusses the prehistoric Indians of the Ohio River Valley who built burial mounds for their leaders and tells how archaeologists have recovered and interpreted the artifacts buried with the dead.

1834 **Tunis, Edwin.** Indians; written and illus. by Edwin Tunis. World, 1959. 157p. $6.95. (I–U)
A lively history of the Indian tribes of the United States, distinguished by meticulously drawn illustrations on every page.

1835 Wellman, Paul I. Indian Wars and Warriors: East; illus. by Lorence Bjorklund. Houghton, 1959. 184p. $2.95. (I)

Reviews the Indian wars east of the Mississippi in a fair, dramatic account of conflicts between the Indian and the white man from the Jamestown Massacre of 1622 to the end of the Seminole Wars in 1844. Illustrated with maps and drawings.

1836 Wellman, Paul I. Indian Wars and Warriors: West; illus. by Lorence Bjorklund. Houghton, 1959. 182p. $2.95. (I)

A companion volume to *Indian Wars and Warriors: East,* above, treating in the same objective, dramatic manner Indian wars west of the Mississippi.

DISCOVERY AND EXPLORATION OF AMERICA

1837 American Heritage. Discoverers of the New World; by the eds. of American Heritage, The Magazine of History. Narrative by Josef Berger, in consultation with Lawrence C. Wroth. American Heritage, 1960. American Heritage Junior Library, distributed by Harper. 153p. $4.95; lib. ed. $4.79 net. (I–U)

Chronicles 300 years of exploration of the American continents by adventurers from many countries. Based on firsthand accounts of the explorers and illustrated with an abundance of rare maps, paintings, prints, and drawings of the period.

1838 American Heritage. Trappers and Mountain Men; by the eds. of American Heritage, The Magazine of History. Consultant, Dale L. Morgan. American Heritage, 1961. American Heritage Junior Library, distributed by Harper. 153p. $4.95; lib. ed. $4.79 net. (U)

The foreword states that this "touches upon some of the highlights of the North American fur trade, while also mirroring something of a unique and unforgettable way of life, together with its heroes, a tough, colorful, sometimes cruel, always superbly skilled breed of men." Profusely illustrated with maps and period paintings and prints.

1839 Buehr, Walter. The French Explorers in America; illus. by Walter Buehr. Putnam, 1961. 93p. $3; lib. ed. $2.97 net. (I)

Briefly describes the explorations of such men as Cartier, Champlain, and La Salle and discusses their influence on the settle-ment of America. Illustrated with maps and drawings.

1840 Buehr, Walter. The Spanish Conquistadores in North America; written and illus. by Walter Buehr. Putnam, 1962. 96p. lib. ed. $2.97 net. (I)

A companion volume to *The French Explorers,* above, tracing Cortes' conquest of Mexico and the explorations of Coronado, Ponce de León, Balboa, and De Soto.

1841 Dalgliesh, Alice. America Begins: The Story of the Finding of the New World; with pictures by Lois Maloy. rev. ed. Scribner, 1958. 64p. lib. ed. $3.12 net. (I)

An introduction to the discovery and exploration of the New World, written simply but conveying the drama and danger of the expeditions.

1842 Duvoisin, Roger. And There Was America; written and illus. by Roger Duvoisin. Knopf, 1938. 75p. lib. ed. $3.39 net. (I)

Illustrations in glowing colors spark this narrative account of the discovery and early settlement of America.

1843 Meredith, Robert K. The Quest of Columbus: A Detailed and Exact Account of the Discovery of America with the Many Dangers and Triumphant Return . . . Ed. and adapted by Robert K. Meredith and E. Brooks Smith; illus. by Leonard Everett Fisher. Little, 1966. 125p. $3.95. (U)

Columbus' first voyage, as recorded by his son Ferdinand, is here adapted and annotated for young people. The writing has the immediacy of the firsthand account, and the notes and dramatic illustrations add to the realism.

1844 Rich, Louise Dickinson. The First Book of New World Explorers; pictures by Cary. Watts, 1960. 79p. $2.65. (I)

An animated first book on the exploration of America, beginning with the Vikings and including Columbus, the Spaniards, and the French. Lists books for further reading.

UNITED STATES

General Works

1845 American Heritage. The Golden Book of America: Stories from Our Country's Past; adapted for young readers by

Irwin Shapiro from the pages of American Heritage, The Magazine of History; with a foreword by Bruce Catton. Golden Pr., 1957. 216p. $4.95. (U)

America's history from its discovery to World War I, told through stories of important people and events.

1846 Brown, Harriett M., (and) Guadagnolo, Joseph F., with the editorial assistance of Howard R. Anderson. America Is My Country: The Heritage of a Free People. Houghton, 1961. 268p. $6.50. (I)

Brings together symbols, documents, quotations, songs, and landmarks which help young people to understand what it means to be an American and to accept their responsibilities as citizens of a democracy. Valuable material for social studies and for the celebration of patriotic holidays.

1847 Cavanah, Frances. Our Country's Story; illus. by Julia Keats. Rand McNally, 1962. rev. ed. 64p. $2.95; lib. ed. $3.08 net. (P–I)

A simply written, well-organized first history of the United States from the Colonial period to the present.

1848 Commager, Henry Steele. The First Book of American History; pictures by Leonard Everett Fisher. Watts, 1957. 62p. $2.65. (I)

An eminent historian summarizes the history of America in a readable, strikingly illustrated account.

1849 Coy, Harold. The Americans; illus. by William Moyers. Little, 1958. 328p. $4.95. (I–U)

American history centered around the people who made it, telling how they lived, felt, and solved their personal problems and the problems of the nation. Includes a reading list.

1850 Earle, Olive L. State Birds and Flowers. Morrow, 1961. 64p. lib. ed. $2.94 net. (I)

An alphabetical arrangement of states, with brief information about each, and a sketch and description of the bird and flower chosen to represent each.

1851 Earle, Olive L. State Trees; written and illus. by Olive L. Earle. Morrow, 1960. unp. $2.95; lib. ed. $2.94 net. (I)

Describes and shows in sketches the shape, leaf, seed, flower, and bark of each

state tree, in presentation similar to State Birds and Flowers, above.

1852 Eggenberger, David. Flags of the U.S.A. enl. ed. Crowell, 1964. 222p. $4.95. (I–U)

All flags which have ever flown over the United States are described and pictured in color.

1853 Faber, Harold. From Sea to Sea: The Growth of the United States. Farrar, 1967. 246p. $4.75. (U)

Traces the territorial expansion of the United States from the Treaty of Paris in 1783 to the acquisition of islands in the Pacific following World War II, describing the circumstances under which each new gain was made. Precise maps illustrate the growth of the nation, and a final chapter gives statistics of each state. Excellent background material for the study of United States history.

1854 Hartman, Gertrude. These United States and How They Came To Be . . . Macmillan, 1960. 340p. $6.95. (U)

A well-organized history of the United States from earliest times to World War I, with emphasis on the various ethnic groups which have contributed to the country's development. Many illustrations from contemporary sources.

1855 Johnson, Gerald W. America Grows Up: A History for Peter; illus. by Leonard Everett Fisher. Morrow, 1960. 223p. $3.75; lib. ed. $3.56 net. (I–U)

The second volume of a trilogy, the other two of which are listed below, recounting the growth of the United States from 1787 to 1917, at the beginning of World War I, and describing and interpreting the important events and personalities of the period.

1856 Johnson, Gerald W. America Is Born: A History for Peter; illus. by Leonard Everett Fisher. Morrow, 1959. 254p. $3.95; lib. ed. $3.78 net. (I–U)

The first of a three-volume history covering the period from the discovery of America by Columbus through the Constitutional Convention of 1787. Clear style, penetrating analyses of events, and dramatic illustrations are combined in an exceptionally readable history.

1857 Johnson, Gerald W. America Moves Forward: A History for Peter; illus. by

Leonard Everett Fisher. Morrow, 1960. 256p. $3.95; lib. ed. $3.78 net. (I–U)

Brings the history up to the Eisenhower administration, with the same direct style and keen interpretation of issues as in the two earlier volumes, listed above.

1858 Lawson, Robert. Watchwords of Liberty: A Pageant of American Quotations; new ed. with text and illus. by Robert Lawson. Little, 1957. 115p. $3.95. (I)

An assemblage of quotations of famous people on important occasions in American history, with background notes and colorful illustrations by the author.

1859 Lehner, Ernest, comp. American Symbols: A Pictorial History; introd. by Roger Butterfield. Tudor, 1957. 95p. $3.50. (I–U)

Describes and illustrates 1000 coats of arms, trademarks, state seals, and other American insignia, ranging from Columbus' coat of arms to the symbols of present-day organizations.

1860 Meadowcroft, Enid La Monte. Land of the Free; illus. by Lee J. Ames. Crowell, 1961. 151p. $3.50. (P–I)

A simply written history of the United States restricted to major events from the discovery of America to the formation of the United Nations. Clear print, action pictures, and easy vocabulary should attract reluctant readers. Bibliography and index.

1861 Miers, Earl Schenck. The Rainbow Book of American History; illus. by James Daugherty. World, 1955. 319p. $5.95. (I–U)

A large, handsomely illustrated book tracing the development of America from earliest explorations to the present, with text focused on highlights of history and the lives of famous people.

1862 National Geographic Society. America's Historylands: Touring Our Landmarks of Liberty . . . National Geographic Soc., 1962. 576p. $9.95. (I–U)

This companion volume to *America's Wonderlands* (see No.1949) describes, pictures, and explains the significance of hundreds of homes, battlefields, restored towns, and other historic sites. Text is by outstanding historians and maps and photographs (most in color) are exceptionally fine.

1863 Petersham, Maud, and **Petersham,**

Miska. An American ABC. Macmillan, 1941. unp. $3.95; lib. ed. $3.74 net. (P)

Twenty-six stories about America, with 26 pictures in color on facing pages, comprise this picture book designed to help young children grasp the meaning of their country.

1864 We, the People: The Story of the United States Capitol, Its Past and Its Promise, (by) the U.S. Capitol Historical Society in cooperation with the National Geographic Society. Grosset, 1964. 143p. $3.95; lib. ed. $4.05 net. (U)

A generously illustrated history and guide to the United States Capitol.

1865 White House Historical Association, Washington, D.C. The White House: An Historic Guide. 4th ed. The Association, 1963. Distributed by Grosset. 141p. $3.95; lib. ed. $4.05 net. (U)

A pictorial tour of the White House at different periods of history and the life of the Presidential families who have occupied it, with special attention to furniture, paintings, and ornaments in the official rooms.

Colonial Period, 1607–1775

1866 Alderman, Clifford Lindsey. The Story of the Thirteen Colonies; illus. by Leonard Everett Fisher. Random, 1966. 187p. $1.95; lib. ed. $2.48 net. (I)

A concise summary of the history of each of the thirteen original colonies up to the Revolution.

1867 American Heritage. The French and Indian Wars; by the eds. of American Heritage, The Magazine of History. Author, Francis Russell; consultant, Lawrence Henry Gipson. American Heritage, 1962. American Heritage Junior Library, distributed by Harper. 153p. $4.95; lib. ed. $4.79 net. (U)

American history from 1690 to 1763 as it was influenced by the war for possession of the Ohio Valley, with graphic descriptions of Indian massacres and famous battles, copiously illustrated with contemporary maps and pictures.

1868 American Heritage. Jamestown: First English Colony; by the eds. of American Heritage, The Magazine of History. Author, Marshall W. Fishwick; consultant, Parke Rouse, Jr. American Heritage, 1965. American Heritage Junior Library, distributed by Harper. 151p. $4.95; lib. ed. $4.79 net. (U)

From the first English settlement at Roanoke Island, to a permanent colony at Jamestown, to the Colonial capital at Williamsburg, the author follows the English settlers as they established themselves in the New World. Notable for scholarly text and a profusion of illustrations of the period.

1869 American Heritage. The Pilgrims and the Plymouth Colony; by the eds. of American Heritage, The Magazine of History; narrative by Feenie Ziner, in consultation with George F. Willison. American Heritage, 1961. American Heritage Junior Library, distributed by Harper. 153p. $4.95; lib. ed. $4.79 net. (U)

Comprehensive coverage of the history of the Pilgrim Fathers from the time of the Reformation to 1692, stressing their character and contributions to the development of America. Excellent period illustrations.

1870 Earle, Alice M. Child Life in Colonial Days; with many illus. from photos. Macmillan, 1899. 418p. $5.95. (I–U)

An entertaining record of the child's place in the Colonial home, with chapters on babyhood, dress, manners, education, games, and toys. Companion volume to *Home Life in Colonial Days,* below.

1871 Earle, Alice M. Home Life in Colonial Days; illus. by photos. gathered by the author, of real things, works and happenings of olden times. Macmillan, 1898. 470p. $5.95. (I–U)

A rich source of material on Colonial family life: houses, lighting, food, crafts, travel, flower gardens, and many other aspects of daily living. Companion volume to *Child Life in Colonial Days,* above.

1872 Fisher, Leonard Everett. The Cabinetmakers; written & illus. by Leonard Everett Fisher. Watts, 1966. 47p. $2.65. (I–U)

One of a series of books by this author, describing Colonial American craftsmen. Each gives a brief history of the craft, explains the terms used in the trade, describes in detail how it was practiced in early America, and illustrates the steps of the process in handsome black-and-white pictures. Excellent background reading for Colonial history.

1873 Fisher, Leonard Everett. The Glass-makers; written & illus. by Leonard Everett Fisher. Watts, 1964. 43p. $2.65. (I)

1874 Fisher, Leonard Everett. The Papermakers; written & illus. by Leonard Everett Fisher. Watts, 1965. 46p. $2.65. (I)

1875 Fisher, Leonard Everett. The Printers; written & illus. by Leonard Everett Fisher. Watts, 1965. 46p. $2.65. (I)

1876 Fisher, Leonard Everett. The Schoolmasters; written & illus. by Leonard Everett Fisher. Watts, 1967. 47p. $2.65. (I)

A brief history of education in Colonial America, describing the dame schools, itinerant schoolmasters, private tutors, and neighborhood schools. Illustrations show a horn book, the New England primer, typical schoolroom scenes, and the schoolmasters and mistresses themselves, some with a comic touch.

1877 Fisher, Leonard Everett. The Shoemakers; written & illus. by Leonard Everett Fisher. Watts, 1967. 44p. $2.65. (I)

1878 Fisher, Leonard Everett. The Tanners; written & illus. by Leonard Everett Fisher. Watts, 1966. 43p. $2.65. (I)

1879 Fisher, Margaret, (and) Fowler, Mary Jane. Colonial America. Fideler, 1967. 132p. $3.48. (I)

Everyday life in Colonial America is described and shown in photographs and drawings: a Colonial home, a New England village, a Southern plantation, the making of soap, spinning and weaving, etc. Includes maps, questions and projects, a pronouncing glossary, and an index.

1880 Hall, Elvajean. Pilgrim Stories, from Margaret Pumphrey's Pilgrim Stories; rev. and expanded by Elvajean Hall; illus. by Jon Nielsen. Rand McNally, 1962. 176p. $2.95. (P–I)

Interestingly told episodes in the lives of the Pilgrims, beginning when they left England, describing their ocean voyage, and following them through their first year of danger and distress in the New World.

1881 Hall-Quest, Olga W. How the Pilgrims Came to Plymouth; illus. by James MacDonald. Dutton, 1946. 115p. $2.95. (I)

A more straightforward account than *Pilgrim Stories,* above, of the Pilgrims' persecution in England, their escape to

Holland, and their hazardous journey to the New World, stressing causes, plans, and preparations.

1882 Hall-Quest, Olga W. Jamestown Adventure; illus. by James MacDonald. Dutton, 1950. 185p. $3.50. (I)

A dramatic account of the first 12 years of the Jamestown Colony, based on original documents and containing much information not found in most other children's books.

1883 Hults, Dorothy Niebrugge. New Amsterdam Days and Ways: The Dutch Settlers in New York; illus. by Jane Niebrugge. Harcourt, 1963. 224p. $3.50. (I–U)

Tells how the Dutch founded the colony of New Amsterdam, how the Dutch people lived in the days of Peter Stuyvesant, and how their settlement grew into New York City. Accurate, well organized, and effectively illustrated. Includes a chronology, a table of money values, a pronunciation guide, and a list of historic sites.

1884 Jackson, Shirley. The Witchcraft of Salem Village; illus. by Lili Réthi. Random, 1956. 176p. $2.50; lib. ed. $2.48 net. (I–U)

An unemotional account of the witchcraft trials of Old Salem at the end of the seventeenth century, showing the terrible injustice done the victims and the public reactions which marked the beginning of the end of belief in witchcraft.

1885 Lawson, Marie. Pocahontas and Captain John Smith: The Story of the Virginia Colony; illus. by William Sharp. Random, 1950. 185p. $2.50; lib. ed. $2.48 net. (I–U)

Combines legend and history of the Virginia Colony, from the attempts to settle at Roanoke Island to the time of Bacon's Rebellion.

1886 Morison, Samuel Eliot. The Story of the "Old Colony" of New Plymouth (1620–1692); illus. by Charles H. Overly. Knopf, 1956. 296p. $3.69 net. (U)

A history of the Plymouth Colony centering on the daily lives of the people.

1887 Smith, E. Brooks, ed. Pilgrim Courage; from a firsthand account by William Bradford, Governor of the Plymouth Colony . . . Adapted and ed. by E. Brooks Smith (and) Robert Meredith and illus. by Leonard Everett Fisher. Little, 1962. 108p. $3.95. (I–U)

Presents selected episodes from Bradford's history of Plymouth Plantation and from the journal of Edward Winslow, skillfully abridged and adapted for easier reading.

1888 Tunis, Edwin. Colonial Craftsmen and the Beginnings of American Industry; written and illus. by Edwin Tunis. World, 1965. 159p. $6.95. (I–U)

The everyday life of Colonial households is reflected in this lucid, superbly illustrated account of crafts and craftsmen and the uses to which their products were put. A book of many values: for history classes, handicraft, art, and browsing.

1889 Tunis, Edwin. Colonial Living; written and illus. by Edwin Tunis. World, 1957. 155p. $6.95. (I–U)

Describes and depicts in detailed drawings the houses, clothes, and furniture of the seventeenth and eighteenth centuries, with clear, often humorous text organized both geographically and chronologically.

1890 Tunis, Edwin. Shaw's Fortune: The Picture Story of a Colonial Plantation; drawn and written by Edwin Tunis. World, 1966. 63p. $3.95; lib. ed. $4.09 net. (I)

From a cabin in a clearing, a Virginia settler built his house and his estate into a self-sufficient plantation by 1752, complete with the outbuildings for the slaves and servants and the crafts and industries needed for his vast domain. An absorbing account of Southern plantation life, presented in picture-book format with beautifully executed drawings on every page.

1891 Weisgard, Leonard. The Plymouth Thanksgiving; written and illus. by Leonard Weisgard. Doubleday, 1967. unp. $3.95. (P)

The author re-creates the voyage of the "Mayflower" and the first year of the Plymouth Colony in a simple text, based on William Bradford's diary, and beautiful illustrations, most of them in color double spreads. The last few pages describe and picture the first Thanksgiving feast. Includes a list of "Mayflower" passengers.

Revolution and Confederation

1892 American Heritage. George Washington and the Making of a Nation; by the eds. of American Heritage, The Magazine of History. Author, Marcus Cunliffe; consultant, Richard B. Morris. American Heritage, 1966. American Heritage Junior Library, distributed by Harper. 153p. $4.95; lib. ed. $4.79 net. (I–U)

George Washington's role in the American Revolution is given the emphasis in this penetrating study of his life and times. An abundance of contemporary illustrations adds information and eye appeal.

1893 American Heritage. Lexington, Concord, and Bunker Hill; by the eds. of American Heritage, The Magazine of History. Author, Francis Russell; consultant, Richard M. Ketchum. American Heritage, 1963. American Heritage Junior Library, distributed by Harper. 153p. $4.95; lib. ed. $4.79 net. (I–U)

Events and personalities of the early months of the Revolution are considered in an unromanticized account, profusely illustrated with period maps, paintings, and prints.

1894 Bliven, Bruce. The American Revolution, 1760–1783; illus. by Albert Orbaan. Random, 1958. 182p. $1.95; lib. ed. $2.48 net. (I)

A concise overview of the causes, battles, and results of the Revolution, presented in pleasing, well-illustrated format.

1895 Commager, Henry Steele. The Great Declaration: A Book for Young Americans; written and ed. by Henry Steele Commager; drawings by Donald Bolognese. Bobbs-Merrill, 1958. 112p. $3.75; lib. ed. $3.25 net. (U)

After discussing the events leading up to the decision of the colonies to break with England, the author describes the writing of the Declaration and the struggle to get it adopted, quoting from the writings of men who helped to draft it.

1896 Hall-Quest, Olga W. The Bell That Rang for Freedom: The Liberty Bell and Its Place in American History; illus. by Christine Price. Dutton, 1965. 184p. $3.75; lib. ed. $3.71 net. (I)

Combines the history of Revolutionary Philadelphia with the story of the Liberty Bell as a symbol of freedom and democracy.

1897 Hall-Quest, Olga W. From Colony to Nation . . . with Washington and His Army in the War for Independence; illus. by Christine Price. Dutton, 1966. 242p. $4.25; lib. ed. $4.21 net. (I–U)

New York City is the setting of this ac-

count of the Revolution, covering events and military leaders on both sides of the skirmishes and battles of the area, enlivened by quotations and period illustrations.

1898 Mason, F. Van Wyck. The Winter at Valley Forge; illus. by Harper Johnson. Random, 1953. 180p. $2.50; lib. ed. $2.48. (I)

The winter of 1777–1778 is made painfully real in this fictionalized story of the ordeal of Valley Forge.

1899 Morris, Richard B. The First Book of the American Revolution; pictures by Leonard Everett Fisher. Watts, 1956. 67p. $2.65. (I)

An introduction to the Revolutionary period, covering causes of the war, battles, leaders, and significance of the results.

1900 Reeder, Red. The Story of the Revolutionary War; illus. and maps by Frederick Chapman. Duell, 1959. 249p. $4.50. (I–U)

Paul Revere's ride, the battles of Lexington and Concord, the campaigns in New York and the South, and the surrender at Yorktown are described, along with military and political leaders, in a compact survey of the Revolution.

Constitutional Period and Nineteenth Century to 1861

1901 Adams, Samuel Hopkins. The Erie Canal; illus. by Leonard Vosburgh. Random, 1953. 182p. $1.95; lib. ed. $2.48 net. (I)

An anecdotal history of the building of the Erie Canal and the changes brought about by this new waterway.

1902 Adams, Samuel Hopkins. The Santa Fe Trail; illus. by Lee J. Ames. Random, 1951. 181p. $2.50; lib. ed. $2.48 net. (I)

Recounts the most dramatic episodes in the first wagon expedition from Franklin, Missouri, to Santa Fe, New Mexico.

1903 American Heritage. The California Gold Rush; by the eds. of American Heritage, The Magazine of History; narrative by Ralph K. Andrist, in consultation with Archibald Hanna. American Heritage, 1961. American Heritage Junior Library, distributed by Harper. 153p. $4.95; lib. ed. $4.79 net. (I–U)

One of the most dramatic chapters in the Westward movement is colorfully described and illustrated in an account which captures the excitement of the gold rush.

1904   American Heritage. Commodore Perry in Japan; by the eds. of American Heritage, The Magazine of History. Author, Robert L. Reynolds; consultant, Douglas MacArthur II. American Heritage, 1963. American Heritage Junior Library, distributed by Harper. 153p. $4.95; lib. ed. $4.79 net. (U)

The many period illustrations of this account of Perry's expedition to Japan in 1852–1854 make it particularly useful for the study of American history or Japanese life in the 1850's.

1905   American Heritage. Cowboys and Cattle Country; by the eds. of American Heritage, The Magazine of History; narrative by Don Ward, in consultation with J. C. Dykes. American Heritage, 1961. American Heritage Junior Library, distributed by Harper. 153p. $4.95; lib. ed. $4.79 net. (I–U)

A realistic picture of cowboys of the western frontier and their life on the range and the cattle drive, enlivened by songs, jokes, and copious illustrations, including color reproductions of paintings by Frederic Remington, Charles M. Russell, and other well-known artists.

1906   American Heritage. The Erie Canal; by the eds. of American Heritage, The Magazine of History. Author, Ralph K. Andrist; consultant, Carter Goodrich. American Heritage, 1964. American Heritage Junior Library, distributed by Harper. 153p. $4.95; lib. ed. $4.79 net. (I–U)

Considers the transportation factors that led to the building of the canal, discusses the engineering and construction problems encountered by the builders, and describes life on the canal boats and along the towpaths. Many period illustrations.

1907   American Heritage. Steamboats on the Mississippi; by the eds. of American Heritage, The Magazine of History; narrative by Ralph K. Andrist, in consultation with C. Bradford Mitchell. American Heritage, 1962. American Heritage Junior Library, distributed by Harper. 153p. $4.95; lib. ed. $4.79 net. (I–U)

The great days of Mississippi River travel are colorfully described and illustrated with numerous contemporary maps and pictures. Facts and legends are mingled in an account of the river itself, the towns along its banks, the steamboats which plied it, and the sometimes bizarre characters who traveled it.

1908   American Heritage. Texas and the War with Mexico; by the eds. of American Heritage, The Magazine of History; narrative by Fairfax Downey, in consultation with Paul M. Angle. American Heritage, 1961. American Heritage Junior Library, distributed by Harper. 153p. $4.95; lib. ed. $4.79 net. (I–U)

Recounts the struggle of Texas to win independence, the political situation which led to the War with Mexico, and the battles and leaders of the war itself in interesting text and many period illustrations.

1909   American Heritage. Westward on the Oregon Trail; by the eds. of American Heritage, The Magazine of History; narrative by Marian T. Place; consultant, Earl Pomeroy. American Heritage, 1962. American Heritage Junior Library, distributed by Harper. 153p. $4.95; lib. ed. $4.79 net. (I–U)

Another in the American Heritage series of accurate, colorfully written, and elaborately illustrated histories focuses on the Oregon Trail in 1843, the year of the great migration, describing the establishment of the 2000-mile route and some of the famous journeys over it.

1910   Berry, Erick. When Wagon Trains Rolled to Santa Fe; illus. by Charles Waterhouse. Garrard, 1966. 95p. $2.39. (P–I)

For the advanced primary reader or the older slow reader, this simply written, fictionalized story of one wagon train's journey over the Santa Fe Trail is recommended. Facts are accurate, episodes are chosen for dramatic appeal, and illustrations, many from contemporary sources, are full of action. (R4–5)

1911   Coit, Margaret L. The Fight for Union. Houghton, 1961. 136p. $3.50. (U)

The political and social developments in the mid-nineteenth century are lucidly described and interpreted—the Webster-Calhoun debates, the Texas revolution, John Brown's raid, and other events of this critical period—along with portrayals of the great men of the era. Important reference reading for older history students.

1912   Daugherty, James. Of Courage Undaunted: Across the Continent with Lewis and Clark. Viking, 1951. 168p. $5. (U)

A fine record of a daring exploit, told with clarity and zest and vigorously illustrated.

1913 Dorian, Edith, and **Wilson, W. N.** Trails West and the Men Who Made Them. McGraw-Hill, 1955. 92p. $3.50; lib. ed. $3.06 net. (I)

Locates and describes each of the famous trails and delineates some of the rugged characters who used them. Illustrated with maps and drawings.

1914 Harmer, Mabel. The True Book of Pioneers; illus. by Loran Wilford. Childrens Pr., 1957. 44p. $2.50. (P)

A simply told story of covered-wagon days and early settlers: their courage, their hardships, the homes they built, and how they lived. (R2-3)

1915 Miers, Earl Schenck. Wild & Woolly West; illus. by Steele Savage. Rand McNally, 1964. 200p. $3.95. (I–U)

An unglamorized history of westward expansion and the people who were part of it: miners and mountain men, homesteaders and adventurers, explorers and cattlemen.

1916 Morris, Richard B. The First Book of the War of 1812; illus. by Leonard Everett Fisher. Watts, 1961. 64p. $2.65. (I–U)

A concise history of America's second war with England: its causes, its heroes, its battles, and the significance of its outcome. Illustrated with drawings and maps.

1917 Neuberger, Richard. The Lewis and Clark Expedition; illus. by Winold Reiss. Random, 1951. 180p. $2.50; lib. ed. $2.48 net. (I)

A simpler, more dramatic account than the Daugherty book, *Of Courage Undaunted*, above, describing the journey and telling how the leaders spent their later lives.

1918 Parish, Peggy. Let's Be Early Settlers with Daniel Boone; illus. by Arnold Lobel. Harper, 1967. 96p. $2.95; lib. ed. $2.92 net. (P–I)

Simple instructions and helpful drawings for making pioneer houses, clothing, weapons, and other objects needed for a project on frontier life or for costumes of the period.

1919 Place, Marian T. American Cattle Trails East & West; illus. by Gil Walker. Holt, 1967. 148p. $3.95; lib. ed. $3.59 net. (I–U)

The American cattle trade as it affected the growth of the country is discussed, and the trails by which the herds were taken to market are described and traced on maps. Of particular importance is the inclusion of some little-known trails, such as the Bay State Cow Path of Colonial New England and Daniel Boone's Wilderness Trace.

1920 Tallant, Robert. The Louisiana Purchase; illus. by Walter Chappell. Random, 1952. 183p. $2.50; lib. ed. $2.48 net. (I)

Reviews the world situation which influenced Napoleon to sell the vast Louisiana territory to the United States and describes the negotiations which preceded the sale.

1921 Tunis, Edwin. Frontier Living; written and illus. by Edwin Tunis. World, 1961. 165p. $6.95. (I–U)

A well-organized and superbly illustrated account of frontier homes, household articles, farming, transportation, and other aspects of pioneer life, following the expansion of the country from east to west. Companion volume to the author's *Colonial Living* (see No.1889).

1922 Wellman, Paul I. Gold in California; illus. by Lorence Bjorklund. Houghton, 1958. 184p. $2.95. (I)

The gold rush of 1849 is recounted in a simpler story than in the American Heritage book, *The California Gold Rush* (see No.1903), animated by anecdotes and lively illustrations.

Civil War

1923 American Heritage. The Battle of Gettysburg; by the eds. of American Heritage, The Magazine of History. Author, Bruce Catton. American Heritage, 1963. American Heritage Junior Library, distributed by Harper. 153p. $4.95; lib. ed. $4.79 net. (I–U)

The foreword of this profusely illustrated story of the greatest battle ever fought on American soil states that it tells "why Gettysburg was fought, how it was fought, and what it all meant . . . The glory and pageantry of battle is here, and so is its horror and tragedy."

1924 American Heritage. The Golden Book of the Civil War; adapted for young readers by Charles Flato from *The Amer-*

ican Heritage Picture History of the Civil War, by the eds. of American Heritage, with narrative by Bruce Catton. Golden Pr., 1961. 216p. $4.95. (I–U)

This skillful adaptation of an adult book gives an overview of the war and its leaders and retains many of the exceptionally fine period illustrations of the original.

1925   American Heritage. Ironclads of the Civil War; by the eds. of American Heritage, The Magazine of History. Author, Frank R. Donovan; consultant, Bruce Catton. American Heritage, 1964. 153p. $4.95; lib. ed. $4.79 net. (U)

A handsomely illustrated and interestingly written account of the building of the ironclads and the battles in which they fought.

1926   Catton, Bruce. This Hallowed Ground: The Story of the Union Side of the Civil War. Doubleday, 1962. 187p. $4.95. (U)

This special edition for young people of an adult book of the same title is skillfully abridged and copiously illustrated with period maps and pictures.

1927   Davis, Burke. Appomattox: Closing Struggle of the Civil War; ed. by Walter Lord; illus. with 29 Civil War photos. and drawings. Harper, 1963. 637p. $3.50; lib. ed. $3.27 net. (U)

A dramatic account of the last battle of the Civil War, the meeting of Lee and Grant, the terms of surrender, and the farewell speeches.

1928   Lincoln, Abraham. Abraham Lincoln's Gettysburg Address; illus., conceived, and designed by Jack E. Levin. Chilton, 1965. unp. $2.95. (I–U)

Photographs taken by Brady, Gardner, and other Civil War photographers illustrate this edition of the address.

1929   Miers, Earl Schenck. Billy Yank and Johnny Reb: How They Fought and Made Up; illus. by Leonard Vosburgh. Rand McNally, 1959. 256p. $4.50. (U)

An objective account of the Civil War centering around the common soldiers on both sides, based on primary sources and including Civil War songs.

1930   Reeder, Red. The Story of the Civil War; illus. by Frederick Chapman. Duell, 1958. 212p. $3.95. (U)

Focuses on the campaigns and battles of the war and the strengths and weaknesses of the commanding generals. Includes a reading list.

Late Nineteenth and Early Twentieth Centuries

For books on World Wars I and II, see pages 148–49.

1931   Castor, Henry. Teddy Roosevelt and the Rough Riders; illus. by William Reusswig. Random, 1954. 152p. $2.50; lib. ed. $2.48 net. (I)

Roosevelt's famous charge up San Juan Hill is the focal point of this account of the Spanish-American War.

1932   Considine, Bob. The Panama Canal; illus. by Fritz Kredel. Random, 1951. 179p. $2.50; lib. ed. $2.48 net. (I)

An interestingly written history of the Panama Canal: the political background, engineering and health problems, personalities involved, and data on the completed project.

1933   McNeer, May. The Alaska Gold Rush; illus. by Lynd Ward. Random, 1960. 186p. $2.50; lib. ed. $2.48 net. (I)

Recounts the adventures of the prospectors who poured into Alaska in the 1890's. Dramatic illustrations.

1934   Reeder, Red. The Story of the Spanish-American War. Duell, 1966. 179p. $3.95. (U)

After discussing the circumstances which led to the war, the author gives a brief overview of the conflict and its effect on the construction of the Panama Canal and the elimination of yellow fever.

United States Today

1935   Ault, Phil. This Is the Desert: The Story of America's Arid Region; illus. by Leonard Everett Fisher. Dodd, 1959. 175p. $3.50. (I–U)

Following a brief history of the American desert, the author describes it as it is today and speculates on its future development. Good material on irrigation projects and atomic sites.

1936   Cleveland, Libra Jan. High Country: The Rocky Mountain and Plateau States . . . illus. by Tom Dunnington. Childrens Pr., 1962. 93p. $3.95. (I)

An easy-to-read, attractively illustrated

geography, covering physical features, natural resources, climate, industries, and people.

1937 Cleveland, Libra Jan. Pacific Shores: The Pacific States . . . illus. by Tom Dunnington. Childrens Pr., 1962. 93p. $3.95. (I)

In presentation and format similar to *High Country,* above, the author describes the Pacific states, including Alaska and Hawaii.

1938 Ferguson, Charles Wright. Getting To Know the U.S.A.; illus. by Leonard Everett Fisher. Coward-McCann, 1963. 95p. lib. ed. $3.69 net. (I)

An informal discussion of national patterns of growth and behavior as affected by the enormous size of the country.

1939 Fergusson, Erna. Hawaii. Fideler, 1966. new ed. 168p. $3.88. (I–U)

Surveys the land, climate, history, people, industries, and customs of the islands; illustrated with well-chosen photographs. Includes a pronouncing glossary and a topical index.

1940 Floethe, Louise Lee. The Islands of Hawaii; with pictures by Richard Floethe. Scribner, 1964. unp. $3.50; lib. ed. $3.31 net. (P)

This beautiful picture book introduces Hawaii and its people to primary pupils.

1941 Havighurst, Walter, ed. Midwest and Great Plains. Fideler, 1967. 384p. $5.96. (I–U)

Treats the section as a whole (climate, people, industries, etc.) and then considers each state separately in readable text reinforced by many photographs and study aids, a pronouncing glossary, and a topical index.

1942 Jennings, Jerry E., ed. The Northeast. Fideler, 1967. 384p. $5.96. (I–U)

A survey of New England, the District of Columbia, and the Middle Atlantic states, similar in coverage and presentation to the Fergusson and Havighurst titles, above.

1943 Jennings, Jerry E., and **Smith, Marion H.** The South. Fideler, 1967. 276p. $4.61. (I–U)

Another in the Fideler series of geographies, giving an overview of the region, followed by information on each of the 11 states.

1944 Kennedy, John F. The First Book Edition of John F. Kennedy's Inaugural Address; proclamation by Lyndon B. Johnson; illus. by Leonard Everett Fisher. Watts, 1964. 39p. $2.65. (I–U)

The address, proclamation, and Robert Frost poem read at the inauguration are given in full, illustrated with appropriate drawings.

1945 Krasilovsky, Phyllis. Benny's Flag; pictures by W. T. Mars. World, 1960. unp. $2.50; lib. ed. $2.53 net. (P–I)

An effectively illustrated true story of an Indian boy whose design for Alaska's flag won a contest.

1946 McCloskey, Robert. Time of Wonder. Viking, 1962. 63p. $3.50; lib. ed. $3.57 net. (P–I)

Summer on a Maine island is sensitively evoked in poetic text and the author's beautiful pictures portraying the beauty of sea and shore, the moods of the weather, and the fury of a hurricane.

1947 Melbo, Irving Robert. Our Country's National Parks, by Irving Robert Melbo, with the assistance of Robert Irving Melbo. 50 states ed. Bobbs-Merrill, 1964. 2v. $5 ea. (I–U)

One chapter is devoted to each of the national parks, describing its history, scenery, flora, and wildlife. Illustrated with photographs and drawings.

1948 Miers, Earl Schenck. Our Fifty States; illus. by Eleanor Mill; maps by Leonard Darwin. Grosset, 1961. 281p. $5.95; lib. ed. $5.25 net. (I–U)

Compact information about each state: history, products, people, cities, etc.

1949 National Geographic Society. America's Wonderlands: The Scenic National Parks and Monuments of the United States . . . National Geographic Soc., 1959. 510p. $9.95. (I–U)

Scenic attractions, wildlife preserves, and national parks are described and illustrated with maps and color photographs.

1950 Reith, John W., ed. California and the West. Fideler, 1968. 384p. $5.88. (I–U)

Maps, charts, photographs, and study guides are helpful features of this geography of the Western states, touching on history and describing in detail the region as a whole and the individual states, devoting special attention to California.

1951   Sasek, M. This Is New York. Macmillan, 1960. 60p. $3.50; lib. ed. $3.74 net. (P–I)

An impressionistic tour of New York City in brief text and the author's gay, colorful pictures.

1952   Sasek, M. This Is San Francisco. Macmillan, 1962. 60p. $3.50; lib. ed. $3.74 net. (P–I)

In the same lighthearted style as in *This Is New York,* above, the author conveys the atmosphere and charm of San Francisco in pictures of Chinatown, the Bay Bridge, the cable cars, and other characteristic scenes.

1953   Smith, Irene. Washington, D.C.; illus. by Emil Weiss. Rand McNally, 1964. 144p. $2.95. (I–U)

History, government, sights to see, and monuments and parks are described and shown in sketches and maps. Useful for history classes and field trips.

1954   Spring, Norma. Alaska: Pioneer State; photos. (by) Bob and Ira Spring. Nelson, 1966. 224p. $3.50; lib. ed. $3.31 net. (U)

The foreword states that this is "a comprehensive description of what our 49th state is like today, who are the diverse people who constitute its citizenry, how it became what it is, and where it is likely to go in the future." A well-organized and informative study, with interesting photographs, a chronology, and an annotated reading list.

1955   Stull, Edith. The First Book of Alaska; illus. with photos. Watts, 1965. 88p. $2.65. (I)

History, geographical features, people, and industries of Alaska are covered in a brief introduction to the 49th state.

1956   Tompkins, Stuart R. Alaska. Fideler, 1966. new ed. 144p. $3.48. (I–U)

A frequently revised geography covering all aspects of life in Alaska in readable text combined with informative photographs, a pronouncing glossary, and study guides.

1957   Wood, Dorothy. Hills and Harbors: The Middle Atlantic States . . . illus. by Vernon McKissack. Childrens Pr., 1962. 93p. $3.95. (I)

The Middle Atlantic states and the District of Columbia are described and pictured in this readable and attractive geography. The following titles in this series are similar in presentation and format:

1958   Wood, Dorothy. New England Country: The Northeastern States . . . illus. by Tom Dunnington. Childrens Pr., 1962. 93p. $3.95. (I)

1959   Wood, Dorothy. Sea and Sunshine: The South Atlantic States . . . illus. by Katherine Grace. Childrens Pr., 1962. 93p. $3.95. (I)

1960   Wood, Frances E. Gulf Lands and Central South . . . illus. by Katherine Grace. Childrens Pr., 1962. 93p. $3.95. (I)

1961   Wood, Frances E. Lakes, Hills, and Prairies: The Middle Western States . . . illus. by Tom Dunnington. Childrens Pr., 1962. 93p. $3.95. (I)

1962   Wood, Frances E. Panoramic Plains: The Great Plains States . . . illus. by Ed Morgan. Childrens Pr., 1962. 93p. $3.95. (I)

CANADA

1963   Barclay, Isabel. O Canada! Illus. by Cécile Gagnon. Doubleday, 1964. 95p. $3.50. (P)

An introductory history of Canada from the time of its discovery and exploration to the present.

1964   Hills, Theo L., and **Hills, Sarah Jane.** Canada. Fideler, 1967. 204p. $4.35. (I–U)

A geography covering history, physical features, natural resources, government, people, and arts and crafts of Canada, illustrated with maps and photographs. Pronouncing glossary and topical index.

1965   McNeer, May. The Canadian Story; with lithographs by Lynd Ward. Farrar, 1958. 96p. $4.25. (I)

A panoramic history of Canada, organized around colorful personalities and dramatic events and illustrated with striking lithographs in color and black and white.

1966   Mason, F. Van Wyck. The Battle for Quebec; illus. by Victor Mays. Houghton, 1965. 184p. $2.95. (I–U)

Graphically describes the Quebec Campaign of 1759: the battles, leaders, and results. Illustrated with maps and dramatic battle scenes.

1967 **Meyer, Edith Patterson.** The Friendly Frontier: The Story of the Canadian-American Border; illus. by W. T. Mars. Little, 1962. 296p. $4.95. (U)

Discusses the establishment and marking of the 3987-mile Canadian-U.S. border and describes the cooperative ventures of the two countries in such projects as the building of the St. Lawrence Seaway and the establishment of defense installations.

1968 **Peck, Anne Merriman.** The Pageant of Canadian History; illus. with photogravures and a map. 2d ed. McKay, 1963. 386p. $6.50. (U)

Comprehensive history of Canada, with interpretation of events and sketches of famous people.

1969 **Ross, Frances Aileen.** The Land and People of Canada; foreword by A. R. M. Lower. rev. ed. Lippincott, 1964. 128p. lib. ed. $2.93 net. (U)

An overview of the land, history, and people of Canada and the relationships of Canada and the United States.

1970 **Wood, Dorothy.** Canada; illus. by Harvey Shelton. Childrens Pr., 1964. 93p. $3.95. (I)

Reviews Canada's history, geography, and people in readable text illustrated with maps and colored pictures. Includes a table of statistics.

Latin America

INDIANS OF MEXICO, CENTRAL
AMERICA, AND SOUTH AMERICA

1971 **Beals, Carleton.** Land of the Mayas: Yesterday and Today; illus. with photos. by Marianne Greenwood. Abelard-Schuman, 1967. 158p. $4.95. (U)

The civilization of the ancient Mayas and its influence on the life of the Mayan Indians today is interestingly described and pictured in excellent photographs.

1972 **Beck, Barbara L.** The First Book of the Aztecs; pictures by Page Cary. Watts, 1966. 72p. $2.65. (I)

An animated introduction to the life of the Aztecs, describing their ancient civilization and giving probable causes of their defeat by the Spaniards. Many of the detailed drawings are reproduced from official sources.

1973 **Beck, Barbara L.** The First Book of the Incas; pictures by Page Cary. Watts, 1966. 78p. $2.65. (I)

Basing her account of Inca civilization on primary sources, the author briefly describes the government, religion, art, and daily life of the people. Many drawings (some based on Inca artifacts and architecture), a chronology, and a list of rulers enhance the value of the book.

1974 **Bleeker, Sonia.** The Aztec Indians of Mexico; illus. by Kisa Sasaki. Morrow, 1963. 160p. lib. ed. $2.94 net. (I)

Reviews the historical background of the Aztecs, describes the fall of the Aztec Empire, and discusses the present-day life of the people.

1975 **Bleeker, Sonia.** The Inca: Indians of the Andes; illus. by Patricia Boodell. Morrow, 1960. 157p. $2.95; lib. ed. $2.94 net. (I)

In a presentation similar to *The Aztec Indians*, above, the author describes the Inca civilization and its destruction by the Spaniards.

1976 **Bleeker, Sonia.** The Maya: Indians of Central America; illus. by Kisa Sasaki. Morrow, 1961. 160p. $2.95; lib. ed. $2.94 net. (I)

Following the pattern of her two books listed above, the author gives an overview of Maya life and culture.

1977 **Von Hagen, Victor W.** The Incas: People of the Sun; illus. by Alberto Beltrán. World, 1961. 127p. $3.95; lib. ed. $3.86 net. (U)

In authoritative narrative style the author reconstructs the Inca civilization preceding the Spanish conquest, stressing the amazing culture which the Incas developed. A reading list and a chronological chart of the Inca world and world events are useful features.

1978 **Von Hagen, Victor W.** Maya: Land of the Turkey and the Deer; illus. by Alberto Beltrán. World, 1960. 127p. $3.95; lib. ed. $3.86 net. (U)

Basing his story on historical documents and archaeological evidence, the author describes life among the ancient Mayas as seen through the eyes of a boy. An absorbing account, enhanced by a chronology, a bibliography, and pronunciation of difficult Mayan words.

1979 Von Hagen, Victor W. The Sun Kingdom of the Aztecs; illus. by Alberto Beltrán. World, 1958. 126p. $3.95; lib. ed. $3.86 net. (U)

Another in this author's excellent series on ancient cultures is a factual account of the world of the Aztecs, presented in semi-fictional form and effectively illustrated.

MEXICO

1980 Epstein, Sam, and **Epstein, Beryl.** The First Book of Mexico. rev. ed. Watts, 1967. 88p. $2.65. (I)

The reader tours Mexican towns and cities, visits a Mexican school, takes part in games and festivals, and learns the highlights of Mexican history. Illustrated with photographs.

1981 Horizon Magazine. Cortés and the Aztec Conquest; by the eds. of Horizon Magazine. Author, Irwin R. Blacker; consultant, Gordon Eckholm. American Heritage, 1965. A Horizon Caravel Book, distributed by Harper. 153p. $4.95; lib. ed. $4.79 net. (U)

Follows Cortés' conquest of Mexico in an absorbing account of his battles, marches, and destruction of the Aztec Empire, stressing the character and personality of Cortés and his companions. Notable for contemporary illustrations and maps.

1982 Larralde, Elsa. The Land and People of Mexico. rev. ed. Lippincott, 1964. 160p. lib. ed. $2.93 net. (U)

From the Aztec civilization to modern Mexico, a well-rounded picture of the country and its people, illustrated with maps and photographs.

1983 McNeer, May. The Mexican Story; with lithographs by Lynd Ward. Farrar, 1953. 96p. $4.25. (I)

An impressionistic, narrative account of the highlights of Mexican history centered around the people involved in them. The color and drama of Mexico are conveyed in descriptions and brilliant illustrations of fiestas, markets, and other characteristic scenes.

1984 Wood, Frances E. Mexico; illus. by Katherine Grace. Childrens Pr., 1964. 92p. $3.95. (I)

A readable, attractively illustrated study of Mexico: physical features, people, history, industries, and customs.

CENTRAL AMERICA

1985 Colvin, Gerard. The Lands and Peoples of Central America: Guatemala, El Salvador, Costa Rica, Honduras, Nicaragua, Panama, British Honduras. Macmillan, 1962. 96p. $2.50. (I–U)

Surveys the countries of Central America in concise text and many photographs. Includes a map and a glossary.

1986 Markun, Patricia Maloney. The First Book of Central America and Panama. Watts, 1963. 90p. $2.65. (I)

A simply written summary of Central American geography, history, and present conditions, illustrated with photographs.

1987 May, Charles Paul. Central America: Lands Seeking Unity. Nelson, 1966. 224p. $3.50; lib. ed. $3.31 net. (U)

After briefly sketching the history of the seven Central American countries, the author concentrates on present conditions and recent problems of inter-American relations and attempts at solutions through cooperation. Maps, photographs, a chronology, and a reading list add to the book's usefulness for social studies.

CARIBBEAN AND WEST ATLANTIC ISLANDS

1988 Augelli, John P., ed. Caribbean Lands. Fideler, 1966. 352p. $5.88. (I–U)

A photographic study of the history, geography, and peoples of Central America, the Greater and Lesser Antilles, and the Bahama Islands, including maps, charts, a pronouncing glossary, and an index.

1989 Bothwell, Jean. By Sail and Wind: The Story of the Bahamas; illus. with photos. and drawings by Omar Davis. Abelard-Schuman, 1964. 152p. $3.50. (I–U)

Traces the history of the Bahamas from their discovery by Columbus to the present and describes the geography, government, industries, and people of the present day.

1990 McGuire, Edna. Puerto Rico: Bridge to Freedom; foreword by Luis Munoz Marin; illus. with photos. Macmillan, 1963. 180p. $4.50; lib. ed. $4.34 net. (I–U)

Special emphasis is given to "Operation

Bootstrap" in this well-organized study of Puerto Rico's history, geography, government, industry, and people.

1991 Manning, Jack. Young Puerto Rico: Children of Puerto Rico at Work and Play; text and photos. by Jack Manning. Dodd, 1962. 64p. $3; lib. ed. $2.79 net. (P–I)

A photographic study of the home life, education, festivals, and games and dances of Puerto Rican children.

1992 Matthews, Herbert L. Cuba; with an introd. by Frank Tannenbaum. Macmillan, 1964. 134p. $2.95; lib. ed. $2.96 net. (U)

Cuba's long history of oppression by Spain, the controversial role of the United States in Cuba's war for independence, the succession of corrupt rulers, and the Castro revolution are examined in a thought-provoking study.

1993 Sherlock, Philip. The Land and People of the West Indies. Lippincott, 1967. 172p. $3.25; lib. ed. $2.93 net. (U)

Discusses the countries of the Caribbean Archipelago, bringing out differences as well as similarities in the islands and their people. Illustrated with photographs.

South America

1994 Bowen, J. David. The Land and People of Chile. Lippincott, 1966. 154p. $3.25; lib. ed. $2.93 net. (I–U)

The tremendous varieties of climate, scenery, and ways of living in Chile's 2600-mile length are emphasized in this photographic overview of the country and its people.

1995 Bowen, J. David. The Land and People of Peru. Lippincott, 1963. 160p. lib. ed. $2.93 net. (I–U)

Discusses the history, geography, and current conditions of Peru in a readable, well-illustrated account.

1996 Brown, Rose. The Land and People of Brazil. rev. ed. Lippincott, 1963. 120p. lib. ed. $2.93. (I–U)

Smoothly written text and well-chosen photographs tell the story of Brazil.

1997 Carter, William E. The First Book of South America. Watts, 1961. 86p. $2.65. (I)

The author first considers the continent as a whole, then briefly describes each country's history, geography, and people.

1998 Fideler, Raymond, ed. South America. Fideler, 1966. 224p. $4.08. (I–U)

A well-organized geography, illustrated with maps and photographs, giving an overview of the continent and a detailed discussion of each country.

1999 Hall, Elvajean. The Land and People of Argentina; illus. from photos. rev. ed. Lippincott, 1962. 128p. lib. ed. $2.93 net. (I–U)

An enthusiastic discussion of Argentina, past and present, with lively vignettes on ranch life, holidays, schools, and other facets of contemporary Argentine life.

Europe

Austria

2000 Gidal, Sonia, and **Gidal, Tim.** My Village in Austria. Pantheon, 1956. 74p. $3.69 net. (P–I)

Typical family and community scenes, centering around Seppi, an Austrian boy, are shown in photographs and described by Seppi.

2001 Hoffman, George, and **Hoffman, Viola.** Austria. Fideler, 1968. 160p. $3.88. (I–U)

A geography covering a broad range of topics about the country and its people, illustrated with many photographs, maps, and charts.

Czechoslovakia

2002 Hall, Elvajean. The Land and People of Czechoslovakia. Lippincott, 1966. 154p. $3.25; lib. ed. $2.93 net. (I–U)

Combines the history and geography of the Czechoslovak Republic in animated text and illuminating photographs.

England

2003 Buehr, Walter. The Spanish Armada; written and illus. by Walter Buehr. Putnam, 1962. 96p. lib. ed. $2.97 net. (I)

A stirring account of the great sea battle in which England defeated the mighty Armada in 1588.

2004 Denny, Norman, & Filmer-Sankey, Josephine. The Bayeux Tapestry: The Story of the Norman Conquest, 1066. Atheneum, 1966. unp. $7.95. (I–U)

Excellent color photographs show the famous tapestry which tells the story of the Norman conquest of England, each page showing a section of the tapestry, with accompanying explanatory text. Interesting both as art and as history.

2005   Duggan, Alfred L. Growing Up with the Norman Conquest; illus. by C. Walter Hodges. Pantheon, 1966. 217p. $3.95; lib. ed. $3.69 net. (U)

An animated picture of everyday life in England as Normans and Saxons learned to live together in the years following the Battle of Hastings.

2006   Hodges, C. Walter. Magna Carta; written and illus. by C. Walter Hodges. Coward-McCann, 1966. 32p. lib. ed. $3.69 net. (I–U)

The author describes the events leading to the signing of the Magna Carta, discusses the meaning of the document as a milestone in man's struggle for freedom, and highlights the story with superb full-color pictures.

2007   Horizon Magazine. Shakespeare's England; by the eds. of Horizon Magazine, in consultation with Louis B. Wright; illus. with paintings, drawings, and engravings of the period. American Heritage, 1964. A Horizon Caravel Book, distributed by Harper. 153p. $4.95; lib. ed. $4.79 net. (I–U)

Sixteenth-century England as Shakespeare knew it is brought to life in a handsomely illustrated survey of the social, political, and theatrical life of the period.

2008   Malmström, Vincent H., (and) **Malmström, Ruth M.** Life in Europe: The British Isles. Fideler, 1967. 192p. $4.08 (I)

Surveys the British Isles, with emphasis on England, in well-organized text and many photographs, maps, and charts.

2009   Sasek, M. This Is London. Macmillan, 1959. 60p. $3.50; lib. ed. $3.74 net. (P–I)

A tour of London's showplaces and a look at her people in brief, informal text and the author's colorful, atmospheric pictures.

2010   Streatfeild, Noel. The First Book of England; pictures by Gioia Fiammenghi. Watts, 1958. 66p. $2.65. (I)

A readable and appreciative introduction to England and the English.

2011   Unstead, R. J. Looking at History: Britain from Cavemen to the Present Day; with 16 colour plates and nearly 1000 illus. in the text. Macmillan, 1956. 351p. $6.95. (I–U)

The introduction to this book states that it is "about the lives of the ordinary people of England . . . how they built their homes and cooked their food, how they dressed, fought, traveled, worked, and enjoyed themselves."

FINLAND AND LAPLAND

2012   Berry, Erick. The Land and People of Finland. Lippincott, 1959. 126p. lib. ed. $2.93. (I–U)

Surveys Finland's history, geography, daily life, and cultural heritage of mythology and folklore in concise text and many illustrations.

2013   Berry, Erick. Men, Moss, and Reindeer: The Challenge of Lapland; map and diagram by Wes McKeown. Coward-McCann, 1959. 96p. $2.60. (I)

Describes the way of life of the Lapps of Finland against a background of history and geography, showing how their lives are dependent upon their herds of reindeer.

2014   Gidal, Sonia, and **Gidal, Tim.** Follow the Reindeer. Pantheon, 1959. 76p. $3.69 net. (P–I)

The reader goes with young Anders and his Lapp family on a trek to summer grazing lands with their herds of reindeer and learns how the Laplanders live and what their country is like. Excellent photographs help to tell the story.

FRANCE

2015   Creed, Virginia. Life in Europe: France. Fideler, 1964. 160p. $3.88. (I–U)

Essential facts about the history, geography, and people of France are presented in straightforward text and numerous photographs, maps, and charts.

2016   Harris, Leon A. Young France: Children of France at Work and Play. Dodd, 1964. 64p. lib. ed. 2.99 net. (P–I)

Well-captioned photographs and brief text take the reader on a tour of French children's homes, schools, and playgrounds.

2017 **Horizon Magazine.** The French Revolution; by the eds. of Horizon Magazine, in consultation with David L. Dowd . . . American Heritage, 1965. A Horizon Caravel Book, distributed by Harper. 150p. $4.95; lib. ed. $4.79 net. (U)

The complex story of the French Revolution—the social and political events leading up to it, the personalities involved, the highlights of the struggle—is told in well-organized text and hundreds of period illustrations.

2018 **Sasek, M.** This Is Paris. Macmillan, 1959. 60p. $3.50; lib. ed. $3.74 net. (P–I)

The character and atmosphere of Paris and its people are captured in a beautiful picture book.

GERMANY

2019 **Gidal, Sonia,** and **Gidal, Tim.** My Village in Germany. Pantheon, 1964. 85p. $3.95; lib. ed. $3.69 net. (P–I)

Unposed pictures and simple text present everyday life in a village of the Bavarian Alps.

2020 **Lobsenz, Norman.** The First Book of West Germany; pictures by Lili Réthi. Watts, 1959. 66p. $2.65. (I)

Brief account of the history, people, landmarks, and social life and customs of West Germany.

2021 **Sasek, M.** This Is Munich. Macmillan, 1961. 60p. $3.50; lib. ed. $3.74 net. (P–I)

A famous German city is presented in a gay picture book by a talented author-illustrator.

2022 **Shirer, William L.** The Rise and Fall of Adolph Hitler. Random, 1961. 185p. $1.95; lib. ed. $2.48 net. (U)

An effective adaptation of the author's adult book, *The Rise and Fall of the Third Reich*, giving a dramatic account of Hitler's life and Nazi Germany under his dictatorship. Based on Shirer's experiences as a war correspondent and on captured Nazi documents. Illustrated with photographs.

2023 **Wohlrabe, Raymond A.,** and **Krusch, Werner.** The Land and People of Germany. Lippincott, 1964. 118p. lib. ed. $2.93 net. (I–U)

Condenses history, geography, and essential facts about the people and culture of East and West Germany. Illustrated with maps and photographs.

GREECE

2024 **Gianakoulis, Theodore.** The Land and People of Greece; illus. from photos. rev. ed. Lippincott, 1965. 160p. $3.25; lib. ed. $2.93 net. (I–U)

Against a background of Greek history, the author conveys a clear picture of Greece today and her place in the modern world.

2025 **Gidal, Sonia,** and **Gidal, Tim.** My Village in Greece. Pantheon, 1960. 76p. $3.69 net. (P–I)

The authors show life in a Greek island village in interesting text and excellent, unstudied photographs.

2026 **Miller, Helen H.** Greece. Scribner, 1965. 190p. lib. ed. $3.63 net. (U)

Presents a firsthand account of Greece today: government, economic conditions, education, arts, and tourist attractions. Illustrated with maps and photographs.

2027 **Sasek, M.** This Is Greece. Macmillan, 1966. 60p. $3.50; lib. ed. $3.74 net. (P–I)

A handsome picture book which takes the reader on a tour of ancient and modern landmarks, shown in full color and succinctly described.

HUNGARY

2028 **Csicsery-Rónay, István.** The First Book of Hungary. Watts, 1967. 89p. $2.65. (U)

Combines a brief history of the country with a more-detailed discussion of Hungary today, including brief sketches of prominent Hungarians and accounts of the Communist take-over and the 1956 revolution.

IRELAND

2029 **Manning, Jack.** Young Ireland: Children of Ireland at Work and Play; text and photos. by Jack Manning. Dodd, 1965. 64p. $3.25; lib. ed. $2.99 net. (P–I)

Human-interest photographs with brief background text show Irish children in many aspects of their life today.

2030 **Quigley, Lillian Fox.** Ireland. Macmillan, 1964. 118p. $2.95; lib. ed. $2.96 net. (U)

Irish character and culture are stressed in this photographic survey of present-day Ireland.

ITALY

2031 Gidal, Sonia, and **Gidal, Tim.** My Village in Italy. Pantheon, 1962. 83p. $3.95; lib. ed. $3.69 net. (P–I)
An Italian boy leads a tour of Tuscany at grape-harvesting time. An appealing picture of Italian village life in informal text and engaging pictures.

2032 Kish, George. Life in Europe: Italy. Fideler, 1968. 160p. $3.88. (I–U)
An overall study of Italy in readable text and numerous maps, charts, and photographs.

2033 Martin, Rupert. Looking at Italy. Lippincott, 1967. 64p. $2.95; lib. ed. $2.93 net. (P–I)
In simple text and abundant excellent photographs, many in color, the author introduces present-day Italy.

2034 Sasek, M. This Is Rome. Macmillan, 1960. 60p. $3.50; lib. ed. $3.74 net. (P–I)
Ancient Rome and present-day Rome are seen in full-color pictures and described in informal text.

2035 Sasek, M. This Is Venice. Macmillan, 1961. 56p. $3.50; lib. ed. $3.74 net. (P–I)
This companion volume to *This Is Rome,* above, catches the romantic atmosphere of old and new Venice in flavorful pictures and humorous descriptions.

THE NETHERLANDS

2036 Barnouw, Adriann J. The Land and People of Holland. Lippincott, 1961. 129p. lib. ed. $2.93 net. (I–U)
Gives a good picture of present-day Holland, with emphasis on the cultural and artistic life of the people. Illustrated with maps and photographs.

2037 Carew, Dorothy. The Netherlands. Macmillan, 1965. 122p. $2.95; lib. ed. $2.96 net. (U)
This more-advanced study of the Netherlands includes, besides the usual geographical and historical information, a discussion of ancient and modern drainage projects and a review of United States–Dutch rela-

tions over the years. Illustrated with maps and many photographs.

2038 Loman, Anna. Looking at Holland. Lippincott, 1966. 63p. $2.95; lib. ed. $2.93 net. (P–I)
A readable introduction to modern Holland, illustrated with maps and numerous photographs in color and black and white.

POLAND

2039 Kelly, Eric P., and **Kostich, Dragoš D.** The Land and People of Poland. rev. ed. Lippincott, 1964. 128p. $2.93 net. (I–U)
Treats Poland's history, geography, and people, with detailed descriptions of Kraków and Warsaw before, during, and after World War II. Illustrated with maps and photographs.

RUSSIA

2040 Nazaroff, Alexander I. The Land and People of Russia. rev. ed. Lippincott, 1966. 190p. $3.25; lib. ed. $2.93 net. (U)
A compact history of Russia from the time of the Czars to the present is combined with a general description of the enormous country and its varied peoples.

2041 Rice, Tamara Talbot. Finding Out about the Early Russians; introd. by Harrison E. Salisbury. Lothrop, 1964. 168p. $3.50. (U)
Russian history from 3000 B.C. to the time of Peter the Great is surveyed with special attention to the Russian influence on world art, architecture, and religion. Maps and numerous photographs and paintings illustrate the text.

2042 Salisbury, Harrison E. Russia. Macmillan, 1965. 138p. $2.95; lib. ed. $2.96 net. (U)
Discusses Russia's rise from a primitive nation to a world power and describes the life of the people today. Enhanced by maps, photographs, and reproductions.

2043 Snyder, Louis L. The First Book of the Soviet Union. Watts, 1965. 48p. $2.65. (I)
In a simply written, effectively illustrated account the author reviews Russian history and present-day life.

2044 Vandivert, Rita. Young Russia: Children of the USSR at Work and at Play;

photos. by William Vandivert; text by Rita Vandivert. Dodd, 1960. 60p. $3. (P–I)

Revealing photographs and carefully researched text provide an interesting view of Russian children.

SCANDINAVIA

2045 **Cary, Sturges F.** Volcanoes and Glaciers: The Challenge of Iceland; maps by Wes McKeown. Coward-McCann, 1959. 94p. $2.60. (I)

Tells how the people of Iceland, descendants of the Vikings, have turned a bleak, volcanic land into the prosperous country it is today and what their lives are like.

2046 **Gidal, Sonia,** and **Gidal, Tim.** My Village in Denmark. Pantheon, 1963. 77p. $3.69 net. (P–I)

Conversational text and fine photographs portray life in a Danish island village as seen through the eyes of a native boy.

2047 **Horizon Magazine.** The Vikings; by the eds. of Horizon Magazine. Author, Frank R. Donovan; consultant, Sir Thomas D. Kendrick . . . American Heritage, 1964. A Horizon Caravel Book, distributed by Harper. 153p. $4.95; lib. ed. $4.79 net. (U)

In lucid, well-organized text and a wealth of excellent illustrations the authors present the Northmen as farmers, traders, and colonizers as well as seafarers and raiders, citing archaeological evidence to support the legendary tales of Viking exploits and discussing Scandinavian contributions to literature and art.

2048 **Malmström, Vincent H.,** and **Malmström, Ruth M.** Life in Europe: Norway. Fideler, 1968. 160p. $3.88. (I–U)

Comprehensive coverage of Norway's history, geography, and people, illustrated with maps, charts, and photographs.

2049 **Nano, Frederic C.** The Land and People of Sweden. rev. ed. Lippincott, 1964. 116p. lib. ed. $2.93 net. (I–U)

Surveys Sweden today and yesterday—historic sites, scenic attractions, people, industries, crafts, etc.—in readable text and maps and photographs.

2050 **Rich, Louise Dickinson.** The First Book of the Vikings; pictures by Lili Réthi. Watts, 1962. 66p. $2.65. (P–I)

An informal story of life among the Vikings, telling how they built their ships,

how they were governed, and what their daily lives were like. Informative illustrations.

2051 **Riwkin-Brick, Anna,** and **Lindgren, Astrid.** Randi Lives in Norway. Macmillan, 1965. unp. $2.95; lib. ed. $2.94 net. (P–I)

Appealing photographs tied together by descriptive text show typical scenes in a Norse fishing village.

2052 **Wohlrabe, Raymond A.,** and **Krusch, Werner E.** The Land and People of Denmark. Lippincott, 1961. 128p. $2.93 net. (I–U)

A photographic travelogue of Denmark covering the most important aspects of the country and its people.

SCOTLAND

2053 **Buchanan, Freda M.** The Land and People of Scotland. rev. ed. Lippincott, 1962. 128p. lib. ed. $2.93 net. (I–U)

An informative overview of Scotland, stressing its variety of geographical features, colorful personalities, and unique customs.

2054 **Sasek, M.** This Is Edinburgh. Macmillan, 1961. 59p. $3.50; lib. ed. $3.74 net. (P–I)

Another in this artist's impressionistic picture books of great cities highlights Edinburgh's famous landmarks.

SPAIN

2055 **Daly, Maureen.** Spain: Wonderland of Contrasts; illus. with photos. Dodd, 1965. 64p. $3; lib. ed. $2.79 net. (I–U)

The author offers a perceptive and appreciative view of contemporary Spain focused on the character and life of the people and touching only lightly on geography and history. Informatively captioned photographs support the interesting text.

2056 **Gidal, Sonia,** and **Gidal, Tim.** My Village in Spain. Pantheon, 1962. 83p. lib. ed. $3.69 net. (P–I)

A young Spanish boy takes the reader on a tour of his Andalusian village and to Córdoba to see a bullfight. Fine photographs tell much of the story.

2057 **Maiques, Gines M.** Life in Europe: Spain: Fideler, 1967. 160p. $3.88. (I–U)

A geography of Spain covering the usual

topics in well-organized text supported by numerous maps, charts, and photographs.

SWITZERLAND

2058 Epstein, Sam, and Epstein, Beryl. The First Book of Switzerland; illus. with photos. Watts, 1964. 85p. $2.65. (I)

Introduces Switzerland in concise text and many photographs.

2059 Gidal, Sonia, and Gidal, Tim. My Village in Switzerland. Pantheon, 1961. 81p. $3.69 net. (P–I)

As in other books by these authors, a native boy conducts a tour of his home and village, and the reader learns many facts about the history, geography, and home life of Switzerland. Excellent photographs add reality to the informal discourse.

2060 Hoffman, George W., (and) Hoffman, Viola. Life in Europe: Switzerland. Fideler, 1967. 160p. $3.88. (I–U)

A general survey of the country, with chapters on resorts, government, and international organizations. Generously illustrated with maps, charts, and photographs.

Africa

GENERAL

2061 Allen, William D. Africa. Fideler, 1968. 176p. $3.88. (I–U)

A recently updated geography covering the continent as a whole and highlighting physical features, climate, animals, and the changing political picture.

2062 Horizon Magazine. Exploration of Africa; by the eds. of Horizon Magazine. Author, Thomas Sterling; consultant, George H. T. Kimble . . . American Heritage, 1963. A Horizon Caravel Book, distributed by Harper. 153p. $4.95; lib. ed. $4.79 net. (U)

Recounts the amazing exploits of the Europeans who explored the great rivers of Africa for science, adventure, and treasure, giving vivid portraits of colorful characters and discussing the slave trade, trade wars, and the Boer settlements. Notable for excellent illustrations of many types.

2063 Hughes, Langston. The First Book of Africa; illus. with photos. Watts, 1964. 82p. $2.65. (I)

An introduction to the history, geography, and people of Africa, with special attention to recent developments.

2064 Lens, Sidney. Africa—Awakening Giant. Putnam, 1962. 192p. $3.50. (I–U)

Discusses the struggle of African peoples to free themselves from colonial domination and gives interesting pictures of the native leaders who have spearheaded the movement.

2065 Nolen, Barbara, ed. Africa Is People: Firsthand Accounts of Contemporary Africa; with an introd. by Mercer Cook. Dutton, 1967. 270p. $6.95; lib. ed. $6.88 net. (U)

An anthology of selections gathered from journals, interviews, eyewitness accounts, and autobiographies of native Africans or others intimately acquainted with the country and its people. Each selection is introduced by explanatory information on the author and the country. Challenging reading for the advanced older pupil and a rich source of read-aloud material.

2066 Thompson, Elizabeth B. Africa: Past and Present. Houghton, 1966. 330p. $5. (U)

Following a brief description of Africa's geographical features and a concise review of its history, the author discusses the emergence of the new Africa. Maps, photographs, and a reading list add to the book's value.

NORTHERN AFRICA

2067 Bleeker, Sonia. The Tuareg: Nomads and Warriors; illus. by Kisa N. Sasaki. Morrow, 1964. 158p. $2.95; lib. ed. $2.94 net. (I)

Introduces the wandering tribes of the Sahara Desert, describes their way of life, and considers how they may be affected by the coming of technology.

2068 Cavanna, Betty. Ali of Egypt; photos. by George Russell Harrison. Watts, 1966. 68p. $3.95. (P–I)

With nine-year-old Ali, the reader visits the Aswan High Dam and learns what it will mean to the people living along the Nile. Excellent photographs show the dam and the surrounding countryside.

2069 Copeland, Paul W. The Land and People of Libya. Lippincott, 1967. 158p. $3.25; lib. ed. $2.93 net. (I–U)

Similar in treatment to other titles of this series, this is a well-rounded survey of Libya's history, geography, and contemporary life, well illustrated with maps and photographs.

2070 Joy, Charles R. Desert Caravans: The Challenge of the Changing Sahara. Coward-McCann, 1960. 119p. $2.60. (I)

An informed discussion of the Sahara: its history, exploration, plant and animal life, and people, and the recent attempts to develop its natural resources. Illustrated with photographs.

2071 Joy, Charles R. Island in the Desert: The Challenge of the Nile; maps by Marian Manfredi. Coward-McCann, 1959. 95p. $2.60. (I)

Discusses the vital importance of the Nile to Egypt and tells how it is being used to solve some of the country's problems.

2072 Mahmoud, Zaki Naguib. The Land and People of Egypt. Lippincott, 1965. 127p. lib. ed. $2.93 net. (I–U)

Combines history, geography, and present-day life of the people in a competent photographic study of Egypt. The two titles following in this series are similar in coverage and format:

2073 Spencer, William. The Land and People of Morocco. Lippincott, 1965. 160p. $3.25; lib. ed. $2.93 net. (I–U)

2074 Spencer, William. The Land and People of Tunisia. Lippincott, 1967. 160p. $3.25; lib. ed. $2.93 net. (I–U)

EAST AND CENTRAL AFRICA

2075 Bernheim, Marc, and **Bernheim, Evelyne.** From Bush to City: A Look at the New Africa. Harcourt, 1966. 96p. $4.50; lib. ed. $4.62 net. (U)

With emphasis on the nations south of the Sahara, this author-photographer team offers a perceptive study of Africa's new nations and the changes in the lives of the people as tribal life and technology come into conflict.

2076 Bleeker, Sonia. The Masai: Herders of East Africa; illus. by Kisa N. Sasaki. Morrow, 1963. 155p. $2.95; lib. ed. $2.94 net. (I)

A straightforward and absorbing account of all phases of life among the Masai, with especially interesting chapters on the training of girls for home life and the boys for warfare.

2077 Donna, Natalie. Boy of the Masai; photos. by Peter Larsen. Dodd, 1964. unp. $2.99 net. (P–I)

Primitive life and customs in a tribal village are contrasted with life in the city of Nairobi in excellent photographs and explanatory text.

2078 Forsberg, Vera. Gennet Lives in Ethiopia; photos. by Anna Riwkin-Brick. Macmillan, 1968. unp. $3.95. (P–I)

A brief story of seven-year-old Gennet, who goes alone through frightening country to get a doctor for her little brother, ties together remarkably expressive photographs of Ethiopian village people in their homes and at their daily tasks. Should help young people to understand and respect a people very different from themselves.

2079 Kaula, Edna Mason. The Bantu Africans; illus. with photos. Watts, 1968. 90p. $2.65. (I)

Introduces the Bantu-speaking people, the largest single-language group in Africa, and discusses their history, customs, art, and the role they are playing in Bantu-occupied countries.

2080 Kenworthy, Leonard S. Profile of Kenya. Doubleday, 1963. 128p. $3.25. (I–U)

A sympathetic picture of Kenya, with vivid descriptions of its magnificent mountains, game preserves, native customs, cities, and the changing life of the people. Illustrated with photographs.

2081 Lauber, Patricia. The Congo: River into Central Africa; illus. by Ted Schroeder; maps by Fred Kliem. Garrard, 1964. 96p. $2.32. (I)

A simply written account of the explorations of the Congo and the Nile and a description of countries and peoples along their banks. (R4–5)

2082 Lobsenz, Norman M. The First Book of East Africa: Kenya, Uganda, Tanganyika, and Zanzibar; illus. with photos. Watts, 1964. 88p. $2.65. (I)

A general description of the four countries of the great East African Plateau, spiced with accounts of native customs, little-known facts, and a glossary of Swahili words.

2083 Riwkin-Brick, Anna. Sia Lives on Kilimanjaro; photos. by Anna Riwkin-Brick; text by Astrid Lindgren. Macmillan, 1959. unp. $2.94 net. (P)

Excellent photographs tell most of the story of a little girl who follows her parents to a feast in honor of the king. A good introduction to life in Tanganyika.

WEST AFRICA

2084 Buckley, Peter. Okolo of Nigeria. Simon & Schuster, 1962. 125p. $3.95. (P–I)

Through easy text and excellent photographs the reader learns of life in Nigeria as a Nigerian boy struggles to get an education so that he can help his people adjust to the modern world.

2085 Davis, Russell, and **Ashabranner, Brent K.** Land in the Sun: The Story of West Africa; illus. by Robert William Hinds. Little, 1963. 92p. $4.50; lib. ed. $4.58 net. (I)

Life in the rain forests, the bush villages, and the cities of West Africa is described in interesting, well-illustrated text covering people, religion, art, industries, animals, and relations with America.

2086 Forman, Brenda-Lu, and **Forman, Harrison.** The Land and People of Nigeria. Lippincott, 1964. 160p. $3.25; lib. ed. $2.93 net. (I–U)

After sketching Nigeria's history and describing its geography and present-day conditions, the authors discuss the efforts of the new nation to maintain its independence and unify its people. Excellent photographs and maps and a pronunciation guide.

2087 Lobsenz, Norman M. The First Book of Ghana; illus. with photos. Watts, 1960. 62p. $2.65. (I)

A fact-filled introduction to Ghana, highlighting important aspects of its history, geography, and present-day life as old ways meet the new.

2088 Sutherland, Efua. Playtime in Africa; photos. by Willis E. Bell. Atheneum, 1962. 56p. $3; lib. ed. $2.77 net. (P)

Lively photographs and rhythmic text catch the children of Ghana at their games and pastimes, revealing the universality of children's play and providing a bridge of understanding for American children.

SOUTH AFRICA

2089 Paton, Alan. The Land and People of South Africa. rev. ed. Lippincott, 1964. 162p. $3.25; lib. ed. $2.93 net. (I–U)

Very relevant to today's events is this study of South Africa by a South African who understands the political and racial situation and analyzes it penetratingly. After discussing the country's history, geography, and contemporary life, the author considers the country's problems and their effects on the present and future of the nation.

2090 Perkins, Carol Morse, and **Perkins, Marlin.** "I Saw You from Afar": A Visit to the Bushmen of the Kalahari Desert. Atheneum, 1965. 56p. $3.25; lib. ed. $3.07 net. (P–I)

An authoritative and sympathetic portrait of South Africa's oldest inhabitants, describing their cultural patterns, their adjustment to a harsh environment, and their gentleness and courtesy as a people. The many photographs are exceptionally beautiful and revealing.

Asia

NEAR EAST

2091 Comay, Joan, and **Pearlman, Moshe.** Israel; with an introd. by Golda Meir. Macmillan, 1964. 120p. $2.95; lib. ed. $2.96 net. (U)

After giving an overview of Jewish history, the authors discuss the formation of Israel as a separate nation and describe the development of the country and the life of the people. With the exception of Chaim Weizmann, no political figure is mentioned and no controversial issue is discussed.

2092 Gidal, Sonia, and **Gidal, Nachum.** Sons of the Desert. Pantheon, 1960. 79p. lib. ed. $3.69 net. (P–I)

The son of a Bedouin sheik takes the reader on a tour of his desert home and describes the life of his people. Excellent photographs and a suggestion of plot hold the reader's attention.

2093 Hinckley, Helen. The Land and People of Iran. Lippincott, 1964. 160p. $3.25; lib. ed. $2.93 net. (I–U)

Begins with a history of the country when it was Persia and continues with a detailed discussion of Iran today, stressing the problems of economic and agricultural development.

2094 **Holisher, Desider.** Growing Up in Israel. Viking, 1963. 180p. $5; lib. ed. $4.53 net. (U)

Home and family life as experienced by a teen-age brother and sister, native-born Israelis, is presented against a background of Jewish history and contemporary places of interest. Many photographs and a map add interest and information.

2095 **Pinney, Roy.** Young Israel; photos. by the author. Dodd, 1963. 64p. lib. ed. $2.99 net. (P–I)

Similar to *Growing Up in Israel,* above, but briefer and designed to appeal to younger children, this shows children at home, in *kibbutz* communities, at work, and at play. Excellent photographs.

2096 **Sasek, M.** This Is Israel. Macmillan, 1962. 60p. $3.50; lib. ed. $3.74 net. (P–I)

An artist views old and new Israeli points of interest in gay pictures and brief, descriptive text.

2097 **Spencer, William.** The Land and People of Turkey. Lippincott, 1964. 128p. lib. ed. $2.93 net. (I–U)

Reviews Turkish history and describes the modern state and its people in informal style, contrasting the old and the new in order to help the reader understand the problems faced by the country today.

2098 **Warren, Ruth.** The First Book of the Arab World; illus. with photos. Watts, 1963. 65p. $2.65. (I)

An introduction to the Arabian peninsula and adjacent areas inhabited by Arabs, giving generalized information about the history and geography of the region and the way of life of its people. Illustrated with photographs and a map.

2099 **Winder, Viola H.** The Land and People of Lebanon. Lippincott, 1965. 160p. $3.25; lib. ed. $2.93 net. (I–U)

Presents Lebanon as the meeting place between East and West and discusses the country's history, geography, and contemporary life.

CHINA AND HONG KONG

2100 **Goldston, Robert C.** The Rise of Red China; illus. with photos. and drawings by Donald Carrick. Bobbs-Merrill, 1967. 256p. $4.95. (U)

After giving an overview of 2000 years of Chinese history, the author discusses the conditions which led to the establishment of the Communist regime in 1949; appraises the aims and accomplishments of Mao Tse-tung's dictatorship; and considers China's present and future relationship to the rest of the world. For the superior older reader.

2101 **Joy, Charles R.** Getting To Know the Two Chinas; illus. by Claudine Nanki-vel. Coward-McCann, 1960. 65p. lib. ed. $2.68 net. (I)

Explains why China has two governments and describes life under each. Effective illustrations, a glossary of foreign words, and a chronology are helpful study aids.

2102 **Kinmond, William.** The First Book of Communist China. Watts, 1962. 85p. $2.65. (I–U)

For less-able readers than is the Goldston book, above, this sketches the history of China, reviews the events leading to the present regime, describes the country's principal physical features, and discusses the life of the people under Communism.

2103 **Sasek, M.** This Is Hong Kong. Macmillan, 1965. 60p. $3.50; lib. ed. $3.74 net. (P–I)

Catches all the variety and flavor of Hong Kong in colorful pictures and amusing comments.

2104 **Seeger, Elizabeth.** The Pageant of Chinese History; illus. by Bernard Watkins. 4th ed. McKay, 1962. 427p. $6.50. (U)

The absorbing story of China's 5000-year history, highlighting dramatic episodes to sustain interest.

2105 **Wiens, Herald J., and Hertel, Margaret Fisher.** China. Fideler, 1966. 260p. $4.61. (I–U)

Discusses China in detail; well organized and generously illustrated with photographs, maps, and charts.

INDIA, PAKISTAN, AND CEYLON

2106 **Bothwell, Jean.** The First Book of India. Watts, 1966. 88p. $2.65. (I)

This introduction to contemporary India provides the essential facts about the country, its people, and its problems. Skillfully organized, smoothly written, and illustrated with photographs and maps.

2107 Bothwell, Jean. The First Book of Pakistan; illus. with photos. and maps. Watts, 1962. 61p. $2.65. (I)
Introduces Pakistan in a readable survey emphasizing the events which led to Pakistan's separation from India in 1947 and the problems and accomplishments of Pakistan as a separate nation.

2108 Bowles, Cynthia. At Home in India; illus. with photos. Harcourt, 1956. 180p. $3.25. (I–U)
A teen-age daughter of the former United States ambassador to India describes her experiences in school and in the homes of her Indian friends and gives her impressions of India's art, music, and sports.

2109 Modak, Manorama R. The Land and People of India. Lippincott, 1960. 128p. $2.93 net. (I–U)
Chapters on India's epics, the Ramayana and the Mahabharata, are interesting sections of this knowledgeable photographic study of ancient and modern India.

2110 Norris, Marianna. Young India: Children of India at Work and at Play; with photos. by Blaise Levai. Dodd, 1966. 64p. $3.25; lib. ed. $2.99 net. (P–I)
Human-interest photographs and informal text show India's children teaching their parents to read, scrubbing an elephant, winding a turban, at their play, and in other situations interesting to American children.

2111 Raman, T. A. India. Fideler, 1968. 200p. $4.08. (I–U)
Well-balanced coverage of India in a geography geared to elementary school children and illustrated with excellent photographs, maps, and charts.

2112 Sucksdorff, Astrid Bergman. Chendru: The Boy and the Tiger; English version by William Sansom; photos. by Arne Sucksdorff. Harcourt, 1960. unp. $3.50. (P–I)
Superb full-color photographs and poetic text are combined to portray the life of a real boy and his pet tiger in a jungle village of India.

2113 Wilber, Donald N. The Land and People of Ceylon. Lippincott, 1963. 157p. lib. ed. $2.93 net. (I–U)
An overview of the history, geography, economic conditions, and social life and customs of Ceylon, now a part of the British Commonwealth of Nations. Illustrated with photographs.

JAPAN

2114 Buell, Hal. Young Japan; photos. by Hal Buell. Dodd, 1961. 64p. lib. ed. $2.79 net. (P–I)
Excellent captioned photographs show children growing up in Japan today.

2115 Pitts, Forest R. Japan. Fideler, 1966. 160p. $3.88. (I–U)
A competent review of Japan's history, geography, government, industries, and culture, with photographs, maps, and charts.

2116 Yashima, Mitsu, & Yashima, Taro. Plenty To Watch. Viking, 1954. 39p. $3.50; lib. ed. $3.37 net. (P–I)
Japanese children on the way home from school stop to watch the many village activities: dye making, rice pounding, printing, making rice cakes, etc. Information and atmosphere are conveyed in descriptive text and full-color pictures by a Japanese artist.

2117 Yashima, Taro. The Village Tree. Viking, 1953. 34p. $3.50; lib. ed. $3.37 net. (P)
In a style similar to *Plenty To Watch*, above, a Japanese author-artist recalls his childhood and the fun he had playing with his companions under a huge tree by the riverbank.

KOREA

2118 Johnston, Richard J. H. Getting To Know the Two Koreas; illus. by Claudine Nankivel. Coward-McCann, 1965. 62p. lib. ed. $2.68 net. (P–I)
Introduces North and South Korea; discusses the roles played by China, Japan, Russia, and the United States in their affairs; and describes the present-day life of the people.

2119 Solberg, S. E. The Land and People of Korea. Lippincott, 1966. 152p. $3.25; lib. ed. $2.93 net. (I–U)
The conflict of East and West in the

history, politics, and lives of the people is the focus for this overview of Korean civilization. Illustrated with photographs and a map.

SOUTHEAST ASIA

2120 **Dareff, Hal.** The Story of Vietnam: A Background Book for Young People. Parents Mag. Pr., 1966. 256p. $4.50; lib. ed. $3.75 net. (U)

Surveys 2000 years of Vietnam's history and analyzes the factors which have led to today's conflict in forceful, objective style. A timely book for advanced older pupils and their teachers.

2121 **Matthew, Eunice S.** The Land and People of Thailand. Lippincott, 1964. 160p. $3.25; lib. ed. $2.93 net. (I–U)

Competently covers history, geography, and life today in well-organized text and numerous illustrations.

2122 **Roland, Albert.** The Philippines. Macmillan, 1967. 138p. $3.95. (I–U)

Briefly describes the geography of the islands and the ethnic backgrounds of the people and treats the four phases of Philippine history in some detail: the Spanish rule; government by the United States, 1900–1942; World War II; and the Philippines as an independent country.

2123 **Smith, Datus C.** The Land and People of Indonesia. Lippincott, 1961. 125p. lib. ed. $2.93 net. (I–U)

Gives a well-rounded picture of Indonesia today in smoothly written text and many illustrations.

2124 **Tooze, Ruth.** Cambodia: Land of Contrasts; illus. with photos. Viking, 1962. 144p. lib. ed. $3.77 net. (I–U)

An American who spent two years in Cambodia gives an appreciative overview of the country and its people.

2125 **Withington, William A.,** and **Fisher, Margaret.** Southeast Asia. Fideler, 1966. 256p. $4.61. (I–U)

A well-illustrated geography covering the essential facts about Cambodia, Indonesia, the Philippines, Burma, Thailand, Vietnam, Laos, and Malaysia.

Australia and New Zealand

2126 **Harris, Leila,** and **Harris, Kilroy.** Australia. Fideler, 1967. 112p. $3.48. (I–U)

Australia's aborigines, sheep and cattle ranchers, cities, and strange birds and animals are among the interesting topics discussed in this generously illustrated geography.

2127 **Kaula, Edna Mason.** The Land and People of New Zealand. Lippincott, 1964. 160p. lib. ed. $2.93 net. (I–U)

After reviewing New Zealand's history, the author discusses the geography, resources, industries, and social life and customs of the country today. Photographs and maps.

Arctic and Antarctic

2128 **Baum, Allyn.** Antarctica: The Worst Place in the World. Macmillan, 1966. 151p. $4.50. (U)

Photographs and text give a vivid view of Antarctica and the men stationed at scientific research centers at the bottom of the world. In addition, the author discusses the early exploration of the region, its wildlife, and its present and future importance to the world.

2129 **Bixby, William.** The Impossible Journey of Sir Ernest Shackleton. Little, 1960. 207p. $4. (I–U)

Recounts the harrowing experiences of the unsuccessful Imperial Trans-Antarctic Expedition, 1914–1917. An inspiring and dramatic story of adventure and heroism.

2130 **Bleeker, Sonia.** The Eskimo: Arctic Hunters and Trappers; illus. by Patricia Boodell. Morrow, 1959. 160p. $2.95; lib. ed. $2.94 net. (U)

A straightforward account of the home life, methods of hunting and fishing, crafts, games, and folklore of a hardy and interesting people.

2131 **Goetz, Delia.** The Arctic Tundra; illus. by Louis Darling. Morrow, 1958. 62p. $2.94 net. (P–I)

Describes the weather, land, and plant and animal life of the Point Barrow region and discusses the changing way of life of the Eskimos and Lapps who live on the tundra.

2132 Herrmanns, Ralph. Children of the North Pole. Harcourt, 1964. unp. $2.75. (P)

Family life among the Eskimos of Greenland, homes, clothing, and the land itself are shown in striking full-color photographs in this story of a boy who goes out alone to hunt food for his family.

2133 Horizon Magazine. Heroes of Polar Exploration; by the eds. of Horizon Magazine. Author, Ralph K. Andrist, in consultation with George J. Dufek. American Heritage, 1962. A Horizon Caravel Book, distributed by Harper. 153p. $4.95; lib. ed. $4.79 net. (I–U)

A profusely illustrated account of polar explorations from the time of Eric the Red and of the men who took part in them, stressing the hardships and hazards of the expeditions.

2134 Liversidge, Douglas. The First Book of the Arctic. Watts, 1967. 74p. $2.65. (I)

After surveying the geography, climate, wildlife, and people of the Arctic region, the author describes the present and potential importance of the area as sites for military, scientific, and industrial centers.

2135 Owen, Russell. The Conquest of the North and South Poles: Adventures of the Peary and Byrd Expeditions; illus. by Lynd Ward. Random, 1952. 181p. $2.50; lib. ed. $2.48 net. (I)

The story of two intrepid explorers and their accomplishments in pushing back the boundaries of the known world.

2136 Pine, Tillie S., and **Levine, Joseph.** The Eskimos Knew; illus. by Ezra Jack Keats. McGraw-Hill, 1962. 32p. $2.95; lib. ed. $2.96 net. (P)

This useful activity book for young children describes how Eskimos solved such problems as protecting their eyes from glare, getting fresh water from the sea, and using snow to build their houses. The principles involved are applied to today's world and accompanied by easy experiments.

2137 Sperry, Armstrong. All about the Arctic and Antarctic; written and illus. by Armstrong Sperry. Random, 1957. 146p. $2.50; lib. ed. $2.48 net. (I)

A fact-filled survey of the two regions and their exploration. Includes information about "Operation Deepfreeze."

2138 Stefansson, Evelyn. Here Is the Far North; illus. with photos. by the author and others; map by Richard Edes Harrison. Scribner, 1957. 154p. lib. ed. $4.05 net. (U)

The wife of an Arctic explorer looks at Iceland, Greenland, and the Arctic region of the Soviet Union in an absorbing account of the area and its people, with special attention to the changes brought by the twentieth century.

Stories for Intermediate and Upper Grades

Included here are individual stories and story collections intended primarily for pupils in grades 4–8. Books suitable for independent reading by children with limited reading skills are indicated by the symbols R3–4 and R4–5 following the annotations.

2139 Agle, Nan Hayden, and **Wilson, Ellen.** Three Boys and a Helicopter; illus. by Marian Honigman. Scribner, 1958. 122p. lib. ed. $2.76 net. (P–I)

When identical triplets—Abercrombie, Benjamin, and Christopher—decide to build a helicopter, they are caught in a flood and rescued by a real helicopter. Engaging little boys have a fine time and learn a great deal about helicopters. (R3–4)

2140 Agle, Nan Hayden, and **Wilson, Ellen.** Three Boys and a Lighthouse; illus. by Marian Honigman. Scribner, 1951. 100p. lib. ed. $2.76 net. (P–1)

The lively triplets and their dog, John Paul Jones, spend an eventful summer in a lighthouse with their father, the lighthouse keeper. (R3–4)

2141 Agle, Nan Hayden, and **Wilson, Ellen.** Three Boys and Space; illus. by Marian Honigman. Scribner, 1962. 159p. lib. ed. $2.76 net. (P–I)

While helping their fifth grade organize a space club, the triplets come down with chicken pox, but recover in time to watch Commander Shepard's space flight and to win honorable mention in a space contest. (R3–4)

2142 Aiken, Joan. The Wolves of Willoughby Chase; illus. by Pat Marriott. Doubleday, 1963. 168p. $3.50. (I)

In this burlesque of a Victorian melodrama, two London children are sent to a country estate while their parents are away. Here they outwit a wicked governess, escape from packs of hungry wolves, and restore the estate to its rightful owner. Excitement and fun for the imaginative reader.

2143 Alcock, Gudrun. Run, Westy, Run; illus. by W. T. Mars. Lothrop, 1966. 158p. $3.50; lib. ed. $3.33 net. (I–U)

The mixed-up emotions of a lonely and unhappy boy are sympathetically portrayed in this story of a delinquent boy who repeatedly runs away from a detention home.

2144 Alcott, Louisa M. Little Men: Life at Plumfield with Jo's Boys; illus. by Reginald Birch. Little, 1901. 354p. $3.75. (I–U)

Among the pupils at the school founded by Jo and Father Bhaer are some of the March grandchildren.

2145 Alcott, Louisa M. Little Women; or, Meg, Jo, Beth, and Amy. Centennial ed. With a new introd. by Cornelia Meigs. Illus. in color by Jessie Willcox Smith. Little, 1968. 444p. $5.95. (I–U)

The story of the four March sisters, based on the life of the Alcotts of Concord, is still a favorite after a hundred years. This centennial edition has been completely reset and redesigned and is illustrated with the well-known Jessie Willcox Smith paintings.

2146 Alexander, Lloyd. The Black Cauldron. Holt, 1965. 244p. $3.95; lib. ed. $3.59 net. (I–U)

In this second of five fantasies set in the imaginary land of Prydain, Taran and his companions vow to destroy the Black Cauldron, source of power of Arawn, the Lord of the Land of Death. The forces of good battle evil in a tale of high adventure blending fantasy, realism, and humor.

2147 Alexander, Lloyd. The Book of Three. Holt, 1964. 217p. $3.75; lib. ed. $3.45 net. (I–U)

The first of five books about the mythical land of Prydain finds Taran, an assistant pig keeper, fighting with Prince Gwydion against the evil which threatens the kingdom. Elements of Welsh mythology are incorporated in a stirring tale, told in literate style and teeming with unusual characters.

2148 Alexander, Lloyd. The Castle of Llyr. Holt, 1966. 201p. $3.95; lib. ed. $3.67 net. (I–U)

In the third book of the series, a romantic note is introduced as Taran goes to the rescue of Princess Eilonwy, held captive by a wicked enchantress.

2149 Alexander, Lloyd. The High King. Holt, 1968. 285p. $4.50; lib. ed. $3.97 net. (I–U)

The fantasy of Prydain comes to a close in this volume, with Taran and Prince Gwydion leading a victorious army against Arawn Death-Lord and bringing an end to the evil which had held the kingdom in thrall.

2150 Alexander, Lloyd. Taran Wanderer. Holt, 1967. 256p. $4.50; lib. ed. $3.79 net. (I–U)

In this story, which follows *The Castle of Llyr,* Taran sets out to learn the truth about his parentage. Though he does not succeed in his quest, he has many adventures and gains much wisdom.

2151 Allen, Merritt Parmalee. Johnny Reb; decorations by Ralph Ray, Jr. Longmans, 1952. 250p. $3.95; lib. ed. $3.59 net. (U)

The tragedy of the Civil War is seen through the eyes of a South Carolina boy fighting with Wade Hampton's troops. Respect for both sides is inherent in a stirring story of hardship and suffering, relieved by the courage and high spirits of the soldiers.

2152 Anckarsvärd, Karin. Doctor's Boy; tr. from the Swedish by Annabelle MacMillan; illus. by Fermin Rocker. Harcourt, 1965. 156p. $3.25. (I)

Sweden in the horse-and-buggy days is the setting for this story of a country doctor and his young son. Determined to follow in his father's footsteps, Jon goes with the doctor on his calls, shares his hardships and satisfactions, and helps him in emergencies.

2153 Annixter, Jane, and **Annixter, Paul.** Windigo. Holiday, 1963. 196p. $3.25. (U)

After his father's death, Andy Cameron follows the family trap lines in spite of his fear of an evil spirit said to haunt the forest, and proves that the ghost is really a band of robbers preying upon the superstitious trappers. An adventure story with a realistic setting of backwoods Quebec, especially recommended for older boys.

2154 Armer, Alberta. Screwball; illus. by W. T. Mars. World, 1963. 202p. $3; lib. ed. $2.96 net. (I–U)

Crippled Andy suffers by comparison with his athletic twin brother, especially after his family moves to a new community. An opportunity to compete in a sport in which he can win comes when he enters a soapbox derby.

2155 Armer, Alberta. Troublemaker; illus. by J. C. Kocsis. World, 1966. 191p. $3.95; lib. ed. $3.86 net. (I–U)

Twelve-year-old Joe Fuller, child of a broken home, is sent against his will to foster parents for the summer. An understanding story of a boy's emotional distress and gradual improvement under the guidance of wise adults.

2156 Armstrong, Richard. Cold Hazard; illus. by C. Walter Hodges. Houghton, 1956. 180p. $3. (U)

Four apprentice seamen and an older sailor, shipwrecked in the North Atlantic, spend six days of misery and fear in an open boat before reaching a barren island and further dangers. Suspense and adventure for older boys.

2157 Arora, Shirley L. "What Then, Raman?" illus. by Hans Guggenheim. Follett, 1960. 176p. $3.95; lib. ed. $3.78 net. (I)

When Raman, the first in his East Indian village to go to school, realizes that education carries responsibilities, he decides to become a teacher in his own village instead of living a life of scholarly seclusion.

2158 Arthur, Ruth M. A Candle in Her Room; illus. by Margery Gill. Atheneum, 1966. 212p. $3.95; lib. ed. $3.81 net. (I–U)

An old house in Wales and a malevolent witch doll, Dido, dominate this story of three generations of the Mansell girls, all of whom come under Dido's spell. Excellent characterization, strong sense of place, and a haunting story of lives lived in an atmosphere of mystery and evil.

2159 Atwater, Richard, and **Atwater, Florence.** Mr. Popper's Penguins; illus. by Robert Lawson. Little, 1938. 138p. $3.50. (P–I)

Straight-faced humor in story and pictures marks this inventive account of the house painter who liked penguins so much that he rearranged his household and his life to accommodate a penguin family.

2160 Aulaire, Ingri d', and **Aulaire, Edgar Parin d'.** Children of the Northlights. Viking, 1935. 37p. $3.95; lib. ed. $3.77 net. (P–I)

One year in the life of two Lapland children is presented in a story replete with interesting characters and customs and illustrated with striking colored lithographs. (R3–4)

2161 Bailey, Carolyn Sherwin. Miss Hickory; with lithographs by Ruth Gannett. Viking, 1946. 120p. $3.25; lib. ed. $3.19 net. (I)

A doll with a hickory-nut head and an apple-twig body, left behind when a New Hampshire family moves away, spends a difficult winter on the farm. Entertaining reading for imaginative girls.

2162 Baker, Betty. Walk the World's Rim. Harper, 1965. 168p. $3.95; lib. ed. $3.79 net. (I–U)

Chakoh, an Indian boy, joins a sixteenth-century Spanish expedition to "walk the world's rim" from Texas to Mexico and back. After ten years of adventure, hardship, and danger, only four of the 600 members of the expedition return, Chakoh and his Negro friend Esteban, among them. Told against an authentic background, the story has much to say about freedom and human dignity.

2163 Ball, Zachary. Bristle Face. Holiday, 1962. 206p. $3.50. (I–U)

The Mississippi back country is the setting for this story of a boy and his dog. Befriended by an understanding storekeeper, both boy and dog make a place for themselves in the community. Humor and pathos are combined in a realistic tale of fox hunts, country picnics, and a mild romance.

2164 **Barrie, J. M.** Peter Pan; illus. by Nora S. Unwin. Scribner, 1950. 242p. $2.95; lib. ed. $2.97 net. (I)

An attractive edition of the classic story of the boy who never grew up.

2165 **Barringer, D. Moreau.** And the Waters Prevailed; illus. by P. A. Hutchison. Dutton, 1965. 188p. $3.95. (I–U)

Andor, a Stone Age youth, believes that the encroaching sea will one day engulf his homeland. Though scorned by his contemporaries, he persists in his belief for many years and saves some of his people when the flood eventually comes.

2166 **Baudouy, Michel-Aimé.** Old One-Toe; illus. by Johannes Troyer; tr. from the French by Marie Ponsot. Harcourt, 1959. 190p. $3. (I–U)

This is the story of young Piet and his two friends: a hunter who teaches him forest lore and a clever fox who outwits the hunter. Vivid French setting, strong characterization, and well-developed plot.

2167 **Baum, L. Frank.** The Wizard of Oz; pictures by W. W. Denslow. Macmillan, 1956. 236p. $2.95; lib. ed. $3.24 net. (I)

Dorothy, blown by a cyclone from her Kansas home to the wonderful Land of Oz, meets the Tin Woodman, the Cowardly Lion, and other strange characters. Pictures are those of the original edition.

2168 **Baumann, Hans.** I Marched with Hannibal; tr. by Katharine Potts; illus. by Ulrik Schramm. Walck, 1961. 226p. $4.50. (U)

Hannibal's famous march across the Alps and the battles that followed are recalled by an old man, who as a boy of 12 drove Suru, the last elephant to survive the hazardous journey. Rich background and much elephant lore make this rewarding reading for history-minded pupils.

2169 **Baumann, Hans.** Sons of the Steppe: The Story of How the Conqueror Genghis

Kahn Was Overcome. Walck, 1958. 273p. $4.50. (U)

The story of two grandsons of Genghis Kahn whose differing philosophies—one the ruthless barbarian, the other beginning to question the cruelties of war—exemplify the changing attitudes of the times. Dramatic storytelling set against a background contrasting the harsh life of the steppes with the civilization of the conquered peoples.

2170 **Beatty, Patricia.** The Nickel-plated Beauty; illus. by Liz Dauber. Morrow, 1964. 255p. $3.50. (I)

A period story with an unusual setting —Washington Territory in 1886. The Kimball children join forces to earn money for a new stove, the Nickel-plated Beauty, as a surprise Christmas present for their mother. A lively story with humor, interesting background details, and warm family relationships.

2171 **Behn, Harry.** The Faraway Lurs. World, 1963. 190p. $3.50. (I–U)

Life among the Stone Age people of Denmark is re-created in this tragic story of the love of two young people of different warring tribes. Suspenseful plot, strong characterization, and imaginative writing in a story with special appeal for older girls.

2172 **Behn, Harry.** The Two Uncles of Pablo; illus. by Mel Silverman. Harcourt, 1959. 96p. $3. (I)

Pablo's two feuding uncles are very different—one gay and slightly disreputable; the other solemn, proper, and rich. Their efforts to win Pablo's affection bring them together in a story of an engaging small boy and two colorful adults. Humor and Mexican flavor add interest for the perceptive reader.

2173 **Bell, Margaret E.** Watch for a Tall White Sail. Morrow, 1948. 222p. $3.50. (U)

A story of love and adventure in Alaska of the 1880's, with special appeal for older girls.

2174 **Bemelmans, Ludwig.** Hansi; story and pictures by Ludwig Bemelmans. Viking, 1934. unp. $3.95; lib. ed. $3.77 net. (P–I)

Hansi spends Christmas at his uncle's home high in the mountains of the Austrian Tyrol. A picture-story book giving vivid impressions of Austrian scenery, costumes, and customs.

2175 Benary-Isbert, Margot. The Ark; tr. by Clara and Richard Winston. Harcourt, 1953. 246p. $3.25. (I–U)

Based on the author's own experiences, *The Ark* tells the story of a German family following World War II. After moving from one refugee camp to another, the Lechows finally establish a home in an old streetcar in West Germany. Courage, endurance, and family solidarity are reflected in a poignant story of displaced people.

2176 Benary-Isbert, Margot. The Wicked Enchantment; illus. by Enrico Arno; tr. from the German by Richard and Clara Winston. Harcourt, 1955. 181p. $3.25. (I–U)

When a new mayor took office in the little German cathedral town of Vogelsang, an evil influence seemed to grip the community. A small girl, her strong-minded aunt, and a dog play a part in breaking the spell. An entertaining fantasy involving present-day characters in an old legend.

2177 Bennett, Anna Elizabeth. Little Witch; illus. by Helen Stone. Lippincott, 1953. 127p. lib. ed. $2.63 net. (I)

A humorous Halloween story about a witch's daughter who wanted to be an ordinary child.

2178 Berna, Paul. The Horse without a Head; illus. by Richard Kennedy; tr. from the French by John Buchanan-Brown. Pantheon, 1961. 180p. lib. ed. $3.07 net. (I)

Ten slum children in a Paris suburb become involved in an exciting mystery. A headless toy horse, the favorite plaything of the gang, is stolen just when police are trying to solve a major crime—theft of a hundred million francs. The children's part in tracking down the robbers and recovering both the money and the horse is told in a fast-paced adventure story with well-drawn characters and a vivid sense of place.

2179 Binns, Archie. Sea Pup; illus. by Robert Candy. Duell, 1954. 215p. $3.50. (I–U)

In spite of his parents' misgivings, Clint Barlow makes a pet of a baby sea lion. Boy and pet become devoted companions and share exciting adventures until the sea pup becomes so troublesome that Clint must give him up. Interesting information about marine life in Puget Sound is skillfully interwoven into an absorbing story of wholesome family life.

2180 Bishop, Claire Huchet. The Twenty and Ten; as told by Janet Joly; illus. by William Pène du Bois. Viking, 1952. 76p. $3; lib. ed. $2.96 net. (I)

France during the German occupation is the setting for this story of 20 Catholic and 10 Jewish refugee children, cared for by a nun in a mountain school. Religious differences are forgotten as the children share their meager rations and connive to outwit the Nazis. A starkly realistic story of courage and unselfishness, lightened by touches of humor.

2181 Bloch, Marie Halun. Aunt America; illus. by Joan Berg. Atheneum, 1963. 148p. $3.50; lib. ed. $3.41 net. (I)

Out of her own experience, the author writes of life under a dictatorship. When Lesya's Aunt Lydia comes from America to visit in the little Ukrainian village, Lesya begins to see that all people do not think alike about freedom, and to understand that her father, in prison because of his political beliefs, is more truly free than those who toady to oppressive government.

2182 Bond, Michael. A Bear Called Paddington; with drawings by Peggy Fortnum. Houghton, 1960. 128p. $2.95. (P–I)

The Brown family find a small bear on the platform at Paddington Station in London and take him home with them. He becomes a favorite member of the household, in spite of his talent for bringing on well-meant but disrupting crises. An amusing fantasy for reading aloud to primary pupils or for independent reading in the middle grades.

2183 Bonham, Frank. Durango Street. Dutton, 1965. 190p. $3.75. (U)

Rufus Henry, paroled from a detention camp, returns to the Negro slums of a large Western city to face the difficulties of going straight. A convincing story of gang life in the ghetto, told with directness and honesty.

2184 Bonzon, Paul Jacques. The Orphans of Simitra; tr. from the French by Thelma Niklaus; illus. by Simon Jeruchim. Criterion, 1962. 160p. $3.50. (I–U)

Orphaned when an earthquake destroys their home in Greece, two children are sent to a foster home in Holland. Here Porphyras adjusts to his new life, but when unhappy Mina runs away, he goes in search of her. Their harrowing adventures are convincingly related in a moving story.

2185 **Boston, L. M.** The Children of Green Knowe; with illus. by Peter Boston. Harcourt, 1955. 157p. $2.75; lib. ed. $2.88 net. (I)

Tolly comes to live with his great-grandmother at Green Knowe, her ancestral mansion in the English countryside. Here the present blends with the past, and the children of another era become his playmates and help him to break the curse put upon the house by a gypsy. Delightful fantasy for reading aloud or for independent reading by the imaginative child.

2186 **Boston, L. M.** A Stranger at Green Knowe; drawings by Peter Boston. Harcourt, 1961. 158p. $3. (I)

The setting of this story is the same as that of *The Children of Green Knowe,* above, but the chief characters are Ping, a Chinese boy, and Hanno, a gorilla who escapes from the zoo and hides in a thicket near Green Knowe. Ping, far from his homeland, understands Hanno's loneliness and goes to great lengths to hide and befriend him. A sensitively written story with strong appeal for animal lovers.

2187 **Boston, L. M.** Treasure of Green Knowe; drawings by Peter Boston. Harcourt, 1958. 185p. $3. (I)

In this sequel to *The Children of Green Knowe,* Tolly meets ancestors from another century and helps to recover a long-lost treasure.

2188 **Bradbury, Bianca.** Two on an Island; illus. by Robert MacLean. Houghton, 1965. 139p. $3.25. (I)

When Jeff, 12, and Trudy, 9, are marooned for three days on an uninhabited island, their courageous fight to survive brings them new respect for each other. A tense, convincingly told story with strong characterization and realistic background.

2189 **Bradley, Duane.** Meeting with a Stranger; illus. by E. Harper Johnson. Lippincott, 1964. 128p. lib. ed. $3.69 net. (I)

The conflict between ancient and modern ways is sympathetically treated in a quiet story of a white American working among the sheepherders of Ethiopia. Young Teffera, left in charge of the family's flocks while his father is in the hospital, mistrusts the white man until a test proves the stranger's good intentions and opens the way for improvement of the flocks.

2190 **Bragdon, Elspeth.** That Jud! Illus. by Georges Schreiber. Viking, 1957. 126p. $3; lib. ed. $3.04 net. (I)

Orphaned Jud, 12, lives with kindly Captain Ben in a little Maine fishing village. Because the neighbors criticize his escapades—running through flower beds, skipping school, breaking windows—Jud feels rejected until friendship with a young priest and a chance to do something constructive save him from delinquency.

2191 **Brink, Carol Ryrie.** Caddie Woodlawn; illus. by Kate Seredy. Macmillan, 1935. 270p. $3.95; lib. ed. $3.79 net. (I)

A New England tomboy has many adventures when her family moves to Wisconsin in the mid-nineteenth century.

2192 **Bro, Margueritte Harmon.** Sarah. Doubleday, 1949. 343p. $3.50. (U)

Sarah knew that her father, had he lived, would have wanted her to be an artist, but her real talent was music. Her conflicting emotions about choice of a career and her struggles to become a concert pianist are sensitively recounted in this serious family story for older girls.

2193 **Brontë, Charlotte.** Jane Eyre; with illus. by Nell Booker and an introd. by May Lamberton Becker. World, n.d. 504p. $2.95; lib. ed. $2.88 net. (U)

An attractive edition of the classic love story.

2194 **Brooks, Walter R.** Freddy the Detective; illus. by Kurt Wiese. Knopf, 1932. 263p. lib. ed. $3.19 net. (I)

Freddy the pig becomes a detective and solves many mysterious cases on Mr. Bean's farm.

2194a **Bruckner, Karl.** The Day of the Bomb; tr. by Frances Lobb. Van Nostrand, 1963. 189p. $3.50. (U)

This story of the Sasaki family before and after the bombing of Hiroshima follows the fortunes of two of the children. Though all survive and are reunited, the sister succumbs to "radiation sickness" ten years later. A moving and thought-provoking semifictionalized story for mature older readers.

2195 **Buck, Pearl S.** The Big Wave; illus. with prints of Hiroshige and Hokusai. Day,

1948. 61p. $3.50; lib. ed. $3.29 net. (I–U)

"Enjoy life and do not fear death—that is the way of the good Japanese." Young Jiya, left an orphan when a tidal wave destroys his village, demonstrates this philosophy when, as a man, he goes back to help rebuild his former home. A good picture of Japanese life and character for the thoughtful reader.

2196   Buff, Mary, and Buff, Conrad. The Apple and the Arrow. Houghton, 1951. 74p. lib. ed. $3.57 net. (I)

The legend of William Tell is retold from the point of view of his son Walter, from whose head Tell shot the apple. The events of the Swiss revolt against Austria in the fourteenth century are made exciting and vivid in story and pictures. (R3–4)

2197   Buff, Mary, and Buff, Conrad. Hah-Nee of the Cliff Dwellers. Houghton, 1956. 71p. lib. ed. $3.57 net. (I)

Because he is different from the other members of his tribe, Hah-Nee is accused of causing the drought which is destroying the crops. His escape with his family makes a dramatic climax to an absorbing story of thirteenth-century American Indian life.

2198   Bulla, Clyde Robert. Eagle Feather; illus. by Tom Two Arrows. Crowell, 1953. 87p. $3.95; lib. ed. $3.76 net. (P–I)

Navaho Indian life today is sympathetically depicted in the story of a boy who must decide whether or not to go to the white man's school. Words and music of three Indian songs and illustrations by an Indian artist add to the book's effectiveness. (R3–4)

2199   Bulla, Clyde Robert. John Billington: Friend of Squanto; illus. by Peter Burchard. Crowell, 1956. 88p. $3.50; lib. ed. $3.40 net. (P–I)

A simple but graphic account of the first year of the Plymouth Colony, centering around the troublesome boy, John Billington, whose friendship with an Indian boy was the means of saving the colony. (R2–3)

2200   Bulla, Clyde Robert. Riding the Pony Express; illus. by Grace Paull. Crowell, 1948. 95p. $3.95; lib. ed. $3.76 net. (I)

Everyday life and adventure in the Old West are made exciting in this story of a boy who carried the mail through in an emergency. (R3–4)

2201   Bulla, Clyde Robert. The Sword in the Tree; illus. by Paul Galdone. Crowell, 1956. 113p. $3.50; lib. ed. $3.40 net. (I)

Eleven-year-old Shan goes to Camelot to seek King Arthur's help when evil days befall. Life in the days of chivalry is vividly presented in a story for pupils not yet ready for the Arthur legend. (R3–4)

2202   Bulla, Clyde Robert. Viking Adventure; illus. by Douglas Gorsline. Crowell, 1963. 117p. $3.95; lib. ed. $3.90 net. (I)

A century after Leif Ericsson discovered Wineland, young Sigurd joins a Viking adventure over the same course. A rousing tale of hardship and courage. (R3–4)

2203   Bunyan, John. Pilgrim's Progress; drawings by Robert Lawson; retold and shortened for modern readers by Mary Godolphen. Lippincott, 1939. 119p. $4.25. (I–U)

Skillful editing and distinguished illustrations make this edition especially attractive for young readers.

2204   Burch, Robert. Queenie Peavy; illus. by Jerry Lazare. Viking, 1966. 159p. $3.50; lib. ed. $3.37 net. (I–U)

Unhappy because her adored father is in jail and resentful of being teased by other children, Queenie expresses her frustration in delinquent behavior. With the help of wise adults, she weathers her emotional crisis and faces her problems with courage and spirit. A good picture of a Georgia community during the Depression.

2205   Burch, Robert. Tyler, Wilkin, and Skee; illus. by Don Sibley. Viking, 1963. 156p. $3; lib. ed. $2.96 net. (I)

Three lively boys living on a Goergia farm during the Depression work, play, quarrel, and make up, but always stick together. A warm story of simple pleasures and family loyalty.

2206   Burchard, Peter. Jed: The Story of a Yankee Soldier and a Southern Boy; drawings by the author. Coward-McCann, 1960. 94p. $3. (I–U)

Sixteen-year-old Jed, fighting for the Union in Mississippi, rescues a small injured Confederate boy, has his leg set, and takes him home. Later, Jed defends the household against a Yankee raiding party. A well-told story of human values in conflict with the horrors of war.

2207 Burnett, Frances Hodgson. The Secret Garden; illus. by Tasha Tudor. Lippincott, 1962. 256p. $5. (I)

An attractive edition of an old favorite, illustrated with suitably sentimental pictures.

2208 Burnford, Sheila. The Incredible Journey; with illus. by Carl Burger. Little, 1961. 145p. $4.50. (I–U)

A Labrador retriever, an old bull terrier, and a Siamese cat make a hazardous 250-mile journey through the wilderness of northwest Ontario. The cooperation of the three very different animals as they encounter the dangers of the trip is the special emphasis of an unusual story.

2209 Butterworth, Oliver. The Enormous Egg; illus. by Louis Darling. Little, 1956. 187p. $3.25. (I)

A truly funny story about a boy who finds an enormous egg which hatches into a dinosaur. His problems of raising this strange creature are described with a straight face and suggested in amusing pictures.

2210 Calhoun, Mary. Katie John; pictures by Paul Frame. Harper, 1960. 134p. $3.50; lib. ed. $3.27 net. (I)

When the Tuckers inherited an old house in a Missouri town, they decided to live in it until they could get it ready to sell. Ten-year-old Katie John was gloomy at the prospect—until she made a new friend, helped to solve a mystery, and learned to love the house. A pleasant family story with a likable main character.

2211 Cameron, Eleanor. A Spell Is Cast; illus. by Beth and Joe Krush. Little, 1964. 271p. $3.95. (I)

Cory Winterslow, troubled because she has never been adopted by the actress with whom she lives, goes to California to visit her grandmother and uncle. Here she finds mystery and aloofness instead of the warmth she had hoped for, but eventually her problems are worked out, and she at last "belongs." Strong character delineation, sensitively evoked background, and credible solutions to the mystery.

2212 Cameron, Eleanor. Stowaway to the Mushroom Planet; with illus. by Robert Henneberger. Little, 1956. 226p. $3.95. (I)

When David and Chuck start on their second voyage to the planet Basidium, they discover an unexpected passenger. A science fantasy combining facts about space ships with magic. Follows *The Wonderful Flight to the Mushroom Planet,* below.

2213 Cameron, Eleanor. The Wonderful Flight to the Mushroom Planet; with illus. by Robert Henneberger. Little, 1954. 214p. $3.75. (I)

David and Chuck help a neighbor to build a space ship and fly to the planet Basidium, where they help to save the lives of the inhabitants.

2214 Carlson, Natalie Savage. A Brother for the Orphelines; pictures by Garth Williams. Harper, 1959. 100p. $3.95; lib. ed. $3.79 net. (I)

When a baby boy is found on the doorstep of a Paris orphanage, the little girl inmates must convince the nuns that it is proper to keep him. The delightful children are shown in humorous illustrations.

2215 Carlson, Natalie Savage. The Empty Schoolhouse; pictures by John Kaufmann. Harper, 1965. 119p. $3.95; lib. ed. $3.79 net. (I)

Ten-year-old Lullah Royall goes to a newly integrated parochial school in New Orleans, only to find that she is the only pupil present. Told in the first person by Lullah's older sister, the story makes the problems of integration very real and moving.

2216 Carlson, Natalie Savage. The Family under the Bridge; pictures by Garth Williams. Harper, 1958. 99p. $3.95; lib. ed. $3.79 net. (I)

Old Armand, a Paris tramp, is indignant when his private spot under a bridge is invaded by a widow and her three children. Gradually the children win him over, and he gets a job to provide for them. A good read-aloud Christmas story.

2217 Carlson, Natalie Savage. The Happy Orpheline; pictures by Garth Williams. Harper, 1957. 96p. $3.95; lib. ed. $3.79 net. (I)

Twenty little girls in a Paris orphanage are so happy that their only worry is that they may be adopted. Lively doings and attractive children in the first of a series of warm stories with delightful illustrations.

2218 Carlson, Natalie Savage. The Talking Cat, and Other Stories of French Canada; retold by Natalie Savage Carlson; pictures by Roger Duvoisin. Harper, 1952. 87p. $3.50; lib. ed. $3.27 net. (P–I)

Spirited retellings of seven stories handed down from the author's French-Canadian great-great uncle. The humor and zest of the tales make them excellent for the story hour.

2219   Carr, Mary Jane. Children of the Covered Wagon: A Story of the Old Oregon Trail; illus. by Bob Kuhn. Crowell, 1957. 318p. $3.95. (I)

Excitement, heroism, and humor in a readable story of three children's trip from Missouri to Oregon in 1844.

2220   Carroll, Lewis. Alice's Adventures in Wonderland, and Through the Looking-Glass; with illus. by John Tenniel; afterword by Clifton Fadiman. Macmillan, 1963. 148p. $3.95; lib. ed. $4.24 net. (I–U)

A much-quoted classic with pictures by its best-known illustrator.

2221   Carroll, Ruth, and **Carroll, Latrobe.** Tough Enough. Walck, 1954. unp. $3.25. (P–I)

Beanie Tatum, his Great Smoky Mountain family, and his dog Tough Enough come to life in an affectionately humorous story with realistic illustrations by Ruth Carroll. (R3–4)

2222   Catherall, Arthur. Prisoners in the Snow; illus. by Victor Ambrus. Lothrop, 1967. 138p. $3.50; lib. ed. $3.35 net. (I–U)

Two Austrian children and their grandfather are trapped by an avalanche set off by a falling plane. They save the animals by bringing them into the house and rescue the pilot, who has fallen on top of the cowshed. Courage, ingenuity, and family solidarity in a gripping and suspenseful tale.

2223   Catherall, Arthur. Yugoslav Mystery. Lothrop, 1964. 158p. $3.50; lib. ed. $3.35 net. (I–U)

The Yugoslav resistance movement is graphically shown in the story of a boy who hides his politically suspect father from the secret police. Unusual background and good characterization in a thrilling story.

2224   Caudill, Rebecca. A Certain Small Shepherd; with illus. by William Pène du Bois. Holt, 1965. 48p. $3.50; lib. ed. $3.27 net. (P–I)

When a church pageant is canceled because of a blizzard, Jamie, a small mute assigned the part of a shepherd, participates in a real Christmas drama. An Appalachian community and its people are shown in softly colored pictures.

2225   Caudill, Rebecca. Tree of Freedom; illus. by Dorothy Bayley Morse. Viking, 1949. 279p. $3.50; lib. ed. $3.37 net. (I–U)

To escape the fighting during the Revolution, a North Carolina family moves to Kentucky. Here Stephanie and Noel prove their devotion to the cause of freedom by acts of courage and loyalty.

2226   Cavanna, Betty. Going on Sixteen. Westminster, 1946. 220p. $3.25. (U)

Motherless Julie, living on a farm near Philadelphia, despairs of becoming an artist. Her dog Sonny plays an important part in Julie's growing up and achieving her ambition.

2227   Cervantes, Miguel de. The Adventures of Don Quixote de la Mancha; adapted from the Motteux translation of the text of Miguel de Cervantes by Leighton Barret and illus. with drawings by Warren Chappell. Knopf, 1960. 307p. lib. ed. $3.59 net. (I–U)

A flavorful version of the addled knight's adventures, amusingly illustrated.

2228   Chapin, Henry, and **Throckmorton, Peter.** Spiro of the Sponge Fleet; illus. by Bertil Kumlien. Little, 1964. 104p. $3.75. (I–U)

On the Greek isle of Kolymnos 16-year-old Spiro longs to become a sponge diver. Good characterization, interesting story, unusual setting.

2229   Christopher, Matt. Baseball Flyhawk; illus. by Foster Caddell. Little, 1963. 127p. $2.95. (I)

Chico, newly arrived in New York City from Puerto Rico, works hard to make the baseball team and to win new friends.

2230   Church, Richard. Five Boys in a Cave. Day, 1951. 180p. $3.95. (I–U)

Each of five boys reacts differently when two are trapped in a cave. The quality of courage is explored in a well-plotted story of adventure and danger.

2231   Chute, Marchette. The Innocent Wayfaring; with decorations by the author. Dutton, 1955. 199p. $3.25. (U)

In revolt against the restraints of convent life, a girl runs away and joins a young poet, also rebelling against restrictions. For three days they wander the roads of Chaucer's England before deciding to go home to marriage and a conventional life. A delightful period piece, with special appeal for older girls.

2232 Clark, Ann Nolan. Little Navajo Bluebird; illus. by Paul Lantz. Viking, 1943. 143p. $3.25; lib. ed. $3.19 net. (I)

A sensitive story of present-day Navaho life and customs, told from the viewpoint of Doli, a little girl loyal to her own people and fearful of the white man's ways until she realizes that the two races can live together in friendship. (R2–3)

2233 Clark, Ann Nolan. Secret of the Andes; with drawings by Jean Charlot. Viking, 1952. 130p. $3; lib. ed. $2.96 net. (I–U)

High in the Peruvian mountains lives Cusi, a young Incan boy who helps the patriarch of his tribe to care for a sacred llama herd. In return, the old man teaches Cusi the lore and mystery of his people. A beautifully written story for the imaginative reader.

2234 Clarke, Pauline. The Return of the Twelves; illus. by Bernarda Bryson. Coward-McCann, 1963. 251p. $3.95. (I–U)

Twelve wooden soldiers come to life and, aided by three present-day children, return to their former home, the Brontë Museum at Haworth. A tense and original fantasy for the reader able to appreciate the allusions to the Brontë family.

2235 Cleary, Beverly. Beezus and Ramona; illus. by Louis Darling. Morrow, 1955. 159p. $3.25; lib. ed. $3.14 net. (I)

Children with younger brothers and sisters will have a fellow feeling for Beezus (short for Beatrice), plagued by four-year-old Ramona's embarrassing behavior. Very funny real-life situations in a wholesome family. (R3–4)

2236 Cleary, Beverly. Ellen Tebbits; illus. by Louis Darling. Morrow, 1951. 160p. $3.25; lib. ed. $3.14 net. (I)

Eight-year-old Ellen and her best friend, Austine, are drawn together by a shameful secret—both wear woolen underwear. Their experiences in the third grade are comical

and very appealing to children in the middle grades. (R3–4)

2237 Cleary, Beverly. Fifteen; illus. by Joe and Beth Krush. Morrow, 1956. 254p. $3.50; lib. ed. $3.32 net. (I–U)

The joy and anguish of a first romance are portrayed with gentle humor in this story of Jane Purdy's sophomore year.

2238 Cleary, Beverly. Henry and Beezus; illus. by Louis Darling. Morrow, 1952. 192p. $3.25; lib. ed. $3.14 net. (I)

Beatrice (Beezus for short) helps Henry Huggins earn money for a bicycle, though four-year-old Ramona and Henry's dog Ribsy complicate their efforts. Both boys and girls will enjoy this lively story. (R4–5)

2239 Cleary, Beverly. Henry and Ribsy; illus. by Louis Darling. Morrow, 1954. 192p. $3.25; lib. ed. $3.14 net. (I)

Henry's father has promised to take him fishing if he can keep Ribsy out of mischief for a month. Hilarious situations develop before the reward is won. (R4–5)

2240 Cleary, Beverly. Henry and the Clubhouse; illus. by Louis Darling. Morrow, 1962. 192p. $3.25; lib. ed. $3.14 net. (I)

Henry and his friends build a boys-only clubhouse in spite of many difficulties. Another genuinely funny story about true-to-life children. (R3–4)

2241 Cleary, Beverly. Henry and the Paper Route; illus. by Louis Darling. Morrow, 1957. 192p. $3.25; lib. ed. $3.14 net. (I)

Henry Huggins, now ten, competes with a rival for a paper route. To his astonishment it is the pest, Ramona, who helps him win. (R3–4)

2241a Cleary, Beverly. Henry Huggins; illus. by Louis Darling. Morrow, 1950. 155p. $3.25; lib. ed. $3.14 net. (I)

This first book about Henry Huggins and his friends introduces a delightfully funny small boy and his long-suffering family in a series of real-life adventures and misadventures. (R3–4)

2242 Cleary, Beverly. Jean and Johnny; illus. by Joe and Beth Krush. Morrow, 1959. 284p. $3.50; lib. ed. $3.32 net. (I–U)

Fifteen-year-old Jean has her first lesson in false values when Johnny, her high school crush, proves to be conceited and selfish. Good characterization and realistic incidents in an understanding treatment of a teen-age problem.

2243   Cleary, Beverly. The Mouse and the Motorcycle; illus. by Louis Darling. Morrow, 1965. 158p. $3.25; lib. ed. $3.14 net. (I)

A fantasy about Ralph, a mouse, who learns to ride a toy motorcycle and goes on wild rides through the corridors of the hotel where he lives. Keith, the boy to whom the motorcycle belongs, becomes fast friends with Ralph and defends him when danger threatens. A successful blend of fact and fancy.

2243a   Cleary, Beverly. Otis Spofford; illus. by Louis Darling. Morrow, 1953. 191p. $3.25; lib. ed. $3.14 net. (I)

When things got dull in the fifth grade, Otis Spofford could always stir up a little excitement. He succeeded almost too well when the school put on its spring fiesta. An amusing story with every detail of elementary school life exactly right, plus insight about the causes of exhibitionist behavior. (R3–4)

2243b   Cleary, Beverly. Ribsy; illus. by Louis Darling. Morrow, 1964. 192p. $3.25; lib. ed. $3.14 net. (I)

Henry's dog Ribsy gets lost and has some very funny adventures before he finds his way home. (R3–4)

2244   Clymer, Eleanor. My Brother Stevie. Holt, 1967. 76p. $3.50; lib. ed. $3.27 net. (I–U)

Twelve-year-old Annie Jenner tells the story of her brother Stevie, eight, left in her care when their mother deserts them. Living in a housing development with a strict grandmother, the children have a bleak home life, and Stevie reacts by getting into trouble with a neighborhood gang. An understanding teacher, a visit in the country, and a softening of the grandmother's attitude promise better times for two appealing children.

2245   Coatsworth, Elizabeth. Away Goes Sally; pictures by Helen Sewell. Macmillan, 1934. 122p. $3.50; lib. ed. $3.44 net. (I)

A small Massachusetts girl travels to Maine in a little house on runners, drawn by twelve oxen. Easy, interesting background reading about the early 1800's.

2246   Coatsworth, Elizabeth. The Cat Who Went to Heaven; illus. by Lynd Ward. Macmillan, 1958. 62p. $4.50. (I–U)

Watched by his little cat, Good Fortune, a Japanese artist paints a picture of the Buddha receiving homage from the animals. By tradition the cat should not be among them, but the artist risks his reputation by adding Good Fortune and is vindicated by a miracle. The inner meaning is best understood when the story is read aloud.

2247   Coatsworth, Elizabeth. First Adventure; illus. by Ralph Ray. Macmillan, 1950. 60p. $3.50. (P–I)

The boy John Billington wanders away from the Plymouth Colony with his dog and is found and adopted by the Nauset Indians. Based on historical records.

2248   Coblentz, Catherine Cate. The Blue Cat of Castle Town; illus. by Janice Holland. Longmans, 1949. 123p. $4.50. (I)

In the Metropolitan Museum of Art in New York City hangs a rug made by a little Vermont girl more than a hundred years ago. This story is a fantasy about the blue cat in the rug's design and his visits to the artisans of Castle Town. A good period story with emphasis on integrity in craftsmanship.

2249   Collodi, Carlo. The Adventures of Pinocchio; illus. by Naiad Einsel; afterword by Clifton Fadiman. Macmillan, 1963. 192p. $3.95; lib. ed. $4.24 net. (I)

An attractive edition of the story about the wooden puppet whose nose grows longer each time he tells a lie.

2250   Constant, Alberta Wilson. Miss Charity Comes To Stay; illus. by Louis Darling. Crowell, 1959. 249p. $4.50. (I–U)

When Miss Charity comes to teach school in Oklahoma in 1893, a handsome cowboy persuades her to stay. Told by 12-year-old Betsy, Miss Charity's favorite pupil, the story is a good picture of pioneer life.

2251   Coolidge, Olivia E. Egyptian Adventures; illus. by Joseph Low. Houghton, 1954. 209p. $3.50. (U)

Twelve short stories about life in Egypt during the period from 1600 to 1100 B.C., with invented characters and action against an authentic background.

2252   Coombs, Patrica. Dorrie and the Blue Witch; illus. and written by Patricia Coombs.

Lothrop, 1964. 37p. $3.25; lib. ed. $3.13 net.
(P–I)

Dorrie, daughter of a witch, wins first prize for witch catching when she shrinks the bad Blue Witch and puts her into a bottle.

2253 **Corbett, Scott.** The Baseball Trick; illus. by Paul Galdone. Little, 1965. 105p. $3.50; lib. ed. $3.27 net. (I)

With the help of his pal Kerby and his Feats o' Magic chemical set, Fenton at last hits a home run and wins the baseball game against unfair competition. Humorous blend of fantasy and realism, with real-life boys, lively dialogue, and a very funny dog.

2254 **Corbett, Scott.** The Lemonade Trick; illus. by Paul Galdone. Little, 1960. 103p. $3.50; lib. ed. $3.27 net. (I)

A little magic from his chemical set added to the lemonade makes all of Kerby's conversation come out in rhymes.

2255 **Corbin, William.** The Golden Mare; illus. by Pers Crowell. Coward-McCann, 1955. 122p. $3.75. (I)

A sensitively written horse story in which a boy has to face the death of his beloved golden mare.

2256 **Credle, Ellis.** Down, Down the Mountain. Nelson, 1961. unp. $2.50; lib. ed. $2.78 net. (P–I)

Life in the Blue Ridge Mountains is sympathetically portrayed in this story of two children who hope to trade the turnips they have raised for new shoes, but whose plan is complicated by the necessity for doing a kind deed. A brief story, with large, open pages and many illustrations by the author.

2257 **Crowley, Maude.** Azor and the Blue-eyed Cow: A Christmas Story; pictures by Helen Sewell. Walck, 1951. 70p. $3.50. (P–I)

Azor, who lives in Marblehead, Massachusetts, writes a letter to Santa Claus and keeps its contents secret to prove that Santa really exists and to save his blue-eyed cow, Clara. A good read-aloud story for primary grades or for independent reading in middle grades.

2258 **Dalgliesh, Alice.** The Bears on Hemlock Mountain; illus. by Helen Sewell. Scribner, 1952. unp. $2.75; lib. ed. $2.76 net. (P–I)

A humorous tall tale, handed down in Pennsylvania, about eight-year-old Jonathan's encounter with bears when he crossed Hemlock Mountain alone one dark night. For reading aloud or storytelling.

2259 **Dalgliesh, Alice.** The Courage of Sarah Noble; illus. by Leonard Weisgard. Scribner, 1954. 55p. $2.75; lib. ed. $2.76 net. (P–I)

Sarah, though only eight, cooked for her father while he made a new home for the family in the Connecticut wilderness of 1707. When Mr. Noble returned to Massachusetts for the rest of the family, leaving Sarah with a friendly Indian, her courage was sorely tested. A well-told, inspiring story, based on a true incident.

2260 **Daly, Maureen.** Seventeenth Summer. Dodd, 1942. 255p. $3.50. (U)

First love comes to Angie Morrow during her seventeenth summer and hastens her growing up.

2261 **Daringer, Helen Fern.** Adopted Jane; illus. by Kate Seredy. Harcourt, 1947. 225p. $2.95. (I)

Jane was not unhappy in the orphanage, but she did long for a family and a dog of her own. After two trial visits to real homes, she realized her dream. A well-handled story of a generation ago with an appealing central character.

2262 **De Angeli, Marguerite.** Bright April. Doubleday, 1946. 86p. $3.50. (I)

Though April's bright disposition usually justified her nickname, the problem of being a Negro in the predominately white Brownies sometimes dampened her spirits. A sympathetic treatment of a sensitive subject. (R4–5)

2263 **De Angeli, Marguerite.** The Door in the Wall. Doubleday, 1949. 120p. $3.95. (I–U)

Robin, crippled son of a thirteenth-century English knight, fears he will never be able to prove his courage. How he overcomes his handicaps and wins his knighthood is an inspiring story, faithful to the period in text and the author's beautiful illustrations.

2264 **De Angeli, Marguerite.** Yonie Wondernose . . . Doubleday, 1944. unp. $3.25. (P–I)

Life among the Pennsylvania Dutch is

affectionately portrayed in this story of a seven-year-old boy with more than his share of curiosity. Left in charge of the farm while his father is away, Yonie proves himself worthy of his father's trust. The author's attractive illustrations add authentic details.

2265 Decker, Duane. Hit and Run. Morrow, 1949. 188p. $3.50. (I–U)

A baseball story with more substance than most. Two players—one white, one Negro—help each other to overcome their problems during their first year in the big leagues. The excitement of games and glimpses of life behind the scenes give the book appeal for older boys.

2266 Defoe, Daniel. Robinson Crusoe; with illus. by N. C. Wyeth. Scribner, 1957. 368p. $5. (I–U)

The most famous shipwreck story of all time is illustrated in color and presented in inviting format.

2276 De Jong, Meindert. Along Came a Dog; pictures by Maurice Sendak. Harper, 1958. 172p. $3.50; lib. ed. $3.27 net. (I)

An abused stray dog protects a little red hen who has lost her toes through frostbite. Distinguished writing and genuine understanding of animals lift the story above the ordinary. Best appreciated when read aloud.

2268 De Jong, Meindert. Far Out the Long Canal; pictures by Nancy Grossman. Harper, 1964. 231p. $3.50; lib. ed. $3.27 net. (I)

In the little Dutch village everybody could skate—everybody, that is, except nine-year-old Moonta, whose illness kept him from learning at the proper time. His persistence in trying, in spite of embarrassment at the teasing of his friends, inspires admiration for the plucky little boy. The background is gay, with young and old in holiday mood skimming over the ice.

2269 De Jong, Meindert. The House of Sixty Fathers; pictures by Maurice Sendak. Harper, 1956. 189p. $3.50; lib. ed. $3.27 net. (I–U)

During the Japanese invasion of China, Tien Pao, a small Chinese boy, is separated from his parents. His reunion with them comes only after terrifying weeks of danger, hunger, and despair.

2270 De Jong, Meindert. Hurry Home, Candy; pictures by Maurice Sendak. Har-

per, 1953. 244p. $3.95; lib. ed. $3.79 net. (I)

A starkly realistic story of the dangers faced by a stray puppy until he at last finds a happy home.

2271 De Jong, Meindert. Shadrach; pictures by Maurice Sendak. Harper, 1953. 182p. $3.50; lib. ed. $3.27 net. (P–I)

A small Dutch boy's excitement as he prepares for the black rabbit promised him by his parents is communicated to the reader in a story distinguished by the author's understanding of a child's intense feeling about a pet. For reading aloud.

2272 De Jong, Meindert. The Wheel on the School; pictures by Maurice Sendak. Harper, 1954. 298p. $3.95; lib. ed. $3.79 net. (I)

Because storks are said to bring good luck, the children of a Dutch village set out to attract a pair to their school. With the help of the schoolmaster, they persist in their efforts until the whole town becomes involved. Vivid characterization, exciting incidents, and fine background details.

2273 Dickens, Charles. A Christmas Carol; illus. by Arthur Rackham. Lippincott, 1966. 147p. $3.50. (I–U)

Illustrations with genuine nineteenth-century English feeling distinguish this edition of the well-loved story.

2274 Dickens, Charles. David Copperfield; illus. by N. M. Bodecker; afterword by Clifton Fadiman. Macmillan, 1962. 850p. $3.95; lib. ed. $4.24 net. (U)

An attractive, well-bound edition of Dickens' autobiographical novel.

2275 Dillon, Eilís. The Coriander; illus. by Vic Donahue. Funk & Wagnalls, 1964. 211p. $3.50. (U)

When a much-needed doctor from the wreck of the "Coriander" is washed ashore on a tiny Irish island, two boys hide him, and the community conspires to keep him against his will. When the time for escape and revenge comes, the doctor surprises the people by his decision. A dramatic story, spiced with humor and suspense and flavored with Irish speech and customs.

2276 Dillon, Eilís. A Family of Foxes; illus. by Vic Donahue. Funk & Wagnalls, 1965. 119p. $3.25. (I–U)

Four Irish lads help to dispel their island people's superstitious fear of foxes when they rescue and hide a pair of silver foxes washed up in a storm. The boys' ingenuity in providing food and shelter for their charges, soon grown to six with the arrival of cubs, and the ever present danger of discovery add suspense to a well-told story.

2277 **Dillon, Eilís.** The Island of Horses. Funk & Wagnalls, 1957. 218p. $3.25. (I–U)

Old Irish tales about a strange island of horses lead two 16-year-old boys to explore its mystery. The sturdy inhabitants of a remote island off the coast of Ireland are colorfully portrayed in a story of high adventure.

2278 **Dodge, Mary Mapes.** Hans Brinker; or, The Silver Skates; with drawings & decorations by George Wharton Edwards. Scribner, 1915. 380. $5. (I–U)

An attractive edition of the story of nineteenth-century Holland in which a mystery and an exciting skating race are the main elements of the plot.

2279 **Doyle, A. C.** The Boys' Sherlock Holmes. new and enl. ed. A selection from the works of A. Conan Doyle arr. with introd. by Howard Haycraft. Harper, 1961. 524p. $4.95; lib. ed. $4.43 net. (I–U)

Contains three full-length novels: *A Study in Scarlet, The Hound of the Baskervilles,* and *The Sign of the Four*; six short stories; and a sketch of Dr. Joseph Bell, the man upon whom Sherlock Holmes is modeled.

2280 **Du Bois, William Pène.** The Great Geppy; written and illus. by William Pène du Bois. Viking, 1940. 92p. $3.75; lib. ed. $3.64 net. (I)

Striped in red and white to match the circus tent, the Great Geppy, a remarkable horse detective, solves the mystery of the Bott Circus.

2281 **Du Bois, William Pène.** The Twenty-One Balloons; written and illus. by William Pène du Bois. Viking, 1947. 179p. $4.95; lib. ed. $4.43 net. (I)

A fabulous tale of Dr. William Waterbury Sherman who decides to take a balloon trip to get a rest from teaching arithmetic. After three weeks of adventure, he is picked up in the Atlantic amid the wreckage of twenty balloons. A diverting and original tale with a background of scientific facts.

2282 **Eager, Edward.** Half Magic; drawings by N. M. Bodecker. Harcourt, 1954. 217p. $3.25. (I)

Four resourceful children have a week of fun and adventure when they discover that their magic coin will bring them only half of what they wish for. The ridiculous but logical situations which result when they double their wishes are highly entertaining.

2283 **Edmonds, Walter D.** Cadmus Henry; illus. by Manning de V. Lee. Dodd, 1949. 137p. $3. (I–U)

The part which reconnaisance balloons played in the Civil War is shown through the experiences of a Confederate soldier. Excitement is added when young Henry's balloon goes out of control and drifts back and forth over the Union and Confederate lines.

2284 **Edmonds, Walter D.** The Matchlock Gun; illus. by Paul Lantz. Dodd, 1941. 50p. $3.50. (I)

New York State during the French and Indian War is the setting for this story of a boy's courage and resourcefulness. In his father's absence, ten-year-old Edward Alstine helps his mother fight off an Indian attack by firing an old Spanish musket. A tale of tragedy and terror, made more graphic by dramatic illustrations. (R3–4)

2285 **Edmonds, Walter D.** Two Logs Crossing: John Haskell's Story; illus. by Tibor Gergely. Dodd, 1943. 82p. $3. (I–U)

With the help of a wise judge and an Indian friend, a teen-age boy makes good in spite of his family's reputation for shiftlessness. A good picture of fur trapping in New York State in 1830.

2286 **Ellsberg, Edward.** "I Have Just Begun To Fight!" The Story of John Paul Jones; illus. by Gerald Foster. Dodd, 1942. 269p. $4 (I–U)

A Nantucket boy sails with John Paul Jones and takes part in his most famous battle. Danger and suspense in a rousing sea story with authentic historical background.

2287 **Embry, Margaret.** The Blue-nosed Witch; pictures by Carl Rose. Holiday, 1956. 45p. $2.75. (P–I)

A young witch with a nose that glows in the dark goes trick-or-treating with a group of real children. A good Halloween read-aloud story.

2288 Emery, Anne. Sweet Sixteen. Macrae, 1956. 188p. $3.50. (I–U)

Overshadowed by a brilliant and popular younger sister, Jane Ellison makes a bad start in her junior year of high school. Not until a sympathetic teacher helps her to understand her own behavior does she make a new beginning.

2289 Enright, Elizabeth. The Four-Story Mistake; illus. by Elizabeth Enright. Holt, 1942. 177p. $3.50; lib. ed. $3.27 net. (I)

A hideous house, source of the title, provides opportunity for exploration and adventure for the Melendy family. Attractive and resourceful children are presented with perception.

2290 Enright, Elizabeth. Gone-Away Lake; illus. by Beth and Joe Krush. Harcourt, 1957. 192p. $3.50. (I)

Vacationing near an abandoned resort area, three children discover once-handsome but now ruined houses and learn the history of the settlement from two unusual inhabitants. Much nature lore is woven into the story.

2291 Enright, Elizabeth. The Saturdays; written and illus. by Elizabeth Enright. Holt, 1941. 175p. $3.50; lib. ed. $3.27 net. (I)

The four motherless Melendy children, encouraged by their father and an understanding housekeeper, pool their allowances and take turns exploring New York City on Saturdays. An entertaining story, useful to arouse interest in New York attractions for children.

2292 Enright, Elizabeth. Thimble Summer; written and illus. by Elizabeth Enright. Holt, 1938. 124p. $3.95; lib. ed. $3.59 net. (I)

Garnet Linden thinks that her summer of fun and adventure on a Wisconsin farm all came because she had found a magic thimble.

2293 Erdman, Loula Grace. The Wind Blows Free. Dodd, 1952. 242p. $3.50. (U)

In the 1890's Melinda Pierce's family staked a claim and established a home in the Texas Panhandle. A well-told pioneer story with a touch of romance.

2294 Estes, Eleanor. Ginger Pye. Harcourt, 1946. 250p. $3.75. (I)

The Pye family consists of diverse individuals: Mr. Pye, an authority on birds; Rachel, also interested in birds; Jerry, who collects rocks; and three-year-old Uncle Benny, the youngest uncle in town. Mystery and adventure enter their lives when their dog, Ginger Pye, disappears. (R3–4)

2295 Estes, Eleanor. The Hundred Dresses; illus. by Louis Slobodkin. Harcourt, 1944. 80p. $3.50. (I)

Children's unthinking cruelty to those who are different is the theme of a poignant story about Wanda Pretonski, teased because she said she had a hundred dresses at home, though she always wore the same shabby dress to school. Best read aloud and discussed for values in human relationships.

2296 Estes, Eleanor. The Middle Moffat, illus. by Louis Slobodkin. Harcourt, 1942. 317p. $3.95. (I)

Janey Moffat, aged ten, considers herself a very mysterious person, though no one except the Oldest Inhabitant recognizes her special quality. The everyday affairs of ten-year-olds are made amusing and entertaining by the author's understanding of children and her keen ear for their speech. (R3–4)

2297 Estes, Eleanor. The Moffats; illus. by by Louis Slobodkin. Harcourt, 1941. 290p. $3.25. (I)

The Moffats—Mama and her four children—have a fun-filled and satisfying life in spite of being poor. Their little house on New Dollar Street in Cranbury, Connecticut, is the scene of constant activity and surprises. A captivating family story with highly individual characters. Each chapter is a separate episode, suitable for reading aloud. (R3–4)

2298 Estes, Eleanor. Rufus M. Harcourt, 1943. 320p. $3.95. (I)

The youngest Moffat, seven, is the central figure in this very funny story of a small boy's ups and downs as the baby of the family. His agonizing efforts to get a library card, his contributions to the war effort, and his many other activities as he goes his own independent way make entertaining reading for children much older than Rufus. (R3–4)

2299 Fall, Thomas. Canalboat to Freedom; illus. by Joseph Cellini. Dial, 1966. 215p. $3.50. (I)

A freed Negro deckhand on a canalboat in the Delaware and Hudson Canal in the 1840's befriends 12-year-old Benja, a redemptioner illegally sold into service. Life on the canalboat, the work of the Underground Railroad, and the value of courage and friendship are interwoven elements in a thought-provoking story.

2300 **Farley, Walter.** The Blood Bay Colt; illus. by Milton Menasco. Random, 1950. 307p. $2.95; lib. ed. $3.09 net. (I–U)

Though sired by the famous racehorse, Black Stallion, Bonfire is trained for harness racing. In addition to the training of Bonfire and of Tom Messenger, a high school boy, as driver, the plot concerns the conflict between county-fair racing and commercial interests.

2301 **Farmer, Penelope.** The Summer Birds; illus. by James J. Spanfeller. Harcourt, 1962. 155p. $2.95. (I)

A magic summer begins for three English children when they meet a strange boy who teaches them to fly. A well-sustained fantasy for the imaginative reader.

2302 **Fast, Howard.** April Morning. Crown, 1961. 184p. $3.50. (U)

The historic events of April 19, 1775, are seen through the eyes of 15-year-old Adam Cooper as the Battle of Lexington materializes. One family's preparation for the conflict, the brief encounter with the British, and the anguished aftermath pass in review as evidence of the folly and tragedy of war.

2303 **Faulkner, Georgene,** and **Becker, John.** Melindy's Medal; illus. by Elton C. Fax. Messner, 1945. 172p. $3.50. (I)

Eight-year-old Melindy's happy year in Boston's new housing project is made perfect when she wins a medal. An understanding story of a Negro family given a new start in a new home.

2304 **Felsen, Henry Gregor.** Boy Gets Car. Random, 1960. 314p. $3.50; lib. ed. $3.59 net. (I–U)

Woody Ahern finds that owning a car brings on many responsibilities. His problems with money, school, romance, and parents are treated realistically and sympathetically, without pat solutions.

2305 **Fife, Dale.** Who's in Charge of Lincoln? Illus. by Paul Galdone. Coward-McCann, 1965. 61p. $2.95; lib. ed. $2.86 net. (P–I)

Through a misunderstanding, eight-year-old Lincoln is left alone in his New York City apartment when his mother goes to the hospital. For the next two days the little Negro boy's adventures include having stolen money thrust upon him and taking a trip alone to the Lincoln Monument in Washington.

2306 **Fisher, Clay.** Valley of the Bear: A Novel of the North Plains Sioux; illus. by Eric von Schmidt. Houghton, 1964. 176p. $3.25. (I–U)

A young Sioux Indian's sympathy for the great bear, Mato, and his heroism in the face of danger make a tense adventure story, lightened by the humor and wit of the grandmother who shares his dangers.

2307 **Fisher, Cyrus.** The Avion My Uncle Flew; pictures by Richard Floethe. Appleton, 1946. 244p. $3.50. (I–U)

After World War II, Johnny Littlehorn goes to France to visit his uncle, who is building an airplane. Here he becomes involved in mystery and adventure with Germans and French collaborationists, regains self-confidence after a crippling accident, and learns to speak and write an ingenious brand of French.

2308 **Fitzhugh, Louise.** Harriet the Spy; written and illus. by Louise Fitzhugh. Harper, 1964. 298p. $3.95; lib. ed. $3.99 net. (I)

Harriet roams her Manhattan neighborhood spying on everyone who interests her and writing down her opinions in a notebook. When fellow sixth-graders find her notes and read her caustic remarks about them, she is ostracized until she finds a way to make a place for herself in the school.

2309 **Fleischman, Sid.** By the Great Horn Spoon! Illus. by Eric von Schmidt. Little, 1963. 193p. $4.50. (I)

A tall tale about a boy who, with his aunt's butler, Praiseworthy, stows away on a ship bound for the California gold fields in 1849. Praiseworthy's versatility takes the pair through many hilarious adventures.

2310 **Fleischman, Sid.** Chancy and the Grand Rascal; illus. by Eric von Schmidt. Little, 1966. 179p. $4.50. (I)

Chancy Dundee's Uncle Will boasted that he could "out-laugh, out-exaggerate, and out-rascal any man." He proves his boast as he and Chancy travel across the Middle West in search of Chancy's long-lost family.

2311   **Fleischman, Sid.** The Ghost in the Noonday Sun; illus. by Warren Chappell. Little, 1965. 173p. $4.50. (I)

A swashbuckling yarn about the villain-ous pirate, Captain Scratch, who shanghais Oliver because the boy is supposed to be able to see ghosts, and Scratch needs some-one to see a ghost which he thinks will lead him to buried treasure.

2312   **Fleming, Ian.** Chitty Chitty Bang Bang: The Magical Car; illus. by John Burningham. Random, 1964. 111p. $3.50; lib. ed. $3.39 net. (I)

An ingenious nonsense tale about an English family and their remarkable old car. Gifted with the ability to navigate land, sea, and air, Chitty-Chitty-Bang-Bang rescues the family from floods, traffic jams, and gangsters.

2313   **Flory, Jane.** One Hundred and Eight Bells. Houghton, 1963. 219p. $3.25. (I)

Setsuko, 12, lives in Tokyo with her art-ist father and her practical mother. Dreamy and forgetful, Setsuko spends her time drawing and painting instead of learning to be a good housekeeper like her mother. An interesting picture of present-day Japa-nese life and of a family's adjustment to differing personalities.

2314   **Foltz, Mary Jane.** Awani; illus. by Mel Silverman. Morrow, 1964. 128p. $3.25. (I)

Orphaned when his parents are killed, Spotted Fawn is adopted by another Indian tribe and renamed Awani. When the leg-endary white gods—Sir Francis Drake and his crew—arrive, Awani is the first to greet them.

2315   **Forbes, Esther.** Johnny Tremain: A Novel for Young and Old; illus. by Lynd Ward. Houghton, 1943. 256p. $3.75. (I–U)

Johnny Tremain, courier for the Revolu-tionary Committee of Public Safety, loses his chance to become a silversmith when his hand is injured, but plays an important part in the affairs of pre-Revolutionary Boston in spite of his handicap. The Bos-ton Tea Party, Paul Revere's Ride, the Battle of Lexington, and many other ex-citing events are included in the plot of this fine historical novel.

2316   **Forman, James.** The Horses of An-ger. Farrar, 1967. 249p. $3.50. (U)

A stark and graphic picture of World War II as it was experienced by a German boy. Hans, an antiaircraft gunner at 15 and a fanatical admirer of Hitler, is proud of his role in the war until he begins to realize the falseness and brutality of his hero and to see the senseless tragedy of the conflict. For the serious older reader.

2317   **Friedman, Frieda.** Dot for Short; illus. by Carolyn Haywood. Morrow, 1947. 207p. $3.25. (I)

A New York City family with very little money but with a great deal of spirit and loyalty solve their problems by working together.

2318   **Friedman, Frieda.** Ellen and the Gang; illus. by Jacqueline Tomes. Morrow, 1963. 191p. $3.25; lib. ed. $3.14 net. (I)

A thought-provoking story of a lonely New York City girl who becomes involved with juvenile delinquents but frees herself through community activity.

2319   **Friedman, Frieda.** The Janitor's Girl; illus. by Mary Stevens. Morrow, 1956. 159p. $3.25. (I)

The four young Langers, children of the building superintendent of a large New York City apartment, wonder how being "the janitor's kids" will affect them. They find that the important thing about being liked is to be worth liking. A brisk, well-told story of urban life with an unobtru-sive moral.

2320   **Fritz, Jean.** Brady; illus. by Lynd Ward. Coward-McCann, 1960. 223p. $3.75. (I)

In 1836 in Washington County, Pennsyl-vania, feeling about slavery is so bitterly divided that Jerry Minton cannot decide what he believes. He is won over to his father's antislavery position and plays an important part in the Underground Rail-road. A good period story with believable characters and exciting events.

2321   **Fritz, Jean.** The Cabin Faced West; illus. by Feodor Rojankovsky. Coward-McCann, 1958. 124p. $3. (I)

Ann is unhappy when her family moves from Gettysburg to the Pennsylvania fron-tier, but she soon finds friends and begins to see that there is much to enjoy about her new home—including a visit from General Washington.

2322 **Fritz, Jean.** Early Thunder; illus. by Lynd Ward. Coward-McCann, 1967. 255p. $4.50. (I–U)

Two months before the Battle of Lexington and Concord, the early thunder of the Revolution was heard in Salem, for a brief time the capital of Massachusetts. Fourteen-year-old Daniel West must choose between the position of his Tory father and his own increasing resentment of British oppression. When the test comes, Daniel takes his stand for freedom. An understanding presentation of conflicting issues, with strong implications for decision-making today.

2324 **Fritz, Jean.** I, Adam; illus. by Peter Burchard. Coward-McCann, 1963. 255p. $3.75. (I–U)

A mid-nineteenth-century boy, uncertain about his future, feels that he must choose between whaling and farming. After a bitter experience on a farm, and after his father loses a leg on a whale hunt, Adam decides to go to college and prepare himself for a different life. Good father-son relationships and interesting period details.

2325 **Gage, Wilson.** Big Blue Island; pictures by Glen Rounds. World, 1964. 120p. $3.50; lib. ed. $3.41 net. (I–U)

City-bred Darrell hates everything about the lonely Tennessee River island where he is sent by the welfare people to live with his great-uncle. Not until he becomes interested in the great blue herons that live on the island does he understand the meaning of the birds' freedom and his uncle's independence. For nature lovers.

2326 **Gage, Wilson.** Miss Osborne-the-Mop; illus. by Paul Galdone. World, 1963. 156p. $3.50; lib. ed. $2.88 net. (I)

Jody and her cousin Dill forget their differences when it is discovered that Jody has magic powers. They have a fine time producing luxuries—like orange cake and a motorcycle—until Jody turns a mop into a person surprisingly like their fourth-grade teacher and then cannot turn her back again into a mop. An original and humorous fantasy.

2327 **Gannett, Ruth Stiles.** Elmer and the Dragon; illus. by Ruth Chrisman Gannett. Random, 1950. 86p. lib. ed. $3.09 net. (I)

Elmer and his baby dragon are forced down on an island inhabited entirely by canaries, all "sick with curiosity." Well-sustained fantasy supported by humorous illustrations.

2328 **Gannett, Ruth Stiles.** My Father's Dragon; illus. by Ruth Chrisman Gannett. Random, 1948. 86p. $2.95; lib. ed. $3.29 net. (I)

Logical nonsense in a fantasy about Elmer Elevator, who rescues a baby dragon being mistreated by wild animals. Imaginatively illustrated.

2329 **Gard, Joyce.** Talargain. Holt, 1965. 251p. lib. ed. $3.45 net. (I–U)

A story-within-a-story about a seventh-century British boy who appears in the guise of a seal and tells his adventures to a present-day English girl. Talargain, who wanders the oceans with the seals, describes his life in the sea and tells of his part in saving the life of his king. The evocation of his life with the seals draws on all the senses for its graphic and poetic effects.

2330 **Garfield, James B.** Follow My Leader; illus. by Robert Greiner. Viking, 1957. 191p. $3; lib. ed. $2.96 net. (I–U)

An 11-year-old blind boy gradually resumes his normal life with the aid of loyal friends and his guide dog, Leader.

2331 **Garfield, Leon.** Devil-in-the-Fog; illus. by Antony Maitland. Pantheon, 1966. 196p. lib. ed. $3.59 net. (I–U)

A suspenseful tale of a strolling player in eighteenth-century England who discovers that he is really the son of a gentleman. Mystery and danger are introduced when he becomes embroiled in a bloody feud.

2332 **Garnett, Eve.** The Family from One End Street, and Some of Their Adventures; written and illus. by Eve Garnett. Vanguard, 1960. 208p. $3.95. (I–U)

This story of a poor English family and their seven independent, individual children is full of good times in spite of hard times.

2333 **Gates, Doris.** Blue Willow; illus. by Paul Lantz. Viking, 1940. 172p. $3.50; lib. ed. $3.37 net. (I)

Janey, daughter of migrant farm workers, cherished a blue-willow plate and dreamed of the day when it would sit on the mantel in a home where she could stay as long as she wanted to. A discerning but unsentimental picture of a displaced American family.

2334 Gates, Doris. The Cat and Mrs. Cary; illus. by Peggy Bacon. Viking, 1962. 216p. $3.50; lib. ed. $3.37 net. (I–U)

A talking cat, the unexpected visit of a convalescent nephew, and involvement with smugglers complicated Mrs. Cary's life in her new home. A refreshingly different blend of fantasy and realism.

2335 Gates, Doris. The Elderberry Bush; illus. by Lillian Obligado. Viking, 1967. 160p. $3.50; lib. ed. $3.37 net. (I)

California in the early 1900's is the setting for this nostalgic story of Elizabeth and Julie Allen. The warmhearted and lively little girls and their strict but loving parents enjoy the modest pleasures of the time: rides in Father's new Peerless automobile, family visits, and last-day-of-school exercises, when Elizabeth and Julie appear on stage without shoes to save a formerly shoeless classmate from embarrassment.

2336 Gates, Doris. Little Vic; illus. by Kate Seredy. Viking, 1951. 160p. $3.50; lib. ed. $3.37 net. (I)

Pony Rivers, son of a jockey, falls in love with Little Vic and follows him from master to master until the colt finally wins a race, with Pony riding him. (R4–5)

2337 Gates, Doris. Sensible Kate; illus. by Marjorie Torrey. Viking, 1943. 189p. $3; lib. ed. $2.96 net. (I)

Kate, orphaned and passed from one relative to another, longs to be cute and attractive instead of just sensible. When she is adopted by her favorite young couple, who need someone with good sense, she realizes that being sensible is, after all, a blessing.

2338 George, Jean. My Side of the Mountain; written and illus. by Jean George. Dutton, 1959. 178p. $3.75; lib. ed. $3.71 net. (I–U)

Sam Gribley tells the story of the winter he spent alone in the Catskill Mountains. His ingenuity in improvising shelter, finding and cooking food, and devising needed implements enables him to live a comfortable and interesting Robinson Crusoe existence until the need for human companionship brings him home. Of special interest to Boy Scouts and nature-study groups.

2339 George, John L., and **George, Jean.** Masked Prowler: The Story of a Raccoon; illus. by Jean George. Dutton, 1950. 183p. $3.75. (I–U)

This story of Procyon, a raccoon born in the Michigan forest, follows him through his days of training in gathering food and protecting himself to the adult adventures which make him a legend in his community. Good writing, a sound knowledge of the subject, and excellent illustrations.

2340 George, John L., and **George, Jean.** Vulpes, the Red Fox; illus. by Jean George. Dutton, 1948. 184p. $3.75; lib. ed. $3.71 net. (I–U)

A well-written and beautifully illustrated story of a Maryland fox and his cunning escapes from the hunters who sought him. An unsentimental appreciation of wildlife pervades the dramatic story.

2341 Gipson, Fred. Old Yeller; drawings by Carl Burger. Harper, 1956. 158p. $3.50; lib. ed. $3.27 net. (I–U)

In the hard summer of 1860, 14-year-old Travis was the man of the family while his father drove his herd of cattle from Texas to Kansas. An ugly yellow dog fought by Travis' side to protect the family from many dangers.

2342 Godden, Rumer. The Dolls' House; illus. by Tasha Tudor. Viking, 1962. 136p. $3; lib. ed. $2.96 net. (I)

Tottie, a hundred-year-old Dutch doll belonging to two little English girls, lives in a Victorian dollhouse, where her adventures include meeting Queen Victoria at an exhibition.

2342a Godden, Rumer. Impunity Jane: The Story of a Pocket Doll; illus. by Adrienne Adams. Viking, 1954. 48p. $3; lib. ed. $3.04 net. (P–I)

Jane was a doll so small that she could be put into a pocket with impunity. In fact, she *was* put into the pocket of a young boy who let her play the role of fireman, sailor, pilot, and other daring characters. An appealing story for reading aloud.

2342b Godden, Rumer. Mouse House; illus. by Adrienne Adams. Viking, 1951. 63p. $3.75; lib. ed. $3.56 net. (I)

When a family of mice outgrow their home in a flower pot, a real mouse house is provided for them.

2342c Godden, Rumer. The Story of Holly and Ivy; illus. by Adrienne Adams. Viking, 1958. 290p. $2.75. (I)

The lives of three lonely characters—a child living in an orphanage, a childless woman, and a doll in a toyshop—are united at Christmas in this tender story.

2343 Goudge, Elizabeth. Linnets and Valerians; illus. by Ian Ribbons. Coward-McCann, 1964. 290p. $3.95. (I–U)

The four lively Linnet children run away from their strict grandmother and go to the home of an uncle who understands them better. Their adventures, including involvement in a mystery concerning the Valerian family, make an unusual story.

2344 Graham, Lorenz B. I, Momolu; illus. by John Biggers. Crowell, 1966. 226p. $4. (I–U)

An informative picture of life in present-day Liberia emerges from this story of 14-year-old Momolu and his father who endure many degrading experiences on a river journey from their remote village to the coastal city of Cape Roberts. Growing understanding between father and son and the impact of industrialization on tribal customs are interesting aspects of the story.

2345 Graham, Lorenz B. North Town. Crowell, 1965. 220p. $3.95. (U)

After race trouble in the South (see *South Town,* below), 16-year-old David Williams and his family move to North Town, only to find that they have not escaped discrimination. David's experiences in an integrated high school, his brush with the juvenile court, and the family's housing problem are handled with unemotional sympathy and a note of optimism.

2346 Graham, Lorenz B. South Town. Follett, 1955. 189p. $3.95; lib. ed. $4.17 net. (U)

In South Town, David's family are victims of the community's racial tension and violence.

2347 Grahame, Kenneth. The Reluctant Dragon; illus. by Ernest H. Shepard. Holiday, 1953. unp. lib. ed. $2.50. (P–I)

A little boy makes friends with a gentle dragon and arranges a match for him with St. George.

2348 Grahame, Kenneth. The Wind in the Willows; illus. by Arthur Rackham; introd.

by A. A. Milne. Heritage, 1962. 190p. $5. (I–U)

Though not for all children, this classic animal fantasy will be enjoyed by many if introduced by an enthusiastic adult.

2349 Gray, Elizabeth Janet. Adam of the Road; illus. by Robert Lawson. Viking, 1942. 317p. $4.50; lib. ed. $4.13 net. (I–U)

Against a richly re-created background of thirteenth-century England the author tells the story of a boy who wanders the countryside searching for his minstrel father. Authentic details of medieval life in story and pictures are especially valuable for the history-minded reader.

2350 Gray, Elizabeth Janet. The Cheerful Heart; illus. by Kazue Mizumura. Viking, 1959. 176p. $3.50; lib. ed. $3.37 net. (I)

Tomi helps her Tokyo family to accept the changes which follow World War II.

2351 Guillot, René. Grishka and the Bear; tr. by Gwen Marsh; illus. by Joan Kiddell-Monroe. Criterion, 1959. 115p. $2.75. (I)

Each year Grishka's Northern Siberian tribe sacrifices a bear to propitiate the forest gods. When Grishka's pet bear is to be sacrificed, the two run away together. A haunting story of friendship, with beautiful descriptions of life in the forest.

2352 Haig-Brown, Roderick. The Whale People; illus. by Mary Weiler. Morrow, 1963. 256p. $3.95. (I–U)

Atlin, a youth of the pre-Columbian Nootka Indian tribe of the Pacific Northwest, replaces his father as whale chief when his father is killed. Atlin's education in the rituals of his people and his gradual development as a leader are balanced with exciting whale hunts to produce a vivid picture of a primitive people.

2353 Hale, Edward Everett. The First Book Edition of The Man without a Country; with an introd. by Van Wyck Brooks and illus. by Everett Fisher. Watts, 1960. 68p. $2.95. (I–U)

An unabridged edition with striking black-and-white illustrations and a brief biographical sketch of the author.

2354 Hale, Lucretia P. The Complete Peterkin Papers; with the original illus.; introd. by Nancy Hale. Houghton, 1960. 302p. $5. (I–U)

Combines *The Peterkin Papers* and *The*

Last of the Peterkins in an attractive edition. The daffy Peterkins and the Lady from Philadelphia are still good fun after a hundred years.

2355 Hall, Natalie. The World in a City Block; story and pictures by Natalie Hall. Viking, 1960. 42p. lib. ed. $2.96 net. (I)

Nick, son of an Italian baker, sees the world in his own New York City street when he delivers bread to customers from many nations.

2356 Hámori, László. Dangerous Journey; tr. from the Swedish by Annabelle Mac-Millan; illus. by W. T. Mars. Harcourt, 1962. 190p. $3.25. (I–U)

The plight of child refugees the world over is represented in the story of 12-year-old Latsi's escape from Russian-occupied Budapest and his hazardous journey to join his parents in Sweden.

2357 Hauff, Wilhelm. Dwarf Long-Nose; illus. by Maurice Sendak. Random, 1960. 60p. $2.95; lib. ed. $3.09 net. (I)

An old German fairy tale about the shoemaker's son, turned into a hunchbacked dwarf with a long nose, who finally breaks the enchantment by his own efforts.

2358 Haugaard, Erik Christian. Hakon of Rogen's Saga; illus. by Leo and Diane Dillon. Houghton, 1963. 132p. $3. (U)

Set in Norway at the end of the Viking period, this story of 13-year-old Hakon's struggle to regain possession of his father's lands, usurped by a treacherous uncle, is stirring and suspenseful.

2359 Haugaard, Erik Christian. The Little Fishes; illus. by Milton Johnson. Houghton, 1967. 241p. $3.50. (I–U)

Three Neapolitan waifs—the "little fishes"—survive the devastation of World War II as indomitable Guido, 12, leads them to safety. A starkly realistic tale dramatizing the effects of war on children.

2360 Haugaard, Erik Christian. A Slave's Tale; illus. by Leo and Diane Dillon. Houghton, 1965. 217p. $3. (U)

The slave girl, Helga, sails with Hakon to return another slave to his homeland. A beautifully written tale of Norse life, filled with war, death, love, and adventure.

2361 Hawes, Charles Boardman. The Dark Frigate . . . with illus. in color by Anton

Otto Fischer. Little, 1934. 247p. $3.95. (U)

A rousing pirate story of seventeenth-century England.

2362 Haycraft, Howard, ed. The Boys' Book of Great Detective Stories. Harper, 1938. 315p. $4.50; lib. ed. $4.11 net. (U)

A selection of tales from master storytellers whose heroes solve their mysteries with brainwork rather than with bludgeons.

2363 Hays, Wilma. Pilgrim Thanksgiving; illus. by Leonard Weisgard. Coward-McCann, 1955. unp. lib. ed. $2.86 net. (I)

Damaris Hopkins finds that the best thing about the first Thanksgiving feast is making friends with the dreaded Indians. A good read-aloud story expressing the true meaning of friendship and thankfulness.

2364 Haywood, Carolyn. "B" Is for Betsy; written and illus. by Carolyn Haywood. Harcourt, 1939. 159p. $3.50. (P–I)

The everyday adventures of a little girl during her first year in school and her vacation on the farm.

This story is typical of Carolyn Haywood's books, which fill a special need in elementary school. They are warm, humorous stories of real children who become involved in all kinds of comical and amusing situations, but who manage to extricate themselves with ingenuity and independence. The books are tremendously appealing to readers who have graduated from picture-story books and are ready for longer stories with more application to themselves. Each chapter is usually a separate episode, suitable for reading aloud or for independent reading in third—or, sometimes, second—grade. Large print, open pages, and numerous amusing illustrations give the books added appeal for seven- to ten-year-olds. (R3–4)

2365 Haywood, Carolyn. Back to School with Betsy; written and illus. by Carolyn Haywood. Harcourt, 1943. 176p. $3.50. (P–I)

Betsy and her friend Billy find third grade full of lively experiences. (R3–4)

2366 Haywood, Carolyn. Betsy and Billy; written and illus. by Carolyn Haywood. Harcourt, 1941. 156p. $3.50. (P–I)

In second grade Betsy becomes fast friends with Billy. (R3–4)

2367 Haywood, Carolyn. Betsy and the Boys; written and illus. by Carolyn Hay-

wood. Harcourt, 1945. 175p. $3.50. (P–I)
Fourth grade brings new friends and new experiences to Betsy and Billy. (R3–4)

2368 **Haywood, Carolyn.** Betsy's Busy Summer; written and illus. by Carolyn Haywood. Morrow, 1956. 189p. $3.75; lib. ed. $3.56 net. (P–I)
Betsy and her friends spend a happy summer earning money by selling cold drinks and enjoying Betsy's summerhouse. (R3–4)

2369 **Haywood, Carolyn.** Betsy's Little Star; written and illus. by Carolyn Haywood. Morrow, 1950. 157p. $3.75; lib. ed. $3.56 net. (P–I)
Star, Betsy's little sister, stirs up excitement while waiting to be old enough for kindergarten. (R3–4)

2370 **Haywood, Carolyn.** Eddie and Gardenia; written and illus. by Carolyn Haywood. Morrow, 1951. 191p. $3.75; lib. ed. $3.56 net. (P–I)
Eddie Wilson and his goat, Gardenia, spend the summer on a Texas ranch, where they create their special brand of confusion. (R3–4)

2371 **Haywood, Carolyn.** Eddie and His Big Deals; written and illus. by Carolyn Haywood. Morrow, 1955. 190p. $3.75; lib. ed. $3.56 net. (P–I)
Eddie, a born collector of "valuable property" (junk to his parents), meets a rival collector and engages in a swapping contest. (R3–4)

2372 **Haywood, Carolyn.** Eddie and the Fire Engine; written and illus. by Carolyn Haywood. Morrow, 1949. 189p. $3.75; lib. ed. $3.56 net. (P–I)
Eddie's father buys an old fire engine at auction and adds it to Eddie's collection of "valuable property," providing further opportunities for hilarious situations and neighborhood fun. (R3–4)

2373 **Haywood, Carolyn.** Eddie Makes Music; written and illus. by Carolyn Haywood. Morrow, 1957. 191p. $3.75; lib. ed. $3.56 net. (P–I)
After hearing himself singing in the bathtub, Eddie decides to become a violinist in the school orchestra. (R3–4)

2374 **Haywood, Carolyn.** Eddie the Dog Holder; written and illus. by Carolyn Hay-

wood. Morrow, 1966. 187p. $3.75; lib. ed. $3.56 net. (P–I)
Eddie holds Annie Pat's dog while she paints his picture and shares profits with her. (R3–4)

2375 **Haywood, Carolyn.** Here Comes the Bus! Written and illus. by Carolyn Haywood. Morrow, 1963. 186p. $3.75; lib. ed. $3.56 net. (P–I)
First-grader Jonathan and his friends provide long-suffering Mr. Riley, the school bus driver, with constant crises. (R3–4)

2376 **Haywood, Carolyn.** Here's a Penny; written and illus. by Carolyn Haywood. Harcourt, 1944. 158p. $3.50. (P–I)
Adopted Penny, in the first grade, loses and then finds his pet kitten. (R3–4)

2377 **Haywood, Carolyn.** Little Eddie; written and illus. by Carolyn Haywood. Morrow, 1947. 160p. $3.75; lib. ed. $3.56 net. (P–I)
Seven-year-old Eddie Wilson is an inveterate collector of stray animals and cast-off "valuables." (R3–4)

2378 **Haywood, Carolyn.** Penny and Peter; written and illus. by Carolyn Haywood. Harcourt, 1956. 160p. $3.50. (P–I)
Penny and Peter, both adopted, enjoy their new family together. (R3–4)

2379 **Haywood, Carolyn.** Two and Two Are Four; written and illus. by Carolyn Haywood. Harcourt, 1940. 171p. $3.50. (P–I)
Four lively children spend an interesting summer on a farm. (R3–4)

2380 **Heinlein, Robert A.** Red Planet: A Colonial Boy on Mars; illus. by Clifford Geary. Scribner, 1949. 211p. lib. ed. $3.31 net. (I–U)
Fifty years after the first earth colonies are established on Mars, two boys discover a plot against the freedom of their own colony and, with the help of friendly Martians, foil the plot and preserve their liberties. Convincingly plotted science fiction.

2381 **Heinlein, Robert A.** Rocket Ship to Galileo; illus. by Thomas W. Voter. Scribner, 1947. 212p. lib. ed. $3.31 net. (I–U)
Two boys collaborating with an inventor of rocket airplanes succeed in reaching the moon. Science fiction with a basis in science.

2382 Henry, Marguerite. Brighty of the Grand Canyon; illus. by Wesley Dennis. Rand McNally, 1953. 222p. $3.95; lib. ed. $3.97 net. (I–U)

An old prospector and his little gray burro are the central characters in a beautifully illustrated story incorporating much information about the history of the Grand Canyon.

2383 Henry, Marguerite. Justin Morgan Had a Horse; illus. by Wesley Dennis. Rand McNally, 1954. 169p. $3.95; lib. ed. $3.97 net. (I–U)

The history of the little Vermont work horse who sired the famous breed of Morgan horses is told through the experiences of a boy who followed his career through many hardships.

2384 Henry, Marguerite. King of the Wind; illus. by Wesley Dennis. Rand McNally, 1948. 172p. $3.95; lib. ed. $3.97 net. (I–U)

When Louis XV of France rejected the gift of an Arabian stallion, he could not have known that the horse was to become the famous Godolphin Arabian, founder of the strain of thoroughbreds and ancestor of Man o' War. This is the story of the stallion and of the little mute groom whose faith and loyalty remained steadfast through many misfortunes. An exciting story, based on fact and illustrated with handsome pictures.

2385 Henry, Marguerite. Misty of Chincoteague; illus. by Wesley Dennis. Rand McNally, 1947. 172p. $3.95; lib. ed. $3.97 net. (I–U)

Each year the wild ponies of Assateague, a small island in Chesapeake Bay, are driven to the neighboring island of Chincoteague to be sold as children's pets. This is the story of one pony, Misty, and the two Chincoteague children who owned her. The atmosphere of the islands and an understanding of the freedom-loving ponies pervade the story and illustrations.

2386 Henry, Marguerite. Sea Star: Orphan of Chincoteague; illus. by Wesley Dennis. Rand McNally, 1949. 172p. $3.95; lib. ed. $3.97 net. (I–U)

A little orphan pony is rescued by two children and saved from starvation by a bereft mare. Another excellent horse story with interesting background, likable children, and an engaging animal character.

2387 Hentoff, Nat. Jazz Country. Harper, 1965. 146p. $3.50; lib. ed. $3.27 net. (U)

Tom Curtis hesitates between becoming a professional jazz musician and going to college. His contacts with established musicians, mostly Negro, convince him that success in jazz must be earned through hard work and perseverance. A candid picture of the jazz world of New York City and a perceptive story of a boy's maturing.

2388 Hicks, Clifford. Alvin's Secret Code; illus. by Bill Sokol. Holt, 1963. 159p. $3.25; lib. ed. $3.27 net. (I)

Alvin Fernald, the Magnificent Brain, becomes a cryptographer and as Secret Agent K 21½ solves the mystery of the buried treasure. An appendix gives entertaining information about codes and ciphers, along with samples and problems.

2389 Hightower, Florence. Dark Horse of Woodfield; illus. by Joshua Tolford. Houghton, 1962. 233p. $3.50. (I–U)

The depression of the 1930's had brought neglect to Woodfield, the Armistead estate in Massachusetts. Maggie and her younger brother Bugsy help to solve the family's financial problems and to buy back a favorite horse. Well-drawn characters, interesting incidents, and humor lift this above the average horse story.

2390 Hodges, C. Walter. The Namesake; illus. by the author. Coward-McCann, 1964. 269p. $4.50. (U)

Crippled Alfred, scribe to his namesake, King Alfred of England, records the dramatic contest between the Saxons and the invading Danes. A fine historical novel, with believable characters and authentic period details.

2391 Hoff, Syd. Irving and Me. Harper, 1967. 226p. $3.95; lib. ed. $3.79 net. (I–U)

Artie Granick, a displaced Brooklynite, dislikes his new home in Florida until he meets Irving, a boy with a genius for attracting disaster. The adventures of the two 13-year-olds are related with humor and spirit.

2392 Holling, Holling Clancy. Paddle-to-the-Sea; written and illus. by Holling Clancy Holling. Houghton, 1941. unp. $4.50; lib. ed. $3.90 net. (I)

A toy canoe, carved and launched by an Indian boy, traverses the Great Lakes and four years later reaches the sea. Excellent full-page illustrations and many marginal drawings show scenes and industries along the shores.

2393 **Holling, Holling Clancy.** Seabird; written and illus. by Holling Clancy Holling. Houghton, 1948. 58p. lib. ed. $3.90 net. (I)

A seagull carved of ivory brought good luck to four generations of a seafaring family. A distinctively illustrated book showing the transition from the whaling vessel to the clipper ship, the steamship, and the seaplane.

2394 **Holling, Holling Clancy.** Tree in the Trail; written and illus. by Holling Clancy Holling. Houghton, 1942. unp. $4.95; lib. ed. $4.20 net. (I)

When a cottonwood tree standing by the Santa Fe trail was struck by lightning in 1834, its wood bore evidence of the history which had occurred in its lifetime. Beautifully illustrated.

2395 **Holm, Anne S.** North to Freedom; tr. from the Danish by L. W. Kingsland. Harcourt, 1965. 190p. $3.50. (I–U)

Twelve-year-old David, whose only memory is of life in a prison camp, escapes and makes his way across Europe alone. Before he is reunited with his mother, his prison-bred fear of people has gradually faded, and he has learned that goodness as well as evil exists in the world.

2396 **Houston, James.** The White Archer: An Eskimo Legend; written and illus. by James Houston. Harcourt, 1967. 95p. $3.50; lib. ed. $3.54 net. (I)

Eskimo character and customs are treated with respect and admiration in this story of Kungo, who spends four years training to avenge the death of his parents, but who, when the moment for vengeance comes, finds that he cannot kill and thus perpetuate hatred. The author, who has lived among the Eskimos, tells a stark and moving story and illustrates it with strong, clean-lined pictures suggesting Eskimo bone carvings.

2397 **Hunt, Irene.** Across Five Aprils. Follett, 1964. 223p. $3.95; lib. ed. $4.17 net. (I–U)

For the duration of the Civil War, young Jethro and his mother ran their Southern Illinois farm and coped with the dangers of a border state.

2398 **Hunt, Irene.** Up a Road Slowly. Follett, 1966. 192p. $3.95; lib. ed. $4.17 net. (I–U)

After her mother's death Julie Trelling was sent to live with her severe but fair schoolteacher aunt. Julie's growing up is followed in a perceptive story peopled with interesting characters.

2399 **Hunt, Mabel Leigh.** Little Girl with Seven Names; illus. by Grace Paull. Lippincott, 1936. 63p. lib. ed. $2.39 net. (I)

Named for two grandmothers and four aunts, a little Quaker girl struggles with seven names rather than hurt anyone's feelings.

2400 **Hunt, Mabel Leigh.** Miss Jellytot's Visit; illus. by Velma Ilsley. Lippincott, 1955. 126p. lib. ed. $3.39 net. (I)

Nine-year-old Katie O'Dea is allowed to be a visitor in her own home for six days, only to find that visiting involves problems as well as privileges. (R3–4)

2401 **Hürlimann, Bettina.** William Tell and His Son; illus. by Paul Nussbaumer. Harcourt, 1967. 36p. $4.25. (P–I)

The story of the Swiss legendary hero is presented in picture-book format with striking full-color illustrations.

2402 **Inyart, Gene.** Susan & Martin; pictures by Gloria Gaulke. Watts, 1965. 130p. $2.95. (I)

For two fourth-graders the week before Easter is crowded with exciting events: a ride down a fire escape, kittens born in the cloakroom, and a baby lost in the bushes.

2403 **Irving, Washington.** The Legend of Sleepy Hollow; illus. by Leonard Everett Fisher. Watts, 1966. 72p. $2.65. (I–U)

Bold black-and-white pictures interpret the classic story admirably. Excellent for reading aloud.

2404 **Irving, Washington.** Rip Van Winkle; illus. by Leonard Everett Fisher. Watts, 1967. 47p. $2.95. (I–U)

A companion volume to *The Legend of Sleepy Hollow,* above, especially useful at Halloween.

2405 **Ish-Kishor, S.** A Boy of Old Prague; drawings by Ben Shahn. Pantheon, 1963. 90p. $4.95; lib. ed. $3.59 net. (I)

Tomás, bound out to a Jew in the Prague ghetto, experiences his first kindness from a once-hated people. A story of the evils of prejudice set against a background of six-teenth-century Bohemia.

2406 **Jackson, Jacqueline.** Julie's Secret Sloth; illus. by Robert Henneberger. Little, 1953. 186p. $3.50. (I)
Julie's efforts to keep her father from finding out about her pet sloth lead to hilarious complications.

2407 **Jackson, Jacqueline.** The Taste of Spruce Gum; illus. by Lillian Obligado. Little, 1966. 212p. $3.95. (I)
Vermont in the early 1900's is the setting for this story of a child's adjustment to a new home and a new father. Libby Fletcher, 11, hates the rough lumber camp to which the family has moved, fears the lumberjacks, and worries because she thinks her step-father dislikes her.

2408 **Jackson, Jesse.** Call Me Charley; illus. by Doris Spiegel. Harper, 1945. 156p. $2.95; lib. ed. $2.92 net. (I-U)
Twelve-year-old Charley is the only Ne-gro boy in his community. His problems of making friends and proving himself are handled with honesty and directness by a Negro author.

2409 **James, Will.** Smoky, the Cow Horse; illus. by the author. Scribner, 1929. 263p. $3.50; lib. ed. $3.31 net. (I-U)
The story of a cowboy and his horse is told in breezy cowboy language and illus-trated with action-filled pen drawings.

2410 **Jarrell, Randall.** The Animal Family; decorations by Maurice Sendak. Pan-theon, 1965. 179p. $3.50; lib. ed. $3.39 net. (I)
A fantasy about a lonely hunter who ac-quires a strange family: a mermaid, a bear cub, a lynx, and a shipwrecked boy. A gen-tle, delicately written story for the imagina-tive reader.

2411 **Jeffries, Roderic.** Against Time! Har-per, 1964. 151p. $3.50; lib. ed. $3.27 net. (I-U)
Peter Dunn, son of a British police detec-tive, is kidnapped and his life threatened unless his father agrees to give false testi-mony at a murder trial. Efforts to rescue the boy make a tense, fast-moving story of police teamwork in an emergency, including absorbing details about the profession of crime detection.

2412 **Jewett, Eleanore M.** The Hidden Treasure of Glaston; illus. by Frederick T. Chapman. Viking, 1946. 307p. $4; lib. ed. $3.77 net. (U)
In the time of King Henry II of England a crippled boy, mysteriously left at Glaston-bury Abbey on a stormy night, discovers and then loses the missing pages of a book about the Holy Grail. A good companion book to the King Arthur stories.

2413 **Jewett, Sarah Orne.** A White Heron: A Story of Maine; illus. by Barbara Cooney. Crowell, 1963. 34p. $3.50; lib. ed. $3.65 net. (I)
Lovely illustrations of the Maine woods enrich this story (from the author's collec-tion of stories, *The Country of the Pointed Firs*) of nine-year-old Sylvy's love of a beautiful white heron, whose nest she re-fuses to reveal to a young ornithologist.

2414 **Johnson, Annabel,** and **Johnson, Ed-gar.** The Bearcat. Harper, 1960. 231p. lib. ed. $3.79 net. (I-U)
Jeff, who has failed eighth grade, goes to work in a Montana mine where he discovers a company spy. The exciting story that fol-lows combines the dangers of mining, the difficulties of the early labor unions, and the problems of a maturing boy.

2415 **Johnson, Annabel,** and **Johnson, Ed-gar.** The Burning Glass. Harper, 1966. 244p. $3.95; lib. ed. $3.79 net. (I-U)
Fifteen-year-old Jeb runs away from a wagon train and joins a French fur trader. During their life together they spend a win-ter as captives of the Absarokee Indians, face many dangers, and come in contact with the colorful characters of the early Western frontier.

2416 **Johnson, Annabel,** and **Johnson, Ed-gar.** The Grizzly. Harper, 1964. 160p. $3.95; lib. ed. $3.79 net. (I-U)
Eleven-year-old David, living with his divorced mother, is doubtful about going on a camping trip with his father. When a griz-zly injures the father and disables the truck, David surprises both himself and his father by his resourcefulness. A perceptive story of father-son relationships.

2417 **Johnson, Elizabeth.** The Little Knight; illus. by Ronni Solbert. Little, 1957. 56p. lib. ed. $3.14 net. (I)
A story about an unusual princess who wanted to be a knight instead of a lady.

When her father proposes the usual tests for her hand, she disguises herself as a knight and sets out to pass them herself.

2418 **Johnson, Margaret S.** Gay: A Shetland Sheepdog; written & illus. by Margaret S. Johnson. Morrow, 1948. 96p. lib. ed. $2.94 net. (P–I)

The training and work of a young sheepdog are simply told and illustrated.

2419 **Johnson, Sally Patrick.** The Princesses: Sixteen Stories about Princesses; with biographical notes on each author; pictures by Beni Montresor. Harper, 1962. 318p. $4.95; lib. ed. $4.79 net. (I)

A handsome book containing many less-familiar stories, useful for storytelling or reading aloud.

2420 **Jones, Elizabeth Orton.** Twig. Macmillan, 1942. 152p. $3.95; lib. ed. $3.74 net. (P–I)

An imaginative child relieves the drabness of her life by inventing an array of delightful playmates: Mr. Elf, Mr. and Mrs. Sparrow, the fairy queen, and Lord Buzzle.

2421 **Jones, Ruth Fosdick.** Boy of the Pyramids: A Mystery of Ancient Egypt; illus. by Dorothy Bayley Morse. Random, 1952. 140p. lib. ed. $3.29 net. (I)

Life in ancient Egypt is pictured in an absorbing story of two children who watch the building of a pyramid, experience the flooding of the Nile, and help capture a tomb robber.

2422 **Kalashnikoff, Nicholas.** The Defender; illus. by Claire and George Louden. Scribner, 1951. 136p. $3.50. (U)

Turgen, a Siberian shepherd, suffers the ill will of his neighbors because he defends the last of the wild rams in the mountains of the area. A poignant plea for conservation of wildlife.

2423 **Kalnay, Francis.** Chúcaro: Wild Pony of the Pampa; illus. by Julian de Miskey. Harcourt, 1958. 126p. $2.95. (I–U)

An atmospheric story of the Argentine Pampa—its gauchos, its *patróns,* its wild pony herds—with the boy Pedro and his gaucho friend Juan as central figures. Juan lassos a beautiful wild pony for Pedro and loses his job to keep the *patrón's* son from claiming it.

2424 **Keith, Harold.** Rifles for Watie. Crowell, 1957. 332p. $4.50. (I–U)

Jefferson Davis Bussey, in spite of his name, was a young Union soldier fighting in Kansas during the Civil War. His experiences as infantryman, cavalryman, and scout reveal the futility of war and show the courage displayed on both sides. The part played by the Cherokee rebel general, Stand Watie, is an interesting sidelight.

2425 **Kelly, Eric P.** The Trumpeter of Krakow; decorations by Janina Domanska; foreword by Louise Seaman Bechtel. Macmillan, 1966. 208p. $3.95. (U)

A new and beautifully illustrated edition of a tale of adventure and heroism in medieval Poland.

2426 **Kendall, Carol.** The Gammage Cup; illus. by Erik Blegvad. Harcourt, 1959. 221p. $3.25. (I)

In the Land between the Mountains live a lost people, the Minnipins, who faithfully preserve their ancient customs until challenged by a few nonconformists. When they are attacked by an enemy race, it is the banished rebels who save the Minnipins from destruction. An inventive fantasy utilizing a play on words for original effects.

2427 **Key, Alexander.** The Forgotten Door. Westminster, 1965. 126p. $3.50. (U)

A boy from a better world slips through a forgotten door into an Appalachian community where he arouses fear and suspicion because he is different. More serious and thought-provoking than most science fiction.

2428 **Kim, Yong-ik.** Blue in the Seed; illus. by Artur Marokvia. Little, 1964. 117p. $3.95. (I)

In Korea, where most eyes are brown, Chun Bok is teased because his eyes are blue. Not until his blue eyes help him to recover his stolen ox does he accept the fact of his difference.

2429 **Kingman, Lee.** The Best Christmas; illus. by Barbara Cooney. Doubleday, 1949. 95p. $2.95. (I)

The quarry region of Cape Ann, Massachusetts, in the early 1900's is the setting of this warm story of Finnish family life. When it is feared that the eldest son will not return from a trip in time for Christmas, ten-year-old Erkki makes presents for all the family.

2430 **Kingman, Lee.** The Year of the Raccoon. Houghton, 1966. 246p. $3.50. (U)

Fifteen-year-old Joey, the middle son in

a brilliant family, considers himself a disappointment to his parents. A pet raccoon helps to tide him over a difficult period in which he proves himself a person of worth and importance. Good characterization and skillful handling of a common problem.

2431 Kipling, Rudyard. Captains Courageous; illus. by Charles McCurry. Doubleday, 1964. 213p. $3.75. (I–U)

Good print and colored illustrations enhance a new edition of the old story of the spoiled boy rescued from the sea by Gloucester fishermen and made into a man by sharing their work.

2432 Kipling, Rudyard. The Jungle Book; illus. by Philip Hays. Doubleday, 1964. 213p. $3.95. (I–U)

The jungle adventures of the boy Mowgli, reared by Bagheera the panther and Baloo the bear.

2433 Kipling, Rudyard. Just So Stories; pictures by Joseph M. Gleeson. Doubleday, 1932. 249p. $3.50. (P–I)

The classic animal stories of the East Indian forest in an attractive edition.

2434 Kjelgaard, Jim. Big Red; illus. by Bob Kuhn. Holiday, 1945. 245p. $3.50. (U)

The story of a champion Irish setter and a trapper's son who grew up together, roaming the Wintape wilderness and sharing the rugged life of the forest.

2435 Kjelgaard, Jim. Fire-Hunter; illus. by Ralph Ray. Holiday, 1951. 217p. $3.50. (I–U)

A boy and girl of prehistoric times, abandoned by their tribe, survive through courage and intelligence and find better ways of living. A dramatic story with authentic background.

2436 Kjelgaard, Jim. Irish Red: Son of Big Red. Holiday, 1951. 224p. $3.50. (I–U)

A satisfying dog story in which the disappointing son of Big Red (see No.2434) eventually proves himself worthy of his father.

2437 Kjelgaard, Jim. Snow Dog; illus. by Jacob Landau. Holiday, 1948. 236p. $3.75. (I–U)

A wild dog survives wilderness dangers and eventually becomes domesticated.

2438 Knight, Eric. Lassie Come-Home; illus. by Marguerite Kirmse. Winston, 1940. 248p. $3.95; lib. ed. $3.79 net. (I–U)

A valuable collie, sold to a master in northern Scotland, makes a 400-mile journey back to her former owners in Yorkshire.

2439 Konigsburg, E. L. From the Mixed-up Files of Mrs. Basil E. Frankweiler; written and illus. by E. L. Konigsburg. Atheneum, 1967. 168p. $3.95; lib. ed. $3.81 net. (I)

Two New York children run away from home and spend a week in the Metropolitan Museum of Art, where a beautiful statue starts them on the trail of a mystery. Delightfully natural children in a bizarre escapade made entirely believable in a logically developed plot.

2440 Krumgold, Joseph. And Now Miguel; illus. by Jean Charlot. Crowell, 1953. 245p. $4.50. (I–U)

Miguel, son of a New Mexican sheepherder, longs to be old enough to go with the men to take the sheep to summer pasture. An introspective story with appealing characters and an interesting setting.

2441 Krumgold, Joseph. Onion John; illus. by Symeon Shimin. Crowell, 1959. 248p. $4.50. (I–U)

Andy Rusch's father cannot understand his son's affection for Onion John, the odd-jobs man who lives by the city dump. The town's well-meant attempt to reform John's ways of living fails, but through it Andy and his father begin to understand each other.

2442 Lamorisse, Albert. The Red Balloon. Doubleday, 1956. unp. $3.50. (P–I)

Superb colored photographs illustrate this story of a boy's adventures as he follows a magical red balloon through the streets of Paris.

2443 Lampman, Evelyn Sibley. Navaho Sister; illus. by Paul Lantz. Doubleday, 1956. 189p. $3.50. (I–U)

"Sad Girl" resented her name, given because she had only her grandmother for a family, because she thought it made people feel sorry for her. When she left the Navaho reservation in Arizona and went to Indian school in Oregon, she found many friends and, eventually, her own family.

2444 Lampman, Evelyn Sibley. The Shy Stegosaurus of Cricket Creek; illus. by Hubert Buel. Doubleday, 1955. 220p. $3.50. (I)

Only Joan and Joey can see a shy little dinosaur named George.

2445 **Langton, Jane.** The Majesty of Grace; illus. by Jane Langton. Harper, 1961. 190p. lib. ed. $3.27 net. (I)

Grace, a selfish, imaginative child, decides that she is the rightful heir to the throne of England and behaves accordingly, in spite of the privations of the Depression. When she finally realizes the foolishness of her pretense, she returns to reality and becomes a very nice child. Patient, understanding parents accept all this with amused tolerance.

2446 **Latham, Jean Lee.** This Dear-bought Land; pictures by Jacob Landau. Harper, 1957. 246p. $3.95; lib. ed. $3.79 net. (I–U)

The early days of the English colony at Jamestown, Virginia, come to life through the experiences of a 15-year-old boy. A thrilling adventure story, valuable to give readers an appreciation of their country's beginnings.

2447 **Lathrop, West.** Keep the Wagons Moving! Illus. by Douglas Duer. Random, 1949. 337p. lib. ed. $3.49 net. (I–U)

Two brothers start for Oregon, one with a wagon train and the other as a captive of an outlaw. Their adventures are told in a long, swift-paced story.

2448 **Lauritzen, Jonreed.** The Ordeal of the Young Hunter; with illus. by Hoke Denetsosie. Little, 1954. 246p. $3.75. (I–U)

Twelve-year-old Jadih lives in a world of two cultures: that of his own Navaho tribe and that of the white man.

2449 **Lavolle, Lois N.** Captain Nuno; illus. by Hans Schwarz. Lothrop, 1963. 128p. $3.25. (I–U)

Forced to help support his family after his father's death, a Portuguese boy outfits an old boat and becomes a fisherman.

2450 **Lawson, Robert.** Ben and Me: A New and Astonishing Life of Benjamin Franklin, as Written by His Good Mouse Amos; lately discovered, ed. & illus. by Robert Lawson. Little, 1939. 113p. $3.95. (I–U)

A mouse living in Ben Franklin's fur hat acts as Franklin's adviser through many historic adventures. A sophisticated blend of fantasy and fact in story and pictures.

2451 **Lawson, Robert.** Mr. Revere and I . . . Set Down and Embellished with Numerous Drawings by Robert Lawson. Little, 1953. 152p. $3.95. (I–U)

Paul Revere's horse describes the events leading up to the Revolution in a humorous, mostly factual, account of the famous ride.

2452 **Lawson, Robert.** Rabbit Hill. Viking, 1944. 127p. $3.50; lib. ed. $3.37 net. (I)

Georgie, a lively young rabbit, investigates the new family moving into the house on the hill and reports to the other animals that they live by the philosophy that "there is enough for all." The author's humorous illustrations enhance the gently whimsical story. (R3–4)

2453 **Leach, Maria.** The Thing at the Foot of the Bed, and Other Scary Tales; illus. by Kurt Werth. World, 1959. 126p. $3.50; lib. ed. $3.41 net. (I)

Good storytelling material by a well-known folklorist. Includes games, notes on the stories, and a list of similar books.

2454 **Leaf, Munro.** Wee Gillis; illus. by Robert Lawson. Viking, 1964. unp. $3; lib. ed. $2.96 net. (P–I)

Wee Gillis solves the problem of whether to live in the Highlands of Scotland and stalk stags or to go to the Lowlands and raise cattle.

2455 **Lee, Mildred.** The Rock and the Willow. Lothrop, 1963. 223p. $3.50. (U)

The bleak Depression years on an Alabama farm are re-created through the story of Enie: her family responsibilities, her dreams of a better life, and her first love affair. Excellent characterization and a starkly realistic picture of the period and place.

2456 **Le Grand.** Cats for Kansas. Abingdon, 1948. unp. $2. (I)

A tall tale about old Gabe Slade, the trader who brought the first cats to Kansas. Appealing to reluctant readers. (R3–4)

2457 **Le Grand.** Why Cowboys Sing in Texas. Abingdon, 1950. unp. $2. (I)

Regional folklore in a tale about Slim Jim Bean who taught cowboys to sing. For reluctant readers. (R3–4)

2458 **Leighton, Margaret.** Judith of France; illus. by Henry C. Pitz. Houghton, 1948. 281p. $3.75. (U)

The contrast between the civilization of

the Franks and the rough life of Saxon England is revealed in this story of Judith, granddaughter of Charlemagne, and her two royal marriages.

2459 L'Engle, Madeleine. Meet the Austins. Vanguard, 1960. 191p. $3.95. (I–U)

When spoiled, ten-year-old Maggie comes to live with the Austins, their happy home life is for a time disrupted. A warm story of a very real and likable family, told by 12-year-old Vicky Austin.

2460 L'Engle, Madeleine. A Wrinkle in Time. Farrar, 1962. 211p. $3.25. (I–U)

Meg and her friends, searching for her scientist father who has mysteriously disappeared, cross over into another world by means of a wrinkle in time. Their exciting adventures with evil powers can be read as science fiction or as an exploration of the conflict between good and evil.

2461 Lenski, Lois. Strawberry Girl; written and illus. by Lois Lenski. Lippincott, 1945. 193p. $4.50; lib. ed. $4.29 net. (I)

A strong sense of place pervades this story of Birdie Boyer, a little Cracker girl who helps her Florida family to raise strawberries and to cope with the shiftless Slaters next door.

2462 Levy, Mimi Cooper. Corrie and the Yankee; illus. by Ernest Crichlow. Viking, 1959. 189p. $3; lib. ed. $3.04 net. (I–U)

Corrie, a little slave girl, rescues a Yankee soldier.

2463 Lewis, C. S. The Lion, the Witch, and the Wardrobe: A Story for Children; illus. by Pauline Baynes. Macmillan, 1950. 154p. $3.95; lib. ed. $3.74 net. (I)

Four English children find their way through a door in a wardrobe into the enchanted land of Narnia, where the wicked white witch has replaced the rightful ruler, the lion Aslan. The children's adventures in destroying the spell of the witch can be read as a fairy tale or for its deeper meaning—the struggle between good and evil. Best understood when read aloud and discussed.

2464 Lewis, Elizabeth Foreman. To Beat a Tiger, One Needs a Brother's Help; decorations by John Huehnergarth. Winston, 1956. 215p. lib. ed. $2.92 net. (I–U)

A band of Chinese youths struggle to

survive the grim circumstances of their lives and to beat the tiger of war.

2465 Lindgren, Astrid. Pippi Longstocking; tr. from the Swedish by Florence Lamborn; illus. by Louis Glanzman. Viking, 1950. 158p. $2.50; lib. ed. $2.57 net. (P–I)

Pippi, though only nine, lives alone with her horse and her money and defies all efforts of her Swedish village to make her reform. Her wild escapades and wilder stories are a delight to children.

2466 Lindquist, Jennie D. The Golden Name Day; pictures by Garth Williams. Harper, 1955. 247p. $3.95; lib. ed. $3.79 net. (I)

A summer with Swedish friends on a New England farm was full of delights for nine-year-old Nancy, except for one thing—the Swedish calendar did not include her name day. When a way was found to allow her to share the Swedish custom of celebrating a name day, all was perfect.

2467 Lippincott, Joseph Wharton. The Wahoo Bobcat; illus. by Paul Bransom. Lippincott, 1950. 207p. $4.75. (I–U)

A great bobcat roamed the swamps of Florida and was hunted by all except Sammy, a boy who became his friend and protector. A dramatic story with vivid background and colorful characters, useful to encourage conservation.

2468 Lippincott, Joseph Wharton. Wilderness Champion: The Story of a Great Hound; illus. by Paul Bransom. Lippincott, 1944. 195p. $3.95. (I–U)

A year after Johnny loses his hound pup in the forests of Alberta, Canada, he reclaims his dog from a wolf pack.

2469 Little, Jean. Home from Far; illus. by Jerry Lazare. Little, 1965. 145p. $3.95. (I)

When her parents bring foster children into the home soon after her twin brother's death, 11-year-old Jenny withdraws from her mother and father because she thinks that they have forgotten Michael. After a difficult period of adjustment for all the children, a pleasant home atmosphere is restored and Jenny comes "home from far" to her loving family.

2470 Little, Jean. Mine for Keeps; with illus. by Lewis Parker. Little, 1962. 186p. $3.95. (I)

Sarah Jane Copeland, home from a cerebral palsy center, is unhappy not to get the pampering she had expected from her parents. In caring for a timid puppy and helping a sick boy, Sarah Jane forgets her self-pity and begins to lead a normal life. An interesting story with insight into the problems of rehabilitating the handicapped.

2471 **Little, Jean.** Spring Begins in March; illus. by Lewis Parker. Little, 1966. 156p. $3.95. (I)

Disappointed because she does not get a room of her own, and worried over failing marks in school, Meg Copeland becomes defiant and resentful, especially toward her grandmother who comes to live with them. The sensible Copeland family, introduced in *Mine for Keeps,* above, helps Meg to face and solve her problems.

2472 **Locke, Elsie.** The Runaway Settlers: An Historical Novel; illus. by Antony Maitland. Dutton, 1966. 190p. $3.75; lib. ed. $3.71 net. (I–U)

New Zealand in the 1860's is the setting for this story of a mother and her six children who run away from a brutal husband and father. A tale of courage and resourcefulness with good background details.

2473 **Lofting, Hugh.** Doctor Dolittle: A Treasury; written and illus. by Hugh Lofting. Lippincott, 1967. 256p. $4.95. (P–I)

Adventures from eight Doctor Dolittle books, with many illustrations, some never before published. Each story is complete in itself, with continuity provided by the Doctor and his animals. Especially recommended for reading aloud.

2474 **London, Jack.** The Call of the Wild; illus. by Karel Kezer; afterword by Clifton Fadiman. Macmillan, 1963. 128p. $2.95; lib. ed. $3.24 net. (I–U)

An attractive, well-bound edition of a favorite American adventure story.

2475 **Lord, Beman.** Bats and Balls; pictures by Arnold Spilka. Walck, 1962. 57p. $3.25. (I)

A baseball story for younger boys. (R3–4)

2476 **Lord, Beman.** Guards for Matt; pictures by Arnold Spilka. Walck, 1960. 64p. $3.25. (I)

A very funny story about Matt's attempts to earn money for guards for his glasses while playing on the elementary school basketball team. (R3–4)

2477 **Lord, Beman.** Quarterback's Aim; pictures by Arnold Spilka. Walck, 1960. 60p. $3.25. (I)

An underweight boy's efforts to gain weight in order to play on the elementary school football team are recounted with sympathy and humor. High interest, low reading level. (R3–4)

2478 **Lovelace, Maud Hart.** Betsy-Tacy; illus. by Lois Lenski. Crowell, 1940. 112p. $3.50; lib. ed. $3.40 net. (P–I)

Two inseparable five-year-olds picnic, play paper dolls, dress up in long dresses, and make up games, like real little girls everywhere.

2479 **McCloskey, Robert.** Centerburg Tales. Viking, 1951. 190p. $3.50; lib. ed. $3.37 net. (I–U)

The small-town characters of *Homer Price,* below, reappear in this story, as funny as ever and still telling tall tales. The author's lively drawings add to the fun.

2480 **McCloskey, Robert.** Homer Price. Viking, 1943. 149p. $3; lib. ed. $2.96 net. (I–U)

An all-American boy keeps Centerburg in a state of hilarious confusion as he operates a nonstop doughnut machine, helps to catch a bank robber, and sneaks his pet skunk into his room. Minor characters are equally as amusing as Homer. Humorously illustrated by the author.

2481 **McCracken, Harold.** The Flaming Bear. Lippincott, 1951. 222p. $3.50; lib. ed. $3.59 net. (I–U)

Against an authentic background of the Aleutian Islands, the author tells the story of Tan, son of an Aleut chief, who sets out to solve the mystery of the ancestral legend of the Flaming Bear. Heroic adventures recounted with suspense and vigor.

2482 **Macdonald, George.** At the Back of the North Wind; with 8 color plates and line drawings in the text by E. H. Shepard. Dutton, 1964. 325p. $3.50. (I)

An attractive edition of the classic fantasy of Diamond, the little son of a coachman, who became friends with the North Wind.

2483 Macdonald, George. The Light Princess; illus. by William Pène du Bois. Crowell, 1962. 48p. $4.50; lib. ed. $4.40 net. (I)

A slightly edited version of the story of a weightless and heartless little princess. Handsome colored illustrations have a modern feeling.

2484 McGinley, Phyllis. The Plain Princess; with pictures by Helen Stone. Lippincott, 1945. 62p. $3.25. (I)

Princess Esmeralda had everything—except beauty. When Dame Goodwit took her to live with her five amiable daughters, the princess lost her bad disposition and became beautiful.

2485 McGraw, Eloise Jarvis. The Golden Goblet. Coward-McCann, 1961. 248p. $3.95. (I–U)

Though Ranofer dreams of being a goldsmith, he is apprenticed as a stonecutter to his cruel half brother. When he proves that his brother is a tomb robber, Ranofer is free to follow his dream. Exciting story, vivid characterization, and excellent recreation of ancient Egypt.

2486 McGraw, Eloise Jarvis. Mara: Daughter of the Nile. Coward-McCann, 1953. 279p. $3.95. (I–U)

When the throne of Egypt was being contested by Queen Hatshepsut and her half brother, Mara the slave girl plays an important part in the outcome. A romantic story of action and intrigue with excellent period atmosphere.

2487 McGraw, Eloise Jarvis. Moccasin Trail. Coward-McCann, 1952. 247p. $3.75. (I–U)

Left for dead after a grizzly's attack, ten-year-old Jim Keath is found and adopted by Crow Indians. After six years of tribal life, a mysterious letter enables him to rejoin his own family. Graphic portrayal of Indian life and penetrating insight into Jim's conflicting loyalties raise this above the level of many adventure stories.

2488 MacGregor, Ellen. Miss Pickerell and the Geiger Counter; illus. by Paul Galdone. McGraw-Hill, 1953. 123p. $2.95; lib. ed. $2.96 net. (I)

Miss Pickerell is a spunky spinster whose adventures are a nice blend of scientific fact and hilarious nonsense. In this story she starts out to the circus with her cow and

her nephew, but before she arrives she has a brush with a steamboat captain, a red-headed sheriff, and an atomic scientist—and discovers an unsuspected source of uranium.

2489 MacGregor, Ellen. Miss Pickerell Goes to Mars; illus. by Paul Galdone. McGraw-Hill, 1951. 128p. $2.50; lib. ed. $2.63 net. (I)

The salty Miss Pickerell, transported to Mars on a rocket ship, proves herself equal to the emergency.

2490 Machetanz, Frederick. Panuck: Eskimo Sled Dog; illus. by the author. Scribner, 1939. 94p. $3.12 net. (I)

Panuck, the lead dog in an Alaskan Eskimo boy's team, brings his master safely home in a raging blizzard. The training of sled dogs and life among the Eskimos are interestingly pictured in a simple story and realistic pictures. (R4–5)

2491 McKellar, William. Wee Joseph; pictures by Ezra Jack Keats. McGraw-Hill, 1957. 76p. $2.95; lib. ed. $2.96 net. (I)

Davie's father considered Wee Joseph, so named because of his small size and coat of many colors, a worthless dog in a poor family. How a miracle saved Joseph, and how he proved that he was worth saving, make a satisfying story and give a good picture of life in a Scottish family.

2492 McLean, Allan Campbell. Master of Morgana. Harcourt, 1959. 222p. $3. (I–U)

The Isle of Skye is the setting for this fast-paced story of smuggling and salmon fishing. Two brothers, introduced in *Storm over Skye,* below, are in dire peril as they defy local superstition to solve a mystery.

2493 McLean, Allan Campbell. Storm over Skye; illus. by Shirley Hughes. Harcourt, 1957. 256p. $3.50. (I–U)

Action-packed and suspenseful tale of mystery and murder on the Isle of Skye, in which two brothers track down sheep stealers.

2494 McMeekin, Isabel McLennan. Journey Cake; illus. by Nicholas Panesis. Messner, 1942. 231p. $3.50. (I–U)

In the 1790's, Juba, a free colored woman, takes six motherless children over the Wilderness Road to rejoin their father in Kentucky.

2495 MacPherson, Margaret. The Rough Road; illus. by Douglas Hall. Harcourt, 1965. 223p. $3.50. (U)

Jim Smith lives with harsh foster parents on the Isle of Skye and despairs of escaping until a fortunate circumstance opens the way. A convincing story of courage and endurance.

2496 McSwigan, Marie. All Aboard for Freedom; illus. by E. Harper Johnson. Dutton, 1954. 249p. $3.95. (I–U)

An exciting story, based on fact, of how a group of liberty-loving Czechoslovakians escaped by train into the United States zone of Germany in 1951.

2497 McSwigan, Marie. Snow Treasure; illus. by Mary Reardon. Dutton, 1942. 179p. $3.75; lib. ed. $3.71 net. (I)

Under the direction of their parents, a group of Norwegian children take gold out of Occupied Norway by fastening it under their sleds and coasting through the German lines. A dramatic account of an actual happening in World War II.

2498 Martin, Patricia Miles. The Greedy One; illus. by Kazue Mizumura. Rand McNally, 1964. 64p. $3.50; lib. ed. $3.08 net. (P–I)

In this interesting introduction to Japanese family life and customs, Kenji's pet cormorant gobbles up the fish prepared for the traditional Boys' Day festival.

2499 Mason, Miriam E. Caroline and Her Kettle Named Maud; with illus. by Kathleen Voute. Macmillan, 1951. 134p. $3.50. (I)

Seven-year-old Caroline found the teakettle which she did not want and the cow which she hated very useful in the family's new home in the wilds of Michigan. Simple story and large print, suitable for early readers. (R3–4)

2500 Mayne, William. Earthfasts. Dutton, 1967. 154p. $3.50; lib. ed. $3.46 net. (I–U)

In an eerie tale of the supernatural, an eighteenth-century English drummer boy returns to earth carrying a candle which causes the past to become confused with the present and sets off a series of fantastic events involving King Arthur, a boggart, and other legendary characters. For the imaginative reader with sufficient background to appreciate the historical allusions.

2501 Mayne, William. A Grass Rope; illus. by Lynton Lamb. Dutton, 1962. 166p. $3.50. (I)

Four children living in the wild Yorkshire hills solve the mystery of a buried treasure and a unicorn. Mary, the youngest, still believes the old legends and weaves a grass rope to lead the unicorn home. For the special reader.

2502 Meader, Stephen W. Boy with a Pack; illus. by Edward Shenton. Harcourt, 1939. 297p. $3.50. (I–U)

Bill Crawford, 17, sets out from New Hampshire in 1837 to peddle "Yankee notions" throughout Vermont, New York, Pennsylvania, and Ohio.

2503 Meader, Stephen W. Red Horse Hill; illus. by Lee Townsend. Harcourt, 1930. 244p. $3.50. (I–U)

Especially for boys is this story of horses and amateur horse racing on a Vermont farm, in which Bud Martin wins a race, finds an old will, and plans his future.

2504 Meader, Stephen W. Whaler 'round the Horn; illus. by Edward Shenton. Harcourt, 1950. 244p. $3.50. (I–U)

Rodney Glenn ships on a whaler and sails around Cape Horn to Honolulu, where he is shipwrecked and cast up on an island inhabited only by a Hawaiian boy. A thrilling sea story with much information about whaling and life in Hawaii. There is a mild romance at the end.

2505 Meadowcroft, Enid La Monte. By Secret Railway; illus. by Henry C. Pitz. Crowell, 1948. 275p. $4.50. (I–U)

Jim Clayton, a free Negro boy, helps to rescue David Morgan's young brother from drowning in Lake Michigan. When Jim is kidnapped and sold to a slaveowner, David helps him escape and make his way back to Chicago by the Underground Railroad.

2506 Means, Florence Crannell. The Moved-outers; illus. by Helen Blair. Houghton, 1945. 154p. $3.25. (I–U)

A sympathetic story of a relocated Japanese-American family after Pearl Harbor.

2507 Medearis, Mary. Big Doc's Girl; with a foreword by Maureen Daly. Lippincott, 1950. 191p. $3.95. (U)

An Arkansas country doctor and his daughter are the central characters in an appealing story for older girls.

2508 Meigs, Cornelia. The Covered Bridge; illus. by Marguerite de Angeli. Macmillan, 1936. 145p. lib. ed. $4.24 net. (I)

In 1788 Connie spent the winter on a Vermont farm where she rescued the neighbor's sheep, helped to save a covered bridge from a flood, and met Ethan Allen.

2509 Menotti, Gian-Carlo. Amahl and the Night Visitors; this narrative adaptation by Frances Frost preserves the exact dialog of the opera; illus. by Roger Duvoisin. McGraw-Hill, 1952. 86p. $3.75; lib. ed. $3.26 net. (I–U)

This story of the crippled shepherd boy who entertained the Wise Men on their way to Bethlehem is excellent for reading aloud in preparation for the Christmas broadcast of the opera.

2510 Merrill, Jean. The Pushcart War; with illus. by Ronni Solbert. W. R. Scott, 1964. 222p. $3.95. (I–U)

When an organization of truckers, in 1976, attempts to control the streets of New York, the pushcart peddlers band together and defeat the plan. A humorous satire on modern city life, in which the reader's sympathies are with the little man.

2511 Miers, Earl Schenck. Pirate Chase; illus. by Peter Burchard. Holt, 1965. 129p. $3.50; lib. ed. $3.27 net. (I–U)

Shanghaied by a villainous pirate crew and forced to sail aboard their ship, 15-year-old Tim Baillie of Williamsburg escapes in time to join Lieutenant Maynard's expedition against Blackbeard.

2512 Miles, Miska. Fox and the Fire; illus. by John Schoenherr. Little, 1966. 40p. $3.50; lib. ed. $3.27 net. (P–I)

The terror of small animals when their world is on fire is graphically pictured in text and illustrations.

2513 Milhous, Katherine. The Egg Tree; story and pictures by Katherine Milhous. Scribner, 1950. unp. $3.25; lib. ed. $3.12 net. (P–I)

A group of children paint eggs in lovely Pennsylvania-Dutch designs and make an egg tree. For reading aloud at Easter or to inspire art work.

2514 Milne, A. A. The House at Pooh Corner; with decorations by Ernest H. Shepard. Dutton, 1961. 180p. $3.50; lib. ed. $3.46 net. (P–I)

A sequel to *Winnie-the-Pooh,* below, in which Christopher Robin and his toy friends continue their diverting adventures. For the story hour.

2515 Milne, A. A. Winnie-the-Pooh; with decorations by Ernest H. Shepard. Dutton, 1961. 161p. $3.50; lib. ed. $3.46 net. (P–I)

To Christopher Robin his toys are real people who talk and play with him in his games of make-believe. Pooh Bear, Piglet, Kanga and her baby Roo, Tigger, and the gloomy donkey, Eyore, are as individual as Christopher Robin himself.

2516 Mirsky, Reba Paeff. Thirty-One Brothers and Sisters; illus. by W. T. Mars. Follett, 1952. 190p. $3.95; lib. ed. $4.17 net. (I–U)

Ten-year-old Nomusa, one of 31 children of the six wives of a Zulu chief, proves that girls can be as brave as boys. An authentic picture of Zulu home life and folkways.

2517 Montgomery, Rutherford. Carcajou; illus. by L. D. Cram. Caxton, 1936. 263p. $3.50. (I–U)

The villain of this story of the northern wilderness is Carcajou, a wolverine, hated and feared by all in a world where wild animals, Indians, and white trappers compete for a livelihood.

2518 Montgomery, Rutherford. Kildee House; illus. by Barbara Cooney. Doubleday, 1949. 209p. $3.50. (I–U)

Jerome Kildee, who built a house on the edge of the forest in order to be alone, soon found that he had more company than ever: raccoons, skunks, and other woodland creatures liked his house better than their own and moved in to stay.

2519 Moore, Lilian. The Snake That Went to School; illus. by Mary Stevens. Random, 1957. 99p. $1.95; lib. ed. $2.29 net. (P–I)

When Hank's mother refused to let him keep a hog-nosed snake at home, he gave it to the science museum at school, where it created some very funny situations.

2520 Morey, Walt. Gentle Ben; illus. by John Schoenherr. Dutton, 1965. 191p. $3.95. (I–U)

The setting is Alaska before statehood, and the chief characters are a cruelly treated captive brown bear and the 13-year-old boy who befriends him. The boy's love for Ben and his determination to save him when the townspeople decide he should be killed make a memorable story.

2521 Mühlenweg, Fritz. Big Tiger and Christian; illus. by Rafaello Busoni. Pantheon, 1952. 592p. lib. ed. $4.99 net. (U)

A long, richly detailed story of a Chinese boy and his white friend who travel across the Gobi Desert on a dangerous mission during China's civil wars of the 1920's. In this engrossing adventure story, teeming with exotic characters and bizarre events, each chapter is a complete episode, suitable for reading aloud or for piecemeal reading by pupils discouraged by the length of the entire book.

2522 Murphy, Robert. The Pond; illus. by Teco Slagboom. Dutton, 1964. 254p. $4.95. (U)

The time is 1917 and the place is a backwoods hunting camp where a Richmond, Virginia, boy spends his holidays. Here, under the guidance of a wise old caretaker, Joey solves some of the problems of growing up and experiences the satisfaction of observing nature rather than destroying it. A keen appreciation of wildlife and respect for people in all walks of life are reflected in a fine nature story for mature readers.

2523 Nesbit, E. The New Treasure Seekers; illus. by C. W. Hodges. Coward-McCann, 1948. 335p. $3.50. (I)

The six irrepressible Bastable children continue their adventures, begun in *The Treasure Seekers,* in their uncle's English country mansion. Good print and open-page design make this edition especially suitable for independent reading in the middle grades.

2524 Neville, Emily Cheney. Berries Goodman. Harper, 1965. 178p. $3.50; lib. ed. $3.27 net. (I–U)

Berries Goodman, nine, meets anti-Semitism for the first time when his family moves from a New York City apartment to the suburbs. Humor, good characterization, and low-keyed style enrich this handling of a serious problem.

2525 Neville, Emily. It's Like This, Cat; pictures by Emil Weiss. Harper, 1963. 180p. $3.95; lib. ed. $3.79 net. (I–U)

Dave's account of his fourteenth year gives a good picture of his parents, his New York City friends and neighbors, and his pet cat. With humor and insight he describes his growing appreciation of his father, his friendship with a troubled boy, and his awakening interest in girls.

2526 Newell, Hope. A Cap for Mary Ellis. Harper, 1953. 200p. $3.50; lib. ed. $3.27 net. (I–U)

As the only Negroes in the nursing school, Mary Ellis and her friend were determined to make good. Routines of their training and problems of adjustment are realistically presented.

2527 Nordstrom, Ursula. The Secret Language; pictures by Mary Chalmers. Harper, 1960. 167p. $2.95; lib. ed. $2.92 net. (I)

A gently humorous story of two eight-year-olds at boarding school, where they become best friends and communicate through a secret language.

2528 Norton, Andre. Star Rangers. Harcourt, 1953. 280p. $3.25. (U)

In the year 8054, the patrol ship "Starfire" crash lands on an unknown planet from which there is no hope of rescue. The crew's struggle for survival makes a dramatic story with a surprise ending.

2529 Norton, Andre. Steel Magic; illus. by Robin Jacques. World, 1965. 155p. $3.50; lib. ed. $3.41 net. (I–U)

Three children go through a door in a mysterious castle into the world of King Arthur, Merlin, and Huon of the Horn. In order to return to their own world, each must perform a feat of courage to redeem Arthur's sword, Huon's horn, and Merlin's magic ring.

2530 Norton, Mary. The Borrowers; illus. by Beth and Joe Krush. Harcourt, 1953. 180p. $3.25. (I)

In a miniature world beneath the floor of an old English country house live the Borrowers, tiny people who "borrow" what they need from "human beans." A delightfully convincing fantasy.

2531 Norton, Mary. The Borrowers Afield; illus. by Beth and Joe Krush. Harcourt, 1955. 215p. $3.25. (I)

When danger threatens, the Borrowers escape from their home in the big house and take up life in a boot discarded in a field.

2532 O'Brien, Jack. Silver Chief: Dog of the North; illus. by Kurt Wiese. Winston, 1933. 218p. $3.50; lib. ed. $3.27 net. (I–U)

Jim Thorne of the Canadian Mounted Police and his faithful husky track their man through the wilds of Northwest Canada.

2533 O'Dell, Scott. The Black Pearl; illus. by Milton Johnson. Houghton, 1967. 140p. $3.25. (I–U)

The natives of La Paz in Baja California believed in the malevolent giant ray, Manta Diablo, who brought disaster to those who angered him. When 16-year-old Ramón Salazar dives for pearls outside the Manta's cave and brings up a huge black pearl, he starts a chain of events fraught with danger from the Manta and from human enemies. A dramatic, economically recounted adventure story with a vividly recreated background.

2534 O'Dell, Scott. Island of the Blue Dolphins. Houghton, 1960. 184p. $3.50. (I–U)

On the bleak island of San Nicolas, off the coast of California, an Indian girl spent 18 years without human companionship. A moving story of courage and resourcefulness, based on historical fact.

2535 O'Dell, Scott. The King's Fifth; decorations and maps by Samuel Bryant. Houghton, 1966. 264p. $3.95. (U)

The disastrous Spanish expedition to the Seven Cities of Cíbolo is brought to life in this story recounted by Estéban de Sandoval, a survivor of the party languishing in a Spanish prison for allegedly withholding the King's Fifth of the treasure. A long, involved story requiring a good background in history for full appreciation.

2536 O'Hara, Mary. My Friend Flicka. Lippincott, 1941. 253p. $4.50. (I–U)

Beautiful descriptions of Wyoming mountains and plains, realistic details of ranch life, and perceptive treatment of family conflicts mark this story of a young boy's love for his colt.

2537 Ormondroyd, Edward. Time at the Top; illus. by Peggie Bach. Parnassus, 1963. 176p. $3.50. (I)

Susan Shaw rides the apartment elevator into another time and place, where she finds two nineteenth-century children in need of her help.

2538 Osborne, Chester G. The First Bow and Arrow; illus. by Richard N. Osborne. Follett, 1961. 87p. lib. ed. $3.12 net. (I)

Great Bear invents the bow and arrow to replace the clubs and spears used by his fellow cave men to hunt food.

2539 Otis, James. Toby Tyler; or, Ten Weeks with a Circus; illus. by Louis S. Glanzman; introd. by May Lamberton Becker. World, 1947. 239p. $2.95; lib. ed. $2.28 net. (I)

An attractive edition of the story of a ten-year-old who runs away to join the circus and after many hardships runs away again —to go back home.

2540 Ottley, Reginald. Boy Alone; illus. by Clyde Pearson. Harcourt, 1966. 191p. $3.50. (I–U)

On an isolated cattle ranch in Australia a nameless boy works as a "wood and water joey." His aloneness, his longing for a dog to call his own, and his relationships with other workers on the ranch are understandingly depicted.

2541 Pearce, A. Philippa. The Minnow Leads to Treasure; illus. by Edward Ardizzone. World, 1955. 253p. $3.50. (I–U)

In their canoe, the "Minnow," two English boys hunt for treasure buried four hundred years ago.

2542 Pearce, A. Philippa. Tom's Midnight Garden; illus. by Susan Einzig. Lippincott, 1959. 229p. $4.25. (I–U)

Only at night does the lovely English garden which Tom discovers exist. There he meets the girl Hatty, who in the present is an old woman to whose stories Tom has listened.

2543 Pedersen, Elsa. Alaska Harvest; illus. by Kurt Werth. Abingdon, 1960. 192p. $3. (I–U)

Through the experiences of a teen-age girl living on an Alaskan fishing boat with her father and brother, the reader gets a vivid picture of life among the fishermen of Cook's Inlet.

2544 Petry, Ann. Tituba of Salem Village. Crowell, 1964. 254p. $4.50. (U)

The Salem witch trials of 1692 form the background of the story of Tituba, a Negro slave from Barbados, accused of bewitching several young girls. The superstition and hysteria of the village and the chief characters in the trial are presented in a quietly dramatic story, based on historical fact.

2545 Peyton, K. M. The Maplin Bird; illus. by Victor G. Ambrus. World, 1963. 237p. $3.75. (U)

Two English teen-agers inadvertently become involved with a gang of smugglers in a fast-paced, adventure-love story of the nineteenth century.

2546 Peyton, K. M. Sea Fever; illus. by Victor G. Ambrus. World, 1963. 240p. $3.50. (U)

After his father is drowned, 15-year-old Matt Pullen must earn money to buy a fishing boat, which he needs to earn a living for a family of five. His adventures in doing so make a rousing good sea yarn, set on the coast of England about a hundred years ago.

2547 Phipson, Joan. The Family Conspiracy; illus. by Margaret Horder. Harcourt, 1964. 224p. $3.50. (I–U)

The Barkers, living on a lonely sheep ranch in Australia, are faced with two disasters: a drought which threatens their flocks and a serious illness for Mrs. Barker. The Barker children conspire to earn money for their mother's operation, in ways both touching and funny.

2548 Poe, Edgar Allan. The Purloined Letter (and) The Murders in the Rue Morgue; illus. by Rick Schreiter. Watts, 1966. 85p. $2.65. (U)

Monsieur Dupin solves two baffling mysteries in these famous stories.

2549 Polland, Madeleine. Beorn the Proud; illus. by William Stobbs. Holt, 1962. 175p. lib. ed. $3.27 net. (I–U)

Beorn, son of a Viking king, captures a young Christian girl in Ireland and takes her back to Denmark, where her gentle nature softens his harsh, arrogant spirit and leads him to Christianity. The contrast between Christian and pagan philosophies is brought out in an exciting period story.

2550 Polland, Madeleine. The Queen's Blessing; illus. by Betty Fraser. Holt, 1964. 176p. $3.50; lib. ed. $3.27 net. (I–U)

Embittered by Scottish soldiers' destruction of her Northumbrian homeland, 11-year-old Merca vows eternal hatred for King Malcolm, but after chance brings her and her little brother under the protection

of Malcolm's Queen Margaret, she learns that love is stronger than hatred.

2551 Pope, Elizabeth Marie. The Sherwood Ring; illus. by Evaline Ness. Houghton, 1958. 266p. $3.75. (U)

Ancestral ghosts appear to Peggy Grahame in Orange County, New York, and tell her stories which help to unravel a mystery involving the forebears of her friend, Pat Thorne. A light love story which moves from the present to Revolutionary times and back again.

2552 Pyle, Howard. Howard Pyle's Book of Pirates; Fiction, Fact & Fancy Concerning the Buccaneers & Marooners of the Spanish Main; from the writing and pictures of Howard Pyle; comp. by Merle Johnson. Harper, 1921. 208p. $3.95; lib. ed. $3.79 net. (I–U)

Seven rousing tales of sea rovers, illustrated with spirited pictures, many in color.

2553 Pyle, Howard. Otto of the Silver Hand; written and illus. by Howard Pyle. rev. ed. Scribner, 1903. 136p. lib. ed. $3.27 net. (I–U)

Otto, son of a robber baron in medieval Germany, spends his childhood in a monastery and returns in later life to his father's castle, where he is captured by enemies and held prisoner. His silver hand, a substitute for a hand struck off by his father's enemy, is the symbol of his motto: "Better a hand of silver than a hand of iron." Illustrations show medieval costumes, castles, and weapons in meticulous detail.

2554 Pyle, Howard. The Wonder Clock; or, Four and Twenty Marvelous Tales, Being One for Each Hour of the Day; written and illus. by Howard Pyle; embellished with verses by Katharine Pyle. Harper, 1915. 318p. $4.50; lib. ed. $4.11 net. (I–U)

Witty and wise tales told by the puppet figures of an old clock found in Time's garret.

2555 Rankin, Louise. Daughter of the Mountains; illus. by Kurt Wiese. Viking, 1948. 191p. $3.25; lib. ed. $3.19 net. (I–U)

A small Tibetan girl makes an incredible journey from her mountain home to Calcutta in search of her dog. Scenes along the way and in a Buddhist monastery are beautifully described without detracting from the drama and suspense of the story.

2556 Ransome, Arthur. Swallows and Amazons; illus. by Helene Carter. Lippincott, 1958. 343p. $5.95. (I–U)

Two groups of independent English children, the Swallows and the Amazons, spend the summer on an island: sailing, hunting for treasure, and becoming involved in a mystery. A long, imaginative story for good readers.

2557 Rawlings, Marjorie Kinnan. The Yearling; with illus. by N. C. Wyeth. Scribner, 1961. 428p. $6. (I–U)

Jody Baxter and his pet fawn, Flag, roam the scrub-pine forests of Florida until Flag's destruction of crops forces the boy to make a man's decision. Descriptions of the place, the people, and, most of all, the pangs of a boy's maturing make this a memorable story. Illustrations in luminous color add drama and atmosphere.

2558 Reese, John. Big Mutt; illus. by Rod Ruth. Westminster, 1952. 190p. $3.25. (I–U)

Abandoned on the edge of the North Dakota Badlands, a big dog killed sheep for food and became a fugitive from the sheepherders of the region. When young Dwight Jerome rescues and trains him, he proves his worth to the herders.

2559 Renick, James, and **Renick, Marion.** Steady: A Baseball Story; illus. by Frederick Machetanz. Scribner, 1942. 137p. lib. ed. $2.97 net. (P–I)

Written especially for the younger baseball fan, *Steady* combines a good story with facts about training and hints on how to become a good player. (R3–4)

2560 Renick, Marion. Boy at Bat; illus. by Paul Galdone. Scribner, 1961. 116p. lib. ed. $3.12 net. (P–I)

A small boy and his dog join in a neighborhood baseball game, with amusing results. (R3–4)

2561 Renick, Marion. Nicky's Football Team; illus. by Marian Honigman. Scribner, 1951. 115p. lib. ed. $2.76 net. (P–I)

Nicky earns money for a football, organizes a team, helps the players get helmets, and sees his team win the first game. (R3–4)

2562 Renick, Marion. Pete's Home Run; illus. by Pru Herrick. Scribner, 1952. 117p. lib. ed. $2.76 net. (P–I)

Pete finds that there is no easy road to being a baseball star and decides to work hard to earn a place on the team. Good social relationships; useful with retarded readers. (R3–4)

2563 Reynolds, Barbara. Pepper; illus. by Barbara Cooney. Scribner, 1952. 169p. $3.25. (I)

Though Pepper, a raccoon adopted by Alec and his family, gets into much amusing mischief, he provides inspiration for a town project.

2564 Rhijn, Aleid van. The Tide in the Attic; tr. by A. J. Pomerans; illus. by Marjorie Gill. Criterion, 1961. 126p. $3. (I–U)

Tells in story form how a Dutch farm family survived the great flood of 1953. The courage and cooperation of the family and their servants, marooned on the roof until rescued by a helicopter, are an inspiring example of human fortitude.

2565 Rich, Louise Dickinson. Mindy. Lippincott, 1959. 188p. $3.50. (U)

Mindy was not sure that she wanted to marry Caspar, even though he had named his new boat for her—sure sign of an engagement among the lobster fishermen of her little Maine village. A summer of family crises forces Mindy to analyze her feelings and to develop a sounder set of values.

2566 Richter, Conrad. The Light in the Forest. Knopf, 1953. 179p. $4.95; lib. ed. $3.99 net. (U)

True Son, stolen in childhood and brought up by the Delaware Indians, is suddenly returned to his white family. He resents his loss of freedom, hates the confinement of living in a house, and finally returns to the Delawares, only to find when the test comes that the ties of blood are stronger than he had thought. A fine picture of outdoor life and a moving story of conflicting loyalties.

2567 Ritchie, Barbara. To Catch a Mongoose; illus. by Earl Thollander; the French translation by Marie Byrne. Parnassus, 1964. 61p. $3.95. (I)

A bilingual book (English-French) with an exotic setting—the Caribbean island of Martinique. Two children catch a mongoose to sell, but become so fond of it that they keep it for a pet. Illustrations show colorful scenes of the island.

2568 **Robertson, Keith.** Henry Reed, Inc. Illus. by Robert McCloskey. Viking, 1958. 239p. $3.50; lib. ed. $3.37 net. (I–U)

Henry Reed, on vacation from the American School in Naples, keeps a record of his research into the American free-enterprise system, to be used as a school report on his return. With a neighbor, Midge Glass, he starts a business in pure and applied research, which results in some very free and wildly enterprising experiences, all recorded deadpan in his journal. Very funny and original escapades.

2569 **Robertson, Keith.** Henry Reed's Baby-sitting Service; illus. by Robert McCloskey. Viking, 1966. 204p. $3.50; lib. ed. $3.37 net. (I–U)

Again partners in free enterprise, Henry and Midge establish a baby-sitting service, in which they solve their many problems with ingenuity and finesse.

2570 **Robertson, Keith.** Henry Reed's Journey; illus. by Robert McCloskey. Viking, 1963. 220p. $3.25; lib. ed. $3.19 net. (I–U)

Henry takes a trip from California to New Jersey with Midge and her family, faithfully recording his unorthodox experiences along the way.

2571 **Robinson, Tom.** Trigger John's Son; illus. by Robert McCloskey. Viking, 1949. 284p. $3.50; lib. ed. $3.37 net. (I–U)

Tom, a lively orphan adopted by a childless couple, joins the Goosetown Gang and engineers some hilarious escapades.

2572 **Robinson, Veronica.** David in Silence; illus. by Victor Ambrus. Lippincott, 1965. 126p. $3.25. (I)

When 12-year-old David, deaf since birth, moves to a new town, only one of the neighborhood children tries to understand and help him. David's problems of adjustment and the varied reactions of the children toward his handicap are treated with understanding in an unsentimental story.

2573 **Rounds, Glen.** The Blind Colt; written and illus. by Glen Rounds. Holiday, 1960. unp. $3.50. (I)

The South Dakota Badlands is the setting for this story of a blind wild colt, tamed and trained by a ten-year-old boy.

2574 **Rugh, Belle Dorman.** Crystal Mountain; illus. by Ernest H. Shepard. Houghton, 1955. 208p. $3.25. (I)

The mystery of an abandoned house and a tree-climbing governess is solved by four American boys and an English girl living near Beirut in Lebanon. Good characterization in an interesting story with implications for international understanding.

2575 **Ruskin, John.** The King of the Golden River; or, The Black Brothers; illus. by Charles Stewart. Watts, 1967. 60p. $2.95. (I)

The complete story of Gluck and his two wicked brothers in an attractive edition.

2576 **Rutgers van der Loeff, Anna.** Avalanche! Illus. by Gustav Schrotter. Morrow, 1958. 219p. $3.50. (I–U)

A tense, dramatic story of a Swiss boy and a group of war orphans caught in an avalanche.

2577 **Salten, Felix.** Bambi; foreword by John Galsworthy. Grosset, 1929. 293p. $1.95; lib. ed. $2.69 net. (I)

The poetic story of a fawn's growing up in an Austrian forest, with a background bringing to life the wilderness and its inhabitants.

2578 **Sandoz, Mari.** The Horsecatcher. Westminster, 1957. 192p. $3.25. (U)

Daily life among the Cheyenne Indians is sympathetically presented in this story of Elk, a peace-loving boy who proves that catching and training wild horses are as important to his tribe as taking scalps.

2579 **Sauer, Julia L.** Fog Magic. Viking, 1943. 107p. $3.25; lib. ed. $3.19 net. (I)

For Greta, the fog blowing in from the sea around Nova Scotia had the power to transport her to a secret village of long ago. A skillful blending of past and present, reality and magic.

2580 **Sauer, Julia.** The Light at Tern Rock; illus. by Georges Schreiber. Viking, 1951. 62p. $3; lib. ed. $2.96 net. (I)

Ronnie, stranded with his aunt in a lighthouse at Christmas time, learns the true meaning of the season.

2581 **Sawyer, Ruth.** The Enchanted Schoolhouse; illus. by Hugh Troy. Viking, 1956. 128p. $3.50; lib. ed. $3.37 net. (I)

An Irish lad brings a leprechaun to

Maine and uses his magic to persuade the town taxpayers to build a new schoolhouse.

2582 Sawyer, Ruth. The Long Christmas; illus. by Valenti Angelo. Viking, 1941. 200p. $4.50; lib. ed. $4.13 net. (I–U)
Old tales, legends, carols, and rhymes express the spirit of Christmas.

2583 Sawyer, Ruth. Maggie Rose: Her Birthday Christmas; pictures by Maurice Sendak. Harper, 1952. 151p. $3.25; lib. ed. $3.11 net. (I)
A sentimental story of a little Maine girl who sells berries to provide a real Christmas celebration for her shiftless family— and for her own Christmas birthday.

2584 Sawyer, Ruth. Roller Skates; illus. by Valenti Angelo. Viking, 1936. 186p. $4; lib. ed. $3.77 net. (I–U)
Lucinda Wyman, ten, skates about New York City in the 1890's, making friends and having adventures.

2585 Schaefer, Jack. Old Ramon; illus. by Harold West. Houghton, 1960. 102p. $2.50. (U)
A young boy sent to learn sheepherding from Old Ramon learns much about life as well. The sensitive relationships between young and old, the philosophy of a wise old man, and the nuances of writing style are best appreciated when read aloud.

2586 Schlein, Miriam. The Snake in the Car Pool. Abelard-Schuman, 1963. 107p. $2.50; lib. ed. $2.52 net. (P–I)
Uproarious situations develop when a boy starts to school with his pet snake.

2587 Scholz, Jackson. Batter Up. Morrow, 1946. 212p. $3.50. (I–U)
Marty Shane learns the hard way what it takes to make a big-league team. Good characterization and plenty of action.

2588 Sechrist, Elizabeth Hough, comp. 13 Ghostly Yarns; newly illus. rev. ed. Macrae, 1963. 211p. $4.25. (I–U)
Ghost stories from all over the world, especially useful for storytelling or reading aloud.

2589 Selden, George. The Cricket in Times Square; illus. by Garth Williams. Farrar, 1960. 151p. $3.50. (I)
Chester, a musical cricket brought by chance from the country to a New York

City newsstand, entertains a mouse, a cat, and a boy with his concerts. A humorous and spontaneous fantasy, excellent for reading aloud.

2590 Seredy, Kate. The Good Master; written and illus. by Kate Seredy. Viking, 1935. 210p. $4; lib. ed. $3.77 net. (I)
Hungarian farm life, fairs, festivals, and folklore are woven into this story of a farm boy and his tomboy cousin Kate from Budapest. Under the wise guidance of Jancsi's father, the Good Master, Kate becomes a gentler, kinder little girl.

2591 Seredy, Kate. The White Stag; written and illus. by Kate Seredy. Viking, 1937. 94p. $3; lib. ed. $2.96 net. (I–U)
Striking illustrations interpret this hero tale of the legendary founding of Hungary, when a white stag and a red eagle led the people to their promised land.

2592 Serraillier, Ian. The Silver Sword; illus. by C. Walter Hodges. Phillips, 1959. 187p. $4.95. (I–U)
Polish refugee children of World War II endure hardships and danger as they trudge from Warsaw to Switzerland to join their parents.

2593 Sharp, Margery. Miss Bianca; with illus. by Garth Williams. Little, 1962. 152p. $4.50. (I)
Miss Bianca is a charming and sophisticated white mouse who, with her sturdy ally, Bernard, leads the Mouse Prisoners' Aid Society to the rescue of a little girl held prisoner by a wicked Grand Duchess. Well-sustained fantasy with mouse personalities engagingly depicted in story and illustrations. Perfect for reading aloud. A sequel to *The Rescuers,* below.

2594 Sharp, Margery. The Rescuers; with illus. by Garth Williams. Little, 1959. 149p. $4.50. (I)
The Mouse Prisoners' Aid Society hears through its elegant spy, Miss Bianca, of a Norwegian poet held captive in the Black Castle of a barbarous country. The heroic adventures of the party sent to rescue him are related and pictured with subtle humor, best brought out by being read aloud.

2595 Shemin, Margaretha. The Little Riders; illus. by Peter Spier. Coward-McCann, 1963. 60p. lib. ed. $2.86 net. (I)
The Little Riders are metal figures which

march around the steeple of a church in a small Dutch town to announce the hours. Johanna, a young American girl living in Holland during the German occupation, conspires with a lonely German officer to save the figures from being melted down for much-needed metal.

2596 Shotwell, Louisa R. Adam Bookout; illus. by W. T. Mars. Viking, 1967. 256p. $3.95; lib. ed. $3.77 net. (I)

With keen insight into the problems of present-day children, the author tells the story of an Oklahoma boy, orphaned by a plane crash and living in Brooklyn with cousins he scarcely knows. In his new home Adam finds friends of many races and nationalities, solves the mystery of a missing dog, and makes an important decision about his own future.

2597 Shotwell, Louisa R. Roosevelt Grady; illus. by Peter Burchard. World, 1963. 151p. $2.95; lib. ed. $2.88 net. (I)

The problems of the Negro migrant farm worker are sympathetically portrayed in this story of nine-year-old Roosevelt Grady, who longs for a place to "stay put" and to belong.

2598 Shura, Mary Francis. Shoe Full of Shamrock; illus. by N. M. Bodecker. Atheneum, 1965. 64p. $3.75; lib. ed. $3.79 net. (P–I)

Davie O'Sullivan meets a leprechaun in New York's Central Park and gets advice which makes his dearest wish come true. Made to order for St. Patrick's Day.

2599 Simon, Mina. Faces Looking Up; pictures by Howard Simon. Harper, 1960. 153p. $3.50; lib. ed. $3.27 net. (I)

Stories of school children in 12 different countries, bringing out the differences in buildings, curriculum, customs, and home backgrounds. Useful in social studies classes.

2600 Simon, Shirley. Best Friend; illus. by Reisie Lonette. Lothrop, 1964. 191p. $3.50; lib. ed. $3.35 net. (I)

When sixth-grader Jenny Jason is deserted by her best friend, she finds many other friends through her new interests and activities. Good values and wholesome relationships.

2601 Singer, Isaac Bashevis. The Fearsome Inn; tr. by the author and Elizabeth Shub; illus. by Nonny Hogrogian. Scribner, 1967. unp. $3.95; lib. ed. $3.63 net. (I)

A quick-witted student of magic saves himself, his two companions, and three girls, all held captive by a witch and her half-devil husband, by trapping the evil pair in a magic circle. The pervasive aura of evil in the story is enhanced by eerie illustrations.

2602 Slobodkin, Louis. The Space Ship under the Apple Tree. Macmillan, 1952. 114p. $4.50. (P–I)

Eddie, on vacation at his grandmother's farm, tracks what seems to be a falling star to the orchard, where he discovers a space ship and a little man from the planet Martinea. An entertaining blend of Boy Scout activities, pseudo science, and country fun.

2603 Snedeker, Caroline Dale. Theras and His Town; illus. by Dimitris Davis. Doubleday, 1961. 237p. $2.95. (I–U)

The contrast between the freedom- and beauty-loving Athenians and the warlike Spartans is brought out in the story of an Athenian boy taken against his will to Sparta and forced to live for a time in a boys' military camp.

2604 Snyder, Zilpha Keatley. Black and Blue Magic; drawings by Gene Holtan. Atheneum, 1966. 186p. $3.95; lib. ed. $3.81 net. (I)

Eleven-year-old Harry Houdini Marco, anticipating a dull vacation, meets a magician who gives him a lotion which grows wings and enables him to make secret nightly flights over San Francisco.

2605 Snyder, Zilpha Keatley. The Egypt Game; drawings by Alton Raible. Atheneum, 1967. 215p. $3.95; lib. ed. $3.81 net. (I)

Sent by her movie-star mother to live with her grandmother in a run-down section of a western city, April Hall relieves her unhappiness by joining with neighborhood children to set up a shrine to ancient Egyptian gods in an abandoned storage yard. Secret rites, mysterious characters, and a murder add excitement to a highly original story marked by natural relationships among children of several races.

2606 Snyder, Zilpha Keatley. Season of Ponies; drawings by Alton Raible. Atheneum, 1965. 216p. $3.25. (I)

A delicately wrought fantasy in which

the loneliness of a little girl is turned into delight by a flute-playing boy who takes her for moonlight rides on magic ponies.

2607 Sommerfelt, Aimée. The Road to Agra; illus. by Ulf Aas. Criterion, 1961. 191p. $3.50. (I)

Lalu takes his half-blind little sister on a 300-mile journey by foot from their village in India to a hospital in Agra. Present-day social conditions among the poor of India form the background for a moving story of courage and perseverance.

2608 Sorensen, Virginia. Miracles on Maple Hill; illus. by Beth and Joe Krush. Harcourt, 1956. 180p. $2.95. (I–U)

Ten-year-old Marly's father returns from the war broken in health and spirit. Hoping that country life will restore him, the family moves from the city to an old Pennsylvania farmhouse, where the miracles of nature and the kindness of neighbors bring back his interest in life.

2609 Sorensen, Virginia. Plain Girl; illus. by Charles Geer. Harcourt, 1955. 151p. $2.95. (I)

Forced by law to attend public school, a little Pennsylvania Amish girl begins to question the strict traditions of her people, but in the end appreciates her family and their religion more than ever.

2610 Southall, Ivan. Ash Road; illus. by Clem Seale. St. Martin's, 1966. 154p. $3.95. (I–U)

The lonely Australian outback is the setting for a dramatic story of a terrifying brush fire. The reader feels the mounting fear and tension of the threatened families as they struggle throughout a long day to avert disaster.

2611 Southall, Ivan. Hills End. St. Martin's, 1963. 174p. $3.75. (I–U)

Seven Australian children, returning to Hills End after exploring a cave, find the town devastated by a flash flood and deserted. Their successful efforts to fend for themselves under harrowing conditions are convincingly recounted.

2612 Speare, Elizabeth George. The Bronze Bow. Houghton, 1961. 255p. $3.50. (I–U)

A young Jewish boy swears vengeance against the Roman soldiers who have killed his father and wrecked his home, but under the influence of Jesus, learns to forgive his enemies. A moving and thought-provoking story, appropriate for discussion.

2613 Speare, Elizabeth George. The Witch of Blackbird Pond. Houghton, 1958. 249p. $3.50. (I–U)

Kit Tyler comes from her luxurious Barbados home to visit a Puritan family in colonial Connecticut. Rebelling against the bigotry of the times, Kit becomes friendly with an old woman thought to be a witch and sets off a terrifying witch hunt. Three romances within the story add appeal for older girls.

2614 Sperry, Armstrong. Call It Courage; illus. by the author. Macmillan, 1940. 95p. $3.50; lib. ed. $3.24 net. (I–U)

Because he fears the ocean, a Polynesian boy is scorned by his people and must redeem himself by an act of courage. His lone journey to a sacred island and the dangers he faces there earn him the name Mafatu, "Stout Heart." Dramatic illustrations add atmosphere and mystery.

2615 Sperry, Armstrong. Frozen Fire; illus. by the author. Doubleday, 1956. 192p. $3.50. (I–U)

Two American boys go on an expedition into the jungles of Brazil to search for the "frozen fire" of diamonds and the treasure of the Incas. Good background material for geography and history.

2616 Spykman, E. C. A Lemon and a Star. Harcourt, 1955. 214p. $3.50. (I–U)

In a country house in Virginia a father tries in a rather abstracted—and unsuccessful—way to keep his four motherless children in line. The children's unorthodox escapades are very funny and original.

2617 Spyri, Johanna. Heidi; illus. by Jessie Willcox Smith. Scribner, 1958. 380p. $5. (I)

The Alpine scenes shown in the illustrations make this an especially beautiful edition of a well-loved story.

2618 Steele, William O. The Lone Hunt; illus. by Paul Galdone. Harcourt, 1956. 176p. $2.95. (I–U)

Eleven-year-old Yancy is the sturdy hero of this tale of a buffalo hunt in the Cumberland Mountains of Tennessee in the 1800's. This and the following titles by Steele are brief, brisk stories of frontier life, especially recommended for older boys with limited reading skills.

2619 **Steele, William O.** The Perilous Road; illus. by Paul Galdone. Harcourt, 1958. 191p. $2.95. (I–U)

A young Tennessee boy, who hates Yankees and cannot understand how his brother can fight in the Union Army, eventually comes to understand that even a Union soldier can be "a good, decent man."

2620 **Steele, William O.** Wilderness Journey; illus. by Paul Galdone. Harcourt, 1953. 209p. $3.25. (I–U)

The story of Flan Taylor's exciting journey in 1782 over the Tennessee Wilderness Trail from the Holston River settlement to the French Salt Lick.

2621 **Steele, William O.** Winter Danger; illus. by Paul Galdone. Harcourt, 1954. 183p. $3. (I–U)

For most of his 11 years, Caje Amis had wandered the Tennessee forests with a father whom he did not understand; then he was left with a settled family to adjust to an entirely new way of life.

2622 **Stephens, Peter John.** Towappu: Puritan Renegade; drawings by William Moyers. Atheneum, 1966. 246p. $4.50; lib. ed. $4.13 net. (I–U)

Young Tommy Morris, adopted son of King Philip of the Algonquins, makes two perilous journeys to Plymouth Town to plead for peace between the Puritan colony and the Indians. Both sides of the conflict are presented in a thought-provoking story.

2623 **Sterling, Dorothy.** Mary Jane; illus. by Ernest Crichlow. Doubleday, 1959. 214p. $3.50. (I–U)

A straightforward treatment of school segregation in which Mary Jane enters a newly integrated junior high school in a Southern town, where she faces her problems with courage and discovers that prejudice is a two-way street.

2624 **Stevenson, Robert Louis.** Kidnapped; illus. by N. C. Wyeth. Scribner, 1913. 306p. $5. (I–U)

David Balfour's involvement with the supporters of Bonnie Prince Charlie is a rousing tale of adventure, made more colorful by the excellent illustrations of this edition.

2625 **Stevenson, Robert Louis.** Treasure Island; illus. by N. C. Wyeth. Scribner, 1911. 250p. $5. (I–U)

Jim Hawkins, Long John Silver, and Captain Flint search for buried treasure in this colorfully illustrated edition of the classic tale of piracy.

2626 **Stevenson, William.** The Bushbabies; illus. by Victor Ambrus. Houghton, 1965. 288p. $3.50. (I–U)

Just as the Rhodes family is about to leave Africa, 13-year-old Jackie goes back to dispose of her pet tarsier (bushbaby). Left behind when the ship sails, Jackie and an elderly African make a hazardous journey to return the bushbaby to the forest, all the while pursued by police who think that Jackie has been kidnapped. An unusual story of friendship between two people of different ages and races and a graphic picture of the African bush.

2627 **Stolz, Mary.** Good-by My Shadow. Harper, 1957. 208p. $3.95; lib. ed. $3.79 net. (U)

Barbara Perry, afflicted with growing pains and at odds with her family, comes through a difficult year with a better understanding of herself and a greater appreciation of her parents. Familiar problems, including the pangs of first love, give the book appeal for older girls.

2628 **Stolz, Mary.** The Noonday Friends. Harper, 1965. 182p. $3.95; lib. ed. $3.79 net. (I)

A realistic story of family relationships and of a girl's need for friendship. Because she must care for her little brother while her mother works, Franny Davis can see her best friend only at lunch hour. The embarrassment of having a free lunch pass and the uncertainties of life when her father is out of work are problems which Franny faces with courage and good sense.

2629 **Stolz, Mary.** A Wonderful, Terrible Time; pictures by Louis S. Glanzman. Harper, 1967. 182p. $3.95; lib. ed. $3.79 net. (I)

Two Negro girls get an unexpected opportunity to spend two weeks at summer camp. Their different reactions to the contrast between life in the streets of Brooklyn and that of the camp are sharply detailed in a discerning story.

2630 **Stong, Phil.** Honk, the Moose; pictures by Kurt Wiese. Dodd, 1935. 80p. $3.50; lib. ed. $3.23 net. (P–I)

When a starving moose decides to spend the winter in a livery stable, none of the officials of the little Minnesota town can dislodge him. A ludicrous situation made funnier by the salty characters involved and by humorous illustrations.

2631 Streatfeild, Noel. Ballet Shoes; illus. by Richard Floethe. Random, 1937. 294p. $2.95; lib. ed. $3.49 net. (I)
Life behind the scenes at the theater is depicted in the story of three little girls training at the Children's Academy of Dancing in London.

2632 Street, James. Good-bye, My Lady. Lippincott, 1954. 222p. $4.95. (I–U)
Depth of characterization and beauty of writing style are the special qualities of this dog story. Skeeter, living in the Mississippi swamp with his wise but shiftless uncle, finds a rare breed of dog, trains and loves it, and then must give it up.

2633 Stuart, Jesse. The Beatinest Boy; illus. by Robert Henneberger. McGraw-Hill, 1953. 110p. $2.75; lib. ed. $2.84 net. (I)
Davy lives with Grandma in her Kentucky mountain home and is very busy possum hunting, bee-tree cutting, and deciding on just the right Christmas present for Grandma.

2634 Stuart, Jesse. A Penny's Worth of Character; illus. by Robert Henneberger. McGraw-Hill, 1954. 61p. $3.25; lib. ed. $3.01 net. (I)
Shan learns the meaning of honesty when trusted with money.

2635 Sutcliff, Rosemary. Dawn Wind; illus. by Charles Keeping. Walck, 1962. 241p. $4.50. (U)
A wonderfully convincing re-creation of sixth-century Britain forms the background of this story of a boy who, after years of thralldom, earns his freedom and joins the forces fighting for a united country.

2636 Sutcliff, Rosemary. The Eagle of the Ninth; illus. by C. Walter Hodges. Walck, 1954. 255p. $4.50. (U)
A young Roman centurion clears his father's name and recovers the bronze eagle, the standard of the lost Ninth. An exciting historical novel faithfully depicting life in the Roman legions.

2637 Sutcliff, Rosemary. The Mark of the Horse Lord. Walck, 1965. 305p. $4.50. (U)

In second-century Scotland a gladiator wins his freedom and helps a deposed king to regain his throne. A memorable story for the mature reader.

2638 Tarry, Ellen, and **Ets, Marie Hall.** My Dog Rinty; illus. by Alexander and Alexandra Alland. Viking, 1946. unp. $3; lib. ed. $2.96 net. (P–I)
Excellent photographs of a Harlem neighborhood illustrate this story of a small Negro boy's efforts to save his mischievous dog from being sold.

2639 Taylor, Sydney. All-of-a-Kind Family; illus. by Helen John. Follett, 1951. 188p. $3.95; lib. ed. $4.17 net. (I)
A Jewish family of five girls, living on New York's Lower East Side just before the first World War, grow up in a happy home atmosphere of Jewish festivals, midnight snacks, and trips to the public library.

2640 Taylor, Sydney. More All-of-a-Kind Family; illus. by Mary Stevens. Follett, 1954. 159p. $3.95; lib. ed. $4.17 net. (I)
The five girls, now two years older and joined by a baby brother, continue their amusing adventures.

2641 Thurber, James. Many Moons; illus. by Louis Slobodkin. Harcourt, 1943. unp. $3.50; lib. ed. $3.50 net. (P–I)
After the king's wise men have failed, the court jester finds a way to get the moon in order to make the little Princess Lenore well again. The humorous, fairy-tale quality of the story is admirably captured in the illustrations.

2642 Titus, Eve. Basil of Baker Street; illus. by Paul Galdone. McGraw-Hill, 1958. 96p. $3.25; lib. ed. $3.01 net. (I)
Basil, the Sherlock Homes of the mouse world, solves a baffling mystery.

2643 Todd, Ruthven. Space Cat; illus. by Paul Galdone. Scribner, 1952. 69p. lib. ed. $2.76 net. (P–I)
Flyball was such a daring cat that his master bought him a space suit and took him on a trip to the moon. Delightful illustrations add to the humor of this story for the youngest science fiction fans. (R3–4)

2644 Tolkien, J. R. R. The Hobbitt; or, There and Back Again; illus. by the author. Houghton, 1938. 315p. $3.95. (I–U)
Though hobbits are small creatures who

love good food, a good home, and a peaceful life, the hobbit Bilbo Baggins goes on a dangerous journey to recover the ill-gotten gold of a wicked dragon. A classic fantasy recommended for reading aloud.

2645 Townsend, John Rowe. Good-bye to the Jungle. Lippincott, 1967. 184p. $3.75. (I–U)

Delinquent adults are the problem in this family which moves from the jungle of an English city slum to a new housing project. Since their parents' death Kevin and Sandra, 15 and 14, have been living with their shiftless uncle and his disreputable companion, Doris. The young people's efforts to hold the family together and to care for two younger cousins are complicated by new neighbors, new debts, and the same irresponsible adults. A vital story of real people, ending without pat solutions but with a note of hope for four courageous children.

2646 Travers, P. L. Mary Poppins; illus. by Mary Shepard. Harcourt, 1934. 206p. $3.50. (I)

When an astonishing nursemaid blew into the Banks family on an east wind, the children were delighted with the magical adventures she planned for them.

2647 Travers, P. L. Mary Poppins Comes Back; illus. by Mary Shepard. Harcourt, 1935. 268p. $3.50. (I)

After mysteriously disappearing from the Banks home, Mary Poppins returns on the end of a kite string, stays for a while, and then vanishes on a merry-go-round horse.

2648 Trease, Geoffrey. Escape to King Alfred. Vanguard, 1958. 251p. $3.95. (U)

A stirring historical novel of ninth-century Britain when only King Alfred of West Saxony held out against the invading Danes.

2649 Treece, Henry. Viking's Dawn; illus. by Christine Price. Criterion, 1956. 252p. $4.95. (U)

In 780 young Harald, sailing on a Viking expedition to Scotland in quest of treasure ships, endures shipwrecks, sea battles, and other disasters before reaching his home again. The wild and brutal life of Viking warriors is portrayed in great detail in a rousing sea story.

2650 Treffinger, Carolyn. Li Lun: Lad of Courage; illus. by Kurt Wiese. Abingdon, 1947. 93p. $3. (I)

A ten-year-old Chinese boy, so fearful of the sea that he refuses to go on his ritual manhood-testing voyage, is required to prove his courage by growing rice alone on a mountaintop.

2651 Treviño, Elizabeth Borton de. I, Juan de Pareja. Farrar, 1965. 180p. $3.25. (I–U)

Against a rich background of seventeenth-century Spanish court life, Juan, Negro slave of the painter Velázquez, tells the story of his friendship with Velázquez and his struggles to become a painter himself.

2652 Tunis, John R. His Enemy, His Friend. Morrow, 1967. 196p. $3.50; lib. ed. $3.32 net. (U)

A young German sergeant and former football star in charge of a village in Occupied France makes friends with the villagers and, whenever possible, eases the harsh conditions of their lives. When an order comes to execute six innocent men in retaliation for the murder of a German officer, the sergeant must decide which is the higher law: duty to his country or duty to the dictates of his conscience. How he decides and how, 20 years later, he meets the son of one of the executed men in a championship soccer match make a combination war-sports story with a powerful antiwar theme.

2653 Tunis, John R. Silence over Dunkerque. Morrow, 1962. 215p. $3.50; lib. ed. $3.32 net. (I–U)

During the confusion of evacuating British troops from Dunkerque in 1940, Sergeant Williams and one of his men are left behind. The suspenseful story of the sergeant's rescue by a young French girl and his eventual reunion with his family is quietly recounted in a tense and moving story.

2654 Turngren, Ellen. Listen, My Heart; decorations by Vera Bock. Longmans, 1956. 194p. $3.75. (U)

Sigrid Almbeck, 15, shares both her father's restless desire for new experiences and her mother's love for their home in a Swedish community in Minnesota. Her satisfying solution to her problem, combined with the story of her love for Eric Dahl, makes appealing reading for mature girls.

2655 Twain, Mark. The Adventures of Huckleberry Finn; illus. by Worth Brehm.

Harper, 1884. 404p. $2.95; lib. ed. $2.92 net. (I–U)

The story of the waif Huck as he drifts down the Mississippi on a raft with the runaway slave, Jim. May be read as an adventure story or for the moral implications of Huck's decisions.

2655a Twain, Mark. The Adventures of Tom Sawyer; illus. by Worth Brehm. Harper, 1875. 307p. $2.95; lib. ed. $2.92 net. (I–U)

An attractive edition of the tale of Tom Sawyer's escapades.

2656 Twain, Mark. A Connecticut Yankee in King Arthur's Court. Holiday ed. Harper, 1889. 450p. $3.95; lib. ed. $3.79 net. (I–U)

A burlesque of the historical romance of King Arthur, showing the evils which existed beneath the surface of chivalry.

2657 Twain, Mark. The Prince and the Pauper: A Tale for Young People of All Ages; illus. by Howard Simon; introd. by May Lamberton Becker. World, [1948]. 274p. $3.95; lib. ed. $3.79 net. (I–U)

This story of a prince and a beggar boy who exchanged places gives a good picture of England during the reign of Henry the Eighth.

2658 Uchida, Yoshiko. The Promised Year; illus. by William M. Hutchinson. Harcourt, 1959. 192p. $3. (I)

Ten-year-old Keiko comes from Japan to spend a year with her aunt and uncle in California, where she helps in carnation growing, learns American ways, and grows up a bit.

2659 Uchida, Yoshiko. Takao and Grandfather's Sword; illus. by William M. Hutchinson. Harcourt, 1958. 127p. $2.95. (I)

A modern Japanese family is warmly depicted in this story of a potter's son who, after his carelessness causes a disaster at the kiln, sacrifices his treasured antique sword to make amends.

2660 Ullman, James Ramsey. Banner in the Sky. Lippincott, 1954. 252p. $3.95. (U)

A 16-year-old Swiss boy, son of a mountain guide who lost his life in an attempt to scale the Citadel, rebels at his dull job as a hotel apprentice and joins an older man on an expedition to conquer the peak. A thrilling story of moral and physical

courage, based on the author's own experiences and on records of the first ascent of the Matterhorn in 1865.

2661 Uttley, Alison. A Traveler in Time; illus. by Christine Price. Viking, 1964. 287p. $4; lib. ed. $3.77 net. (U)

Visiting an ancestral estate in Derbyshire, Penelope Cameron travels back in time to become involved in Anthony Babington's plot to free Mary Queen of Scots from imprisonment. Convincing fantasy, keenly evocative of Elizabethan England.

2662 Valens, Evans G. Wildfire; pictures by Clement Hurd. World, 1963. unp. $3.95; lib. ed. $3.86 net. (I)

The terrors of a forest fire are described in poetic text supported by dramatic illustrations. Suspense mounts from the time a bolt of lightning starts the fire until the fleeing animals reach safety and the flames burn themselves out.

2663 Van Stockum, Hilda. The Cottage at Bantry Bay; written and illus. by Hilda Van Stockum. Viking, 1938. 252p. $3.50; lib. ed. $3.37 net. (I)

The O'Sullivans live in a little cottage in Ireland, where the children enjoy Father's stories, rescue a dog from gypsies, and have other simple pleasures.

2664 Van Stockum, Hilda. Mogo's Flute; drawings by Robin Jacques. Viking, 1966. 88p. $3.50; lib. ed. $3.37 net. (I)

Modern Kenya is the setting for the story of a frail little boy's determination to overcome his handicaps and join in the normal life of his village.

2664a Van Stockum, Hilda. The Winged Watchman; written and illus. by Hilda Van Stockum. Farrar, 1962. 204p. $3.25. (I–U)

By using the vanes of a windmill as signals, two Dutch boys help the resistance movement to conceal a British flier during the German occupation of Holland in World War II. An exciting tale of courage and patriotism.

2665 Verne, Jules. Around the World in Eighty Days; tr. by Geo. M. Towle; with biographical illus. and drawings reproduced from early eds., together with an introd. and captions by Anthony Boucher. Dodd, 1956. 244p. $3.95. (U)

The famous journey of Phileas Fogg and his valet Passepartout in the 1870's.

2666 **Verne, Jules.** Twenty Thousand Leagues under the Sea; with biographical illus. and drawings reproduced from earlier eds., together with an introductory biographical sketch of the author and anecdotal captions by Allen Klots, Jr. Dodd, 1952. 363p. $3.95. (U)

More than a hundred years ago a French author anticipates the submarine.

2667 **Viereck, Phillip.** The Summer I Was Lost; illus. by Ellen Viereck. Day, 1965. 158p. $3.75. (I–U)

While lost four days in a mountain wilderness, eighth-grader Paul Griffin gains new respect for his own courage and resourcefulness.

2668 **Viksten, Albert.** Gunilla: An Arctic Adventure; tr. by Gustaf Lannestock. Nelson, 1957. 160p. $2.95; lib. ed. $2.92 net. (I–U)

The stark beauty of the Arctic regions is the setting for this story of a Spitsbergen trapper who spent two years alone except for the company of a wolfhound and a pet polar bear, Gunilla, who is the central figure of this dramatic story.

2669 **Waldeck, Theodore J.** Lions on the Hunt; illus. by Kurt Wiese. Viking, 1942. 251p. $3.75; lib. ed. $3.56 net. (I–U)

Against a wonderfully realistic evocation of the South African veldt, the story follows the life of a young lion: his training for the hunt, the dangers he faces from man and nature, and his eventual assertion of leadership in the pack.

2670 **Waldeck, Theodore J.** The White Panther; illus. by Kurt Wiese. Viking, 1941. 193p. $3.75; lib. ed. $3.56 net. (I–U)

Vivid writing and authentic descriptions of wildlife in the jungles of British Guiana bring to life the setting of this story of a young panther, left to fend for himself in a hostile world.

2671 **Warner, Gertrude Chandler.** The Boxcar Children; illus. by L. Kate Deal. Whitman, 1950. 156p. $2.75. (I)

A family of orphans set up housekeeping in an old boxcar. For retarded readers in upper grades. (R3–4)

2672 **Weber, Lenora Mattingly.** Meet the Malones; illus. by Gertrude Howe. Crowell, 1943. 218p. $3.75. (I–U)

Mary Fred, eldest of a family of mother-less children, finds it difficult to play the dual role of substitute mother at home and popular leader in high school. Humor and pathos are nicely blended in a realistic story for older girls.

2673 **Weik, Mary Hays.** The Jazz Man; woodcuts by Ann Grifalconi. Atheneum, 1966. 42p. $3.50; lib. ed. $3.41 net. (I)

Abandoned by his parents in a Harlem tenement, lame Zeke found comfort in the music of the jazz man across the court until he could hope for happier times. A poignant story of a ghetto child, interpreted by striking illustrations.

2674 **Weil, Ann.** Red Sails to Capri; drawings by C. B. Falls. Viking, 1952. 56p. lib. ed. $2.73 net. (I–U)

In 1826 a young boy helps to dispel the superstitions about the Island of Capri and to prove it a place of beauty instead of evil.

2675 **Wenning, Elisabeth.** The Christmas Mouse; drawings by Barbara Remington. Holt, 1959. unp. $2.95; lib. ed. $3.27 net. (P–I)

A fanciful story of how Franz Gruber came to write "Silent Night, Holy Night" after Kasper Kleinmaus ate the bellows and silenced the organ of the little Austrian church. Younger children will enjoy hearing the story read at Christmas time.

2676 **White, Anne H.** Junket: The Dog Who Liked Everything "Just So"; illus. by Robert McCloskey. Viking, 1955. 183p. $3.50; lib. ed. $3.37 net. (I)

Junket, a clever Airedale, teaches a city family how a farm should be run and makes his new owner change his mind about "positively no animals." Humorously believable antics, complemented by amusing illustrations.

2677 **White, E. B.** Charlotte's Web; pictures by Garth Williams. Harper, 1952. 184p. $3.95; lib. ed. $3.79 net. (P–I)

A little girl who talks to animals and a spider who can both talk and write save the life of Wilbur the pig. The delicate charm of the fantasy is best brought out by being read aloud to primary pupils; older children enjoy reading the book for themselves.

2678 **White, T. H.** The Sword in the Stone. Putnam, 1939. 311p. $4.95. (U)

An unorthodox account of a medieval

boy's training in the code of knighthood, and of how he eventually became the legendary King Arthur. Life at court is picturesquely re-created. For mature readers.

2679 Whitney, Phyllis A. Step to the Music. Crowell, 1953. 256p. $4.50. (U)

In this fast-paced romance of Civil War days on Staten Island the daughter of a Northern father and a Southern mother experiences firsthand the divided loyalties that brought on the war. Of special relevance today is the rebellion against the nation's first attempts to draft men into the army.

2680 Wibberley, Leonard. John Treegate's Musket. Farrar, 1959. 188p. $2.95. (I–U)

The first in a series of stories about the Treegate family's part in the Revolutionary War begins in Boston in 1767. Eleven-year-old Peter, puzzled by the turmoil of the times, sees his father's Tory sympathies fade as he embraces the Patriot cause and takes his son to fight beside him in the Battle of Bunker Hill.

2681 Wibberley, Leonard. Peter Treegate's War. Farrar, 1960. 156p. $2.95. (I–U)

In the second book of this series Peter recounts his experiences during the first year of the Revolution when he fights with the Patriots and struggles to resolve a personal conflict between loyalty to his real father and loyalty to his Tory foster father.

2682 Wibberley, Leonard. Sea Captain from Salem. Farrar, 1961. 186p. $2.95. (I–U)

The sequel to *Peter Treegate's War*, above, is the story of Peace of God Manly, a sea captain who saved Peter's life in the earlier book and who now, under orders by Benjamin Franklin, harasses British shipping in the English Channel in rousing sea battles.

2683 Wibberley, Leonard. Treegate's Raiders. Farrar, 1962. 218p. $3.25. (I–U)

In the last volume of the series Peter raises a force of Scotch Highlanders in the Carolinas and leads them in the fighting at King's Mountain and Cowpens. The series ends with Peter present at the surrender at Yorktown. Authentic historical background, excellent characterization, and thrilling plots recommend these stories equally for recreational or supplementary reading.

2684 Wier, Ester. The Barrel; decorations by Carl Kidwell. McKay, 1966. 136p. $3.50; lib. ed. $3.24 net. (I–U)

Chance Reedy, 12, goes to live with a grandmother and a brother he has never known and in their Florida Everglades home has a chance to prove his courage to himself and to his brother.

2685 Wier, Ester. The Loner; illus. by Christine Price. McKay, 1963. 153p. $3.75; lib. ed. $3.44 net. (I–U)

Befriended by a lonely woman sheepherder on the Montana plains, a nameless orphan earns the right to the name David and to the home for which he longs. An emotionally charged but quietly told story with penetrating characterization and unusual setting.

2686 Wilder, Laura Ingalls. By the Shores of Silver Lake; illus. by Garth Williams. Newly illus., uniform ed. Harper, 1953. 290p. $3.50; lib. ed. $3.27 net. (I)

This and the other "Little House" books listed below form a well-loved and useful series on the settlement of the Middle West. Based on the author's own experiences, they re-create in homely and dramatic detail a period in United States history often considered dull. Readers identify with the characters in the story and grow up along with them; therefore, it is desirable that the books be read in sequence. The simply told stories, presented in attractive format, lend themselves equally well to independent reading, reading aloud, or classroom activities.

Fourth in the series, *By the Shores of Silver Lake* finds the family in North Dakota, where Pa has a job in a railroad building camp and Laura, the central character in the story, is now 13. Followed by *The Long Winter*, below.

2687 Wilder, Laura Ingalls. Farmer Boy; illus. by Garth Williams. Newly illus., uniform ed. Harper, 1953. 371p. $3.50; lib. ed. $3.27 net. (I)

This story takes the reader to New York State in the 1860's, when Almanzo Wilder, later to appear in the "Little House" stories, is nine years old. His life on a farm is described in humorous, realistic detail.

2688 Wilder, Laura Ingalls. Little House in the Big Woods; illus. by Garth Williams. Newly illus., uniform ed. Harper, 1953. 237p. $3.50; lib. ed. $3.27 net. (I)

In this first book of the series the Ingalls family is living in a little log house in Wisconsin in the 1870's. Ma, Pa, six-year-old Laura, Mary, and baby Carrie are snug and safe in spite of blizzards, wolves, and the lonely forest.

2689 Wilder, Laura Ingalls. Little House on the Prairie; illus. by Garth Williams. Newly illus., uniform ed. Harper, 1953. 334p. $3.50; lib. ed. $3.27 net. (I)

From the *Little House in the Big Woods* the family move west by covered wagon and build another house, only to find that they are in Indian Territory and must move on. Followed by *On the Banks of Plum Creek,* below.

2690 Wilder, Laura Ingalls. Little Town on the Prairie; illus. by Garth Williams. Newly illus., uniform ed. Harper, 1953. 304p. $3.50; lib. ed. $3.27 net. (I–U)

After the long winter the Ingalls continue to live in town, and Laura, now 14, enjoys school, a job, and a boy friend. Followed by *These Happy, Golden Years,* below.

2691 Wilder, Laura Ingalls. The Long Winter; illus. by Garth Williams. Newly illus., uniform ed. Harper, 1953. 334p. $3.50; lib. ed. $3.27 net. (I)

From Silver Lake the family move into Pa's store in a little South Dakota town, where they face the terrible winter of 1880–81. To save the village from starvation, Almanzo Wilder, met in *Farmer Boy,* above, makes a hazardous journey to find food. Followed by *Little Town on the Prairie,* above.

2692 Wilder, Laura Ingalls. On the Banks of Plum Creek; illus. by Garth Williams. Newly illus., uniform ed. Harper, 1953. 338p. $3.50; lib. ed. $3.27 net. (I)

Sequel to *Little House on the Prairie,* this third book in the series tells of the Ingalls family's experiences living in a sod house in Minnesota, where they cope with a flood, a blizzard, and a grasshopper invasion.

2693 Wilder, Laura Ingalls. These Happy, Golden Years; illus. by Garth Williams. Newly illus., uniform ed. Harper, 1953. 288p. $3.50; lib. ed. $3.27 net. (I–U)

In the last book about the Ingalls family Laura, not quite 16, teaches school for a year and then marries Almanzo Wilder.

2694 Willard, Barbara. Charity at Home; illus. by Douglas Hall. Harcourt, 1966. 187p. $3.25. (I–U)

Fourteen-year-old Charity lives happily with an aunt and uncle until she discovers that she has a talent for sculpture and feels that her family do not sympathize with her ambition to be an artist. An English story of adolescence with good characterization and interesting subplots.

2695 Willard, Barbara. Storm from the West; illus. by Douglas Hall. Harcourt, 1963. 189p. $3.25. (I–U)

Two English children resented their mother's remarriage to an American with four children and were especially unhappy when the Americans joined them in their cottage in Scotland. When the parents left them to work out their problems alone, they did so with humorously interesting results.

2696 Williams, Jay, and **Abrashkin, Raymond.** Danny Dunn and the Homework Machine; illus. by Ezra Jack Keats. McGraw-Hill, 1958. 141p. $2.95; lib. ed. $2.96 net. (I)

When Professor Bullfinch leaves Danny in charge of his miniature computer, Danny and his friend program it to do their homework. Amusing and ingenious.

2697 Wilson, Leon. This Boy Cody; with illus. by Ursula Koering. Watts, 1950. 234p. $3.50. (I)

Cody is a Tennessee mountain boy, ten on the day the story opens, and ready as usual to add excitement to any situation. Each chapter tells a funny episode in one year of Cody's life.

2698 Winterfeld, Henry. Castaways in Lilliput; tr. from the German by Kyrill Schabert; illus. by William M. Hutchinson. Harcourt, 1960. 188p. $3. (I)

Three Australian children, adrift on a rubber raft, are cast ashore on an island where all the people are very tiny. Their adventures as giants among the miniature natives make a diverting tale.

2699 Witheridge, Elizabeth P. Dead End Bluff; drawings by Charles Geer. Atheneum, 1966. 186p. $3.95; lib. ed. $3.81 net. (I–U)

In spite of an overprotective father, an eighth-grade blind boy learns to lead a near-normal life. A believable, unsentimental story of a plucky youngster.

2700   Wojciechowska, Maia. Shadow of a Bull; drawings by Alvin Smith. Atheneum, 1964. 165p. $3.50; lib. ed. $3.41 net. (I–U)

Everyone in the little Spanish town thought that Manolo, son of a famous matador, should follow in his late father's footsteps. Because Manolo did not wish to kill, he thought himself a coward until he found a way to prove his courage. A fine story of a boy's inner struggle, set in the exciting world of the bull ring.

2701   Woolley, Catherine. Ginnie and Geneva; illus. by Iris Beatty Johnson. Morrow, 1954. 159p. $3.25. (I)

When Ginnie at last found a way to cope with Geneva's teasing, the two girls became best friends. Good family and school relationships in a lighthearted story of nine-year-old problems.

2702   Woolley, Catherine. Ginnie and the New Girl; illus. by Iris Beatty Johnson. Morrow, 1954. 159p. $3.25. (I)

Ginnie resented the attention Geneva was paying the new girl, Marcia, but soon found other fourth-grade friends and interests to replace her dependence on one friend.

2703   Wormser, Richard. Ride a Northbound Horse; illus. by Charles Geer. Morrow, 1964. 190p. $3.50. (I–U)

Cav Rand, 13, is equal to the dangers and hardships of a Texas cattle drive in the 1870's. An eventful Western with good characterization, humor, and smooth writing style.

2704   Worth, Kathryn. They Loved To Laugh; illus. by Marguerite de Angeli. Doubleday, 1942. 269p. $3.95. (U)

A North Carolina Quaker family of five boys and an adopted girl are the lively members of this generous, fun-filled household of the 1830's. Especially recommended for older girls.

2705   Wrightson, Patricia. Down to Earth; illus. by Margaret Horder. Harcourt, 1965. 222p. $3.75. (I–U)

Science fiction about a young Martian who comes to earth and has to be protected by two Australian boys. The view of the earth people through the eyes of the boy from Mars is humorous and thought-provoking.

2706   Wuorio, Eva-Lis. The Island of Fish in the Trees; illus. by Edward Ardizzone. World, 1962. 59p. $3.50; lib. ed. $3.41 net. (P–I)

Two children of the Balearic Islands wander off in search of El Medico to cure their mother's toothache and are everywhere received with warmth and helpfulness by the people they meet. A tale of human kindness among simple people in an interesting setting. Suggested for reading aloud.

2707   Wyndham, Lee. Candy Stripers. Messner, 1958. 191p. $3.50. (U)

Though Bonnie Schuyler, 15, enrolls as a junior hospital aide just to have something to do, she soon realizes the importance of the work done by volunteers. Realistic details of hospital routines and a light love interest give the book appeal for older girls.

2708   Wyss, Johann. The Swiss Family Robinson; ed. by William H. G. Kingston; illus. by Lynd Ward. Grosset, 1949. 388p. $2.95; lib. ed. $3.49 net. (I–U)

The improbable adventures of a shipwrecked family are still enthralling after more than 50 years.

2709   Yashima, Taro. Crow Boy. Viking, 1955. 37p. $3.50; lib. ed. $3.37 net. (P–I)

An understanding teacher helps Crow Boy to demonstrate an unusual talent and to take his place as an important person in his Japanese village school. A moving story interpreted by the author's distinctive illustrations, valuable for human relations and for its picture of Japanese school life.

2710   Yashima, Taro, and **Muku, Hatoju.** The Golden Footprints; illus. by Taro Yashima. World, 1960. 50p. $2.95; lib. ed. $2.88 net. (I)

A young Japanese boy conspires with a pair of foxes to feed their captive baby and eventually saves it from destruction by his father. A sensitive story for reading aloud.

2711   Yates, Elizabeth. Carolina's Courage; illus. by Nora S. Unwin. Dutton, 1964. 94p. $2.95; lib. ed. $2.92 net. (I)

In a pioneer story for younger girls, Carolina gives up her beloved doll to an Indian child and thus secures safe passage for her family on their journey from New Hampshire to Nebraska.

Picture Books and Stories for Primary Grades

Listed here are picture books, including alphabet and counting books; stories to be used primarily by or with pupils in grades K–3; and stories for independent reading by pupils with reading levels of grades 1–3. Books of information for primary children are listed with other books on the same subjects.

Books for independent reading were selected from lists prepared especially for primary pupils with limited reading skills and are characterized by lively action, amusing illustrations, open pages, limited vocabulary, short sentences, and large print. Approximate reading levels are indicated by the symbol R1–2 or R2–3 following the annotation, to suggest that pupils reading on grade levels 1–2 or 2–3, respectively, can probably read the books for themselves. But since no mechanical device can positively predict readability, the symbols here used merely narrow the field and make it somewhat easier to fit a particular book to a particular child.

2712 Adshead, Gladys L. Brownies—Hush! With pictures by Elizabeth Orton Jones. Walck, 1938. unp. $3.25. (P)

The playful Brownies help an old couple with their work, but run away when seen and rewarded with new clothes. Gentle humor and sprightly illustrations make this version of an old story especially appealing to kindergarten and first-grade pupils.

2713 Adshead, Gladys L. Brownies—It's Christmas! With pictures by Velma Ilsley. Walck, 1955. unp. $3.25. (P)

The Brownies return to help the old couple decorate their Christmas tree.

2714 Alexander, Anne. Noise in the Night; pictures by Abner Graboff. Rand McNally, 1960. unp. $2.75; lib. ed. $3.08 net. (P)

Sherri is reassured when she discovers that a frightening nighttime noise is only Daddy snoring. (R2–3)

2715 Aliki. Three Gold Pieces; a Greek folktale retold and illus. by Aliki. Pantheon, 1967. unp. $3.50; lib. ed. $3.39 net. (P–I)

A peasant who exchanges his entire fortune—three gold pieces—for three pieces of advice finds wealth and good fortune. Pictures, some in brilliant color, reflect the moods of the story and show typical Greek scenes and characters. For the story hour.

2716 Ambrus, Victor G. The Three Poor Tailors. Harcourt, 1965. unp. $3.50; lib. ed. $3.60 net. (P)

Three poor tailors, riding on a nanny-goat, run away from an inn to avoid paying their bill. A droll Hungarian folktale retold with a straight face and illustrated with the author's comical full-color pictures.

2717 Anderson, C. W. Billy and Blaze. Macmillan, 1962. 48p. $2.95; lib. ed. $2.94 net. (P)

Billy has many adventures riding his birthday pony, Blaze. The author's realistic pen drawings—one for each sentence—enhance a popular story. (R2–3)

2718 Anderson, C. W. Blaze and the Lost Quarry; story and pictures by C. W. Anderson. Macmillan, 1966. 46p. $2.95; lib. ed. $2.94 net. (P)

Billy and Blaze discover a lost quarry and rescue a dog from drowning. (R2–3)

2719 Anglund, Joan Walsh. The Brave Cowboy. Harcourt, 1959. unp. $2.25. (P)

A small boy becomes a hero in imaginative play. The author's illustrations show the pretended adventures in red and the real activities in black. (R1–2)

2720 Anglund, Joan Walsh. A Friend Is

225

Someone Who Likes You. Harcourt, 1958. unp. $1.95. (P)

In words and pictures the author presents the concept of friendship and tells the many kinds of friends a young child may have. A small book with delicate, stylized illustrations and rhythmic text.

2721 Ardizzone, Edward. Little Tim and the Brave Sea Captain. Walck, 1961. unp. $3.50. (P)

Tim runs away to sea, is shipwrecked, and becomes a hero. The author's seascapes are just as full of salt and action as the story.

2722 Association for Childhood Education International. Told under the Blue Umbrella: New Stories for Children; sel. by the Literature Committee of the Association for Childhood Education; illus. by Marguerite Davis. Macmillan, 1933. 161p. $2.95; lib. ed. $2.94 net. (P)

Thirty-eight imaginative and realistic stories for young children, arranged by age levels.

2723 Association for Childhood Education International. Told under the Green Umbrella: Old Stories for New Children; sel. by the Literature Committee of the International Kindergarten Union; pictures by Grace Gilkison. Macmillan, 1930. 188p. $2.95; lib. ed. $3.44 net. (P)

Twenty-six favorite fairy tales for kindergarten and first-grade story hour.

2724 Association for Childhood Education International. Told under the Magic Umbrella: Modern Fanciful Stories for Young Children; sel. by the Literature Committee of the Association for Childhood Education; illus. by Elizabeth Orton Jones. Macmillan, 1939. 248p. $2.95; lib. ed. $3.44 net. (P)

For upper primary grades, 33 stories arranged by age appeal.

2725 Aulaire, Ingri d', and Aulaire, Edgar Parin d'. Don't Count Your Chicks. Doubleday, 1943. unp. $3.50. (P)

This author-artist team tells the story of an old woman who counted her chickens before they were hatched. A humorous story illustrated with large lithographs showing colorful country scenes.

2726 Aulaire, Ingri d', and Aulaire, Edgar Parin d'. Ola. Doubleday, 1932. unp. $3.50. (P)

A little Norwegian boy takes the reader on a visit to many interesting places in his country: a Lapp settlement, a fishing village, a bird colony. Large lithographs in color and black and white show authentic details of Norse scenery and costumes.

2727 Austin, Margot. William's Shadow. Dutton, 1954. unp. $2.50. (P)

A sleepy-headed groundhog almost brings on 40 days of bad weather. A good read-aloud story for February 2. (R1–2)

2728 Averill, Esther. The Fire Cat; story and pictures by Esther Averill. Harper, 1960. 63p. $1.95; lib. ed. $2.19 net. (P)

Pickles is rescued from a tree and taken to live in a firehouse, where he becomes a brave firefighter. (R2–3)

2729 Averill, Esther. Jenny's Adopted Brothers; written and illus. by Esther Averill. Harper, 1952. 32p. $1.95; lib. ed. $2.19 net. (P)

Jenny Linsky is a little black cat who adopts two homeless cats and then becomes jealous of them.

2729a Ayer, Jacqueline. Nu Dang and His Kite. Harcourt, 1959. unp. $3. (P–I)

The author's pictures, full of the exotic color of Siam, extend a simple story about a small boy's search for his kite.

2730 Baker, Betty. Little Runner of the Longhouse; pictures by Arnold Lobel. Harper, 1962. 63p. $1.95; lib. ed. $2.19 net. (P)

A little Iroquois Indian convinces his mother that he is big enough to join the older boys in the New Year's celebration. An engaging small boy and authentic details of Indian life. (R2–3)

2730a Balet, Jan B. The Gift: A Portuguese Christmas Tale; pictures by the author. Delacorte, 1967. unp. $3.25. (P)

Stiff little figures dressed in traditional Portuguese costume illustrate this story of a small boy who finds the perfect gift to bring the Christ Child at the Christmas festival.

2731 Beim, Jerrold. Andy and the School Bus; illus. by Leonard Shortall. Morrow, 1947. unp. lib. ed. $2.94 net. (P)

Andy at last gets a ride on the school bus. Large, clear type and many illustrations. (R2–3)

2732 Beim, Jerrold. Country Fireman;

illus. by Leonard Shortall. Morrow, 1948. unp. lib. ed. $2.94 net. (P)

Ricky's adventures with the village fire department will appeal to small boys and will add to their understanding of an important community service. (R2–3)

2733 **Beim, Jerrold.** Country Garage; pictures by Louis Darling. Morrow, 1952. unp. lib. ed. $2.94 net. (P)

Seth, allowed to help in his uncle's filling station, learns about cars and how they are kept rolling. (R2–3)

2734 **Beim, Jerrold.** Country School; pictures by Louis Darling. Morrow, 1955. 47p. lib. ed. $2.94 net. (P)

Tony, unhappy when the little country school was replaced by a large modern building, finds that he likes his new school, after all. (R2–3)

2735 **Beim, Jerrold.** Kid Brother; illus. by Tracy Sugarman. Morrow, 1952. 48p. lib. ed. $2.94 net. (P)

Frankie surprises everyone when he makes his first appearance in a school assembly program.

2736 **Beim, Jerrold.** The Smallest Boy in the Class; illus. by Meg Wohlberg. Morrow, 1949. unp. lib. ed. $2.94 net. (P)

Jim resents being called Tiny until he learns that he can be important in spite of his small size. (R2–3)

2737 **Beim, Jerrold.** Swimming Hole; pictures by Louis Darling. Morrow, 1951. unp. lib. ed. $2.94 net. (P)

Color prejudice around the swimming hole dissolves when children of both races learn that color is not important in friendship. A light and humorous treatment of a serious problem. (R2–3)

2738 **Beim, Lorraine,** and **Beim, Jerrold.** Two Is a Team; pictures by Ernest Crichlow. Harcourt, 1945. unp. $2.75. (P)

Two six-year-old friends—one white, one Negro—play happily together until they disagree about making a coaster. A quiet lesson in cooperation which young children can understand.

2739 **Bemelmans, Ludwig.** Madeline; story and pictures by Ludwig Bemelmans. Viking, 1939. unp. $3.50; lib. ed. $3.37 net. (P)

Madeline is a nonconformist in a regimented world—a Paris convent school. This

rhymed story tells how she made an adventure out of having appendicitis. Authentic Paris atmosphere in text and pictures.

2740 **Bemelmans, Ludwig.** Madeline's Rescue; story and pictures by Ludwig Bemelmans. Viking, 1953. 56p. $3.50; lib. ed. $3.37 net. (P)

Madeline is rescued from the Seine by a dog which becomes the school pet. When the trustees object, the dog herself solves the problem in a surprising way. Distinguished watercolors show Paris landmarks.

2741 **Benchley, Nathaniel.** Oscar Otter; illus. by Arnold Lobel. Harper, 1966. 64p. $1.95; lib. ed. $2.19 net. (P)

A disobedient little otter is almost eaten by his enemies. A mildly exciting story with amusing illustrations. (R2–3)

2742 **Benchley, Nathaniel.** Red Fox and His Canoe; pictures by Arnold Lobel. Harper, 1964. 62p. $1.95; lib. ed. $2.19 net. (P)

The adventures of a little Indian who gets a big surprise when three bears, two otters, a raccoon, and a moose join him in his canoe. Fun in story and pictures. (R2–3)

2743 **Bennett, Rainey.** The Secret Hiding Place; written and illus. by Rainey Bennett. World, 1960. unp. $3.50; lib. ed. $3.41 net. (P)

Little Hippo, the pet of the herd, wants to escape his adoring relatives. His first hiding place is rather frightening, but finally he finds a spot where he can be alone, but not too much alone. A gentle story about a common childhood problem, told in simple text and the author's beautiful colored pictures.

2744 **Berg, Jean Horton.** There's Nothing To Do, So Let Me Be You; illus. by Madeline Marabella. Westminster, 1966. unp. $2.95. (P)

A baby raccoon who trades places with his mother and father runs into some difficulties as he works while they play.

2745 **Beskow, Elsa.** Pelle's New Suit; picture book by Elsa Beskow; tr. by Marion Letcher Woodburn. Harper, [1929]. unp. $3.25; lib. ed. $3.27 net. (P)

Beautiful colored pictures show Swedish scenes and costumes as Pelle does errands to earn his new suit. All the processes needed to produce a suit are explained and depicted.

2746 Bishop, Claire Huchet, and Wiese, Kurt. The Five Chinese Brothers. Coward-McCann, 1938. unp. $2.50; lib. ed. $2.52 net. (P)
Each of five identical Chinese brothers has a special talent which he uses to save the lives of all. Rhythm, repetition, and humorously exaggerated pictures by Kurt Wiese make this tale excellent for the story hour. (R2–3)

2747 Bishop, Claire Huchet. The Man Who Lost His Head; illus. by Robert McCloskey. Viking, 1942. unp. $3; lib. ed. $2.96 net. (P)
A man without a head tries several substitutes but finds none satisfactory. Droll illustrations match the absurdity of the story.

2748 Bonsall, Crosby. The Case of the Cat's Meow. Harper, 1965. 64p. $1.95; lib. ed. $2.19 net. (P)
Four boys, members of a no-girls-allowed club, become private eyes to search for a missing cat. Believable characters, lively dialog, and humorous pictures. (R2–3)

2749 Bonsall, Crosby. The Case of the Dumb Bells. Harper, 1966. 64p. $1.95; lib. ed. $2.19 net. (P)
An easy-to-read mystery about the problems which develop when Skinny mistakenly connects the boys' clubhouse telephone to his friend's doorbell wires. (R2–3)

2750 Bonsall, Crosby. Tell Me Some More; pictures by Fritz Siebel. Harper, 1961. 64p. $1.95; lib. ed. $2.19 net. (P)
Andrew converts Tim to the joys of the library by describing it as a place where he can hold an elephant, pat a lion, and do other astonishing things. An original idea, extended in amusing illustrations. (R1–2)

2751 Bonsall, Crosby. Who's a Pest? Harper, 1962. 64p. $1.95; lib. ed. $2.19 net. (P)
Homer knows he is not a pest, but he must prove his point to his sisters and to the animals he has teased. How he does this makes a very funny story for independent reading. (R2–3)

2752 Bontemps, Arna, and Conroy, Jack. The Fast Sooner Hound; illus. by Virginia Lee Burton. Houghton, 1942. 28p. lib. ed. $3.23 net. (P–I)
A tall tale about a hound who could out-run a train. The excitement of the story is intensified by rhythmic action pictures.

2752a Borack, Barbara. Grandpa; pictures by Ben Shecter. Harper, 1967. 64p. $2.95; lib. ed. $2.92 net. (P)
A little girl tells about her perfectly delightful grandfather who knows just how to play with a five-year-old.

2753 Bright, Robert. Georgie. Doubleday, 1944. unp. $2.95. (P)
Georgie is a friendly little ghost who lives in Mr. and Mrs. Whittaker's attic and tells them when to go to bed by squeaking a step. When he gets his feelings hurt and leaves home, both he and the Whittakers are unhappy. (R2–3)

2754 Bright, Robert. Georgie to the Rescue; written and illus. by Robert Bright. Doubleday, 1956. unp. $2.95. (P)
Georgie accompanies the Whittakers to a city hotel and finds something to squeak so that they will feel at home. (R2–3)

2755 Bright, Robert. Georgie's Halloween; written and illus. by Robert Bright. Doubleday, 1958. unp. $2.95. (P)
Georgie enters the village contest for the best Halloween costume and comes home to a big surprise. (R2–3)

2755a Bright, Robert. My Red Umbrella. Morrow, 1959. unp. lib. ed. $1.98 net. (P)
A good read-aloud story for very young listeners, about a little girl whose red umbrella grew to accommodate all the creatures who sought shelter under it. Cheerful colored pictures by the author.

2756 Brooke, L. Leslie. Johnny Crow's Garden; a picture book drawn by L. Leslie Brooke. Warne, 1903. unp. $2.95. (P)
Nonsense rhymes about the animals who come to Johnny Crow's garden are enlivened by humorous pictures.

2757 Brown, Marcia. Henry—Fisherman: A Story of the Virgin Islands. Scribner, 1949. unp. $3.50. (P)
Henry has a wonderful adventure when he goes on his first fishing trip with his father. The author's illustrations provide an excellent introduction to the scenery and people of the islands.

2758 Brown, Marcia. The Little Carousel. Scribner, 1946. unp. lib. ed. $3.12 net. (P)

A lonely little boy is made happy when he earns a ride on a carousel. New York City street scenes are vividly depicted in the author's illustrations.

2759 Brown, Margaret Wise. Country Noisy Book; with illus. by Leonard Weisgard. Harper, 1940. unp. $2.95; lib. ed. $2.92 net. (P)

Little dog Muffin visits the country and learns the meaning of new sounds. A springboard for listening activities in the classroom. (R1–2)

2760 Brown, Margaret Wise. The Golden Egg Book; illus. by Leonard Weisgard. Golden Pr., 1963. unp. $1; lib. ed. $2.19 net. (P)

A lonely bunny finds a friend when a mysterious egg hatches into a duck. Brilliantly colored pictures show small animals and flowers on each large page. (R1–2)

2761 Brown, Margaret Wise. Goodnight Moon; pictures by Clement Hurd. Harper, 1947. unp. $2.95; lib. ed. $2.92 net. (P)

The coming of night is shown in pictures which change from bright to dark as a small rabbit says good night to the familiar things in his nest. Useful for young children's rest periods. (R1–2)

2762 Brown, Margaret Wise. The Indoor Noisy Book; pictures by Leonard Weisgard. Harper, 1942. unp. $2.95; lib. ed. $2.92 net. (P)

Another listening book, in which a little dog identifies sounds he hears indoors. (R1–2)

2763 Brown, Margaret Wise. The Sleepy Little Lion; photos. by Ylla. Harper, 1947. unp. $3.50; lib. ed. $3.27 net. (P)

A very simple text is interpreted by exceptionally appealing photographs showing a lion cub as he gets acquainted with other young animals and children.

2764 Brown, Margaret Wise. Wait till the Moon Is Full; pictures by Garth Williams. Harper, 1948. unp. $2.95; lib. ed. $2.92 net. (P)

A young raccoon eagerly awaits the full moon when his mother will allow him to go abroad at night for the first time. (R2–3)

2765 Brown, Margaret Wise, and **Gergely,**

Tibor. Wheel on the Chimney. Lippincott, 1954. unp. $3; lib. ed. $3.11 net. (P–I)

Each year the storks return from Africa to nest on the chimney of a Hungarian house and bring good luck to the family. Story and pictures make the migration of the great birds dramatic and inspiring. (R2–3)

2766 Brown, Margaret Wise. Young Kangaroo; illus. by Symeon Shimin. W. R. Scott, 1955. unp. $3.50. (P)

Lovely sepia pictures illustrate this brief story of a baby kangaroo who leaves his mother's pouch to see what the world is like.

2767 Brown, Myra Berry. Benjy's Blanket; illus. by Dorothy Marino. Watts, 1962. unp. $2.95. (P)

Benjy loves his blanket and hates to give it up. A gently humorous story about a common experience of childhood.

2768 Brown, Myra Berry. Company's Coming for Dinner; pictures by Dorothy Marino. Watts, 1959. unp. $2.95. (P)

Stevie helps prepare for company and is rewarded by being allowed to stay up and meet the guests. (R2–3)

2768a Brown, Myra Berry. First Night Away from Home; pictures by Dorothy Marino. Watts, 1960. unp. $2.95. (P)

Stevie packs his suitcase and goes to spend the night with his friend down the street—only to find that he needs his teddy bear to keep him from feeling homesick. (R2–3)

2769 Brown, Myra Berry. Pip Camps Out; pictures by Phyllis Graham. Golden Gate, 1966. unp. $3.50; lib. ed. $3.27 net. (P)

Pip finds that sleeping in the family orchard is not much fun until Daddy joins him. (R2–3)

2770 Brown, Myra Berry. Pip Moves Away; illus. in color by Polly Jackson. Golden Gate, 1967. unp. $3.50; lib. ed. $3.27 net. (P)

Moving to a new place and making new friends is not so bad as Pip thought it would be. A familiar childhood experience treated with understanding and humor. (R2–3)

2771 Brown, Palmer. Something for Christmas. Harper, 1958. 32p. $2.50. (P)

A small mouse wants to give a very special present to a very special person—his mother. He finds that the best gift of all is love. A tender story reflecting the true spirit of Christmas and illustrated with endearing pictures by the author.

2772 Brunhoff, Jean de. The Story of Babar, the Little Elephant; tr. from the French by Merle S. Haas. Random, 1960. 47p. $1.95. (P)

Babar runs away from the jungle and goes to live with an old lady in Paris, where he adapts quickly to French amenities. Later he returns to the jungle and becomes king. Much of the charm of the story is contributed by the author's gay pictures.

2773 Buckley, Helen E. The Little Boy and the Birthdays; illus. by Paul Galdone. Lothrop, 1965. unp. $3.25; lib. ed. $3.13 net. (P)

A little boy discovers the pleasure of remembering other people's birthdays. Warm family situation, natural dialog, and bright pictures.

2774 Burningham, John. John Burningham's ABC. Bobbs-Merrill, 1967. unp. $4.95. (P)

Strikingly handsome pictures in bold color are the unique feature of this alphabet book.

2775 Burton, Virginia Lee. Choo Choo: The Story of a Little Engine Who Ran Away. Houghton, 1937. unp. lib. ed. $3.73 net. (P)

The author's dramatic black-and-white pictures add to the excitement of Choo Choo's adventures.

2776 Burton, Virginia Lee. Katy and the Big Snow; story and pictures by Virginia Lee Burton. Houghton, 1943. 32p. $3.50; lib. ed. $3.23 net. (P)

Katy is a crawler tractor who saves the city when it is snowed in by a blizzard. Though personified, Katy is presented accurately in the author's colored illustrations.

2777 Burton, Virginia Lee. The Little House; story and pictures by Virginia Lee Burton. Houghton, 1942. 40p. $3.50; lib. ed. $3.23 net. (P)

The great city swallowed up a little house that once stood in the country; then it was moved back to the country, where it was

happy again. Rhythmically illustrated in clear colors which suggest day and night and seasonal changes.

2778 Burton, Virginia Lee. Maybelle, the Cable Car. Houghton, 1952. 42p. lib. ed. $3.73 net. (P)

Based on fact, this story tells how the people of San Francisco saved the picturesque cable cars from the inroads of progress. The atmosphere of the city is captured in story and the author's illustrations.

2779 Burton, Virginia Lee. Mike Mulligan and His Steam Shovel; story and pictures by Virginia Lee Burton. Houghton, 1939. unp. $3.25; lib. ed. $3.07 net. (P)

Mike and his old-fashioned steam shovel prove that they can do some things better than the new-fangled bulldozers. Lively crayon drawings.

2780 Cameron, Polly. "I Can't" Said the Ant: A Second Book of Nonsense; words and pictures by Polly Cameron. Coward-McCann, 1961. unp. lib. ed. $2.52 net. (P)

Nonsense rhymes tell how the ants, the spiders, and the kitchen utensils help to put poor broken Miss Teapot back on the shelf. Each helper is shown in an amusing picture.

2781 Carroll, Ruth. What Whiskers Did. Walck, 1965. unp. $3. (P)

Action pictures without text encourage children to tell the story of a runaway puppy befriended by a rabbit family.

2782 Caudill, Rebecca. Did You Carry the Flag Today, Charley? Illus. by Nancy Grossman. Holt, 1966. 94p. $3.75; lib. ed. $3.45 net. (P)

It was a great surprise when five-year-old Charley subdued his high spirits sufficiently to earn the privilege of carrying the flag at school. A good picture of Appalachian Mountain life and a sympathetic treatment of a lively little boy's problems.

2782a Caudill, Rebecca. A Pocketful of Cricket; illus. by Evaline Ness. Holt, 1964. unp. $3.50; lib. ed. $3.27 net. (P–I)

An understanding teacher prevents a crisis when Jay takes his pet cricket with him on his first day in school. A perceptive nature story with distinctively designed pictures of farm life. Excellent for reading aloud.

2783 Clark, Ann Nolan. Looking-for-Something: The Story of a Stray Burro of Ecuador; illus. by Leo Politi. Viking, 1952. 53p. $3; lib. ed. $2.96 net. (P–I)
A little gray burro leaves his mother and goes out to see the world. His journey across Ecuador shows typical scenes and characters.

2784 Clark, Ann Nolan. Tía María's Garden; illus. by Ezra Jack Keats. Viking, 1963. 47p. $3; lib. ed. $3.04 net. (P–I)
Tía María's garden is the desert where she and her small nephew go walking to look at the strange animals and plants that live there. A mood piece which evokes the wonder of the desert in poetic text and sensitive illustrations.

2785 Clark, Margery. The Poppy Seed Cakes; illus. by Maud and Miska Petersham. Doubleday, 1924. unp. $3.25. (P)
A read-aloud story for kindergarten and early primary pupils, telling of Auntie Katushka who came from Russia and told wonderful stories to four-year-old Andrewshek.

2786 Cohen, Miriam. Will I Have a Friend? Pictures by Lillian Hoban. Macmillan, 1967. unp. $3.50. (P)
Jim's chief worry about starting to school is that he may not have a friend, but before the first day is over, he has many friends. Realistic illustrations show a racially mixed group in an urban school.

2787 Collier, Ethel. The Birthday Tree; pictures by Honoré Guilbeau. W. R. Scott, 1961. unp. $3.50. (P)
A little girl, watching while her birthday tree is dug up and replanted, dreams of the time when it will have hundreds of leaves instead of just ten. (R1–2)

2788 Collier, Ethel. I Know a Farm; illus. by Honoré Guilbeau. W. R. Scott, 1960. unp. $3.50. (P)
A very simple story of a city child's first visit to a farm, illustrated with clear, realistic pictures. (R1–2)

2789 Collier, Ethel. Who Goes There in My Garden? Illus. by Honoré Guilbeau. W. R. Scott, 1963. unp. $3.50. (P)
Many insects and animals come to visit a little boy's first garden. (R1–2)

2790 Cooney, Barbara. Chanticleer and the Fox; by Geoffrey Chaucer; adapted and illus. by Barbara Cooney. Crowell, 1958. unp. $3.50; lib. ed. $3.40 net. (P–I)
A prose version of "The Nun's Priest's Tale" distinguished by richly colored pictures with a medieval flavor. For reading aloud or storytelling.

2791 Craig, M. Jean. The Dragon in the Clock Box; illus. by Kelly Oechsli. Norton, 1960. unp. $3.25; lib. ed. $3.03 net. (P)
A read-aloud story about Joshua and his mysterious box which he said contained a dragon's egg. Delightful small boy and understanding parents.

2792 Dalgliesh, Alice. The Little Wooden Farmer; pictures by Anita Lobel. Macmillan, 1968. unp. $3.95. (P)
New illustrations reinterpret the old story of the little wooden farmer and his wife who acquire the animals they need to make their farm complete. A repetitive story with stiff, patterned illustrations that perfectly maintain the illusion of the little wooden world.

2793 Daugherty, James. Andy and the Lion. Viking, 1938. unp. $3; lib. ed. $3.04 net. (P)
A modern version of *Androcles and the Lion,* in which Andy befriends a lion, who later reciprocates. Large, lion-yellow-and-black illustrations by the author extend the fun and action. (R2–3)

2794 Dawson, Rosemary, and **Dawson, Richard.** A Walk in the City. Viking, 1950. 39p. $3; lib. ed. $2.96 net. (P)
The sights a small boy sees when he goes for a walk with his mother in New York are described in rhyme and pictured in gay colors.

2795 De Jong, David Cornel. The Happy Birthday Egg; illus. by Harvey Weiss. Little, 1962. unp. $3; lib. ed. $2.97 net. (P)
An easy-to-read mystery story in which David and his friends find a dinosaur egg. Sequel to *The Happy Birthday Umbrella,* below. (R2–3)

2796 De Jong, David Cornel. The Happy Birthday Umbrella; illus. by Harvey Weiss. Little, 1959. unp. lib. ed. $2.79 net. (P)
A gay little story in which David's friends add their birthday presents to David's yellow umbrella. (R2–3)

2797   Dennis, Wesley. Flip; story and pictures by Wesley Dennis. Viking, 1941. unp. $2.75; lib. ed. $2.73 net. (P–I)

Encouraged by dreaming he has wings, a little colt finds that he can jump a brook in his pasture. A simple story in which excellent black-and-white illustrations carry the action. (R2–3)

2798   Dennis, Wesley. Flip and the Cows; story and pictures by Wesley Dennis. Viking, 1942. unp. $3; lib. ed. $2.96 net. (P–I)

Flip, the little colt, overcomes his fear of cows. Both Flip and the cows are shown in lifelike illustrations. (R2–3)

2799   Dennis, Wesley. Flip and the Morning; story and pictures by Wesley Dennis. Viking, 1951. unp. $2.75; lib. ed. $2.73 net. (P–I)

Willie, the goat, finds a way to keep Flip from waking everybody up too early. Illustrations show realistic farm scenes. (R2–3)

2800   De Regniers, Beatrice Schenk. A Little House of Your Own; drawings by Irene Haas. Harcourt, 1954. unp. $2.25; lib. ed. $2.36 net. (P)

Gently whimsical text and pictures show many secret "houses" (under the dining-room table, behind a large chair) where a small child can find privacy and peace. Has possibilities for dramatization. (R2–3)

2801   De Regniers, Beatrice Schenk. May I Bring a Friend? Illus. by Beni Montresor. Atheneum, 1964. unp. $3.50; lib. ed. $3.41 net. (P)

A long-suffering king and queen, who tactfully accept the difficult animal friends a little boy brings to tea, are rewarded by being invited to tea at the zoo. Elaborate and richly colored illustrations accent the absurd situations. (R1–2)

2802   De Regniers, Beatrice Schenk. The Snow Party; illus. by Reiner Zimnik. Pantheon, 1959. unp. lib. ed. $3.09 net. (P–I)

A lonely little old woman gets her wish to have a party when dozens of people stop in out of the snow and a snowbound bakery truck provides refreshments. (R2–3)

2803   Du Bois, William Pène. Bear Party. Viking, 1963. 48p. $3; lib. ed. $2.96 net. (P)

A wise old koala bear gave a costume party to reunite all of his quarreling neighbors. Full-color pictures by the author.

2804   Du Bois, William Pène. Lion. Viking, 1956. 36p. $3.75; lib. ed. $3.56 net. (P)

An artist in the Sky Workshop decides to create a new animal and, after much trial and error, produces a lion. The author's stunning color illustrations suggest original art activities for the classroom. (R2–3)

2805   Duvoisin, Roger. A for the Ark. Lothrop, 1952. unp. $3.50; lib. ed. $3.35 net. (P)

Two by two, the author's amusingly drawn animals march in alphabetical order into Noah's Ark.

2806   Duvoisin, Roger. The House of Four Seasons. Lothrop, 1956. unp. $3.50; lib. ed. $3.35 net. (P)

When each member of the family wanted to paint a new house to harmonize with a different season, Father mixed his paints into a color that pleased everybody. Duvoisin's illustrations skillfully extend the pleasant story into a lesson in color combinations. (R2–3)

2807   Duvoisin, Roger. Petunia; written and illus. by Roger Duvoisin. Knopf, 1950. unp. lib. ed. $3.09 net. (P)

Petunia, the silly goose, creates havoc in the barnyard by pretending that she can read. Hilarity in story and pictures. Useful for reading readiness.

2808   Duvoisin, Roger. Petunia's Christmas; written and illus. by Roger Duvoisin. Knopf, 1952. unp. lib. ed. $3.09 net. (P)

A romance develops when Petunia rescues Charles, a handsome gander earmarked for the farmer's Christmas dinner.

2809   Duvoisin, Roger. Veronica; written and illus. by Roger Duvoisin. Knopf, 1961. unp. lib. ed. $3.29 net. (P)

Veronica, a hippopotamus who wanted to be different, left the herd and went to the city, where her unfriendly reception convinced her that the mudbank was best for her, after all. The droll situation is made funnier by laughable illustrations.

2810   Eastman, P. D. Are You My Mother? Written and illus. by P. D. Eastman. Beginner Books, 1960. 63p. $1.95; lib. ed. $2.29 net. (P)

Funny pictures and easy text tell of a little bird's efforts to find his mother. (R1–2)

2811 Eichenberg, Fritz. Ape in a Cape: An Alphabet of Odd Animals. Harcourt, 1952. unp. $3; lib. ed. $3.24 net. (P)

Animals are arranged in alphabetical order, described in nonsense rhymes, and shown in the author's amusing illustrations.

2812 Eichenberg, Fritz. Dancing in the Moon: Counting Rhymes. Harcourt, 1955. 20p. $3.25; lib. ed. $3.30 net. (P)

Numbers from 1 to 20 are accompanied by nonsense rhymes and illustrated by the author with humorous pictures of animals in silly situations.

2813 Elkin, Benjamin. The Loudest Noise in the World; illus. by James Daugherty. Viking, 1954. 64p. $3.50; lib. ed. $3.37 net. (P)

Prince Hulla-Baloo of Hub-Bub asks for the loudest noise in the world for his sixth birthday but gets a very different present. (R2–3)

2814 Emberley, Barbara, adapter. Drummer Hoff; illus. by Ed Emberley. Prentice-Hall, 1967. unp. $4.25. (P)

A cumulative folk rhyme is adapted in spirited style and illustrated with arresting black woodcuts accented with brilliant color. The characters who participate in the building and firing of a cannon—"Sergeant Crowder brought the powder, Corporal Farrell brought the barrel," etc.—are hilariously rugged characters, while "Drummer Hoff who fired it off" stands by, deadpan, waiting to touch off the marvelously satisfying explosion.

2815 Emberley, Ed. The Wing on a Flea: A Book about Shapes; written and illus. by Ed Emberley. Little, 1961. 48p. $3.50; lib. ed. $3.27 net. (P)

Rhymes and colored pictures help a child to recognize triangles, rectangles, and circles in everyday objects. (R2–3)

2816 Ets, Marie Hall. Bad Boy, Good Boy. Crowell, 1967. 49p. $3.95; lib. ed. $3.76 net. (P)

A rather long story about five-year-old Roberto, middle child in a poor Spanish-speaking family in California, who gets into trouble because he is neglected and bewildered in a strange world. When his mother leaves home, he is put into a day-care center where he learns constructive activities and becomes the means of bringing his mother back. Illustrated with realistic drawings by the author.

2817 Ets, Marie Hall. Gilberto and the Wind. Viking, 1963. 32p. $3; lib. ed. $2.96 net. (P)

A little Mexican boy finds that the wind makes a good playmate. The author's pictures, in subdued colors, show an attractive child.

2818 Ets, Marie Hall. In the Forest; story and pictures by Marie Hall Ets. Viking, 1944. unp. $2.50; lib. ed. $2.57 net. (P)

Wearing his paper hat and blowing his new horn, a small boy calls up a parade of imaginary animals to follow him in the forest. (R2–3)

2819 Ets, Marie Hall. Just Me; written and illus. by Marie Hall Ets. Viking, 1965. 32p. $2.50; lib. ed. $2.57 net. (P)

Imitating the way the animals walk is fun, but it is even more fun to run just like a little boy to meet Daddy.

2820 Ets, Marie Hall. Mister Penny's Circus. Viking, 1961. 64p. $3.25; lib. ed. $3.19 net. (P)

Mr. Penny adds a bear and a chimpanzee to his farm animals and starts a circus. Black-and-white pictures by the author add humor to this read-aloud story.

2821 Ets, Marie Hall, and **Labastida, Aurora.** Nine Days to Christmas; illus. by Marie Hall Ets. Viking, 1959. 48p. $3.50; lib. ed. $3.37 net. (P–I)

Mexico City at fiesta time is shown in colorful detail as Ceci enjoys her first Christmas *posada,* a special party given each night for nine nights. A springboard for social studies and art activities.

2822 Ets, Marie Hall. Play with Me; story and pictures by Marie Hall Ets. Viking, 1955. 31p. $2.75; lib. ed. $2.73 net. (P)

A little girl longs to play with the small creatures in the meadow, but they all run away until she sits quietly and waits for them to come near. (R2–3)

2823 Falls, Charles Buckles. The ABC Book. Doubleday, 1923. unp. $3.50. (P)

The author's brilliantly colored woodcuts show animals from Antelope to Zebra.

2824 Fatio, Louise. The Happy Lion; pictures by Roger Duvoisin. McGraw-Hill, 1954. unp. $2.95; lib. ed. $2.96 net. (P)

A lion in a zoo in France is everybody's favorite—until he escapes. Then his only friend is a little boy who leads him back to his cage. Gay illustrations show a lovable lion and an engaging little boy. (R2–3)

2825 Fatio, Louise. The Happy Lion in Africa; pictures by Roger Duvoisin. McGraw-Hill, 1955. 30p. $2.95; lib. ed. $2.96 net. (P)

The Happy Lion goes to Africa, where he is frightened by the wild animals and longs for home in the zoo. (R2–3)

2826 Felt, Sue. Rosa Too-Little; story and pictures by Sue Felt. Doubleday, 1950. unp. $2.95. (P)

At last the day comes when Rosa can write her name and get her own library card. A good read-aloud story.

2827 Fischer, Hans. The Birthday: A Merry Tale with Many Pictures. Harcourt, 1954. unp. $4.50. (P)

Distinguished six-color illustrations by the author tell how the animals celebrated Old Lizette's seventy-sixth birthday.

2828 Fischer, Hans. Pitschi: The Kitten Who Always Wanted To Be Something Else; A Sad Story but One Which Ends Well. Harcourt, 1953. unp. $4.95. (P)

A foolish kitten tries being a rooster, a duck, and a rabbit only to find that it is better to be oneself. Sophisticated lithographs in six colors.

2829 Flack, Marjorie. Angus and the Cat; told and pictured by Marjorie Flack. Doubleday, 1931. unp. $2.95. (P)

The little Scottie learns the hard way that it is best to make friends with a cat. Humor and surprise in a simple, brightly illustrated story just right for the youngest listeners.

2830 Flack, Marjorie. Angus and the Ducks; told and pictured by Marjorie Flack. Doubleday, 1930. unp. $2.95. (P)

Curiosity leads a little Scottie into trouble. A simple read-aloud story with attractive illustrations in clear primary colors.

2831 Flack, Marjorie. Ask Mr. Bear; story and pictures by Marjorie Flack. Macmillan, 1932. unp. $2.95. (P)

Though Danny asked many animals what to give his mother for her birthday, only Mr. Bear knew the right answer. Repetition invites audience participation in storytelling. (R2–3)

2832 Flack, Marjorie. The Boats on the River; pictures by Jay Hyde Barnum. Viking, 1946. 31p. $4.95; lib. ed. $4.53 net. (P–I)

Rhythmic text and dramatic pictures in bright colors are combined in a large book about the many kinds of boats on the river. (R3–4)

2833 Flack, Marjorie, and **Wiese, Kurt.** The Story about Ping. Viking, 1933. unp. $2; lib. ed. $2.19 net. (P)

Ping, a little duck who lives on a houseboat in the Yangtze River, always gets a spanking to hurry him aboard. One night he stays ashore and almost comes to grief. A suspenseful story complemented by pictures full of humor, atmosphere, and action.

2834 Flack, Marjorie. Wait for William. Houghton, 1935. unp. $3; lib. ed. $2.90 net. (P)

Because William, aged four, got lost when he went with his older brother and sister to see the circus parade, he got a ride on the elephant's head. Gaily colored pictures catch the fun and excitement of the parade.

2835 Flack, Marjorie. Walter the Lazy Mouse; illus. by Cyndy Szekeres. Doubleday, 1963. 95p. $3.50. (P)

Walter is so lazy that he gets left behind when his family moves. Trying to find them, he has many adventures, including teaching frogs to play leapfrog.

2836 Floethe, Louise Lee. The Cowboy on the Ranch; with pictures by Richard Floethe. Scribner, 1959. unp. lib. ed. $3.31 net. (P)

Bright pictures showing realistic details and simple text take the young cowboy to a ranch to see a round-up, branding, feeding, and other range activities.

2837 Flora, James. Sherwood Walks Home; story and pictures by James Flora. Harcourt, 1966. unp. $3.25; lib. ed. $3.36 net. (P)

Sherwood is a wind-up bear who is left in the park and must find someone to wind his motor and then try to walk home before it runs down. How he accomplishes this makes a very funny story.

2838 Foster, Doris Van Liew. A Pocketful of Seasons; illus. by Talivaldis Stubis. Lothrop, 1960. 37p. $3.50; lib. ed. $3.35 net. (P)

The changing seasons bring different re-actions to a farmer and a little boy. Illustrations effectively show changing moods and colors.

2839 Foster, Doris Van Liew. Tell Me, Mr. Owl; illus. by Helen Stone. Lothrop, 1956. 23p. $3.75; lib. ed. $3.52 net. (P)
A wise owl explains the mysteries of Halloween to Little Boy in rhyming text, illustrated with suitably scary pictures.

2840 The Fox Went Out on a Chilly Night: An Old Song illus. by Peter Spier. Double-day, 1961. unp. $3.50. (P)
Myriad details of the New England coun-tryside are included in the illustrations of this story of the fox who raided the farm-er's poultry yard and escaped the farmer's wrath on the way home to Mrs. Fox and the babies. Includes music.

2841 Françoise. Jeanne-Marie Counts Her Sheep. Scribner, 1951. unp. lib. ed. $3.12 net. (P)
A French author-illustrator offers a counting book in gay colors showing Jeanne-Marie counting her sheep and plan-ning how she will spend the money from their wool.

2842 Françoise. Noel for Jeanne-Marie. Scribner, 1953. unp. lib. ed. $3.12 net. (P)
Jeanne-Marie tells her pet sheep, Pata-pon, all about Christmas and decides how Patapon can help to celebrate. Lovely col-ored pictures show a crèche, *santons* (small images of saints), and other details of the Christmas season in the south of France.

2843 Françoise. Springtime for Jeanne-Marie. Scribner, 1955. unp. lib. ed. $3.12 net. (P)
Soft springtime colors create atmosphere as Jeanne-Marie and her little white sheep search for the lost duck, Madelon. (R2–3)

2844 Françoise. The Thank-You Book. Scribner, 1947. unp. lib. ed. $3.12 net. (P)
Softly colored pictures are the important feature of this book in which a French child gives thanks to the people, animals, and things that he loves.

2845 Françoise. What Time Is It, Jeanne-Marie? Scribner, 1963. unp. $3.25; lib. ed. $3.12 net. (P)
A few French words are sprinkled through this account of what Jeanne-Marie is doing

at each hour of the day. The simple text and gay pictures help Jeanne-Marie and the reader-listener to tell time.

2846 Freeman, Don. Fly High, Fly Low. Viking, 1957. 58p. $3.50; lib. ed. $3.37 net. (P)
High up over San Francisco, a pigeon and his mate build a nest in a neon sign. Suspense develops as the sign is about to be torn down. Spacious views of the city are provided in colorful illustrations by the author.

2847 Freeman, Don. The Guard Mouse; story and pictures by Don Freeman. Vi-king, 1967. 47p. $3.50; lib. ed. $3.37 net. (P)
When cousins visit Clyde, the handsome guard at Buckingham Palace, he gives them a mouse-eye view of the city from several unusual vantage points.

2848 Freeman, Don. Mop Top; story and pictures by Don Freeman. Viking, 1955. 48p. $3; lib. ed. $3.04 net. (P)
A funny story about a boy who would not get his hair cut, until a lady mistook him for a mop.

2849 Freeman, Don. Norman the Door-man. Viking, 1959. 64p. $3.75; lib. ed. $3.56 net. (P)
Norman, the mouse doorman at the base-ment of the museum, wins an award with a "sculpture" made from mousetrap parts. Full-color lithographs by the author are as full of fun as the imaginative text.

2850 Freeman, Don. A Rainbow of My Own. Viking, 1966. unp. $3; lib. ed. $2.96 net. (P)
Failing to catch the rainbow in the sky, a little boy imagines one, then is delighted to find a rainbow at home—made by sun shining through the water in his goldfish bowl. A fanciful and satisfying story with lovely colored pictures by the author.

2851 Freeman, Don. Space Witch. Viking, 1959. unp. $2.50; lib. ed. $2.57 net. (P)
Here is something different in Halloween stories. A witch builds a space ship and, with her cats, spends the evening scaring whatever there is in outer space.

2852 Friedrich, Priscilla, and Friedrich, Otto. The Easter Bunny That Overslept; illus. by Adrienne Adams. Lothrop, 1957. unp. $3.50; lib. ed. $3.35 net. (P)

The bunny who slept through Easter had trouble giving away his eggs on other holidays, until Santa Claus solved his problem. An original idea presented in simple text and soft, springtime colors.

2853 Gág, Wanda. The ABC Bunny; hand-lettered by Howard Gág. Coward-McCann, 1933. unp. $3.50; lib. ed. $3.29 net. (P)

Original lithographs by Wanda Gág are the outstanding feature of an alphabet book which tells in rhyme the adventures of a small rabbit.

2854 Gág, Wanda. Millions of Cats. Coward-McCann, 1928. unp. $2.95; lib. ed. $2.86 net. (P)

Repetitive story and rhythmic illustrations by the author make this story of a little old couple who wanted a cat perfect for the story hour with young children. (R2–3)

2855 Garten, Jan. The Alphabet Tale; illus. by Muriel Batherman. Random, 1964. unp. lib. ed. $2.69 net. (P)

A picture of an animal's tail and a descriptive verse provide clues for guessing the animal shown on the following page. Though the animals are listed in alphabetical order, this is more a participation book than a device for teaching the alphabet.

2856 Goudey, Alice E. The Day We Saw the Sun Come Up; illus. by Adrienne Adams. Scribner, 1961. unp. $3.25; lib. ed. $3.12 net. (P)

From sunrise to sunset, two children watch the changes in light and shadow, then at bedtime their mother explains why night and day occur. Accurate information presented in poetic text and softly colored illustrations.

2857 Gramatky, Hardie. Hercules: The Story of an Old-Fashioned Fire Engine; written and illus. by Hardie Gramatky. Putnam, 1940. unp. lib. ed. $3.29 net. (P)

The adventures of an old horse-drawn fire engine who becomes a hero, told with zest and illustrated in bright colors. (R2–3)

2858 Gramatky, Hardie. Little Toot; pictures and story by Hardie Gramatky. Putnam, 1939. unp. $3.50; lib. ed. $3.29 net. (P)

A conceited little tugboat learns a lesson when it is caught at sea in a storm. Humor and suspense in story and pictures. (R2–3)

2859 Grifalconi, Ann. City Rhythms. Bobbs-Merrill, 1965. unp. $4.95; lib. ed. $4.25 net. (P)

A small Negro boy absorbs the rhythms of a big city and repeats them on his homemade musical instruments. Children, especially those in an inner-city school, will find much that is familiar in the simple story and brightly colored pictures.

2860 Guilfoile, Elizabeth. Have You Seen My Brother? Illus. by Mary Stevens. Follett, 1962. 29p. $1; lib. ed. $1.89 net. (P)

The tables are turned when the little brother looks for the older one. (R1-2)

2861 Guilfoile, Elizabeth. Nobody Listens to Andrew; illus. by Mary Stevens. Follett, 1957. 27p. $1; lib. ed. $1.89 net. (P)

Nobody believed Andrew when he told them there was a bear in his bed—but there really was! (R1-2)

2862 Hader, Berta, and **Hader, Elmer.** The Big Show. Macmillan, 1948. unp. lib. ed. $4.50. (P-I)

Large, colorful pictures by the authors show the birds and animals which come for the food put out by an old couple after a big snow. Useful for nature study. (R2–3)

2863 Hader, Berta, and **Hader, Elmer.** Reindeer Trail: A Long Journey from Lapland to Alaska. Macmillan, 1959. unp. $4.95. (P-I)

A story based on an actual event, telling how Lapp herders brought their reindeer to Alaska to provide food and clothing for the Eskimos. Realistic colored pictures by the authors show details of Eskimo life.

2864 Hader, Berta. The Story of Pancho and the Bull with the Crooked Tail; written and illus. by Berta and Elmer Hader. Macmillan, 1942. unp. $3.95; lib. ed. $3.74 net. (P)

A small Mexican boy unexpectedly becomes a hero when he captures a dangerous bull. An amusing glimpse of Mexico in story and illustrations.

2865 Handforth, Thomas. Mei Li. Doubleday, 1938. unp. $3.50. (P-I)

Traditional Chinese life is interestingly portrayed in story and pictures of Mei Li's day at the New Year's fair in North China and her return home to meet the Kitchen God at midnight. (R2–3)

2866 **Harris, Isobel.** Little Boy Brown; illus. by André François. Lippincott, 1949. 44p. lib. ed. $2.93 net. (P)

The contrast between city and country life is inherent in an engaging story of a small city boy's visit to the country.

2867 **Heilbroner, Joan.** The Happy Birthday Present; pictures by Mary Chalmers. Harper, 1962. 63p. $1.95; lib. ed. $2.19 net. (P)

Peter and Davy have adventures when they go shopping for a ten-cent present for their mother's birthday. (R1–2)

2868 **Heyward, Du Bose.** The Country Bunny and the Little Gold Shoes, as told to Jenifer; pictures by Marjorie Flack. Houghton, 1939. unp. $3.50; lib. ed. $3.23 net. (P)

A brave mother rabbit earns the right to be one of the five special Easter bunnies. Her 21 delightful babies are shown in clear spring colors. For the story hour.

2869 **Hill, Elizabeth Starr.** Evan's Corner; illus. by Nancy Grossman. Holt, 1967. unp. $3.95; lib. ed. $3.59 net. (P–I)

Evan, one of a family of eight living in a two-room flat, wants a place of his own. When his wise mother assigns him a corner, he at first enjoys arranging it just for himself, but eventually finds that it is more fun to help his little brother with his corner. An appealing picture of a Negro slum family, illustrated with realistic scenes of inner-city life.

2870 **Hoban, Russell.** A Baby Sister for Frances; pictures by Lillian Hoban. Harper, 1964. unp. $2.95; lib. ed. $2.92 net. (P)

When a new baby arrives in the badger family, Frances feels neglected and decides to run away. A familiar family situation treated with understanding and humor. (R2–3)

2871 **Hoban, Russell.** Bedtime for Frances; pictures by Garth Williams. Harper, 1960. unp. $2.95; lib. ed. $2.92 net. (P)

Father Badger proves more than a match for Frances when she tries to postpone bedtime. (R2–3)

2872 **Hoban, Russell.** Bread and Jam for Frances; pictures by Lillian Hoban. Harper, 1964. 31p. $2.95; lib. ed. $2.92 net. (P)

Frances' decision to eat only bread and jam weakens when her parents grant her wish. (R2–3)

2873 **Hoban, Russell.** The Little Brute Family; pictures by Lillian Hoban. Macmillan, 1966. unp. $3.50. (P)

The manners of the five disagreeable little Brutes are transformed when Baby Brute brings home a little lost good feeling. An amusing cautionary story for the very youngest.

2874 **Hoff, Syd.** Chester; story and pictures by Syd Hoff. Harper, 1958. 64p. $1.95; lib. ed. $2.19 net. (P)

Amusing story of a wild horse who wants to be caught and loved. Easy reading, large print, and cartoon-like pictures in this book and the titles following attract independent beginning readers. (R1–2)

2875 **Hoff, Syd.** Danny and the Dinosaur; story and pictures by Syd Hoff. Harper, 1958. 64p. $1.95; lib. ed. $2.19 net. (P)

A dinosaur comes out of the museum and goes with Danny on a tour of the town. A popular subject treated with humor and imagination in simple story and funny pictures. (R1–2)

2876 **Hoff, Syd.** Grizzwold; story and pictures by Syd Hoff. Harper, 1963. 64p. $1.95; lib. ed. $2.19 net. (P)

When lumbermen cut down his forest, an enormous bear finds a home in a national park. (R1–2)

2877 **Hoff, Syd.** Julius; story and pictures by Syd Hoff. Harper, 1959. 64p. $1.95; lib. ed. $2.19 net. (P)

Davy and his father bring Julius, the gorilla, to America, where he becomes the star in a circus. (R1–2)

2878 **Hoff, Syd.** Oliver; story and pictures by Syd Hoff. Harper, 1960. 64p. $1.95; lib. ed. $2.19 net. (P)

The story of a dancing circus elephant, told in simple text and amusing illustrations. (R1–2)

2879 **Hoff, Syd.** Sammy the Seal; story and pictures by Syd Hoff. Harper, 1959. 64p. $1.95; lib. ed. $2.19 net. (P)

Sammy, permitted to leave the zoo for a sightseeing tour of the city, creates havoc among its human inhabitants. (R1–2)

2880 **Hoff, Syd.** Stanley; story and pictures by Syd Hoff. Harper, 1962. 64p. $1.95; lib. ed. $2.19 net. (P)

A cave man with advanced ideas leaves

his cave and invents a house to live in. (R1–2)

2881 Holl, Adelaide. The Rain Puddle; pictures by Roger Duvoisin. Lothrop, 1965. unp. $3.25; lib. ed. $3.13 net. (P)
Each of the silly barnyard animals sees his reflection in a rain puddle and thinks that one of his own kind is drowning. When the sun dries up the puddle, the animals are relieved, thinking that everyone has been saved. An absurd, repetitive story with a folktale quality in style and illustrations, suitable for the story hour. (R2–3)

2882 Holl, Adelaide. The Runaway Giant; illus. by Mamoru Funai. Lothrop, 1967. unp. $3.50; lib. ed. $3.35 net. (P)
Consternation reigns in the forest when each of four animals reports that he has seen a giant, with no two agreeing on his size. When the giant snowman melts, the animals celebrate their courage in scaring him away. An ingenious and colorfully illustrated bit of fun.

2883 Hurd, Edith Thacher. Last One Home Is a Green Pig; pictures by Clement Hurd. Harper, 1959. 63p. $1.95; lib. ed. $2.19 net. (P)
A duck and a monkey use many ingenious means of transportation when they race each other home. (R1–2)

2884 Ipcar, Dahlov. Brown Cow Farm: A Counting Book. Doubleday, 1959. unp. $3.25. (P)
A pleasant lesson in counting, adding, and multiplying the animals and their young on the author's brightly pictured farm.

2885 Ipcar, Dahlov. I Like Animals; written and illus. by Dahlov Ipcar. Knopf, 1960. unp. lib. ed. $3.39 net. (P)
A small boy's love of animals is shown in colorful pictures of animals of the zoo, pet shop, farm, and forest. Very brief text.

2886 Ipcar, Dahlov. The Wonderful Egg. Doubleday, 1958. unp. $3.25. (P)
A fanciful story of what prehistoric animal might have hatched out of a wonderful egg laid in the jungles of long ago. The author suggests several species of ancient animals and presents them in bright colors. Includes a table of comparative sizes and a pronunciation guide.

2887 Johnson, Crockett. Harold and the

Purple Crayon. Harper, 1955. unp. $2.50; lib. ed. $2.57 net. (P)
As Harold goes for a moonlight walk, he uses his purple crayon to draw a path and the things he sees along the way, then draws himself back home. A fantasy useful to stimulate imaginative activities in young children. (R1–2)

2888 Johnson, Crockett. Will Spring Be Early? or Will Spring Be Late? Crowell, 1959. 48p. $3.50; lib. ed. $3.30 net. (P)
A funny story about a little groundhog who was a poor weather prophet.

2889 Johnston, Johanna. Edie Changes Her Mind; illus. by Paul Galdone. Putnam, 1964. unp. lib. ed. $2.68 net. (P)
Because Edie made a scene every night about going to bed, her parents took her bed apart and put it away. After one night of sleeping on the floor, Edie was glad to go to bed without a fuss. A pleasant story with a gentle lesson.

2890 Joslin, Sesyle. Brave Baby Elephant; pictures by Leonard Weisgard. Harcourt, 1960. unp. $2.50; lib. ed. $2.56 net. (P)
Baby Elephant's big adventure is going to bed by himself for the first time. His preparations, as if for a long and dangerous journey, will amuse young children. Pictures show a beguiling little elephant behaving just like a little boy.

2891 Kahl, Virginia. Away Went Wolfgang! Written and illus. by Virginia Kahl. Scribner, 1954. unp. lib. ed. $3.31 net. (P)
Wolfgang, the noisiest dog in a little Austrian village, becomes a surprising asset when hitched to a milk cart. Tyrolean atmosphere in story and pictures.

2892 Kahl, Virginia. The Duchess Bakes a Cake; written and illus. by Virginia Kahl. Scribner, 1955. unp. lib. ed. $3.12 net. (P)
When the duchess puts too much baking powder into her cake, it rises to the housetops, taking the duchess with it. How she gets down makes a fine nonsense story, told in lively rhymes and illustrated with bright pictures.

2893 Kahl, Virginia. Plum Pudding for Christmas; written and illus. by Virginia Kahl. Scribner, 1956. unp. lib. ed. $3.12 net. (P)
The king, who likes plum pudding, is coming to Christmas dinner with the duch-

ess, but little Gunhilde has eaten all the plums. The ever resourceful duchess solves the problem in a gay picture book with rhyming text and amusing illustrations.

2894 **Kay, Helen.** An Egg Is for Wishing; pictures by Yaroslava. Abelard-Schuman, 1966. unp. $2.95; lib. ed. $2.89 net. (P)
A little boy who is afraid of chickens has trouble finding an egg to be decorated for Easter. Ukrainian customs and costumes are shown in the pictures.

2895 **Kay, Helen.** One Mitten Lewis; illus. by Kurt Werth. Lothrop, 1955. unp. $3.25; lib. ed. $3.13 net. (P)
Lewis just couldn't seem to help losing one of each pair of mittens. Finally his mother solved his problem in a most ingenious way.

2896 **Kay, Helen.** Snow Birthday; illus. by Barbara Cooney. Farrar, 1955. 46p. $3.75. (P)
The snow that Stephen wished for almost —but not quite—spoiled his birthday party. A suspenseful story in a happy family setting.

2897 **Keats, Ezra Jack.** Peter's Chair. Harper, 1967. unp. $3.95; lib. ed. $3.79 net. (P)
Peter took his little blue chair and ran away because his parents were taking all his furniture for a baby sister; but when he found that the chair was too small for him, he realized that he was big enough to help his father get ready for the new baby. An understanding treatment of a familiar problem; interesting collage illustrations by the author.

2898 **Keats, Ezra Jack.** The Snowy Day. Viking, 1962. 32p. $3; lib. ed. $2.96 net. (P)
In a simple story and striking collage illustrations the author perfectly captures a small boy's delight as he plays in the snow. (R1–2)

2899 **Keats, Ezra Jack.** Whistle for Willie. Viking, 1964. 33p. $3.50; lib. ed. $3.37 net. (P)
Peter longs to whistle for his dog Willie, but finds that whistling is not so easy as it looks.

2900 **Kepes, Juliet.** Lady Bird, Quickly. Little, 1964. 47p. $3; lib. ed. $2.97 net. (P)
All the insects pass the word along to Lady Bird when her house seems to be on fire. In this variation of the old nursery rhyme, "Lady Bug, Lady Bug, fly away home," the house is not on fire but is filled with fireflies. The author's pictures of insects, each kind on a different color of paper, are simple and pleasing.

2901 **Kessler, Leonard.** Here Comes the Strikeout. Harper, 1965. 64p. $1.95; lib. ed. $2.19 net. (P)
By dint of much effort, the worst player on the team finally becomes an asset. A popular subject, easy vocabulary, and the author's humorous action pictures entice reluctant readers in intermediate grades as well as independent readers in primary grades. (R2–3)

2902 **Kessler, Leonard.** Kick, Pass, and Run. Harper, 1966. 64p. $1.95; lib. ed. $2.19 net. (P)
After watching a football game, some animals decide to have a game of their own—with hilarious results. Information about football is included with the nonsense. May appeal to the older reluctant reader. (R2–3)

2903 **Kingman, Lee.** Peter's Long Walk; with pictures by Barbara Cooney. Doubleday, 1953. 47p. $3.25. (P)
Left alone when the older children go to school, Peter goes in search of playmates. Repetition, rhythm, and colorful illustrations make this just right for reading to young children.

2904 **Knight, Hilary.** Where's Wallace? Story and panoramas by Hilary Knight. Harper, 1964. 40p. $3.50; lib. ed. $3.47 net. (P)
A kindly zookeeper cooperates with Wallace, a little orangutan who likes to explore the city occasionally. Detailed color spreads invite readers and listeners to find Wallace in unlikely places.

2905 **Koch, Dorothy.** When the Cows Got Out; pictures by Paul Lantz. Holiday, 1958. 36p. lib. ed. $2.75 net. (P)
Tim, on a visit to his grandfather's farm, leaves a gate open and the cows get out. His difficulties in getting them back make an exciting story. (R1–2)

2906 **Krasilovsky, Phyllis.** The Cow Who Fell in the Canal; illus. by Peter Spier. Doubleday, 1957. unp. $3.50. (P)
Hendrika, a cow who lived in Holland,

sometimes got bored with just giving milk; but after she fell into the canal and floated down the river on a raft, she was never bored again. Dutch scenes are delightfully depicted in color.

2907 Krauss, Ruth. The Big World and the Little House; pictures by Marc Simont. Harper, 1949. unp. $3.95; lib. ed. $3.79 net. (P)
A family moves into a deserted house and makes it a home.

2908 Krauss, Ruth. The Carrot Seed; pictures by Crockett Johnson. Harper, 1945. unp. $2.50; lib. ed. $2.57 net. (P)
A little boy's faith that his carrot seed will come up is finally rewarded. A very simple story for the youngest gardeners and nature lovers.

2909 Krauss, Ruth. The Growing Story; pictures by Phyllis Rowand. Harper, 1947. unp. $3.25; lib. ed. $3.11 net. (P)
Though he watches other things grow, a little boy does not realize that he himself is growing, until he puts on last year's clothes. (R2–3)

2910 Langstaff, John. Frog Went A-Courtin'; retold by John Langstaff; with pictures by Feodor Rojankovsky. Harcourt, 1955. unp. $2.95; lib. ed. $3.26 net. (P)
Equally good for storytelling or singing, a composite version of the old Scottish ballad illustrated with large, lively pictures. Includes music.

2911 Langstaff, John. Over in the Meadow; with pictures by Feodor Rojankovsky. Harcourt, 1957. unp. $3.50; lib. ed. $3.57 net. (P)
A counting book based on the old song about the meadow animals and their babies. Rhyming, repetitive text and softly colored pictures showing animals and flowers make this excellent for use with young children. Includes the tune of the song.

2912 La Rue, Mabel G. Tiny Toosey's Birthday; pictures by Mary Stevens. Houghton, 1958. 128p. $3.50. (P)
Tiny Toosey, the youngest of seven, is taken to the city for a day of fun and misadventure on his birthday. (R2–3)

2913 La Rue, Mabel G. Tiny's Big Umbrella; pictures by Mary Stevens. Houghton, 1963. 127p. $3.50. (P)

When all seven of the Tooseys arrived home from school dripping wet, it was clear that they needed umbrellas. How to get seven new umbrellas was a problem requiring ingenuity and family cooperation. (R2–3)

2914 Laskowski, Jerzy. Master of the Royal Cats; illus. by Janina Domanska. Seabury, 1965. unp. $3.50. (P–I)
When the dogs of ancient Egypt refused to guard the Pharaoh's grain, cats came to his rescue. Handsome stylized pictures recreate scenes from Egyptian life.

2915 Leaf, Munro. The Story of Ferdinand; illus. by Robert Lawson. Viking, 1936. unp. $2.50; lib. ed. $2.57 net. (P–I)
Ferdinand, thought to be the most ferocious bull in Spain, was really a gentle soul who liked to sit and smell the flowers. His fiasco in the bull ring is told in a hilarious story and delightfully humorous pictures.

2916 Lefévre, Félicité. The Cock, the Mouse, and the Little Red Hen: An Old Tale Retold by Félicité Lefévre; with 24 illus. by Tony Sarg. Macrae, 1947. unp. $3.95; lib. ed. $3.73 net. (P)
An old favorite with young children, retold with humor and illustrated with bright, amusing pictures.

2917 Lenski, Lois. Cowboy Small. Walck, 1949. unp. $2.75. (P)
Cowboy Small does all the things a real cowboy would do. Stylized pictures show cowboy outfit and gear for the horse. (R1–2)

2918 Lenski, Lois. I Like Winter. Walck, 1944. unp. $2.50. (P)
The joys of winter are reviewed in simple rhymes and gay pictures by the author. Like the three titles following, this is a small book for small children. (R1–2)

2919 Lenski, Lois. Now It's Fall. Walck, 1948. unp. $2.50. (P)
Bright fall colors accent verses telling the fun of gathering nuts, raking leaves, and Halloween. (R1–2)

2920 Lenski, Lois. On a Summer Day. Walck, 1953. unp. $2.50. (P)
The freedom of summertime play makes this season best of all. (R1–2)

2921 Lenski, Lois. Spring Is Here. Walck, 1945. unp. $2.50. (P)

The flowers return, kites fly, Easter comes —all seen from a child's viewpoint. (R1–2)

2922 Le Sieg, Theo. Come Over to My House; illus. by Richard Erdoes. Beginner Books, 1966. 62p. $1.95; lib. ed. $2.29 net. (P)
Home is home the world around—this is the theme of a rhymed introduction in easy vocabulary to homes, customs, and games in many places. (R2–3)

2923 Lexau, Joan M. Benjie; illus. by Don Bolognese. Dial, 1964. unp. $3; lib. ed. $2.97 net. (P–I)
A little Negro boy is surprised to find that his shyness disappears when he goes out to search for his grandmother's earring.

2924 Lexau, Joan M. The Homework Caper. Harper, 1966. 64p. $1.95; lib. ed. $2.19 net. (P)
Junior private eyes solve the mystery of the missing homework paper in a humorous, easy-to-read detective story. (R2–3)

2925 Lexau, Joan M. Olaf Reads; illus. by Harvey Weiss. Dial, 1961. 53p. $2.75; lib. ed. $2.78 net. (P)
Three funny, easy-to-read stories tell the trouble Olaf has because he does not read. Good for reading readiness or to encourage independent reading. (R2–3)

2926 Lifton, Betty Jean. The Cock and the Ghost Cat; illus. by Fuku Akino. Atheneum, 1965. 32p. $3.50; lib. ed. $3.41 net. (P–I)
Koko, a brave red cock, saves his beloved master from the demon ghost cat. Fine literary style and imaginative illustrations distinguish this tale of old Japan.

2927 Lifton, Betty Jean. Joji and the Dragon; illus. by Eiichi Mitsui. Morrow, 1957. unp. lib. ed. $3.32 net. (P–I)
Though Joji was a scarecrow, the crows loved him and came to his rescue in his time of need. Gentle humor and Japanese atmosphere in story and brush drawings.

2928 Lindgren, Astrid. Christmas in the Stable; text by Astrid Lindgren; pictures by Harald Wiberg. Coward-McCann, 1962. unp. $3.50; lib. ed. $3.29 net. (P)
A mother tells the Christmas story to her little girl, who sees the events as if they were happening in the present. There is dignity and reverence in the story and in the softly colored illustrations.

2929 Lindgren, Astrid. The Tomten; adapted from a poem by Viktor Rydberg; illus. by Harald Wiberg. Coward-McCann, 1961. unp. $3.50; lib. ed. $3.29 net. (P)
The tomten is a Swedish folklore character who makes his nightly rounds to see that all is well in farmhouse and stable. Beautiful illustrations perfectly evoke frosty, starlit winter scenes.

2930 Lindgren, Astrid. The Tomten and the Fox; adapted by Astrid Lindgren from a poem by Karl-Erik Forsslund; illus. by Harald Wiberg. Coward-McCann, 1966. unp. $3.50; lib. ed. $3.29 net. (P)
When the sly fox comes on Christmas Eve to raid the henhouse, the tomten shares food left for him by the children and sends the fox away content to spare the hens. The contrast between the snowy barnyard and the warm, bright kitchen is well captured in the illustrations.

2931 Lionni, Leo. Frederick. Pantheon, 1967. unp. $3.50; lib. ed. $3.39 net. (P)
Frederick is a field mouse with the heart of a poet. While his brothers store up food for the winter, he stores up the beauty and warmth of summer to brighten dark days. Delightful collage illustrations by the author.

2932 Lionni, Leo. Swimmy. Pantheon, 1963. unp. $3.50; lib. ed. $3.39 net. (P)
Swimmy is a small black fish who teaches the larger red fish how to protect themselves from their enemies. A fantastic underwater world is depicted in the author's stunning illustrations.

2933 Littlefield, William. The Whiskers of Ho Ho; pictures by Vladimir Bobri. Lothrop, 1958. 33p. $3.95; lib. ed. $3.70 net. (P–I)
In this Chinese version of the origin of Easter eggs, Ho Ho, the rabbit, collaborates with his master and a hen to paint eggs which they take to countries where Easter is being celebrated. An original story told with grace and illustrated with beautifully designed Easter eggs.

2934 Lobel, Anita. Sven's Bridge; story and pictures by Anita Lobel. Harper, 1965. unp. $2.95; lib. ed. $2.92 net. (P)
A charmingly illustrated book about a bridge blown up by an impatient king. Sven, the bridgekeeper, and all the townspeople were unhappy until the bridge was rebuilt.

2935   Lobel, Anita. The Troll Music; story and pictures by Anita Lobel. Harper, 1966. unp. $2.95; lib. ed. $2.92 net. (P)

A mischievous troll casts a spell upon a group of traveling musicians, causing animal sounds to come from their instruments. How a clever flutist breaks the spell makes a delightful story, illustrated with gay pictures.

2936   Lopshire, Robert. Put Me in the Zoo. Beginner Books, 1960. 58p. $1.95; lib. ed. $2.29 net. (P)

An easy-to-read story about a large dog who joins a circus. (R1–2)

2937   McCloskey, Robert. Blueberries for Sal. Viking, 1948. 54p. $3.50; lib. ed. $3.37 net. (P)

Sal and a baby bear find themselves with the wrong mothers as they pick blueberries on a Maine hillside. Delightful pictures (by the author) of pine woods and sea. (R2–3)

2938   McCloskey, Robert. Lentil. Viking, 1940. unp. $3.50; lib. ed. $3.37 net. (P–I)

Scenes and activities in a small Midwestern town come to life in McCloskey's humorous story and pictures of Lentil, the boy who substituted for the town band on an important occasion.

2939   McCloskey, Robert. Make Way for Ducklings. Viking, 1941. unp. $3.50; lib. ed. $3.37 net. (P)

When a mallard family tries to cross a busy Boston street, a kindly policeman comes to their rescue. The author's full-page lithographs are full of action and humor.

2940   McCloskey, Robert. One Morning in Maine. Viking, 1952. 64p. $3.50; lib. ed. $3.37 net. (P)

Warm family life is reflected in this story of how Sal lost her first tooth.

2941   McCrea, James, and **McCrea, Ruth.** The King's Procession. Atheneum, 1963. unp. $3.25; lib. ed. $3.07 net. (P)

A boy's loyalty to his shabby little donkey is the subject of this pleasant picture book.

2942   MacDonald, Golden. The Little Island; with illus. by Leonard Weisgard. Doubleday, 1946. unp. $3.75. (P)

Richly colored pictures show a little is-land in changing seasons and weathers as a kitten tries to discover the secret of what makes an island. A simple, poetic story for the imaginative child.

2943   MacDonald, Golden. Little Lost Lamb; with illus. by Leonard Weisgard. Doubleday, 1945. unp. $3.95. (P)

In this modern version of the old Bible story, the only little black lamb in the flock wanders away and the shepherd boy searches for him through the night.

2944   McGinley, Phyllis. All around the Town; illus. by Helen Stone. Lippincott, 1948. unp. $3.50; lib. ed. $3.39 net. (P)

Lively rhymes and gay illustrations about the sights and sounds of New York City.

2945   McLeod, Emilie Warren. One Snail and Me; illus. by Walter Lorraine. Little, 1961. 32p. $3.25; lib. ed. $3.14 net. (P)

A counting book about a little girl who shares her bathtub with many animals.

2946   Marino, Dorothy. Where Are the Mothers? Lippincott, 1959. unp. lib. ed. $2.93 net. (P)

While kindergarten and first-grade children are at school, their mothers are busy in many different places. A simple story to help young children understand family responsibilities and activities.

2947   Martin, Patricia Miles. Calvin and the Cub Scouts; drawn by Tom Hamil. Putnam, 1964. 47p. $3; lib. ed. $2.86 net. (P–I)

A truly funny story about how Calvin acquired a pet for the Cub Scout pet show.

2948   Martin, Patricia Miles. The Rice Bowl Pet; illus. by Ezra Jack Keats. Crowell, 1962. 30p. $3.50; lib. ed. $3.76 net. (P–I)

When Ah Jim's mother tells him that he may have a pet only if he can find one small enough to fit into a rice bowl—and into the family's tiny apartment in San Francisco's Chinatown—Ah Jim solves his problem in a most amusing way.

2949   Matsuno, Masako. Chie and the Sports Day; illus. by Kazue Mizumura. World, 1965. unp. $3.50; lib. ed. $3.41 net. (P)

A small Japanese girl finds a way to help her inept brother on sports day. The four-color illustrations are typically Japanese, and there is a list of Japanese words.

2950 **Matsuno, Masako.** A Pair of Red Clogs; illus. by Kazue Mizumura. World, 1960. unp. $3; lib. ed. $2.96 net. (P)
A Japanese grandmother reminisces about how, as a small child, she broke her red clogs and tried to conceal the accident. Quietly makes the point that deception can bring unhappiness. Story and pictures are rich in Oriental feeling.

2951 **Matsuno, Masako.** Taro and the Tofu; illus. by Kazue Mizumura. World, 1962. unp. lib. ed. $3.41 net. (P–I)
When Taro goes back through the dark and cold to return the extra 40 yen the peddler gave him when he bought bean curd for supper, the good feeling of having done right rewards him for his trouble. Present-day life in Japan is portrayed in story and beautifully colored pictures.

2952 **Matthiesen, Thomas.** ABC: An Alphabet Book; photos. in color by Thomas Matthiesen. Platt & Munk, 1966. unp. $2.50. (P)
Familiar objects—shoes, a clock, a balloon—represent the 26 letters of the alphabet. The appealing photographs and brief text should be useful with very young children.

2953 **Matthiesen, Thomas.** Things To See: A Child's World of Familiar Objects; photos. in color by Thomas Matthiesen. Platt & Munk, 1966. unp. $2.50. (P)
More excellent color photographs presented as in the *ABC* book, above.

2954 **Miles, Betty.** A House for Everyone; illus. by Jo Lowrey. Knopf, 1958. 44p. lib. ed. $3.39 net. (P)
A picture book about the different kinds of houses in which different kinds of people live.

2955 **Minarik, Else Holmelund.** Father Bear Comes Home; pictures by Maurice Sendak. Harper, 1959. 62p. $1.95; lib. ed. $2.19 net. (P)
A beguiling small bear waits for his father to come home from the sea. Tenderness and humor in family relationships pervade both story and pictures. (R1–2)

2956 **Minarik, Else Holmelund.** Little Bear; pictures by Maurice Sendak. Harper, 1961. 63p. $1.95; lib. ed. $2.19 net. (P)
Four stories in which Little Bear and his mother have a happy day together. Delightful illustrations. (R1–2)

2957 **Minarik, Else Holmelund.** Little Bear's Friend; pictures by Maurice Sendak. Harper, 1961. 57p. $1.95; lib. ed. $2.19 net. (P)
After playing all summer with his human friend, Emily, Little Bear is sad when she must go back to school, until Father Bear shows him a way to keep in touch with her. (R1–2)

2958 **Minarik, Else Holmelund.** Little Bear's Visit; pictures by Maurice Sendak. Harper, 1960. unp. $1.95; lib. ed. $2.19 net. (P)
On a wonderful day with his grandparents, Little Bear hears a story about his mother when she was a little girl, has lots of good things to eat, and plays games, until he falls asleep. (R2–3)

2959 **Mizumura, Kazue.** I See the Winds. Crowell, 1966. unp. $2.95; lib. ed. $2.65 net. (P)
The wind in all its moods is portrayed in poetic text and lovely watercolor pictures.

2960 **Mosel, Arlene.** Tikki Tikki Tembo; retold by Arlene Mosel; illus. by Blair Lent. Holt, 1968. unp. $4.50; lib. ed. $3.97 net. (P)
An amusingly retold Chinese folk tale about a first son with a very long name. When Tikki Tikki Tembo-No Sa Rembo-Chari Bari Ruchi-Pip Peri Pembo fell into the well, it took his little brother so long to say his name and get help that Tikki almost drowned. Handsome illustrations in gay, rich colors enhance the tongue-in-cheek humor and add Chinese flavor to the repetitive story.

2961 **Munari, Bruno.** ABC. World, 1960. unp. $3.95; lib. ed. $3.86 net. (P)
An original and stunning alphabet book. Each letter, printed in heavy black, is represented by two or more familiar objects, shown in brilliant color.

2962 **Munari, Bruno.** Zoo. World, 1963. unp. $3.95; lib. ed. $3.86 net. (P)
Big, handsomely designed animals on double-page spreads are characterized by brief, witty statements.

2963 **Myller, Rolf.** How Big Is a Foot? Atheneum, 1962. unp. $2.95; lib. ed. $2.74 net. (P)
A nonsense book for the youngest, show-

ing the confusion which results when there is no standard system of measurement. (R1–2)

2964 Myrick, Mildred. The Secret Three; drawings by Arnold Lobel. Harper, 1963. 64p. $1.95; lib. ed. $2.19 net. (P)

A seaside mystery story in which a coded message leads to the formation of a club. Fun for would-be sleuths. (R2–3)

2965 Ness, Evaline. Josefina February; written and illus. by Evaline Ness. Scribner, 1963. unp. lib. ed. $3.12 net. (P)

Striking wood-block prints in an unusual color combination carry the simple story of a little Haitian girl who finds a baby donkey but gives him up in exchange for a pair of shoes for her grandfather.

2966 Ness, Evaline. Sam, Bangs, & Moonshine; written and illus. by Evaline Ness. Holt, 1966. unp. $3.95; lib. ed. $3.59 net. (P–I)

Sam—short for Samantha—is a motherless child who confuses truth with "moonshine." Only after her make-believe almost brings tragedy to her friend Thomas and Bangs, her cat, does Sam realize the difference between truth and fantasy. Illustrations in pale watercolors are imaginative and beautiful.

2967 Newberry, Clare Turlay. Marshmallow; story and pictures by Clare Turlay Newberry. Harper, 1942. unp. $4.95; lib. ed. $4.79 net. (P)

Soft, furry illustrations show a white rabbit and a black kitten whose friendship develops in spite of a bad beginning. A large picture book with simple text.

2968 Newberry, Clare Turlay. Mittens; story and pictures by Clare Turlay Newberry. Harper, 1936. 28p. $3.50; lib. ed. $3.27 net. (P)

Mittens, a kitten with six white toes on each paw, is lost and then found. Six-year-old Richard is shown with his new pet in remarkably realistic and appealing illustrations.

2969 Nodset, Joan L. Who Took the Farmer's Hat? Pictures by Fritz Siebel. Harper, 1963. unp. $2.95; lib. ed. $2.92 net. (P)

When Farmer Brown's hat blew away, the animals found many amusing uses for it. (R1–2)

2970 Orgel, Doris. Cindy's Snowdrops; illus. by Ati Forberg. Knopf, 1966. unp. $3.25; lib. ed. $2.99 net. (P)

Five-year-old Cindy follows all the steps of a true gardener as she selects bulbs, plants them carefully, and watches through the seasons until they come up in the spring. (R2–3)

2971 Ormondroyd, Edward. Theodore; illus. by John M. Larrecq. Parnassus, 1966. unp. $3.25. (P)

When Lucy carelessly let her teddy bear, Theodore, get mixed up with the laundry, he came out so clean she did not recognize him. A good read-aloud story for kindergarten and first grade.

2972 Parish, Peggy. Amelia Bedelia; pictures by Fritz Siebel. Harper, 1963. unp. $2.50; lib. ed. $2.57 net. (P)

Amelia Bedelia is a maid whose talent for interpreting instructions literally results in comical situations, such as dressing the chicken in fine clothes.

2973 Parkin, Rex. The Red Carpet; story and pictures by Rex Parkin. Macmillan, 1948. unp. $4.25. (P)

The red carpet surprises everyone by running away to meet a celebrated visitor. Action and excitement in rhymed story and bright pictures.

2974 Payne, Emmy. Katy No-Pocket; pictures by H. A. Rey. Houghton, 1944. unp. $3.50; lib. ed. $3.23 net. (P)

A carpenter solves a problem for Katy Kangaroo, who had no pocket in which to carry her baby. A funny story with a surprise ending.

2975 Peet, Bill. Huge Harold; written and illus. by Bill Peet. Houghton, 1961. 45p. $3.50; lib. ed. $3.23 net. (P)

A rhymed story of a rabbit who outgrew his home. The author's droll illustrations are perfectly suited to the tall tale.

2976 Peet, Bill. The Pinkish, Purplish, Bluish Egg; written and illus. by Bill Peet. Houghton, 1963. 46p. $3.50; lib. ed. $3.23 net. (P)

Myrtle, the turtledove, defies her friends and hatches a strange egg into a strange creature—a griffin.

2977 Piatti, Celestino. Animal ABC. Atheneum, 1965. unp. $4.95. (P)

The author's striking illustrations in bold color show animals from alligator to zebra, with a witty four-line rhyme for each.

2978 Piatti, Celestino. The Happy Owls. Atheneum, 1964. unp. $4.95. (P)

A moral tale about two wise owls who bring harmony to their quarrelsome neighbors. Handsomely designed and richly colored pictures by the author.

2979 Piper, Watty. The Little Engine That Could; the complete original edition; retold by Watty Piper; illus. by George & Doris Hauman. Platt & Munk, 1961. unp. $1.50. (P)

When a train carrying good things to children breaks down, the little blue engine proves his courage and determination. The rhythmic, repetitive text encourages children to help tell the story.

2980 Platt, Kin. Big Max; with pictures by Robert Lopshire. Harper, 1965. 64p. $1.95; lib. ed. $2.19 net. (P)

Humor and mystery are combined in a detective story for beginning readers. (R2–3)

2981 Politi, Leo. A Boat for Peppe. Scribner, 1950. unp. lib. ed. $3.12 net. (P)

Monterey, California, is the setting for this story of a Sicilian-American boy who longs for a boat of his own. The author's pictures are fresh and bright.

2982 Politi, Leo. Juanita. Scribner, 1948. unp. lib. ed. $3.12 net. (P)

At Easter the Mexican-American children of Los Angeles parade their pets to the mission to be blessed by the padre. Juanita is the central character in a gentle story, vitalized by the author's pictures of the colorful festival.

2983 Politi, Leo. Moy Moy. Scribner, 1960. unp. lib. ed. $3.12 net. (P)

Moy Moy participates in the exciting New Year festival in the Chinese community of Los Angeles. Traditional games, dances, and costumes are shown in gay pictures.

2984 Politi, Leo. Pedro: The Angel of Olvera Street. Scribner, 1946. unp. lib. ed. $2.76 net. (P)

Because Pedro sings so beautifully, he is chosen to lead La Posada, a Mexican street celebration, at Christmas time. The

Mexican section of Los Angeles comes to life in story and pictures. Words and music of two carols are included.

2985 Politi, Leo. Rosa. Scribner, 1963. unp. $3.25; lib. ed. $3.12 net. (P)

Everyday life in Mexico is depicted in lavish color in this story of Rosa, who longed for a doll and got a baby sister instead.

2986 Politi, Leo. Song of the Swallows. Scribner, 1949. unp. $3.25; lib. ed. $3.12 net. (P)

Each year the swallows return to the Mission of Capistrano on St. Joseph's Day. Pictures in lovely springtime colors show Juan and his old friend as they wait to welcome the swallows. Words and music of the swallow song are included.

2987 Potter, Beatrix. The Tailor of Gloucester. Warne, 1931. 85p. lib. ed. $1.50 net. (P)

When a poor tailor falls ill just at Christmas, little mice finish a beautiful embroidered coat for his richest customer. A read-aloud classic in polished style, perfectly complemented by the author's exquisite watercolor illustrations, as are all of Beatrix Potter's small books for small hands.

2988 Potter, Beatrix. The Tale of Benjamin Bunny. Warne, 1932. 58p. lib. ed. $1.50 net. (P)

Benjamin and his cousin Peter pay dearly for their exciting adventure in Mr. McGregor's garden.

2989 Potter, Beatrix. The Tale of Jemima Puddle-Duck. Warne, 1936. 84p. lib. ed. $1.50 net. (P)

A silly duck, determined to hatch her own eggs, chooses the wrong place for a nest.

2990 Potter, Beatrix. The Tale of Peter Rabbit. Warne, n.d. 58p. lib. ed. $1.50 net. (P)

Disobedient Peter learns why his mother told him not to go into Mr. McGregor's garden.

2991 Puner, Helen. Daddies—What They Do All Day; illus. by Roger Duvoisin. Lothrop, 1946. 30p. $3.25; lib. ed. $3.13 net. (P)

Big, bright pictures and simple text show daddies at work as doctors, office workers, miners, window washers, etc. Useful in the primary unit on home and family.

2992   Raskin, Ellen. Nothing Ever Happens on My Block. Atheneum, 1966. unp. $2.95; lib. ed. $2.74 net. (P)

Chester misses the excitement going on around him while he sits wishing for adventure. The author's illustrations are full of action and fun.

2993   Rey, H. A. Curious George. Houghton, 1941. 56p. $3.25; lib. ed. $3.07 net. (P)

Curious George, introduced in humorous text and the author's lively pictures, is a monkey who gets himself and his owner into one scrape after another, all because of his curiosity. (R2–3)

2994   Rey, H. A. Curious George Learns the Alphabet. Houghton, 1963. 72p. $3.25; lib. ed. $3.07 net. (P)

When the man in the yellow hat decides to teach his little monkey the alphabet, everybody has fun. The author's ingenious device of drawing the letters right into his pictures makes a game of the lesson. (R2–3)

2995   Rey, H. A. Curious George Rides a Bike. Houghton, 1952. 45p. $3.25; lib. ed. $3.07 net. (P)

George starts out on his bike to deliver papers and ends up as a circus performer. (R2–3)

2996   Rey, Margret. Curious George Flies a Kite; pictures by H. A. Rey. Houghton, 1958. 80p. $2.95; lib. ed. $2.90 net. (P)

More escapades of George who is, as usual, in hot water. Limited vocabulary makes this book easier to read than the other stories about the curious little monkey. (R1–2)

2997   Rey, Margret, and Rey, H. A. Curious George Goes to the Hospital; in collaboration with the Children's Hospital Medical Center, Boston. Houghton, 1966. 48p. $3.25; lib. ed. $3.07 net. (P)

When George goes to the hospital to have a piece of jigsaw puzzle removed from his stomach, he behaves very well until the last day, when curiosity again gets him into trouble. Hospital routines are accurately followed in an amusing story which should help to dispel children's fear of going to the hospital. (R2–3)

2998   Sandburg, Helga. Joel and the Wild Goose; illus. by Thomas Daly. Dial, 1963. unp. $3.50; lib. ed. $3.39 net. (P–I)

A lonely boy makes a pet of a lonely wild goose, only to let it fly away and join its own kind. A poignant story interpreted by sensitive colored pictures.

2999   Sauer, Julia L. Mike's House; illus. by Don Freeman. Viking, 1954. 31p. $2.75; lib. ed. $2.73 net. (P)

Because *Mike Mulligan* is his favorite book, four-year-old Robert loves the public library—"Mike's House"—and never misses a story hour there. One day he gets lost in a snowstorm and is helped by many kindly people before arriving at the library. An appealing main character, attractive illustrations, and an amusing story. For kindergarten and first-grade story hour. (R2–3)

3000   Scheer, Julian, and **Bileck, Marvin.** Rain Makes Applesauce. Holiday, 1964. unp. $4.95. (P)

A book of original nonsense, illustrated with intricate drawings. Small children love the refrains, "Rain makes applesauce" and "You're just talking silly talk," and enjoy the fantastic details in the pictures.

3001   Schlein, Miriam. City Boy, Country Boy. Childrens Pr., 1955. unp. $2.75. (P)

A small boy discovers that both city and country are pleasant places in which to live. (R2–3)

3002   Schneider, Nina. While Susie Sleeps; pictures by Dagmar Wilson. W. R. Scott, 1948. unp. $3.25. (P)

Shows small children that many community helpers work through the night to bring comfort and safety to each home.

3003   Schulz, Charles M. A Charlie Brown Christmas. World, 1965. unp. $2.50. (P–I)

Good Old Charlie Brown, beloved by young and old, is frustrated even at Christmas.

3004   Scott, Ann Herbert. Big Cowboy Western; pictures by Richard W. Lewis. Lothrop, 1965. unp. $2.95; lib. ed. $2.84 net. (P)

Nobody but Mr. Arrico, the fruit-and-vegetable man, will believe that five-year-old Martin is a big cowboy. Realistic illustrations show an attractive Negro family and an appealing small boy in imaginative play.

3005 **Scott, Ann Herbert.** Sam; drawings by Symeon Shimin. McGraw-Hill, 1967. unp. $3.95; lib. ed. $3.26 net. (P)
Sam is an engaging Negro child trying desperately to get his busy family to notice him. Not until he bursts into tears of frustration do his parents and brother and sister realize his need to be a part of the group. A simple story with warm, attractive illustrations.

3006 **Sendak, Maurice.** Alligators All Around: An Alphabet. Harper, 1962. unp. $2.95; lib. ed. $2.19 net. (P)
This, and the three small books following, are rhymed nonsense tales with the author's amusing illustrations.

3007 **Sendak, Maurice.** Chicken Soup with Rice: A Book of Months. Harper, 1962. unp. $2.95; lib. ed. $2.19 net. (P)
"I told you once / I told you twice / All seasons of the year are nice / For eating chicken soup with rice!"

3008 **Sendak, Maurice.** One Was Johnny: A Counting Book. Harper, 1962. unp. $2.95; lib. ed. $2.19 net. (P)
Johnny finds a surprising way to get rid of the queer creatures who overrun his house.

3009 **Sendak, Maurice.** Pierre: A Cautionary Tale in Five Chapters and a Prologue. Harper, 1962. unp. $2.95; lib. ed. $2.19 net. (P)
Pierre gets his just deserts for always saying, "I don't care."

3010 **Sendak, Maurice.** Where the Wild Things Are; story and pictures by Maurice Sendak. Harper, 1963. unp. $3.95; lib. ed. $3.79 net. (P)
Max, sent supperless to bed, escapes in imagination to the land where he is king of the "wild things." Imaginative illustrations show playfully horrendous creatures cavorting in a never-never land of great beauty.

3011 **Seuss, Dr.** And To Think That I Saw It on Mulberry Street. Vanguard, 1937. unp. $2.95. (P–I)
Dr. Seuss's uninhibited rhymes and weird and wonderful drawings are well loved by children of all ages. In this book, a small boy's imagination converts a plain horse and wagon into a circus parade led by an elephant and two giraffes.

3012 **Seuss, Dr.** The Cat in the Hat. Random, 1957. 61p. $1.95; lib. ed. $2.29 net. (P)
First and second graders can read this zany story for themselves. Nonsense verses and rollicking pictures tell how a fantastic cat entertains two children one rainy day. (R1–2)

3013 **Seuss, Dr.** The Cat in the Hat Comes Back! Beginner Books, 1958. 61p. $1.95; lib. ed. $2.29 net. (P)
More antics of the astonishing cat in the hat. (R1–2)

3014 **Seuss, Dr.** The 500 Hats of Bartholomew Cubbins. Vanguard, 1938. unp. $2.95. (P)
A read-aloud story telling what happened to Bartholomew Cubbins when he couldn't take his hat off before the king.

3015 **Seuss, Dr.** Horton Hatches the Egg. Random, 1940. unp. $2.95; lib. ed. $3.07 net. (P)
An unobtrusive moral emerges from these hilarious verses about a faithful elephant who hatches an egg for the lazy bird Mazie. (R2–3)

3016 **Seuss, Dr.** How the Grinch Stole Christmas. Random, 1957. unp. $2.95; lib. ed. $3.07 net. (P–I)
A queer creature who tries to abolish Christmas gets his comeuppance.

3017 **Seuss, Dr.** If I Ran the Circus. Random, 1956. unp. $2.95; lib. ed. $3.07 net. (P–I)
Morris McGurk assembles an array of fabulous animals in his Circus McGurkus, along with an intrepid performer, Sneelock.

3018 **Seuss, Dr.** McElligot's Pool; written and illus. by Dr. Seuss. Random, 1947. unp. $2.95; lib. ed. $3.07 net. (P–I)
In spite of warnings that there are no fish in McElligot's Pool, a boy continues to fish and to imagine the rare and wonderful denizens of the deep which he just *might* catch.

3019 **Seuss, Dr.** Thidwick, the Big-hearted Moose; written and illus. by Dr. Seuss. Random, 1948. unp. $2.95; lib. ed. $3.07 net. (P–I)
When a colony of free-loaders takes up residence in Thidwick's antlers, he finds a novel way to solve his problem.

3020 **Sewell, Helen.** Blue Barns: The Story of Two Big Geese and Seven Little Ducks. Macmillan, 1933. unp. $3.50; lib. ed. $3.74 net. (P)

Engaging lithograph drawings by the author extend a simple story about Andrew the gander and his seven adopted ducklings. For story hour in kindergarten and first grade.

3021 **Sherman, Nancy.** Gwendolyn, the Miracle Hen; illus. by Edward Sorel. Golden Pr., 1961. unp. $3.95. (P)

Gwendolyn, who lays beautifully colored and designed eggs, saves kind Farmer Brown's farm from Mr. Meany. Rhymed text and delightful colored illustrations.

3022 **Shulevitz, Uri.** One Monday Morning. Scribner, 1967. unp. $3.95; lib. ed. $3.63 net. (P)

On a rainy morning a small tenement dweller sits dreaming of a procession of playing-card characters who come to visit him each day of the week until they at last find him at home. Beginning with the king, a new member of the court is added each morning until the little boy's room is full of make-believe characters who "just dropped in to say hello." Repetitive text and humorous, stylized illustrations by the author.

3023 **Simon, Mina.** If You Were an Eel, How Would You Feel? Illus. by Howard Simon. Follett, 1963. unp. $3.50; lib. ed. $3.48 net. (P)

An eel's-eye view of the world, illustrated with appropriate pictures.

3024 **Slobodkina, Esphyr.** Caps for Sale: A Tale of a Peddler, Some Monkeys & Their Monkey Business; told and illus. by Esphyr Slobodkina. W. R. Scott, 1947. unp. $2.75. (P)

While a cap peddler is napping, monkeys steal his caps. How he gets them back makes a very funny story, excellent for dramatization.

3025 **Stolz, Mary.** Emmett's Pig; pictures by Garth Williams. Harper, 1959. 61p. $1.95; lib. ed. $2.19 net. (P)

Even though he lives in a city apartment, Emmett's wish for a real, live pig is finally granted. (R1–2)

3026 **Swift, Hildegarde H.,** and **Ward, Lynd.** The Little Red Lighthouse and the Great Gray Bridge. Harcourt, 1942. unp. $3.25; lib. ed. $3.38 net. (P)

After the great beacon atop the new George Washington Bridge was installed, the little red lighthouse feared he would no longer be useful; but when an emergency arose, the little lighthouse proved that he was still important.

3027 **Taylor, Mark.** Henry the Explorer; illus. by Graham Booth. Atheneum, 1966. unp. $4.95; lib. ed. $4.75 net. (P)

One snowy day Henry takes his dog Angus and sets out on an exploring expedition. Though lost for a time, they manage to reach home ahead of the search party.

3028 **Titus, Eve.** Anatole; pictures by Paul Galdone. McGraw-Hill, 1956. 32p. $3.75; lib. ed. $3.26 net. (P)

Anatole is a mouse who has a job as taster in a Paris cheese factory. Humorous story and pictures with a French flavor.

3029 **Tresselt, Alvin.** Autumn Harvest; illus. by Roger Duvoisin. Lothrop, 1951. unp. $3.25; lib. ed. $3.13 net. (P)

Rhythmic text and bright autumn colors show the coming of fall. Good nature-study material for the early primary grades.

3030 **Tresselt, Alvin.** Follow the Wind; pictures by Roger Duvoisin. Lothrop, 1950. unp. $3.25; lib. ed. $3.13 net. (P)

Breezy story and pictures tell how the wind can be both fierce and gentle.

3031 **Tresselt, Alvin.** Frog in the Well; illus. by Roger Duvoisin. Lothrop, 1958. unp. $3.50; lib. ed. $3.35 net. (P)

Marvelous green, shiny frogs in many froggy positions are the special feature of this brief story about a frog who learned that his particular well was not the whole world.

3032 **Tresselt, Alvin.** "Hi, Mister Robin!" Pictures by Roger Duvoisin. Lothrop, 1950. unp. $3.25; lib. ed. $3.13 net. (P)

After Mr. Robin arrives, a little boy finds many other signs that the dreary winter is changing into spring. Lovely country scenes in delicate color encourage the young child to do his own looking for signs of spring.

3033 **Tresselt, Alvin.** Hide and Seek Fog; illus. by Roger Duvoisin. Lothrop, 1965. unp. $3.50; lib. ed. $3.35 net. (P)

Only the children enjoyed the heavy fog which enveloped the Cape Cod village for three days. A mood piece with poetic text and beautiful, misty pictures.

3034 **Tresselt, Alvin.** I Saw the Sea Come In; illus. by Roger Duvoisin. Lothrop, 1954. unp. $3.50; lib. ed. $3.35 net. (P)

On his first visit to the seashore a little boy gets up early to watch the tide inch up the white beach.

3035 **Tresselt, Alvin.** Rain Drop Splash; pictures by Leonard Weisgard. Lothrop, 1946. unp. $3.50; lib. ed. $3.35 net. (P)

Brief text and striking illustrations follow the raindrops into a puddle, a stream, and finally to the sea.

3036 **Tresselt, Alvin.** Sun Up; pictures by Roger Duvoisin. Lothrop, 1949. unp. $3.25; lib. ed. $3.13 net. (P)

Author and artist follow the activities of farm life from cockcrow to sunset.

3037 **Tresselt, Alvin.** Wake Up, City! Pictures by Roger Duvoisin. Lothrop, 1957. unp. $3.25; lib. ed. $3.13 net. (P)

From the small sounds of early morning to the clatter of people going to work, the city comes to life each day.

3038 **Tresselt, Alvin.** Wake Up, Farm! Pictures by Roger Duvoisin. Lothrop, 1955. unp. $3.25; lib. ed. $3.13 net. (P)

On the farm the animals are first to begin the day, then the farmer and his wife, and, finally, the little boy.

3039 **Tresselt, Alvin.** White Snow, Bright Snow; illus. by Roger Duvoisin. Lothrop, 1947. 32p. $3.50; lib. ed. $3.35 net. (P)

Arresting pictures effectively convey the frosty beauty of a heavy snowfall and depict the fun and work that come with it. Brief, poetic text.

3040 **Tresselt, Alvin.** The World in the Candy Egg; illus. by Roger Duvoisin. Lothrop, 1967. unp. $3.75; lib. ed. $3.57 net. (P)

Each of the toys in a toyshop peeks into a spun-sugar Easter egg and sees the things that please him most, and a little girl sees the whole "magic world, little world, made for a child's delight." A charming seasonal picture book illustrated in gay springtime colors.

3041 **Tudor, Tasha.** 1 Is One. Walck, 1956. unp. $3.75. (P)

A counting book in which the author-artist introduces the numbers from 1 to 20 in simple rhymes and whimsical illustrations.

3042 **Tworkov, Jack.** The Camel Who Took a Walk; pictures by Roger Duvoisin. Dutton, 1951. unp. $3.50; lib. ed. $3.46 net. (P)

A suspense story with a surprise ending about how a beautiful young camel escaped a fierce tiger, a monkey, a squirrel, and a bird. Enjoyable nonsense in text and pictures.

3043 **Uchida, Yoshiko.** Sumi's Prize; pictures by Kazue Mizumura. Scribner, 1964. unp. lib. ed. $3.12 net. (P–I)

A small Japanese girl fails miserably to win a prize for kite flying, but wins a special prize for rescuing the mayor's silk hat. Japan at festival time is the background for an amusing story and lively pictures.

3044 **Uchida, Yoshiko.** Sumi's Special Happening; pictures by Kazue Mizumura. Scribner, 1966. unp. $3.50; lib. ed. $3.31 net. (P–I)

Instead of a present, Sumi gives her 99-year-old friend a "happening"—an unforgettable ride on a fire engine.

3045 **Udry, Janice May.** Let's Be Enemies; pictures by Maurice Sendak. Harper, 1961. unp. $1.95; lib. ed. $2.19 net. (P)

John, annoyed because James is entirely too bossy, decides that he no longer wants him for a friend and goes to tell him so. Instead of becoming enemies, they agree that it would be more fun to go skating. An artless little treatise on childhood friendships, with illustrations that exactly suit the story.

3046 **Udry, Janice May.** A Tree Is Nice; pictures by Marc Simont. Harper, 1956. unp. $2.95; lib. ed. $2.92 net. (P)

The importance and fun of trees is the theme of a simple story and clear, beautiful pictures.

3047 **Udry, Janice May.** What Mary Jo Shared; illus. by Eleanor Mill. Albert Whitman, 1966. unp. $2.95. (P–I)

Mary Jo, attending an integrated school for the first time, can think of nothing different to bring for "show and tell," until she decides to share her father. Warm relationships and realistic illustrations.

3048 **Ungerer, Tomi.** Crictor. Harper, 1958. 32p. $3.50; lib. ed. $3.27 net. (P)

Gay nonsense about a boa constrictor who became the pet and assistant of a French schoolteacher. Crictor's unusual activities—teaching the children to spell, serving as a sliding board and a jump rope, capturing a burglar—provide fun in the story and the author's pictures.

3049 **Waber, Bernard.** The House on East 88th Street. Houghton, 1962. 48p. $3.50; lib. ed. $3.23 net. (P)

When the Primms move into their new house, they find Lyle, a performing crocodile, in the bathtub. How Lyle ingratiates himself into the family makes a daffy read-aloud story, augmented by the author's fun-filled, colored pictures.

3050 **Waber, Bernard.** Lyle and the Birthday Party. Houghton, 1966. 48p. $3.25; lib. ed. $3.07 net. (P)

Lyle, sick with jealousy because he gets no attention on Joshua's birthday, is sent to the hospital, where he recovers from his bad humor by helping others.

3051 **Ward, Lynd.** The Biggest Bear. Houghton, 1952. 84p. $3.50; lib. ed. $3.23 net. (P–I)

A handsome picture book about a boy who gets a bear cub for a pet. Lively humor in the story and in the author's monochrome illustrations.

3052 **Watson, Nancy Dingman.** Sugar on Snow; illus. by Aldren A. Watson. Viking, 1964. 43p. $3; lib. ed. $2.96 net. (P–I)

Cammie gets her wish to have pickles and sugar on snow for her birthday. Maple sugaring is described in a quiet read-aloud story, with chilly blue-and-white illustrations showing all the steps in the process.

3053 **Weil, Lisl.** The Busiest Boy in Holland. Houghton, 1959. 38p. $2.75; lib. ed. $2.73 net. (P)

Toontje, a boy with ideas, goes to Amsterdam for the Flower Festival and there becomes a minor hero. The author-artist has created an attractive picture book showing colorful scenes of Dutch life.

3054 **Wersba, Barbara.** Do Tigers Ever Bite Kings? Illus. by Mario Rivoli. Atheneum, 1966. unp. $3.50; lib. ed. $3.41 net. (P)

A rhymed story about a timid king and an equally timid tiger who collaborate to make the king seem brave. An amusingly different story with elaborate colored illustrations.

3055 **Wiese, Kurt.** Fish in the Air; story and pictures by Kurt Wiese. Viking, 1948. unp. $3.50; lib. ed. $3.37 net. (P–I)

A huge fish-shaped kite proves too much for a small Chinese boy in a funny story, perfect for reading aloud.

3056 **Wildsmith, Brian.** ABC. Watts, 1963. unp. lib. ed. $3.95 net. (P)

Glowing watercolors depict familiar objects set on brilliantly colored pages and named in both capital and lower-case letters. Useful in art classes as well as in story-hour discussions with young children.

3057 **Wildsmith, Brian.** Brian Wildsmith's Birds. Watts, 1967. unp. $4.95. (P)

Similar to the artist's *Wild Animals*, below, in quality, originality, and usefulness. Implications of the group terms, such as a "stare of owls" and a "rafter of turkeys," are suggested in witty pictures.

3058 **Wildsmith, Brian.** Brian Wildsmith's Wild Animals. Watts, 1967. unp. $4.95. (P)

Imaginatively designed and beautifully colored pictures of animals in groups (a pride of lions, a skulk of foxes) stimulate appreciation of color and awareness of new words.

3059 **Will.** Finders Keepers; by Will and Nicolas. Harcourt, 1951. unp. $3.25. (P)

Two quarrelsome dogs join forces to fight off a common enemy. Illustrations by Nicolas Mordvinoff are dramatic and humorous.

3060 **Will.** Two Reds; by Will and Nicolas. Harcourt, 1950. unp. $3.75. (P)

Red predominates in the vigorous pictures showing a redheaded boy and a red cat who have adventures together in a big city.

3061 **Williams, Garth.** The Big Golden Animal ABC. Golden Pr., 1957. unp. lib. ed. $2.39 net. (P)

A tiny rabbit gamboling across pages showing an animal for each letter of the alphabet adds interest to appealing pictures.

3062 **Williams, Gweneira.** Timid Timothy: The Kitten Who Learned To Be Brave; illus. by Leonard Weisgard. W. R. Scott, 1944. unp. $2.75. (P)

Timid children may identify with Timothy, who learns that courage comes through facing up to frightening experiences.

3063 **Wright, Ethel.** Saturday Walk; pictures by Richard Rose. W. R. Scott, 1954. unp. $2.50. (P)

Brief text and bright, uncluttered pictures of things that small boys admire tell of one boy's Saturday walk with his father.

3064 **Yashima, Mitsu,** and **Yashima, Taro.** Momo's Kitten. Viking, 1961. 33p. $3.50; lib. ed. $3.37 net. (P)

Momo, a little Japanese-American girl, adopts a stray cat who promptly produces five kittens. The author-artist team has produced an appealing picture book with a Japanese flavor in the illustrations.

3065 **Yashima, Taro.** Seashore Story. Viking, 1967. unp. $4.95; lib. ed. $4.53 net. (P)

Urashima, the Japanese Rip Van Winkle, befriends a turtle who rewards him by taking him to a wonderful place beneath the sea. Upon his return, many years later, his whole village is strange and he has become an old man. In this version of the tale a group of present-day children visit the lonely seashore where Urashima might have disappeared and wonder about the mystery. The author's misty illustrations have the same haunting quality as the story.

3066 **Yashima, Taro.** Umbrella. Viking, 1958. 30p. $3; lib. ed. $2.96 net. (P)

Momo, given an umbrella and a pair of red boots on her third birthday, is overjoyed when at last it rains and she can wear her new rain togs.

3067 **Yolen, Jane H.** The Emperor and the Kite; pictures by Ed Young. World, 1967. unp. $3.95; lib. ed. $3.86 net. (P–I)

Tiny Djeow Seow, the Chinese emperor's insignificant eighth child, is the only one clever and loving enough to rescue her father from his enemies. Illustrated with beautiful colored pictures cut from paper.

3068 **Zion, Gene.** Dear Garbage Man; pictures by Margaret Bloy Graham. Harper, 1957. unp. $3.25; lib. ed. $3.11 net. (P)

The new garbage man cannot bear to grind up the useful objects which he finds in the trash, until he discovers that his garbage can help to make land for a playground.

3069 **Zion, Gene.** Harry by the Sea; pictures by Margaret Bloy Graham. Harper, 1965. unp. $3.25; lib. ed. $3.11 net. (P)

Harry, a friendly little dog on a visit to the seashore with his family, creates havoc on the beach when a wave covers him with seaweed and makes him look like a sea monster. A farcical story supported by very funny illustrations.

3070 **Zion, Gene.** Harry the Dirty Dog; pictures by Margaret Bloy Graham. Harper, 1956. unp. $3.25; lib. ed. $3.11 net. (P)

Like many small children, Harry hated to take baths, so he hid the scrubbing brush and went to play in delightfully dirty places. When he came home, no longer a white dog with black spots but a black dog with white spots, he is frightened into reforming when his family does not recognize him.

3071 **Zion, Gene.** The Plant Sitter; pictures by Margaret Bloy Graham. Harper, 1959. unp. $3.25; lib. ed. $3.11 net. (P)

Tommy takes such good care of the neighbors' plants while they are on vacation that his house becomes a jungle. A bit of nature study and a good deal of fun in story and pictures.

3072 **Zion, Gene.** The Summer Snowman; pictures by Margaret Bloy Graham. Harper, 1956. unp. lib. ed. $2.92 net. (P)

Henry surprises his older brother by producing a tiny snowman (kept in the deep-freeze since winter) on the Fourth of July. A good read-aloud story for young children.

3073 **Zolotow, Charlotte.** Do You Know What I'll Do? Pictures by Garth Williams. Harper, 1958. unp. $3.25; lib. ed. $3.11 net. (P)

In a tender story and sensitive pictures a little girl tells her baby brother how she will express her love for him. For the quiet hour.

3074 **Zolotow, Charlotte.** Mr. Rabbit and the Lovely Present; pictures by Maurice Sendak. Harper, 1962. unp. $2.95; lib. ed. $2.92 net. (P)

A friendly rabbit helps a little girl find just the right present for her mother who likes colors—a basket of red apples, yellow bananas, green pears, and blue grapes. The quiet story, told in dialogue, is illustrated in richly colored pictures which exactly fit the fanciful mood.

3075 **Zolotow, Charlotte.** Over and Over; pictures by Garth Williams. Harper, 1957. unp. $3.50; lib. ed. $3.27 net. (P)

When a little girl blows out the candles on her birthday cake, she wishes that all the happy holidays she remembers will happen over and over again.

3076 Zolotow, Charlotte. The Storm Book; pictures by Margaret Bloy Graham. Harper, 1952. unp. $2.95; lib. ed. $2.92 net. (P)

The beauty of a storm rather than its frightening aspects is caught in a poetic story and handsome pictures of a storm that sweeps over city, country, mountains, and seashore. Good read-aloud nature material.

3077 Zolotow, Charlotte. A Tiger Called Thomas; pictures by Kurt Werth. Lothrop, 1963. unp. $3.50; lib. ed. $3.35 net. (P)

Fall colors and fanciful costumes make this Halloween story attractive to children. Shy Thomas, new to the neighborhood, goes out in his tiger suit and finds that he already has many friends.

Professional Tools
for Building Book Collections

The professional tools listed below are the editor's choice of first-purchase aids for selecting and using elementary school library materials. As the library develops, more extensive lists of aids will be helpful; four such bibliographies are noted on page 257.

Abridged Readers' Guide to Periodical Literature . . . Author and Subject Index to a Selected List of Periodicals . . . Wilson. Annual. $11.

Issued monthly, except in June, July, and August, with bound annual cumulations. Useful as a guide to building a file of magazines for reference, as well as for locating articles on current topics after a file has been established.

American Association of School Librarians, of the American Library Association, and Department of Audiovisual Instruction, of the National Education Association. Standards for School Media Programs. A.L.A., 1969. 84p. $2.

This revision of *Standards for School Library Programs* (A.L.A., 1960) was prepared by a joint committee of the American Association of School Librarians, of the American Library Association, and the Department of Audiovisual Instruction of the National Education Association. Its purpose is to coordinate the standards for school library and audiovisual programs into media programs designed to serve the instructional program of the school more effectively than separate programs. Objectives of the media center program are stated, and the staff, resources, and facilities needed to implement the program are described. The standards are intended to apply at the building level to all schools with 250 or more pupils, in any combination of grades, and to programs at the system and area level.

American Association of School Librarians, of the American Library Association, and National Commission for Teacher Education and Professional Standards Coordinating Committee for the Teachers' Library Project. The Teachers' Library: How To Organize It and What To Include. National Education Assn., 1968. 208p. Paper. $1.50.

Sets up standards for a teachers' library and offers practical suggestions for organizing and adminstering a wide range of professional materials. Following the text is an extensive annotated bibliography of books, pamphlets, films, filmstrips, and journals, selected by 44 national organizations and arranged by areas of the curriculum and other subjects of interest to educators. Indexed by author and title.

Arbuthnot, May Hill. Children and Books. 3d ed. Scott, Foresman, 1964. 688p. $9.25.

An invaluable guide to children's interests in reading; criteria for selecting books in many areas; penetrating discussions of books, authors, and illustrators; lists of award books; extensive subject bibliographies; and chapters on using books with children.

The Booklist and Subscription Books Bulletin. American Library Assn. Semi-monthly, except monthly in August. $10.

Authoritative reviews of recent books recommended for adults, young people, and children, along with periodic lists of new editions, award books, paperbacks and pamphlets, and U.S. government documents. Each issue carries a detailed evaluation of one or more reference works (titles not recommended as well as those recommended), prepared by the Subscription Books Committee of the American Library Association.

Books for Children, 1960–1965; as sel. and reviewed by *The Booklist and Subscription Books Bulletin,* September, 1960 through August, 1965. American Library Assn., 1966. 447p. $10.

More than 3000 reviews, arranged by a modified Dewey Decimal Classification, giving full buying information, grade levels, suggested subject headings, and evaluative notes.

Books for Children, 1965–1966; as sel. and reviewed by *The Booklist and Subscription Books Bulletin,* September, 1965 through August, 1966. American Library Assn., 1966. 119p. Paper. $2.

Reviews 770 titles.

Books for Children, 1966–1967; as sel. and reviewed by *The Booklist and Subscription Books Bulletin,* September, 1966 through August, 1967. American Library Assn., 1967. 128p. Paper. $2.25.

Reviews 802 titles.

Books for Children, 1967–1968; as sel. and reviewed by *The Booklist and Subscription Books Bulletin,* September, 1967 through August, 1968. American Library Assn., 1968. 145p. Paper. $2.50.

Reviews 913 titles.

Children's Books—1967. Comp. by Virginia Haviland and Lois Watt. Govt. Print. Off., 1968. 16p. $.15.

An annual listing of about 200 outstanding books for children, arranged by broad subjects, annotated, and graded.

Children's Catalog. 11th ed. Ed. by Rachel Shor and Estelle A. Fidell. Wilson, 1966. 1024p. $17.

More than 4000 titles, arranged by the Dewey Decimal Classification, with full bibliographic information, annotations, grade levels, and suggested subject headings. An extensive index includes authors, illustrators, titles, subjects, and analytics for collections of fairy tales, folklore, collective biography, short stories, plays, and other parts of books. Price includes four annual supplements.

Crosby, Muriel, ed. Reading Ladders for Human Relations. 4th ed. (by) Muriel Crosby, ed. and the Committee on Reading Ladders for Human Relations of the National Council of Teachers of English. American Council on Education, 1963. 242p. $4.

More than 1000 books for children and young people, grouped around six human relations themes and listed in order of difficulty within each group. Includes chapters on how to conduct discussions of human relations topics.

Deason, Hilary J., comp. The AAAS Science Book List for Children. 2d ed. Comp. under the direction of Hilary J. Deason. Consultant, Nora Beust. Published with the assistance of a grant from the National Science Foundation. American Association for the Advancement of Science, 1963. 201p. $2.50. Paper. $1.50.

Approximately 1300 science books for recreational and collateral reading by elementary pupils through grade 8. Arranged by Dewey classes, annotated, and coded for three reading levels: primary, intermediate, and advanced. Eighty-one titles are double-starred for first purchase, 278 single-starred for second priority.

Eakin, Mary K., comp. Good Books for Children: A Selection of Outstanding Children's Books Published 1950–1965. 3d ed. Univ. of Chicago Pr., 1966. 407p. $7.95.

More than 1300 titles chosen from books reviewed in the *Bulletin of the Center for Children's Books,* arranged alphabetically by author and fully described and evaluated. Grading combines probable difficulty level with subject interest, and potential usefulness of each title is suggested. Includes an excellent chapter on criteria for book selection and a subject and title index.

Enoch Pratt Free Library, Baltimore. Stories To Tell: A List of Stories with Annotations. 5th ed. rev. and ed. by Jeanne B. Hardendorff. Enoch Pratt Free Library, 1965. 83p. Paper. $1.50.

A classified list of stories chosen from titles used in Enoch Pratt story hours.

Gaver, Mary, ed. The Elementary School Library Collection: Phases 1-2-3. 3d ed. Bro-Dart, 1967. 1210p. $20.

A book catalog, arranged by Dewey classes, of approximately 6000 titles, designed to describe a collection of materials meeting the standards set in *Standards for School Library Programs* (American Library Assn., 1960). Unique features include: an excellent selection policy; lists of recordings, filmstrips, and other nonbook materials; lists of periodicals and professional tools; a graded listing of books for beginning readers; and a sample catalog card for each title. First- , second- , and third-purchase titles are indicated by the symbols P1, P2, and P3, respectively. Kept up to date by annual supplements and frequent revisions.

George Peabody College for Teachers, Nashville. Division of Surveys and Field Services. Free and Inexpensive Learning Materials . . . George Peabody College for Teachers. Frequently revised. Paper. $2.

A carefully screened list of more than 3000 items useful to schools, classified by subject and accompanied by full order information. An excellent source of information for starting a vertical file collection.

Guilfoile, Elizabeth. Books for Beginning Readers; illus. by Norma Phillips. National Council of Teachers of English, 1962. 73p. Paper. $1.

More than 400 books for independent reading in primary grades, arranged alphabetically by author and keyed to exact reading levels. Introductory chapters give excellent criteria for selecting books in this field. No annotations.

Heller, Frieda M. I Can Read It Myself! Some Books for Independent Reading in the Primary Grades; comp. and annotated by Frieda M. Heller. rev. ed. College of Education, Ohio State Univ., 1965. 46p. Paper. $1.25.

An annotated list organized in three parts: books for the child just beginning to read independently; books for the child reading "a little better"; and books for the child reading well.

The Horn Book Magazine. Horn Book. Bimonthly. $6.

Perceptive reviews of books for children and young people and articles on authors, illustrators, children's literature, and science books. Annual listing of outstanding books.

Huck, Charlotte S., and **Kuhn, Doris Young.** Children's Literature in the Elementary School. 2d ed. Holt, 1968. 792p. $10.

An excellent guide for teachers and librarians, covering criteria for selection of books in many fields, children's characteristics and interests at various ages, ways of using books with children, and extensive subject bibliographies. Supplementary material includes children's book awards, children's book clubs, and other topics related to children's books.

Junior High School Library Catalog . . . Ed. by Rachel Shor and Estelle A. Fidell. Wilson, 1965. 768p. $20.

Lists 3278 books, arranged by Dewey, with buying information, subject headings, and annotations. A detailed index includes analytics for composite books. Price includes four annual supplements.

Katz, William Loren. Teachers' Guide to American Negro History. Quadrangle, 1968. 192p. Paper. $2.25.

The author's preface states that the purpose of this list is to give the classroom teacher the basic tools necessary to integrate his American history course by placing the Negro in appropriate places in the curriculum, unit by unit of study. This he does by listing "Dates to Remember" at the beginning of each unit and then providing an annotated list of related materials, both print and audio-visual, to help pupils and teachers understand the part Negroes played in each event. Special features of the list include a core reference library, a list of historic landmarks associated with Negroes, locations of Negro history museums and libraries, and lists of paperbacks and free or inexpensive materials. Along with these rich sources of materials, the author suggests approaches to teaching Negro history which make it a natural part of American history in general. Basically a secondary school list, the *Teachers' Guide* provides also much help for teachers of grades 5–8.

Let's Read Together: Books for Family Enjoyment. 2d ed. Sel. and annotated by a Special Committee of the National Congress of Parents and Teachers and the Children's Services Division, American Library Association. A.L.A., 1964. 91p. Paper. $1.50. New edition in preparation.

Though directed to parents, this bibliography is equally useful to the librarian or teacher guiding a child's reading. Includes approximately 500 titles, grouped by subject and age level.

New York Library Asssociation. Children's and Young Adult Services Section. Recordings for Children: A Selected List. 2d ed. rev. Prepared by New York Library Association. Children's and Young Adult Services Section . . . The Association, 1964. 43p. Paper. $1. Order from Office of Children's Services, New York Public Library.

Lists recordings of games, songs, foreign languages, poetry, stories, and documentaries, selected as "a cross section of the best recordings now available with stress on those best suited for the home and recreational collection."

Paperback Goes to School: A Selected List of High & Junior High School Titles . . . BIPAD. Annual. Free.

Prepared by a joint committee of the National Education Association and the American Association of School Librarians and distributed by the Bureau of Independent Publishers and Distributors. A subject list of more than 4000 titles considered suitable for pupils of high and junior high school age. Each entry includes author, title, price, and source, but no annotation. Indexed by author and title.

Paperback Goes to School, Elementary Edition: A Selected List of Pre-School and Elementary Titles. BIPAD. Annual (?). Free.

A companion list to the entry above, similarly prepared and distributed. Approximately 600 titles are arranged by subject in two categories, "For Lower Elementary Grades" and "For Upper Elementary Grades," and coded to indicate books for advanced readers. Included at the end of the listings are "some basic materials specifically designed for classroom use." No index.

Rollins, Charlemae, ed. We Build Together: A Reader's Guide to Negro Life and Literature for Elementary and High School Use. National Council of Teachers of English, 1967. 71p. Paper. $1.50.

An excellent introduction calls attention to recent changes in books about Negroes and sets up criteria for judging books in this area. A bibliography follows, arranged by broad subjects and with annotations pointing out strengths and weaknesses in the titles evaluated.

School Library Journal: The Journal of Library Work with Children and Young People. Bowker. Monthly, September through May. $5.

Brief reviews, both favorable and adverse, of books for grades K–12; articles of interest to school librarians and teachers; reviews of professional books, recordings, filmstrips, and 8mm films. Occasional special lists.

Science Books: A Quarterly Review. American Assn. for the Advancement of Science. Paper. $6.50.

A periodical edited by Hilary J. Deason, reviewing trade books, textbooks, and reference works for elementary grades through junior college. Reviews, written by scientists or others with special competencies, include both recommended and not recommended titles and are arranged by Dewey.

Strang, Ruth; Phelps, Ethlyne; (and) Withrow, Dorothy. Gateways to Readable Books: An Annotated Graded List of Books in Many Fields for Adolescents Who Find Reading Difficult. 4th ed. Wilson, 1966. 245p. $5.

More than 1000 books in 28 subject categories, with estimated reading levels from first to seventh grades. Brief annotations and author, title, and grade-level-of-difficulty indexes. Very useful to the librarian or teacher coping with problem readers.

Subject Index to Books for Intermediate Grades. 3d ed. Comp. by Mary K. Eakin. American Library Assn., 1963. 308p. $7.50.

Approximately 1800 books indexed by more than 4000 subjects in a bibliography "designed as a reference tool to be used by classroom teachers and librarians in identifying books that have value as teaching materials in Grades 4–6." Books indexed are listed alphabetically by author, with buying information; index includes many new subject headings, reflecting the changing needs of classroom instruction, and suggested grade levels.

Subject Index to Books for Primary Grades. 3d ed. Comp. by Mary K. Eakin. American Library Assn., 1967. 113p. $4.

Similar in purpose and organization to the entry above, with both independent-reading and interest levels indicated for many books. Includes more than 900 trade books and readers, with some designated for teacher use.

Subscription Books Bulletin Reviews, 1960–1962. Reprinted from *The Booklist* *and Subscription Books Bulletin,* Volumes 57–58, September 1, 1960—August, 1962. Prepared by the American Library Association Subscription Books Committee. A.L.A., 1962. 94p. Paper. $1.50.

Subscription Books Bulletin Reviews, 1962–1964. Reprinted from *The Booklist and Subscription Books Bulletin,* Volumes 59–60, September 1, 1962—August, 1964. Prepared by the American Library Association Subscription Books Committee. A.L.A., 1964. 146p. Paper. $2.

Subscription Books Bulletin Reviews, 1964–1966. Reprinted from *The Booklist and Subscription Books Bulletin,* Volumes 61–62, September 1, 1964—August, 1966. Prepared by the American Library Association Subscription Books Committee. A.L.A., 1967. 136p. Paper. $2.25.

The 185 detailed reviews included in the three volumes listed above provide an invaluable guide to reference books published within the last nine years. Reviews of both recommended and not recommended titles, which are fully documented and aim "to be scrupulously fair to both publisher and probable purchaser," serve not only as an aid to selection but as a guide to the use of reference books.

Sutherland, Zena, comp. History in Children's Books: An Annotated Bibliography for Schools and Libraries. McKinley, 1967. 248p. $8.50.

A semiselective subject list geared to grades K–8, providing buying information and brief but informative annotations. Within each section the arrangement is chronological, with biography, history, and fiction combined and with separate listings for grades K–5 and 6–8. Out-of-print and easy-to-read books are designated by symbols, and there is an author and title index.

University of Chicago. Graduate Library School. Bulletin of the Center for Children's Books. Univ. of Chicago Pr. Monthly. $4.50.

Discriminating reviews, both favorable and unfavorable, of children's books, and lists of articles about children's books and reading of interest to parents, teachers, and librarians.

For libraries needing a more extensive listing of professional tools, the following are recommended:

Aids to Choosing Books for Children. Children's Book Council, 1968. 6p. $.35.

A selected list of bibliographies and review media, prepared by Mrs. Ingeborg Boudreau, librarian of the Children's Book Council, in consultation with school and children's librarians. Includes general lists, lists in special areas, and sources of reviews for audio-visual materials.

Periodicals for School Libraries: A Guide to Magazines, Newspapers, and Periodical Indexes. Comp. and ed. by Marian H. Scott, Chairman, Periodicals List Subcommittee of the American Library Association Editorial Committee. A.L.A., 1969. 235p. $3.50.

Intended as a buying guide to more than 400 periodicals and newspapers for school library purchase. Covers all grade levels, kindergarten through twelfth grade.

Selecting Materials for Children and Young Adults; prepared by the Children's Services Division and the Young Adult Services Division of the American Library Association. A.L.A., 1967. 24p. $.25.

A list of general and specialized selection aids for books and nonbook materials.

Selecting Materials for School Libraries: Guidelines and Selection Sources To Insure Quality Collections; prepared by the American Association of School Librarians, a Division of the American Library Association and a Department of the National Education Association. A.L.A., 1967. rev. ed. 8p. Single copy free.

An extensive bibliography listing aids for the selection of all types of school library materials.

Directory
of Publishers and Distributors

A.L.A. American Library Association, Publishing Dept., 50 E. Huron St., Chicago, Ill. 60611

Abelard-Schuman. Abelard-Schuman, Ltd., 6 W. 57th St., New York, N.Y. 10019

Abingdon. Abingdon Press, 201 Eighth Ave. S., Nashville, Tenn. 37202

Abrams. Harry N. Abrams, Inc., 6 W. 57th St., New York, N.Y. 10019

American Assn. for the Advancement of Science. American Assn. for the Advancement of Science, 1515 Massachusetts Ave. N.W., Washing, D.C. 20005

American Council on Education. American Council on Education, 1785 Massachusetts Ave., N.W., Washington, D.C. 20036

American Heritage. American Heritage Publishing Co., Inc., 551 Fifth Ave., New York, N.Y. 10017

Appleton. Appleton-Century-Crofts, 440 Park Ave. S., New York, N.Y. 10016

Atheneum. Atheneum Publishers, 122 E. 42d St., New York, N.Y. 10017

Barnes. A. S. Barnes & Co., Inc., Forsgate Dr., Cranbury, N.J. 08512

Barrows. M. Barrows & Co., Inc., Publishers, 425 Park Ave. S., New York, N.Y. 10016

Basic Books. Basic Books, Inc., 404 Park Ave. S., New York, N.Y. 10016

Beginner Books. Beginner Books, 457 Madison Ave., New York, N.Y. 10022

BIPAD. Bureau of Independent Publishers and Distributors, 122 E. 42d St., New York, N.Y. 10017

Bobbs-Merrill. Bobbs-Merrill Co., Inc., 4300 W. 62d St., Indianapolis, Ind. 46206

Bowker. R. R. Bowker Co., 1180 Ave. of the Americas, New York, N.Y. 10036

Branford. Charles T. Branford Co., 28 Union St., Newton Centre, Mass. 02159

Bro-Dart. Bro-Dart Foundation, 113 Frelinghuysen Ave., Newark, N.J. 07101

Bruce. Bruce Publishing Co., 400 N. Broadway, Milwaukee, Wis. 53201

Capitol. Capitol Publishing Co., Inc., 850 Third Ave., New York, N.Y. 10022

Caxton. Caxton Printers, Ltd., Caldwell, Idaho 83605

Children's Book Council. Children's Book Council, Inc., 175 Fifth Ave., New York, N.Y. 10010

Childrens Pr. Childrens Press, 1224 W. Van Buren St., Chicago, Ill. 60607

Chilton. Chilton Book Co., 401 Walnut St., Philadelphia, Pa. 19106

College of Education, Ohio State Univ. Ohio State University, Publications Office, 242 W. 18th St., Columbus, Ohio 43210

Compton. F. E. Compton Co., 1000 N. Dearborn St., Chicago, Ill. 60610

Comstock. Comstock Publishing Associates, 124 Roberts Pl., Ithaca, N.Y. 14850

Coward-McCann. Coward-McCann, Inc., 200 Madison Ave., New York, N.Y. 10016

Creative Educ. Soc. Creative Educational Society, Inc., 515 N. Front St., Mankato, Minn. 56001

Criterion. Criterion Books, Inc., 6 W. 57th St., New York, N.Y. 10019

Crowell. Thomas Y. Crowell Co., 201 Park Ave. S., New York, N.Y. 10003

Crowell-Collier. P. F. Collier & Son Corp., 866 Third Ave., New York, N.Y. 10022

Crown. Crown Publishers, Inc., 419 Park Ave. S., New York, N.Y. 10016

Day. John Day Co., 200 Madison Ave., New York, N.Y. 10016

Delacorte. Dell Publishing Co., Inc., 750 Third Ave., New York, N.Y. 10017

Dial. Dial Press, Inc., 750 Third Ave., New York, N.Y. 10017

Dodd. Dodd, Mead & Co., 79 Madison Ave., New York, N.Y. 10016

Donohue. M. A. Donohue & Co., 711 S. Dearborn St., Chicago, Ill. 60605

Doubleday. Doubleday & Co., Inc., 277 Park Ave., New York, N.Y. 10017

Duell. Duell, Sloan & Pearce, 250 Park Ave., New York, N.Y. 10017

Dutton. E. P. Dutton & Co., Inc., 201 Park Ave. S., New York, N.Y. 10003

Enoch Pratt Free Library. Enoch Pratt Free

Library, 400 Cathedral St., Baltimore, Md. 21201

Farrar. Farrar, Straus & Giroux, Inc., 19 Union Sq. W., New York, N.Y. 10003

Fideler. Fideler Co., 31 Ottawa Ave. N.W., Grand Rapids, Mich. 49502

Field Enterprises. Field Enterprises Educational Corp., 510 Merchandise Mart Plaza, Chicago, Ill. 60654

Follett. Follett Publishing Co., 1010 W. Washington Blvd., Chicago, Ill. 60607

Forest. Forest Press, Inc., Lake Placid Club, N.Y. 12946

Four Winds. Four Winds Press, 50 W. 44th St., New York, N.Y. 10036

Friendship Pr. Friendship Press, 475 Riverside Dr., New York, N.Y. 10027

Frontier Pr. Frontier Press Co., 50 W. Broad St., Columbus, Ohio 43215

Funk & Wagnalls. Funk & Wagnalls, 380 Madison Ave., New York, N.Y. 10017

Garden City. Garden City Books, 277 Park Ave., New York, N.Y. 10017

Garrard. Garrard Publishing Co., 1607 N. Market St., Champaign, Ill. 61820

George Peabody College for Teachers. George Peabody College for Teachers, Division of Surveys and Field Services, Nashville, Tenn. 37203

Ginn. Ginn & Co., Statler Bldg., Back Bay P.O. 191, Boston, Mass. 02117

Golden Gate. Golden Gate Junior Books, Box 398, San Carlos, Calif. 94070

Golden Pr. Golden Press, 850 Third Ave., New York, N.Y. 10022

Govt. Print. Off. U.S. Government Printing Office, Division of Public Documents, Washington, D.C. 20402

Grolier. Grolier Incorporated, 575 Lexington Ave., New York, N.Y. 10022

Grosset. Grosset & Dunlap, Inc., 51 Madison Ave., New York, N.Y. 10010

Hammond. Hammond, Inc., Maplewood, N.J. 07040

Harcourt. Harcourt, Brace & World, Inc., 757 Third Ave., New York, N.Y. 10017

Harper. Harper & Row, 49 E. 33d St., New York, N.Y. 10016

Hart. Hart Publishing Co., Inc., 510 Ave. of the Americas, New York, N.Y. 10011

Harvey House. Harvey House, Inc., 5 South Buckhout St., Irvington-on-Hudson, N.Y. 10533

Hastings. Hastings House, Inc., 10 E. 40th St., New York, N.Y. 10016

Hawthorn. Hawthorn Books, Inc., 70 Fifth Ave., New York, N.Y. 10011

Heritage. Heritage Press. See Dial.

Hill & Wang. Hill & Wang, Inc., 141 Fifth Ave., New York, N.Y. 10010

Holiday. Holiday House, 18 E. 56th St., New York, N.Y. 10022

Holt. Holt, Rinehart & Winston, Inc., 383 Madison Ave., New York, N.Y. 10017

Horn Book. Horn Book, Inc., 585 Boylston St., Boston, Mass. 02116

Houghton. Houghton Mifflin Co., 2 Park St., Boston, Mass. 02107

International. International Publishers Co., Inc., 381 Park Ave. S., New York, N.Y. 10016

Knopf. Alfred A. Knopf, Inc., 501 Madison Ave., New York, N.Y. 10022

Ktav. Ktav Publishing House, Inc., 120 E. Broadway, New York, N.Y. 10002

Lippincott. J. B. Lippincott Co., E. Washington Sq., Philadelphia, Pa. 19105

Little. Little, Brown & Co., 34 Beacon St., Boston, Mass. 02106

London House. London House & Maxwell, Inc., 122 E. 55th St., New York, N.Y. 10022

Longmans. See McKay.

Lothrop. Lothrop, Lee & Shepard Co., Inc., 381 Park Ave. S., New York, N.Y. 10016

Luce. Robert B. Luce, Inc., 1244 19th St., N.W., Washington, D.C. 20036

McGraw-Hill. McGraw-Hill Book Co., 330 W. 42d St., New York, N.Y. 10036

McKay. David McKay Co., Inc., 750 Third Ave., New York, N.Y. 10017

McKinley. McKinley Publishing Co., Brooklawn, N.J. 08030

Macmillan. The Macmillan Co., 866 Third Ave., New York, N.Y. 10022

Macrae. Macrae Smith Co., 225 S. 15th St., Philadelphia, Pa. 19102

Medical Books for Children. Medical Books for Children Publishing Co., 940 Upper Midwest Bldg., Minneapolis, Minn. 55401

Melmont. Melmont Publishers, Inc., 1224 W. Van Buren St., Chicago, Ill. 60607

Meredith. Meredith Press, 250 Park Ave., New York, N.Y. 10017

Merriam. G. & C. Merriam Co., 47 Federal St., Springfield, Mass. 01101

Messner. Julian Messner, 1 W. 39th St., New York, N.Y. 10018

Morrow. William Morrow & Co., Inc., 425 Park Ave. S., New York, N.Y. 10016

National Council of Teachers of English. National Council of Teachers of English, 508 S. Sixth St., Champaign, Ill. 61820

National Geographic Soc. National Geographic Society, 17th & M Sts., N.W., Washington, D.C. 20036

Natural History. Natural History Press, Central Park West & 79th St., New York, N.Y. 10024

Nelson. Thomas Nelson & Sons, Copewood & Davis Sts., Camden, N.J. 08103

New Amer. Lib. New American Library, Inc., 1301 Ave. of the Americas, New York, N.Y. 10019

New York Public Library. New York Public Library, Fifth Ave. & 42d St., New York, N.Y. 10018

Norton. W. W. Norton & Co., Inc., 55 Fifth Ave., New York, N.Y. 10003

Odyssey. Odyssey Press, 55 Fifth Ave., New York, N.Y. 10003

Oxford Univ. Pr. Oxford University Press, Inc., 200 Madison Ave., New York, N.Y. 10016

Pantheon. Pantheon Books, Inc., 437 Madison Ave., New York, N.Y. 10022

Parents Mag. Pr. Parents' Magazine Press, 52 Vanderbilt Ave., New York, N.Y. 10017

Parnassus. Parnassus Press, 2422 Ashby Ave., Berkeley, Calif. 94705

Phillips. S. G. Phillips, Inc., 305 W. 86th St., New York, N.Y. 10024

Platt & Munk. Platt & Munk, Inc., 200 Fifth Ave., New York, N.Y. 10010

Plays. Plays, Inc., 8 Arlington St., Boston, Mass. 02116

Prentice-Hall. Prentice-Hall, Inc., 70 Fifth Ave., New York, N.Y. 10011

Putnam. G. P. Putnam's Sons, 200 Madison Ave., New York, N.Y. 10016

Quadrangle. Quadrangle Books, Inc., 12 E. Delaware Pl., Chicago, Ill. 60611

Rand McNally. Rand McNally & Co., P.O. Box 7600, Chicago, Ill. 60680

Random. Random House, Inc., 457 Madison Ave., New York, N.Y. 10022

Reilly & Lee. Reilly & Lee Co., 114 W. Illinois St., Chicago, Ill. 60610

Ronald. Ronald Press Co., 79 Madison Ave., New York, N.Y. 10016

Roy. Roy Publishers, Inc., 30 E. 74th St., New York, N.Y. 10021

St. Martin's. St. Martin's Press, Inc., 175 Fifth Ave., New York, N.Y. 10010

W. R. Scott. William R. Scott, Inc., 333 Ave. of the Americas, New York, N.Y. 10014

Scott, Foresman. Scott, Foresman & Co., 1900 E. Lake Ave., Glenview, Ill. 60025

Scott Publications, Inc. Scott Publications, Inc., 461 Eighth Ave., New York, N.Y. 10001

Scribner. Charles Scribner's Sons, 597 Fifth Ave., New York, N.Y. 10017

Seabury. Seabury Press, Inc., 815 Second Ave., New York, N.Y. 10017

Silver Burdett. Silver Burdett Co., Park Ave. & Columbia Rd., Morristown, N.J. 07960

Simon & Schuster. Simon & Schuster, Inc., 630 Fifth Ave., New York, N.Y. 10020

Sloane. William Sloane Associates. *See* Morrow.

Sterling. Sterling Publishing Co., Inc., 419 Park Ave. S., New York, N.Y. 10016

Time. Time, Inc., Book Division, Time & Life Bldg., Rockefeller Center, New York, N.Y. 10020

Tudor. Tudor Publishing Co., 221 Park Ave. S., New York, N.Y. 10003

Tuttle. Charles E. Tuttle Co., Inc., 28 S. Main St., Rutland, Vt. 05701

Univ. of Chicago Pr. University of Chicago Press, 5750 Ellis Ave., Chicago, Ill. 60637

Vanguard. Vanguard Press, Inc., 424 Madison Ave., New York, N.Y. 10017

Van Nostrand. D. Van Nostrand Co., Inc., 120 Alexander St., Princeton, N.J. 08540

Viking. Viking Press, Inc., 625 Madison Ave., New York, N.Y. 10022

Walck. Henry Z. Walck, Inc., 19 Union Sq. W., New York, N.Y. 10003

Warne. Frederick Warne & Co., Inc., 101 Fifth Ave., New York, N.Y. 10003

Watts. Franklin Watts, Inc., 575 Lexington Ave., New York, N.Y. 10022

Webster. Webster Publishing Co., Manchester Rd., Manchester, Mo. 63011

Westminster. Westminster Press, Witherspoon Bldg., Philadelphia, Pa. 19107

Albert Whitman. Albert Whitman & Co., 560 W. Lake St., Chicago, Ill. 60606

Wilson. H. W. Wilson Co., 950 University Ave., Bronx, N.Y. 10452

Winston. *See* Holt.

World. World Publishing Co., 2231 W. 110th St., Cleveland, Ohio 44102

Index

Numbers listed refer to entries and not to pages, except for numbers within parentheses which represent dates.

Index

Index

Index

Index

Index

Mandell, M. Make Your Own Musical Instruments, 1039
Manley, S. Rudyard Kipling, 1593
Mann, M. How Things Work, 524
Manners Can Be Fun, 160
Manners Made Easy, 155
Manners To Grow On, 161
Manning, J. Young Ireland, 2029; Young Puerto Rico, 1991
Manning-Sanders, R. Book of Dragons, 1345
Man's Way from Cave to Skyscraper, 93
Mantle, Charles Mickey, 1624
Many Moons, 2641
Many Worlds of Benjamin Franklin, 1546
Map drawing, 1714
Maple sugar, 3052
Maplin Bird, 2545
Maps, 1710, 1713–14
Mara: Daughter of the Nile, 2486
Marblehead, Massachusetts: stories, 2257
Marco Polo's Adventure in China, 1661
Marconi, Guglielmo, 1625
Marcus and Narcissa Whitman, 1706
Margaret, Queen of Scotland: stories, 2550
Marguerite de Angeli's Book of Nursery and Mother Goose Rhymes, 1379
Marian Anderson, 1459
Marine animals, 759, 825, 837
Marine at War, 1798
Marine biology, 611, 614–15, 621, 657–58, 677
Marine resources, 629
Marino, D. Where Are the Mothers? 2946
Marion, Francis, 1626
Mark of the Horse Lord, 2637
Markun, P. M. First Book of Central America and Panama, 1986; First Book of Mining, 543
Marmots: stories, 2727, 2888
Marquette, Jacques, 1627
Mars (Planet), 455; stories, 2380
Marshall, John, 1628
Marshmallow, 2967
Martha, Daughter of Virginia, 1704
Martin, P. M. Calvin and the Cub Scouts, 2947; Greedy One, 2498; Rice Bowl Pet, 2948

Martin, R. Looking at Italy, 2033
Martin de Porres, 1629
Martin Luther, 1619
Martin Luther King, 1590
Martinique: stories, 2567
Mary Jane, 2623
Mary McLeod Bethune, 1470
Mary Poppins, 2646
Mary Poppins Comes Back, 2647
Mary Stuart, Queen of the Scots, 1630; stories, 2661
Maryland: stories, 2340
Masai (African tribe), 2076–77
Masers, 508
Masers and Lasers, 508
Masked Prowler, 2339
Masks (for the face), 1011
Masks and Mask Makers, 1011
Mason, B. S. Book of Indian Crafts and Costumes, 1830; Junior Book of Camping and Woodcraft, 1090
Mason, F. V. Battle for Quebec, 1966; Winter at Valley Forge, 1898
Mason, G. F. Animal Clothing, 761; Animal Homes, 762; Animal Sounds, 763; Animal Tails, 764; Animal Tools, 765; Animal Tracks, 766; Animal Weapons, 767
Mason, M. E. Caroline and Her Kettle Named Maud, 2499
Massachusetts: history, 1869, 1886–87, 1891, 1893; stories, 2247, 2389, 2429
Massoglia, E. T. Fun-Time Paper Folding, 1014
Master of Morgana, 2492
Master of the Royal Cats, 2914
Master Surgeon, 1614
Matchlock Gun, 2284
Mathematics, 433; history, 442, 447; poetry, 1199
Mathews, F. S. Field Book of American Trees and Shrubs, 743
Matsuno, M. Chie and the Sports Day, 2949; Pair of Red Clogs, 2950; Taro and the Tofu, 2951
Matthew, E. S. Land and People of Thailand, 2121
Matthews, H. L. Cuba, 1992
Matthiesen, T. ABC, 2952; Things To See, 2953
May, C. P. Central America, 1987

May I Bring a Friend? 2801
Maya: Indians of Central America, 1976
Maya: Land of the Turkey and the Deer, 1978
Mayas, 1971, 1976, 1978
Maybelle, the Cable Car, 2778
"Mayflower" (Ship), 1881
Mayne, W. Earthfasts, 2500; Grass Rope, 2501
Mayo, Charles Horace, 1631
Mayo, William James, 1631
Mayo Brothers, 1631
Mays, Willie Howard, 1632
Mead, M. Anthropologists and What They Do, 94; People and Places, 95
Meader, S. W. Boy with a Pack, 2502; Red Horse Hill, 2503; Whaler 'round the Horn, 2504
Meadowcroft, E. L. By Secret Railway, 2505; Crazy Horse: Sioux Warrior, 1518; Gift of the River, 1765; Land of the Free, 1860; On Indian Trails with Daniel Boone, 1474
Meaning of Music, 1047
Means, F. C. Moved-outers, 2506
Mechanical engineering, 524
Mechanics, 519, 524, 531–32
Medal of Honor, 368, 370
Medal of Honor Heroes, 370
Medearis, M. Big Doc's Girl, 2507
Medicine: biography, 1427; history, 961, 963, 965, 1410; research, 965, 967, 1439, 1452, 1464
Medicine as a profession, 962, 967
Medicine in Action, 967
Medicine Man (Indian), 1822a
Medieval Days and Ways, 1776
Mediterranean region: history, 1785
Meeks, E. M. Jeff and Mr. James' Pond, 623
Meet the Austins, 2459
Meet the Malones, 2672
Meeting with a Stranger, 2189
Mehdevi, A. S. Persian Folk and Fairy Tales, 1346
Mei Li, 2865
Meigs, C. Covered Bridge, 2508; Invincible Louisa, 1453
Melbo, I. R. Our Country's National Parks, 1947
Melindy's Medal, 2303

298

Index

Index